THE VICTORIA HISTORY
OF THE
COUNTIES OF ENGLAND

———

A HISTORY OF
SHROPSHIRE

VOLUME IV

THE VICTORIA HISTORY
OF THE
COUNTIES OF ENGLAND

EDITED BY C. R. ELRINGTON

DIEU ET MON DROIT

THE UNIVERSITY OF LONDON
INSTITUTE OF
HISTORICAL RESEARCH

Oxford University Press, Walton Street, Oxford OX2 6DP
Oxford   New York   Toronto
Delhi   Bombay   Calcutta   Madras   Karachi
Petaling Jaya   Singapore   Hong Kong   Tokyo
Nairobi   Dar es Salaam   Cape Town
Melbourne   Auckland
and associated companies in
Berlin Ibadan

Oxford is a trademark of Oxford University Press

Published in the United States by
Oxford University Press, New York

British Library Cataloguing in Publication Data
A History of Shropshire.—(The Victoria
history of the counties of England)
Vol. 4
Agriculture
1. Shropshire, History
I. Baugh, G.C.
II. University of London
Institute of Historical Research
III. Series
942.4'5
ISBN 0-19-722775-9

Printed in Great Britain by
H Charlesworth & Co Ltd,
Huddersfield, West Yorkshire

INSCRIBED TO THE

MEMORY OF HER LATE MAJESTY

QUEEN VICTORIA

WHO GRACIOUSLY GAVE THE TITLE TO

AND ACCEPTED THE DEDICATION

OF THIS HISTORY

JUNE
weeding

AUGUST
reaping

SEPTEMBER
threshing

LABOURS OF THE MONTHS
Mid 15th-century English glass roundels (*c.* 165 mm in diameter)
from Lower Pulley Farm (demolished 1964), Meole Brace.

A HISTORY OF

SHROPSHIRE

EDITED BY G. C. BAUGH

VOLUME IV

AGRICULTURE

PUBLISHED FOR

THE INSTITUTE OF HISTORICAL RESEARCH

BY

OXFORD UNIVERSITY PRESS

1989

Distributed by Oxford University Press until 1 January 1992
thereafter by Dawsons of Pall Mall

CONTENTS OF VOLUME FOUR

CONTENTS OF VOLUME FOUR

LIST OF ILLUSTRATIONS

For permission to reproduce material in their copyright, custody, or possession and for the loan of prints, thanks are offered to Acton Scott Working Farm Museum; Mr. Arnold Baker; the Committee for Aerial Photography of the University of Cambridge; Mrs. G. S. O. Colthurst; the Department of Defence; Mrs. J. Griffiths; Mr. R. D. Griffiths; Mr. C. H. Hand; Mr. T. H. Leath; the National Monuments Record (N.M.R.) of the Royal Commission on Historical Monuments (England); the Institute of Agrarian History and Museum of English Rural Life, University of Reading; Dr. D. H. Robinson; Shrewsbury and Atcham Borough Museums; Shropshire County Council Property and Planning Services Department; Shropshire Record Office; Sotheby's; and Times Newspapers Ltd.

LIST OF MAPS AND OTHER FIGURES

The figures were drawn by K. J. Wass from drafts by R. C. Hill (Figs. 13–20), R. Perren (Figs. 21–2), and P. A. Stamper (Figs. 1–12).

LIST OF TABLES

EDITORIAL NOTE

VOLUME IV is the sixth volume of the *Victoria History of Shropshire* to be published, and the fifth since the revival of the project outlined in the Editorial Note to Volume VIII (1968). The partnership between the Shropshire County Council (with the generously maintained support of the Walker Trust) and the University of London has continued, supervision of the *History*'s work being devolved by the Council's Leisure Activities (from 1988 Leisure Services) Committee on the Victoria County History Advisory Board. From 1981 to 1985 Mr. V. M. E. Holt chaired the Committee and the late Sir Jasper More chaired the Board. Mr. A. Freudmann chaired the Committee and the Board from 1985 to 1988, when he was succeeded in both chairs by Mr. N. L. Pickering. It is sad to record Sir Jasper More's death in 1987 and sad also to record that of Sir Philip Magnus-Allcroft, Bt., C.B.E., in 1988. It was Sir Philip who first approached the University on the County Council's behalf in 1959, suggesting the revival of the Shropshire *History*, and from that time until his death he maintained his interest in it, serving as a member—for considerable periods as chairman or vice-chairman—of the committees charged with its local supervision.

The local staff mentioned in the Editorial Note to Volume XI (1985) have continued in their posts, Mr. G. C. Baugh as County Editor and Dr. D. C. Cox and Dr. P. A. Stamper as Assistant County Editors. Mrs. M. B. Key, who had typed Volumes III and XI and was appointed part-time secretary to the *History* in 1984, left in 1987 when she was succeeded by Mrs. J. M. Day.

For many years the progress of the Shropshire *History* was very greatly assisted by the voluntary work of Mr. H. D. G. Foxall and Mrs. J. McFall, both of whom, it is recorded with great regret, died in 1989. Between 1962 and 1988 George Foxall produced, besides some more general maps, about 500 field-name maps, mainly from tithe apportionments and maps but some from estate records. This great labour, liberally undertaken to help forward the work of the Shropshire *History*, has increasingly proved generally valuable, and George Foxall has left all future students of Shropshire history, topography, and place names greatly in his debt. In 1980 Jessie McFall began to write the Education sections of parish histories that were included in Volume XI. She went on to write similar sections for three more volumes, as yet unpublished. In 1988 she had to give up the work for reasons of health, but the contribution which she so generously made will become apparent as future volumes appear.

During the planning of this volume valuable advice was given by Professor F. M. L. Thompson and Dr. Joan Thirsk. For help received during its research and writing thanks are rendered to the staffs of the Shropshire Record Office under Mrs. L. B. Halford, County Archivist, and of the Local Studies Library, Shrewsbury, under Mr. A. M. Carr. Shropshire Libraries' Information Service has also given valuable assistance. Mr. Fred Powell kindly gave much help with the search for illustrations. As for some previous volumes Sir Michael Leighton, Bt., has readily given access to his family papers at Loton, and once again a special debt of gratitude is due to him. Other people who have helped with particular articles are named in appropriate footnotes.

The *General Introduction* to the *History* (1970) outlines the structure and aims of the series as a whole.

LIST OF CLASSES OF DOCUMENTS
IN THE PUBLIC RECORD OFFICE
USED IN THIS VOLUME WITH THEIR CLASS NUMBERS

Board of Trade

BT 31   Files of Dissolved Companies

Chancery

Proceedings
C 1   Early
C 3   Series II
C 66   Patent Rolls

Inquisitions post mortem
C 132   Series I, Hen. III
C 133   Edw. I
C 134   Edw. II
C 135   Edw. III
C 141   Ric. III
C 145   Miscellaneous Inquisitions

Duchy of Lancaster

DL 39   Forest Proceedings

Exchequer, Treasury of the Receipt

E 32   Forest Proceedings

Exchequer, King's Remembrancer

E 134   Depositions taken by
             Commission
E 142   Ancient Extents
E 149   Inquisitions post mortem, Series I
E 179   Subsidy Rolls, etc.

Exchequer, Augmentation Office

E 135   Miscellaneous Books

Exchequer, Lord Treasurer's Remembrancer's
and Pipe Offices

E 356   Customs Accounts
E 358   Miscellaneous Accounts

Ministry of Agriculture, Fisheries and Food

MAF 68   Various, Agricultural Returns,
                Parish Summaries

Probate

Prerogative Court of Canterbury
PROB 4   Parchment Inventories post
                1660

Special Collections

SC 2   Court Rolls
SC 6   Ministers' and Receivers'
             Accounts
SC 12   Rentals and Surveys

Court of Star Chamber

Proceedings
STAC 2   Hen. VIII
STAC 3   Edw. VI

SELECT LIST OF ACCUMULATIONS AND COLLECTIONS IN THE SHROPSHIRE RECORD OFFICE

USED IN THIS VOLUME

Official Archives

207	Shropshire War Agricultural committees
294, 3898	Much Wenlock parish
356	Ludlow corporation
1335	Shifnal parish
1831	Shrewsbury Drapers' Co.
1900	Newport urban district council
2106	Ruyton in the Eleven Towns parish
2151	Chetwynd parish
2280	Madeley parish
3067	Stockton parish
3365	Shrewsbury corporation
	Shropshire (formerly Salop) County Council
3763	Victoria History of Shropshire
4449	County Valuer and Land Agent
3916	Archdeacon of Salop
4001	Bridgnorth corporation
4687	West Felton parish

Family and Estate Archives

2	Sandford of Sandford
5	Walcot, formerly of Walcot and Bitterley
20	Oakly Park estate
38, 972	The duke of Sutherland
81	Leeke of Longford
93	Edwards of Great Ness
99	Wakeman of Yeaton Peverey
103	LLoyd of Leaton Knolls
112	Noel-Hill of Attingham
167, 168	Lord Barnard
212, 611	Bridgwater estate
231	Woodcote Hall estate
322	Corbet of Acton Reynald
327, 1096	Corbet of Adderley
465	Sandford of the Isle
482	Cholmondeley of Condover
513	Cure of Badger
552, 1043, 1635	The earl of Powis
567	Corbett of Longnor
631	Price-Davies of Marrington
665	Eyton of Eyton upon the Weald Moors
735	Montford estate
807	Bright of Totterton

809	Benson of Lutwyche
840	Tyrwhitt-Jones of Stanley Hall
894	Hanmer of Pentre-pant
946	Shavington estate
1037	More of Linley
1093	Aldenham Park estate
1224	Lord Forester
1514	Bruce-Smythe of Acton Burnell
1696	Borough of Chetwynd Park
1952	Kenyon-Slaney of Hatton Grange
2028, 2029	Boycott of Rudge
2713	Davenport House estate
2868	Leighton of Sweeney
2919	Corser of Bletchley
2922	Lady Labouchere
3075	Silvington estate
3320	Childe of Kinlet
3657	Weston Park estate

Solicitors' Accumulations

426	Norris & Miles of Tenbury
497	G. H. Morgan & Sons of Shrewsbury
731	Henry Lee, Bygott & Eccleston of Wem
783	G. H. Morgan & Sons of Ludlow
933	Peele & Aris of Shrewsbury
938	Curtler & Hallmark of Worcester
1011	Salt & Sons of Shrewsbury
1190	Pitt & Cooksey of Bridgnorth
1681	Cooper & Co. of Broseley
3651	Salt & Sons (later Wace, Morgan & Salt) of Shrewsbury

Other Archives

3510	Benson & Rogers-Coltman
4531	National Farmers' Union Shropshire County Branch
4752	Nock, Deighton & Son

Artificial Collections

89	Hardy & Reckitt
566	Coalbrookdale Archives Association
837	British Records Association
3195	Sir Thomas Phillipps
3375, 4064	Mr. H. D. G. Foxall

NOTE ON ABBREVIATIONS

Among the abbreviations and short titles used the following may require elucidation:

Ag. Hist. Eng.	*The Agrarian History of England and Wales*, i–ii, iv–v, viii, ed. H. P. R. Finberg and J. Thirsk (1967–88)
Agric. H.R.	*Agricultural History Review*
Ann. Mon. (Rolls Ser.)	*Annales Monastici*, ed. H. R. Luard (5 vols., Rolls Ser. 1864–9)
Arch. Jnl.	*Archaeological Journal*
B.L.	British Library
B.M.	British Museum
Bk. of Fees	*The Book of Fees* (3 vols. H.M.S.O. 1920–31)
Bodl.	Bodleian Library, Oxford
Brit. Arch. Rep.	British Archaeological Reports
Bull. Inst. Hist. Res.	*Bulletin of the Institute of Historical Research*
Burke, *Land. Gent.*	J. and J. B. Burke and others, *A Genealogical and Heraldic Dictionary* (later *History*) *of the Landed Gentry* (1843–1972)
Burke, *Peerage*	J. Burke and others, *A General* (later *Genealogical*) *and Heraldic Dictionary* (later *History*) *of the Peerage* (1826–1970)
Bye-Gones	*Bye-Gones relating to Wales and the Border Counties* (Oswestry, [1871–1940])
Cal. Chart. R.	*Calendar of the Charter Rolls preserved in the Public Record Office* (H.M.S.O. 1903–27)
Cal. Close	*Calendar of the Close Rolls preserved in the Public Record Office* (H.M.S.O. 1892–1963)
Cal. Inq. Misc.	*Calendar of Inquisitions Miscellaneous (Chancery) preserved in the Public Record Office* (H.M.S.O. 1916–69)
Cal. Inq. p.m.	*Calendar of Inquisitions post mortem preserved in the Public Record Office* (H.M.S.O. 1904–in progress)
Cal. Pat.	*Calendar of the Patent Rolls preserved in the Public Record Office* (H.M.S.O. 1891–in progress)
Camd. Soc.	Camden Society
Census	Census report (printed)
Close R.	*Close Rolls of the Reign of Henry III preserved in the Public Record Office* (H.M.S.O. 1902–75)
Complete Peerage	G. E. C[okayne] and others, *The Complete Peerage* (2nd edn., 13 vols. 1910–59)
Compton Census, ed. Whiteman	*The Compton Census of 1676: a critical edition*, ed. A. Whiteman (British Academy Records of Social and Economic History, N.S. x, 1986)
D.N.B.	*Dictionary of National Biography*
Dict. Welsh Biog.	*The Dictionary of Welsh Biography down to 1940* (Honourable Society of Cymmrodorion; 1959 edn.)
E.H.R.	*English Historical Review*
Econ. H.R.	*Economic History Review*
Eyton	R. W. Eyton, *Antiquities of Shropshire* (12 vols. 1854–60)
G.E.C. *Baronetage*	G. E. C[okayne], *Complete Baronetage* (6 vols. 1900–9)
Gent. Mag.	*The Gentleman's Magazine* (1731–1867)
H.W.R.O.(H.)	Hereford and Worcester Record Office (Hereford)
Hist. Parl., Commons	*The History of Parliament: The House of Commons*, 1509–58, ed. S. T. Bindoff (3 vols. 1982); 1558–1603, ed. P. W. Hasler (3 vols. 1981); 1715–54, ed. R. Sedgwick (2 vols. 1970); 1754–90, ed. L. Namier and J. Brooke (3 vols. 1964)
I.G.M.T.	Ironbridge Gorge Museum Trust
Ind. Arch. Rev.	*Industrial Archaeology Review*
Inq. Non. (Rec. Com.)	*Nonarum Inquisitiones in Curia Scaccarii*, ed. G. Vanderzee (Record Commission, 1807)

NOTE ON ABBREVIATIONS

J.R.A.S.E.	*Journal of the Royal Agricultural Society of England*
Jnl. Brit. Arch. Assoc.	*Journal of the British Archaeological Association*
L. & P. Hen. VIII	*Letters and Papers, Foreign and Domestic, of the Reign of Henry VIII* (H.M.S.O. 1864–1932)
L.J.	*Journals of the House of Lords*
L.J.R.O.	Lichfield Joint Record Office
Leland, *Itin.* ed. Toulmin Smith	*The Itinerary of John Leland*, ed. L. Toulmin Smith (5 vols. 1906–8)
Lond. Gaz.	*London Gazette*
Med. Arch.	*Medieval Archaeology*
Mont. Colln.	*Montgomeryshire Collections: Journal of the Powysland Club*
N.L.W.	National Library of Wales, Aberystwyth
O.S.	Ordnance Survey
Orders of Q. Sess.	*Abstract of the Orders made by the Court of Quarter Sessions for Shropshire*, ed. R. Ll. Kenyon and Sir Offley Wakeman (Shropshire County Records nos. 2–5, 7, 9, 11–17 [Shrewsbury, 1901–16])
P.R.O.	Public Record Office (see p. xvi)
P.R.S.	Pipe Roll Society
Pipe R.	*Pipe Rolls*
R.H.S.	Royal Historical Society
R.O.	Record Office
Rec. Bucks.	*Records of Buckinghamshire*
Rot. Hund. (Rec. Com.)	*Rotuli Hundredorum temp. Hen. III et Edw. I in Turri Londinensi et in Curia Receptae Scaccarii West. asservati*, ed. W. Illingworth and J. Caley (2 vols. Record Commission, 1812–18)
Rot. Parl.	*Rotuli Parliamentorum* (6 vols. [1783])
S.C.C.	Shropshire (formerly Salop) County Council
S.M.R.	Shropshire Sites and Monuments Record, S.C.C. Property and Planning Services Department. Information cited by primary record number prefixed with SA
S.P.L.	Local Studies Library, Shrewsbury (formerly Shrewsbury Public Library)
S.P.R.	*Shropshire Parish Registers*
S.R.O.	Shropshire Record Office (see p. xvii)
SA	See above, S.M.R.
T.C.S.V.F.C.	*Transactions of the Caradoc and Severn Valley Field Club*
T.S.A.S.	*Transactions of the Shropshire Archaeological and Historical Society*
Tax. Eccl. (Rec. Com.)	*Taxatio Ecclesiastica Angliae et Walliae auctoritate P. Nicholai IV, circa A.D. 1291*, ed. T. Astle, S. Ayscough, and J. Caley (Record Commission, 1802)
V.C.H.	*Victoria History of the Counties of England*
Visit. Salop. 1623	*The Visitation of Shropshire, taken in the Year 1623* (Harleian Society, xxviii–xxix, 1889)
W.S.L.	William Salt Library, Stafford
Yr. Bk.	*Year Book*

AGRICULTURE

NOTWITHSTANDING its important role in the 18th-century Industrial Revolution,[1] Shropshire was mainly an agricultural county until recent times. From the first practice of agriculture in Neolithic times until the later 20th century the county's population was predominantly rural, though long before the 1960s it was a dwindling minority that earned its livelihood or drew its rents from the profits of farming.[2] Even in the later 20th century, when *c.* 44 per cent of Shropshire people lived in the two main towns of Shrewsbury and Telford, the county's landscape remained largely rural and agricultural.[3]

The main crises in the long history of Shropshire agriculture and rural landed society naturally coincided with those that affected the nation. The severest crises were those that came most suddenly, as in 1066 when the English landowning class was largely dispossessed, in 1349 when the Black Death brought demographic disaster and the beginnings of profound social and economic change, in 1536–40 when the monasteries were dissolved and their great landed estates confiscated, in the 1870s when cereal prices collapsed, and *c.* 1910–25 when many great landlords, to their tenants' alarm, sold off their estates. The consequences in Shropshire of such crises, and of the secular changes that they engendered, are among the themes treated below. Of necessity the story is not continued beyond *c.* 1985, a date which, though fortuitous, is by no means an unsatisfactory point at which to break off. In the mid 1980s, as perhaps never before, farming was subject to strong and bewilderingly contrary political, social, and technological pressures, some explicit, some subtle. The perspectives of the 1980s, too short to yield any confident prediction of the resolution of those pressures, have nevertheless suggested that some of the more important of them—themes for a future historian of agriculture—result from a faltering of confidence in the immediate economic future of farming and from a redefinition of relationships between agriculturists and the general public over the exploitation and conservation of the countryside.[4]

The prosperity of British agriculture was continuously fostered by successive governments after the Second World War,[5] and for a decade after 1973, when the United Kingdom became a member of the European Economic Community (E.E.C.),[6] the community's common agricultural policy (C.A.P.) seemed to promise a continuation of that support. The farmer was supported so that he might maximize his output. In the spring of 1984, however, the E.E.C. set limits to milk production by introducing quotas. In Shropshire, as elsewhere, the immediate practical effects were not dramatic: the number of registered milk producers in the county, for example, fell from 1,382 to 1,347 in the year 1986–7 but 11 million (2 per cent) more litres of milk were sold off Shropshire farms in 1986–7 than in 1985–6.[7] The quotas, however, were a psychological shock, and one not merely to

[1] *V.C.H. Salop.* xi, 1, 22–3; B. Trinder, *Ind. Rev. Salop.* (1981).

[2] In 1961 almost 51 per cent of the co. pop. lived in boros. or U.D.s but M. Wenlock boro. included several rural pars.: *V.C.H. Salop.* ii. 219–29; iii. 179. In 1881 just 11.1 per cent of the Salop. working pop. was employed in agric.: *Census.*

[3] Inf. from S.C.C. Property and Planning Services Dept. But cf. *The Independent Mag.* 26 Nov. 1988, pp. 62, 64, 66.

[4] J. Blunden and N. Curry, *A Future for Our Countryside* (1988).

[5] B. A. Holderness, *Brit. Agric. since 1945* (1985).

[6] European Communities Act, 1972, c. 68.

[7] Inf. from Milk Marketing Bd.

milk producers but to the whole farming community.[8] For the first time in a generation some farmers were being asked to restrain production, and those who were building the E.E.C.'s wheat mountain had reason to fear that they, like contributors to the butter mountain, would in due course have to reverse direction. In the western half of England dramatically increased yields from new strains of wheat and high C.A.P. intervention prices had made winter wheat a reliable and profitable crop to be stored in intervention warehouses[9] like those at Prees Heath. In the 1980s, however, the C.A.P. was under attack throughout Europe and, despite the apparent impossibility of its reform, it seemed to offer the farmer progressively less certainty for the future as the 'single European market' planned for 1992 drew nearer.[10] British farm incomes began to falter about the same time. In 1982 they increased by a record 45 per cent, but at the end of 1984 they were said to be 8 per cent below the 1982 level. In 1988 the government introduced a 'set-aside' scheme intended to reduce arable crop surpluses, and particularly the growing of cereals on relatively marginal land. For a five-year period payments of up to £200 a hectare were to be available to farmers who took at least 20 per cent of their arable land out of production. Land set aside had either to be left fallow, planted as woodland, or used for certain specified non-agricultural purposes mostly linked with leisure and tourism. In 1988 the set-aside premiums offered were not high enough to induce the county's farmers to take land out of production immediately; nevertheless many farmers did register their land for possible set-aside in the course of the five-year period, seeing it as a useful option in the event of cereal prices falling.[11]

As farm incomes were checked and the value of agricultural land fell in the mid 1980s[12] farmers were coming to feel that they were increasingly under pressure from the advocates of 'green', conservationist, or environmental policies.[13] The use of fertilizers and weedkillers, for example, aroused particular alarm from time to time, and in 1986 the Shropshire Association of Parish and Town Councils called for a tightening of the regulations concerning crop spraying.[14] Large-scale drainage schemes enhancing the value of farm land were resented by some as unwarranted interference with the landscape at public expense and evidence of a 'cosy relationship between the Ministry of Agriculture and the water authorities to grow crops for which there is no market'.[15] Nevertheless it was by no means true that relations between the water authorities and the farmers were inevitably cosy: the Severn–Trent Water Authority's Shropshire Groundwater Scheme, developed from 1981, was at first very vigorously opposed by the county branch of the National Farmers' Union.[16] Nor was it the case that issues raised by conservationist policies automatically divided farmers and conservationists into opposing camps. On the one hand there were conservationists who were unhappy with the working of the 1981 Wildlife and Countryside Act[17] while on the other hand there were farmers and landowners who welcomed conservationist policies out of regard for

[8] As was evident at the 96th Salop. & W. Midlands Agric. Soc. show 16–17 May 1984.

[9] Demonstration on 'The Farm 1934–84' at 96th Salop. & W. Midlands Agric. Soc. show; *The Changing Countryside*, ed. J. Blunden and N. Curry (1985), 29, 37.

[10] Inf. (1988) from Mr. R. D. Park, principal of Salop. Fm. Inst., Walford, 1949–79.

[11] *Sunday Times*, 27 Feb. 1983, p. 13; *The Guardian*, 16 Jan. 1985, p. 3; *Set Aside* (Min. of Agric., Fish. and Food 1988); inf. from Min. of Agric. and N.F.U.

[12] Inf. from S.C.C. Property and Planning Services Dept.

and from local land agents.

[13] The results of a movement that had been growing in strength since the appearance of Rachel Carson's *Silent Spring* (1962): *The Guardian*, 30 Jan. 1986, p. 19.

[14] *Shropshire Star*, 25 Nov. 1986, p. 15.

[15] *Co. Councils Gaz.* Oct. 1983, 228; *Shrews. Chron.* 27 July 1984, p. 15; *Shropshire Star*, 26 Feb. 1985, p. 14.

[16] *Shropshire Star*, 23 Sept. (p. 11), 1 Dec. 1978; *Shrews. Chron.* 20 July 1984, p. 37.

[17] *The Guardian*, 30 July 1984.

their land[18] and as a way of increasing their incomes or diversifying their sources of income.[19] By 1988 Shropshire contained *c*. 80 sites of special scientific interest (S.S.S.I.s) and some two dozen farmers or landowners in the county had by then received payments or compensation ('for profits forgone') under the 1981 Act for managing or not disrupting areas in those sites: typical payments were those for agreed methods of woodland management, for leaving grassland unploughed or wetlands undrained, and for relinquishing the use of pesticides and fertilizers.[20]

There were of course from time to time straightforward conflicts between conservationists and farmers when particular sites were ploughed or drained, perhaps because the 1981 Act was being put into effect too slowly to bring prompt protection to many of the S.S.S.I.s. Efforts were, however, made to bring farmers and conservationists together regularly, and by 1984 the Shropshire Farming and Wildlife Advisory Group had been formed to that end.[21] What seemed to hold out hope of some eventual success for such efforts was the fact that in a period of economic uncertainty two related and increasingly urgent questions were acknowledged to require answers from both agriculturists and conservationists: how intensively should resources of land and water be exploited for agriculture when too much food was being produced, and how could some proportion of those same resources be put to profitable, non-agricultural uses? Some possible answers were beginning to emerge in practice. Agricultural diversification[22] was one, and there was increasing local evidence of it.[23] At the Lynches farm, Yockleton, for example, 'Butterfly World' opened in 1984, and by 1988 (renamed 'Country World') it attracted thousands of visitors a year not only to see butterflies but to study old livestock and poultry breeds and areas of conserved meadow on the edge of the working farm.[24] Flower and herb farming was being tried in more and more places,[25] and by 1988 there was deer farming at Webscott farm near Myddle and at Walford College of Agriculture, and milking ewes were kept at Wackley farm, Petton;[26] Shropshire then had at least one snail farm too.[27]

Another way in which conservationist policies and the interests of agriculturists were beginning to come together was evident from the many conversions of redundant farm buildings for domestic or tourist accommodation.[28] Increasingly during the 1980s those concerned with conserving the countryside's architectural heritage had been expressing concern at the loss of old farm buildings.[29] By 1988, however, many Shropshire landowners and farmers were realizing much additional capital or income from their surplus buildings, then at last recognized as very considerable assets.[30]

The Shropshire countryside is varied and diverse. No form of agriculture has ever been predominant throughout the country, and in recent centuries the county's traditions of mixed husbandry have engendered flexible responses to even the

[18] e.g. the Wykes of Foxhill Fm., Shelve: ibid. 17 Nov. 1983, p. 16.

[19] For the local hill farmers' disappointment when the Clun valley failed to secure designation as an environmentally sensitive area see *Shropshire Star*, 15 Aug. 1986, p. 14.

[20] Inf. from Nature Conservancy, Attingham.

[21] Cf. *The Guardian*, 17 Nov. 1983, p. 16; *Shrews. Chron.* 20 July 1984, p. 37.

[22] Practised in earlier periods of economic uncertainty: *Eng. Landscape, Past, Present, and Future*, ed. S. R. J. Woodell (1985), 129-47.

[23] In 1988 the Farm Diversification competition organized by the Salop. & W. Midlands Agric. Soc. attracted a 'huge entry': *West Mid 100* (Salop. Weekly Newspapers special suppl. May 1988), p. 4.

[24] *Shrews. Chron.* 19 Apr. 1984, p. 2; local inf.

[25] e.g. at Laundry fm., Nesscliff (*Shropshire Star*, 10 Nov. 1984, pp. 20-1), and at Lydbury North (*West Mid 100*, pp. 1, 4). Daffodils were being grown in Lilleshall by 1979: *V.C.H. Salop.* xi. 160.

[26] Local inf. [27] Inf. from Mr. Park.

[28] Abundant local evid. Cf. the remarks of A. E. H. Heber-Percy, pres. Salop. & W. Midlands Agric. Soc. 1988, on tourism and the farming world: *West Mid 100*, p. 3.

[29] See e.g. *Shropshire Star*, 10 Nov. 1984, p. 13, for rep. of seminar on fm. bldgs. past, present, and future, organized by S.C.C. Planning Dept. and attended by representatives of many organizations. The Country Landowners' Assoc. ran a fm. bldgs. award scheme: see e.g. ibid. 6 Feb. 1986, p. 14.

[30] Abundant local evid. Cf. Dept. of Environment planning policy guideline note 7 (Jan. 1988).

severest crisis. There were some signs in the mid 1980s of a similar flexibility of effort to ensure that the prosperity of farming and the manifold life of the countryside should continue to flourish.

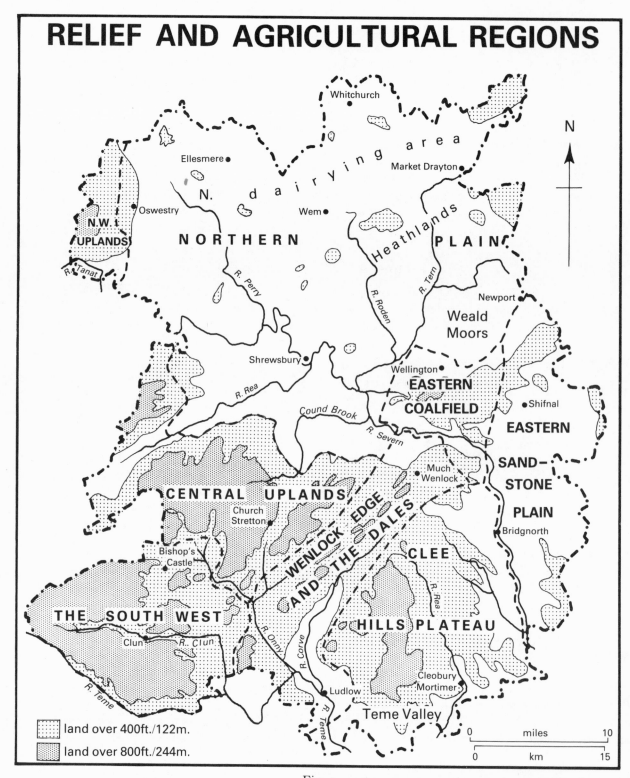

Fig. 1

The county boundary is modern (pre-1965). Regions based on sources for following article: see especially E. J. Howell, *Salop.* (Land of Britain, lxvi), 246; cf. W. W. Watts, *Salop.: Geog. of the Co.* (Shrews. 1919), 17; W. J. Slack, 'Hist. Agric. and Enclosure in Salop.' (*c.* 1953), cap. i (TS. in S.R.O. 3763/19/1); S.R.O. 3763/20/4; *Domesday Geog. of Midland Eng.* ed. H. C. Darby and I. B. Terrett (1971), 155; T. Rowley, *Salop. Landscape* (1972), 23.

THE PHYSICAL
ENVIRONMENT

SHROPSHIRE divides naturally into two halves whose contrasting physical characteristics[31] provide the controlling conditions for agriculture. The Severn, flowing south-east through the county from Melverley to Alveley, drains virtually all Shropshire[32] and almost everywhere[33] marks a convenient boundary between the two halves. South and west of the river is an upland country of Palaeozoic rocks, forming the greater part of the Welsh border hills and in the west including the eastern edge of the central Welsh plateau. It is a land of hills and ridges ('edges') separated by dales and drained by rivers and brooks for the most part of no great size; in the west it gives way to the plateau dissected by the river Clun. By contrast the eastern and northern regions of the county are part of the wide rolling plain formed by the foundering of the Palaeozoic floor in early Mesozoic time; it extends into mid Staffordshire and Cheshire and forms one of the principal lowland interruptions of highland Britain. The Shropshire portion of the plain, like the Staffordshire and Cheshire portions, is interrupted here and there by sandstone hills[34] which do not, however, alter the essentially gentle landscape characteristics which link it with the English midlands. In north-west Shropshire the plain runs up to the foothills of the Berwyn Mountains and an abrupt change to a Welsh upland landscape.

Rich in the great variety of its geology, Shropshire features most of the geological periods, and in more recent geological times glaciation has had profound effects. During the last major glaciation, from about 40,000 B.C., two great ice sheets, known as the Irish Sea Ice and the Welsh Ice, were active in the Shropshire area. By erosion, deposition of debris (gathered from as far as Scotland and the Lake District), and drainage diversions, important modifications of the landscape occurred. Though the upper soil coverage often closely reflects the underlying solid or drift geology, the effects of climate, relief, and vegetation sometimes

[31] Except where otherwise stated, this article is based on evidence from the rest of this volume and on the following main sources: J. R. Earp and N. A. Hains, *Welsh Borderland* (Brit. Regional Geol. 1971); R. Millward and A. Robinson, *Welsh Marches* (1971); idem, *Welsh Borders* (1978); T. Rowley, *Salop. Landscape* (1972); A. E. Trueman, *Geol. and Scenery in Eng. and Wales* (1971); J. E. Wright, *Geol. of Ch. Stretton Area* (Mem. Geol. Surv. 1968); D. C. Greigg and others, *Geol. of Country around Ch. Stretton, Craven Arms, Wenlock Edge and Brown Clee* (Mem. Geol. Surv. 1968); I. D. Mercer, 'Geog. of Alberbury Breccia', *Field Studies*, i (1), 102-15; D. L. Dineley, 'Salop. Geol.: Outline of the Tectonic Hist.' ibid. i (2), 86-108; C. A. Sinker, 'N. Salop. Meres and Mosses: a Background for Ecologists', ibid. i (4), 101-38; C. P. Burnham and D. Mackney, 'Soils of Salop.' ibid. ii (1), 83-113, with map 'Soil Assocs. of Salop.'; P. Toghill and K. Chell, 'Salop. Geol.: Stratigraphic and Tectonic Hist.' ibid. vi. 59-101; J. Norton, *Geol. of Ludlow Area of Salop.–Herefs. Border* (Salop. Co. Mus. Publn. ii, 1975); idem, *Geol. of Wenlock Edge Dist.* (Co. Mus. Publn. iv, 1980); D. Mackney and C. P. Burnham, *Soils of W. Midlands* (Soil Surv. Bull. ii, Harpenden, 1965); J. M. Hodgson, *Soils of the Ludlow Dist.* (*Sheet 181*) (Mem. Soil Surv. of Gt. Brit. 1972). Mr. A. A. Kean is thanked for his comments on this article.

[32] Small northern areas drain to the Dee and (via the Weaver) Mersey; two very small eastern areas in Donington and Tong, and possibly an even smaller area in Albrighton, drain to the Trent system: *V.C.H. Salop.* i. 58-60, and map facing p. 51; *T.S.A.S.* 4th ser. vi. 123-6.

[33] Geologically and scenically the Wrekin and the E. Salop. coalfield seem an extension of S. Salop. over the Severn, and the N. plain includes an area S. of the river running W. from Cressage to Westbury: E. J. Howell, *Salop.* (Land of Britain, lxvi), 207; *V.C.H. Salop.* viii. 1, 178; xi. 104; W. J. Slack, 'Hist. Agric. and Enclosure in Salop.' (c. 1953), cap. i, p. 4 (TS. in S.R.O. 3763/19/1); below. W. J. Slack (1897-1954) was a successful farmer until his retirement in 1947 and from c. 1935 also studied the county's agrarian hist.; at the time of his death he was writing the hist. of agric. and inclosure cited above: *T.S.A.S.* lv. 106-8 (obit. listing his published work); S.R.O. 3763/18/1, corresp. Slack's drafts (versions of which survive in S.R.O. 2118/168; 3763/19/1), notes, and collections of material (S.R.O. 2321; 3763/18/1; 3763/20/1-14) have been of considerable value during the preparation of this vol.

[34] *V.C.H. Ches.* i. 2-4; *V.C.H. Salop.* i, maps facing p. 1 and betw. pp. 22-3; *V.C.H. Staffs.* i, maps facing p. 1 and betw. pp. 24 and 25.

5

produce different soils on similar rocks. Western Shropshire, mostly in the upland regions, has significantly higher rainfall than the eastern parts of the county[35] and the lighter, better drained soils are found mainly in the east too. In terms of soil types, agricultural use, and settlement pattern therefore the county cannot be divided into natural regions simply on the basis of relief. A consideration of geology, relief, soils, climate, and drainage, however, enables a more accurate picture of the Shropshire environment to emerge and reveals eight major regions with a number of sub-regions.

SOUTH SHROPSHIRE

South Shropshire seems capable of minute division into sub-regions: 'every ridge and dale...is highly individual in both its structure and relief, as are the Clee Hills to the east and the mass of Clun Forest to the south-west. Innumerable *pays* here form perfect examples of the French concept of small sub-regions.'[36] Despite the area's complexity, however, a broad division does seem possible, and the regions between the Worcestershire boundary and the Stretton Hills may be distinguished from those further west extending to the Welsh border.

The Clee Hills plateau

In the Devonian period the recent closure of the Iapetus Ocean left a continental mass with mountains over central and northern Britain, and to the south a retreating sea. Old Red Sandstone, the non-marine facies of the Devonian, forms a wide triangular plateau around the peaks of the Clee Hills. The Clees are the eastern outpost of the Welsh border hills towards the midland plains. Two table-topped masses rise from the broad Old Red Sandstone plateau. They are the Titterstone Clee (533 m.) and, to the north, the Brown Clee with its twin knolls of Clee Burf and Abdon Burf (545 m.), the highest land in Shropshire. Outcrops of Carboniferous Millstone Grit and Lower and Middle Coal Measures form the base of the Clee Hills, which are capped by thick layers of volcanic dolerite or basalt (the black 'Dhu Stone').[37] At Titterstone Clee a narrow band of Carboniferous Limestone encompasses the northern and southern flank of the hill. The sandstone plateau tilts down to the south-east where, in the valley of the Borle brook, the Lower and Middle Coal Measures are encountered again at Highley and Kinlet on the northern edge of Wyre forest.[38]

The plateau supports a large area of leached brown soils, sometimes with gleying, which can cause waterlogging. There is little drift on the plateau, however, and the sandstone decomposes and weathers easily into marl producing silty loam over silty clay loam. The porosity of the underlying rock and the undulating landform provide some natural drainage,[39] and rich brown earths are found as high as 335 m. on the Brown Clee.[40] Early settlers favoured both the defensible summits of the Clee Hills (crowned with forts in the Iron Age) and the loams of the alluvial silts and clays in the valleys.[41] The plateau itself, however, was capable of cultivation,

[35] Howell, *Salop.* 211–15.

[36] D. Sylvester, *Rural Landscape of the Welsh Borderland: A Study in Historical Geog.* (1969), 319.

[37] *V.C.H. Salop.* i. 34, and map facing p. 1.

[38] Ibid. 23 sqq., 33–4, and map facing p. 1; Howell, *Salop.* 238, 246.

[39] Slack, 'Hist. Agric. in Salop.' cap. i, pp. 11–12 (copy in S.R.O. 3763/19/1).

[40] R. T. Rowley, 'Hist. of S. Salop. Landscape 1086–1800' (Oxf. Univ. B.Litt. thesis, 1967), 6.

[41] *V.C.H. Salop.* i. 359, 371–2; *Domesday Geog. of Midland Eng.* ed. H. C. Darby and I. B. Terrett (1971), 157.

though more adapted to grass and cereals than to fruit or roots. The predominant soil types on the outcrop of Coal Measures to the east are acid-brown and surface-water gley soils; those soils also occur on the slopes of Titterstone Clee where fine-textured head containing occasional dolerite boulders occurs. The soil is poorly drained and of a sandy loam or loam or clay texture. The summits of the Clees show areas of well drained acid-brown soils and podzolized soils, but altitude, slope, and the thin, shallow, infertile soils, often wet or stony, produce only poor vegetation and rough moorland grazing, much of it still uninclosed in the 1980s.[42] The platforms surrounding the summits tend to support surface-water gley soils or peaty gley podzols. The Brown Clee is pocked with small spoil banks of coal shale and waterlogged man-made holes. The heavy leaching of the podzols and acid-brown soils restricts their agricultural use, though grass and cereals can be grown. In south Shropshire generally the cattle–corn economy flourished mainly in the valleys until the late 18th century but during the wars of 1793–1815 the need for more home-grown cereals caused a great extension of arable in the region[43] and gained for it the name 'Wheatland'; the name—used in Bridgnorth c. 1740 to distinguish lands west of the Severn from those on the east (the Ryeland)—indicated that wheat was the chief cereal that could be grown in the area.[44] The fall in corn prices after the 1870s caused most of the area's arable to be laid down to grass by c. 1900, primarily for the raising of store cattle. By the late 1930s a sparse though fairly even distribution of small arable fields did not detract from the region's character as a major stretch of improved grassland.[45] It is the flatter lands over the sandstone plateau that tend to be used for arable, while the steeper valley sides are fit only for rough grazing. Thin arms of richer brown warp and ground-water gley soils intrude into the plateau wherever riverine alluvial silts and clays have built up.

A significant sub-region is formed by the southern slopes of the plateau dropping down to the Teme valley. The area eventually became a small extension of the Herefordshire and Worcestershire cereal and fruit-growing region. The area's geology and soil are the same as those of the plateau to the north and the advance of mixed farming that was achieved by c. 1750, with good cereal acreages (including winter corn), the spread of hopyards, and the growth of new crops like clover and turnips, doubtless owed much to the southern aspect of the land. Orchards were spread over some 10–20 per cent of the farm land by the late 1930s.[46] Oast houses remained a common feature of the landscape in the early 1950s but only a very small acreage of hops was then grown.[47] The meadows and pastures of the Teme and the South Rea valleys also favoured some dairying.

Wenlock Edge and the dales

The region, encompassing all the land between the Clee Hills plateau in the east and the south Shropshire uplands and south-west Shropshire in the west, is one of very varied relief, an undulating landscape composed of the ridge of Aymestry Limestone bounding Corve Dale on the west and the parallel Wenlock Edge, with Corve Dale, Hope Dale, and Ape Dale intervening. A picturesque and well settled

[42] Howell, *Salop.* 237, 246, 252; S.C.C. Ch. Exec.'s Dept., commons reg. nos. CL 4, 8, 10–13, 17, 20, 49, 72.

[43] Howell, *Salop.* 280–1; W. Watkins-Pitchford to H. D. G. Foxall 2 Sept. 1936 (copy in S.R.O. 3763/123/3).

[44] Howell, *Salop.* 253; Slack, 'Hist. Agric. in Salop.' cap. ii, pp. 4–5 (copy in S.R.O. 2118/168); *T.S.A.S.* ix. 204–5.

Hunting men adopted the name for the area in the earlier 19th cent.: *V.C.H. Salop.* ii. 171, 175–6.

[45] Howell, *Salop.* 225–6, 232, 252–3.

[46] Ibid. 240–1, 246, 253, 255.

[47] Slack, 'Hist. Agric. in Salop.' cap. ii, p. 6 (copy in S.R.O. 2118/168).

area, a regular belt of scarp and vale topography running SSW.–NNE. in line with the Church Stretton Fault, it is broken at its southern end by the plunging Ludlow anticline. Corve Dale runs down almost 20 km. south-west from its head near Bourton, in Much Wenlock, to Stanton Lacy; there it opens into a plain between Onibury and Ludlow, where the Onny and the Corve flow into the Teme. Westwards the intermontane plain and Corve Dale are bounded by the Upper Silurian Ludlow beds which form the limestone hills of Stokesay and Onibury parishes and the long escarpment of Wenlock Edge.[48] Much visited and well recorded by geologists, the area displays a folding of the limestone and shale beds forming curving infacing escarpments surrounding the lowland Wigmore Basin, just in Herefordshire; it contains classic Silurian outcrops whose fossils have led to significant discoveries in the geological and tectonic history of southern Britain. The succession of SSW.–NNE. scarps and dales is based on underlying Silurian rocks of varying hardness. All are beds of a shallow-water shelf facies formed under marine conditions, with the sea gradually retreating at the end of the period. Southern Britain then lay south of the equator but was drifting north. Some of the region's fossil beds have yielded important insights into the climatic and marine conditions then affecting Britain.

At the western escarpment[49] of the Clee Hills plateau the Old Red Sandstone is thrown down to form the floor of Corve Dale. The redness of the ploughed fields on the dale's eastern side derives from the non-marine Downtonian sandstones and marls before the Silurian Upper Ludlow siltstones and limestones emerge; those formations have been reclassified as Leintwardinian and Whitcliffian Beds, mainly through the identification of their fossils. There is a change from marine to non-marine facies at the top of the Upper Ludlow Shales or Whitcliffe Beds as witnessed by the appearance of gastropods and bivalves in the area. Immediately above the Upper Whitcliffe Beds lies the famous Ludlow Bone Bed, once viewed as the Devonian base but now placed at the end of the Silurian. The bed is made almost entirely of organic remains and contains the earliest sizeable grouping of British vertebrate fossils.

On the west Corve Dale is bounded by the escarpment of emerging Aymestry Limestone now known as the Bringewood Beds. Owing to faulting the scarp is frequently dissected by the valleys of streams. Beyond, to the west, lies Hope Dale, a valley or step feature based on the older, softer beds of Lower Ludlow Shales, now reclassified as Eltonian Beds. The Bringewood Beds contain thick shell banks in places but only solitary corals; Wenlock Edge, however, the succeeding parallel ridge of richly fossiliferous Much Wenlock Limestone, contains corals built up into a patch reef facies. The Wenlock Limestone has resisted erosion longer than the softer shales which (topographically and in geological time) lie either side of it. Wenlock Edge therefore stands proud of Hope Dale (Eltonian shales) and Ape Dale (Buildwas and Coalbrookdale shales), forming a straight ridge running 40 km. north-east from Craven Arms to Much Wenlock. It is unbroken for many kilometres, though in places dissected by valleys of streams draining (through the more frequent gaps in the Aymestry Limestone ridge) to the Corve. Both limestone scarps have been quarried and both are extensively wooded, though with bare grey crags on the summits.

The wooded scarp of Wenlock Edge is regarded as an outstandingly beautiful

[48] Ibid. For the dist.'s relief and drainage see O.S. Map 1/25,000, SJ 50, 60; ibid. SO 47–9, 57–9, 69 (1956–7 edns.); for its geol. see *V.C.H. Salop.* i, map facing p. 1.

[49] Esp. pronounced at the N. end: Rowley, 'S. Salop. Landscape', 2.

part of the county; nevertheless its heights, even though they rise to no more than *c.* 300 m., can be severe and inhospitable. On the upper slopes of Wenlock Edge and in Ape Dale and the Plaish brook[50] valley the typical soils, derived from silty shales and naturally poorly or imperfectly drained, are brown silt loams over silty clay loam.[51] In Corve Dale the valley floor is alluvial over the Old Red Sandstone[52] and there are silty loams and good heavy red soils. The central raised sandstone ridge offers drier sites for settlement, situated as it is above the damp river pastures. In the region as a whole there are few obvious signs of prehistoric lowland settlement, though there is evidence of prehistoric settlement on the alluvium around Bromfield and there was Roman settlement in Ape Dale and the Plaish brook valley and perhaps in Corve Dale too. Saxon settlement, possibly based on a residual Romano-British settlement pattern with Corfham (later a royal estate) as a nucleus, probably dates from the 7th or early 8th century[53] and most settlement in Corve Dale is on marl and gravel ridges.[54] Corve Dale is one of the more favoured parts of south Shropshire and in the mid 17th century, when there were large arable acreages, mixed farming was taking hold despite the persistence of open fields (albeit perhaps fragmented) on one large estate there. By the 1820s the Corve Dale farmers were prosperous by comparison with those on the Clee plateau.[55] Imperfect drainage gave rise to long-surviving areas of open waste,[56] but underdrainage, installed by one large Corve Dale landowner in the 1830s and 1840s,[57] enables good cereal crops to be grown and excellent grass,[58] and the area has rich fattening pastures and some very good arable land.[59]

Also of the Silurian era is the double horseshoe-shaped escarpment just west of Ludlow, caused by folding of the rocks during late Ludlovian times. The movement created uplift in the earth's surface in the area and is known as the Caledonian Orogeny. The corresponding syncline, or dip feature, is north-west of Ludlow.

The east Shropshire coalfield

The geology and relief of the coalfield and the Wrekin associate the region with south Shropshire rather than the north. The region's undulating plateaux, mostly over 122 m. and rising to 407 m. at the Wrekin summit, and its productive Coal Measures extend north from Shirlett across the Severn Gorge to Lilleshall and interpose a distinctive landscape between the plains of east and north Shropshire. On the east, near Kemberton and Priorslee, the Upper Coal Measures disappear beneath the Carboniferous (Permian) sandstones and marls that form the fringe of the eastern plain. On the north-west the Lower and Middle Coal Measures run up against the volcanic rocks of the Wrekin and its Cambrian and Silurian foothills; farther south they are faulted against the Silurian Upper Ludlow Shales. The western edge of the region, beyond the productive coalfield, is formed by the major Church Stretton Fault and the lesser Brockton Fault, and to the south-east lies another lesser fault, the Wrekin Fault. The Church Stretton Fault, like the Pontesford–Linley Fault farther west, was initiated during the Pre-Cambrian

[50] Named also from the villages it drains (Hughley, Harley, and Sheinton), the brook seems earlier to have been named, as low as Wigwig, from Plaish (cf. *V.C.H. Salop.* viii. 85; S.P.L., Deeds 18670), where it rises.

[51] The Speller and Stanway ser.: Rowley, op. cit. 4–6, fig. 3.

[52] Ibid 2; below, Early Agriculture. Continuing analysis of aerial photography of the 1980s is beginning to suggest extensive prehistoric use of lowland and gravel areas.

[53] Rowley, op. cit. 12–17; *V.C.H. Salop.* i. 261, 278; viii. 86.   [54] Rowley, op. cit. 5–6.

[55] J. P. Dodd, 'High Farming in Salop. 1845–70', *Midland Hist.* viii. 151.

[56] e.g. Balaam's Heath, Vernolds Common, Shortwood, and Oldfield Common: Rowley, op. cit. 5–6.

[57] The Hon. R. H. Clive.   [58] Rowley, op. cit. 4.

[59] Slack, 'Hist. Agric. in Salop.' cap. ii, p. 5 (copy in S.R.O. 2118/168).

period, and all Shropshire's Pre-Cambrian outcrops occur along the line of, or between, those two great fault systems. The metamorphic Rushton Schists, south-west of the Wrekin, are only a small outcrop but could be the basement to a larger area of Shropshire; they are probably older than the Pre-Cambrian volcanics and Longmyndian sedimentary rocks found west of the coalfield. An even smaller area of Pre-Cambrian metamorphics at the south-western end of the Wrekin displays Primrose Hill Gneisses and Schists similar to the Malvernian Gneisses. Later in the Pre-Cambrian sequence comes the igneous complex of Uriconian Volcanics occurring in two belts across the county. The eastern belt runs SSW.–NNE. along the Church Stretton Fault line. The northernmost outcrop is at Lilleshall, and more volcanic rocks occur on the Wrekin and the Ercall and also near Wrockwardine along the Brockton Fault.

During the Cambrian period Shropshire contained the shoreline of a still widening Iapetus Ocean, and the rocks of that period are mainly a shallow-water marine sequence. Like the Pre-Cambrian rocks, the Cambrian rocks are closely associated with the major fault systems running through the coalfield. The Cambrian period in the region is represented by the Wrekin quartzite and a large area of Shineton Shales extending from a point south of the Severn to the south-west end of the Wrekin. There is also a small outcrop of Cambrian Lower Comley sandstone at Lilleshall. The northern end of the belt of marine Silurian rocks known as Wenlock Edge also runs into the coalfield, comprising shallow-water shelf sediments left by the retreating Iapetus Ocean.

The onset of the Carboniferous period brought a return to marine conditions followed by a gradual change to terrestrial sedimentation. It was during that phase that the coalfield's rich natural resources were laid down: coal, ironstone, refractory clays, and limestone.

The hummocky terrain of the plateaux either side of the Severn Gorge, particularly visible at Windmill Hill, represents drumlins formed of boulder clay during the glaciation of north Shropshire. Valleys such as Coalbrookdale were etched across the plateau on the fringe of the Irish Sea Ice. As the ice retreated to the plains of north Shropshire and Cheshire, Lake Lapworth was formed. Owing to the northerly drainage being blocked by ice the entire lake had to drain over the watershed between Benthall Edge and Lincoln Hill to a tributary of the river Stour. The meltwaters then gouged out the deep gorge that became the course of the Severn, whose upper catchment area had formerly drained north. The soft clays and sandstones through which the Severn Gorge is cut make its sides unstable, as testified by continuing landslips. Smaller tributary streams, cutting down slower than the Severn, created hanging valley effects above the Severn valley floor. The rapid streams in the side valleys provided industrial power from the 17th century.

The main drift cover is boulder clay.[60] Acid-brown and surface-water gley soils cover much of the area, usually resting on the Coal Measures. Drainage varies from good to poor and the soil is generally a sandy loam. A siltier loam mix characterizes the leached brown soils found mostly in the east. Smaller patches of well drained acid-brown and podzolized soils also occur, overlying Pre-Cambrian volcanic rocks. In the Middle Ages the district was heavily wooded, with a wood–pasture economy; even today large areas of wood remain. Increasing industrialization from the late 17th century transformed the landscape, especially

[60] V.C.H. Salop. i, maps facing pp. 1, 23; xi. 1, 3, 104, 198; Inst. Geol. Sciences Map 1/25,000, Telford (1978 edn.).

in the central area around Dawley and Oakengates, with mining spoil, clay workings, and sprawling settlements, and over the next two centuries agriculture gradually became a relatively less important part of the region's economy. Away from the central parts of the coalfield, however, the region's landscape remained largely agricultural and rural. Even in the central area agriculture survived. In the 1930s there was a considerable amount of dairying, and some of the farming around Willey, Broseley, Madeley, and Stirchley was arable. In places there was rough grazing on levelled pit mounds or between surviving ones as, with the ebb of industrial prosperity after the 1840s, agriculture was reinstated in areas from which it had been displaced. In the 1960s and 1970s, as Dawley (later Telford) new town was built, agriculture virtually ceased in the central part of the coalfield region north of the Severn.[61]

The central uplands

The central uplands contain perhaps the most varied and spectacular scenery in Shropshire and some of Britain's oldest rocks. The region runs from the western watershed of Ape Dale and the Plaish Brook valley to the Welsh border west of the Shelve Plateau, and from Linley and Wistanstow in the south to Pontesbury in the north. Most of it lies over 183 m. and many parts over 300 m. The topography ranges from the line of whale-backed volcanic hills along the Church Stretton Fault through the fertile valleys either side of the Long Mynd to the bleak open plateau lands of the Long Mynd and the Shelve district and the jagged skyline of the Stiperstones ridge; its diversity reflects to a great degree the underlying rock beds.

Glacial deposits apart, the region's geological sequence is almost entirely early, starting with the Pre-Cambrian (4,600 million to 570 million years ago) and continuing through the succeeding Cambrian, Ordovician, and Silurian periods. All the Pre-Cambrian outcrops lie between, or along the line of, two great SSW.-NNE. fault systems, the Church Stretton and the Pontesford-Linley faults, and the major part of both runs through the region. The fault systems played a fundamental role in the process of sedimentation in the region, as can be seen from the way that the geological strata follow the direction of the fault lines. The igneous suite of Uriconian volcanics is divided into two belts (the Eastern and Western Uriconians) along the line of the two faults. They form a line of hills and comprise a great variety of volcanic rock types, varying from basalt and rhyolite lavas to coarse- and fine-grained tuffs (ashes). The Eastern Uriconians appear as a line of hog-backed hills on the eastern flank of the Long Mynd: Ragleth, Hazler, Helmeth, Caer Caradoc, and the Lawley. The outcrop is found again north of the Severn, and east of Helmeth and Caer Caradoc it continues with the large mass of the Hope Bowdler, Willstone, and Cardington hills. The Western Uriconians start in the south at Linley and, after a 5-km. gap, continue with the ancient masses of Earl's Hill, Pontesford Hill (possessing important dolerite intrusions), and Plealey. Newer, but still Pre-Cambrian, are the Longmyndian sedimentary rocks. They are late Pre-Cambrian shallow-water sediments deposited in a subsiding shallow marine trough between the two fault systems, close to the shore line of the widening Iapetus Ocean when Shropshire lay just within the continental mass on its south-

[61] *V.C.H. Salop.* xi. 1, 14, and *passim*, esp. (for the disappearance of agric. in Telford) 44, 105, 118, 184, 190; Slack, op. cit. cap. i, p. 11 (copy in S.R.O. 3763/19/1); cap. ii, p. 3 (copy in S.R.O. 2118/168); [1st] Land Util. Surv. Map, sheet 61; Howell, *Salop.* 266-7.

eastern margin. The Longmyndian group is divided into the higher Wentnor Group of purple sandstones and conglomerates and the lower Stretton Group of sandstones, siltstones, and shales. The whole sequence forms *c.* 8,000 m. of sediments. The major outcrop is the massive smooth-topped Long Mynd plateau formed of slates and sandstone. It covers *c.* 50 sq. km. and rises to 517 m.; most of it remains uninclosed pasture.[62] Its uncompromising outline is interrupted by deeply cut narrow valleys, known locally as batches or hollows.

A complete Cambrian sequence, including Comley sandstones and limestones and also shales, outcrops east of the Lawley and around Hill End on the eastern side of the Cardington hills. On the western flank of the Long Mynd, however, the line of Cambrian beds following the Pontesford–Linley Fault forms a very different landscape of deep open valleys and long ridges. Thick boulder clay covers the higher spots, and Ice Age lake deposits are found lower down. The landscape is based on a long narrow outcrop of Shineton Shales deposited in a thin shallow-water marine environment.

A great belt of Ordovician strata runs SSW.–NNE. between Wenlock Edge and the Church Stretton Fault, extending from the Onny valley in the south and running north on the eastern side of the Stretton Hills and Caer Caradoc. The outcrop is called the Caradoc Sequence and is entirely a shallow-water deposit with abundant shelly fauna. Various limestones, sandstones, shales, flags, and grits are included in the group, some of them folded and faulted by movements along the Church Stretton Fault. The igneous type Ordovician rocks found farther west are practically non-existent but the Shelve Plateau contains the full Ordovician sequence, igneous and sedimentary: 4,500 m. of shallow-water sandstones, deeper-water shales and siltstones, some limestones, and beds of volcanic ashes and lavas. There are also pockets of intrusive and extrusive andesites, basalts, and dolerites, notably the great rounded dolerite cone of Corndon Hill (Mont.), rising to 513 m. All the underlying geology gives rise to wild bleak upland scenery punctuated by rugged peaks formed of the harder beds. Most pronounced of the SW.–NE. ridges, the Stiperstones are formed of tilted Arenig quartzite eroded into the sort of jagged hill-top crowns seen on Dartmoor. The Stiperstones slopes are strewn with great quartzite boulders resulting from Ice Age action. The local volcanoes responsible for the (relatively thin) Ordovician igneous beds were situated in or near the Shelve area. The Shelve Plateau lies at *c.* 365 m., with the Stiperstones rising 150 m. higher. It is an inhospitable land supporting only rough uninclosed pasture.[63] Lead was formerly mined from Late Ordovician mineralization.

The last geological era represented in the region (apart from the recent Pleistocene) is the Silurian, whose strata appear west of the Church Stretton Fault as a thick basin facies like those of the Long Mountain on the region's western edge; the Long Mountain is composed of soft sedimentary Upper Silurian strata folded into a syncline. Most of the area is formed of marine Silurian, though there is a small pocket of Downtonian near Vennington. The Long Mountain attains 408 m., and the effect of folding is to give it a softer relief than the Shelve and Long Mynd plateaux to the east. Boulder clay from Ice Age frost action overlies the sedimentary beds.

Over the region's highest areas, such as the Shelve Plateau, and over the steep valleys and scarp of the Long Mynd and the belt of volcanic hills by the Church Stretton Fault, the soils are largely acid-brown and podzolized. They overlie the

[62] S.C.C. Ch. Exec.'s Dept., commons reg. nos. CL 9, 55–6, 63, 109.   [63] Ibid. nos. CL 57, 80.

Pre-Cambrian volcanics, sandstones, and siltstones, and the Ordovician beds. The extensive acid-brown soils tend to be well drained and a silt loam or loamy sand. Leaching on such soils, with loss of important nutrients, can be severe and is worst on the infertile, highly podzolized soils of exposed areas like the Stiperstones or the bleaker ridges of the western Shelve area. Many such areas support only heath, open moorland, or rough pasture. On the Long Mountain surface layers have been disturbed by landslips and solifluxion, producing scree and some large blocks of rock. The well drained, stony, acid-brown soils are head, derived by colluvial processes from the Silurian strata beneath. The acid-brown soils in the western Shelve area tend to be siltier and deeper, except for the steeper slopes where the soil is thinner.

Surface-water gley soils and leached brown soils with gleying predominate on the region's lower land and at the feet of the ridges. They mostly rest on Ordovician or Silurian beds, themselves sometimes overlain by glacial boulder clay. Natural drainage on such soils is often poor and their use may depend on artificial drainage. Most soils of the type, however, can grow good wheat; they vary from a silt loam to a sandy clay loam or a sandy loam. Impermeable boulder clay often fills valleys west of the Stiperstones, as it does in the upper reaches of the West Onny. Where layers of glacial sands or gravels occur, as in the northern section of the Long Mynd, the soil type is a sandy acid-brown soil of a sandy loam quality. The river courses usually support ground-water gley soils or brown warp soils (formed from the recent build-up of alluvial silts), clays, and possibly some glacial drift deposits. Drainage varies.

Much of the region is bleak wild upland interspersed with heath and moorland, but there are fertile valleys, such as Stretton Dale and the upper Rea valley, and land successfully supporting mixed farming. Mainly, however, it is stock rearing country[64] with an emphasis on sheep. The region's villages, as in most upland areas, are usually small and widely scattered, and the region has never been highly populated.

South-west Shropshire

South-west Shropshire is a remote upland region of grass pasture and moorland. Much of it was part of Wales in the Middle Ages and many of the place names are Welsh. Morphologically the region is an extension of the Welsh Plateau and a continuation of the Kerry Hills (Mont.). The Clun and Teme river systems have deeply dissected the plateau, forming a series of broad-backed ridges divided by steep narrow valleys. The Teme and the Clun drain the region in the south and centre, the Onny and the Camlad in the north. Slopes vary from moderate to steep, and the higher summits join up with the old plateau surface. The highest point, Beacon Hill (Radnors.), rises to 547 m. The landscape becomes softer in the east, breaking into a series of isolated rounded hills.

The region is based entirely on Silurian beds, namely the marine Silurian and sizeable outcrops of Downtonian. The Silurian rocks represent sedimentation left as the Iapetus Ocean finally retreated west in southern Britain. The thick basin facies Silurian deposits are the same as those of the Long Mountain farther north. The beds in the basin are all of the Ludlow and Downton series in age and are mostly graptolitic. A deep layer of siltstones and mudstones, c. 2,000 m. thick,

64 V.C.H. Salop. viii. 1, 178 (referring to the N. edge of the dist.).

makes up the Ludlow series and a thinner layer of mudstones, shales, and siltstones, *c.* 600 m. deep, the Downton series. The latter are situated around Clun and in a large block on the region's western border. Both series contain fossil-rich silty beds, the basic beds of the Downton Castle sandstone. Some time after the Downton beds were deposited Caledonian folding affected the area.

Most of the region supports well drained acid-brown soils of a silt loam texture. The underlying Silurian rocks are all either non-calcareous or only slightly calcareous. The surface layers of the beds have been disturbed by landslips or solifluxion, as is shown by the build-up of scree-like material or head. Consequently the overlying soils are largely developed from colluvium and head; colluvial soils predominate on the steep slopes, head on the lower slopes. Boulder clay occurs infrequently but is more likely to be found in the east, particularly around river terraces and alluvial deposits. Acid-brown soils in the upland areas are most suited to grass for sheep grazing and in their natural state usually support bracken and dry heath grassland. Leaching of such soils is intense, but not as intense as with the podzolized acid-brown soils found on the gentler hill slopes of summits over 365 m. Those imperfectly or well drained soils often support heather and bilberry. Where there are patches of boulder clay or head, peaty gleyed podzols may occur. The presence of fairly impermeable boulder clay beneath subsoils often produces a waterlogged peaty surface layer. Such areas generally remain semi-natural moorland. On other slopes of hills above the 365-m. contour, pockets of surface-water peaty gley soils occur. They are usually very poorly or imperfectly drained, and of a silty clay loam texture. Again such areas are more particularly suited to sheep grazing because the combination of high acidity, high rainfall, and poor drainage makes successful agriculture very difficult. The semi-natural vegetation may be heather and bilberry, and in the wetter areas moor grass, rushes, and cotton grass. Groups of rushes mark the presence of flushes where springs keep the soils wet. Long thin arms of brown warp soils and ground-water gley soils intrude into the uplands and mark the courses of the Clun and Teme. This silty clay loam mix is based on alluvial silts and clays.

The upland soils, brown, naturally free-draining silt loams, mostly between 245 m. and 365 m., are generally suitable for cultivation and there is much evidence of prehistoric settlement.[65] In medieval times the valleys of the Teme and its tributaries gave access to a remote upland section of the middle march[66] where Clun and Bishop's Castle became the main settlements. Population and settlement figures have never been high and the commonest form of settlement remains the isolated farmstead. Much of the area is heath or moorland. Trees and hedges are oftener found in the valleys than on the windy uplands, though from 1924 the western part of the area was extensively planted by the Forestry Commission, and by 1939 *c.* 1,200 ha. were growing conifers.[67] In the 1930s there was a higher proportion of arable in the region, mostly in the eastern part, than elsewhere in south Shropshire,[68] and there was a certain amount of dairying. Sheep farming, however, remains the area's most characteristic enterprise.

[65] Slack, op. cit. cap. ii, pp. 5–6 (copy in S.R.O. 2118/168); *V.C.H. Salop.* i. 197, 199, 202, and map facing p. 351; *T.S.A.S.* xi. 211 sqq.; S.M.R.

[66] C. P. Lewis, 'Eng. and Norman govt. and lordship in Welsh borders 1039–87' (Oxf. Univ. D. Phil. thesis, 1985), 150–1.

[67] Mostly European larch, Douglas fir, and Scots pine: Howell, *Salop.* 239.

[68] [1st] Land Util. Surv. Map, sheet 70; Slack, 'Hist. Agric. in Salop.' cap. ii, pp. 5–6 (copy in S.R.O. 2118/168); S.R.O. 3763/20/4.

NORTH SHROPSHIRE

Compared with south Shropshire the regions largely east and north of the Severn appear much more uniform in terms of geology and relief and there is little land over 122 m. Yet there too sub-regions can be identified, perhaps more easily indeed than in the more complex south.

The eastern sandstone plain

Geologically and scenically the eastern sandstone plain belongs to the west midlands. The rich red sandstone countryside, most of it below 122 m., combines wide tracts of flat land, cut by deeply bedded streams, with gently rolling hills and patches of hummocky glacial terrain. The underlying Carboniferous, Permian, and Triassic deposits are the same as those in the west midlands. In 1086 much of the region was in Staffordshire, and in terms of geology and soil coverage it has little in common with Shropshire's upland regions to the west. The annual rainfall is lower than in western Shropshire, annual hours of sunshine are greater, and average temperatures are somewhat higher.

Upper Coal Measures fringe the plain to the west and south. Near Bridgnorth lies the northern end of the Wyre Forest coalfield, positioned over the Symon Fault where the lower layers have eroded. Most of the plain is floored by Bunter deposits of the intermediary Permo-Trias age. The Bunter sandstone, a useful reservoir of underground water,[69] is found extensively in the region; now known as the Bridgnorth or Lower Mottled sandstone, it is part of the Permo-Triassic New Red Sandstone, which underlies large areas of east and north Shropshire but in both regions is thickly overlain by glacial clay or sand and gravel. The Bunter Pebble Beds, now known as the Kidderminster formation, represent the base of the succeeding Triassic period in east Shropshire. They contain many quartz and quartzite pebbles and were probably laid down in a delta environment at the end of the Permian age 280–225 million years ago. The period was marked by sub-aerial erosion of the local highlands and deposition in the developing graben system. The breccia formation of that time, such as the Clent breccia exposed 4 km. south of Claverley, consists of angular calcareous scree material plucked from the limestone uplands and deposited in a mix of red marl in a red sandstone matrix. Evidence for the continuation of such airborne deposition, with some intermontane lake deposition, is provided by the Bridgnorth sandstone already referred to.

After the formation of the intermediary Permo-Trias Bunter sandstone and pebble beds the Triassic period proper (225–190 million years ago) began, when the stretch of Keuper sandstones and marls, found in the extreme east of the plain, was deposited. The Keuper sandstone (now known as the Wilmslow Sandstone) and the succeeding Keuper marls (now known as the Mercia Mudstone group) were both formed in largely non-marine, semi-arid conditions. The terrestrial landscape was subject to narrow horst and graben structures, which directed sedimentation, including intensive fluvial deposition, in east Shropshire. The finer-textured Wilmslow Sandstone of east and north Shropshire probably signifies a slowing down of some of the river systems, caused by the erosion of the nearby uplands. After a short-lived marine incursion, the former terrestrial environment

[69] *V.C.H. Salop.* i. 38.

was restored and the saliferous marls of the Mercia Mudstone group were then deposited. These impermeable red-brown marls, layered with other rocks like sandstone, quartz, and shales, were formed by deposition in shallow water.

East Shropshire, like the northern plain, bears distinctive reminders of Pleistocene glacial activity. Near the eastern county boundary, by Weston under Lizard (Staffs.), the low swell of boulder-clay end moraines represents the halt of the Irish Sea Ice in its northerly retreat. Other glacial mounds of sand and gravel are particularly prominent near Blymhill (Staffs.) and Boscobel and along the valley of the Back brook near Newport. The mounds may be worn down eskers or kames deposited at right angles to the ice sheet. Of course the main impact of glacial action in the region is the general blanket of glacial deposits which often obscures all earlier geological formations.

Because there is so much underlying sandstone and overlying sands and gravels, a very large proportion of the region exhibits light, sandy, acid-brown and podzolized soils with poor water retention properties; there is almost no surface water and there are few shallow wells. Properly managed, the soils are well suited to market gardening and intensive agriculture, though the danger of drought makes them less suited to permanent pasture. Particularly sandy and more sterile soils usually occur over the mounds of glacial sands and gravels, and coniferous trees are often the only vegetation they support. Such poor podzolized soils once supported great stretches of natural heath, some of which has been reclaimed for conifer plantations. The old areas of scrub-heath, themselves the product of still earlier woodland clearance, usually denoted underlying beds of Bunter pebbles. Over the Keuper (Wilmslow) Sandstone the soil is noticeably moister and richer than it is over the Bunter pebbles and sandstones. The belt of Keuper marls at the eastern edge of the region displays an opposite extreme in soil coverage. There, as with the areas thickly covered by glacial boulder clay, the drainage is poor or imperfect, and the often impermeable nature of the deposit creates frequent surface streams. The soil is generally a sandy clay loam or a loam over clay loam or clay. In the extreme southern and western parts of the region, over the Coal Measures, siltier leached brown soils predominate, with a more variable free or imperfect drainage. Finally the flood plain of the Severn, particularly near Bridgnorth, has a build-up of alluvial silts and clays, and imperfectly drained gley soils are common there.

Originally almost the whole region was occupied by a great extent of woodland stretching from Staffordshire to Worcestershire. The creation of the royal forest of Morfe in Norman times inhibited the spread of settlement but there had been earlier settlement, often in the valleys or in the form of isolated farmsteads and hamlets. The shrunken villages and small moated medieval farms found to the south speak of restricted settlement and small-scale land reclamation in a marginal forest or heathland environment. Nevertheless there are also a few notably large and prosperous villages, such as Alveley, Claverley, and Worfield, of a type not found in the more extreme marginal environment of the meres and mosses of the northern plain. By the 18th century Morfe forest had lost its woodland character and was more or less scrub-heath. At inclosure (1812) the cleared land that had remained common waste was formed into regular fields. In many parts, however, the eastern plain still displays remnants of a more ancient landscape, marked by smaller irregular fields and high-banked winding lanes. By the early 18th century the region was known as the Ryeland from the suitability of its fine, dry sandy soils for rye and barley,[70] and in recent centuries the region has been more distinctly arable than any other part of Shropshire.[71]

The northern plain

In terms of relief the northern plain forms a very distinct region of Shropshire. It lies between 80 m. and 110 m., an extensive level region interrupted here and there by low red sandstone hills forming a gently undulating lowland landscape. The effects of glaciation, the soils, and the present landscape, however, are varied. The plain encompasses both arable and pastoral areas, as well as extremes of wild fenland vegetation and heathlands. The Severn, moreover, winds its way across the southern part of the plain, cutting into the eastern coalfield through the Severn Gorge, a legacy of glaciation. The fertile deposits of the Severn flood plain make a distinctive southern sub-region of the plain, both in terms of soils and of the resulting settlement and agriculture.

Much of the plain is based on Triassic or Permo-Triassic rocks, mostly sandstone and marls, but they are in turn heavily overlain by glacial drift and more recent deposits. The extensive area of Bunter (now called Bridgnorth) Sandstone was deposited in terrestrial conditions on a semi-arid continent 280–225 million years ago. It results from the sub-aerial, or wind-blown, erosion of the Varsican uplands and is typically red and lacking in fossils. Next in geological sequence are the Triassic Keuper sandstones and marls laid down under similar terrestrial conditions interrupted by marine incursions. Those deposits, occurring extensively in the central and northern parts of the plain, comprise a series of cross-stratified orange-red sandstones, such as the Sherwood sandstone and the Wilmslow sandstone (originally called Keuper sandstone) and silts and mudstones like the Mercia Mudstone (originally known as the Keuper marl). Less extensive outcrops in the area are the Upper Coal Measures to the far south, around Shrewsbury, and the far east and west, and a patch of more recent Jurassic Lower and Middle Lias clays and silts south-east of Whitchurch. Lastly a spur of the much earlier Pre-Cambrian Longmyndian sedimentary rocks intrudes into the plain, outcropping at Longden, Lyth Hill, Bayston Hill, and Sharpstone Hill and dividing the Cound and Rea drainage systems; north of the Severn it outcrops again east of Shrewsbury as Haughmond Hill.

Most of north Shropshire is covered by glacial drift and fluvio-glacial deposits, a legacy of the Welsh and the Irish Sea ice sheets. The Irish Sea Ice left the bulk of the drift and it is usually reddish brown in colour and composed of boulder clay intermixed with sands and gravels and rocks from the Lake District and south-west Scotland. The plain also shows the physical marks of glaciation more clearly than other parts of Shropshire: its varied topography of glacial or morainic hills, smaller drumlins, and boggy meres and mosses was created by late Pleistocene glaciation.

Discontinuous ranges of morainic hills running from Ellesmere and Cockshutt towards Whitchurch, evident for example at Breaden Heath, represent accumulated debris left by the retreating ice. Hills on the crest of the moraine can be quite steep sided, in contrast to the gentler slopes of the drumlins, as shaped and elongated by the slow-moving ice. The low drumlins provide useful islands of drier land in a generally damp area, and some farms are sited eligibly on them.

---

[70] *T.S.A.S.* ix. 205.   *Salop.* 224 sqq.; S.R.O. 3763/20/4.
[71] [1st] Land Util. Surv. Map, sheets 61, 71; Howell,

Where hollows occurred in this glacial drift (possibly the result of pockets of slower melting ice) small meres have developed, as around Ellesmere, and some of them have developed into wet peaty hollows. Such shallow hollows contain the mosslands of the plain. Thick beds of fen peat began to accumulate as the hollows silted up; tests on Whixall Moss indicate that the process began soon after 8000 B.C. In the early modern period those inhospitable marginal lands accommodated a number of squatter settlements. Despite some 19th-century reclamation, the wetter mosses like Whixall Moss have retained their wild fenland character[72] and are still used for peat cutting.

Drift largely determines the nature of the region's soils. The boulder clay areas are capped by surface-water gley soils and leached brown soils with some gleying. They tend to be heavy textured loamy soils with imperfect or poor drainage, suitable for extensive cultivation only if effectively drained. Traditionally such soils, which cover large parts of north Shropshire, have been used for pasture, though with careful management wheat can be grown. The northernmost arc of land in the county, extending from Market Drayton by Grinshill to Oswestry and centring on Whitchurch, was increasingly notable from the 17th century as a dairying district with pig feeding as an important subsidiary enterprise until c. 1940.[73] Where the boulder clay is more intermixed with sands and gravels, as it is around Ellesmere, Cockshutt, and Welshampton, the soil tends to be somewhat loamier, more organic in the upper layers, and so more fertile; that has allowed successful arable cultivation.

Where the drift is mostly sands and gravels, lighter textured acid-brown soils or podzolized soils occur. They are sandy loams, usually greyish brown in colour and well drained. They are widespread over the plain, but the two largest areas lie in its north-eastern and north-western parts: one between Market Drayton and Ercall Magna with extensions north through Prees to Whitchurch and south to the lower Tern valley around Upton Magna, the other between Oswestry and the Severn (at Montford). The light sandy soils found on sandstone hills such as Nesscliff, Pim Hill, Grinshill, and Hawkstone attracted prehistoric settlement. Iron Age earthworks like Oliver's Point and Bury Walls cap the hills or (as at the Berth) lie in the low ground between them. Organic deficiency means that such soils are not inherently fertile, but they respond to treatment and are well suited to roots or oats. The north-eastern area was fitted for arable in the early modern period as sheep and cattle fattening developed, and the extensive remaining heaths[74] of the north-east and north-west were inclosed at the end of the 18th century when wartime cereal prices brought them into cultivation. The north-east, long retaining its identity as an area of improved heathland, contains smaller areas of podzols, gley podzols, and leached brown soils. The podzols tend to be sandy soils sitting on the glacial sands and gravels, and the leached brown soils, mainly along the northern edge of the improved heathlands, form a richer silty loam based on the Keuper marls and sandstones and the Coal Measures. There, in the 1920s and 1930s, dairying spread from the northern part of the plain.[75]

Areas of pure peat and peaty soils with poor or blocked drainage are found in the glacial morainic country to the north-west and in the east, notably in the Weald Moors. Their agricultural and settlement potential is severely limited without the aid of artificial drainage. From the late 16th century, when landowners were

[72] V.C.H. Salop. xi. 104.
[73] P. R. Edwards, 'Farming Econ. of NE. Salop.' (Oxf. Univ. D.Phil. thesis, 1976), 8, 71–88; Howell, Salop. 246, 255–8.
[74] Evident on J. Rocque, Map of Salop. (1752).
[75] Edwards, op. cit. 116–28; Howell, Salop. 246, 263–5.

beginning to inclose and improve thousands of acres there, the Weald Moors were specializing as a livestock-fattening area.[76] In the later 18th century some of the ill drained peaty areas of the north-west, such as the Baggy Moor, were drained and cultivated.

Valleys like those of the Severn, the Tern, and the Rea give rise to rich alluvial silts and clays which form brown warp and ground-water gley soils of variable drainage. The light loamy soils of the Severn flood plain have attracted some of the earliest and most intense agricultural activity in Shropshire. Settlement has been severely limited on the flood plain itself, but in the river valley abundant crop marks signify both settlement and agricultural activity as far back as the Bronze Age. The flood plain of the Vyrnwy also yields evidence of prehistoric settlement. The southern part of the plain, south-east and south of Shrewsbury, includes the lowland valleys of the Bullhill and Cound brooks; south-west and west of Shrewsbury it includes the lowland parts of Pontesbury and Westbury parishes (the lower Rea valley) and the parishes to the north bordering the river. Those two southern extensions of the plain[77] were early occupied by relatively prosperous settlements with large open fields in Alberbury, Cardeston, and Ford on the free-draining soils of the breccia outcrop between Loton and Cardeston, an area where arable cultivation (with an emphasis on barley) remained notable even in the 1930s.[78] East of the county town as far as the lower Tern valley and including the Cound brook valley south of the Severn, light free-draining soils occur more frequently, and on the lower land correspondingly large arable fields are found from an early date;[79] the range of that area's arable enterprises was increased by the cultivation of sugar beet after 1927.[80] Mixed farming was widespread over the southern fringe of the plain in modern times, though here and there local conditions produced a different emphasis.[81]

Settlers in the north Shropshire plain have conspicuously taken advantage of the islands of higher and drier ground. Between the scattered nucleated villages lie isolated farms and hamlets, and man's recent efforts in the way of inclosure, drainage, and land reclamation have made an impact on the landscape. That is particularly noticeable in the formerly ill drained and inhospitable fenlands east of Ellesmere. Eighteenth-century inclosure left a rash of small squatter settlements which were often eradicated by the reclamation of large areas for cultivation in the next century. The whole area remains largely rural in character, thinly populated, and with remnants of a more ancient landscape in the wild fens and heathlands.

The north-west uplands

More than any other part of Shropshire the north-west uplands west of Oswestry bear a distinctly Welsh character with a hilly terrain, scattered pastoral farms, and small stone cottages. Tectonically the region is part of the Welsh system and on the far western edge of the region the underlying Ordovician sedimentary and igneous rocks represent the easternmost fringe of the Berwyn Mountains. A thick sequence of those earlier Ordivician rocks passes under the Carboniferous Limestone, and farther east the region is dominated by stretches of Carboniferous

[76] Edwards, op. cit. 8, 100–15; *T.S.A.S.* lxiii. 1–10; Howell, *Salop.* 246, 260–3.

[77] Divided by the outcrop of Longmyndian sedimentary rocks noted above.

[78] *V.C.H. Salop.* viii. 182–3, 185–6, 210, 224–5, 233; Howell, *Salop.* 258.

[79] Howell, *Salop.* 246, 260; *V.C.H. Salop.* viii. 4.

[80] When the Allscott sugar factory opened: *V.C.H. Salop.* xi. 141, 226, 232, 315; Howell, *Salop.* 260.

[81] As when the Minsterley creamery opened: *V.C.H. Salop.* viii. 1, 178; Howell, *Salop.* 246, 258–9.

Millstone Grit (basically grits, sandstones, and shales) and the Lower and Middle Coal Measures. Those deposits were laid down under returning marine conditions followed by a slow change to terrestrial sedimentation when deltaic and swamp material built up, eventually forming the sandstone and Coal Measures found today. Marine layers with distinctive fossil fauna can be found extensively through the Coal Measures.

The region represents an eastern extension of the Welsh Plateau, which ends in steep scarp slopes just north of the region, beyond the county boundary. The land rises from 80 m. in the east to over 300 m. in the west at the Welsh border. Intensive glaciation over the last few million years affected the whole of north and central Shropshire and in the north-west uplands a reddish brown drift of boulder clay, gravels, and silts left by the Irish Sea Ice covers the solid geology. Particularly thick glacial deposits lie on the broad valley bottoms, on ledges on the valley slopes, and on the flatter hilltops. Glaciation also resulted in common rocky outcrops on valley sides.

The resulting topography is an irregular hilly terrain with deeply incised, broad-bottomed valleys. The region has a higher than average rainfall for the county, 30-40 in. a year being recorded, with the highest figure reached in the west. Because of the porous nature of the rocks surface drainage takes the form of deeply engraved water courses such as the Morlas brook, the river Morda, and the river Tanat and its tributaries.

The soils based on the Carboniferous Sandstones are largely acid-brown. They tend to be shallow and strong but relatively well drained on the ridges and steepest slopes. The good drainage enables them to produce a good grass crop, generally used for rearing stock. On the more exposed summits infertile leached podzols support only poor rough grazing. The well drained leached brown and calcareous soils found in the Carboniferous Limestone areas tend to be shallow, subject to summer drought, and of limited agricultural value. Finally surface-water gley soils and leached brown soils with some gleying are also found in patches (over boulder clay deposits) throughout the region. They are poorly drained and often waterlogged in autumn or winter, though potentially good agricultural land if properly drained.

Because of the relief and the often infertile nature of the soils, the area has not seen intense agricultural activity and has been characterized by mixed woodland and rough grazing. The settlement pattern of isolated farmsteads and small hamlets has also been affected by the limitations of the physical environment, though in the warmer periods of prehistory there may have been more extensive use of the upland areas.

EARLY AGRICULTURE

AGRICULTURE began to be adopted as the predominant mode of subsistence in Britain some time after c. 3500 B.C.,[82] replacing the way of life that hunter–gatherer communities had practised over the previous six or seven millennia.[83] How the change came about, whether for example it was through colonization, indigenous

[82] Dates thus expressed are in calendar years. Uncalibrated radio carbon dates appear as 'b.c.'.
[83] T. Darvill, *Prehistoric Brit.* (1987) is cited frequently below on general points. The bk. has a thematic bibliography providing an up-to-date guide to the diverse literature on prehist. Brit. Dr. Darvill is thanked for his comments on this article.

development, or acculturation (the transference of ideas, beliefs, traditions, and sometimes artefacts by contact between societies), remains obscure. In what is now Shropshire little data has yet been found to contribute to the discussion, though there is enough to indicate that small communities of hunter–gatherers occupied the area before the introduction of farming.[84] Woods then covered most of the land, apart perhaps from the highest hill tops,[85] with thick, wet alder carr and willow on the flood plains and in the river valleys and broad leaved species, especially lime, dominant on the higher, drier ground.[86]

Evidence of Neolithic man's activities and his impact on the environment comes from three main sources: pollen sequences that show vegetational changes, the archaeological investigation of sites, and stray finds. Together they show that over much of Britain there was patchy clearance of woodland in the later 4th millennium b.c. as the pioneer farming communities began to establish themselves, herding animals, especially cattle, and growing cereals, mostly wheat and barley. It was at that time that the first permanent settlements began to be built, along with enclosed fields, and funerary monuments. The equipment necessary for farming, such as axes, sickles, quernstones, storage pits, and pottery containers, also appears for the first time.[87] In the Shropshire area early Neolithic activity was apparently fairly restricted. The pollen evidence from Crose Mere, Baschurch Pools, and other sites suggests that clearances were small in scale and relatively short lived, and that, while they may have altered the forest structure locally, with birch and ash increasing as the amount of lime decreased, the total tree cover was not substantially reduced.[88] The archaeological evidence seems to tell the same story for very few sites of this period are known. Settlements at Sharpstone Hill near Shrewsbury and at Bromfield may possibly belong to the early (3500-2900 b.c.) rather than the middle Neolithic. Neolithic pits at Bromfield contained grains of barley (*Hordeum vulgare*) and seed from ivy speedwell (*Veronica hederifolia L.*), a common weed on cultivated ground. Hazel nuts were also found at Bromfield, evidence of the part that woodland resources continued to play in the economy.[89] Hunting too probably remained important.[90] Even less is known of activity in the county in the middle Neolithic period (2800-2400 b.c.), to which a possible occupation site at the Roveries near Bishop's Castle can perhaps be assigned and some of the flint implements found in south Shropshire.[91] In the succeeding late Neolithic and Beaker periods (2400-1800 b.c.) the pattern of land use was changing, and by c. 2000 b.c. agriculture had expanded in various parts of the country, especially upland areas. Specialized practices seem to have developed, notably short range transhumance involving the movement of pastoralists and their animals to upland summer grazing.[92] Such a pattern is suggested, for instance, by evidence from

[84] e.g. W. Britnell, 'A barbed point from Porth-y-waen, Llanyblodwel', *Proc. Prehist. Soc.* l. 385-6; *T.S.A.S.* lix. 198-210.

[85] *Environment in Brit. Prehist.* ed. I. Simmons and M. Tooley (1981), 105, 202.

[86] *Palaeohydrology in Practice: A River Basin Analysis*, ed. K. J. Gregory, J. Lewin, and J. B. Thornes (1987), 226-8; *Archaeological Aspects of Woodland Ecology*, ed. S. Limbrey and M. Bell (Brit. Arch. Rep. International Ser. cxlvi), 23-55; inf. from Dr. A. G. Brown, who is thanked, on unpubl. work in the Perry catchment area. Mr. J. B. Innes is also thanked for help.

[87] Darvill, *Prehist. Brit.* cap. 3; Simmons and Tooley, *Env. in Brit. Prehist.* cap. 4.

[88] Gregory, Lewin, and Thornes, op. cit. 228-32; S. Twigger, 'Differential Human Impact in later Prehistory:

Vegetational Clearances in N. Salop.', *Circaea*, iv. 21-6; P. W. Beales, 'Late Devensian and Flandrian Vegetational Hist. of Crose Mere', *New Phytologist*, lxxxv. 133-61; D. Pannett and C. Morey, 'The origin of the Old River Bed at Shrews.' *Bull. Salop. Conservation Trust*, xxxv. 7-12; P. H. Rowlands and F. W. Shotton, 'Pleistocene deposits of Ch. Stretton and its neighbourhood', *Jnl. Geological Soc.* cxxvii. 612-17.

[89] S. C. Stanford, 'Bromfield—Neolithic, Beaker, and Bronze Age Sites, 1966-79', *Proc. Prehist. Soc.* xlviii. 288; *W. Midlands Arch. News Sheet*, viii. 14; ix. 13-14; x. 21-2; inf. from Dr. Darvill.

[90] Darvill, *Prehist. Brit.* 53-4.

[91] T. C. Darvill, 'The Neolithic of Wales and the Mid West of Eng.' (Southampton Univ. Ph.D. thesis, 1983), 319-422.

[92] Darvill, *Prehist. Brit.* 105.

Trelystan, just across Shropshire's western border near Welshpool, where the excavator of one of four barrow groups on the Long Mountain suggested that the hill provided summer grazing for the barrow builders whose settlements probably lay on the lower land.[93] Occupation of that date on Pontesford Hill is also indicative of upland exploitation.[94]

The arrival of metal working c. 2000 b.c., and the start of the period traditionally called the Bronze Age, had little immediate effect on farming. Nevertheless evidence, particularly from burials, indicates a highly stratified society in which prestige goods, often changing in fashion, were important. Prerequisites for the development of such a society would seem to be the evolution of landownership and the control of resources.[95] It is thought that in middle and late Bronze Age Britain more land than ever before was under cultivation, with extensive farming of areas little used today, such as the North York Moors and Dartmoor.[96] Numerous round barrows on the uplands of south and west Shropshire, such as the Long Mynd,[97] and 'Celtic fields', such as those on the sides of Caer Caradoc near Church Stretton,[98] indicate the extent to which man was using the higher land in the area at that time. The pollen evidence from Crose Mere, Whixall Moss, and Baschurch Pools confirms the importance of the Bronze Age, rather than the Neolithic, for the expansion of agriculture in the area, with major long term clearances being made for the first time.[99] Nevertheless it is likely that especially on the wetter, heavier soils very extensive woods remained uncleared throughout the Bronze Age.[1]

In the early 1st millennium B.C., the late Bronze Age, signs of stress appear in society, caused perhaps either by climatic deterioration[2] and the resulting difficulty in farming the higher ground or by soil exhaustion brought about by heavy exploitation over several centuries. Upland areas, particularly those under arable cultivation, were abandoned, while settlements began to be enclosed—defended it seems—by palisades, ramparts, and walls. In some parts of the country boundaries were created which defined large territories, perhaps associated with a new emphasis on pastoralism. In some areas pit alignments, that is rows of closely spaced pits running for hundreds of metres or more, seem to have been used to divide the land.[3] Several such alignments are known in Shropshire, though of unknown date.[4] The emergence of the bulk salt trade from the Worcestershire and Cheshire areas in the early 1st millennium B.C., evidenced by finds of briquetage salt containers from sites including Sharpstone Hill,[5] may have been at least partly due to the pastoralists' demand for salt. It would have been needed both as licks for the animals and to preserve their meat.[6]

About 650 b.c. iron began to be exploited more extensively than before, an innovation which traditionally marks the beginning of the Iron Age. Within 300 or 400 years iron was in common use in a way that bronze had never been, with even basic farming equipment and tools being made of iron rather than wood or

[93] W. Britnell, 'Two Round Barrows at Trelystan, Powys', *Proc. Prehist. Soc.* xlviii. 183–91.

[94] *Prehistoric Man in Wales & the West*, ed. F. Lynch and C. Burgess (1972), 345–53.

[95] Darvill, *Prehist. Brit.* 85–106; Simmons and Tooley, *Env. in Brit. Prehist.* 240–9.

[96] Darvill, *Prehist. Brit.* 105.   [97] Inf. in S.M.R.

[98] Clwyd–Powys Arch. Trust, air photo. colln. 87-MB-99, 100.

[99] Gregory, Lewin, and Thornes, *Palaeohydrology in Practice*, 228–32, 242; *Environmental Archaeology: a Regional*

Review, ii, ed. H. C. M. Keeley (1987), 113.

[1] Below.

[2] Simmons and Tooley, *Env. in Brit. Prehist.* 256–61.

[3] Darvill, *Prehist. Brit.* 106, cap. 5.

[4] e.g. SA 600, 2269; T. Rowley, *Landscape of Welsh Marches* (1986), 30.

[5] E. Morris, 'Prehist. Salt Distributions: Two Case Studies from W. Brit.' *Bull. Bd. Celtic Studies*, xxxii. 336–79; Darvill, *Prehist. Brit.* 129–30.

[6] J. Clutton-Brock, *Nat. Hist. of Domesticated Mammals* (1987), 67.

other less durable materials.[7] That may have had a considerable effect on the speed with which agricultural tasks could be performed, and in turn on the amount of land that might be worked. In fact, according to the pollen evidence, in the Shropshire area the Iron Age saw intensive campaigns of woodland clearance, with large-scale fellings first of broad-leaved woods and probably slightly later of the alder and willow woods on the lower flood plains. Palaeo-environmental data from a number of sites in the Severn basin have shown that such vegetational clearances in the mid 1st millennium B.C. were sufficient to cause extensive erosion and a consequent increase in flood-plain alluviation.[8]

By c. 800 b.c. hill forts were being built, striking testimony to the wider changes affecting society. About the 4th century B.C. there was what seems to have been a process of centralization; many hill-top sites were abandoned, whereas those that remained had heavy new defences added in the form of additional ramparts, ditches, and outworks. Shropshire's uplands have one of the highest concentrations of hill forts in the country. Few, however, have been investigated archaeologically. The basis of their economy therefore remains uncertain, especially the degree to which their inhabitants were personally engaged in farming the forts' hinterlands as opposed to drawing goods, rents, or tributes from a tenant or subject population in a wider territory.[9] Excavations at the Wrekin yielded carbonized grains of wheat, lesser amounts of barley, and some wild oats and hazel nuts. A cow bell was also found.[10] It appears likely that, at least for upland Iron Age communities, stock rearing remained of primary importance, the uplands being largely devoid of boundaries other than occasional and often major territorial ones which seem to have served to divide the grazing lands. Such may be the purpose of the dykes cutting across Stapeley Hill near Chirbury.[11]

A different landscape and economy was found on the lower lands, especially on the well drained soils along the Severn and its tributaries. Similar contrasts between upland and lowland have been noted in other parts of the country.[12] Along the rivers, as aerial photographs show, farmsteads were numerous, each surrounded by its own fields in which both arable and pastoral farming was practised.[13] The grain produced was stored above ground in structures supported on four main posts, rather than in underground storage pits.[14] Usually the farmstead was surrounded by a substantial ditch, and probably a bank and palisade as well; the scale suggests a defensive function, further evidence, with the hill forts, of the unsettled nature of the times and the competition for resources. At Sharpstone Hill Site A an unenclosed settlement with associated field system was replaced c. 800 × 300 b.c. by a small square enclosure, c. 35 × 40 m. internally, which contained at least one round house. Nearby, at Site B, a larger enclosure was increasingly well defended after the later 1st millennium B.C., at first by a palisade, then by a single ditch, and finally by a double ditch.[15] Until more sites have been examined, however, it is difficult to talk of typologies, chronologies, hierarchies, or the farming economy, and studies elsewhere have stressed the complexity and

[7] Darvill, Prehist. Brit. 153-5; S. C. Stanford, Arch. of Welsh Marches (1980), 85.

[8] Gregory, Lewin, and Thornes, Palaeohydrology in Practice, 239, 242. See also Simmons and Tooley, Env. in Brit. Prehist. 267-71.

[9] Darvill, Prehist. Brit. 133-44.

[10] S. C. Stanford, 'Wrekin Hillfort Excavations 1973', Arch. Jnl. cxli. 74, 80-3.

[11] SA 3967, 4122; cf. G. Guilbert, 'Ratlinghope/Stitt Hill: Earthwork Enclosures and Cross-Dykes', Bull. Bd. Celtic Studies, xxvi. 363-73 and pl. II.

[12] Gregory, Lewin, and Thornes, Palaeohydrology in Practice, 264; Aspects of Iron Age in Central S. Brit. ed. B. Cunliffe and D. Miles (1984), 78-85; Pragmatic Archaeology: Theory in Crisis, ed. C. F. and V. L. Gaffney (Brit. Arch. Rep. Brit. Ser. clxvii), 95-9.

[13] e.g. G. Webster, The Cornovii (1975), 90-2.

[14] Stanford, Arch. of Welsh Marches, 108.

[15] Webster, op. cit. 92.

variety of systems that may lie behind site-types superficially alike.[16] Generally it seems probable that during the Iron Age expansion of settlement and possibly aggressive competition led to greater economic specialization and so to more clearly defined farming regions.

Roman military power had reached the area by c. A.D. 52,[17] the conquest rapidly and permanently altering the local power structure. The hill forts were either abandoned or taken—the gate and internal buildings of that on the Wrekin were burnt, never to be rebuilt[18]—and it must be assumed that the native aristocrats either professed allegiance to Rome or were replaced. Otherwise, compared with much of Britain, the conquest had relatively little effect on the Shropshire area. Perhaps most remarkable is how little apparent change there was in the organization and farming of land, at least as evidenced by the construction of villas. Fewer than ten are known in Shropshire, and the enclosed 'native' farms seem to have continued in use as before.[19] It must be stressed, however, that the evidence is slight, and that those conclusions are somewhat at variance with orthodox opinions. Those maintain that the Roman conquest introduced or strengthened the impetus to produce a surplus, either by necessity through the exaction of taxes or by choice as people sought to acquire the means to pay for new types of luxury goods.[20] The likeliest explanation for that variance may be geographical, that the Shropshire area was on the western edge of what was anyway a peripheral province of the Roman empire, and that there, even in the 1st and 2nd centuries, Roman administration, organization, and influence was less effective than in more central areas.

The only towns established were *Viroconium Cornoviorum* (Wroxeter) and *Mediolanum* (Whitchurch).[21] In fact there were probably fewer large nucleated settlements in the county in the Roman period than in the late Iron Age when several of its hill forts may have had a population of a few hundred. Modern excavations of *Viroconium* have produced firm evidence about the food processed and consumed in the town. Most of it was presumably produced locally. Cattle provide the one possible exception, and it has been suggested that the cattle trade may have been the town's economic basis, rather as Oswestry's was at a later period, funnelling the trade between the highland and the lowland zone.[22] Excavation of 1st-, 2nd-, and 5th-century levels at Wroxeter has shown that cattle bone, always in the vast majority, increased over time at the expense of sheep, a trend visible on many other Romano-British sites.[23] Two other gradual changes were noted: an increasing proportion of the cattle bones were those of immature animals, probably reared specially for meat; and both the cattle and the sheep increased in size. Moreover there was a greater genetic difference between animals of the 1st and 2nd centuries than between those of the 2nd and 5th. Those facts suggest that the native stock was improved or replaced in the 1st and 2nd centuries by imported animals. Pork was also eaten in *Viroconium*, and red deer bone was present at all dates but in very small quantities.

Archaeological investigation has also revealed the main crops sold and consumed

[16] Cunliffe and Miles, *Aspects of Iron Age*, 73.
[17] Webster, op. cit. 28-9.
[18] *Arch. Jnl.* cxli. 85.
[19] Stanford, *Arch. of Welsh Marches*, 154-5.
[20] *Romano-Brit. Countryside: Studies in Rural Econ. and Soc.* ed. D. Miles (Brit. Arch. Rep. Brit. Ser. ciii), 25-7.
[21] SA 2702.
[22] Inf. from Mr. P. A. Barker, who is thanked for his comments on Wroxeter.
[23] B. Noddle in *Integrating the Subsistence Econ.* ed. M. Jones (Brit. Arch. Rep. International Ser. clxxxi), 211-38, and in *Husbandry in Europe*, ed. C. Grigson and J. Clutton-Brock (Brit. Arch. Rep. International Ser. ccxxvii), 105-24. Miss Noddle is thanked for commenting on the bones from the excavations of Mr. Barker and Dr. G. Webster.

in *Viroconium*.[24] Wheat was the dominant cereal; the main species were spelt wheat (*Triticum spelta*) and emmer wheat (*T. diococcum*). The compact bread wheat *T. aestivo-compactum* was also present, but in small quantities that may cause its use to be underestimated: in such free-threshing wheats (unlike the glume wheats, spelt and emmer) the ears do not have to be parched before threshing and casual depositions are thus fewer. Barley occurs less frequently than wheat, and is the six-rowed hulled type (*Hordeum sativum* or *H. sativum hexastichum*). Rye and oats were relatively rare. Weed seeds found in the town are typical of those from cereal fields. The only other field crop represented was the pea (*Pisum sativum*). Also noted were hazel nuts, blackberries, and elderberries, which may also have been gathered for sale or consumption.

Some time after the formal end of Roman rule *Viroconium* and *Mediolanum* fell into disuse, and it seems that the few villas did also. Generally it is likely that the end of Roman rule had relatively little impact on farming in the county, and that there was essentially a continuity in rural settlement and farming patterns and practices from perhaps the middle of the 1st millennium B.C. to some time after the middle of the 1st millennium A.D.

What forms of landownership obtained and how estates were organized before the Norman Conquest necessarily remain speculative. Nevertheless there are clear indications that in Shropshire, as elsewhere, some, if not all, settlements were grouped in units of administration or lordship. Domesday Book records 25 instances, mostly on the estates held by Earl Roger in 1086, of manors with berewicks, outlying and subsidiary settlements. Two other manors had 'members', and three more manors were said to be berewicks of other, unspecified, manors. *Lege*, probably Longnor, was subject to an unnamed 'head manor'.[25] Manors with berewicks were spread fairly evenly across the whole county apart from the Clun area, where their absence may not be significant. Such estate organization is found in most of pre-Conquest England. It shared characteristics with arrangements described in considerable detail in Welsh law tracts of the 12th century and later, the central concept of which is the support of head settlements by a hierarchy of subsidiary ones owing rents, tributes, or services. Such 'multiple' estates may have origins in pre-Roman Celtic times.[26] By 1086 it appears that in Shropshire that form of estate organization was disappearing, not least in the face of Norman manorial reorganization. How widespread it had once been, and when it had evolved are questions impossible to answer. No hint of local estate hierarchies is given, for instance, in the few Saxon charters dealing with lands in Shropshire.[27]

An intriguing, and unanswerable, question concerns the relationship between estate organization and the fundamental change in the rural settlement pattern and farming systems that occurred at some stage in the 400 years preceding the Norman Conquest. Nucleated settlements began to replace dispersed farms, and a part of the land associated with such settlements began to be subdivided in some fashion among those who had (or thus acquired) a share in it. That seems, on the available evidence, to be the context in which open fields began to evolve, though there is no documentary evidence for the process and the archaeological evidence that is available is slight. Medieval occurrence of the name 'old field' as at Bromfield,

[24] Mr. M. Charles is thanked for inf. on work done by himself and Mr. M. Monk.
[25] C. P. Lewis, 'Intro. to Salop. Domesday', *Salop. Domesday*, ed. A. Williams and R. W. H. Erskine (forthcoming). Dr. Lewis is thanked for sight of his unpubl. wk.
[26] e.g. *Medieval Settlement*, ed. P. H. Sawyer (1976),

15–40; Wendy Davies, *Wales in Early Middle Ages* (1982), 43–7; cf. N. Gregson, 'The multiple estate model: some critical questions', *Jnl. Hist. Geog.* xi. 339–51.
[27] H. P. R. Finberg, *Early Charters of W. Midlands* (1972), 147–50.

Chetton, Coton, Madeley, and Smethcott[28] may indicate remaining memories of the original open-field nuclei in those places.[29]

Little is known of late Saxon Shropshire beyond the image of it preserved in the Conqueror's survey of 1086. It appears likely that a growing population and demand for food—perhaps the pressures that had generated the emergence of nucleated settlements and open fields—continued to mould the countryside, bringing new land into cultivation and reordering the methods of cultivation on the older-settled lands. The landscape that Domesday Book records was an ancient one, formed by man's exploitation of it over several millennia. Nevertheless it was a landscape that was in the middle of a period of unusually rapid change in the face of intensified land use. As has been seen that was but the most recent of a series of major changes over the previous 5,000 years in how the land was cultivated. Those changes, resulting from the interplay of environmental, social, and technological developments, were just as dynamic as those in later, better documented times.

DOMESDAY BOOK TO 1300

THE two and a half centuries extending from Edward the Confessor's reign to the last years of Edward I form a period of growth: of population, of food production, and of the area under cultivation.[30] Most modern commentators regard the last two phenomena as responses to the increase in the country's population, from perhaps c. 2 million in 1086 to 5 or 6 million in 1347.[31] Those responses, and indeed the ability to respond in terms of the available resources, varied greatly across England. In some parts of the country agriculture, particularly arable farming, was already intensive by the time of the Norman Conquest, and there opportunities for expansion, as opposed to further intensification, were few. Elsewhere large tracts of lightly populated land survived in the late 11th century where the characteristic agriculture was pastoral and widely dispersed: by and large they were in the areas with poorer soils and less immediate agricultural potential. Shropshire was such an area except for a few fairly small and discrete areas, particularly on the lighter and well drained soils associated with the county's main watercourses. In the two centuries up to 1300 the agriculture of the county changed considerably. The county never had great areas with prairie-like expanses of open field land surrounding large nucleated villages, but by the early 14th century more of it was under arable cultivation than ever before. Moreover the land not under the plough comprising the woods, moors, and pastures, often on the uplands, was more widely grazed, and more closely managed and regulated, than at any stage in the past. It was a full and busy landscape, of hamlets and villages each with its own small open fields and a patchwork of closes; of woods full of grazing animals as well as people collecting and cutting wood; of heaths and uplands walked by flocks of sheep several hundred strong; and of rivers and ponds yielding heavy catches. For those with an adequate share in the resources—the lords, and a few of the richer freeholders and peasants—those were by and large

[28] T. Rowley, *Salop. Landscape* (1972), 137; *V.C.H. Salop.* xi. 42; S.P.L., Deeds 3666.

[29] *Origins of Open Field Agric.* ed. R. T. Rowley (1981), 89.

[30] Dr. C. C. Dyer and Mr. J. B. Lawson are thanked for their comments on this article.

[31] E. Miller and J. Hatcher, *Med. Eng.: Rural Soc. and Econ. Change 1086-1348* (1978), 28-9.

good centuries, providing opportunity and profit. For the mass of the peasantry there was no hope of any economic advance beyond subsistence, and hunger and hardship were never far away.

The sources which reveal that story, as for the rest of the country, are relatively few before the mid 13th century, and even in the later 13th century no substantial archive has survived from a single estate or institution in the county. The account which follows is therefore based largely on impression and inference rather than on a statistically reliable body of data.

Lords and tenants

The first systematic account of the landowning class is given by Domesday Book. In the later 11th century several national magnates are recorded as owning Shropshire estates: King Edward and Queen Edith, Earl Leofric (d. 1057) and his wife Godiva (fl. 1080), King Edward's brother-in-law (and successor) Earl Harold, and Earls Edwin (d. 1071) and Morcar (d. after 1087). The bishops of Hereford and of Chester also held important estates in the county and the church of Wenlock claimed an ancient endowment. In 1066 two outstandingly rich thegns among the Shropshire landowners[32] were Edric the wild, nephew of Eadric Streona, ealdorman of Mercia, and Edric's distant kinsman Siward, a son of King Edward's kinsman Aethelgar. Siward's brother Ealdred was also a Shropshire landowner. Edric and Siward were probably sufficiently important to be independent of the Mercian earls, but the many second-rank thegns of Shropshire and the smaller landowners were probably all the earl's men.

By 1086 there was virtually no *terra regis*, and the predominance of Roger of Montgomery, earl of Shrewsbury, was the main feature of Shropshire landed society. Apart from Earl Roger, the bishops of Hereford and Chester, and the abbot of St.-Remi, there were only five other tenants in chief in the county, most of whose lands held in chief lay in south Shropshire. Earl Roger's leading position was forfeited by his son in 1102,[33] and thereafter there was no earl with a title from the county until 1442. The families who emerged as leading Shropshire landowners in the 12th and 13th centuries were the FitzAlans, their tenants the Stranges, and the Chetwynds, Corbets, FitzWarins, Mortimers, and Pantulfs. Some of those families founded cadet lines (the Eytons of Eyton upon the Weald Moors, for example, were probably cadets of the Pantulfs), some eventually died out in the male line but transmitted their lands to heiresses, and some—notably the FitzAlans from their acquisition of Arundel in 1243—became families of national standing. By the end of the 12th century the ranks of the leading Shropshire landowners had been joined by half a dozen monasteries: Buildwas, Combermere (Ches.), Haughmond, Lilleshall, and Shrewsbury abbeys and the priory of Wenlock. Beneath the leading landowners were the ranks of the gentry, lords of one or two manors, whose family fortunes and vicissitudes have been amply chronicled for the period.[34] Many of them—the Eytons, Ercalls, Foresters, Gatacres, Hodnets, Plowdens, and Sandfords for example—transmitted their estates to heirs who held them for many generations after the close of the period. Nevertheless landowning society was by no means static. In the 13th century families such as the Audleys, the Burnells, the Charltons, the Erdingtons, and the Ludlows joined the ranks of

[32] C. P. Lewis, 'Eng. and Norman govt. and lordship in Welsh borders 1039-87' (Oxf. Univ. D.Phil. thesis, 1985), cap. 3.

[33] *V.C.H. Salop.* i. 279-349; iii. 10.

[34] For this see Eyton, i-xii. For the monasteries cf. *V.C.H. Salop.* ii. 18 sqq.

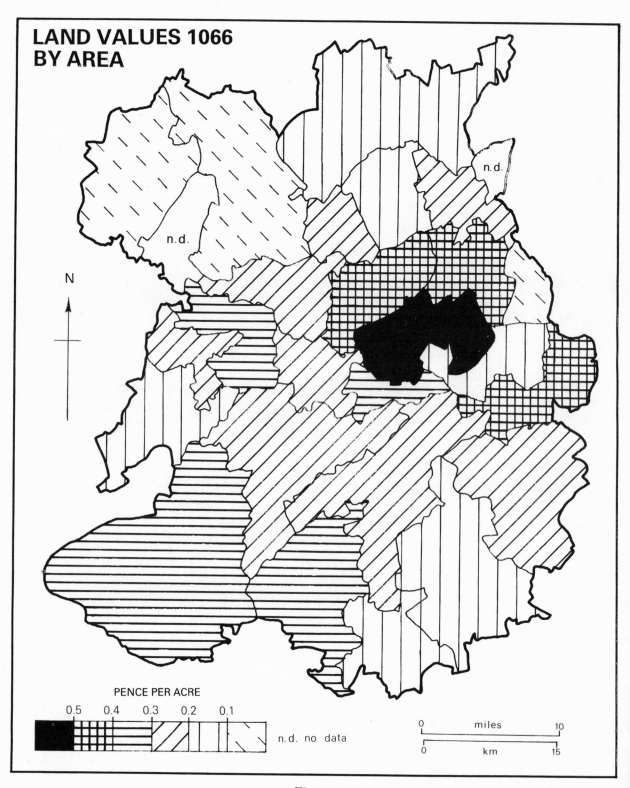

Fig. 2
Based on inf. in *V.C.H. Salop*. i. 309–49. For the regions see *Domesday Geog. of Midland Eng.* ed.
H. C. Darby and I. B. Terrett (1971), 131.

Shropshire landowners as a result of successful years spent in royal service or in trade. There is little evidence that such newcomers had any impact on agricultural practices—any more than the 11th-century Norman conquerors had. It is, however, the record of their landholdings that provides much of the documentary history of agriculture during the two centuries or more that followed the Norman Conquest.

A fairly consistent picture emerges from the Domesday survey about regional variations in the evolution of agriculture within the county in the late 11th century. As revealing as any of the more widely used figures are those of 'land value', which were not plotted in the *Domesday Geography* series[35] but which, as recent work suggests, do record in a reasonably consistent fashion the income which the lord could expect to receive from his manor, whether as rent if the manor was leased or in revenue if exploited directly.[36] That value was required, if possible, to be recorded in triplicate: for 1066, 1070, and 1086. The Conqueror's devastation of eastern Shropshire in 1070 left economic production disrupted and manorial values depressed both in 1070 (as can be seen in the relatively few cases where precise figures for that year were recorded) and 16 years later. The Shropshire estates described as 'waste' in 1066 lay mainly in the west: those around Chirbury may have been thus understood to be exempt from geld because of their owners' extensive hunting rights, analogous to the later forest laws; the 'waste' estates around Oswestry may have been given reduced geld assessments after the area was regained from the Welsh in the mid 1060s.[37] In other areas the 1066 values may be taken as representing fairly accurately the wealth of the various parts of the county in the mid 11th century.

The most valuable manors were clearly concentrated east of Shrewsbury, between it, Edgmond, and Albrighton, and to a lesser extent west of Shrewsbury (Figs. 2 and 3). That concentration of highest values is also reflected in the numbers both of ploughteams at work in 1086 and of ploughlands, a new fiscal assessment of 1086-7,[38] although the relative rankings of the regions differ from one method of assessment to another. The differences are due not least to the fact that the three methods of assessment reflect different things: numbers of ploughteams reflect arable production whereas manorial values, and probably numbers of ploughlands too, reflect total agricultural production. In a county such as Shropshire, where animal husbandry dominated the economy in some areas, the differences may be considerable. The contribution of sheep husbandry may well explain the high value of land in the Clun region in 1066 when it is compared with the small number of ploughteams at work and the low density of recorded population. Another contribution to the value of manors in pastoral areas such as Clun may have been rents paid by minor tenants. As with the rent paying *censarii* on Burton abbey's estate, such tenants may not have been recorded in 1086.[39] Land values, ploughteams, and ploughlands all indicate the relative poverty and lack of agricultural development in the northern third of the county.

The numbers of ploughteams in 1086 allow some very broad conclusions to be drawn about how the 500-odd manors in the county were worked, whether solely by demesne teams, or by a mixture of demesne and peasant teams, or by peasant teams alone. Most numerous, comprising a little more than half of those manors,

[35] *Domesday Geog. Mid. Eng.* ed. H. C. Darby and I. B. Terrett (1971), 130-1; H. C. Darby, *Domesday Eng.* (1977) 380-1.

[36] J. McDonald and G. D. Snooks, *Domesday Economy: New Approach to Anglo-Norman Hist.* (1986); *Field and Forest: Hist. Geog. of Warws. and Worcs.* ed. T. R. Slater and P. J. Jarvis (Norwich, 1982), 105-24.

[37] Darby and Terrett, op. cit. 130-1, 144-9; Lewis, 'Eng. and Norman govt. 1039-87', cap. 5 and p. 178.

[38] *Domesday Bk.: A Reassessment*, ed. P. Sawyer (1985), 86-103.

[39] J. F. R. Walmsley, 'The *censarii* of Burton abbey and the Domesday pop.' *N. Staffs. Jnl. Field Studies*, viii. 73-80.

were those with both demesne and peasant teams, apparently the precursors of the typical manor of the 12th and 13th centuries. They lay thickest in some of the best agricultural land, in east Shropshire and especially in the Severn valley below Shrewsbury and the area between the Severn and the Clee Hills. About a tenth of the county's manors had only a home farm, while about twice that number had no ploughs owned by the lord and were apparently worked solely by the peasantry. Manors of those two types lay thickest in, and west of, the Roden valley and in the Severn valley about Shrewsbury, with smaller groups in north-east Shropshire, east of Madeley, and in some of the southern valleys.[40] About a tenth of the county's manors were still reckoned to be at least partly 'waste' in 1086, and 36 were wholly waste with no recorded population or value. It is clear, however, that the county had undergone a remarkable economic recovery in the 16 years since c. 1070 when c. 120 vills lay 'waste', most as a result of the king's devastation of districts which had supported Edric the wild's revolt, but some probably owing to earlier upheavals, notably the suggested recovery of territory from the Welsh.[41]

The extent of the arable land of manorial demesnes in the 13th century was frequently recorded in carucates rather than acres. The usual Exchequer reckoning was 120 a. to the carucate,[42] and that can be taken as a reasonable working figure for Shropshire. It was used, for instance, when Peter Corbet's demesne lands were listed on his death in 1300,[43] although carucates of 108 a., 104 a. and 100 a. were also recorded.[44] The size of the carucate was recognized as varying: in a survey of 1301 the demesne at Newcastle, in Clun, was said to comprise two small carucates.[45] Accepting the carucate as c. 120 a., it is probably a fair estimate that over half of the demesnes in hand in the county in the 13th century comprised between 100 and 250 a. of arable, of which two thirds would have been under cultivation each year.[46] Few were smaller, while demesnes of 3 or 4 carucates were not unusual. It was rare for more than 4 carucates to be in hand on a single manor: of the six examples noted, three were demesne manors of Wenlock priory,[47] one was a grange of Buildwas abbey,[48] and one belonged to the earl of Arundel.[49] The other was at Pontesbury where 6 carucates, or c. 720 a., were in hand on the lord's death in 1286.[50]

The lack of Shropshire estate records for the period makes it difficult to assess how far landlords followed national trends of estate management. It is impossible to ascertain whether there was a renewed emphasis on the direct exploitation of demesnes in the early 13th century as commodity prices soared and landlords sought to increase their profits,[51] although that is suggested by evidence from some of the county's monastic estates: Haughmond abbey, for instance, clearly had a policy of expanding both its demesne lands and its rent roll in the early 13th century.[52] A century or so later there is slightly more evidence of a reverse trend when landlords began to prefer the security of cash rents as the economic situation

[40] What follows based on C. P. Lewis, 'Intro. to Salop. Domesday', Salop. Domesday, ed. A. Williams and R. W. H. Erskine (forthcoming). Dr. Lewis is thanked for sight of his unpubl. wk.

[41] Darby and Terrett, Domesday Geog. Mid. Eng. 144-7; V.C.H. Salop. iii. 7; above.

[42] F. W. Maitland, Domesday Bk. and Beyond (1960), 459. 555. [43] P.R.O., C 133/7, no. 8.

[44] At Albrighton and Pitchford in 1284: P.R.O., C 133/41, no. 14; at Forton in 1300: Cal. Inq. p.m. iii, p. 451.

[45] Two Est. Surveys of Earls of Arundel (Suss. Rec. Soc. lxvii), p. 64.

[46] Estimate based on figs. in Cal. Inq. p.m. i-iii; c. 60 inq.

p.m. in P.R.O., C 132-3 and E 149; P.R.O., SC 12/14/23-4; Two Est. Surveys of Earls of Arundel; Tax. Eccl. (Rec. Com.), 163-4.

[47] Oxenbold (7 carucates), M. Wenlock (5), Madeley (5): Tax. Eccl. 164.

[48] Meole Brace (5): S.P.L., MS. 28.

[49] Two Est. Surveys of Earls of Arundel, p. 65.

[50] P.R.O., C 133/45, no. 2; V.C.H. Salop. viii. 272.

[51] P. D. A. Harvey, 'Eng. Inflation of 1180-1200', Past & Present, lxi. 3-30; C. Dyer, Lords and Peasants in a Changing Soc.: Est. of Bpric. of Worc. 680-1540 (1980), 52.

[52] Cart. of Haughmond Abbey, ed. U. Rees (1985), pp. 8-14; below, 1300-1540 (Assarting and inclosure).

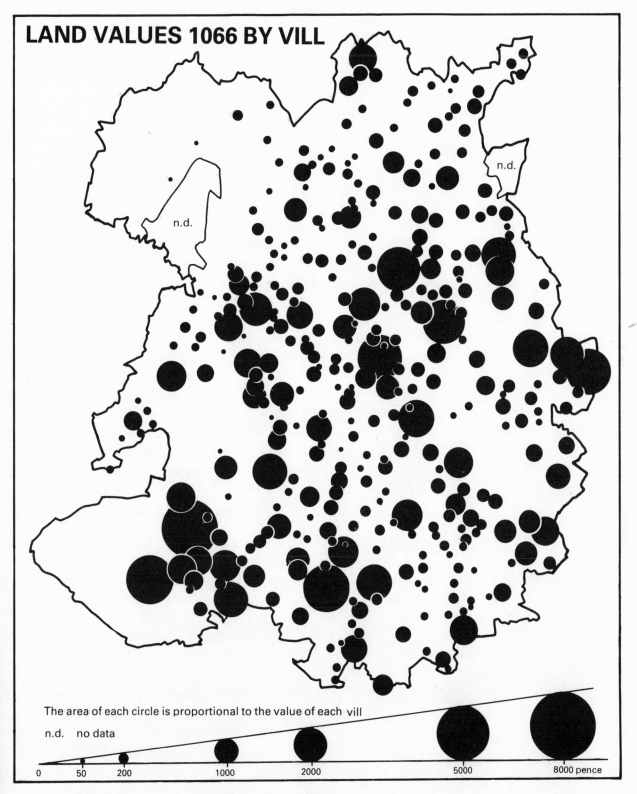

LAND VALUES 1066 BY VILL

n.d.

n.d.

The area of each circle is proportional to the value of each vill

n.d.   no data

| 0 | 50 | 200 | 1000 | 2000 | 5000 | 8000 pence |

Fig. 3
Based on inf. in *V.C.H. Salop.* i. 309–49.

became less certain,[53] and there are many instances of demesnes being leased by the end of the 13th century. In 1301, for instance, on the FitzAlan estates in the county the demesnes at Acton Round (*c.* 200 a.) were in the villeins' hands, as were 3 virgates (*c.* 180 a.) of demesne at Acton, in Clun, and *c.* 100 a. at Westhope, in Diddlebury.[54] In the lordship of Oswestry the demesne comprised 4 carucates, or up to 480 a., in 1272, 140 a. in 1302, and had been completely leased by 1362–3.[55] Wenlock priory ceased to cultivate its Little Wenlock demesne *c.* 1300 and let it in small lots to the customary tenants; that probably marked the beginning of the retreat from the high point of demesne farming which had been reached in the late 13th century.[56] Shrewsbury abbey too began to move rapidly away from demesne farming soon after 1300,[57] and Haughmond abbey a little later, the first recorded lease of demesne being dated 1316.[58]

A profitable appurtenance on many demesnes by the later 11th century was a mill, and Domesday Book records 98 mills in the county.[59] Although it can be assumed that most, if not all, were water rather than horse mills,[60] the type can only be guessed. Even in the 13th century, by which time their number had greatly increased, few details are found of the mills themselves, unlike their pools and watercourses which gave rise to frequent complaint from the the owners or occupants of adjoining land. One of the few technical details to have survived concerns Hope Bagot mill, where in 1292 the miller was dragged to his death by the inner of two waterwheels.[61] Winnowing places adjoined some mills in the 13th century,[62] and most mills probably had eel and fish traps set in their water channels, some Domesday mills owing their rents wholly or partly in eels.[63]

Windmills began to appear in England in the late 12th century,[64] but none is noticed in Shropshire until 1267 when there was one in Shrewsbury, apparently within the town walls and built by the burgesses.[65] The only other 13th-century windmill known in the county was at Wem; in 1281 it was said to be worth 10s. a year, compared with the two watermills there worth £2 13s. 4d.[66] Wellington had one by 1315,[67] and one was destroyed at Wrockwardine by 1349.[68] Generally it appears that their adoption in a county with ample watercourses was slow.

By 1267 in addition to their windmill, the burgesses of Shrewsbury had also built three horsemills in the town and three in the suburbs.[69] As with the windmill, the intention was clearly to circumvent the abbey, which owned three watermills in Shrewsbury and since 1121 had had the right to the multure of the whole town.[70] Another horsemill was recorded at Buildwas abbey's grange at Monkmeole in 1279.[71]

Of the various classes under which Domesday Book groups the rural population the largest was villeins, 1,985 of whom were recorded in Shropshire, that is 37 per cent of its total population.[72] They were unfree tenants who owed rents and services for their share of the manor's lands. On two of Roger de Lacy's manors, Stanton

---

[53] M. M. Postan, *Med. Economy and Soc.* (1972), 110–18; Miller and Hatcher, *Med. Eng.* cap. 8; J. Z. Titow, *Eng. Rural Soc. 1200–1350* (1969), 43–54; below, 1300–1540 (Leasing of demesnes).

[54] *Two Est. Surveys of Earls of Arundel*, pp. 58, 63, 79–80.

[55] W. J. Slack, *Lordship of Oswestry 1393–1607* (Shrews. 1951), 25; Llinos O. W. Smith, 'The Lordships of Chirk and Oswestry, 1282–1415' (Lond. Univ. Ph.D. thesis, 1970), 118, 120.

[56] *V.C.H. Salop.* ii. 42–3; xi. 82.

[57] Ibid. ii. 32.

[58] *Cart. Haughmond*, p. 15.

[59] Darby and Terrett, *Domesday Geog. Mid. Eng.* 147–51.

[60] Darby, *Domesday Eng.* 270.

[61] Eyton, iv. 365.

[62] *Cart. Haughmond*, pp. 115, 149.

[63] Darby and Terrett, *Domesday Geog. Mid. Eng.* 148.

[64] *New Hist. Geog. of Eng.* ed. H. C. Darby (1973), 94.

[65] *Cart. of Shrews. Abbey*, ed. U. Rees (1975), i, pp. 136–8.

[66] P.R.O., C 133/27, no. 9.

[67] *V.C.H. Salop.* xi. 226.

[68] Ibid. 316.

[69] *Cart. Shrews.* i, pp. 136–8.

[70] Ibid. pp. 49, 136–8; *T.S.A.S.* 2nd ser. vi. 341–57.

[71] S.P.L., MS. 28, p. 44.

[72] Darby and Terrett, *Domesday Geog. Mid. Eng.* 129.

Lacy and Onibury, nine 'half villeins' were noted, an indication that in 1086, as later, villein holdings might be divided.[73] The next largest Domesday group, totalling 1,198, comprised the bordars.[74] Their status has been much debated, although it seems that they were smallholders, some of whom were freed slaves settled on parcels of demesne.[75] Their holdings were probably smaller than the villeins'. Bordars probably also had different obligations to their lords, and in Shropshire bordars occur much more frequently than villeins on manors where the only ploughteams were on the lord's home farm.[76]

The lowest group of the population in 1086 was the *servi*, serfs or slaves, and Shropshire, particularly the south-eastern part of the modern county (largely in Staffordshire in 1086), had one of the highest proportions of slaves (*c.* 19 per cent of the population)[77] of any county in England.[78] They probably worked on the demesne for their keep but had no other remuneration or any land of their own. Oxmen (*bovarii*), of whom there were 361 (7.5 per cent of the population) in the county,[79] were confined to the counties along the Welsh border. Employed in looking after and driving the demesne plough beasts, their legal status was probably similar to that of the *servi*.[80] In most parts of England the number of *servi* was already in decline in the late 11th century, and in the following century or so they were to disappear altogether, merging with the bordars and cottars into the class of unfree smallholder or becoming *famuli* or wage labourers.[81]

Apart from those four classes Domesday Book records 440 tenants in Shropshire. Of them 171 were radmen, tenants who, anciently at least, owed riding services for their lands, acting as messengers and officials around a lord's estates. Again, the class is little heard of after 1086 and it is difficult to define either their legal or economic position. Generally, as in Cheshire, it seems likely that they occupied a position above the villeins and that they occupied separate agricultural holdings and owned their own plough beasts. In that respect their position was analogous to that of freemen, 20 of whom were noted in the county. Among the 15 or so other broad classes in which Shropshire's men and women were described in 1086 the two largest were ethnic: Welshmen (64), and Frenchmen (34). Most of the remaining groups were occupational and included 55 priests, 8 smiths, 7 reeves, a beekeeper, and a miller.[82]

In the 12th and 13th centuries the usual customary tenant holding in Shropshire was the virgate or a fraction thereof. Virgate size differed considerably between counties and areas,[83] not least because a virgate was a share in the resources rather than a set acreage. Moreover the possibility of calculating virgate size in terms of statute acres is limited by the likely use in the 12th century of field acres as a measure. Nevertheless, in the few instances where virgate size seems to be reliably given, a surprisingly high figure of 50–60 a. is consistently found.[84] In addition to that 50 or 60 a. of arable, possibly originally held entirely in the open fields, each virgate had other rights or shares in the vill's woods and commons, which provided the essential grazing beyond that in the fallow field and the peasant's own croft.

[73] Ibid. 127.
[74] Ibid. 129.
[75] *Med. Settlement*, ed. P. H. Sawyer (1976), 197–9; R. Lennard, 'Econ. position of bordars and cottars in Domesday Bk.' *Econ. Jnl.* lxi. 342–71; *Ag. Hist. Eng.* ii. 58–64.
[76] Lewis, 'Salop. Domesday'.
[77] Darby and Terrett, *Domesday Geog. Mid. Eng.* 127.
[78] Darby, *Domesday Eng.* 76–7.
[79] Darby and Terrett, op. cit. 149.
[80] Ibid. 127–8.

[81] Ibid.; Darby, *Domesday Eng.* 72–4; Miller and Hatcher, *Med. Eng.* 24–5.
[82] Darby and Terrett, *Domesday Geog. Mid. Eng.* 128; *V.C.H. Ches.* i. 331; *T.S.A.S.* lix. 95–6.
[83] I. H. Adams, *Agrarian Landscape Terms: Glossary for Hist. Geog.* (1976), 11.
[84] H. L. Gray, *Eng. Field Systems* (1915), 68; Eyton, iii. 111; *Two Est. Surveys of Earls of Arundel*, p. 58; *Cart. Shrews.* ii, p. 312; S.R.O. 3195/1, f. 6; S.P.L., Deeds 370, 6948; P.R.O., C 145/20, no. 1.

Thus a late 13th-century extent of Claverley noted that there were 22 virgates in villeinage, each worth 8s. a year with its pasture and other rights.[85] Meadow was scarce and valuable in most Shropshire vills,[86] and there is little evidence about how much, if any, it was usual for a virgate to have, or whether doles were fixed or regularly realloted. That virgate holdings could include set amounts of meadow, and also of woodland, is indicated both by a survey of Prees in 1298, where a regular 1 a. of meadow to each 17 a. of arable bond land in Prees and ½ a. to every 11½ a. at Darliston is suggested,[87] and by a case of 1319 concerning '4 virgates [of arable land], 4 a. of meadow, 4 a. of wood and 4s. rent' in Ellesmere, apparently a division of a hide of land granted to Haughmond abbey in the mid 12th century.[88] Furthermore where assarting was continuing it was usual for virgaters to hold a few acres of such land, normally as small parcels of enclosed arable, meadow, or pasture accounted for separately from their main holding.[89]

There are many indications of the division of a settlement's arable land into equal-sized virgates in a single operation.[90] It is notable that in almost every case where virgates were divided it was into halves or quarters. The one clear exception was at Barlow, in Hopesay, where in 1301 all 13 holdings were of either ⅓ or ⅙ virgate,[91] but even that reinforces the clearly discernible regularity with which old arable lands were allocated among a vill's tenants.

Nowhere, however, is the division into virgates actually documented, and it seems generally, or perhaps always, to have been made in the county by the end of the 12th century. In Cardington parish in 1185, for instance, the Templars' tenants held 17¾ virgates: 16½ in ½-virgates and the remainder as ¼-virgates. There were 10 virgates in Cardington township, 3½ in Enchmarsh, 2¼ in Chatwall, and 2 in 'Botelegee'. The rental value of each ½ virgate varied from place to place: 60d. in 'Botelegee', 48d. in Enchmarch, 27½d. in Chatwall, and either 40d., 36d., or 24d. in Cardington. The general uniformity of value within a township combined with the variation between townships suggests that the division into virgates was made at different times from place to place and perhaps before the estates came under a single lord, which was before 1066.[92]

In the 13th century about half of the county's landed peasants had ½ virgate or its equivalent, that is 30 a. or a little less.[93] Only c. 15 per cent of the landed peasants held a full virgate, while the rest held ¼ virgate (a nook) or less. It is difficult to subdivide the last group and to reckon how many were cottagers with just a few acres. On the earl of Arundel's manors in the county in 1301 c. 19 per cent of the tenantry held a nook and c. 20 per cent were cottagers, some of the cottagers being on manors in welshries where the law of partible inheritance tended to decrease the size of holdings.[94] Even on manors unaffected by Welsh custom there could be as many cottagers, with just a garden and a few acres of assart land, as there were men who had a share of the open fields. That seems to be implied, for instance, by surveys of Cheswardine and Child's Ercall in 1280[95] and of Hope and Shrawardine in 1301.[96] The bishop of Coventry and Lichfield's estate at Prees,

[85] P.R.O., SC 12/14/24.
[86] Below (Livestock and pastoral farming).
[87] Staffs. R.O., D.(W.) 1734/J/2268, ff. 26-8.
[88] Cart. Haughmond, pp. 57-8.
[89] Two Est. Surveys of Earls of Arundel; below.
[90] Origins of Open Field Agric. ed. R. T. Rowley (1981), 130-44.
[91] Two Est. Surveys of Earls of Arundel, pp. 53-4.
[92] V.C.H. Salop. i. 322; ii. 85-6; Rec. of Templars in Eng. ed. B. A. Lees (1935), 37-9.

[93] e.g. Two Est. Surveys of Earls of Arundel; Lees, Rec. of Templars in Eng. 37-9; Bk. of Fees, ii. 1241-2; Eyton, v. 91-100; vi. 145-6; V.C.H. Salop. viii. 126; P.R.O., C 133/7, no. 8; C 133/15, no. 3; C 133/98, no. 30; P.R.O., SC 12/14/23. Cf., however, the pertinent remarks in Miller and Hatcher, Med. Eng. 140-1.
[94] Two Est. Surveys of Earls of Arundel. Cf. Dyer, Lords and Peasants, 89; below.
[95] T.S.A.S. 3rd ser. viii. 362-7.
[96] Two Est. Surveys of Earls of Arundel, pp. 54, 81-2.

in north-east Shropshire, was described in some detail in a survey of 1298.[97] In Prees township there were 19 neifs who held *c.* 126 a. altogether, most holdings including a tenement, arable, and meadow held by 'old tenure', and a little 'new' land assarted from the extensive common heaths, moors, and woods around the village. At Darliston, about 3 miles east, there were seven neifs with holdings of a similar size, four of the better endowed holding 11½ a. 'old' arable and ½ a. 'old' meadow each. Prees had 25 cottagers, Darliston three. Most had a cottage and ½-a. croft, and about half also had an acre or two of either 'old' or assart land. To the cottagers can perhaps be added five *conventionarii* at Prees, four of whom held 1½ a. or less and one 6 a., and 13 holders of small parcels of new land who do not appear to be listed elsewhere. Generally, of the bishop's 72 or so customary tenants, about two thirds held 5 a. or less, about a dozen 5–10 a., and 7 or so 10–20 a. The reckoning by virgates makes assessment of the size of the 13 freeholds in Prees and Darliston difficult, although clearly they varied greatly, between ¼ and 2 virgates; most freeholders in Prees probably held about as much land as the wealthier customary tenants. Small holdings were especially a feature of those areas of western Shropshire where land was held by Welsh tenure.[98] Thus in 1301 at Newcastle, in Clun, where, perhaps significantly, the 2 carucates of demesne were described as small, the 21 tenants held a total of just 75 a. and one meadow. In the same year in Llanhedric, in Clun, the six tenants held a total of 75 a., while 37 a. and an assart, previously held by five men, were listed as vacant.[99] The inference is that in such communities agriculture was principally pastoral on the upland commons.

The foregoing observations are based almost exclusively on manorial records which because of their limited purpose make no mention of three matters fundamental to the size of peasant holdings and the quality of peasant life. First, the landless, who might include younger sons, widows, and *famuli*, were not enumerated. Secondly, such records largely ignore the workings of the peasant land market, particularly subletting for terms that varied from a year to life, which is known to have been widely practised in the 13th century.[1] The old or infirm, to take an obvious example, might let all or part of their holding to another peasant for a term, either for cash or for food, clothing, and housing.[2] Such land might be taken up by the opportunistic rich peasant, who in turn might employ 'undersettles' to work it. Thirdly, the records are invariably silent on the size and composition of the household on any holding. A man with only a wife to support or with several working children was obviously far better off than one with unproductive young children or old relatives living in his household. Thus to some extent manorial surveys and extents give an artificially regular picture of peasant life, and a village such as Wattlesborough, composed entirely of ½-virgate holdings,[3] would probably have had a highly stratified peasant society in both economic and social terms.

When attempting to identify and define social classes in the 12th and 13th centuries contemporaries and later writers concur that there are no clear dividing lines or nomenclature. The main division among the peasantry was between those of servile status who held their land of the lord in return for specified rents,

[97] Staffs. R.O., D.(W.) 1734/J/2268, ff. 26–8. Some slightly ambiguous entries prevent absolute precision.
[98] Below.
[99] *Two Est. Surveys of Earls of Arundel*, pp. 59, 64. Cf. also for Braggington evidence *V.C.H. Salop.* viii. 208; *T.S.A.S.* lviii. 130.
[1] Miller and Hatcher, *Med. Eng.* 141; Postan, *Med. Econ.*

and Soc. 152. For examples of leases cf. e.g. *Roll of Salop. Eyre 1256* (Selden Soc. xcvi), pp. 3, 14, 49, 51, 67, 80, 91, 120, 129; S.P.L., Deeds 16283; S.R.O. 322, med. deed no. 39; 1093/2/530; 1514/151, 214, 255; 4651/1; Staffs. R.O., D. 593/A/2/34/15.
[2] Below.
[3] P.R.O., C 133/98, no. 30.

obligations, and, most crucially, labour services on the demesne, and freemen who held their land free of all exactions but a money rent.[4] Many instances can be cited where custom and practice differed from lawyers' theory. In Much Wenlock township in 1247 the prior's free tenants were subject to exactions that included terciary, that is the payment of one third of chattels on death, and one owed ploughing and mowing services.[5] In Shropshire, as in the rest of the west midlands, it seems that it was normal for free tenants to owe heriot, and on High Ercall and Whittington manors it was only the free tenants who owed such dues.[6]

Servile tenants appear variously as customary tenants, neifs and, most commonly, villeins. Most manors also had a number of cottagers who held and usually lived on an acre or two of what was often former waste land and owed only a money rent to the lord of the manor. In Prees and perhaps elsewhere there were also *conventionarii*, conventionary tenants, who held their few acres 'at the bishop's will' for money rents.[7] Nothing else is known of the nature of that tenure at Prees, but in other counties it involved a seven-year lease for which a money rent and perhaps an entry fine and heriot were due but no labour service.[8] Technically villeins were the lord's property and could be bought or sold together with their goods, chattels, and family (but not a man's wife if she were free born) and either with or without the land they held. About 1240 Robert de Girros, lord of Fitz manor, granted one of his villeins to Haughmond abbey with all his goods and chattels[9] and in 1300 Simon of Alveley gave to his daughter and son-in-law ½ virgate of land together with its tenant, his chattels, his brother, sister, nephew, and the rest of his family (*sequela*).[10] A villein might not leave his land without his lord's permission. About 1250 Robert de Rollisword quitted his holding on the earl of Warwick's land; when caught and presented to the justices in eyre in 1256 Robert admitted that he was the earl's villein and the justices ordered that he and his chattels be returned to the earl.[11] When the abbot of Halesowen was faced with 'rebel villeins' at Oldbury in 1284 he did what he argued he was entitled to do in seizing the men's goods and chattels and imprisoning the men at the abbey.[12] Servile tenants were subject to various other disabilities, restrictions, and obligations. Most burdensome, and indeed recognized by the courts as an indication of servile status, was the liability to perform regular labour services for the lord.[13] Other burdens might include the payment of heriot, tallage, lairwite, and merchet,[14] the last mentioned, paid by a man when his daughter married, becoming increasingly significant to lawyers as a test of whether he was villein or free.[15] In the welshries bond tenants faced burdens and exactions peculiar to Welsh law.[16]

A villein might become free in several ways. His lord might grant a charter of freedom or he himself might flee to a privileged town and remain undetected there for a year and a day. Perhaps the most usual way was buying manumission. As in law the villein's goods and chattels were the lord's property the purchase money had, technically, to be provided by a third party, the recognizer.[17] By granting a

---

[4] For background see Miller and Hatcher, *Med. Eng.* 111-21; A. L. Poole, *Obligations of Soc. in 12th and 13th Cent.* (1946), cap. 2; M. M. Postan, *Essays on Med. Agric. & Gen. Problems of the Med. Econ.* (1973), cap. 13.

[5] B.L. Harl. Ch. 45 A 33.

[6] *T.S.A.S.* lxii. 14; inf. from Dr. Dyer.

[7] Staffs. R.O., D.(W.) 1734/J/2268, ff. 26-8; above.

[8] J. Hatcher, 'Non-manorialism in med. Cornw.' *Agric. H.R.* xviii. 1-16; C. R. Straton, 'An Eng. manor in the time of Eliz.' *Wilts. Arch. and Nat. Hist. Mag.* xxxii. 302-3.

[9] *Cart. Haughmond*, p. 80.

[10] S.R.O. 2029/1; cf. *T.S.A.S.* lxii. 24.

[11] *Roll of Salop. Eyre 1256*, p. 16; Eyton, iv. 150-1.

[12] *Sel. Bills in Eyre* (Selden Soc. xxx), pp. lviii-lix, 25-6.

[13] Below.

[14] All, for instance, owed by the neifs at Prees in 1298: Staffs. R.O., D.(W.) 1734/J/2268, f. 27.

[15] Miller and Hatcher, *Med. Eng.* 117; Poole, *Obligations of Soc.* 18-19.

[16] Below.

[17] Poole, op. cit. 28-32; F. Pollock and F. W. Maitland, *Hist. Eng. Law* (1898), i. 429.

man his freedom a lord might be surrendering considerable future income from the man's works, tallages, and so forth, and it was no doubt those losses that were reflected in the sums paid for manumission by five villeins or their representatives at Hodnet in 1240. Two brothers rendered £1 6s. 8d. together, another two men £4 each, and the fifth man £1.[18] In another case, at Wem in 1272, the price was 6s. 8d. to the lord and a sore hawk to the recognizers.[19] On the whole, instances of manumission are rare, probably not least because a villein gained so little by what was a fairly expensive process when commutation of labour services for a relatively small sum was commonly available. Moreover a lord might be unwilling to contemplate manumission, and indeed there was a general tightening of servile ties and a closer definition of servile status c. 1200.[20]

It was in no one's interest for a holding to be in the hands of an old or infirm tenant, perhaps a widow, not properly self-supporting or unable to fulfil communal obligations and perform labour services.[21] A few maintenance agreements and champart leases survive as evidence of what may well have been usual practice, with tenants retiring and passing on their holdings in return for being fed, housed, and clothed. In the late 13th century Robert of Bold (Bold was a freehold and hamlet in Willey), granted all his land to William of Willey and Margery his wife. In return they were to supply him for the rest of his life with food and drink of the standard they provided in their own household, and 4 ells of russet cloth, 2 pairs (paria, possibly undergarments rather than sheets)[22] of linen cloth, and 3s. shoe money a year. In addition they were also to pay £1 6s. 8d. dower when Robert's daughter married.[23] About 1295 Adam, a man from Rossall, near Shrewsbury, gave a champart lease of all his land, except 13 a. otherwise leased, to two men, probably brothers, also of Rossall. They were to plough and prepare the land; if Adam supplied half of the seedcorn he would receive half of the threshed crop, whereas if he failed to supply any seedcorn he would receive only a third of it.[24] A similar lease was made in 1269 when a Brockton woman surrendered her land there to Wombridge priory. The priory was to give her a third of the grain it grew on the land after the tithe had been taken, and a quarter of rye if it did not till her garden croft.[25]

In general the labour services owed by bondmen were apt to be heaviest on large and ancient manors.[26] Thus on the royal manor of Condover, probably c. 1267, the tenants of each 60-a. virgate owed an annual rent of 14d., four days' week work throughout the year, four days' ploughing, and the harrowing of the land ploughed. Such services may have been exceptionally heavy for the bailiff there seems to have allowed 17 of the virgaters to do less service than was supposedly due.[27]

Labour services on monastic estates also tended to be relatively heavy,[28] and it may have been that which in 1163 caused the villein tenants of Wenlock priory to 'throw down their ploughshares' and to cease tilling the priory's lands.[29] By the 13th century labour services on the priory's manors were moderate: each year in Little Wenlock, for instance, half-virgaters owed three days' ploughing, four days' reaping and a day's mowing, carriage services, and pool work. Nevertheless the tenants also owed rents in kind, while at death both terciary and a heriot were

[18] Eyton, ix. 330.
[19] Ibid. 170-1.
[20] Postan, *Essays on Med. Agric.* 283-4; Dyer, *Lords and Peasants*, 104-5.
[21] Miller and Hatcher, *Med. Eng.* 136-7; Titow, *Eng. Rural Soc.* 82-3.
[22] Suggestion owed to Dr. Dyer.
[23] S.R.O. 1093/2/500.
[24] S.R.O. 1514/388.
[25] Staffs. R.O., D. 593/A/2/29/10.
[26] Miller and Hatcher, *Med. Eng.* 123.
[27] *V.C.H. Salop.* viii. 45; P.R.O., C 145/20, no. 1.
[28] *V.C.H. Wilts.* iv. 8.
[29] R. Graham, 'Hist. of Alien Priory of M. Wenlock', *Jnl. Brit. Arch. Assoc.* 3rd ser. iv. 124-5.

payable. Terciary, but no other service, was also owed in Shropshire on the Templars' manor of Lydley, in Cardington.[30]

Heavy services, often laid on the whole township rather than on specific holdings, had come to be demanded by the 13th century in some townships in the lordship of Oswestry, though the reasons for that are obscure.[31] Before commutation the four nook-holders at Cotton owed an improbable[32] 928 works between Michaelmas and Lammas and 218 works in the autumn, while at Maesbury and Treflach nine villeins owed 478 works between Lammas and Michaelmas. Such heavy services were not unusual in Oswestry: in 1301 the holders of the five bondlands at Weston nominally owed a man each to work on the demesne for each working day throughout the year, although by then such services were probably commuted throughout the lordship. Additionally they owed, apparently collectively, two days' ploughing 'at the two seasons if they have a plough'. Similarly Middleton's bondmen had to supply eight men a day throughout the year to work on the demesne and a man every other day, each tenant with a plough owing in addition four days' ploughing.

Generally, however, where they existed at all by the 13th century, customary services and obligations in the county were relatively light, as in much of west and north England.[33] On the Corbet manor of Wattlesborough (including Cardeston and Loton) in 1300 the holders of ½-virgate tenancies each owed 3 days' ploughing, a day's reaping, and a day's weeding,[34] and very similar services were owed, for instance, nominally at least, at Corfham, Culmington, and Siefton,[35] at Meole Brace,[36] and at Child's Ercall.[37] At Westbury in 1267 the only service owed by each of the 14 half-virgaters was one day in autumn.[38] It is impossible to assess whether there was any general move in the county in the 13th century to reimpose labour services;[39] by and large it seems[40] that the commutation of labour services for cash was then usual. At Wotherton, in Chirbury, in the late 13th century, for instance, the tenants paid the lord a total of 18s. 9d. at Christmas in lieu of ploughing, reaping, mowing, weeding, and carting services.[41]

Another potentially burdensome obligation which the bondman faced was that of acting as one of the lord's agents or officers: in particular the more prominent villagers had to undertake the duties of reeve, woodward, hayward, and the like from time to time. For many reasons such duties were usually unpopular, and in 1248 the refusal of Herbert of Corfton to act as reeve for William FitzJohn, lord of the manor of Heath, clearly had something to do with a dispute between the two men.[42] The only benefit customarily attached to the reeve's office was relief from labour services during the period of duty.[43]

Far less well documented than men's obligations to their lords are, as has already been seen, the relationships, contracts, and bonds between peasants. It is clear, though little documented in Shropshire, that labour services might be undertaken by someone other than the customary tenant himself. Indeed when labour services are set down it is often in the form that each holding owes a man for so many days. Thus in 1239 Henry the smith, of Rushbury, held a nook and 3 a. in Hope

---

[30] V.C.H. Salop. xi. 81; T.S.A.S. lviii. 68–76.
[31] Para. based on Two Est. Surveys of Earls of Arundel, pp. 70–3; P.R.O., C 132/35, no.18; Smith, 'Lordships of Chirk and Oswestry', 118–19.
[32] Assuming a 6-day week and making no allowance for feast days, each tenant worked 286 out of 313 available days in the year. But cf. below, for how the tenant's obligations might be fulfilled by his fam. or hired help.
[33] Miller and Hatcher, Med. Eng. 123–4.

[34] P.R.O., C 133/98, no. 30.
[35] Ibid. /91, no. 2.   [36] Ibid. /2, no. 7.
[37] T.S.A.S. 3rd ser. viii. 365–7.
[38] P.R.O., C 133/35, no. 18.
[39] Postan, Essays on Med. Agric. 89–106.
[40] Most inf. is contained in extents attached to inq. p.m.
[41] P.R.O., C 133/76, no. 1.
[42] Eyton, iv. 14–15; Dyer, Lords and Peasants, 114–15.
[43] Staffs. R.O., D.(W.) 1734/J/2268, f. 27.

Bowdler for 2s. a year and for finding two men for a day's harvesting.[44] If a holding supported a family the tenant's sons might undertake the services due, or else a wage labourer might be hired.

In the early Middle Ages western Shropshire was very much a border zone.[45] The boundary between England and Wales, traditional and often violent enemies, remained uncertain and fluctuating, albeit approximately on the line established in the later 8th century by Offa.[46] To some extent, however, the precise border was an irrelevance, given the existence of such semi-autonomous marcher lordships as Oswestry, Caus, Montgomery, and Clun.[47] It was in that area that the two separate cultures, with different languages, customs, mores, and laws met but rarely mixed.

The separation was recognized by contemporaries, and in the marches an area was deemed either an englishry or a welshry. In Shropshire there were welshries in Caus,[48] Clun,[49] Knockin,[50] and Oswestry.[51] The Welsh written sources define a hierarchy of settlements and obligations, clear indications of which remained in the welshries at the end of the 13th century although by then some of the old distinctions, perhaps always partly theoretical, had become blurred. According to those sources[52] the four ancient provinces of Wales were divided in *cantrefi*, each of which was supposed to comprise 100 *trefi*, or townships. In time commotes superseded *cantrefi*, of which they were divisions, as units of organization and jurisdiction. In each commote two *trefi* were allocated to the lord, one for his *hafod dir*, or summer pasture, the other for the *maerdref* or demesne, occupied and cultivated by bondmen relieved of most of the burdens suffered by other unfree tenants. The remaining *trefi* were either free or unfree. In the unfree the inhabitants paid food renders and supported the ruler's servants, horses, and hounds. Those *trefi* would be subject to a yearly circuit by the commote's court and officers. Most of the *trefi*, however, were free, with the land being held in *gwelyau*, family holdings. Those holdings were partible amongst male heirs, including paternally acknowledged bastards, but female descent was generally prohibited.[53] Thus in time the original holding came to be split between a group or clan of related families, a *gwelygordd*. Each *tref* owed a fixed food render to the ruler; later that was commuted to a payment called *tunc*. Unlike English custom which permitted the alienation of free land, Welsh custom permitted only its mortgaging for fixed terms under licence from the lord.[54]

The various surveys and extents of the later 13th and 14th century which are the main sources for the practice, as opposed to the theory, of Welsh tenure in the Middle Ages, show that by 1300 much of the clarity had been lost. One contributory factor was undoubtedly that not all the welshries in Shropshire were of the same antiquity; gwelyau are not found in the eastern part of the lordship of Oswestry in 1086, and it seems possible that they were founded there in the mid 12th century during the Welsh resurgence under Madog ap Maredudd.[55] During the period various townships were annexed to or withdrawn from the welshry of Caus.[56] Only occasionally in the late 13th or 14th century can the Welsh townships be identified

[44] Eyton, iv. 364; *T.S.A.S.* 4th ser. iv. 176-7.
[45] R. R. Davies, *Lordship and Soc. in the March of Wales 1282-1400* (1978). A useful discussion of Welsh influence in Salop. comprises cap. 7 of W. J. Slack, 'Hist. Salop. Agric.' (unpubl. TS.; copy in S.R.O. 3763/19/1).
[46] Davies, op. cit. 15.
[47] Ibid. 20-6.
[48] Ibid. 23; *V.C.H. Salop.* viii. 202, 325.
[49] *Two Est. Surveys of Earls of Arundel.*
[50] Eyton, x. 370.
[51] Smith, 'Lordships of Chirk and Oswestry'; Slack, *Lordship of Oswestry.*
[52] Slack, op. cit. 22-4; Smith, op. cit. 263-74.
[53] Davies, *Lordship and Soc.* 313.
[54] Ibid. 143-4; *Cart. Haughmond*, pp. 13-14.
[55] Smith, 'Lordships of Chirk and Oswestry', 264-5; inf. from Dr. Smith, who is thanked for comments on welshries.
[56] *V.C.H. Salop.* viii. 202, 325.

as anciently free or unfree: the obligation, for instance, of Trefonen township, in Oswestry, in 1272 to keep the lord's hounds[57] and the payment of a similar render by men in Obley, near Clun,[58] indicate unfree status.

In Oswestry lordship by the late 13th century Welsh tenants owed three customary payments: *tunc*; *kant morkie*, a payment in lieu of military service; and *kant tydion* (etymologically '100 cows'), a biennial autumn cattle render. As in Clun they also owed *amobyr*, a marriage payment. In other Welsh areas additional customary payments were owed.[59]

There were cases where arbitrary changes of lordship transferred a whole township from an englishry to a welshry or vice versa;[60] on the whole, however, lords, both English and Welsh, sought to ensure that Welshmen, that is Welsh speakers of Welsh blood, should hold their land by Welsh tenure and Englishmen by English tenure.[61] Although there were few intrinsic differences between English and Welsh townships in their agricultural arrangements, both having open fields, meadows, and commons, inevitably the variations of law and custom produced distinctions. Especially notable was the influence of partible inheritance which fragmented Welsh holdings and inevitably led to an emphasis on subsistence rather than the production of a surplus for sale. Thus in those western parts of the county where English and Welsh townships, or even individual tenancies, lay adjacent, the superficially homogeneous agricultural landscape in fact concealed the considerable differences between the two cultures which extended to agricultural life.

Woodland, assarting, and commons

Woodland was usually recorded in Shropshire in 1086, though less systematically than in some counties.[62] Moreover, detail given is not easy to interpret and comparisons within the county are made difficult by the differing methods of reckoning the extent of woodland.[63] In nine of the hundreds each wood was described in terms of a number of swine that could be fattened on its acorns and beech nuts, though whether that number was then, or ever had been, a realistic estimate is uncertain. On the other hand, in four hundreds the length and breadth of each wood were given, or at least one of its dimensions. Woodland on Earl Roger's demesne manors, which were perhaps exempt from ordinary hundredal jurisdiction, was invariably recorded by the second method.[64] Where the later extent of a wood mentioned in Domesday Book is known, a single linear measurement in Domesday seems to represent maximum length.[65] Relating number of swine to woodland area is impossible.

The location of the woodlands mentioned in Domesday Book is less straightforward than records suggest. Many woods were detached, often at some distance from the vill that owned them. As in other parts of the country,[66] blocks of woodland might be common to a number of surrounding vills. In some cases pressure on resources had already led to the partition of a wood between communities that had previously intercommoned it, a tendency that was to become more pronounced in the 12th and 13th centuries.[67] Already by 1086, for example, the large tract of woodland, *c.* 5 km. by 2 km., east of Wellington had been divided

---

[57] Slack, *Lordship of Oswestry*, 25.
[58] *Two Est. Surveys of Earls of Arundel*, p. 61.
[59] Ibid. 65; Slack, op. cit. 26-8; Smith, 'Lordships of Chirk and Oswestry', 226-31; Eyton, x. 331.
[60] *V.C.H. Salop.* viii. 202, 325.
[61] Davies, *Lordship and Soc.* 314.

[62] Darby, *Domesday Eng.* 184.
[63] Darby and Terrett, *Domesday Geog. Mid. Eng.* 136-9.
[64] Lewis, 'Salop. Domesday'.
[65] e.g. *V.C.H. Salop.* xi. 328 n. 64.
[66] *Countryside of Med. Eng.* ed. G. Astill and A. Grant (1988), 130.
[67] Below.

between the vills with rights in it, including Wrockwardine, 7 km. to the west.[68]

Apart from its recitation of the swine pasture of certain woods Domesday Book reveals little of woods' use, though an entry for Eaton Constantine, that 'the underwood renders 5d.',[69] acts as a reminder that three types of vegetation were to be found in woods: grass and other growth which animals could graze and browse; underwood, usually coppiced and the source of most material for building, fencing, and fuel; and a relatively few mature standards, most usefully oak, reserved to the lord of the soil who would use, sell, or grant them for use as major structural timbers.

Extensive woodland clearance was a feature of the early Middle Ages.[70] By the 13th century some woods were very small; on the three demesne manors of John FitzAer (d. 1293) there were three woods, of just 3 a., 2 a., and 1 a., the last also being detached from its manor.[71] The pressures on an increasingly scarce resource produced clearer definitions of rights. Not all woods, for instance, were of the same status. Some were private, usually to the lord of the manor, whereas others were common for specific communities.[72] Nevertheless even in private woods commoners might enjoy certain rights.[73] Frodesley, a fairly typical example of a well wooded manor, had three inclosed woods: the lord's wood, a park, and a common wood.[74]

The physical character of the county's early medieval woods is difficult to assess, though oak-dominated pasture woods seem to have been most prevalent. In some places enclosed coppice woods were found,[75] while 'Timber wood' in Little Wenlock and Madeley suggests a different specialization.[76] Between 1246 and 1254 James de Audley permitted Richard Pride of Shrewsbury to fell 1,000 oaks in Ford,[77] which hints not only at the dominance of oak in the medieval timber trade but also at the existence of specialist timber merchants. In a few cases a species other than oak was dominant: c. 1250 Robert Corbet inclosed a 5-a. birch wood, probably in Moreton Corbet;[78] in the wooded area of north-west Shifnal was a holly wood;[79] and at Longnor there was an alder grove.[80] The capital reserve represented by mature trees and underwood was fully appreciated by their owners, and occasionally that value is recorded in inquisitions post mortem. In 1274 an 8-a. wood called Haywood in Meole Brace was valued at 20d. an acre,[81] and a 4-a. wood at Faintree at 10s. an acre.[82] Such a valuable asset was liable to be stripped if a manor came temporarily into a custodian's hands, and 1,700 oaks were said in 1235 to have been sold from Worfield wood in the troubles of Henry III's minority.[83] Similarly the depredations of lessees had to be guarded against; about 1290, for instance, the lessee of a 100-a. wood at Great Berwick was accused by its owner of having felled 100 oaks.[84]

As with swine and other pasture, the rights of commoners to take underwood, deadwood, and timber varied widely. By and large the usual entitlements to housebote, firebote, hedgebote, and ploughbote were permitted, often in return for customary annual payments. Such payments could be in cash, although renders in kind, particularly of poultry, were probably more usual. In the late 13th century Clive village paid 8 qr. of oats a year for entry into Wem's woods, besides 300

[68] Astill and Grant, op. cit. 130.
[69] Darby and Terrett, *Domesday Geog. Mid. Eng.* 138.
[70] Miller and Hatcher, *Med. Eng.* 33–5; Below.
[71] P.R.O., C 133/65, no. 12.
[72] Astill and Grant, *Countryside of Med. Eng.* 133–5.
[73] Below.   [74] *V.C.H. Salop.* viii. 80.
[75] Eyton, viii. 109; Staffs. R.O., D. 593/A/2/32/1.

[76] *V.C.H. Salop.* xi. 41, 81–3.   [77] Ibid. viii. 224.
[78] *Roll of Salop. Eyre 1256*, p. 40.
[79] Hollinswood: *V.C.H. Salop.* xi. 286.
[80] *Cart. Haughmond*, pp. 144, 149.
[81] P.R.O., C 133/2, no. 7.
[82] P.R.O., C 133/4, no. 14.
[83] Eyton, iii. 215.   [84] Ibid. x. 222.

hens probably as part of the same payment, and 29 ploughshares for pasture rights.[85] Those without common rights had to buy wood, ensuring a ready market for sellers like the lord of Wem, who in 1290 sold 46s. worth of wood without making waste.[86] Occasionally lords made gifts of firewood and timber to religious communities, such as the lepers of St. Giles in Shrewsbury, who in 1232 were granted a daily horseload of firewood from Buriwood in Condover.[87]

Wood, timber, and grazing were only the main products of woodland. Others included leaved branches, especially of holly, for winter browse;[88] birds and other minor game, fungi, berries, and nuts. Again the right to take such things was limited to certain communities or even households. In 1281, for instance, Lawrence of Ludlow granted Haughmond abbey's tenants in Newton, in Stokesay, the right to have common and to collect nuts in Newton wood according to the size of their tenements.[89] Charcoal was manufactured, for burning in more well-to-do households.[90] Large quantities of oak bark were taken to the tanning industries in towns like Shrewsbury[91] and Ludlow, where in 1290 it was apparently brought into town on horse back.[92] Another product was often honey, important as the only locally produced sweetener and the main ingredient in mead, while beeswax was used to make fine candles.[93] Some was gathered from the nests of wild swarms, and some from purpose-built hives; 32 'bee stalls' were among the deficiencies of stock listed at Worfield in 1202 (Table I).[94] At Ludlow tolls were payable from 1290 on each horse load (1d.) and cask (3d.) of honey and on each cart load ($\frac{1}{4}d.$ or $\frac{1}{2}d.$ according to size) and horse load ($\frac{1}{4}d.$) of honeycomb sold.[95] Further potential income came from the capture and sale of sparrowhawks and other birds of prey, and three hawks' nests were noted in Shropshire in 1086.[96] Many later examples are known; c. 1250 the lord of Donington wood, near Brewood, had a sparrowhawk eyrie,[97] while sparrowhawks and honey worth 20s. came from Wem's woods in 1290.[98]

TABLE I: DEFICIENCIES OF STOCK ON ROYAL MANORS
IN 1202

	ox teams	cows	sheep	sows	bee skeps
Claverley	4	24	300	15	—
Condover	—	24	—	24	—
Edgmond	4	30	140	24	—
Ford	5	72	—	40	—
Worfield	6	24	600	30	32

Source: Pipe R. 1202 (P.R.S. N.S. xv), 47.

Domesday Book records 36 hays in Shropshire, apparently enclosures in or close to woodland where deer would be bred or gathered before their release for hunting;[99] that at Corfton was actually described as being for the catching of roe deer.[1] As after the Conquest, deer hunting in late Saxon England was essentially the preserve of the Crown and the aristocracy, and Domesday Book records that, in King

[85] P.R.O., C 133/57, no. 3; E 149/1/10.
[86] P.R.O., E 149/1/10.
[87] V.C.H. Salop. ii. 106.
[88] J. Radley, 'Holly as a winter feed', Agric. H.R. ix. 89–92.
[89] Cart. Haughmond, p. 167. See also Eyton, xi. 265.
[90] P.R.O., C 66/109, m. 35; Astill and Grant, Countryside of Med. Eng. 139.
[91] S.R.O. 3365/152, 158.
[92] P.R.O., C 66/109, m. 35.
[93] McDonald and Snooks, Domesday Econ. 85; Cart.

Haughmond, pp. 114, 148; Wendy Davies, An Early Welsh Microcosm: Studies in the Llandaff Charters (1978), 48.
[94] Eyton, iii. 68; below, 1300–1540 (Demesne agriculture).
[95] P.R.O., C 66/109, m. 35. See also T.S.A.S. 3rd ser. v. 172.
[96] Darby, Domesday Eng. 205–7.
[97] Roll of Salop. Eyre 1256, p. 131.
[98] P.R.O., E 149/1/10; cf. C 132/17, no. 1; T.S.A.S. 2nd ser. xi. 263; Cart. Haughmond, p. 142.
[99] Darby, Domesday Eng. 204–5.
[1] Darby and Terrett Domesday Geog. Mid. Eng. 140–1.

Edward's time, the sheriff had to find 36 men for eight days, presumably to beat, whenever the king was at 'Marsetelie', probably Marsley in Habberley.[2] Under the Norman kings the Crown's prerogative to hunt deer was greatly extended by the imposition of forest law across large parts of the countryside. In Shropshire, as in other counties, both the names and the bounds of forests altered with time, but the main Norman forests were Brewood, the Long Forest, Morfe, Mount Gilbert or the Wrekin, and Shirlett.[3] Also probably under forest law in early times were the various chases in the county such as Clee and Wyre.[4] No part of north Shropshire was under forest law. Another Norman introduction was the fallow deer which, not least because it will graze alongside cattle, is well suited to park life and may fatten better on poor land than the red deer.[5]

Lesser lords who wished to keep deer for the hunt and for the table generally did so by creating parks, enclosing woodland and pasture with a high pale or fence to prevent the deer's escape. Little is known of the county's earliest parks, which were perhaps few in number. Ruyton park was enlarged by John le Strange (II) in 1195,[6] while on the county boundary the bishop of Coventry was permitted to make a deer-leap into his new park at Brewood by the king in 1206.[7]

In the later 13th century, and especially from the 1270s, many new parks were created throughout England, and at least 26 in Shropshire between 1270 and 1310.[8] Most were of 50–100 a.: Acton Burnell park was enlarged from 40 a. to 80 a. in 1280,[9] and Yockleton was said in 1300 to comprise 70 a.[10] Of larger parks Minsterley was estimated in 1300 at 300 a.[11] In some respects the imparkment of demesne woodland caused little change; grazing[12] and other common rights might continue to exist in them and the wood was probably managed as before. The lord himself might continue to put in his oxen or pigs to feed, while in Condover park in 1298 there were wild pigs (*porcos silvestres*).[13] Nevertheless imparkment was a heavy undertaking. A licence might have to be bought from the king and, particularly in retrospective cases, that could prove expensive: the prior of Wenlock in 1251 paid 300 marks to retain his previously unlicensed park at Oxenbold.[14] Other expenses might be required for the extinction of common rights in the park through legal action and compensation awards, for constructing a bank, ditch, and pale, and for obtaining stock. Once a park had been created its owner was likely to find that maintenance of its pale and stock was a constant burden.[15] Even on large and relatively wealthy manors maintenance was at times neglected. At Wem in 1281 there were two parks: the uninclosed park, not surprisingly, contained no beasts of the chase, and the inclosed park just eleven.[16] Many of the minor lords who made parks probably did so in direct emulation of their betters, but whatever the motive for imparkment, the result was the same: a greater emphasis in the demesne economy on rearing deer.

Over the country as a whole it is clear that the centuries leading up to the agrarian and demographic reverses of the earlier 14th century were ones which saw massive inroads into wood and waste land by agriculturists.[17] In 1086 bordars formed about a quarter of the recorded population of Shropshire,[18] and although

[2] *V.C.H. Salop.* i. 309; viii. 239, 241; F. Barlow, *Wm. Rufus* (1983), 22–3.

[3] Eyton, ii. 185–6; iii. 212–19, 295–9; vi. 335–47; ix. 143–9.   [4] Ibid. iv. 276–9; v. 196–202.

[5] *Environmental Arch.: a Regional Review*, ed. H. C. M. Keeley, i (1984), 217.

[6] *T.S.A.S.* 3rd ser. i. 226.

[7] Eyton, ii. 186.

[8] L. Cantor, *Med. Parks of Eng.: a Gazetteer* (Loughbor-ough, 1983), 63–4.

[9] *V.C.H. Salop.* viii. 3.   [10] Ibid. 320.

[11] *Cal. Inq. p.m.* iii, pp. 451–2.   [12] e.g. Eyton, ix. 84.

[13] *Cal. Pat. 1292–1301*, 383.

[14] *Close R. 1247–51*, 567; *Cal. Chart. R. 1226–57*, 369.

[15] Astill and Grant, *Countryside of Med. Eng.* 141.

[16] P.R.O., C 133/27, no. 9.

[17] Miller and Hatcher, *Med. Eng.* esp. 33–41, 53–63.

[18] Cf. Darby and Terrett, *Domesday Geog. Mid. Eng.* 129.

the equation in individual settlements of Domesday bordars with continuing, rather than past, assarting is unsound, such a large element in the county's population does suggest that the 11th century was a period of considerable clearances.[19] Nevertheless attribution of a rise in a manor's recorded value between 1066 and 1086 to woodland clearance[20] is speculative.

In the 13th century it becomes possible to assess the progress of assarting, although accurate quantification is impossible apart from at the very local and usually short-term level. Probably the most crucial influence on the course of clearance was the lord's attitude. Most lords, in a period of rising prices and profits, seem to have been keen to convert as much woodland and waste as possible to arable land, or at least to inclosed pasture, either to add to their demesne or, more usually, to let to tenants. Some lords undertook the clearance themselves. In 1256 the abbot of Lilleshall complained, as a commoner with the right of estovers, of the actions of William de Harcourt, who had cleared 300 a. and disposed of 6,000 oaks from Tong wood.[21] Alternatively, as especially in Ford and Condover hundreds, the lord allowed or encouraged pioneering settlement. To the settler the main inducement was the free tenure that was offered, as at Oaks in the 12th century and Berrington, Longnor, Smethcott, and Woolstaston in the 13th.[22] The lord could enlarge his rent roll in the long term. At Great Wytheford in 1293, for instance, 28s. 10d. of annual rent came from newly broken waste.[23] Many of the holdings in Ford and Condover hundreds were worked from houses built in the woodland itself, as at Frodesley in 1235,[24] rather than from new houses in existing villages. The more substantial assarted farms were often moated; it is not clear to what extent a moat was intended to be a practical deterrent to malefactors, rather than a visual display of the owner's standing and substance.[25]

At the same time more intensive cultivation was being introduced on the county's heaths, moors, and wetlands, which like that cleared from woodland was mostly land of poor quality. At Ellesmere 68s. 4½d. was paid in 1250 for the farm of 'new' assarts, probably made in the preceeding 20 or so years and totalling c. 200 a.[26] At Calverhall 30 a. of heath, formerly common pasture, was cleared in the years before 1256, probably by the tenants of houses built on it by the lord of the manor specifically for that purpose.[27] On the bishop of Coventry and Lichfield's estate at Prees in 1298 c. 127 a. of tenant land were described as 'new' and there were also c. 90 a. of recently approved demesne land.[28] Just how important seigneurial initiative could be is evident at High Ercall where, it has been suggested, the Middle Ages saw a constant enlargement of the cultivated area, which at times was striking, with new open fields and townships being created from former heathland.[29]

Monastic houses played a special role as approvers. Of the Benedictine houses, Shrewsbury abbey seems mainly to have concentrated on the acquisition of urban property,[30] whereas Wenlock priory actively extended its lands by assarting, not least into Shirlett, Wrekin, and Clee forests.[31] The later foundations were even more active. In the 1130s and 1140s Buildwas, a Savigniac house, and the

[19] Sawyer, *Medieval Settlement*, 197–9; Lewis, 'Salop. Domesday'.
[20] e.g. *V.C.H. Salop.* viii. 14, 22.
[21] *Roll of Salop. Eyre 1256*, pp. 45–6; Eyton, ii. 222.
[22] *V.C.H. Salop.* viii. 15, 108, 111, 147, 154, 247, 276.
[23] P.R.O., C 133/65, no. 12.
[24] *V.C.H. Salop.* viii. 80.
[25] *T.S.A.S.* lxv. 1–11; D. Wilson, *Moated Sites* (1985), 17–23.
[26] *Ag. Hist. Eng.* ii. 266; Eyton, x. 243. The 195 a. of

assarts noted 1280 accords well with the 1250 fig. if that was based on a rent of 4d. an acre.
[27] *Roll of Salop. Eyre 1256*, p. 29; Eyton, x. 10–11.
[28] Staffs. R.O., D.(W.) 1734/J/2268, ff. 26–8.
[29] *T.S.A.S.* lxii; but cf. *Local Historian*, xvii. 55–7. For similar examples of the forces argued to be involved cf. *Land, Kinship and Life Cycle*, ed. R. M. Smith (1984), 13–14.
[30] *V.C.H. Salop.* ii. 31–2.
[31] Ibid. 41; *T.S.A.S.* 4th ser. i. 391; *Pipe R.* 1190 (P.R.S. N.S. i), 127; *Cal. Chart. R.* 1327–41, 488.

Augustinian houses of Haughmond, Lilleshall, and Wombridge were all founded in secluded, undeveloped, and well wooded locations according to the usual preferences of those orders.[32] They prospered largely because of their expansionist policies: demesne lands were enlarged, granges founded, grazing rights obtained, and rent rolls enlarged. In the 13th and early 14th centuries Haughmond abbey greatly expanded its holdings around the abbey itself, in north Shropshire, and in the pastoral areas between the Long Mynd and Leebotwood and near Bridgnorth. Around Leebotwood, for instance, where the abbey gained the nucleus of an estate 1163–70, it quickly set about enlarging its holding by assarting, for which licences from the Crown were obtained in 1179, 1232, and 1283. Boundaries with adjoining lordships were fixed in the early 13th century, and a grange was established at

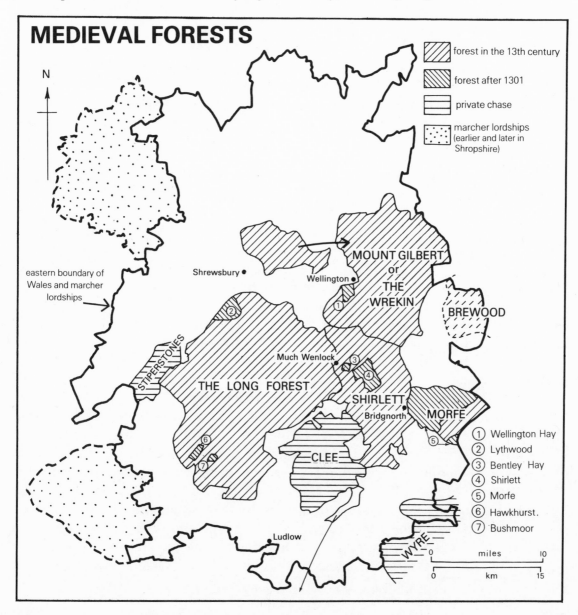

Fig. 4

Small areas disafforested in the late 12th and 13th centuries are not shown, nor are private woods called 'forest' (such as Hogstow forest). Brewood was disafforested between 1204 and 1209. See Eyton *passim*; cf. for Clee *T.S.A.S.* lviii. 50; for Stiperstones *V.C.H. Salop.* viii. 129, 295, 298; and for Wyre R. Morden, *Map of Worcs.* [1695].

[32] G. C. Baugh and D. C. Cox, *Monastic Salop.* (1982), 7, 17–18.

Mickelwood by 1255.[33] Wombridge, like Haughmond founded in a wooded, extra-parochial area, developed its estates in a similar way and assarted extensively around the priory itself and its granges.[34] Also active in woodland clearance were the knights Templar, who had a preceptory at Lydley, between the forest of Botwood and Lawley hill.[35]

A major determinant on the course of the assarting movement was the Crown's attitude to its forest lands, for forest law, administered through special officials and courts, could prohibit or seriously inhibit colonization. The forest reached its maximum extent under Henry II, when perhaps a third of the realm, including about a third of Shropshire, was forest (Fig. 4). By the end of Henry II's reign, however, the king's need for money was greater than his obsession with hunting,[36] and in Shropshire, as in other counties, the forest began to be reduced. It was probably in Henry II's time that Clee forest passed into private hands to become a chase.[37] In 1190 the prior of Wenlock paid 20 marks to have his part (c. 900 a.) of Shirlett taken out of the regard, and by 1235 John FitzAlan's part (probably c. 400 a.) was also removed.[38] In 1209 'the knights and men who live in Brewood' paid 100 marks for it to be disafforested in confirmation of the charter to that effect made by the king in 1204.[39] Equally important in terms of the total acreage involved were the small assarts and purprestures around forest-edge vills. The fines paid in forest courts for such clearances were in effect licences; by 1129 there were set rates according to the use to which the land was put, and there is little evidence that, by the late 12th century, the Crown objected to such initiatives.[40] As can be seen from the records of successive forest regards, most assarts were small, of an acre or less, and most were claimed to be growing oats,[41] for which the fine was 6d. an acre, as opposed to wheat for which the fine was double.[42]

During Henry III's reign forest resources, temporarily at least, were further reduced as the Crown drew heavily from its demesne woods. Particularly in the mid 13th century deer, wood, and timber were taken in large quantities whether for the Crown's own use, for sale, or for grant to others, especially the religious.[43] In Shropshire the examples are provided by Lythwood, a royal hay of c. 800 a. in the Long forest 3 miles south of Shrewsbury,[44] and Shirlett forest, where the Crown's demesne woods probably comprised c. 1,000 a. (Fig. 5).[45] Although Lythwood seems to have contained few deer, the distribution of timber products in particular, often to destinations many miles away and nearer to other royal forests, indicates that the exploitation of those forests followed the typical pattern of the time. That was to be expected, for to some extent forest administration was on a national scale; in 1281, for instance, 24 roe deer were sent from Hampshire to stock the Long forest.[46]

Forest law had always been hated, and in the later 1290s a major reduction of the forests was forced on the Crown.[47] The new perambulations, confirmed in 1301, left little forest in Shropshire beyond the king's demesne woods, and only Morfe survived at anything like its previous extent.[48]

[33] V.C.H. Salop. ii. 63-4; viii. 102; Cart. Haughmond, pp. 9-11. [34] V.C.H. Salop. ii. 80-1.
[35] Ibid. 85; ibid. x (forthcoming, Cardington parish).
[36] Miller and Hatcher, Med. Eng. 34-5.
[37] Eyton, v. 196-7.
[38] Ibid. iii. 296; V.C.H. Salop. x (forthcoming, Barrow parish).
[39] Eyton, ii. 185-6; V.C.H. Staffs. ii. 337. For similar cases see Miller and Hatcher, Med. Eng. 35.
[40] Miller and Hatcher, op. cit. 34-5.
[41] P.R.O., E 32/143-5, 147.
[42] Miller and Hatcher, op. cit. 35.
[43] e.g. P. A. Stamper, 'Medieval Forest of Pamber, Hants', Landscape Hist. v. 45-6; J. Steane, 'Bernwood forest—past, present and future', Arboricultural Jnl. ix. 47-8.
[44] Eyton, vi. 346; V.C.H. Salop. viii. 29.
[45] V.C.H. Salop. x (forthcoming, Barrow parish); Eyton, iii. 295-9. [46] V.C.H. Salop. i. 491.
[47] C. R. Young, Royal Forests of Med. Eng. (1979), 135-40. [48] Cart. Shrews. ii, pp. 245-51.

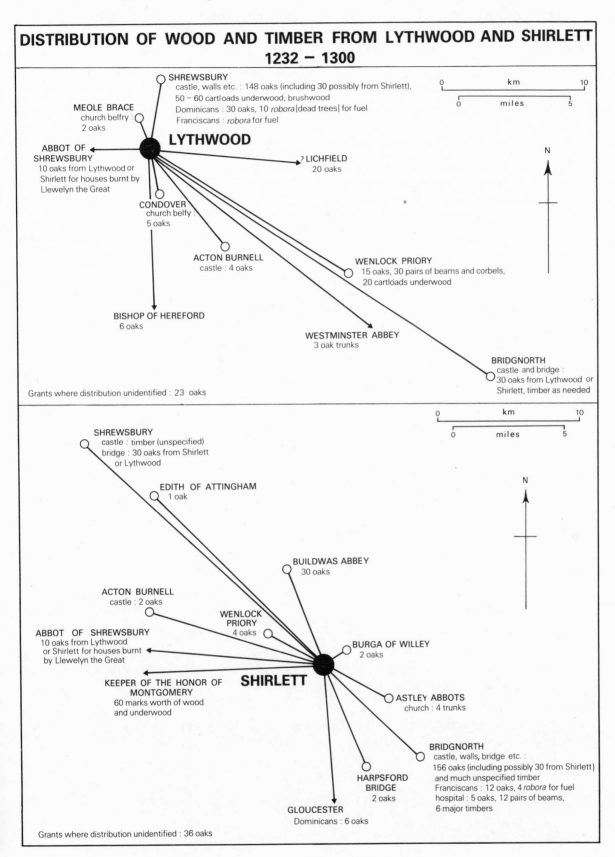

DISTRIBUTION OF WOOD AND TIMBER FROM LYTHWOOD AND SHIRLETT 1232 – 1300

SHREWSBURY
castle, walls etc. : 148 oaks (including 30 possibly from Shirlett),
50 – 60 cartloads underwood, brushwood
Dominicans : 30 oaks, 10 *robora* [dead trees] for fuel
Franciscans : *robora* for fuel

MEOLE BRACE
church belfry :
2 oaks

LYTHWOOD

ABBOT OF
SHREWSBURY
10 oaks from Lythwood or
Shirlett for houses burnt by
Llewelyn the Great

? LICHFIELD
20 oaks

CONDOVER
church belfry :
5 oaks

ACTON BURNELL
castle : 4 oaks

WENLOCK PRIORY
15 oaks, 30 pairs of beams and corbels,
20 cartloads underwood

BISHOP OF HEREFORD
6 oaks

WESTMINSTER ABBEY
3 oak trunks

BRIDGNORTH
castle and bridge :
30 oaks from Lythwood or
Shirlett, timber as needed

Grants where distribution unidentified : 23 oaks

0   km   10
0   miles   5

N

SHREWSBURY
castle : timber (unspecified)
bridge : 30 oaks from Shirlett
or Lythwood

EDITH OF ATTINGHAM
1 oak

BUILDWAS ABBEY
30 oaks

ACTON BURNELL
castle : 2 oaks

WENLOCK
PRIORY
4 oaks

ABBOT OF SHREWSBURY
10 oaks from Lythwood
or Shirlett for houses burnt
by Llewelyn the Great

BURGA OF WILLEY
2 oaks

KEEPER OF THE HONOR OF
MONTGOMERY
60 marks worth of wood
and underwood

SHIRLETT

ASTLEY ABBOTS
church : 4 trunks

BRIDGNORTH
castle, walls, bridge etc. :
156 oaks (including possibly 30 from Shirlett)
and much unspecified timber
Franciscans : 12 oaks, 4 *robora* for fuel
hospital : 5 oaks, 12 pairs of beams,
6 major timbers

HARPSFORD
BRIDGE
2 oaks

GLOUCESTER
Dominicans : 6 oaks

Grants where distribution unidentified : 36 oaks

0   km   10
0   miles   5

N

Fig. 5
Based on *Close R.* 1231–72; *Cal. Close,* 1272–1302.

One of the clearest indications of the growing pressure on land is the number of disputes over, and divisions of, commons. As more and more land was approved the amount of common grazing and of land from which such materials as brushwood, bracken, turf, and peat might be taken[49] was reduced. At Hisland, near Oswestry, for instance, by 1314 only a part of the vill's moors and pastures remained uninclosed and common.[50] Nationally the problem was so serious and recurrent by the mid 13th century that legislation[51] was necessary to confirm lords' rights over the waste provided that their inclosures left sufficient pasture for freeholders' use.[52]

In Shropshire that pressure on the land is most frequently detected by agreements between lords which divided commons previously intercommoned. Most cases involved woodland. In 1190, in one of the earliest recorded instances, Shrewsbury abbey and Wenlock priory divided the woods on the Wrekin which their tenants had previously intercommoned.[53] Such boundaries often took the form of trenches, or linear clearances, and in 1234 Little Wenlock's common rights in the Wrekin's woods were redefined by perambulation and the trenches were renewed.[54] In the Leebotwood area in the 1220s and 1230s there was a series of agreements between parties with interests in the area's extensive woods which led to their subdivision.[55] Similar examples in the mid 13th century can be cited from the areas around Hortonwood,[56] Buildwas,[57] Much Wenlock,[58] Cound,[59] Sheinton,[60] Edgton,[61] Shawbury,[62] and Hadnall,[63] and from the early 14th century from near West Felton.[64] By the early 14th century landlords clearly preferred, wherever possible, to hold land unencumbered by the rights of other lords and their tenants, and at Smethcott in 1340 the holders of the three portions of the manor partitioned not only the manorial wood but also the arable land and the commons.[65] Similar pressures presumably also lay behind 13th-century boundary agreements on the Weald Moors.[66]

Arable farming

There was great variety in the county in the organization and working of arable land. Such differences are to be expected between geophysical regions, and are compounded in Shropshire which not only straddles the highland and lowland zones and contains several distinct regions[67] but also lies on the border between England and Wales, each of which had not only its own language but also its own system of law, tenure, and agricultural and settlement organization.[68]

On an estimate of 100 a. (40 ha.) for each recorded Domesday ploughteam[69] it appears that c. 22 per cent of the county was under arable cultivation,[70] compared with over 50 per cent of much of the midlands and East Anglia and over 70 per cent of the most intensively cultivated parts of the country such as east Norfolk and north Gloucestershire.[71] Within Shropshire there was considerable regional

[49] T.S.A.S. 4th ser. vi. 191.
[50] Cart. Haughmond, p. 19.
[51] Statute of Merton, 20 Hen. III, c. 4; Statute of Westminster II, 13 Edw. I, c. 46.
[52] V.C.H. Leics. ii. 180; Miller and Hatcher, Med. Eng. 39; J. Birrell, 'Common Rts. in Med. Forest: Disputes and Conflicts in 13th cent.' Past & Present, cxvii. 22–4, 44–9.
[53] V.C.H. Salop. xi. 222.
[54] Ibid. 81.
[55] Ibid. ii. 85; viii. 146; Cart. Haughmond, pp. 143–4.
[56] V.C.H. Salop. xi. 142, 176.
[57] Ibid. ii. 52; S.R.O. 1224/2/11.
[58] Roll of Salop. Eyre 1256, pp. 138–9.
[59] V.C.H. Salop. viii. 14–15.
[60] Roll of Salop. Eyre 1256, p. 57.
[61] S.R.O. 465/69; Eyton, xi. 261.
[62] Cart. Haughmond, pp. 25–6.
[63] Ibid. p. 90.
[64] Cart. Haughmond, pp. 30–1, 38.
[65] V.C.H. Salop. viii. 147, 153.
[66] Ibid. xi. 141, 155.
[67] Above, Physical Environment.
[68] Cf. Studies of Field Systems in Brit. Isles, ed. A. R. H. Baker and R. A. Butlin (1973), 189.
[69] R. Lennard, Rural Eng. 1086–1135 (1959), 393.
[70] Calculated from figs. in Darby and Terrett, Domesday Geog. Mid. Eng. 126; Census, 1831, i. 526–7.
[71] Astill and Grant, Countryside of Med. Eng. 16.

differentiation in the number of ploughteams at work. The areas with the highest density of teams, over two to the square mile, lay east and west of Shrewsbury in the Severn lowlands and Ercall–Cound regions and around Bromfield at the southern end of the Scarplands and the Clee Hills platform. The regions with the lowest densities, of less than one plough to the square mile, were in the northern part of the county, and the south-central uplands and the Clun regions in the south-west.[72]

No mention of open-field land occurs in the few Saxon documents from the county[73] and by the mid 13th century, when the evidence is more plentiful, the open fields were apparently as fully developed in form, if not always in extent, as they were ever to be. All villages and most hamlets seem to have had some open-field land, evidenced by mention of strip holdings. Where the medieval landscape can be reconstructed, it is clear that what mainly determined how much of a settlement's land lay open in strips was the inherent quality of the land: those places with the best land, affording easily worked soils and level terrain, had far more open-field land than those with poor or heavy soils or extensive areas of upland or waterlogged soils. Thus around Wellington there were wide expanses of open-field land between the southern boundary of the Weald Moors and the heavily wooded higher land which extended south to the Severn, whereas within that wooded area the many open fields attached to individual hamlets were small and discrete.[74] Survivals of ridge-and-furrow are so few as to suggest that the prominent ridging of arable lands was not practised in the county.[75]

Documentary sources allow some conclusions to be drawn about the layout of open-field land. Where there was a sufficient area of good land, and possibly where there was a strong lord or active manorial community, three extensive open fields might lie around the settlement. It was usual for them to be named either in terms of the direction in which they lay from the settlement, hence 'North field' or 'South field', or in terms of the neighbouring settlement towards which they extended. Thus in 1298 the three main areas of open-field land in Prees appear to have been called the field towards Willaston, the field towards Darliston, and the Middle field.[76] In about 30 instances the documents concerning 12th- and 13th-century open fields are full enough to allow the type of layout to be assessed, and in every certain case it is in three fields, not two. Such a layout is documented more frequently in the eastern part of the county than the west; no evidence of a three-field layout has been found in the Clun area.

Evidence of three open fields, however, does not necessarily mean that all a settlement's open-field land lay within three large and separate fields. Especially where the terrain was irregular or wooded, a village's open-field land might lie in a variety of enclosures: one or more open fields of the classic type, with strips grouped into *culturae* or furlongs, often lying at right angles to each other, might be combined with any number of hedged, walled, fenced, or ditched closes scattered about, each divided into strips of the usual type and in multiple tenure. Administratively, however, in such cases all the settlement's open-field land, whether in large open fields or small closes, was considered together, and it was divided into three 'seasons' for cropping purposes. Thus as Prees in 1298[77] in

[72] Darby and Terrett, op. cit. 132; Darby, *Domesday Eng.* 132.

[73] Above, Early Agriculture.

[74] *V.C.H. Salop.* xi, fig. facing p. 1; 1, 3.

[75] For early medieval ridge and furrow see P. Barker and J. Lawson, 'A pre-Norman field-system at Hên Domen,

Montgomery', *Medieval Arch.* xv. 58–72; SA 165, incl. air photos. apparently showing the motte and bailey castle at Culmington astride ridge and furrow.

[76] Staffs. R.O., D.(W.) 1734/J/2268, ff. 26–8; S.R.O. 3763/125/4 A.

[77] Staffs. R.O., D.(W.) 1734/J/2268, ff. 26–8.

addition to the three main open fields there were strips in a number of closes whose names, with the elements 'hay', 'stocking', and 'bruches', indicate that they were relatively late products of clearance from wood or waste.[78] Each 'season' of the demesne included lands in four or five separate fields or closes, and within each of those the demesne was divided into 'divers pieces' or strips, interspersed with the tenants' lands.

Some conclusions can also be drawn about the internal organization of open fields, especially about the regularity with which holdings were divided between the three fields or 'seasons'. More often than not a fairly close tripartite division can be seen.[79] Among the lords Adam of Faintree held 90 a. in his vill's three fields at his death in 1274, 34 a. in one, 30 a. in another, and 26 a. in the third,[80] while in the same year in Meole Brace the demesne holdings in the three fields totalled 42½ a., 40½ a., and 30 a.[81] Virgate holdings exhibit some of the most precise divisions: in 1199–1200 the greater part of ⅓ virgate at Darliston comprised 6 a. in each of the three fields, and a ¼ virgate at Romsley had 8 a. in each of two fields and 6 a. in the third.[82] The concept of regular apportionment can also be seen in the way in which a virgate at Woofferton was split in 1221 into holdings of ⅔ and ⅓ of a virgate, 2 a. in every 3 being allotted to the former holding; the 2 a. in every 3 were those which lay 'towards the sun'.[83] Although such phraseology is reminiscent of the *solskifte* or 'sun division' system of strip allocation, it cannot be taken as evidence of its presence at Woofferton.[84] The preference for an equal tripartite division of a holding between the open fields can also be seen in grants to the religious: in the 13th century, for instance, John of Balderton granted 2 a. in each of the village's three fields to Haughmond abbey.[85]

The second major characteristic of open-field agriculture, along with the equal division of strip holdings, was the annual allotment of one of the fields as fallow grazing for all the commoners. The need or desire to ensure grazing land in that way has been shown as the essential reason behind the adoption of open-field agriculture.[86] Specific mention of regular fallows in the county are rare, though the usual tripartite division of lands, discussed above, is in itself strongly indicative of their use. One mention is at Charlton, in Shawbury, where it was agreed in 1249 that the abbot of Lilleshall's men were not to have common before Michaelmas except in the arable land during fallow.[87] Another mention is at Nash, close to the southern border of the county. There in 1256 a man complained that he had been prevented from commoning in a field of *c.* 34 a. as he used to, all the year round every third year when the field lay fallow, and after the hay and corn harvests in the other two years when it was sown.[88]

Medieval farmers were well aware of the need to retain soil fertility both by fallowing and by the application of what may broadly be termed fertilizers.[89] Occasionally 'weak' or 'worn out' land (*terra debilitata*) is noted: 2 carucates of demesne at Great Wytheford, in Shawbury, were so described in 1292–3,[90] as was ½ carucate of demesne at Woolstaston in 1292; in the latter case that condition was reflected in the very low valuation of the land at 6s. 8d.[91] Soil exhaustion was a particular problem where assarting brought land of inherently poor quality into

[78] Rowley, *Origins of Open Field Agric.* 67, 74, 92; Dyer, *Lords and Peasants*, 68–9.   [79] Cf. Rowley, op. cit. 73–4.
[80] P.R.O., C 133/4, no. 14.
[81] P.R.O., C 133/2, no. 7.
[82] Gray, *Eng. Field Systems*, 68.
[83] *T.S.A.S.* 3rd ser. vi. 174.
[84] Rowley, *Origins of Open Field Agric.* 109–10, n. 51.
[85] *Cart. Haughmond*, p. 43.
[86] Rowley, op. cit. 74–5.
[87] S.R.O. 322, med. deed no. 26.
[88] *Roll of Salop. Eyre 1256*, p. 35.
[89] Miller and Hatcher, *Med. Eng.* 214–15.
[90] P.R.O., C 133/65, no. 12.
[91] P.R.O., C 133/63, no. 32.

cultivation, and in Linley, in More, assarts lay fallow in the years before 1309, presumably to allow the soil to recover.[92] In the welshries the combination of partible inheritance and often limited amounts of good quality arable land produced very small holdings in the townships' open fields.[93] Those were supplemented by plots of waste which were ploughed and had two or three crops taken from them before soil exhaustion led to their abandonment.[94] While it can be assumed that as much manure, both human and animal, as was available was spread on the land,[95] only rarely, as at Walford, in Baschurch, where an overflowing fishpond washed manure from the land in 1256, is the practice actually noted.[96] Manure was gathered from middens, from pens, or from animal houses such as the new byre (*bostarium*), 80 ft. by 40 ft., built at Chirbury c. 1250.[97] It was also deposited directly on fallows by animals, especially sheep, deliberately run there for that purpose. Indeed tenants were often compelled to fold their animals on the lord's demesne rather than their own land. Those animals would either feed on the fallow field itself, or else on nearby commons, being driven back to the field at the end of the day to dung it.[98] At night sheep seem usually to have been kept in a fold, either a temporary one which could be moved about the field, or a permanent one, such as Wombridge priory had at Brockton,[99] where straw was regularly spread to build up a layer of manure. Thus in 1236 Roger of Onslow granted Buildwas abbey common grazing on Onslow heath, west of Shrewsbury. In return 120 of his sheep were to be cared for by the abbey's shepherd there and folded in its sheepfold; Roger was to supply hay and straw for his sheep, but was to receive back their dung.[1]

In the 13th century marl came to be widely applied to arable land in Shropshire, presumably to improve soil texture. Marl was believed to be beneficial to the soil for a longer period than dung, and it was probably for that reason that it was added to dung before manuring took place.[2] Marl is a type of subsoil consisting primarily of clay with lime carbonate, the argillaceous (clayey) and calcareous ingredients being found in varying proportions appropriate to the lightening of clay soils or the strengthening of sandy soils to improve their fertility. Historically a wide range of subsoils was used to dress land.[3] Of the two dozen early medieval, mostly mid 13th-century marlpits of which mention has been found, two thirds lay in the northern half of the county. Too few are located precisely enough to enable assessment of the soil type, but it is clear that certain local subsoils were favoured. About 1250, for instance, Haughmond abbey was granted an acre in the field land of Preston Boats and access to it to get marl for its land in Uffington and elsewhere.[4] The marl pits at Whitchurch were so extensive that by the mid 16th century they were flooded and a notable topographic feature.[5] Some marl pits were common rather than private, as at Edgton,[6] Hisland,[7] and apparently Roden where a 'great marl pit' lay in or close to open-field land.[8] The amount of land, whether demesne or tenant, that was regularly marled was probably limited by the considerable effort or expense involved: invariably marling cost over 1s. and

[92] *Cart. Haughmond*, p. 148.
[93] Above (Lords and tenants).
[94] Slack, *Lordship of Oswestry*, 23.
[95] e.g. *V.C.H. Wilts.* iv. 12.
[96] *Roll of Salop. Eyre 1256*, p. 58.
[97] *Cal. Anct. Corresp. Concerning Wales*, ed. J. G. Edwards (1935), p. 17.
[98] B. M. S. Campbell, 'Agric. Progress in Med. Eng.: Evidence from E. Norfolk', *Econ. H.R.* 2nd ser. xxxvi. 35; *V.C.H. Cambs.* ii. 67; *V.C.H. Wilts.* iv. 22.

[99] Staffs. R.O., D. 593/A/2/31/7.
[1] *T.S.A.S.* 4th ser. iv. 162.
[2] *Walter of Henley and other Treatises on Est. Management*, ed. D. Oschinsky (1971), 329, 339.
[3] J. Thirsk, *Eng.'s Agric. Regions and Agrarian Hist. 1500-1750* (1987), 63.
[4] S.R.O. 3763/125/4B; *Cart. Haughmond*, p. 179.
[5] *Ag. Hist. Eng.* ii. 439.
[6] Eyton, xi. 261.
[7] *Cart. Haughmond*, p. 26.
[8] S.R.O. 322/29.

sometimes, in the late 13th century, 3s. 6d. an acre.[9] It was also dangerous: eleven deaths in the county caused by collapses and drowning in marl pits were reported to the justices in eyre in 1256;[10] they had presumably occurred since the previous eyre of 1248.[11]

Liming too may have been undertaken where calcareous rock and fuel to burn it were readily available. In the mid 13th century limekilns were noted at Cound,[12] at Bullhill hear Harnage Grange,[13] under the Wrekin, and in Wellington hay,[14] although the lime they produced may, at least in part, have been for building work rather than agriculture.

Ploughing was the main task in the agricultural round. The 13th-century treatises recommended that, in addition to the ploughing of land for sowing crops in winter and spring, the fallow should be ploughed twice to reduce weed infestation. As a single team would do well to plough as much as an acre a day and might manage only $\frac{1}{2}$ a., it has been argued that in the west midlands, given the resources available, fallow ploughing was done hurriedly, if at all.[15] The only detailed notice found of the type of plough used in Shropshire in the period occurs in a bailiff's account of 1280-1 for Aston, in Oswestry.[16] There the cost of making several pairs or sets of plough wheels (*paria rotarum pro carrucis*) shows that it was the wheeled plough that was used, as was often the case in the county in the later Middle Ages.[17] The account also notes the costs of making and sharpening ploughshares, of making iron fittings for the plough feet, and of supplying new timbers for harrows. In many manors rents owed in kind included ploughshares, an exceptional case being that of William the smith, who in 1301 held his freehold in Upton Magna by providing the lord with ironwork for the demesne ploughs, namely ploughshares, coulters, and iron swingletrees, the trace holders and associated furniture on the cross bars of the plough yoke.[18]

The cereal crops grown in the Middle Ages can be divided into those sown in the autumn (winter corn) and those in the spring. The former comprised wheat, the chief bread corn, and rye, occasionally used alone for bread but more often mixed with other grains. The spring corns were barley, used mainly for malting but also for bread and fodder, and oats, used to feed horses and as porridge. Oats could be grown on relatively poor land, and frequently occur in the lists of forest assarts made in the 13th century.[19] Mixed corns were also sown: maslin (wheat and rye) and dredge (barley and oats).[20] Peas and beans were also grown in the open fields; they are quick growing, food for men and animals, and good for the soil as they are nitrogen-fixing. Only one detailed account roll which included grainstuffs has been located, from Haughmond abbey's grange of Aston, in Oswestry, for 1280-1. There the emphasis was on winter corn, especially wheat: twice as much wheat was grown as either rye or oats. The other crops comprised relatively small amounts of barley, peas, and beans.[21] Otherwise references are fleeting, as in the case of Maud Gnat, 'an evil doer and thief', who c. 1256 was killed by a watchman sleeping in the barn from which she fled after stealing a quarter of wheat.[22]

[9] Miller and Hatcher, *Med. Eng.* 214-15; *Econ. H.R.* 2nd ser. xxxvi. 34.

[10] *Roll of Salop. Eyre 1256*, pp. 205, 222, 250, 252, 276-7, 282, 286, 288.   [11] Ibid. p. xi n.

[12] *V.C.H. Salop.* viii. 68.

[13] *T.S.A.S.* liv. 116.

[14] *V.C.H. Salop.* ii. 92; xi. 231.

[15] Dyer, *Lords and Peasants.* 126-7; inf. from Dr. Dyer.

[16] N.L.W., Aston Hall 5300. Dr. U. Rees is thanked for supplying transcript.

[17] Below, 1300-1540 (Demesne agriculture).

[18] *Two Est. Surveys of Earls of Arundel*, p. 64.

[19] P.R.O., E 32/143-5, 147.

[20] See *V.C.H. Cambs.* ii. 62.

[21] N.L.W., Aston Hall 5300.

[22] *Roll of Salop. Eyre 1256*, p. 213.

Besides cereals,[23] crops such as flax, hemp,[24] mustard,[25] and particularly household vegetables, were also grown in crofts and gardens attached to houses. For everyone the vegetables and fruit—brassica, broad beans, onions, leeks, garlic, herbs, apples, and pears—represented a welcome variety to the diet. More importantly, vegetables and herbs were the main ingredients of pottage, a mess that was a staple element in the medieval diet, especially for the peasantry.[26] There was also the prospect of a little cash from the sale of any surplus,[27] very necessary for the peasantry in an age when ever-increasing numbers of cash fines and dues were demanded by the king, the church, and the lord of the manor.[28] The importance of gardens is shown by the tithe income they provided to the vicar of Stokesay in 1252—10s., the same amount as the parish's wool tithe.[29] The gardens attached to manor houses are frequently mentioned in contemporary documents. At Stirchley in 1247, for instance, there were apparently two distinct manorial gardens: a 'great garden', at least partly taken up with an orchard, and a second outside the *curia*.[30] Apples and pears were particularly important as they could be kept through the winter, and the apples used to make cider.[31] Until the later 13th century, when climatic change including a lowering of the mean temperature occurred,[32] the gardens of the county's richer inhabitants may also have included vines, whose grapes were used to make wine, or more probably verjuice, a kind of vinegar.[33] No vineyards were recorded as far north as Shropshire in Domesday Book,[34] but in the 13th century there may have been a vineyard belonging to Shrewsbury abbey on the banks of the Severn at Shrewsbury.[35]

Livestock and pastoral farming

Any evidence collected by the Domesday inquiry of meadow land in Shropshire was omitted from the final record, although at six of the places later in the county but then in Staffordshire and (if Domesday Book is to be believed) Warwickshire, meadow land in amounts of between 1 and 16 a. was recorded.[36] As so often, no record was preserved of other permanent grassland.[37]

In the 13th century in most parts of the county the demesne plough beasts and other hay-eating stock were supported by quite small amounts of meadow. Only about 6 per cent of manors had more than 10 a. of meadow to each carucate (120 a.) of arable. It was exceptional for a manor to be as well supplied as Prees, where in 1298, in addition to 342½ a. of arable land, the demesne included 75 a. of meadow and 46 a. of pasture, 30 a. of which had recently been approved from the waste.[38] About 31 per cent of manors had between 5 and 10 a. of meadow to each carucate, while 63 per cent had under 5 a. In the last group by far the largest number of manors had 2 a. or less of meadow for every carucate of arable.[39]

[23] Staffs. R.O., D. 593/A/2/29/10.
[24] *V.C.H. Cambs*. ii. 70; Astill and Grant, *Countryside of Med. Eng*. 114, 122; *T.S.A.S*. lxii. 26; S.R.O. 1514/59 (flax pool field name).
[25] S.R.O. 3365/158 (Edw. le Mostardmaker, whose goods incl. mustard seed worth 4s.).
[26] J. H. Harvey, 'Vegetables in Middle Ages', *Garden Hist*. xii. 89-97.
[27] Miller and Hatcher, *Med. Eng*. 88; E. Britton, *The Community of the Vill* (1978), 157-9.
[28] Dyer, *Lords and Peasants*, 73, 100-3, 106.
[29] *Cart. Haughmond*, p. 213.   [30] Eyton, viii. 118-19.
[31] S.R.O. 322/52; *Cal. Inq. Misc*. i, pp. 359-60; Oschinsky, *Walter of Henley*, 429.
[32] H. H. Lamb, 'The early medieval warm epoch and its

sequel', *Paleogeography, Paleoclimatology, Paleoecology*, i. 13-37; *Palaeohydrology in Practice: a River Basin Analysis*, ed. K. J. Gregory, J. Lewin, and J. B. Thornes (1987), 121-3.
[33] Astill and Grant, *Countryside of Med. Eng*. 117.
[34] Darby, *Domesday Eng*. 277.
[35] H. Owen and J. B. Blakeway, *Hist. Shrews*. (1825), ii. 45.
[36] Darby and Terrett, *Domesday Geog. Mid. Eng*. 141-2. For arguments for and against Warws. cf. *T.S.A.S*. lvii. 157-60; *Domesday Bk.: Salop*. ed. F. and C. Thorn (1986), n. EW.
[37] Darby, *Domesday Eng*. 149, 151.
[38] Staffs. R.O., D.(W.) 1734/J/2268, f. 26v.
[39] Sample size of 85 manors: sources as above, p. 30 n. 46.

That disparity, approached only in a few other parts of the country,[40] was reflected in the relative values attached to arable and meadow land. In Shropshire in the 13th century arable was usually estimated to be worth 2*d.* to 4*d.* an acre[41] whereas meadow was rarely reckoned at less than 1*s.* an acre, and was often valued at 2*s.* or 3*s.* An extreme case was the manor of Ellesmere in 1280, where the demesne comprised 324 a. arable and just 3½ a. meadow, valued at 4*d.* and 7*s.* 7*d.* an acre respectively.[42] Those figures should not necessarily be taken as accurate reflections of the rates that could be obtained for land on the open market, and the rents paid were often much higher.[43] Occasionally work on demesne meadows was mentioned as a labour service, and in 1276 in Oswestry the demesne servants included a reaper and a watchman.[44] At Upton Magna in 1301 meadow was left fallow one year in three.[45] Virtually nothing else is revealed by the sources for the period about the management of meadows in Shropshire.

It was the county's extensive permanent grassland, moorland, and woodland pastures that enabled relatively large numbers of animals to be kept. In south and west Shropshire upland grazing was the predominant type of common, and townships sometimes had pasture rights on hills some distance from the settlement. In the lordship of Oswestry, for instance, the lowland townships of Crickheath and Maesbury had upland pastures on the other side of the lordship, respectively at Cynynion and Cefn-y-maes (probably 'hill of Maesbury'). There transhumance clearly played a part in the local economy.[46] In much of central and south-east Shropshire grazing was in woodland[47] and in the north and north-east on moorland or heath, often waterlogged. Prees is an example of a manor in the north-east that still retained extensive commons in the late 13th century despite a vigorous assarting movement and apparently a considerable population growth.[48] In 1298 the 95 or so households on the bishop of Coventry and Lichfield's estate there farmed *c.* 1,300 a. of open arable land and inclosed fields, most of the households being those of peasant farmers with an acre or less of several grassland; they also had access to *c.* 1,180 a. common heath and moorland (on which the villagers of Hawkstone, Kenstone, Marchamley, Sandford, and Weston-under-Redcastle also had rights) and *c.* 920 a. woodland.

Broad conclusions can be drawn about the types of animals kept, their numbers and proportions on farms of different types, and their use. The most important animal in the farming economy was the ox, the main draught beast. Generally, medieval cattle were of a fairly primitive short-horned variety, with an average withers height of no more than 1.10 m.[49] Although on light soils a team of oxen could work only half as fast as a team of horses, it coped much better with wet and heavy soils and slow pulling.[50] In the 12th and 13th centuries horse teams or mixed horse and ox teams began to be used for ploughing on some farms in eastern England; otherwise, and especially in western England and Wales, all ploughing and most heavy haulage in the early Middle Ages was done by oxen.[51] In the early 13th century when the royal manors in Shropshire were restocked, the incoming stock included 120 oxen but no horses (Table I).[52] Forty of those oxen were for

[40] Cf. *V.C.H. Cambs.* ii. 59, 65; *V.C.H. Leics.* ii. 162; Miller and Hatcher, *Med. Eng.* 98; G. Platts, *Land and People in Med. Lincs.* (Lincoln, 1985), 106–7; Astill and Grant, *Countryside of Med. Eng.* 16–18.

[41] The 1291 val. of Wenlock priory's lands at *c.* ½*d.*–2*d.* an acre is improbably low: *Tax. Eccl.* (Rec. Com.), 164.

[42] *T.S.A.S.* 2nd ser. xi. 252.[43] Cf. *V.C.H. Cambs.* ii. 59.

[44] Smith, 'Lordships of Chirk and Oswestry', 119.

[45] *Two Est. Surveys of Earls of Arundel*, p. 78.

[46] Slack, *Lordship of Oswestry*, 22–3; cf. *Two Est. Surveys of Earls of Arundel*, p. 72 s.v. Cottone, for another possible instance of transhumance.

[47] Above (Woodland, assarting, and commons).

[48] Staffs. R.O., D.(W.) 1734/J/2268, ff. 26–8.

[49] Astill and Grant, *Countryside of Med. Eng.* 176.

[50] J. Langdon, *Horses, Oxen and Technological Innovation* (1986), 19, 21.   [51] Ibid. 22, 29, 46–7, 52–3, 61; below.

[52] *Pipe R.* 1209 (P.R.S. N.S. xxiv), 146.

Ford manor; the oxen there seem to have been the main target of a Welsh band which raided in 1260, killing, wounding, or taking prisoner 28 men and carrying off from the neighbourhood 260 oxen, 80 sheep, and 57 horses.[53]

The optimum size of ploughteam seems consistently to have been regarded as eight beasts[54] and, nominally at least, that was the composition of each of the 1,833⅜ ploughteams recorded in the area of the modern county in 1086.[55] Certainly eight was the number in the few later references which specify or suggest ploughteam size, as when the royal manors in the county were restocked between 1202 and 1209 (Table I),[56] and in the mid 13th century at Corfton,[57] at Adstone, in Wentnor, and at Hopton, in Hodnet.[58] In the early 13th century a grant of ½ virgate in Stanton Lacy carried with it the right to pasture four oxen and one heifer,[59] which may hint at a local theoretical relationship between the virgate as a land unit and the eight-ox team as the means of working it. In 1086 by far the largest number of ploughteams, well over 100 in all, was owned by Roger of Montgomery, earl of Shrewsbury. Ford was exceptional in having ten teams; the rest of his demesne manors had between one and six teams, with four being the most common.[60] Generally on Earl Roger's estates there is considerable evidence of his interest in profitable demesne farming, and one important facet of that seems to be the generous provision of ox teams.[61] The second largest landowner in the county in 1086, Reynold the sheriff, had fewer than 40 teams; the best-endowed monastery, Wenlock priory, had under 20; and on the home farms of the lesser lay lords there were usually at most ten teams.[62] Comparison of the recorded numbers of Domesday peasants and their teams makes it clear that few peasants owned a full ox team,[63] and suggests that the compilation of full teams for ploughing involved either hiring animals or co-operation.[64] That kind of arrangement is indicated at Moreton Corbet c. 1250, where tenants who did not own enough beasts to plough their lands were permitted to receive 'foreign' beasts according to the size of their tenements.[65] The peasant might perforce put cows or heifers into his team, while the smallholder, whose lands might lie outside the open fields, may have struggled to plough his lands with perhaps as few as two beasts.[66]

The numbers of cows recorded as stocked and stinted suggest that manors had, at most, sufficient to provide the demesne with ox calves and the household with dairy products. In the early 13th century a herd of 24 or 30 cows was apparently usual at four of the five royal manors in the county then being restocked. The exception was Ford, where 72 were reported as lacking in 1202 and 67 were sent in 1208–9.[67] Relatively small herds were also recorded on the manors of the county's larger monastic houses in 1291 (Table II). Early in the 13th century Haughmond abbey had developed a farm near Cothercott called *Boveria* to which animals were brought from Oswestry and Wales by the abbey's two drovers. Despite its name, however, the surviving records suggest that cattle played only a minor role in its economy; those there were primarily young oxen.[68] The minor

[53] *V.C.H. Salop.* viii. 231.
[54] Langdon, *Horses, Oxen and Tech. Innovation*, 31; Darby, *Domesday Eng.* 125-6.
[55] Darby and Terrett, *Domesday Geog. Mid. Eng.* 126.
[56] *Pipe R.* 1202 (P.R.S. N.S. xv), 47; 1209 (P.R.S. N.S. xxiv), 146.
[57] *Roll of Salop. Eyre 1256*, p. 220; Eyton, iv. 14-15.
[58] *Cart. Haughmond*, pp. 126, 174.
[59] Heref. Cathedral, Dean & Chapter Archive 3226.
[60] Lewis, 'Salop. Domesday'.
[61] *Social Relations and Ideas: Essays in Honour of R. H.*

Hilton, ed. T. H. Aston and others (1983), 45-72.
[62] Lewis, 'Salop. Domesday'.
[63] Ibid.
[64] Langdon, *Horses, Oxen and Tech. Innovation*, 236-7.
[65] S.R.O. 322/26.
[66] Langdon, op. cit. 242. For peasant ownership of oxen see also *Rolls of Just. in Eyre 1221-2* (Selden Soc. lix), pp. 59, 533-4.
[67] *Pipe R.* 1202 (P.R.S. N.S. xv), 47; 1209 (P.R.S. N.S. xxiv), 146.
[68] *Cart. Haughmond*, pp. 10-11; N.L.W., Aston Hall 5300.

TABLE II: STOCK RECORDED IN 1291 ON
MONASTIC PROPERTIES IN SOUTH SHROPSHIRE

	horses	cows	sheep
Alberbury priory	—	6	60
Buildwas abbey	—	32	300[a]
Haughmond abbey	—	—	186
Preen priory	—	2	—
Ratlinghope priory	—	4	10
Shrewsbury abbey	—	32	300
Wenlock priory	19	25	974

Source: Tax. Eccl. (Rec. Com.), 163–5, covering those parts of Shropshire in Hereford diocese. There is no comparable information for the parts of Shropshire in Lichfield and St. Asaph dioceses.

[a] Besides 10 goats and their young.

place that dairying had is also suggested by records of stints. About 1268 the Condover demesne had common for only 6 cows compared with 12 oxen, 30 pigs, and 120 sheep; the cow pasture was valued, per beast, at twice that of the oxen,[69] perhaps because the oxen would usually be taken out to work during the day. About 1245 at Worfield the animals pastured in Soudley wood were 12 cows, 18 oxen, 15 pigs and their litters, and 500 sheep; again, it cost twice as much to pasture a cow as an ox.[70]

Milk yields were poor, especially where there was a shortage of good grazing. Moreover cows' milk, like sheep's, was available for only part of each year, cows that give milk throughout the year being a product of modern breeding.[71] Over a year a medieval cow produced c. 90 lb. (40 kg.) of milk products compared with 1,000 lb. from a modern animal.[72] Generally milk production was probably less important than the production of oxen and, for richer households, beef,[73] with dairy produce forming a much more important component of poor people's diet than rich people's.[74]

Specialist beef production increased in importance in the later Middle Ages.[75] There is little evidence of it in the county before 1300, although it is often impossible to tell the age and sex of recorded cattle. Conceivably it was beef animals that the 13th-century villagers of Loughton pastured 2 miles away in the Clee forest,[76] or that were kept by Buildwas abbey at Ruckley grange and pastured at Donington,[77] or that were bred by the lords of Pontesbury;[78] it seems far likelier, however, to have been plough beasts and breeding stock in all those cases. While there is no independent evidence of it from Shropshire, most beef eaten in the Middle Ages came from weak, old, and surplus plough beasts and dairy cattle. 'Ox meat' is frequently mentioned in early 14th-century lay subsidy records for Shrewsbury. Hide and horns too had a market, as perhaps did bones, and in the 13th and 14th centuries Shrewsbury was a renowned tanning centre.[79] An old or dead cow was thus a marketable commodity, far more than a horse whose flesh was rarely, if ever, eaten.[80] In certain parts of the county, however, herds of young

[69] P.R.O., C 145/20, no. 1.
[70] P.R.O., SC 12/14/24; Eyton, iii. 111.
[71] Astill and Grant, Countryside of Med. Eng. 29; R. Hellier and S. Moorhouse, Medieval Dairying (Medieval Section, Yorks. Arch. Soc. [1980]), 2.
[72] Aston, Social Relations and Ideas, 211.
[73] Astill and Grant, Countryside of Med. Eng. 155–6.
[74] Aston, op. cit. 211.
[75] Below, 1300–1540 (Demesne agriculture).
[76] Eyton, v. 201.   [77] T.S.A.S. 4th ser. vi. 188–9.
[78] V.C.H. Salop. viii. 272.
[79] S.R.O. 3365/152, 156, 158; Eng. Hist. Doc. 1189–1327, ed. H. Rothwell (1975), p. 882.
[80] W. Levison, Eng. and the Continent in the 8th Cent. (1946), 101; Astill and Grant, Countryside of Med. Eng. 160, 174.

beef stock were a common sight from the 13th century, as the practice grew of driving Welsh-bred animals to midland pastures before taking them on to London for sale and slaughter.[81] Commercial breeding is suggested, for instance, by the grant to Chirbury priory of pasture at Montgomery by the king in 1227 for 100 cows and their calves and 50 mares and their foals, the calves and foals being removed when they were three and two years old respectively.[82]

The horse was probably rarely used to plough in medieval Shropshire.[83] Nevertheless large numbers of horses were employed in agriculture, for instance for harrowing[84] and particularly in the distribution of produce.[85] Some time before 1274 the Templars, lords of Holdgate, sent 6 qr. of oats to Ludlow on horseback. The party was ambushed by men described as bailiffs of the lord of Corfham, who stole the grain and immediately sowed it, and then harrowed it in using the horses which they had also taken.[86] Horses were ridden by all classes of society from the richer peasantry upwards.[87] In the late 14th century there were wild horses, presumably a type of hill pony, in the Preston Brockhurst area.[88] Such animals may have been suitable for some purposes, such as general packing and hauling, but better bloodstock and breeding were required to produce the larger, specialist riding[89] and war horses required by the aristocracy.[90] Lay subsidy records of the early 14th century reflect the wide range of horses available. In the valuation of 1306 for Shrewsbury 75 affers, or workhorses,[91] were listed, usually valued at between 3s. and 6s. 8d. Forty animals were valued as 'horses'; all but three were worth between 7s. and 20s., with the majority (25) being valued at between 10s. and 14s. The three horses whose valuations were exceptional, especially given the tendency for goods to be undervalued by the assessors,[92] were two owned by the leading wool merchant John of Ludlow (50s. each), and one owned by William of Harley (53s. 4d.).[93] Most horses were small compared with modern animals, and few stood as high as 1.60 m. (15.75 hands) at the withers.[94] Large landowners often kept their own studs. In 1175 Henry II granted Haughmond abbey pasture on the Long Mynd for its herds of horses,[95] and in 1232 Wenlock priory had horses from a stud commoned in Clee forest, presumably under supervision.[96] Horse breeding seems to have been widely practised in the Welsh marches. The earl of Arundel (d. 1302) had important studs at Bromhurst park (near Oswestry) and at Clun,[97] while Roger de Mortimer apparently had a stud at Hopton Wafers in south-east Shropshire: mares worth 200 marks that were being sent there from Chirk were seized in 1302 by Wenlock priory as they passed through priory lands.[98] Horse and fatstock production in general was not confined to lordly households. Where there were sufficient commons it was sometimes undertaken by the peasantry, as on another of the earl of Arundel's manors in west Shropshire, Shrawardine, where horses were bred and sold by the tenantry.[99] The same activity is indicated by the

[81] H. P. R. Finberg, 'An Early Ref. to the Welsh Cattle Trade', *Agric. H.R.* ii. 12–14; B. M. Campbell, 'Towards an Agric. Geog. of Med. Eng.' ibid. xxxvi. 97.
[82] Eyton, xi. 59.
[83] No refs. to horses being so used noted in Langdon, *Horses, Oxen and Tech. Innovation*, 46, 61, 90.
[84] Ibid. 34, 59.   [85] Below (Marketing).
[86] *Rot. Hund.* (Rec. Com.), ii. 101.
[87] Peasants pres. rode their affers.
[88] Owen and Blakeway, *Hist. Shrews.* ii. 26.
[89] For palfreys cf. *Cart. Haughmond*, p. 237.
[90] *Horses in European Econ. Hist.* ed. F. M. L. Thompson (1983), 4–20; H. le Strange, *Le Strange Records* (1916), 162.
[91] Cf. Oschinsky, *Walter of Henley*, 267, and Langdon,

Horses, Oxen and Tech. Innovation, 293–7, for terminological problems.
[92] *Lay Subsidy of 1334*, ed. R. E. Glassock (1975), p. xxii.
[93] S.R.O. 3365/152.
[94] Astill and Grant, *Countryside of Med. Eng.* 178.
[95] *V.C.H. Salop.* ii. 63; *Cart. Haughmond*, p. 149.
[96] *T.S.A.S.* 4th ser. i. 392.
[97] Smith, 'Lordships of Chirk and Oswestry', 148; below, 1300-1540 (Demesne agriculture). Gerald of Wales attributed the quality of marcher horses to Spanish bloodstock imported by Rob. of Bellême c. 1100: *T.S.A.S.* 3rd ser. iii. 40.
[98] *Cal. Pat. 1301-7*, 95.
[99] *Two Est. Surveys of Earls of Arundel*, p. 81.

frequent issue in the early 14th century of licences to sell foals in Halesowen, a large predominantly wood–pasture manor on the borders of Shropshire, Stafford-shire, and Worcestershire.[1]

By far the commonest animal kept in Shropshire in the early Middle Ages was the sheep. Where flocks were large wool production had gained primacy by the 12th century, whereas for peasants with just a few animals milk remained the main product.[2] If, as seems likely, livestock other than ploughteams was recorded in the hundredal and county returns in 1086, it was omitted from the final Exchequer copy.[3] Thus almost all the surviving information about sheep husbandry in the county dates from the 13th century onwards, by which time it dominated Shropshire's pastoral economy. Almost certainly, however, that dominance was of long standing, the woods and uplands of much of the county being ideally suited to sheep husbandry, always an attractive farming proposition because of the small amount of labour needed and the sheep's ability to survive on relatively poor land.

The best medieval data concern the flocks of the county's religious houses. At least the larger ones derived a considerable income from wool, though only Buildwas appears in Pegolotti's late 13th-century list of monasteries supplying wool to Italian merchants. He reckoned its annual clip at 20 sacks; to judge from the price it was good quality wool.[4] Certainly in the 14th century and later Shropshire's wool was reckoned among the best in the country.[5] Individual medieval fleeces weighed between 1 lb. and 2 lb., a third of the modern figure.[6] Therefore, at a conservative estimate of 240 fleeces to the sack,[7] Pegolotti's figure suggests that Buildwas's clip came from c. 4,800 animals. It is possible that Buildwas's own flocks sufficed to provide that clip,[8] though it is perhaps likelier the abbey was buying wool from other local producers.[9] When 'good quality' wool is spoken of it is in contemporary terms; analysis of preserved wool fragments has demonstrated a variety of early medieval fleece types, though a 'primitive hairy generalized medium' type predominated. In general modern wool types were not found in the Middle Ages despite the introduction, probably in the 14th century, of longwools.[10] Buildwas abbey probably had large flocks on most or all of its granges. In 1236 it was granted extensive common pasture on Onslow heath, where it had a sheepfold and shepherd, apparently mainly for sheep from the abbey's grange at Monkmeole, west of Shrewsbury,[11] and in 1247 it was granted pasture near the adjoining Bicton heath for 300 head.[12] In 1291 it had 300 sheep on its estates in Hereford diocese, including Wentnor and Kinnerton, and in the early 13th century the abbey was granted the right to take its sheep from its grange at Harnage to wash them in the Severn.[13]

The house with the largest number of sheep in 1291 in the Shropshire part of Hereford diocese was Wenlock priory: it had 976 sheep, 209 of them breeding ewes (Table II). With such large flocks wethers, ewes, and hogs might be kept separately.[14] Haughmond abbey was also involved in the commercial production of wool.[15] In the 1230s pasture for 860 sheep was granted to it at Acton Reynald and Grinshill, and at about the same time for 300 sheep together with pannage for

[1] R. H. Hilton, *Eng. Peasantry in Later Middle Ages* (1974), 19.
[2] M. L. Ryder, *Sheep & Man* (1983), 444, 447.
[3] Darby, *Domesday Eng.* 4–5, 162–70.
[4] W. Cunningham, *Growth of Eng. Ind. and Commerce during Early and Middle Ages* (5th edn. 1922), i. 628, 632; *V.C.H. Salop.* ii. 52.
[5] Below, 1300–1540 (Demesne agriculture).
[6] Ibid.; Ryder, *Sheep & Man*, 449.

[7] *V.C.H. Staffs.* vi. 9; Titow, *Eng. Rural Soc. 1200–1350*, 45.
[8] Dr. Dyer's suggestion.
[9] *V.C.H. Salop.* ii. 53, 57. Buildwas owned few tithes.
[10] Ryder, *Sheep & Man*, 472–6.
[11] *T.S.A.S.* 4th ser. iv. 162.
[12] Ibid. 4th ser. vi. 191.
[13] *V.C.H. Salop.* ii. 52–3.
[14] Oschinsky, *Walter of Henley*, 188, 277.
[15] Following acct. based on *Cart. Haughmond*, pp. 10–11.

100 pigs in Hadnall, Haston, Shotton, and Smethcott. Soon afterwards pasture rights for 50 sheep were purchased at Hopton, in Hodnet, which had a grange and sheepfold by the early 14th century. By 1250 Haughmond had a grange at Aston, in Oswestry, which a bailiff's account of 1280–1 suggests was a gathering place for stock, perhaps Welsh animals, purchased at Oswestry market. Stock was sent both to flocks on the abbey's other properties and as meat for the abbey's kitchens: 120 sheep were driven to the Long Mynd and c. 30 each to Sundorne, Caldicott, and Hisland, and 147 sheep and a calf were forwarded for an episcopal visit. Shrewsbury abbey, like Buildwas, had 300 sheep noted in 1291 (Table II), though 847 were washed and sheared in 1333.[16] At least some of the abbey's sheep were probably pastured in High Ercall and Osbaston, where it had the right to pasture 440 sheep and 2 milch cows.[17]

Among the other religious houses with notable flocks in the county were Aconbury priory (Herefs.), given pasture c. 1250 for 200 ewes at Great Ness;[18] Wombridge priory, which apparently had a large flock at Brockton in the early 13th century;[19] and the Templars' preceptory at Lydley, at the foot of the Lawley hill, which in 1308 got 254 fleeces from its 280 sheep and 96 lambs.[20]

Evidence from lay estates confirms the general dominance of sheep in the pastoral economy. When the royal manors in Shropshire were restocked in the early 13th century six times as many sheep as cows were supplied and eight times as many sheep as pigs. Especially notable were the deliveries of 600 head to Worfield and 300 to Claverley, neighbouring manors on the south-eastern border of the county.[21] About 1245 in Worfield 40s. a year came from the beasts pastured in Soudley wood: 12 cows, 18 oxen, 15 pigs with their litters, and 500 sheep.[22] At Condover, another royal manor, to which no sheep had been sent in the early 13th-century restocking, there was common pasture available to the demesne c. 1268 for 120 sheep, 12 oxen, 6 cows, and 30 pigs.[23] In 1301 the demesne sheep stints were recorded on some of the earl of Arundel's manors, giving an indication of the importance that sheep were to have on Arundel manors in the county in the 14th century:[24] in the west of the county, 300 head at both Shrawardine and Bicton, in Clun, and in east-central Shropshire 200 each at Acton Round, Upton Magna, and Wroxeter.[25] In 1280 each of the 9 neifs and 2 cottars listed in an extent of the manor of Child's Ercall, which included extensive heathlands, owed the service of washing the lord's sheep.[26] On the nearby manor of High Ercall there may have been as many as 2,100 sheep in the later 13th century.[27]

A particularly striking example of the sheep's dominance of the pastoral economy, at least in the southern uplands, is provided by an analysis of the vicar of Stokesay's income in 1252. He received 10s. from the tithe of wool and 10s. from that of lambs. By comparison, the tithe of foals, calves, and piglets generated just 2s. 6d., dairy products (to which, again, sheep's milk may have made a considerable contribution) 5s., and hay 8s. 4d.[28]

There is much less information about the size of separate flocks, some clearly considerable, owned by minor lords or the peasantry. A Callaughton man had 70

[16] *Cart. Shrews.* i, p. xxi n. 7.
[17] Ibid. ii, pp. 270, 362; Eyton, ix. 83, 107.
[18] Eyton, viii. 276.
[19] Staffs. R.O., D. 593/A/2/31/7.
[20] *V.C.H. Salop.* ii. 86.
[21] *Pipe R. 1202* (P.R.S. N.S. xv), 47; 1209 (P.R.S. N.S. xxiv), 146; Eyton, iii. 67–8.
[22] Eyton, iii. 111.

[23] P.R.O., C 145/20, no. 1.
[24] Below, 1300–1540 (Demesne agriculture).
[25] Though not stated in every case to be demesne stints, it seems likely that all are: *Two Est. Surveys of Earls of Arundel*, pp. 59, 74, 76, 79, 81.
[26] P.R.O., SC 12/14/23; *T.S.A.S.* 3rd ser. viii. 365–7.
[27] *T.S.A.S.* lxii. 27.
[28] *Cart. Haughmond*, p. 213.

sheep stolen in 1274[29] and a villein at Tasley owned a flock of 16 ewes (worth 32s.) and 11 wethers (22s.) in 1291-2.[30] In 1248 Herbert of Corfton, clearly an exceptionally rich villein, claimed to have been robbed of 8 draught animals, 6 rams, 5 wainloads of corn, 6 bu. of wheat flour and 3 of oatmeal, 4 ells of cloth, 9 linen sheets, and 4 napkins.[31] In 1306 ten of the 251 people from Shrewsbury and its liberties who were assessed to the lay subsidy owned sheep; five had flocks of 5 to 10 head, three of 20-25, and two of c. 40.[32] Such men were presumably minor wool producers, although they almost certainly were milking the animals. Medieval ewes produced 7 to 12 gallons of milk during a lactation, and according to Walter of Henley 20 lactating ewes gave enough milk to make 4 pints of butter and 250 round flat cheeses a week.[33]

The importance of sheep in the county's economy is demonstrated by the leading role played by its wool merchants in the international market. In 1271-4 twelve merchants from Shrewsbury and six from Ludlow were among those who obtained export licences for wool. In the earlier 13th century Shrewsbury was undoubtedly the main centre of the wool trade in the western counties and the marches and it retained its trade in the latter part of that century when other centres began to lose theirs to London.[34] Shrewsbury was, for instance, the base of Nicholas of Ludlow, one of the greatest English merchants of the 1260s[35] and founder of what was at the time the country's leading dynasty of wool merchants. In 1265, when the goods of Englishmen were seized at Bruges and Damme he lost wool worth £158 13s. 9d., and in 1270 when a similar seizure was made in Flanders he had 330 sacks, valued at £1,828 11s. 5d. taken.[36] Nicholas's business was carried on after his death by his son Lawrence, the builder of Stokesay castle, whose standing was such that in 1294 he headed the consortium of the country's leading wool merchants that agreed to the king's demand for an extra export duty on wool, the maletot. The levy was heavy and unpopular, and Lawrence's death in 1294 on a Channel crossing was seen, at least by the Dunstable priory annalist as divine retribution: 'and because he sinned against the wool mongers he was drowned in a ship laden with wool'.[37] His business was carried on into the 14th century by his widow and younger kinsmen, several of whom were wool exporters.[38] Other leading Shrewsbury wool mongers included Roger Pride, a kinsman of the Burnells, who lost 32 sacks of wool worth £203 8s. 4d. in 1270 and who received an export licence for 120 sacks in 1273, and Richard Stury who exported 61 sacks in 1297-8 and was later the first mayor of the compulsory staple at St.-Omer.[39]

Two developments in the county in the 13th century indicate that by then a buoyant cloth industry had developed, stimulated and facilitated by the local wool trade. The first was the gaining in 1227 by Shrewsbury's merchants of a county-wide monopoly to purchase undressed cloth. Thereafter, nominally at least, control of the dyeing, finishing, and distribution of cloth within the county was in their hands.[40] The second development was the introduction of the fulling mill. Fulling, the cleansing of surplus oil and grease from wool and the pounding of cloth made from short wools to produce a closer woven, felted cloth, was traditionally done by the fuller or walker, beating, kneading, or walking on the materials. In the late

[29] Rot. Hund. ii. 101.
[30] Eyton, i. 95.
[31] Ibid. iv. 14-15; Roll of Salop. Eyre 1256, p. 220.
[32] S.R.O. 3365/152.
[33] Ryder, Sheep & Man, 448.
[34] T. H. Lloyd, Eng. Wool Trade in Middle Ages (1977), 132-3.
[35] Ibid. 274.
[36] Ibid. 55, 322 n. 50.
[37] Ibid. 76, 78; E. Power, Wool Trade in Eng. Med. Hist. (1941), 7, 9; Ann. Mon. (Rolls Ser.), iii. 389.
[38] Lloyd, Eng. Wool Trade, 55, 87, 133, 294. The fam.'s genealogy is obscure: cf. Eyton, v. 36-8; ix. 334.
[39] Lloyd, op. cit. 55, 133.
[40] U. Rees, 'Leases of Haughmond Abbey', Midland Hist. viii. 18; Cart. Haughmond, p. 11.

12th century one or two fulling mills, with water-driven wooden mallets for beating, began to be built in the north of England and the Cotswolds. It took, however, one or two generations before they were spread widely across the country as a whole.[41] The earliest fulling mill known in Shropshire formed part of the foundation grant in the 1220s to St. John's hospital, Ludlow. It stood close to the town on the Teme, and by 1241 the hospital had the exclusive right to full the cloth produced in Ludlow.[42] Religious houses seem to have played a significant role in the construction of fulling mills. By the mid 13th century Lilleshall abbey had one on the Severn at Atcham;[43] Haughmond abbey was granted the right to build one on the Perry at Adcote between 1240 and 1263;[44] and Combermere abbey (Ches.) had one on the Tern at Ternhill in 1255.[45] In the later 13th century fulling mills owned by the laity begin to be recorded in the county: at Pitchford (by 1284),[46] Charlcotte (by 1290),[47] Longnor (by 1300),[48] and Clun (by 1301).[49] There may have been at least one other fulling mill close to Ludlow.[50]

In the upland, wooded, and often marginal areas of south Shropshire goats probably played an important part in the peasant economy of the early Middle Ages. Goats can subsist on marginal land, and have a remarkable ability to convert underwood and rough and moorland grazing into milk and meat. Their versatile diet enables them to be kept on terrain unsuitable for sheep, although it seems likely that wherever possible the more profitable wool-producing sheep was replacing the goat in the 11th and 12th centuries. Goats were not recorded for Shropshire in the Exchequer version of Domesday Book, but where they were noted, as in East Anglia and south-west England, goats were numerous in 1086. Although Shropshire provides no evidence before the early 13th century it seems likely that in 1086 there were large numbers of goats in the south of the county.[51] Whether by then sheep had already ousted goats from the farming economy of north Shropshire is unknown; certainly by the 13th century goats are rarely found.

In 1255 both Peter of Minton, the keeper of forest hays near Stretton, and the poor people of Stretton kept goats on the manor's hills and in its woods. Goats were said to be the poor's sole means of livelihood, and it seems likely that they herded goats on the hills and produced cheese and meat.[52] In 1255 in the adjacent walk of the Long forest on Wenlock Edge the forester, although he kept no goats himself, permitted lords to keep goats in their own woods except during the fence month,[53] the period in midsummer when the deer were fawning.[54] At Westhope pannage of goats comprised part of the manor's profits in 1301.[55]

On the northern limits of the Long forest it was assumed c. 1268 in the customs of Condover that the villeins there would own goats,[56] and in 1292 when it was proposed to inclose 200 a. in the forest there it was alleged that the lord would lose the profit from impounding goats in the fence month.[57] At the north end of Wenlock Edge in the manor of Kenley the lord impounded the goats belonging to the men of the neighbouring manor of Hughley in 1231 during a dispute over common rights, kept them until they died, and then sold their meat and hides.[58]

[41] R. H. Hilton, *A Medieval Society: W. Midlands at End of 13th Cent.* (1967), 209–13.
[42] *V.C.H. Salop.* ii. 102; Eyton, v. 297; Dugdale, *Mon.* vi. 681.
[43] B.L. Add. MS. 50121, p. 93.
[44] *Cart. Haughmond*, p. 21.
[45] Eyton, viii. 203.
[46] *V.C.H. Salop.* viii. 121; P.R.O., C 133/41, no. 14.
[47] S.R.O. 1756/4.
[48] *Two Est. Surveys of Earls of Arundel*, p. 52.
[49] *V.C.H. Salop.* viii. 112.
[50] S.R.O. 356/MT/1131–3; cf. *T.S.A.S.* lxii. 28, for a walkmill at Weeseland, in Ercall Magna, possibly est. c. 1256.
[51] Darby, *Domesday Eng.* 163–4. Mr. Lawson is thanked for much useful inf. on goats.
[52] *Rot. Hund.* ii. 84.
[53] Ibid. 73.
[54] *Royal Forests of Northants.* (Northants. Rec. Soc. xxiii), 39.
[55] *Two Est. Surveys of Earls of Arundel*, p. 63.
[56] P.R.O., C 145/20, no. 1.
[57] Eyton, vi. 17.
[58] *V.C.H. Salop.* viii. 95. Goat hides were among tanners' stocks in early 14th-cent. Shrews.: S.R.O. 3365/152, 158.

Goats were probably singled out in the last case because of the damage which they caused to the vert, and that was presumably also the reason why the foresters of Clee sought to exclude the goats of the prior of Wenlock's tenants from the woods in Ditton Priors and Stoke St. Milborough in 1232.[59] At much the same time the abbot of Shrewsbury obtained specific confirmation of his right to pasture goats in the same forest for his manor of Loughton.[60] It is likely that transhumance, or straking, was practised on the Clee hills at that time although it is not expressly documented until the 17th century.[61]

Evidently as late as *c.* 1280 some goat herds in south-west Shropshire were large; about then the lord of Whitcot granted Walter of Minton the right to pasture 50 goats and their followers in Whitcot.[62] On the southern border of the Stiperstones forest Gatten, where the Corbets had a hay first mentioned in 1226,[63] means 'the clearing for goats in the long valley'.[64] North of that forest at Aston Rogers a man had a herd of 24 goats in 1273,[65] and to the south at Little Rhadley the men of Mucklewick were granted common except for their goats in 1291.[66]

Away from the southern uplands, in Morfe forest the underwood of Claverley wood was said to be much damaged by goats in 1235.[67] The exclusion of goats was increasingly usual as common rights were formalized.

A notable element of the county's economy, expecially in those better wooded parishes where there was extensive pannage or mast available for autumn fattening, was pig rearing. Pigs need little supervision, are extremely efficient converters to meat of a wide range of organic matter (some like acorns or beech nuts otherwise inedible or poisonous), are relatively prolific, and produce meat that can be readily preserved to last the winter.[68] The records reveal virtually nothing about the physical appearance of the animal, probably thin legged and a fraction of the size of the modern one;[69] the record of William Tuppe's stabbing in Sandford wood, in Prees, in 1254 by a thief who stole his seven black pigs is unusually revealing.[70] Pigs, like sheep, probably only reached maturity after two years.[71]

In 1086 much of the county's woodland was described in terms of the number of pigs that it was said could be fattened there, the largest total, of 600, being at Longnor.[72] In the 13th century pannage payments, sometimes called wormtack,[73] were either in cash, as at Condover *c.* 1268 where pigs, like sheep, were charged at $\frac{1}{2}d.$ each a year,[74] or in kind. At Edgton in the late 13th century a nook carried the right to pasture 10 swine free of pannage, although *c.* 1275 those who fattened eight beasts or more in the lord's wood owed the third best beast, and those with fewer than eight 2*d.* for each mature pig and 1*d.* for younger swine.[75] In 1282 one pig in every 10 was due from those fattened in Linley wood, in More.[76] About 1230 a virgate at Webscott near Myddle carried the right to pasture 24 pigs,[77] and at Aston Rogers in 1273 a man had 20 pigs.[78] While peasant herds of that size may have been slightly larger than usual, in well wooded areas a lord's income from pannage payments could be considerable. At Wem in 1290 it was £8, equal to the combined income from agistment, herbage, and wood sales, and probably

[59] *T.S.A.S.* 4th ser. i. 392.
[60] *Cart. Shrews.* i, p. 13.
[61] *T.S.A.S.* lviii. 58–64.
[62] Eyton, xi. 217.
[63] Ibid. 134.
[64] Inf. from Dr. M. Gelling.
[65] *Sel. Bills in Eyre*, p. 10.
[66] *Cart. Haughmond*, p. 148.
[67] Eyton, iii. 215.
[68] Astill and Grant, *Countryside of Med. Eng.* 157–9.
[69] Ibid. 177.
[70] *Roll of Salop. Eyre 1256*, p. 262.
[71] *Ag. Hist. Eng.* ii. 126.
[72] Darby and Terrett, *Domesday Geog. Mid. Eng.* 136;
V.C.H. Salop. viii. 107.
[73] *V.C.H. Salop.* viii. 59; *Two Est. Surveys of Earls of Arundel*, pp. xxxvii, 52, 65, 76, 79; *Cal. Anct. Petitions Relating to Wales*, ed. Wm. Rees (1975), p. 170. In Wem by 1564 wormtack was a payment made to the lord when the mast failed: S. Garbet, *Hist. Wem* (Wem, 1818), 119.
[74] P.R.O., C 145/20, no. 1.
[75] S.R.O. 465/72; Eyton, xi. 265.
[76] *Cart. Haughmond*, p. 148 n.
[77] Eyton, x. 76.
[78] *Sel. Bills in Eyre*, p. 10.

represented payments for at least 1,000 pigs.[79] Pigs were often fattened in woods, like those on the Wrekin,[80] several miles from the owner's home. In such cases a sty or piggery might be provided, such as Buildwas abbey had in Brewood wood on the Staffordshire border in 1247.[81] All the evidence from Shropshire contradicts the view that the woodland pasturing of pigs had been replaced either by more intensive methods of production or by open-country pig keeping well before the 13th century.[82] In Shropshire considerable amounts of wood pasture survived, and pig husbandry remained woodland based and an important element in the peasant economy throughout the Middle Ages.

Two types of animal were reared exclusively by lords of manors: deer and rabbits. As forests and woodland were reduced in the Middle Ages deer seem to have been increasingly kept in parks;[83] accordingly they were more subject than previously to management and selective breeding. Rabbits, introduced into the British Isles in the later 12th century, were kept in specially constructed enclosed warrens consisting of artificial mounds of usually sandy soil, sometimes containing man-made stone burrows.[84] In 1274 a warren at Weston-under-Redcastle was worth 13s. 4d.,[85] and in 1301 the earl of Arundel had warrens at Oswestry and Shrawardine, each worth 5s. a year.[86] Nevertheless such early references to warrens are rare in Shropshire.

Many aristocratic households also kept birds of prey to take small birds and game, while swans and the produce of heronries might be among the perquisites of the lord of the manor.[87] Many manors had a cockshoot (*volatus*) in their woods where birds such as woodcock would be taken.[88] Surprisingly cockshoots were not solely manorial properties, and *c.* 1225 a property in Haston, in Myddle, comprised a messuage with virgate, selion, 22 a. of land, and a cockshoot.[89] One species of bird kept exclusively by lords of manors and churchmen was the domesticated rock dove (*Columba livia*). Doves can be kept in holes in domestic or agricultural buildings, but most characteristic are freestanding dovecots or pigeon houses.[90] In Shropshire they were recorded from the later 13th century, not surprisingly mainly on large manors such as Acton Burnell,[91] Caus,[92] Holdgate,[93] and Tong.[94] They are also found at monastic houses,[95] and at a few smaller lay manors such as Chetton[96] and Nordley, in Astley Abbots.[97]

Even the most modest peasant holding probably included some poultry, particularly chickens. Archaeological evidence suggests that backyard fowl were kept primarily for their eggs and were eaten only when old.[98] That hens were commonly kept is shown by their frequent mention as rents, especially in return for woodland rights. In the late 13th century the villagers of Clive paid a total of 300 hens each Christmas to the lord of Wem,[99] and the lord of Corfham received 84 hens a year worth 7s. in rents and renders.[1] In 1301 the lord of Upton Magna received at least 33 hens and 170 eggs (or their cash equivalents) from his tenants at Upton Magna and Haughton in return for woodland and grazing rights.[2] In 1252

[79] P.R.O., E 149/1/10.
[80] *Cart. Shrews.* ii, p. 354.
[81] Oschinsky, *Walter of Henley*, 286; *T.S.A.S.* 4th ser. vi. 189.
[82] O. Rackham, *Hist. of Countryside* (1986), 75–8.
[83] Above (Woodland, assarting, and commons).
[84] E. Veale, 'The Rabbit in Eng.' *Agric. H.R.* v. 85–90.
[85] P.R.O., C 133/15, no. 3.
[86] *Two Est. Surveys of Earls of Arundel*, pp. 65, 81.
[87] *T.S.A.S.* 2nd ser. xi. 263; P.R.O., C 132/17, no. 1.
[88] Eyton, vi. 52; x. 276; xi. 372.
[89] *Cart. Haughmond*, p. 111; cf. ibid. p. 122.

[90] *Ag. Hist. Eng.* ii. 882–5.
[91] Two dovehos. worth 5s. in 1292: P.R.O., C 133/63, no. 32.
[92] P.R.O., C 133/7, no. 8.
[93] Eyton, iv. 69.
[94] P.R.O., C 133/75, no. 1.
[95] *Tax. Eccl.* 163–5.
[96] P.R.O., C 133/56, no. 25.
[97] P.R.O., C 133/9, no. 1.
[98] Astill and Grant, *Countryside of Med. Eng.* 163.
[99] P.R.O., C 133/57, no. 3.
[1] P.R.O., C 133/91, no. 2.
[2] *Two Est. Surveys of Earls of Arundel*, pp. 78–9.

the vicar of Stokesay's income included 9d. from eggs at Easter and 9d. from geese.[3] Millers, whose premises contained grain that had been spoilt or spilled, were particularly well placed to keep poultry, perhaps on a semi-commercial basis. About 1280 the miller at Ryton was permitted to keep cocks, hens, capons, geese, ganders, chickens, and ducks around the mill.[4] Peasants, however, were not the only ones to keep poultry, and in 1280-1 a house (*cottagium*) for hens and geese was made at Haughmond abbey's grange at Aston at a cost of 7d.[5]

Fish were important in the medieval diet both nutritionally and increasingly as a means of mitigating the religious prohibition of meat-eating during days and seasons of fast. By the 13th century many of the clergy and well-to-do laity avoided meat by eating fish every Friday and Saturday, for the season of Lent, and on the vigils of the main feasts. Additionally many households also observed Wednesday as a fish day.[6] The late 13th-century stallage receipts from Shrewsbury market regularly rose to a peak during Lent, a reflection, it has been argued, of the copious fish sales.[7] Some of the fish sold were presumably freshwater, taken mainly from within the county. Richer households had access to a very wide range of fish, the more usual freshwater varieties being, in order of preference, eel, bream, perch, pike, roach, and tench,[8] and the quantities consumed in the larger households were often enormous.[9] Carp were a later introduction, of the 14th or 15th century.[10]

There were three types of freshwater fisheries: in rivers, in open water, and in ponds that were usually constructed specially for pisciculture. At least 18 separate fisheries were recorded in Shropshire in 1086. Most were on rivers, distributed across the centre of the county on the Perry, Roden, Severn, and Tern and their tributaries.[11] Those rivers drained several wet, peaty, basins which provided an ideal habitat for fish. The notices of eel renders in 1086, such as 1,502 great eels from Ercall Magna, 1,600 eels from Chetwynd, and 1,000 from Crudgington,[12] indicate the importance of that fish, and the Tern especially, draining the Weald Moors, was an ideal eel river. Most fisheries probably comprised some form of weir with openings in which nets, baskets, and traps could be suspended. The evidence suggests, as later, that river traffic was able to pass the weir by means of a bylet or bypass channel, either natural or artificial. On the tributaries of the main rivers many fisheries were associated with mills, whose narrow channels facilitated the placing of traps, as at Duncot mill, in Atcham, c. 1180.[13] While eel were apparently the staple catch many other species were present. Salmon were almost certainly taken from the Severn and were among the fish eaten by Bishop Swinfield and his household when they were in south Shropshire in 1290. They also ate lampreys, which could perhaps be bought in Shrewsbury and Ludlow markets in the late 13th century.[14]

There were several major open-water fisheries in the county. The meres and

[3] *Cart. Haughmond*, p. 213.
[4] Eyton, ii. 86; cf. *Cart. Haughmond*, p. 149, for a 14th-cent. example.
[5] N.L.W., Aston Hall 5300.
[6] A. S. Littler, 'Fish in Eng. Econ. and Soc. down to the Reformation' (Univ. of Wales Ph.D. thesis 1979), 1-3; *Medieval Fish, Fisheries and Fishponds in Eng.* ed. M. A. Aston (Brit. Arch. Rep. clxxxii), 28.
[7] W. A. Champion, 'Shrews. Tolls and Commerce, 1259-1638', 9-10 (TS. 1986; copy in S.R.O. 5012/1).
[8] *Medieval Fish*, 30-2. For Salop. examples cf. *Roll of Salop. Eyre 1256*, p. 9; Eyton, ix. 105.
[9] *Household Roll of Bp. Swinfield* (Camd. Soc. [1st ser.], lxii), 75-84.
[10] *Medieval Fish*, 32.

[11] Darby and Terrett, *Domesday Geog. Mid. Eng.* 142-3.
[12] Ibid. 142; *Domesday Bk.: Salop.* ed. F. and C. Thorn (1986), entries 4.1.21, 4.6.5, 4.19.2; *T.S.A.S.* lxii. 5.
[13] *Cart. Haughmond*, pp. 56, 179; Darby, *Domesday Eng.* 280-1; Darby and Terrett, op. cit. 142-3; Lennard, *Rural Eng.* 248-9 n.; Eyton, viii. 237; *Roll of Salop. Eyre 1256*, p. 237; S.R.O. 938/3-5; *Medieval Fish*, 170-8, 371-89; D. J. Pannett, 'Fish Weirs of the River Severn', *Folk Life*, xxvi. 54-64. Mr. Pannett is thanked for inf. on fisheries.
[14] Champion, 'Shrews. Tolls and Commerce', 9-10; *Household Roll of Bp. Swinfield*, 75-84; P.R.O., C 66/109, m. 35. But for tolls as representative of goods sold cf. warning remarks of C. M. Fraser, 'Pattern of Trade in NE. Eng. 1265-1350', *Northern Hist.* iv. 45-7 and app.

lakes around Ellesmere and between Baschurch and Myddle were intensively fished, and in the early Middle Ages the burgesses of Newport owed carriage of fish from the king's vivary there to the royal court, wherever in the country it was.[15] Besides fish for immediate consumption or preservation the lakes supplied livestock for transfer to other ponds, a surprisingly commonplace practice in the Middle Ages, the fish being packed in wet grass in canvas-lined barrels to keep them alive for a day or more.[16] In 1275, for instance, the sheriff was ordered to have 100 live female bream carried *c*. 30 miles from Ellesmere to the king's fishponds at Brockhurst castle, Church Stretton.[17] The construction of fishponds seems to have begun in England in the mid 12th century,[18] and by 1300 most lords of manors and some wealthy freeholders had dug their own or had created one by damming a stream. For security and convenience they were usually sited near the manor house or within an enclosed park. In some cases the moats around houses, an increasingly widespread feature from the later 12th century,[19] were themselves used as fishponds, as at Sheriffhales in 1294.[20] It was possible, perhaps even usual, for ponds to be stocked with young fish for fattening either from the large fisheries in rivers and open water or from special hatching and breeding stations; the 13 small fisheries (*stankinges*) in Worfield parish *c*. 1240, eight at Burcote and five at Bradney, may have been such stations.[21]

Incidental profits and benefits accrued from ponds. They could be used to water stock and to keep wildfowl and swans,[22] while their edges provided lush grazing and hay, or rushes for thatching.[23] When ponds were drained, as they regularly were for cleaning, a catch crop of cereals could be grown on the rich pond bottom before the mud was dug out and spread on the fields to improve fertility.[24]

Sea fish were widely available. In the mid 13th century, for example, Haughmond abbey was granted the right to fish the river Dee and to buy 6,000 herrings in Chester free of toll.[25] Sea fish were normally dried, salted, or smoked to preserve them, and some varieties, like herring, were cheap enough to be enjoyed by at least the richer peasantry.[26] Sea fish, including herrings, were probably available at Ludlow market in the late 13th century, delivered by cart and packhorse.[27] In Shrewsbury in the early 14th century there were six or eight merchants who dealt in dried fish and herrings, such as Nicholas of Grimsby and John of Kent.[28]

Marketing

A feature of the period is the growth in the number and size of markets and fairs. Domesday Book records no market in the county, not even in either of the two Shropshire boroughs, Shrewsbury and Quatford.[29] Markets, however, certainly existed. Informal buying and selling of produce is rarely recorded[30] but local opportunities for trade at times when people gathered for other reasons may be surmised from the frequent location of market places in or near churchyards; such

---

[15] S.R.O. 938/3-5; 1900/2/1; P.R.O., C 133/35, no. 3; Eyton, ix. 132-3, 137-9.
[16] B. K. Roberts, 'Medieval Fishponds', *Amateur Historian*, vii. 123.
[17] *Cal. Anct. Petitions Relating to Wales*, p. 321; *Medieval Fish*, 438-40.
[18] J. M. Steane, 'Med. fishponds of Northants.' *Northants. Past and Present*, iv. 299-310; J. McDonnell, *Inland Fisheries in Med. Yorks.* (Borthwick Papers, lx), 14.
[19] *La Maison Forte an Moyen Âge*, ed. M. Bur (Paris, 1986), 24. [20] *Cal. Inq. p.m.* iii, p. 104.
[21] Eyton, iii. 111.

[22] E. Roberts, 'Bp. of Winchester's Fishponds in Hants', *Proc. Hants Field Club and Arch. Soc.* xlii. 135.
[23] *Cart. Shrews.* ii, pp. 369-70.
[24] Slater and Jarvis, *Field and Forest*, 257-80, and refs. there cited; *Amateur Historian*, vii. 123.
[25] *Cart. Haughmond*, p. 60. [26] *Medieval Fish*, 31-3.
[27] P.R.O., C 66/109, m. 35. But cf. warning cited above, n. 14. [28] S.R.O. 3365/152, 158.
[29] Darby, *Domesday Eng.* 318-19; Darby and Terrett, *Domesday Geog. Mid. Eng.* 152-3.
[30] D. Postles, 'Mkts. for Rural Produce in Oxon. 1086-1350', *Midland Hist.* xii. 19-21.

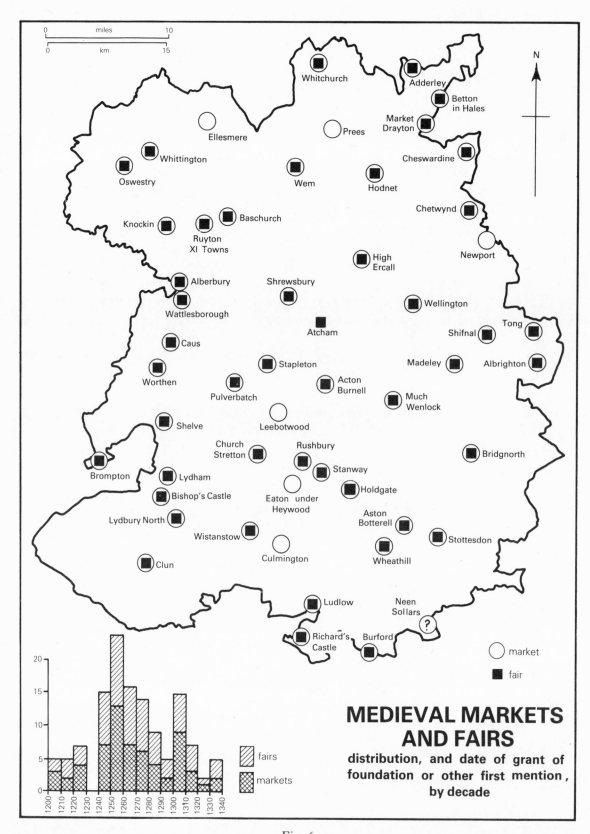

Fig. 6
Some markets were held before 1200 by prescription. Most grants of market or fair were by charter, letters patent, etc., and are noted by Eyton and *V.C.H. Salop. passim.* Clun, Knockin, Oswestry, and Whittington lay in marcher lordships outside the medieval county.

arrangements may first be detected in the 13th century but the topography of individual settlements hints at a much earlier connexion between churchgoing and trade. At Much Wenlock the Sunday market was probably in the churchyard[31] and at Wellington an area (later the Green) immediately north of the churchyard was probably the early market place.[32] Shrewsbury's earliest market place was almost certainly the area between the churchyards of St. Julian's, St. Alkmund's, and St. Mary's.[33] Such links suggest that some of the Saxon minsters, and perhaps some manors serving as administrative centres for wider areas, attracted market business.[34]

Markets almost certainly increased in number as new towns were founded in the late 11th and the 12th centuries: Bishop's Castle, Bridgnorth, Caus, Ludlow, Newport, and Oswestry.[35] Not until the 13th century, however, does the foundation of markets appear to have been sufficiently formalized to leave a written record.

The 13th century witnessed many attempts in Shropshire by manorial lords to promote the urban and commercial development of existing towns and villages. Often the plan seems to have consisted of a carefully designed addition of streets, burgage plots, and open space to the settlement and the purchase of market rights from the Crown. That happened at Wellington,[36] Market Drayton,[37] Madeley,[38] and Baschurch,[39] and those places were among the more successful 13th-century promotions; rather less successful, because of its remote situation, was Clun.[40] By

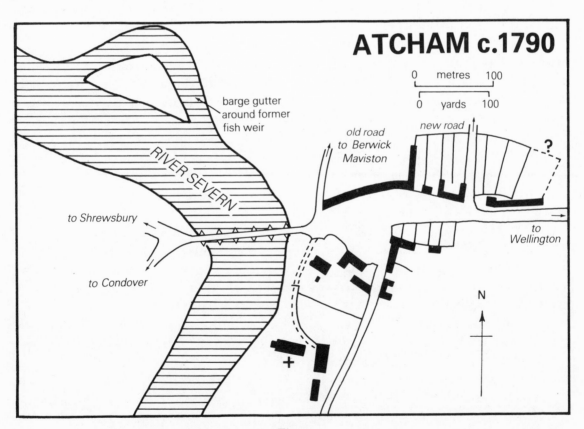

Fig. 7
Based on S.R.O. 112, maps 2–3.

[31] V.C.H. Salop. x (forthcoming).   [32] Ibid. xi. 204.   D. Lloyd and P. Klein, Ludlow: Historic Town in Words and
[33] J. L. Hobbs, Shrews. Street-Names (Shrews. [1954]),   Pictures (1984), 13, 16.   [36] V.C.H. Salop. xi. 204.
26–7.   [34] Rowley, Salop. Landscape, 174.   [37] Trinder, Hist. Salop. 36.
[35] M. Beresford, New Towns of Middle Ages (1967),   [38] V.C.H. Salop. xi. 55.
479–83; for Newport, Eyton, ix. 129–30; B. Trinder,   [39] Trinder, op. cit. 36; Beresford, New Towns of Middle
Hist. Salop. (1983), 35; cf. also V.C.H. Salop. viii 310;   Ages, 479.   [40] Trinder, op. cit. 35–6.

the end of the 13th century promotions were becoming more and more speculative, some standing very little chance of success (Fig. 6).[41] Among the failures may be noticed Burford and Lydham, granted free borough status in 1266 and 1270 respectively;[42] New Ruyton, an attempted borough foundation of the first years of the 14th century;[43] and Atcham (Fig. 7) where, surprisingly, a Severnside village which the abbot of Lilleshall equipped with a bridge, fulling mill, two fairs, and probably burgage plots and a market place, failed to develop into a town.[44] Such speculations, natural in a period of economic expansion, were encouraged by the fairly small capital outlay involved. The least ambitious promotions, involving no expansion of settlement, required probably no more than the provision of a market place and the cost of buying the market privilege from the Crown. Such may have been the plan at High Ercall, granted a market charter in 1267.[45] At Wattlesborough where a grant of a Tuesday market was obtained in 1272, Market piece remained the site of a fair until the 19th century although no memory remained of any market[46] and probably no expansion of settlement had ever been planned. The price of a royal charter was probably not very great and the lord of Holdgate's payment of 5 marks and a palfrey in 1222[47] may have been abnormally expensive.

The Crown speculated too but in those cases there was no expenditure on privileges. Hence in 1214 the new Wednesday market and one-day August fair at the royal manor of Stretton were merely advertised by the Crown, whereas in 1251-3 and 1337, when the market and fair days there were altered, charters had to be purchased for by then the manor had passed from the king's hands.[48]

Lords' incomes from market tolls naturally varied widely. At Oswestry income from tolls and market fees produced £9 13s. 4d. in 1267[49] and £20 in 1271,[50] while in 1276 'tolls of the borough' yielded £27 11s. 11½d.[51] At Clun, a similar border town with 85 burgesses in 1302, the Saturday market produced £10 in 1272.[52] Smaller markets are suggested by the toll incomes of £2 in 1285-6 at Albrighton,[53] 10s. in 1283 at Newport,[54] and 6s. 8d. in 1284 at Holdgate.[55] Other markets were worth so little to the lord, or indeed had ceased to be held (if they ever had been), that no account was made of income from them at the lord's death.[56]

A few incidental references confirm that the main goods sold at market were staple commodities such as corn and salt,[57] and in the larger towns firewood. Animals were also sold, especially in autumn when farmers were reducing stocks against winter.[58] Items such as vegetables and eggs were presumably also on offer everywhere from peasant producers. Dearer goods, however, such as cloth and wine,[59] may have been sold only at the larger markets in towns, such as Ludlow.[60] From 1290 tolls were payable there on a wide range of goods both raw and manufactured. Animal products came in either on the hoof or as salted meat, hides, pelts, or fleeces. Vegetable products included grain, flour, pulses, onions, and garlic. From the district's woods came boards, charcoal, and bark. Cheese, butter, and honey were other local products, whereas wine, cumin, fish, and salt came from farther afield. Manufactured goods included various types of cloth, metal and

[41] Beresford, op. cit. 328-31.
[42] Eyton, iv. 318; xi. 280. [43] Beresford, op. cit. 483.
[44] Rolls of Just. in Eyre 1221-2, p. 563; V.C.H. Salop. ii. 63.
[45] T.S.A.S. lxii. 15, 20 n. 17, 67, where, however, the laying-out of burgage plots also is supposed.
[46] V.C.H. Salop. viii. 211. [47] Eyton, iv. 64.
[48] Ibid. xii. 20-2; Close R. 1251-3, 321; Cal. Chart. R. 1327-41, p. 421; S.R.O. 2833/1-3.
[49] P.R.O., C 132/35, no. 18.
[50] P.R.O., C 132/42, no. 5. [51] Eyton, x. 331.
[52] Ibid. xi. 231-2; Rowley, Salop. Landscape, 175-7.
[53] P.R.O., C 133/41, no. 14.
[54] P.R.O., C 133/35, no. 3. [55] P.R.O., C 133/39, no. 8.
[56] But cf. V.C.H. Leics. ii. 161-2, for comments on poss. concealment of true val. of est. by heirs or escheators.
[57] Cart. Haughmond, p. 170.
[58] Owen and Blakeway, Hist. Shrews. i. 96 n.; cf. S.R.O. 3365/153, 156, 158, for firewood valuations in early 14th-cent. Shrews. [59] Below.
[60] Beresford, New Towns of Middle Ages, 482.

earthenware vessels, millstones, nails and horseshoes. Iron and lead were available to local plumbers and smiths.[61]

From 1200 grants of markets and fairs contained a clause which made them conditional on the new franchise not damaging an existing one. The minimum distance between markets was reckoned at just over 6 miles, a spacing that allowed time to travel to and fro in a day and do business.[62] A new market could damage an existing one, and John le Strange's foundation of a market and fair at Knockin in 1249 led to prolonged litigation with his overlord, John FitzAlan, who considered them likely to harm his own market and fair at Oswestry, 6 miles away.[63] In general, however, as in other counties,[64] the distribution of markets suggests that little notice was taken of the distance between them. For instance Eaton-under-Heywood, Rushbury, Nether Stanway, and Holdgate each had the right to hold a Thursday market in the later 13th century, though all lay within 3 or 4 miles of each other.[65]

In contrast with markets, where mainly local goods were offered for sale on a weekly basis, fairs drew merchants from a whole region, or even more widely, for a once-yearly meeting over several days at which they bought in bulk and sold relatively exotic goods. Shropshire's fairs lay too far west to be regularly visited by foreign merchants, whose presence made the 13th-century fairs of Boston, St. Ives, Stamford, Northampton, and Winchester the greatest in the country.[66] Many of Shropshire's wool merchants, however, were active in the European market and presumably did much of their buying at the county's fairs. That activity has left no written record, and the only reference to fair business in the period is from Clun, whose fair was visited c. 1300 by Worcester merchants who wished to buy stock.[67]

No Shropshire fairs were recorded in 1086,[68] although it may be suspected that wool fairs were already a feature of the annual round in the south of the county. To lords, the attraction of a fair was the profit that might accrue. Although the monks claimed that the right to hold a fair in Shrewsbury had been granted by Earl Roger, it was more probably Henry I who gave the first grant of a three-day fair.[69] The first formal grant to the burgesses of the right to hold a fair was made in 1205 for 1 to 3 June.[70] In 1227 Shrewsbury abbey was holding its three-day fair in Abbey Foregate on 1-3 August, extended in that year to include 31 July,[71] and by 1256 the abbey had a second annual fair on 20-23 September.[72] When in 1267 the burgesses obtained a grant for a second fair of their own, on 24-7 July, the abbey claimed that it was to the detriment of its August fair.[73] The parties reached agreement at the end of the century: the abbey was to pay the burgesses 38s., and in return at the time of the Abbey Foregate fair all shops, except those selling wine and ale, were to be closed, murage and pavage were not to be levied, and the abbey's servants were to be allowed to supervise the fair and to take all profits from it.[74] The influx of goods and traders at fair times was considerable; in

[61] P.R.O., C 66/109, m. 35. But cf. warning cited above, n. 14.
[62] Miller and Hatcher, *Med. Eng.* 77; M. Reed, 'Mkts. and Fairs of Med. Bucks.' *Rec. Bucks.* xx. 564.
[63] Eyton, x. 369. For another complaint cf. ibid. xi. 53.
[64] *Rec. Bucks.* xx. 567-9, and refs. there cited in n. 2; *Midland Hist.* xii. 16-17; Platts, *Land and People in Med. Lincs.* 135-40; P. A. Stamper, 'Med. Hants: Studies in Landscape Hist.' (Southampton Univ. Ph.D. thesis, 1983), 36-9.
[65] Eaton (*Cal. Chart. R.* 1226-57, 17), Rushbury (ibid.

1257-1300, 266), Stanway (ibid. 166), Holdgate (Eyton, iv. 64).
[66] E. W. Moore, *Fairs of Med. Eng.: Introductory Study* (Toronto, 1985), 1, 10.
[67] Hilton, *W. Midlands at End of 13th Cent.* 261.
[68] Moore, *Fairs of Med. Eng.* 142.
[69] *Cart. Shrews.* i, p. xii.
[70] Owen and Blakeway, *Hist. Shrews.* i. 89.
[71] *Cart. Shrews.* i, p. 57.   [72] Ibid. p. 55.
[73] *Yr. Bk.* 4 Edw. II (Selden Soc. xxiv), 93-7.
[74] *Cart. Shrews.* ii, pp. 238-42.

1263, for instance, five times as much was paid in murage on goods coming into the town during fair time as at other times.[75] Precise figures showing the profits of fairs are rare, and only one Shropshire example is known: £6 in 1272 from the three-day May and November fairs at Clun.[76]

As with markets, the earliest documented fairs were mainly associated with towns: at Shrewsbury (by 1135), Much Wenlock (1138),[77] Clun (1204),[78] Shrewsbury (1205), Church Stretton (1214),[79] Richard's Castle (1216),[80] and Bridgnorth (1226).[81] By the later 13th century the lords of rural manors were seeking the right to hold fairs, as at Nether Stanway in 1271[82] and nearby Rushbury, where Hugh Burnell obtained a grant of market and fair soon after buying the manor in 1283.[83] Unusually both fairs (if they were ever held) were two-day events. Most of the county's fairs lasted three days while a few lasted four or five. None officially lasted longer than six days. As elsewhere,[84] most fairs were held in August and September when harvested produce, wool, and fatstock were ready. At least two fairs, however, were held in each month between the start of the county's fair cycle at Acton Burnell and Burford, both of which had fairs on 24–6 March from the 1260s,[85] and its end with Clun's Martinmas (11–13 November) fair,[86] where it was presumably mainly fattened pigs and surplus stock that were sold for slaughter and salting. Within the general constraints imposed by the agricultural round there are indications that, wherever possible, fair dates were chosen to coincide with the wakes and other activities which marked the local church's patronal feast.[87]

The distribution of produce was limited by the means of transport available. Most efficient for the long distance carriage of bulk goods was the navigable river and in the early 13th century, as perhaps for long before, barges plied the Severn between Bristol and Shrewsbury.[88] In 1220 Henry III granted murage to the burgesses of Bridgnorth and Shrewsbury and included the right to tolls on vessels bringing goods for sale into those towns.[89] Gascon wine was brought up river to Bridgnorth from Bristol in the 13th and 14th centuries for the king,[90] the bishop of Coventry and Lichfield,[91] and lesser churchmen like the rector of Pattingham (Staffs.).[92] The Severn has also been an obstacle to road traffic. In places it is fordable but elsewhere crossing had to be by ferry or one of the few bridges. Below Bridgnorth in the Middle Ages there were only two bridges, at Worcester and Gloucester.[93] At Bridgnorth a new bridge had been built by the 13th century replacing an earlier crossing at 'Cwatbridge', in Quatford, while in Shrewsbury the bridges later known as the English and Welsh bridges existed by the early 12th century.[94] A third crossing in the county was provided between 1200 and 1222 at Atcham by the abbot of Lilleshall; it superseded the two ferry boats from which he had previously profited.[95] A fourth bridge, at Preston Montford, was in use by the 1240s.[96] Bridge building and urban growth tended to go hand in hand,[97] and

[75] Champion, 'Shrews. Tolls and Commerce', 52, 63–4.
[76] Eyton, xi. 231–2.
[77] Clywd R.O., DD/WY/4466.
[78] Eyton, xi. 229.   [79] Above.
[80] Eyton, iv. 314.
[81] Ibid. i. 307.
[82] Cal. Chart. R. 1257–1300, 166.
[83] Ibid. 1257–1300, 266; Eyton, iv. 97.
[84] Rec. Bucks. xx. 572.
[85] V.C.H. Salop. viii. 10; Eyton, iv. 317.
[86] Eyton, xi. 229. From 1330 Ludlow had a fair 24–8 Nov.: Cal. Chart. R. 1327–41, 94.
[87] Eyton, i. 340 n.; vi. 202; x. 33 n.; for a later example, V.C.H. Salop. ii. 129.
[88] Hilton, W. Midlands at End of 13th Cent. 9, 254; V.C.H.

Salop. ii. 52.
[89] Owen and Blakeway, Hist. Shrews. i. 96 n.; Eyton, i. 299–300.
[90] Eyton, i. 266.
[91] J. Isaac, 'Two Med. Accts. for Lichfield', Trans. S. Staffs. Arch. & Hist. Soc. xviii. 61, 63.
[92] J. F. A. Mason, Boro. of Bridgnorth 1157–1957 (Bridgnorth, 1957), 16.
[93] Hilton, W. Midlands at End of 13th Cent. 9.
[94] Mason, op. cit. 5, 15; A. Blackwall, Hist. Bridges of Salop. (Shrews. 1985), 91, 97.
[95] V.C.H. Salop. ii. 73.
[96] Cal. Pat. 1232–47, 252; Eyton, x. 164.
[97] Beresford, New Towns of Middle Ages, 109–11, 115–19, 137.

at Ludlow it seems that the first bridge (over the Teme) was built by Joce de Dinan, probably lord and castellan of Ludlow, to promote the success of the newly founded town by bringing travellers and trade into it.[98]

Bridge building, one of the necessary labours with which the Saxon landowner was burdened,[99] is the best recorded form of medieval road improvement,[1] but the roads themselves, whose maintenance went largely unrecorded,[2] were of great economic importance. Road traffic increased greatly during the 12th and 13th centuries and the economic self-sufficiency of that region of western England which is drained by the Severn may have owed as much to the great road that ran north from Bristol (via Worcester) to Chester (and beyond to Liverpool) as it did to the river itself. In Shropshire the road passed through Bridgnorth, Shrewsbury, and Ellesmere.[3] About 1102 Henry I levelled and widened it, cutting back trees, probably near Wenlock Edge.[4] In other parts of the county there were what seem to have been alternative routes between market towns: one that pack horses could tackle, and another which avoided steep gradients and so—in dry weather at least— was more suited to carts. Such perhaps were the alternative routes between Shrewsbury and Newport: the Watling Street with steep gradients at Overley Hill, and the Port Way via Admaston and Shawbirch.[5] The great importance of Shropshire roads in the cattle droving season is illustrated by the levy of *stretward* in the 13th century to maintain an elaborate system of road guards.[6] Another indication of the quality of the roads and the average speed of commercial traffic is provided by the general presuppositions about the spacing of markets and fairs.[7]

Much long-distance trade, for instance of salt, was by packhorse, mentioned in Shrewsbury's murage grant of 1220.[8] Packhorses were used about the same time by Haughmond abbey to carry loads in sacks and small wooden kegs,[9] and at Ludlow in 1290 tolls were levied by the horse load on salt, cloth, fish, cumin, garlic, honey, bark, and charcoal.[10] Bulkier carriage necessitated the use of horse- or ox-drawn vehicles.[11] Carts called *carectae* were drawn by one[12] or two horses;[13] hay and wood carts had two horses in the mid 13th century.[14] The *carra* was a heavier, ox-drawn vehicle; examples are noted in the 13th century at Glazeley,[15] Shelderton,[16] and in the Morville area.[17] They were probably commoner in the 12th century than *carectae*, though in the 13th century horse haulage became more widespread,[18] and in the early 14th century *carectae* seem to have been ubiquitous in and around Shrewsbury.[19] The ox-drawn wain called a *plaustrum* had usually, but not invariably, two wheels.[20] Heavy or long-distance haulage required large teams. When Abingdon abbey was rebuilt in the early 12th century Welsh timber was brought from Shrewsbury on six *plaustra*, each drawn by twelve oxen.[21] The round trip, of *c.* 226 miles, took six or seven weeks. For short-haul work sledges, without wheels and cheap to produce, were used.[22]

[98] Lloyd and Klein, *Ludlow,* 16.
[99] F. M. Stenton, *Anglo-Saxon Eng.* (3rd edn. 1971), 289.
[1] Many well recorded bridges were maintained by piety and charity.
[2] The Eng. road 'made and maintained itself': *Public Wks. in Medieval Law,* ii (Selden Soc. xl), p. xvi.
[3] F. M. Stenton, 'Road System of Medieval Eng.' *Econ. H.R.* vii. 3–8, 17–19; E. J. S. Parsons, *The Gough Map: intro. to the facsimile* (Bodl. map reproductions, i; corr. reprint [1970]), 16; B. P. Hindle, *Medieval Roads* (1982), 19.
[4] *V.C.H. Salop.* viii. 86, and source there cited.
[5] Ibid. xi. 200–1. Even as late as the 1790s wet weather made steep roads preferable to level ones: S.P.L., MSS. 6860–5 *passim.*
[6] *V.C.H. Salop.* iii. 21.
[7] Above.

[8] Owen and Blakeway, *Hist. Shrews.* i. 96 n.; Darby, *Domesday Eng.* 261, 263.
[9] *Cart. Haughmond,* p. 56. [10] P.R.O., C 66/109, m. 35.
[11] Langdon, *Horses, Oxen and Technological Innovation,* 76–8.   [12] *Rolls of Just. in Eyre 1221–2,* p. 551.
[13] *Roll of Salop. Eyre 1256,* pp. 198, 299.
[14] Ibid. p. 198; *Cart. Haughmond,* p. 206.
[15] *Roll of Salop. Eyre 1256,* p. 214.
[16] Rees, *Cal. Anct. Petitions Relating to Wales,* p. 294.
[17] *Roll of Salop. Eyre 1256,* p. 212.
[18] Langdon, *Horses, Oxen and Tech. Innovation,* 77, 95–6.
[19] S.R.O. 3365/152, 158.
[20] *Roll of Salop. Eyre 1256,* p. 539; Langdon, op. cit. 78.
[21] *Chron. Mon. de Abingdon* (Rolls Ser.), ii. 150.
[22] *Roll of Salop. Eyre 1256,* p. 285.

1300–1540

THE later Middle Ages, in particular the period from the mid 14th century to the last quarter of the 15th century, have traditionally been seen as a time of depression in agrarian society, punctuated by crises. Recent interpretations, however, have drawn attention to signs of adaptation to changed conditions and to elements of innovation.[23] The geographical position and physical make-up of Shropshire meant that it was affected by agrarian depression in different ways from other midland counties and that there was perhaps less need for readjustment and less scope for growth or innovation. A series of crises did indeed cause considerable short-term distress and disruption but not abrupt changes of direction. The predominantly mixed nature of demesne exploitation in the county meant that the policies of the major landowners, and in particular the balance between arable and pastoral farming or between direct exploitation and leasing of the demesnes, depended more on individual circumstances or inclination than on market forces. Although the sources are weighted towards the landlords there is considerable evidence of peasant poverty, caused more by political factors such as the Crown's financial demands and Welsh raids than by population pressures. There was still plenty of room for the expansion of settlement and there is evidence throughout the period of assarting and the continued clearance of forest and woodland; that expansion was often under the control of the landlords, especially in the earlier 14th century.[24]

However the later 14th and 15th centuries are perceived, whether as a time of depression or of opportunity, there is no doubt that the early 14th century was a turning point. The lay subsidy of 1327 can be taken as a guide to differing regional levels of prosperity at that time, albeit an imperfect one. Apart from imperfections common to tax records generally, perhaps the principal uncertainty arises from concentrations of urban wealth in Shrewsbury, Bridgnorth, Ludlow, and Newport[25] and their possible weighting of calculations for the regions around those towns (Fig. 9). It should also be noted that the subsidy was taken only five years after a disruptive and damaging sequence of agricultural crises. In 1327 the wealthiest area of the county was the Severn lowland around and to the west of Shrewsbury. Also relatively prosperous were the Bridgnorth area and lower Corve Dale, and perhaps the small area around Newport on the eastern border of the county. The poorest areas were the uplands of the south and south-west.

The impact on Shropshire of the agrarian crisis of 1315–22[26] can be traced most fully in the bailiffs' accounts of the manor of Adderley, which was then in the king's hands.[27] In 1316–17 twenty of the villein tenants and cottagers left their lands 'because of their poverty and the dearth of corn', and the number of vacant holdings had risen to 34 by 1321–2 when decayed rents amounted to 25 per cent of a total rental of nearly £52. Villein land was kept in hand and cultivated and 39 a. of such land was sown in 1322–3, compared with 115 a. of demesne. Under royal management the manor was being developed to provide pasture for cattle and horses from other manors and a small dairy herd was established,[28] but the enterprise was cut short by the arrival of the cattle murrain. In January 1319 a

[23] *V.C.H. Staffs.* vi. 35, 45–8; C. Dyer, *Warws. Farming 1349–c. 1520* (Dugdale Soc. Occasional Paper xxvii).
[24] *T.S.A.S.* lxii. 10–12; *Cartulary of Haughmond Abbey,* ed. U. Rees (1985), 9–10, 15; cf. below (Assarting and inclosure).
[25] Newport cannot be supposed as rich as the other three

towns, but it is situated in a small region, made even smaller by the lack of data for Sheriffhales; its weighting effect may therefore be relatively greater.
[26] I. Kershaw, 'The gt. famine and agrarian crisis in Eng. 1315–22', *Past & Present,* lix. 3–50.
[27] *T.S.A.S.* xlvi. 105–6. [28] Below (Demesne agriculture).

AGRICULTURAL DEPRESSION CAUSES ALLEGED IN 1341

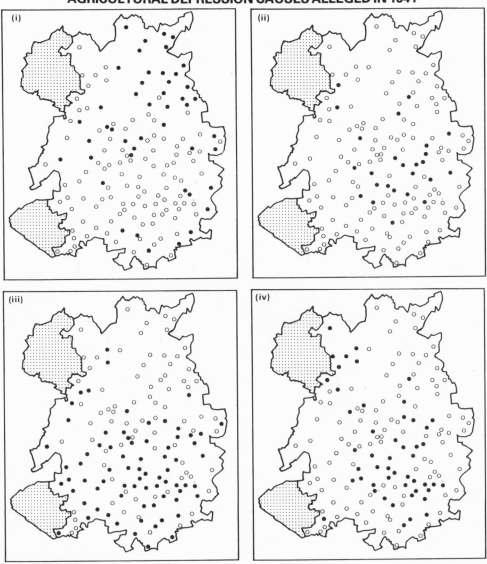

Fig. 8

The circles represent the places assessed to the 1340 lay subsidy: *Inq. Non.* (Rec. Com.), 182–94. The solid black circles represent places where (i) no claim for reduction in assessment on the basis of agricultural adversity was made, (ii) crops were destroyed by storms, (iii) land was lying untilled, and (iv) there was sheep murrain or insufficient stock. The stippled areas show marcher lordships not reunited to Shropshire until the 16th century.

bull and 20 cows were driven to Adderley from Beverley (Yorks. E.R.) but 6 of the cows were dead by Michaelmas and during the next accounting year the bull and 8 cows died and the remaining 14 cows on the manor were sold because they were ill or sterile. In 1321–2 receipts from pannage and the sale of pasture, including that of a meadow formerly used for demesne cattle, were sharply reduced because of the great murrain of the previous year, and it was necessary to buy 10 oxen at a cost of £7 4s. 8d. to replace animals that had died or been sold at the first sign of weakness.[29] The accounts of the earl of Arundel's manor of Ruyton-XI-Towns confirm that 1319–20 was one of the worst years of the crisis: all 17 of the demesne oxen died of the murrain and 60 of the 192 sheep on the manor that year died or had to be sold. The demesne arable of *c.* 90 a., which had been

[29] P.R.O., SC 6/965/2–5.

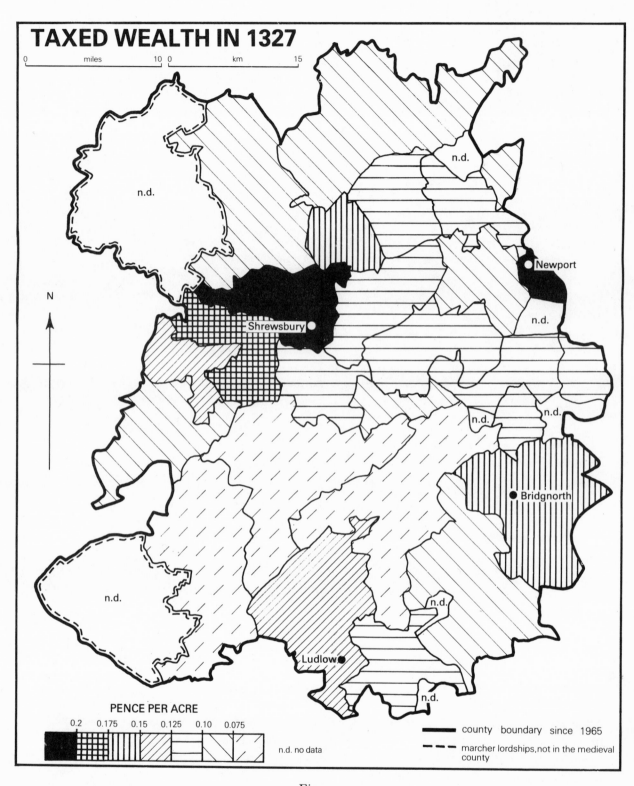

Fig. 9
Based on refs. cited in *T.S.A.S.* 3rd ser. vii. 375–8. For the regions see *Domesday Geog. of Midland Eng.* ed. H. C. Darby and I. B. Terrett (1971), 131.

extended in the previous year by a 13½-a. assart, produced in 1320 only 296 bu. of wheat on a sowing of 117 bu. and only 466 bu. of oats on a sowing of 332 bu.[30] The years of crisis may have persuaded some Shropshire landlords to reduce or abandon completely the direct exploitation of their arable demesnes: by 1336 the abbot and convent of Lilleshall had leased some of their lands which they had been unable to cultivate on account of cattle murrain and other adversities, and the Ruyton demesne was leased by the early 1340s.[31]

The lay subsidy of 1340, which records valuable evidence of agricultural conditions,[32] reveals continued and widespread poverty and distress in the county.[33] For over 100 vills (out of a total of 161) the assessors reported a lower return from the ninth sheaf, the ninth fleece, and the ninth lamb than that which the Crown expected on the basis of the valuation of the benefice in 1291, adducing (from the verdicts of local jurors) a variety of reasons for the shortfall. Some of the distress had been caused by recent disasters such as a sheep murrain which was specifically noted in the returns for 20 vills and was presumably the cause of the low flock sizes mentioned in another 35, and the storms and floods which were said to have caused harvest failure in 25 vills. Shropshire is one of four areas from which large-scale abandonment of arable land was reported.[34] The reports are vague and inconsistent as to the amount of land lying uncultivated, but in over 70 vills, predominantly on the uplands south and west of the Severn, land was said to have been abandoned, usually because the tenants were too poor to cultivate it. In some cases that may indicate a short-term and possibly temporary retreat of settlement from marginal land caused by unfavourable conditions and the pressure of royal taxation; at Cold Weston, for example, it was reported that all but two of the tenants had absconded to avoid paying the ninth, 'as many throughout the *patria* have done'.[35] Nevertheless the extent of the shortfall in the value of the ninths, on average about 60 per cent, and the vehemence of the complaints of poverty point to a more fundamental malaise and to a chronically impoverished and unstable population, especially in the south of the county. In over 20 vills the tenants were said to have deserted their holdings: at Cardington, which was affected in 1340 by sheep murrain and harvest failure, 20 tenants had left; at Stoke St. Milborough the land of 11 tenants lay fallow and at Tugford it was reported that the tenants did not cultivate their lands because of poverty and that six of them went begging.[36] Though the evidence is mainly from south Shropshire, it cannot be assumed that conditions were better in the north.[37]

Death rather than dearth or destitution was the cause of the next fall in the value of land. The Black Death reached Shropshire in the early spring of 1349. In May 2 carucates of demesne arable at Harley which had been worth 60s. a year could not be valued 'because of the pestilence', and income from assize rents had fallen from £4 to 10s., while at Yockleton the mills were of no value 'for lack of grinding' and rents from free tenants had fallen from £8 to 30s.[38] Similar reductions in value were reported by jurors in inquisitions post mortem during the summer and autumn of 1349; at Ellesmere 6 a. of meadow were halved in value to 6s.; at

[30] S.P.L., Deeds 7323.
[31] Llinos O. W. Smith, 'The Lordships of Chirk and Oswestry, 1282–1415' (Lond. Univ. Ph.D. thesis, 1970), 120–3; *Cal. Pat.* 1334–8, 248.
[32] B. Waites, 'Medieval Assessments and Agric. Prosperity in N.E. Yorks.: 1292–1342', *Yorks. Arch. Jnl.* xliv. 142; cf. C. R. Elrington, 'Assessments of Glos.' *Trans. Bristol and Glos. Arch. Soc.* ciii. 7–13.

[33] The following para. is based on an analysis of Salop. returns in *Inq. Non.* (Rec. Com.), 182–94.
[34] *Geographical Interpretations of Hist. Sources*, ed. A. R. H. Baker *et al.* (1970), 89–90.
[35] *Inq. Non.* 188.
[36] Ibid. 186–8.
[37] Baker, *Geog. Interpretations of Hist. Sources*, 88.
[38] P.R.O., C 135/96, no. 14.

Whittington two water mills were said to be worth only 20s. because the tenants had died of the plague; at Dodington 2 carucates of demesne arable which had formerly been worth 60s. could not be valued because the farm servants and labourers were dead and no one was willing to rent the land.[39] Evidence from court rolls confirms that the plague was at its height during the summer and autumn: at Kinnerley 14 tenements, amounting to a quarter of the customary land, were vacant by Michaelmas[40] and at Prees there were 22 admissions to vacant holdings at a court held in October 1349 when there were seldom more than two admissions recorded in normal times.[41]

The impact of the plague varied in intensity and duration. At Ruyton the bailiff accounted for 35 heriot cattle between Michaelmas 1349 and Michaelmas 1350 and in the following year was allowed £4 15s. 4d. for vacant tenements, but by 1357-8 the rent roll had risen above pre-plague levels.[42] At Wrockwardine the value of demesne arable and meadow had been halved by Michaelmas 1349 and assize rents had been reduced from £20 to £2 and the perquisites of court from 40s. to 5s. 'because the tenants are dead'; by 1367, however, income from the manor had recovered fully.[43] On Shrewsbury abbey's manor of Betton in Hales, however, 33 virgates of land were still lying uncultivated and in common in 1355 after the deaths of their tenants in the pestilence, and at Quatt a fall of two thirds in the value of 2 carucates of demesne was still being blamed on the pestilence in 1357.[44] Some of the land in the manor of Nordley was uncultivated in 1362 'on account of the past and present pestilences', and it was difficult to find tenants at Kenley after the second visitation of the plague in 1361-2.[45] After the third visitation in 1369 one court at Prees recorded 11 heriots of dead tenants and entry fines were lower than those levied in 1349.[46] Although the 25 per cent reduction in the amount of land held in demesne by Wenlock priory between 1291 and 1370 has been ascribed to stagnation during a period of royal custody rather than to economic adversity,[47] plague accelerated the decline in arable cultivation of the demesnes of Lilleshall abbey which was already under way before 1349: in 1353 the value of Lilleshall and its four granges was only 60 per cent of what it had been in 1330, and there was a further 60 per cent decline in value between 1353 and 1375.[48] By the beginning of the 15th century, however, Lilleshall's income had recovered to pre-plague levels, probably owing to increased concentration on stock rearing,[49] and elsewhere, such as in the lordship of Oswestry and on the Talbot (formerly le Strange) estate around Whitchurch, the last quarter of the 14th century was a time of prosperity for landlords.[50]

That precarious period of prosperity was shattered in many parts of the county by the events of the first decade of the 15th century. Oswestry was burnt in 1400 by Owen Glendower[51] and the Shropshire lowlands began to feel the effects of rebellion from 1403. Donnington, in Wroxeter, close to Henry IV's route to Shrewsbury, was worth nothing in 1403-4 'because of the rebellion'.[52] In April 1404 the inhabitants of Shropshire complained that a third of the county had been sacked by the Welsh rebels and many of them had been forced to abandon their

[39] P.R.O., C 135/95, no. 7; C 135/98, no. 2; C 135/101, no. 6; T.S.A.S. 4th ser. i. 217.
[40] S.P.L., Deeds 7532.   [41] S.P.L., MS. 340.
[42] Smith, 'Lordships of Chirk and Oswestry', 211-12; S.P.L., Deeds 7280.
[43] P.R.O., C 135/98, no. 3; V.C.H. Salop. xi. 308, 314.
[44] B.L. Add. MS. 6165, p. 82; Cal. Inq. p.m. x, p. 311; xi, p. 195.   [45] Cal. Inq. p.m. xi, pp. 195, 410.
[46] S.P.L., MS. 342.

[47] V.C.H. Salop. ii. 43.
[48] Ibid. 75; xi. 156; B.L. Add. MS. 6165, pp. 69, 77, 93.
[49] V.C.H. Salop. xi. 156-7.
[50] Smith, 'Lordships of Chirk and Oswestry', 222-3; A. J. Pollard, 'Fam. of Talbot, Lds. Talbot and Earls of Shrews. in the 15th Cent.' (Bristol Univ. Ph.D. thesis, 1968), 394-6.
[51] J. E. Lloyd, Owen Glendower (1931), 32, 72, 86-7, 128, 141-2, 153-4.
[52] S.R.O. 552/1A/2.

homes.[53] The area around Oswestry suffered badly: at Aston the grange and sheepfold were burnt in 1403–4 and only small parcels of land could be cultivated; next year no rents could be collected because the tenants, their homes destroyed and their cattle abducted, had left in search of food.[54] At Sandford all the tenants abandoned their holdings and no rents could be collected between 1403 and 1405,[55] and at Ruyton the damage inflicted caused nearly £50 to be written off the revenues of the manor in 1406–7.[56] Whitchurch and the surrounding area were sacked in 1404 and rents were still being remitted five years later.[57] In 1405 the keeper of Caus castle reported that 100 of the Welsh tenants of the lordship had been driven out in a retaliatory raid from Baschurch, and Caus and the surrounding townships were granted exemption from taxation in 1405–6.[58] There was another destructive raid on Shropshire at the end of 1406 and tenants in 22 places around Shrewsbury were reported to have fled 'on account of the frequent attacks of the rebel Welshmen';[59] in 1407 the burgesses of Shrewsbury complained to parliament that all the sheep in the area had been killed or driven off by the rebels.[60] In 1410, the year of Glendower's final raid into Shropshire, pasture at Church Pulverbatch could not be let because the tenants were afraid that their animals would be taken by the Welsh rebels.[61]

The effects of the rebellion continued to be felt later in the 15th century: in 1430 the lands of Hugh Burgh, which included the manors of Yockleton and Stoney Stretton, were given a low valuation because they had been devastated by the rebel Welshmen and were still mostly waste 'on account of pestilence and robbery prevailing there in the marches'.[62] In neighbouring Minsterley the lapse of labour services was blamed on the rebellion, and some houses destroyed by Glendower had not been rebuilt by 1445.[63] Farther north, in the lordship of Oswestry, there was a fairly rapid recovery from the worst effects of the raids but rents in several of the manors were reduced to attract tenants back into a seriously underpopulated area.[64] Recovery after the 1404 raid was slower on the Talbot estate around Whitchurch: in 1407–8 it produced only 42 per cent of the revenues coming in before the raid and by 1436–7 the income was still only 74 per cent of what it had been in 1399–1400.[65] In spite of the adverse local conditions the demesnes of the estate were extensively exploited between 1413 and 1422, probably a reflection of the Talbots' personal interest in agriculture. All forms of direct exploitation were, however, stopped after 1422 and the estate stagnated until rising population in the 1520s led to a revitalization of the administration and an increase in rent income which had remained remarkably stable during the 15th century.[66] There, as elsewhere in the county, it was the landowners who suffered financially as the structure of seigneurial privilege and monopoly disintegrated, and it was tenants who were able to take advantage of the stable agrarian conditions.[67]

Landlords

The FitzAlans, earls of Arundel, were undoubtedly the county's greatest and richest landlords in the first half of the period. The family's estate had long been

[53] *Procs. and Ordinances of Privy Council* (Rec. Com.), ii. 77–8.　[54] N.L.W., Aston Hall 5319.
[55] Ibid. 5788.　[56] S.P.L., Deeds 7277.
[57] A. J. Pollard, 'Est. Management in the Later Middle Ages: the Talbots and Whitchurch, 1383–1525', *Econ. H.R.* 2nd ser. xxv. 560.
[58] *Cal. of Anct. Corresp. Concerning Wales*, ed. J. G. Edwards (1935), p. 197; *V.C.H. Salop.* viii. 316.
[59] P.R.O., E 179/166/48.　[60] *Rot. Parl.* iii. 618–19.

[61] Lloyd, *Glendower*, 141; S.R.O. 665, box 33, bailiff's acct. 10–11 Hen. IV.
[62] G. T. O. Bridgeman, 'The Princes of Upper Powys', *Mont. Colln.* i. 92, 190.　[63] *V.C.H. Salop.* viii. 316.
[64] Smith, 'Lordships of Chirk and Oswestry', 424–32.
[65] Pollard, 'Fam. of Talbot in 15th cent.' 359–60.
[66] Ibid. 362–7, 398–400.
[67] Ibid. 409–10; Smith, 'Lordships of Chirk and Oswestry', 432; below (Leasing of demesnes; Peasants).

among the most extensive in Shropshire[68] but in the mid and later 13th century they also became great landowners in southern England: their acquisition of part of the d'Aubigny inheritance in 1243, of the d'Aubigny earldom of Arundel by 1291, and of a large share of the estates of the last Warenne earl of Surrey (d. 1347) with that earldom (1361),[69] made them one of the greatest magnate dynasties in the kingdom. Richard FitzAlan, earl of Arundel 1330-76, used his vast landed income thriftily, settled his inheritance carefully, and increased his wealth by lending to his fellow noblemen and the Crown. Profits were invested in land,[70] mainly outside Shropshire[71] though the Shropshire estates did increase between the late 13th century and the early 15th century.[72] The forfeiture of 1397 was quickly reversed in 1400 and only on the childless Earl Thomas's death in 1415 was the inheritance reduced, unsettled estates passing to his three sisters.[73] Though the FitzAlans' political interest in Shropshire collapsed after 1415,[74] the earl of Arundel's Shropshire inheritance remained one of the four or five greatest landed estates in the county for a further century and a half.[75]

The other estates on a par with Arundel's in Shropshire[76] were those of the Corbets of Caus, some of which passed in 1347 to the Stafford family, earls of Stafford from 1351 and dukes of Buckingham 1444-1521;[77] those of the Mortimers, earls of March 1328-30 and 1354-1425, which passed to the duke of York after 1425 and to the Crown in 1461 when York's son became king as Edward IV;[78] those of the Talbots, a line of Herefordshire landowners to whom the title and estates of the Stranges of Blakemere came in 1383 and on whom the earldom of Shrewsbury was conferred in 1442;[79] those of the Stranges of Knockin, one of the greatest landed families never to receive an earldom[80] but whose lands passed c. 1480 to the Stanleys, earls of Derby from 1485;[81] and the barony of Wem, with its three extensive demesne manors of Wem, Loppington, and Hinstock which passed from the Botilers through the Lords Greystoke to the Lords Dacre of Gilsland.[82]

Such large estates, together with those of the more important monasteries—Buildwas, Combermere (Ches.), Haughmond, Lilleshall, Shrewsbury, and Wenlock,[83] whose estates bore local comparison with those of the aristocracy—were the dominant features of the medieval landowning pattern in Shropshire.[84] At a lower economic level were the gentry. Throughout the period their estates were being built up and consolidated or divided among heiresses. Families like the Corbets of Moreton Corbet and the Newports of High Ercall steadily increased their acreages, furnishing themselves with the means of joining the ranks of the leading

[68] Above, Domesday Book to 1300 (Lords and tenants).

[69] *Complete Peerage*, i. 237, 240-1; xii (1), 512; C. Given-Wilson, *Eng. Nobility in Late Middle Ages: the 14th-Cent. Political Community* (1987), 31, 135-6.

[70] Cf. *V.C.H. Salop.* iii. 34; Given-Wilson, op. cit. 45, 47, 125-6, 153, 156, 158; G. A. Holmes, *Estates of Higher Nobility in 14th-Cent. Eng.* (1957), 7, 39-40, 50-1.

[71] Earl Ric. spent over £4,000 on the acquisition of Suss. properties: *Two Est. Surveys of the FitzAlan Earls of Arundel* (Suss. Rec. Soc. lxvii), p. xxvi.

[72] *V.C.H. Salop.* ii. 86; xi. 220; *T.S.A.S.* 3rd ser. i. 43; *S.P.R. Heref.* xix (5), p. v; Eyton, iv. 17-19; *Cal. Chart. R.* 1327-41, 353; Smith, 'Lordships of Chirk and Oswestry', 55-62.

[73] Among whom the earldom of Surrey fell in abeyance. See *Complete Peerage*, i. 246; xii (1), 512; *V.C.H. Salop.* xi. 220.

[74] *V.C.H. Salop.* iii. 54, 57, 234, 236; Pollard, 'Fam. of Talbot in 15th Cent.' 228-9; E. Powell, 'Procs. bef. J.P.s at Shrews. in 1414', *E.H.R.* xcix. 536-41.

[75] Below, 1540-1750 (Landlord and tenant).

[76] Pollard, 'Fam. of Talbot in 15th Cent.' 227 and map V.

[77] Holmes, *Estates of Higher Nobility*, 39-40, 49-50; *Complete Peerage*, xii (1), 174 sqq.; *V.C.H. Salop.* viii. 311; *T.S.A.S.* 3rd ser. vi. 97.

[78] Holmes, op. cit. 10-19, 40, 45-7, 51-3; *Complete Peerage*, viii. 453-4; *V.C.H. Salop.* iii. 44 and n. 58, 54.

[79] Pollard, 'Fam. of Talbot in 15th Cent.' *passim*; *Complete Peerage*, xi. 698; xii (1), 345-6, 616 sqq.; H. le Strange, *Le Strange Records* (1916), 288, 321-2.

[80] Given-Wilson, *Nobility in Late Middle Ages*, 64.

[81] *Complete Peerage*, iv. 205 sqq.; xii (1), 356-7. The earldom did not actually pass to the owner of the Strange est. until 1504.

[82] S. Garbet, *Hist. Wem* (Wem, 1818), 34-48; cf. *V.C.H. Salop.* iii. 51-2.

[83] *V.C.H. Salop.* ii. 18 sqq.

[84] M. D. G. Wanklyn, 'Landed Soc. and Allegiance in Ches. and Salop. in 1st Civ. War' (Manchester Univ. Ph.D. thesis, 1976), 16-17.

gentry and the new aristocracy after the close of the Middle Ages.[85] Large inheritances extending far beyond the county, like that of the Burghs of Mawddwy (Merion.) and Wattlesborough, were built up by marriage only to be divided among heiresses in a later generation: the estates of Sir John Burgh (d. 1471) were partitioned among his four married daughters and served to increase the landed endowments of the Leightons, the Newports, the Lingens, and the Myttons.[86] Similarly the considerable inheritance enjoyed by William Burley, of Broncroft, passed after his death in 1458 to the families of his daughters Lady Trussell and Lady Littleton.[87] Despite the seeming inevitability of such changes in the long run, some modest estates of one or two manors continued in the same families, neither increasing nor greatly diminishing as generation succeeded generation. Such, for example, were those of the Eytons of Eyton,[88] the Gatacres of Gatacre,[89] the Lutwyches of Lutwyche,[90] and the Plowdens of Plowden.[91] Sometimes changes of family obscure an essential continuity. The Chetwynds maintained themselves at Chetwynd for five generations but then, c. 1354, an heiress carried it to the Peshalls, and in the next century a Peshall heiress carried it to the Pigotts.[92] Hodnet is a rare case of an estate which, though it passed from family to family, was never sold between 1086 and the 20th century.[93]

Sales of estates seem to have been less common in the later Middle Ages than they were from the mid 16th century onwards,[94] though aristocrats whose main interests lay elsewhere occasionally sold marginal properties[95] or Shropshire windfalls. Thus in 1425 the duchess of Norfolk sold the third of Wellington Hay that had come to her as part of the unsettled estates of her brother, the earl of Arundel (d. 1415),[96] and in 1448 the duke of York sold Cressage, an escheat, to his adviser William Burley.[97] Towards the end of the period there are signs of the purchasing of land by successful townsmen and lawyers. In 1462–3 Lord Lovel sold Norton and Pitchford to the Shrewsbury merchant Thomas Stone,[98] and about the same time the Londoner Hugh Stapleton acquired the manor of Oaks[99] and part of Minton.[1] In the later 15th century too the Needhams, a Cheshire family of successful lawyers, began to buy up considerable quantities of Shropshire land around Shavington, eventually their seat.[2]

The pre-eminence of a few large lay and ecclesiastical landowners over more numerous, but less well endowed, gentry families suffered no fundamental change before the Crown's dispersal of monastic estates after the Dissolution.[3] Family vicissitudes did not alter the general pattern. Evidence for the management of the gentry estates during the later Middle Ages, however, is almost entirely lacking. The considerable changes to the ways in which the land was exploited can be charted only on the estates of the marcher aristocracy who dominated the county.

[85] V.C.H. Salop. xi. 97, 101; A. E. C[orbet], The Fam. of Corbet: its Life and Times, ii [1918], caps. 12 sqq. and pedigree facing p. 368; Eyton, ix. 95–7.
[86] T.S.A.S. 4th ser. v. 211, 214–18; V.C.H. Salop. viii. 197. [87] T.S.A.S. lvi. 263–4, 271–2.
[88] V.C.H. Salop. xi. 114, 139–40.
[89] Eyton, iii. 86 sqq.; Visit. Salop. 1623, i (Harl. Soc. xxviii), 197–8; Shrews. Chron. 15 July 1927, p. 6; Daily Express, 17–18 July 1961.
[90] Eyton, iv. 113–16; Visit. Salop. 1623, ii (Harl. Soc. xxix), 345–7; J. B. Blakeway, Sheriffs of Salop. (Shrews. 1831), 189–90; S.P.L., MS. 6865, p. 163.
[91] Eyton, xi. 218; Burke, Land. Gent. (1914), 1514–17; The Field, Dec. 1987, p. 39.
[92] H. E. Chetwynd-Stapylton, The Chetwynds of Ingestre (1892), 1–42; S.P.L., MS. 2792, pp. 166, 172; Eyton, viii.

81–9.
[93] Shrews. Chron. 19 May 1911, p. 5 (obit. of A. Heber-Percy); cf. Country Life, 16 Apr. 1987, p. 116.
[94] Cf. V.C.H. Salop. viii and xi; L. Stone, Crisis of the Aristocracy (1965), 144 sqq.
[95] For the earl of Shrewsbury's sale of Alberbury in 1500 see below, 1540–1750 (Landlord and tenant).
[96] V.C.H. Salop. xi. 220.
[97] Ibid. viii. 75; T.S.A.S. lvi. 264.
[98] V.C.H. Salop. viii. 41, 119. [99] Ibid. 266.
[1] S.R.O. 665/2, box 42, deeds of 1478–84; P.R.O., C 141/2, no. 19.
[2] H. D. Harrod, Hist of Shavington (Shrews. 1891), 18–23.
[3] Wanklyn, 'Landed Soc. and Allegiance in Ches. and Salop.' 16–17.

Even for those estates bailiffs' accounts, the most informative sources for landlord farming, have survived only for isolated and exceptional years and only for parts of the far-flung estates of families such as the Mortimers and FitzAlans.

In spite of the deficiencies of the evidence, certain trends are apparent, notably the continued advance of settlement into the forests and wastes, usually with the encouragement and, at least at the beginning of the period, under the active direction of the landlords. Cereal production for the market became less and less important; amounts of demesne arable were small and contracting. On some estates the arable demesne had been leased before 1300[4] and that trend continued during the 14th century. Landlords preferred where possible to concentrate on the more profitable and less labour intensive activities of sheep farming and cattle rearing, but even that form of direct involvement in agricultural production had virtually ceased by the mid 15th century and the major families had come to rely on income from rents and other indirect profits of lordship.

Assarting and inclosure

There is evidence throughout the central and northern parts of the county during the period for the continued clearing of woodland and forest and for the improvement of wastes. For a variety of reasons assarting, though a continuous process, was a piecemeal one. It was still conducted, however, under the landlords' direction, or with their encouragement. Only in the 1530s are there signs that squatters were beginning to encroach on the commons.[5] The pace of advancing cultivation depended on the extent of the demand for new land, the availability of labour for clearing the land and preparing it for use, and above all on the desire of lords to add to their demesnes or to increase their income from rents and entry fines. For those reasons the most active direction by the lords or their officers came in the early years of the 14th century when there was still pressure from an expanding population and when many lords were still engaged in the direct exploitation of their estates.[6]

Some fragmentary information can be found in bailiffs' accounts for the cost of breaking up new land before it was leased or incorporated in the demesne and cultivated. At Ruyton in 1319–20 it cost 6s. an acre to break up an assart of 12½ a. in woodland by piece work; preparing a parcel of waste for sowing in 1338 involved removing stones and cleaning the ground; in 1343 assarting some moorland cost 53s. 1½d. and in 1346 breaking up a meadow for cultivation cost 67s. 7d.[7] The earl of Arundel's bailiff at Wroxeter in the early 14th century employed two men for 13 days on assarting work, while the bailiff of Shrawardine paid out 33s. for the making of two assarts by piece work and also employed extra labour to ditch the assarts and inclose them with thorns, and at Upton Magna an *assartator* was employed for part of the year. At Adderley in 1318 six men were hired for 4 days' ditching on an assart.[8] At Dodington 6d. was spent on a ploughshare for breaking new land in 1342 and considerable labour costs were incurred for marling the land.[9] Newly broken land was usually sown with oats, but rye was also regarded as a suitable crop: a demesne assart at High Ercall was called Rye furlong.[10] Oats sown on an assart in woodland at Ruyton in 1319–20 yielded 5:2 and at Dodington

---

[4] Above, Domesday Book to 1300 (Lords and tenants).
[5] D. G. Hey, *An Eng. Rural Community: Myddle under the Tudors and Stuarts* (1974), 10.
[6] See in particular *T.S.A.S.* lxii. 1, 10–12.

[7] S.P.L., Deeds 7188, 7192, 7265, 7323.
[8] P.R.O., SC 6/965/2; S.P.L., Deeds 7531.
[9] S.R.O. 212, box 80, bailiffs' accts. 15–16, 17–18 Edw. III; below (Demesne agriculture). [10] *T.S.A.S.* lxii. 25.

in 1342 newly broken land was sown with 2 qr. 3 bu. of oats and another new assart in 1344 with 7 qr. of rye.[11]

Haughmond abbey provides a good example of how the direction of assarting of waste and woodland could form part of a policy of systematic extension of the cultivated area on a large estate.[12] In 1308 the abbot negotiated the partition of the wastes of Hadnall, Hardwick, and Grinshill, and the abbey's portions were inclosed and brought under cultivation.[13] A royal licence was obtained in 1313 to inclose and cultivate 60 a. of Haughmond wood and in 1318 Hadnall wood was divided and inclosed.[14] In 1297 the abbot and convent had been given permission by John le Strange (V), lord of Knockin, to inclose their grange of Caldicott within the demesne of Knockin and to build houses on the heath or waste and grant them out to tenants.[15] That policy was followed by the abbey on its own newly inclosed land: small portions of waste were granted to tenants for life on condition that they built houses or cultivated and marled the land at their own expense.[16] The demand for such land, and the ability to pay high entry fines, began to fall off in the mid 14th century, and some tenants in financial difficulties conveyed their assarts back to the abbey by way of mortgage.[17]

There is evidence, though not usually so detailed, that other lords, lay and ecclesiastical, were aware of the importance of controlling the assarting of waste land. The lords of the manor of High Ercall, it has been argued, balanced alienations of their demesne in the form of grants to the church or members of their families by a progressive policy of inclosure of the waste. In the final stage of the process, between 1278 and 1345, the wastes that separated Ercall from its neighbours were converted to arable or meadow, leaving barely enough common pasture in the manor. The improved land was leased to free tenants: cleared woodland fetched 1s. and heathland 6d. an acre. In addition the customary tenants were encouraged to make 'bruches' or assarts on marginal land for which they were charged nominal rents.[18] Elsewhere in the county, for example at Woolstaston and Smethcott, free tenancies were created to encourage the clearance of woodland.[19] In Condover land assarted from Buriwood was known as 'purchase land' and could be bought and sold without restriction. The process of clearing Buriwood began under the lord's direction, and in 1307 Edward Burnell granted out part of his waste at a rent of 25s. a year with the stipulation that if any cottages were built on the improved land their holders should pay him rent and owe suit to his court of Condover. Clearance was completed by the tenants of later, non-resident, lords who could easily obtain licences to hold assarts in severalty.[20] Assarting in the lordship of Oswestry was carefully regulated from the early 14th century. Assarts that were not taken into the demesne and cultivated directly were kept as separate units; unlike earlier assarts they were kept distinct from land held as part of a *gwely* and the holders were charged economic rents. Incursions into the waste help to explain the increase in the annual income from rents in the lordship from £60 in 1301 to £112 in 1362. The lord's financial interest in the increase of cultivated land culminated in the establishment of a seigneurial right to regulate incursions into waste land in the lordship by the sale of licences. In 1341 three men accused of

[11] S.P.L., Deeds 7323; S.R.O. 212, box 80, bailiffs' accts. 15-16, 17-18 Edw. III.
[12] U. Rees, 'Leases of Haughmond Abbey', *Midland Hist.* viii. 16.
[13] *Cart. Haughmond*, pp. 83 (no. 350), 115 (nos. 535-6).
[14] Ibid. pp. 91 (no. 397), 95 (no. 426).
[15] Ibid. p. 59 (nos. 207-10).
[16] Ibid. pp. 86 (no. 364), 108-9 (no. 491), 136 (no. 653), 137 (no. 655), 166 (no. 820).
[17] Ibid. pp. 92 (no. 405), 97 (no. 440).
[18] *T.S.A.S.* lxii. 1-3, 10-12.
[19] *V.C.H. Salop.* viii. 154, 170. Cf. above, Domesday Book to 1300 (Woodland, assarting, and commons).
[20] S.P.L., Deeds 6640A; *V.C.H. Salop.* viii. 28, 45-6.

appropriating the waste of Eardiston township were called to answer in the court of Ruyton.[21] In the neighbouring lordship of Ellesmere Roger le Strange was found in 1319 to have made many grants of waste at rents ranging from 1d. to 6d. an acre.[22]

Assarting in royal manors, woods, and forests in the county continued under licences granted by the king. In 1346 the abbot and convent of Shrewsbury were granted 240 a. of Lythwood, a royal hay in Condover, at a rent of 3d. an acre and by 1364 clearance of the wood by the abbey and its tenants was well under way.[23] Earlier in the century Haughmond abbey had been granted 'Skyneresmore' in Morfe forest and agreed to pay the arrentors of the royal waste an entry fine of 6s. 8d. an acre and a rent of 6d. an acre.[24] At the same time 8 a. of waste in the royal manor of Claverley was rented at 4d. an acre;[25] some 30 years later Sir William of Shareshill was licensed to bring into cultivation 200 a. of waste and pasture in the same manor and to lease them to tenants.[26] Records of the regards of Morfe and Shirlett forests in 1356 and 1360 show the extent to which the woodland was being reduced by hundreds of assarts, ranging in size from under 1 a. to 80 a., but most under 5 a. Included were the assarts, licensed and unlicensed, made by Shareshill and his tenants, and at King's Nordley John Astley held 80 a. himself and had leased 42 a. to tenants at a rent of 1d. an acre. Those assarts were being cultivated regularly and many had cottages erected on them.[27]

The clearing of woodland and improvement of the waste was not a steady, continuous process and it is not an easy one to chart accurately but evidence for it can be found throughout the period. On Wenlock priory's estates, where there had been vigorous expansion into woodland and waste in the 13th century, 'new land', often held in separate, inclosed plots, could still command rents of up to 1 s. an acre in the first half of the 14th century, and, on one occasion at least, ½ a. of newly assarted land was offered as an incentive to encourage a tenant to take a holding at Derrington in Ditton Priors.[28] In 1345 Isabel de Ferrers made extensive grants out of the waste in her manor of Stoke upon Tern; she had no difficulty in finding tenants who were willing to pay 1 s. an acre (measured by the perch of 24 ft. as was usual with assarts on the Welsh border) for inclosed holdings. In one case the tenants, two brothers, took on 120 a., paid an entry fine of 10d. an acre, promised an annual rent of 12d. an acre, and undertook to find other tenants who would take 80 a. more on the same terms and build on their holdings. Ten years later, however, Isabel's son William reduced the rents for those assarts by a third.[29] On the neighbouring manor of Prees there was still a brisk market in holdings approved from the waste in the later 14th century.[30] Assarts were still being made in the late 14th century in Habberley, Westbury, and Betton in Hales and during the 15th century in Condover, Pontesbury, Cound, and Kenley.[31] As much of the late assarting was from poor and unproductive heath land, it was often necessary to offer incentives in the form of favourable leases and low rents; in Eyton upon the Weald Moors, for example, the lord granted long leases rent free for the first eight years while the scrubland was being cleared.[32]

[21] Smith, 'Lordships of Chirk and Oswestry', 201, 210–11, 275–7; N.L.W., Aston Hall 6918; S.P.L., Deeds 7295.
[22] Eyton, x. 245.
[23] V.C.H. Salop. viii. 29; Cal. Pat. 1345–8, 73; P.R.O., E 32/308/4.
[24] Cart. Haughmond, p. 49 (no. 154).
[25] Cal. Pat. 1301–7, 360.
[26] Ibid. 1334–8, 525, 535.
[27] P.R.O., E 32/149–50.
[28] V.C.H. Salop. ii. 41; xi. 82; S.R.O. 1037/19/1; 1224/2/10.
[29] S.R.O. 327, box 11, deeds 2 Oct. 1345, 2 July 1355 (copies); Cart. Haughmond, p. 95 (no. 428).
[30] S.P.L., MS. 340, esp. ct. r. 6 Ric. II; MS. 343, esp. ct. r. 14 Ric. II; Staffs. R.O., D.(W.) 1734/1/5/1, f. 1.
[31] V.C.H. Salop. viii. 59, 93, 238, 247, 299; S.P.L., Deeds 6172, 9136; S.R.O. 327, box 14, agreement betw. abbots of Combermere and Shrews. 1376; 665, box 33, bailiff's acct. 8–9 Hen. IV.
[32] V.C.H. Salop. xi. 141.

The scattered nature of settlement over much of the county, the predominantly pastoral or mixed character of agriculture, and the availability of pasture resources combined to lend flexibility to agrarian practice during the period. That flexibility can be seen in the varied treatment of assarts taken from the wastes and woodland. In some cases the open fields were extended: at Poynton in 1412 each of the three fields included a number of 'bruches' and in Alberbury, Cardeston, and Smethcott the amount of open-field land was extended by assarting during the later Middle Ages.[33] Those renting assarted land were frequently allowed to inclose and cultivate it provided that the lord and his tenants had common pasture rights.[34] Land improved from waste or woodland and held in severalty was often used for private pasture with the occasional arable interval. Land newly taken from the waste in Prees manor in 1391 carried a rent of 9d. an acre for pasture and 12d. for each acre cultivated; it was to be completely inclosed but the lord was to have access for pigs in time of pannage.[35] There was a similar flexibility of practice in the use of 'old' land. Open fields, it has been shown, were established over most of the county long before the end of the 13th century,[36] but there is evidence of considerable variety. Holdings could be part open and part inclosed, and extents and rentals of the period reveal a complicated mix of holdings in the open fields combined with closes, assarts, and meadows held in severalty.[37] At Little Wenlock in the 1320s there were apparently no common meadows, but some meadows were held in severalty and licences were issued to inclose both assarts and selions in the common fields; later in the 14th century fines were being levied for holding closes in severalty and for putting animals in a private field (*in campum separale*) after prohibition by the manor court.[38]

The proportion of open to inclosed land depended on the policies of individual landlords and the character of manorial arrangements, but there is considerable evidence of an increase in the amount of inclosed pasture and meadow to allow specialist livestock farming not possible in the common fields. Demesne pasture and meadow was highly valued; in the lordship of Oswestry the meadows were the last pieces of the demesne to be leased.[39] Meadow which could supply hay for winter feed or whose agistment could be sold was worth the expense of maintaining inclosures;[40] in Sutton upon Tern manor in 1367 tenants were amerced for allowing their animals to stray into the lord's inclosed pastures.[41] Meadow could also be broken up and cropped; income from agistment payments was reduced in Cleobury Barnes manor in the 1370s because one of the meadows was regularly sown with wheat and oats and in 1378–9 half of the manorial park was sold for pasture and the rest sown with oats.[42] At Ruyton it cost £3 7s. 7d. to break up two meadows in 1346–7 and at Ercall Magna two thirds of Holtesmoor was under the plough in 1424.[43] As landlords gave up the direct exploitation of their demesnes, leases of pasture with licence to inclose were made more frequently.[44] Sometimes such leases resulted in considerable increases in value; an inquiry into rents in the manor

[33] *Cart. Shrews.* ii. 265–7; *V.C.H. Salop.* viii. 148, 184–5.
[34] e.g. *Cart. Haughmond*, p. 45 (no. 140); S.R.O. 465/14; 2919/2/13.
[35] S.P.L., MS. 343, ct. 27 Apr. 1391.
[36] H. L. Gray, *Eng. Field Systems* (1915), 37–9, 66–9; *T.S.A.S.* lii. 15–16; D. Sylvester, *Rural Landscape of the Welsh Borderland* (1969), 302, 307, 332, 334–6, 339, 345.
[37] e.g. *T.S.A.S.* 2nd ser. xi. 252 sqq. (Ellesmere 1280); S.P.L., Deeds 9114 (Condover 1421); S.R.O. 1224/2/298 (Chelmarsh 1455).
[38] S.R.O. 1037/19/1; 1224/2/1; *V.C.H. Salop.* xi. 81–2; W. F. Mumford, *Wenlock in the Middle Ages* (Shrews. 1977),

162–3, 171.
[39] Smith, 'Lordships of Chirk and Oswestry', 117; S.P.L., Deeds 7260; below (Demesne agriculture).
[40] e.g. S.R.O. 212, box 14, bailiffs' accts. 8–9, 19–20 Ric. II; S.P.L., Deeds 7245, 9766; P.R.O., SC 6/965/5, m. 5; SC 6/967/10.   [41] S.P.L., Deeds 5454.
[42] P.R.O., SC 6/965/15, 17, 21, 24.
[43] S.P.L., Deeds 7192; *T.S.A.S.* lxii. 26.
[44] e.g. S.R.O. 665, box 33, Ch. Pulverbatch extracts from ct. r. 28 Hen. VI; S.P.L., Deeds 9136, Condover ct. r. 7 Hen. VI; Staffs. R.O., D. 593/A/1/18/13; /B/2/2/1A/8; *T.S.A.S.* liv. 58–63.

of Ruyton in 1393–4 found that the value of two meadows had been doubled by their tenants who had drained and inclosed them and rooted up thorns and brambles; Rednal meadow, which was then worth 8s. a year held in severalty, was said to be potentially worth 20s. but it would cost at least £10 to inclose it with hedges and ditches.[45]

A further indication of the flexible use of land in the period is the appearance of grassland within the arable fields. Field land could be laid down to grass temporarily or permanently and field names containing 'leasow' or 'ley' occur frequently.[46] There was meadow at the head of all the furlongs of Moortown, a township in Ercall Magna, in 1479 and in the manor of Oaks mention is made in 1407 of 'Kneriseleye', a permanently inclosed grass strip.[47] References to 'frisc' or uncultivated land need not imply that such land was derelict. Assarts were often allowed to lie fallow for some years before being brought back into cultivation.[48] In 1383 Bromfield manor court recorded an agreement of the tenants to cultivate part of the land lying frisc in one of the open fields.[49] Land which went out of cultivation was often put to other profitable uses: at Stanton Lacy and Cleobury Barnes in the 1370s uncultivated demesne was leased for sowing or sold as pasture, and the bailiff of Stokesay manor accounted in 1424–5 for 59s. 7d. received from the sale of the herbage of several closes and of frisc land in one of the common fields.[50]

The flexible treatment of pasture and meadow was accompanied by efforts to consolidate holdings in the open fields. There is evidence from the early 14th century of the piecemeal and largely peaceful inclosure which has been said to characterize Shropshire and which led writers in the 16th century to regard the county as largely inclosed.[51] Holdings in the common fields were exchanged and licences were obtained to inclose the consolidated strips, resulting in a complicated mixture of closes in the open fields: evidence comes from all parts of the county— south (Larden 1409, Stoke St. Milborough 1321–2),[52] east (Lilleshall 1345, Longford 1358, Madeley 1449–50, and Posenhall 1445),[53] central (Harley 1338 and 1359 and Longnor 1346 and 1454),[54] west (the Oswestry area and Picklescott in the 1520s),[55] and north (Hadnall 1471).[56] In some instances the process of consolidation led to complete inclosure of the open fields. At Kenley the open fields, which were still in use in the early 15th century, appear to have been inclosed by the end of the Middle Ages. At Allfield, in Condover, a man who was inclosing part of the open fields c. 1430 eventually bought out the remaining copyholders and the whole township was inclosed by 1595.[57] Despite apparently extensive piecemeal inclosure of open fields in Shropshire from the 14th century there was no large-scale conversion of arable to pasture, with associated depopulation and agrarian discontent, such as occurred in some other parts of the country.[58]

The returns of the commissioners appointed under the Tillage Act of 1515,[59] which made it an offence to convert land from tillage to pasture, are of little use in charting the progress of inclosure in the county. Although the commissioners

[45] T.S.A.S. 3rd ser. i. 63–4; ii. 391.
[46] T.S.A.S. lxii. 26, 36, 38, 40; H. D. G. Foxall, Salop. Field-Names (Salop. Arch. Soc. 1980), 4–5, 9, 35–8, 52.
[47] T.S.A.S. liv. 31–2; lxii. 26.
[48] e.g. Cart. Haughmond, p. 148 (no. 717).
[49] S.R.O. 20/1/7.
[50] P.R.O., SC 6/965/12, 17, 21, 24–5; SC 6/967/27, mm. 2, 8, 10–11; S.P.L., Deeds 9733.
[51] Ag. Hist. Eng. iv. 203, 246.
[52] T.S.A.S. liv. 235–6; Eyton, iv. 9.
[53] V.C.H. Salop. xi. 156; Staffs. R.O., D. 938/726; S.R.O. 1224/2/9; /3/109.

[54] Staffs. R.O., D. 938/710, 713; Eyton, viii. 210; S.R.O. 567/2A/30.
[55] Smith, 'Lordships of Chirk and Oswestry', 281; V.C.H. Salop. viii. 148.
[56] Cart. Haughmond, p. 91 (no. 400).
[57] V.C.H. Salop. viii. 30, 93; T.S.A.S. l. 142.
[58] V.C.H. Salop. viii. 1, 4–5, 62, 115, 117, 142, 163, 178, 182, 192–3, 305–6; Deserted Medieval Villages: Studies, ed. M. W. Beresford and J. G. Hurst (1971), 203; T. Rowley, Villages in the Landscape (1978), 119; T.S.A.S. lviii. 46–7, 122, 130–1.
[59] 7 Hen. VIII, c. 1.

reported in 1517 that 58 ploughs had been put down and 344 people deprived of their livelihood from the land as a result of conversion to pasture over the previous 20 years, their survey was unsystematic and of doubtful accuracy.[60] They started with Hopesay where they reported that Richard Rychard had inclosed 40 a. of arable and converted it to pasture in 1516, but they also found that seven inclosures totalling only 18 a. and not involving conversion of arable had been made in 1504. After a detailed survey of part of Purslow hundred the return becomes summary and casual; 35 of the 55 inclosures and conversions listed are said to be of 20 a. The largest inclosure reported was of 80 a. at Kenley in 1513 and may represent the former open fields.[61] All that the returns can safely be taken to indicate is an increase in the amount of inclosed pasture in the southern uplands at the end of the Middle Ages, and that appears to have been achieved, as in Cheshire and Herefordshire, without excessive disruption and depopulation.[62]

Demesne agriculture

It is possible to build up a picture of the nature of demesne agriculture in the county in the later Middle Ages. The picture will inevitably be incomplete because the most informative source, bailiffs' accounts, survive for large and untypical estates and often only for isolated years. There are, however, accounts for most parts of the county and they cover the period from the early 14th century, when the retreat from direct exploitation had already begun, to the early decades of the 15th century, after which all the major landlords had leased out their demesnes, apart from some home farms, and ceased to be directly involved in agriculture.

At the heart of every demesne was the home farm or grange. Differing farm sizes, a greater or lesser emphasis on arable or pastoral farming, and varying local building traditions would all have contributed, as later, to a wide variety of building types. Similarly, on the demesne farms of the great estates individual buildings might be larger and more substantial than on smaller manors. Thus in 1468 Haughmond abbey's great barn at Homebarn Grange was of 11 bays[63] rather than the more usual 3 or 4.[64]

Although there was variety, the same basic elements appear consistently when farms were described. Chelmarsh and High Ercall were probably typical of larger demesne farms in the 15th century. At High Ercall in 1424 the complex was large and probably moated, being entered across a bridge that led to a 3-storey gatehouse. A separate stone tower was presumably defensive. Attached to the hall were a number of residential chambers; kitchen, larder house, brewhouse, and bakehouse stood separate. The agricultural buildings, probably roughly grouped around one or more yards, comprised 2 barns, 3 stables, ox and cow houses, a dovecot, a barleyrick tower, a garner, and a hay loft.[65] The manorial buildings at Chelmarsh in 1454–5 were slightly fewer: a hall with 2 cross chambers, chapel, another chamber, kitchen, gatehouse, 2 stables, barn, oxhouse, cowhouse, and dovecot.[66] On smaller demesnes and on granges there were probably still fewer buildings. At Haughmond abbey's grange at Nagington in 1474, for instance, there was a 3-bay house, 3-bay barn, and a sheepfold.[67]

[60] J. A. Yelling, *Common Field and Enclosure in Eng. 1450–1850* (1977), 20–1. The Salop. returns are printed in *Trans. R.H.S.* N.S. viii. 310–31, and discussed in *T.S.A.S.* 4th ser. xi. 207–12. Cf. *V.C.H. Salop.* iii. 88.
[61] *V.C.H. Salop.* viii. 93.
[62] M. Beresford, *Lost Villages of Eng.* (1954), 384; Sylves-ter, *Rural Landscape of Welsh Borderland*, 327 n.
[63] *Cart. Haughmond*, p. 123 (no. 581).
[64] e.g. ibid. pp. 159 (no. 783), 216 (no. 1176); *V.C.H. Salop.* viii. 307.
[65] *T.S.A.S.* lxii. 32.
[66] S.R.O. 1224/2/598, m. 2d.
[67] *Cart. Haughmond*, p. 159 (no. 783).

In general the Shropshire demesnes were not large. Of the eight FitzAlan manors in Shropshire and the march[68] surveyed in 1301, only Oswestry with 5 carucates and Shrawardine with 4 carucates had over 250 a. of demesne arable, and in the four townships in the lordship of Clun where there were over 20 a. of demesne meadow there was no arable at all in demesne. The importance attached to demesne meadow is clear from the values given in the survey: meadow is valued at between 1s. and 3s. an acre, while arable is valued at between 2d. and 6d. an acre or between £1 and £2 a carucate.[69] The same pattern of small arable demesnes and highly valued meadow is found in inquisitions post mortem during the 14th century. In 1300 a jury reported that Peter, Lord Corbet, had in demesne at Caus 3 carucates of arable, each of 120 a., worth 3d. an acre and 2 a. of meadow worth 3s., at Worthen 4 carucates of arable worth 4d. an acre and 15 a. of meadow worth 1s. an acre, and at Minsterley 3 carucates of arable worth 6d. an acre and 24 a. of meadow worth 1s. 6d. an acre.[70] In 1310 the 60 a. of arable belonging to a third of the manor of Broseley were valued at 15s., and 40 a. of arable at Billingsley were worth only 1½d. an acre.[71] Two carucates of demesne arable at Wrockwardine which were valued at only £2 in 1324 because the land was very infertile had fallen to £1 in 1349; the demesne meadow was also halved in value after the plague but was still worth 1s. an acre.[72] In 1378 200 a. of field land (*acrae campestrales*) were valued at 2d. an acre because the land was sandy and lay in common, but 20 a. of meadow were worth 1s. an acre.[73]

The demesnes of the larger monastic houses in the county tell a similar story. The 21 carucates of arable held in demesne in Shropshire by Shrewsbury abbey in 1291 had shrunk to 12 carucates by 1355 and the 2 carucates in Astley manor that were valued at £3 in 1355 had fallen in value to £2 5s. in 1361, while the abbey's meadow continued to be valued at 1s. an acre.[74] In 1291 Wenlock priory had arable demesnes totalling 43 carucates; in 1370 there were 30 carucates divided between 13 manors and granges and valued at between 6s. 8d. and 13s. 4d. a carucate; by 1390 there had been a further reduction to 25 carucates in demesne.[75] At the Dissolution only the home farm of 286 a., valued at nearly 4d. an acre, was still cultivated directly but the convent had retained 25 a. of meadow valued at 28s. 4d.[76] At Lilleshall in 1330 the abbey had 10 carucates of demesne arable attached to four granges and managed in a three-year rotation with the two parts under cultivation valued at £15; by 1375 there were 9 carucates of which the two cultivated parts were valued at £10. There had also been a reduction in demesne meadow from 40 a. in 1330 to 24 a. in 1375 but the value remained constant at 1s. an acre.[77] At the Dissolution the Lilleshall demesnes consisted of 157 a. of arable valued at just over 5d. an acre, 35½ a. of meadow valued at 64s., and 331½ a. of pasture valued at 9d. an acre.[78]

The small size of the arable demesnes reveals that cereal production was on a minor scale and almost invariably subordinate to pastoral farming. Oats was the chief crop and is found on every estate for which accounts of cereal production survive. Wheat was the main winter-sown crop and was sometimes grown mixed

---

[68] Acton Round, Heath, Holdgate, Shrawardine, Upton Magna, and Wroxeter in Salop., Clun and Oswestry in the march.

[69] *Two Est. Surveys of Earls of Arundel*, pp. xxiii, xxix-xxx, 51-2, 54, 56-9. 62, 64-5, 74, 76, 79, 81, 84, 88-9. Cf. above, Domesday Book to 1300 (Livestock and pastoral farming).

[70] P.R.O., C 133/94, no. 6.

[71] S.R.O. 1224/3/288.

[72] *T.S.A.S.* 4th ser. viii. 157; P.R.O., C 135/98, no. 3.

[73] *Cal. Inq. Misc.* iv, pp. 23-4.

[74] *V.C.H. Salop.* ii. 32; B.L. Add. MS. 6165, pp. 81-3, 89.

[75] *V.C.H. Salop.* ii. 42-3; B.L. Add. MS. 6165, pp. 97-100.

[76] P.R.O., E 315/400, pp. 7-8.

[77] B.L. Add. MS. 6165, pp. 69, 77, 93.

[78] P.R.O., E 315/400, pp. 1-2.

with rye as maslin; barley was grown but only in small quantities and sometimes mixed with oats as dredge.[79] Also found in small quantities throughout the 14th century are peas, vetch, and beans. When the forfeited estates of the recently executed Roger Mortimer, earl of March, were valued in April 1331, just before the spring sowing, 80 a. of the 200 a. of demesne arable at Earnwood were sown with wheat, as were 40 a. of 120 a. of arable at Highley and 60 a. of 200 a. of arable at Cleobury Barnes. The granaries of the Shropshire manors contained 117 qr. of wheat, valued at between 4s. 4d. and 6s. 8d. a quarter, and just over 100 qr. of oats, valued at between 2s. and 4s. 4d. a quarter; there were also small quantities of rye, peas, and vetch but no barley.[80] Oats and wheat were the main crops in 1313–15 on the earl of Arundel's manors of Shrawardine, Upton Magna, Acton Round, and Ruyton, but barley, rye, and peas were also grown at Wroxeter, and peas and vetch at the former Templar manor of Lydley on which there had been found 125 qr. 5 bu. of oats, 47 qr. 5 bu. of wheat, and 44 qr. of maslin in January 1308.[81] The demesne arable at Ruyton continued to be cultivated directly until the early 1340s and in 1341–2 wheat, oats, and small quantities of rye, barley, and vetch were sown.[82] Cultivation of the demesne arable ceased at the same time at neighbouring Kinnerley where oats and beans were being sown together in small quantities as dredge in 1338–9.[83] Wheat and oats were the only crops sown on the c. 100 a. of demesne arable in Caus lordship, which were leased to tenants in 1383.[84] Records survive for the sporadic exploitation between 1331 and 1422 of part of the demesne arable on the estate around Whitchurch held successively by the Strange and Talbot families, and there oats was the main crop, but wheat, barley, rye, peas, and beans were also grown.[85]

The preponderance of oats and wheat is shown by the comparison in Table III of acreages sown at Adderley, a manor in the north of the county in the king's hands during the crisis years 1318–27, and on the southern manors of Cleobury Barnes and Stanton Lacy during the declining years of demesne farming at the end of the 14th century. At Adderley oats were sown at 4 bu. an acre, wheat at 2 bu., barley and beans at 3 bu., rye at 2 bu., and peas and vetch at 1½ bu. Sowing rates at Cleobury Barnes and Stanton Lacy were slightly lower for the major crops: oats at between 3 and 4 bu. an acre and wheat at between 1½ and 2 bu. an acre, and slightly higher for the minor crops: barley at 4 bu., peas between 2 and 3 bu., and vetch at 2 bu. an acre. Yields, impossible to estimate accurately, do not seem to have been good. The wheat yield at Adderley between 1322 and 1324 was just over 3:1, and it was 5:1 at Cleobury Barnes in 1378–9, the only year for which it can be estimated there. Oats yielded 2:1 at Adderley between 1322 and 1324 and only slightly better at Cleobury Barnes between 1377 and 1380 (Table III). On the Talbot lordship of Blakemere oats yielded 7:2 in 1384 but dropped to under 2:1 in 1388; in 1419 wheat yielded nearly 4:1.[86]

In 1392–3 the bailiff at Stanton Lacy noted that the seed was of poor quality that year.[87] Seed corn was usually taken from the previous harvest but occasionally it was mixed with purchased seed. Wheat was bought for sowing at prices ranging from 13d. a bushel at Adderley in 1322–3 to 6d. a bushel at Cleobury Barnes in 1378–9;[88] oats was rarely bought for sowing but in 1313 both wheat and oats were bought at Shrewsbury for sowing at Ruyton and 9 bu. of rye and 10 bu. of barley

[79] P.R.O., SC 6/965/12 (2 parts oats to 1 part barley).
[80] P.R.O., E 142/68–9.
[81] S.P.L., Deeds 7531; P.R.O., E 358/18, m. 4; V.C.H. Salop. ii. 86.
[82] S.P.L., Deeds 7190.
[83] Ibid. 7235.
[84] V.C.H. Salop. viii. 317.
[85] Pollard, 'Fam. of Talbot in 15th cent.' 346–50.
[86] Ibid. 348.
[87] P.R.O., SC 6/967/27, m. 12.
[88] P.R.O., SC 6/965/5, m. 5; SC 6/965/24.

TABLE III: ACREAGES SOWN ON THREE MANORS

	wheat	rye	oats	barley	dredge	vetch	peas	beans	TOTAL
Adderley									
1318–19	48	3	59	8	—	15	—	—	133
1319–20	51	4½	48½	5	—	8	—	—	117
1321–2	57	—	77	9	—	15	3	3	159
1322–3	51	—	71	10	—	8	7	5	154
1323–4	60	2	67	4½	—	6	4	10	149½
Cleobury Barnes									
1372–3	36	—	50	—	4	2½	3	—	94
1375–6	29	—	25	—	—	3	—	—	57
1377–8	24	—	35	—	—	3	—	—	62
1378–9	33	—	22	—	—	3½	—	—	58½
1379–80	27½	—	27	—	—	4	—	—	59½
Stanton Lacy									
1377–8	81	—	57	—	—	6	4	—	148
1379–80	74	—	87	—	—	5	4	—	170
1385–6	40	—	28	—	—	16[a]	—	—	84
1387–8	46	—	40	—	—	—	3	—	89
1389–90	38	—	38	3	—	—	2	—	79[b]
1392–3	40	—	38	4	—	—	5	—	87

Sources: P.R.O., SC 6/965/3–5 (Adderley); SC 6/965/12, 15, 17, 21, 24–5 (Cleobury Barnes); SC 6/967/27 and SC 6/1304/17 (Stanton Lacy).

[a] Actually 16 a. of vetch and peas.

[b] The totals are the totals harvested and do not necessarily correspond exactly to the sum of the acres sown. Unusually the Stanton Lacy account for 1389–90 also gives the total acreage sown, 81.

were bought at Shrewsbury in 1341–2 for sowing at Ruyton.[89] In 1343 the bailiff at Dodington went with two carters to collect wheat for sowing and in 1384 the bailiff of husbandry at Myddle bought 3 qr. of seed wheat at Shrewsbury.[90] The treasurer of Lilleshall abbey bought seed wheat at Wenlock and seed rye at Newport in 1437–8, and in 1446–7 on the abbey's manor of Atcham 20 bu. of purchased seed was sown with 8 qr. 5 bu. of wheat from the previous year's harvest.[91]

It is unusual for accounts to note vegetables and fruits, both commonplace in medieval gardens. Leeks and cabbages, two of the staple vegetables, were grown at Adderley in the early 14th century, and at Myddle a century later onions, another staple, were grown, and leeks. The reeve of Kinnerley accounted for the sale of apples in 1335–6 and for the sale of 45 gallons of cider in 1346–7.[92] Apples were sold from the garden at Stanton Lacy in 1377–8 and in the following year the reeve at Earnwood bought tar to paint on the trees in the garden to stop the rabbits eating them.[93] There were several manorial orchards at High Ercall in 1424.[94]

The major part of the crops produced on the demesnes was consumed by livestock, including the oxen and other draught animals necessary for the cultivation

[89] S.P.L., Deeds 7190, 7322.
[90] S.R.O. 212, box 14, bailiff's acct. 8–9 Ric. II; box 80, bailiff's acct. 17–18 Edw. III.
[91] L.J.R.O., B/C/5, Lilleshall abbey acct. r. 1428–9; S.P.L., Deeds 4426.
[92] P.R.O., SC 6/965/2–4; S.P.L., Deeds 7233, 7238; *Ag. Hist. Eng.* ii. 473.
[93] P.R.O., SC 6/967/4; SC 6/967/27, m. 4.
[94] *T.S.A.S.* lxii. 32.

of the land. The chief plough beast remained the ox which was usually worked in teams of eight, although numbers varied from year to year as debilitated animals died or were sold and replaced by beasts purchased or brought from other manors.[95] There was considerable movement of animals between the manors of the large estates both for winter feeding and to make up the necessary ploughing numbers. There were 45 oxen at Clun in the early years of the 14th century and 39 at Caus in 1374 but only 16 in 1382 when the demesne arable was leased.[96] During 1343–4 there were 41 oxen on Ruyton manor: 6 from the previous year, 2 received as heriots, and 33 sent by the receiver of Chirk; 13 were handed over to the bailiffs of other manors, leaving 28 at the end of the year.[97] At Michaelmas 1373 there were 16 oxen on Cleobury Barnes manor but during the preceding year 8 oxen had come from Stanton Lacy and 8 had been handed over to the parker of Earnwood. During 1387–8 there were 14 oxen at Stanton Lacy: 8 remained from the previous year, 2 were sent from Orleton (Herefs.), 2 received as heriots, 2 purchased, 4 sold, and 4 slaughtered, leaving 8 at the end of the year.[98] In the later 14th century black, grey, brown, and red oxen were all noted on Wenlock priory's estate, and that hints at the mixed nature of the stock available to farmers.[99]

Affers—draught horses—are found in most of the surviving accounts, usually one horse for every seven or eight oxen, and the scant evidence does not suggest that the proportion of horses increased during the 14th century.[1] Although horses cost less to buy, they were more expensive to keep than oxen. It is unusual to find oxen being fed on vetch and peas as they were at Stanton Lacy for six weeks in the winter of 1377 when the hay and straw were said to be poor and the oxen weak, but affers regularly required additional rations of oats during heavy work, such as harrowing.[2] Although 21s. 6d. was spent on a horse for the plough at Adderley in 1323–4, that was at the height of the cattle murrain when the cost of oxen rose to between 15s. and 17s.[3] In 1331 the 66 oxen on the estates forfeited by the earl of March were valued at between 6s. 8d. and 8s. each and the 9 affers at between 3s. 4d. and 5s. each.[4] Horses were mainly used for harrowing and carting rather than ploughing (which was the ox's preserve) but two oxen were bought to pull the wool wagons at Clun in 1386–7.[5]

Regular outlay was necessary to maintain ploughs and other equipment. The 'cost of ploughs' at Adderley in the early 14th century was between 11s. and 15s. a year and included the repair of a wheeled plough.[6] The latter was not such a rarity in the county as has recently been claimed, and wheeled ploughs were also used on the demesnes at Ruyton, Upton Magna, Dodington, and Cleobury Barnes.[7] In 1331 ploughs with harrows on the manors forfeited by the earl of March were valued at 12d. or 16d., and at Ruyton a plough to break new land was bought in 1336–7 for 4d. and also a harrow (3d.), a seed basket (3d.), and a two-wheeled wain (*plaustrum*) at 3s. for the same assarting work.[8] Three of the burgages in Oswestry in 1301 owed the service of making a pair of ploughshares, valued at 1s. 6d., with the lord providing the iron.[9] In 1343–4 at Dodington a smith was paid 1s. 1d. for

[95] J. Langdon, *Horses, Oxen and Technological Innovation* (1986), 110–11, 127; P.R.O., SC 6/965/5, m. 1; SC 6/965/17, 24; S.P.L., Deeds 7531 (Upton Magna and Haughmond).
[96] S.R.O. 1093, box 1, view of acct. of lands of earl of Arundel, ?1310–13; *V.C.H. Salop.* viii. 317.
[97] S.P.L., Deeds 7265.
[98] P.R.O., SC 6/965/12; SC 6/1304/17.
[99] *T.S.A.S.* lviii. 73–6.
[1] Cf. Langdon, *Horses, Oxen and Tech. Innovation*, 88, 99.

[2] S.P.L., Deeds 7531 (Acton Round); P.R.O., SC 6/967/27, mm. 1–2, 4.   [3] P.R.O., SC 6/965/2, m. 6.
[4] P.R.O., E 142/68.   [5] S.R.O. 552/1A/8.
[6] P.R.O., SC 6/965/2–6.
[7] Langdon, *Horses, Oxen and Tech. Innovation*, 128–9, 133; S.P.L., Deeds 7323, 7531; P.R.O., SC 6/965/24; S.R.O. 212, box 80, bailiffs' accts. 7–8, 43–4 Edw. III; Staffs. R.O., D. 641/1/2/240. Cf. also above, Domesday Book to 1300 (Arable farming). [8] P.R.O., E 142/68; S.P.L., Deeds 7271.
[9] *Two Est. Surveys of Earls of Arundel*, 67.

dressing a pair of plough irons for the third plough newly set up (*de novo levato*) for the winter and spring sowings.[10] On the same estate 75 years later 2s. 10d. was spent on a set of new implements: a mattock (7d.), a seed basket (5d.), 8 hoes (8d.), a fork (2d.), 6 iron teeth for a fork (4d.), 3 plough staves (3d.), and 5 plough feet (5d.).[11] Carts and wagons were expensive pieces of equipment which required the attention of both smiths and carpenters. At Myddle 8s. 9½d. was spent on the ploughs in 1384–5 and 15s. 5d. on the wains and carts, including 11s. for a new wain.[12] A dung wain was forfeited as a deodand at Purslow in 1512. The 'draght' constructed at Cleobury Barnes in 1372–3 is thought to have been a sled or a harrow.[13]

As well as being spread as farmyard manure dung was also dropped directly on the soil by folding. In 1373 all 240 sheep remaining at Clunton and Kempton were sent after shearing to the reeve of Bicton, who grazed them on Weston's open-field land throughout September, presumably to prepare the ground for sowing with winter wheat.[14]

The principal chemical fertilizer in the Middle Ages was marl, which was being widely applied in Shropshire by the later 13th century, albeit in restricted quantities because of the expense of its extraction, transport, and spreading.[15] It was probably in north Shropshire that marl was most commonly applied, and the costs of marling assarts at Dodington in the 1340s show the esteem in which it was held. In preparation for the operation carts were repaired and fitted out and three-tined forks and a mattock bought. The work was done by farm servants, by tenants paid on a piecework basis, and by day labourers. About 32,500 heaped baskets of marl were dug, carried, and spread in 1342 and *c.* 13,400 in 1344; the costs of carriage and spreading totalled £9 13s. 7d. in 1342 and £4 11s. 8d. in 1344. In addition men had to be paid to dig the marl, two being so employed for six weeks in November and December 1343, and to drain the marl pit if it was flooded.

Lime too was applied to the soil, although its use in the later Middle Ages apparently remained restricted. At Dodington in the 1340s lime dressing seems to have accompanied the marling, and in 1342 two carters were paid 1s. for bringing lime from Corfham, a property of the same lord over 65 km. away.[16]

Arable farming was labour-intensive and the needs of the estates involved in arable cultivation were met in various ways, of which labour services were, by the beginning of the 14th century, the least significant.[17] The 1301 survey of the lordship of Oswestry records mainly seasonal services such as haymaking and reaping at harvest, and the performance of services was likely to be haphazard; the holders of five bondlands in Weston, for example, owed two days' ploughing at the two seasons, if they had a plough.[18] Commutation was already far advanced in many parts of the county by the beginning of the period: a holding in Little Wenlock which had carried ploughing, mowing, reaping, and carting services was leased at the beginning of the 14th century for three lives and an annual rent of 13s.[19] In 1328 at Ash Magna 11 bond tenants could pay 4d. instead of performing plough works and were given an allowance of 2d. instead of food by the lord.[20] At Ruyton in 1361–2 even the payment instead of customary works was relaxed in

[10] S.R.O. 212, box 80, bailiffs' accts. 15–16, 17–18 Edw. III.
[11] Ibid. box 81, bailiff's acct. 6–7 Hen. V.
[12] Ibid. box 14, bailiff's acct. 8–9 Ric. II.
[13] P.R.O., SC 6/965/12; S.R.O. 552/1/53.
[14] *Ag. Hist. Eng.* ii. 434.
[15] Above, Domesday Book to 1300 (Arable farming).

Rest of para. based on *Ag. Hist. Eng.* ii. 439–40.
[16] *Ag. Hist. Eng.* ii. 441.
[17] Above, Domesday Book to 1300 (Lords and tenants).
[18] *Two Est. Surveys of Earls of Arundel*, 65–7, 70, 72–3, 75.
[19] S.R.O. 1224/2/10, holding of Thos. Crasset.
[20] S.R.O. 212, box 17, extent of Whitchurch, 2 Edw. III.

case the tenants gave up their holdings; at Minsterley 9 of the tenants still performing labour services were allowed to commute them in 1378 for lack of plough beasts, and all services had been commuted by 1388.[21] At High Ercall all work services, apart from one day's love reap at harvest, had been commuted for money rents by 1399.[22] Even where customary labour services were still exacted they had to be supplemented by paid labour. At Kinnerley ploughs were hired in 1340–1 to 'repair the defects' in the winter and spring ploughing and harrowing that had been done by boon work. Customary tenants at Dodington were paid 2d. for each ploughing and 1d. for each harrowing and their reaping at harvest was supervised by an overseer (messor) who was paid 1½d. a day for 28 days.[23]

On each manor there was a small staff of full-time farm servants (famuli) and wage labour was recruited when necessary to help with seasonal and specialized work. The farm servants were paid in cash and food, carefully graded according to the job. The men who guided the ploughs (tentatores) were better paid than those who drove the oxen (fugatores). Large teams of ploughmen are found at Lydley in 1308 when half of the 16 farm servants were ploughmen, and there were four drivers and four ploughmen at Caus in 1374.[24] The ploughman at Ruyton in 1313 was paid 6s. a year and the driver 3s. 6d. Typically other farm servants would include carters, cowmen, shepherds, swineherds, dairymaids, and poultry-maids.[25] Casual labour was used for many tasks and paid at varying rates. At Stanton Lacy and Cleobury Barnes between 1373 and 1394 the cost per acre of harvesting, which involved reaping, collecting, tying, and carrying, was calculated at between 6d. and 11d.[26] Forty-three reapers, mostly women and several with Welsh names, were paid 2d. a day at Stanton Lacy in 1381; at Bicton in 1355 reaping by 60 Welsh customary tenants was paid at ½d. a day and the reapers at Stokesay in 1424–5 were women or Welsh or both.[27] Hoeing and haymaking were also done by piecework, sometimes supplemented by labour services. At Blakemere in 1418–19 the wheat was hoed and the meadows mown by wage labour but the hay was lifted and carried by customary tenants who were paid ½d. for each boon work.[28] Wage labour was also used for threshing and winnowing when the farm servants were not available to do the work.[29] In 1374–5 an extra ox driver was hired for the winter sowing at Cleobury Barnes because the farm servant was watching the sheep, and at Dodington in 1343–4 extra labour was employed to help the farm servants carry and spread marl.[30] Casual labour, usually women's or boys', was employed to sow peas and beans and scare birds from new seed.[31]

On most of the estates for which records survive arable cultivation was subordinate to animal husbandry and was intended to serve it by producing grain and hay for consumption by the livestock rather than for the market. Cattle rearing and dairying, horse breeding, and sheep farming and wool production were better suited to conditions over most of the county, required less labour, and were more amenable to central supervision than arable farming. Criminal records give some idea of the scale of stock rearing in the county: in 1327 Sir Hugh Mortimer complained that 28 horses, 60 oxen, 40 sheep, and 80 swine had been stolen from

[21] S.P.L., Deeds 7333; V.C.H. Salop. viii. 318.
[22] T.S.A.S. lxii. 23.
[23] S.P.L., Deeds 7236; S.R.O. 212, box 80, bailiffs' accts. 15–16, 43–4 Edw. III.
[24] V.C.H. Salop. ii. 86; viii. 317.
[25] S.P.L., Deeds 7322; P.R.O., E 358/18, m. 4; SC 6/965/2; SC 6/965/5, m. 1.
[26] P.R.O., SC 6/965/12, 15, 17, 21–5; SC 6/967/27; SC 6/1304/17.
[27] P.R.O., SC 6/967/27, m. 7; S.R.O. 552/1A/3; S.P.L., Deeds 9733.
[28] S.R.O. 212, box 81, bailiff's acct. 6–7 Hen. V.
[29] Ibid. box 14, bailiff's acct. 8–9 Ric. II; box 80, bailiff's acct. 51 Edw. III–1 Ric. II; P.R.O., SC 6/965/12.
[30] P.R.O., SC 6/965/15; S.R.O. 212, box 80, bailiff's acct. 17–18 Edw. III.
[31] e.g. P.R.O., SC 6/965/5, m. 4; S.P.L., Deeds 7190, 7234.

his manor of Chelmarsh and in 1331 Sir Fulk FitzWarin claimed to have lost 5 horses, 100 mares, 100 colts, 48 oxen, 40 bullocks, 40 cows, 40 heifers, 500 sheep, and 100 swine, valued at £1,000, as the result of a raid on Whittington.[32] A quarter of the cases recorded in the Shropshire peace roll between 1400 and 1414 are concerned in some way with cattle and, although the county was particularly vulnerable at that time to Welsh cattle thieves,[33] it is clear that cattle were very important in the agrarian economy of the county.[34] Cattle were brought into the county for rearing and fattening and the main point of entry from Wales was Oswestry, the chief cattle market for the region in the later Middle Ages.[35] Haughmond abbey used its grange at Aston to pasture animals bought at Oswestry before they were distributed to its other granges and cattle farms.[36] Shrewsbury, Whitchurch, Ludlow, Bridgnorth, Wem, and Newport also had markets specializing in the cattle trade.[37]

Although the earl of Arundel had begun to specialize in sheep farming in his marcher lordships by the beginning of the 14th century, there were 45 oxen, 1 bull, 44 cows, 7 steers, and 20 calves at Clun in the first decades of the century, and oxen and cows were moved round the Shropshire estates both for ploughing and for fattening for sale and the larder.[38] The earl's officials were still buying cows in the 1330s, and in 1350 there were 160 oxen and 121 cows on the earl's estates in Shropshire, including 19 oxen, 1 bull, and 17 cows at Kinnerton.[39] The manor of Adderley was used for a short-lived experiment when it came into the king's hands in 1318. That year 24 cattle were purchased for pasturing in the small park and sold at a profit of £3 5s. Next year 41 cattle were fattened at a profit of £4 13s. and a dairy herd was built up from a bull and 20 cows sent from Beverley (Yorks. E.R.) in January (a journey of 7½ days) and 6 cows purchased with their calves for £2 15s. 11d. A cowman was engaged at a wage of 4s. 9d. and a dairy was equipped with a churn, a tub, a bucket, 2 stone pots, a brass pan, 2 cheese vats, 2 presses, and a supply of linen and salt. The cheese and milk products of the herd were sold for £2 1s. in 1318–19 and £1 11s. 10d. in 1319–20 but then the cattle murrain struck and the remnants of the herd were sold off because they were weak or sterile, and the pasture of the small meadow was sold once more.[40] At Cleobury Barnes in the 1370s a small herd of cows was kept on the manor but other animals were brought in for fattening; in 1372–3 the pasture in Rowley park was used for 11 cattle brought from other manors and 23 animals brought from Wales, and in 1375–6 five of the 40 oxen and young beasts received from the household died of murrain in July and August before the remainder were handed back in November. The cattle were looked after by a herdsman who was paid 5s. a year, and when necessary another herdsman was hired for part of the year. Milch cows were leased out if they were strong enough after separation from their calves but in 1378–9 no one could be found to hire the five milch cows so they were left with their calves.[41]

Similar arrangements are found on estates in the northern part of the county. During 1368–9 there were on Whittington manor 3 bulls, 18 oxen (of which 11 were sold), 13 cows (of which 6 were sold), and 20 steers and heifers (of which 17 were sold); 6s. 8d. was received in milk rent for two of the cows.[42] Before the Black

[32] Cal. Pat. 1327–30, 215; 1330–4, 134.
[33] Above, pp. 76–7.
[34] Salop. Peace Roll, 1400–14, ed. E. G. Kimball (1959), 46–7; E.H.R. xcix. 549.
[35] Smith, 'Lordships of Chirk and Oswestry', 371.
[36] Cart. Haughmond, p. 11.   [37] Ag. Hist. Eng. iv. 492.
[38] S.P.L., Deeds 7531; S.R.O. 1093, box 1, view of acct. ?1310–13.
[39] S.R.O. 552/1/5; ibid. /1A/1.
[40] P.R.O., SC 6/965/3–5.
[41] P.R.O., SC 6/965/12, 15, 17, 21, 24.
[42] N.L.W., Aston Hall 5820.

Death a herd of cattle, 30 in 1341–2, was kept at Dodington and used mainly to produce meat for the lord's larder but there was a small income from milk rents and at the end of the 14th century Ankaret, the widowed Lady Talbot, revived the tradition of cattle rearing in the lordship of Blakemere. The grange at Yockings Gate was reconstructed and a small herd of dairy cattle, 25 in 1402, was established there under a dairymaid who was paid 7s. a year; the cows produced butter, cheese, and milk worth £2 8s. in 1402–3. That, however, was another ill-fated venture as 14 head of cattle were stolen in 1400 and in 1404 the whole herd was lost to the Welsh rebels.[43] Cattle rearing began again at Blakemere under Gilbert, Lord Talbot, and in 1418–19 there was a large herd consisting of 2 bulls, 35 oxen, 65 cows, 13 steers, 17 young oxen, 30 yearlings, and 41 calves, looked after by a cowman, but the herd was sold when exploitation of the demesne ceased in 1422.[44] A few years later the herd at Myddle, which had been kept at over 30 in 1422–4, was also sold.[45] There was still a demesne herd of some 30 head of cattle at Gatten in 1446–7, when the reeve accounted for £3 2s. 4d. for the farm of 17 milch cows, and also what seems to be a herd of wild cattle (*animalia silvestria*) consisting of a bull, 21 cows, 4 oxen, 10 bullocks, 16 steers, and 8 calves.[46] Cattle were kept by the canons of Lilleshall until the Dissolution. During the 15th century the bailiffs of their granges paid half-yearly milk rents and there were two dairies run by dairymaids. In October 1538 there were 18 oxen, a bull and 15 milch cows, 20 young steers and heifers, and 8 weaning cows at the home grange and 10 cows and a bull in Lubstree park, and 40 cheeses in the canons' dairy house.[47]

Shropshire demesnes were also used for the feeding and breeding of horses. Adderley manor played host to 11 of the king's cart horses, together with their carts and carters, between 1318 and 1324. Apart from a few months' absence on the Scottish campaign of 1322 and short periods when they were hired out for ploughing and carting (such as carrying wool from Newport to London in 1319–20), they spent most of the year at Adderley and were maintained on the manor. They were expensive guests as they were fed twice-daily rations of oats and their carters were paid at the rate of 4d. a day. During their stay at Adderley two of the horses died of murrain and another had to be sold because it became so weak.[48]

Several of the marcher lords maintained studs on their Shropshire lands: in the 1320s the Mortimer stud was wintered at Earnwood and the lords of Caus had a stud farm in Minsterley park during the later 14th century.[49] The earl of Arundel was, in this as in other matters, the most enterprising of the marcher lords and had four studs, two of them in Clun and Oswestry lordships.[50] In 1301 the stud of 40 mares at Clun was valued at £5 and that of 30 mares at Oswestry at £2 10s.[51] In 1302 Edward I ordered the studs to be seized and the better mares retained for his own use in part payment of a debt.[52] By the end of the 14th century there were two studs at Clun, one in Clun forest and the other in 'the park of Boror', and the Oswestry stud was divided between the upper and lower parks at

[43] Pollard, 'Fam. of Talbot in 15th cent.' 352–3; S.R.O. 212, box 80, bailiffs' accts. 15–16, 17–18 Edw. III; box 81, bailiff's acct. 3–4 Hen. IV; *Salop. Peace Roll 1400–14*, 60.

[44] Pollard, op. cit. 353–4; S.R.O. 212, box 81, bailiff's acct. 6–7 Hen. V.

[45] S.R.O. 212, box 14, bailiffs' accts. 9 Hen. V–1 Hen. VI, 1–2, 3–4, 5–6 Hen. VI.

[46] S.P.L., Deeds 6173, reeves' accts. 25–6 Hen VI.

[47] *V.C.H. Salop.* xi. 156–7; M. E. C. Walcott, 'Inventories and Valuations of Religious Houses', *Archaeologia*, xliii.

208–9; L.J.R.O., B/C/5, Lilleshall abbey acct. r. 1428–9, 1436–7. For milk rents and cow hiring see also S.R.O. 552/1/7, ct. 3 Mar. 1337; *T.S.A.S.* xliii. 44; below, 1540–1750 (Livestock and dairy farming).

[48] P.R.O., SC 6/965/3–5.

[49] P.R.O., SC 6/965/10–11; *V.C.H. Salop.* viii. 317.

[50] R. R. Davies, *Lordship and Society in the March of Wales 1282–1400* (1978), 120.

[51] *Two Est. Surveys of Earls of Arundel*, 52, 65.

[52] *Cal. Close 1296–1302*, 513.

Oswestry and Bromhurst park in Aston, near Oswestry.[53] There was a total of 26 great horses (6 of them stallions), 55 mares, 32 colts, and 33 foals on Arundel's marcher estates in the mid 14th century, and 214 horses were among his son's forfeited possessions at Clun and Oswestry in 1397.[54] Horses were moved between the studs; the largest numbers were kept in the forest stud at Clun, and the keeper of the stud there in 1400–1 accounted for 245 animals, including 151 mares, at the start of the year, of which 47 were carried off by the Welsh rebels, 11 were sold, and 8 died of murrain.[55] The horses ate large amounts of hay and oats and 'at the time of leaping the mares' the stallions were fed a bread made from peas.[56] Considerable sums were spent on the care of the horses in the studs: in 1362–3 the receiver of Oswestry accounted for £18 9s. 8½d. spent on the horses, including candles for the stables in winter, cloth for blankets, and sulphur, fur, and honey for treating mares with mange.[57] Horses from the studs were occasionally quartered on other Shropshire manors and cannot have been welcome guests. In 1313–14 the earl's destrier, Morel Lestrange, and a dozen or so colts spent varying periods at Ruyton, Wroxeter, Lydley, and Shrawardine and were fed oats and bran. The farrier of the lord of Great Ness was called in at Ruyton to treat the war horse and some of the colts for mange; he used pig fat, olive oil, and honey.[58] During the 14th century the receiver of Ruyton accounted regularly for the cost of looking after horses on their way between Oswestry and Clun; in 1360–1 the reeve of Wroxeter fed 12 cart horses which had come from London and in 1363–4 the reeve of Kinnerley spent 73s. 4d. on 8 war horses during a stay of 98 days: the sum covered the hire of a stable, 2 bu. of oats a day, and 2s. spent on medicine for a sick horse.[59]

Sheep were the most profitable stock reared on Shropshire demesnes. Evidence for sheep farming can be found in most parts of the county during the period but the poor soils of the Clee hills plateau, the south-west and central uplands, and parts of the north-west plain provided the best environment for the Clun or mountain sheep, a light-weight breed with polled head and white or mottled face which produced a fine, short-woolled fleece.[60] Most evidence for the size and management of flocks and the marketing of wool comes from the demesnes of the marcher lords, in particular the earl of Arundel's estates. For the FitzAlans sheep farming was big business, amenable to much closer central supervision than arable demesne farming, and much more profitable.[61] In 1301 the FitzAlans' Shropshire demesnes provided grazing for 900 sheep, with 460 more in the adjoining marcher lordships of Clun (300) and Oswestry (160); the figure for Clun, however, can hardly be accurate, representing only what was available at Bicton; in 1349 over 3,000 of Arundel's 5,385 sheep in Shropshire and the march were in the lordship of Clun.[62] In 1371–2 a bailiff or stock keeper at Clun directly managed nine flocks, each of about 240 sheep, kept in seven places; he was responsible for buying and selling sheep, supplying cart loads of hay to the flocks, paying the wages of seven shepherds, and arranging the washing and shearing of 1,945 sheep at the rate of 1d. for every ten sheep. In addition he organized transfers of sheep between flocks kept on other manors under the care of demesne officials.[63] Flocks were frequently

[53] Cal. Inq. Misc. iv, pp. 112–13.
[54] Ibid.; S.R.O. 552/1A/1.
[55] N.L.W., Aston Hall 5318; S.P.L., Deeds 9777; S.R.O. 552/1A/8, 11.
[56] N.L.W., Aston Hall 6918; S.P.L., Deeds 9777.
[57] N.L.W., Aston Hall 6918.
[58] S.P.L., Deeds 7322, 7531.

[59] Ibid. 5922, 7244, 7325, 7327, 9766.
[60] R. Trow-Smith, Hist. of Brit. Livestock Husbandry to 1700 (1957), 164.
[61] Davies, Lordship and Society, 118.
[62] Two Est. Surveys of Earls of Arundel, 59, 65, 74, 76, 79, 81; S.R.O. 1093, box 1, view of acct. 28 Sept. 1349; cf. S.R.O. 552/1A/1.   [63] S.R.O. 552/1A/10.

moved between manors: in 1313-14, for example, a flock spent the winter months at Wroxeter before being driven to Clun, and in 1372-3 the bailiff of Clunton and Kempton handed over 240 sheep to the reeve of Bicton to stock a new grange there but received in his turn 237 hoggets (yearling sheep) from the reeve of Clunbury.[64] Sheep could be kept on manors where there was no longer any demesne arable. At Upton Magna, where the demesne had been leased before 1300, a new sheepcot was built in 1313-14 and 24 a. were assarted to provide oats and straw for a flock of sheep sent from Clun; in 1381 the farmer of the demesnes at 'Neuton' and Bicton in Clun (where four flocks totalling 981 sheep were pastured in 1371-2) was ordered to provide enough litter for the sheep kept there.[65]

In 1349 the earl of Arundel had 422 sheep in the lordship of Oswestry and 452 in Ruyton. The Oswestry flock, which was kept at Llwyn-y-mapsis in Sweeney township, was maintained at just over 500 sheep in the early 1360s; in 1394-5 there were 260 sheep in the flock but by then there was another flock at Sandford.[66] Sheep had been kept at Sandford before the manor was acquired by the earl of Arundel in the 1360s but were reintroduced only when it proved difficult to find tenants for the demesnes in the late 1370s; a flock of about 300 was kept there until the spring of 1397 when the remaining sheep were sold, the shepherd paid off, and the sheepcot leased.[67] The most detailed accounts survive for the flock at Ruyton. There was an inauspicious start to sheep farming there in 1319-20 when 176 sheep were sent from Kempton, in Clunbury, and a shepherd engaged to look after the new flock; 30 of the sheep died of murrain and another 30 had to be sold. No more sheep are recorded at Ruyton until 1335-6 when there were 232 left at the end of the year after 32 had been killed for the larder.[68] The flock was then increased by purchase and transfer from Oswestry to a peak of 969 sheep in 1344-5; after that it was reduced by sales and natural wastage to between 400 and 450 in the late 1340s and early 1350s. In 1354-5 murrain reduced the flock by 35 per cent to 252 and it was maintained at that level for the rest of the 14th century (Table IV).[69]

There is little detailed information on the size and management of other demesne flocks. When Lydley Hayes demesne was leased in 1316 the stock leased with it comprised 240 sheep, 22 oxen, and 22 cows. In 1374 there were 879 sheep at Caus

TABLE IV: RUYTON-XI-TOWNS: THE FLOCK IN SELECTED YEARS

	beginning of year	bought	sold	died	end of year	fleeces
1336-7	232	190	26	12	406	467
1339-40	622	120	54	175	513	315
1344-5	721	236	151	16	769	720
1346-7	515	6	225	182	421	461
1352-3	480	64	79	31	444	441
1356-7	254	40	25	20	248	248
1366-7	240	147	95	56	220	232
1379-80	246	137	18	80	285	293
1386-7	261	72	60	12	261	269

Sources: S.P.L., Deeds 7189, 7192, 7203, 7266, 7271, 7327, 7334, 7338, 7340.

[64] Ibid. /1A/4; S.P.L., Deeds 7531.
[65] S.P.L., Deeds 7531; S.R.O. 552/1/20; ibid. /1A/10.
[66] S.R.O. 1093, box 1, view of acct. 28 Sept. 1349; N.L.W., Aston Hall 6918; S.P.L., Deeds 9777; Smith,
'Lordships of Chirk and Oswestry', 144-5.
[67] N.L.W., Aston Hall 5308, 5348, 5769, 5771, 5784; Smith, op. cit. 464. [68] S.P.L., Deeds 7186, 7323, 7328-9.
[69] Ibid. Deeds 7266, 7335.

and Wallop of which 352 died of murrain during the year and the flock had shrunk to 439 when it was recorded for the last time in 1402; in 1385 the demesne meadows at Cound supported over 300 sheep but none remained by 1416 when the hay from the meadows was being sold annually.[70] The Stranges kept sheep on their manors of Dodington and Blakemere during the 14th century and there was close co-operation between the manors. In 1341–2 there was a flock of 247 milking ewes at Dodington of which 89 were sent to Blakemere and the rest died of murrain before shearing and lambing. During 1343–4 Blakemere sent 271 lambs to Dodington, and the 134 hoggets which remained at Dodington at the end of the year were handed over to the bailiff of Blakemere. In 1369–70 the 420 wethers kept at Blakemere were sold off after shearing but there were 241 sheep on the manor in 1379–80 and 210 in 1381–2.[71] Small flocks of sheep are found on the Mortimer manors of Cleobury Barnes and Stanton Lacy in the last quarter of the 14th century as part of a mixed farming enterprise. At Cleobury Barnes 200 sheep were fattened for the household in 1375–6, and in May 1380 the bailiff of Stanton Lacy bought 227 sheep at Knighton and sold 72 of them to the household after shearing. No tithes were due on sheep bought and sold in the same year and in 1376 the bailiff of Stanton Lacy bought 260 sheep for £15 15s. 5½d. in May and sold 240 of them to a Leominster merchant for £14 after shearing; by 1390 the number purchased had risen to 302, of which 294 were sold after shearing to a Hereford dealer, but in 1393 that enterprise ended with the 'sale' of the 184 sheep remaining on the manor to the receiver of Wigmore.[72]

Sheep farming remained important to the economies of the larger religious houses in the county after the decline of the arable demesnes, but little evidence survives.[73] They continued to keep sheep long after the great lay lords had abandoned their demesne flocks. When the abbot and convent of Haughmond leased Downton grange in 1465 they reserved the use of the sheepfold and half a croft and common pasture for their sheep, and the lessee had to cart six loads of hay a year to the sheepfold and provide enough straw for the sheep.[74] During the 15th century a small flock was kept on the home grange at Lilleshall: 20 wethers were bought for it in 1428–9 and in 1436–7 a man was paid 2s. to look after the lambs which were fed on milk from the dairy at Atcham; there were 40 sheep and lambs on the grange at the Dissolution.[75]

Daily custody and care of the sheep was in the hands of shepherds, engaged by the flock managers or manorial officials. One shepherd could look after a flock of about 250, as at Ruyton in the later 14th century, but two or three shepherds were employed earlier in the century when between 700 and 900 sheep were kept on the manor, and the flock manager paid six shepherds to look after 2,000 sheep at Clun in 1371–2.[76] The shepherds were sometimes provided with additional help during lambing, and the cost of washing and shearing was accounted for separately, according to the number of sheep.[77] On manors where there were no permanent flocks shepherds were taken on temporarily and paid by the week.[78] Shepherds employed all year were paid between 3s. and 10s., usually with an allowance of oats. There was no standard wage for shepherds on the Arundel estates. Shepherds

[70] S.R.O. 567, box 10, deed of 20 Nov. 1316; *V.C.H. Salop.* viii. 66, 317.

[71] S.R.O. 212, box 80, bailiffs' accts. 15–16, 17–18, 43–4 Edw. III, 2–3 Ric. II.

[72] P.R.O., SC 6/965/17; SC 6/967/27, mm. 8, 10–12; SC 6/1304/17. [73] *V.C.H. Salop.* ii. 20.

[74] *Cart. Haughmond*, p. 75 (no. 300).

[75] *V.C.H. Salop.* xi. 157; L.J.R.O., B/C/5, Lilleshall abbey acct. r. 1428–9, 1436–7.

[76] S.R.O. 552/1A/10; S.P.L., Deeds 7190, 7267, 7341.

[77] S.R.O. 212, box 80, bailiff's accts. 17–18 Edw. III; 552/1A/10; S.P.L., Deeds 7335, 7531 (Upton Magna).

[78] P.R.O., SC 6/967/27, mm. 8, 10; SC 6/1304/17; S.P.L., Deeds 7531 (Wroxeter).

at Ruyton were paid 4s. in 1313, 3s. in 1335–6, 5s. in 1347–8, 6s. in 1361–2, and 6s. 8d. in 1387–8; those at Oswestry 5s. in 1362–3 and 6s. 8d., with a livery of 4 bu. of rye, in 1394–5; and the shepherd at Sandford was paid 7s. in 1380–1.[79] Most generously treated was Richard Perkyn who was engaged as a shepherd by the abbot of Lilleshall in 1398; he was to be paid 10s. a year, with 2 ells of Welsh cloth, 4 qr. 2 bu. of rye, and salt and oats for his pottage, and he was promised a place in an almshouse when he could no longer carry out his duties.[80] Sometimes a house was provided for the shepherd in the grange or on the sheep walk; 40s. was spent at Ruyton in 1386–7 to make a new grange and shepherd's house at Coton, and expenditure on a new pinfold and sheep pens followed.[81]

The demesne flocks were pastured on hills and heaths and any arable land when it was common or fallow; in winter they were fed with hay and sometimes with peas and vetches, and with oats for milking ewes and milk and bran for lambs.[82] Apart from extra attention during lambing, such as the provision of fern or pea straw litter, care was rudimentary.[83] The accounts record frequent purchases of red stone for marking the sheep, and a sheep bell costing 3d. was bought for Stanton Lacy in 1385–6 after some sheep had been killed by dogs.[84] Tallow and oil were bought to waterproof the sheep; 'tarpitch' and verdigris for treating cuts, sheep scab, and foot rot; and considerable amounts of ointment for unspecified ailments.[85] Disease took a heavy toll of flocks, and the recorded deaths in individual flocks confirm the evidence in the 1340 lay subsidy of the devastating effects of sheep murrain in the county. The bailiff at High Ercall reported the deaths of 16 rams, 21 ewes, 2 hogs, and 9 lambs in 1338–9; 146 of the 169 ewes in the demesne flock at Dodington in 1341–2 died of murrain before lambing and 28 per cent of the flock at Ruyton died in 1339–40.[86] In the 30 years between 1319 and 1394 for which deaths are recorded in the dry, non-breeding flock at Ruyton an average of 14 per cent a year died of disease and, in addition to 1339–40, losses were exceptionally high in 1346–7, 1348–9, 1354–5, 1358–9, and 1379–80.[87] Thirty-six per cent of the flock at Sandford in 1396–7 died before it was sold off.[88] Deaths were carefully recorded as either before or after shearing, and in the lordship of Clun the casualty figures were checked by the inspectors of the carcasses of the lord's sheep (cadaveratores).[89] Most of the demesne flocks for which records survive were non-breeding and numbers were made up by purchase while weak and surplus sheep were sold off. At Stanton Lacy the flock was increased by sheep bought at Knighton and animals were sold to dealers from Hereford and Leominster; as well as purchasing the tithe lambs of Clun, the flock manager at Clun in 1371–2 was buying sheep at Knighton and in 1341–2 the bailiff of Ruyton sent sheep to be sold at the new fair at Shrewsbury.[90]

The short-woolled sheep of the Shropshire demesne flocks did not produce heavy fleeces. Fleeces sold from the flock at Stanton Lacy between 1385 and 1393 weighed on average between 1.3 lb. and 1.9 lb.[91] There is insufficient evidence to show how far disease may have affected fleece weights but at Ruyton fleece weights

[79] S.P.L., Deeds 7322, 7330, 7333, 7341, 9777; N.L.W., Aston Hall 5771, 6918.
[80] S.R.O. 972, box 219, deed 9 Oct. 1398.
[81] S.P.L., Deeds 7338, 7341–2; V.C.H. Salop. viii. 133.
[82] S.P.L., Deeds 7190, 7266, 7330, 7531 (Upton Magna); S.R.O. 212, box 80, bailiffs' accts. 5–6, 43–4 Edw. III; 522/1A/10. [83] S.P.L., Deeds 7330, 7531 (Upton Magna).
[84] P.R.O., SC 6/967/27, m. 10; S.R.O. 552/1A/2, 10.
[85] e.g. S.R.O. 212, box 80, bailiff's accts. 5–6, 15–16 Edw. III; 552/1A/10; S.P.L., Deeds 7266, 7325; N.L.W., Aston

Hall 5784.
[86] T.S.A.S. lxii. 28; S.R.O. 212, box 80, bailiff's acct. 15–16 Edw. III; S.P.L., Deeds 7189.
[87] S.P.L., Deeds 7192, 7268, 7321, 7335, 7340.
[88] N.L.W., Aston Hall 5784.
[89] S.R.O. 552/1/26 (cts. 27 Sept., 19 Dec. 1397), 27 (cts. 18 Oct. 1396, 9 and 30 May 1397).
[90] Ibid. /1A/10; P.R.O., SC 6/967/27, mm. 8, 10–11; S.P.L., Deeds 7190.
[91] P.R.O., SC 6/967/27, mm. 10–12; SC 6/1304/17.

of 1.5 lb. in 1336–7 had risen to 1.8 lb. in 1370–1.[92] The market value of the fleeces was high: in the surviving wool price schedules for the 14th and 15th centuries Shropshire wool was second in value only to Herefordshire wool.[93] In 1337 the king ordered the purchase for export of 1,500 sacks of wool in Shropshire at a price of £7 a sack, compared with £8 a sack for Herefordshire wool.[94]

Price schedules give an idea of the comparative value of Shropshire wool but the price actually received by the producers varied according to the amount of wool available for sale and the way in which it was marketed. Buildwas abbey may have been exporting its wool directly at the beginning of the period but most of the wool produced by the Shropshire monasteries was probably sold locally in the later Middle Ages. Shrewsbury was emerging in the period as the centre of the wool trade along the English border and in the Welsh marches, and in 1326 it was named as a staple town.[95] In 1339 merchants from Bridgnorth and Ludlow as well as from Shrewsbury are found exporting wool through London.[96] By the 15th century monastic marketing of wool was on a very modest scale: in 1428–9 and 1436–7 the treasurer of Lilleshall abbey sold about £10 worth of wool a year, mostly in small amounts to women for spinning.[97] Stanton Lacy in the last quarter of the 14th century is an example of a manor where wool from a demesne flock was marketed directly. Between 177 and 300 fleeces a year were sold to merchants from Hereford or Leominster at prices varying between 3½d. and 4d. a lb., or up to £6 13s. 4d. a sack. Three hundred fleeces (1¼ sacks) were sold for £5 16s. 8d. in 1389–90; that represented a profit for the year of £2 13s. or 2d. a sheep.[98]

It was more usual on the larger estates for the fleeces, after the deduction of tithes, to be sent to a centre where the sale of large quantities of wool could be negotiated; only the lockets and skins of dead sheep were sold off the individual manors. In the early 14th century fleeces from the bishop of Coventry and Lichfield's manor of Prees were sent to Haywood in Staffordshire; in 1307–8 over 8 sacks of wool, to which Prees had contributed over 300 fleeces, were sold for c. £8 a sack.[99] Clun was the collection centre for wool produced on the earl of Arundel's extensive manors. After deduction of tithes and sometimes a rough calculation of their value (see Table V), the fleeces were carried to Clun where the wool was weighed and sorted, a task that took the steward and auditor three days to supervise in 1387.[1] That year there were 2,505 fleeces, weighing 9 sacks 9 stones, to be dealt with and added to 10 sacks which had been kept in store from the previous year.[2] Few details survive of the mechanics of sale but the wool was probably taken up to London. In 1395 the receiver of Oswestry was informed from Arundel that 2,143 fleeces from the flocks at Ruyton, Sandford, and Llwyn-y-mapsis, which had been collected at Oswestry over the previous three years, had been sold to a London merchant.[3] The profit level is difficult to gauge: in the early years of Edward II's reign wool sales from Clun were nearly £400 a year with the clear profit estimated at over £170 a year, and in 1376 wool from the FitzAlan estates in Surrey, Sussex, and the march was sold for £2,041 6s. 8d.[4] For

[92] S.P.L., Deeds 7271, 9766. The weights are calculated on a stone of 8 lb. (S.P.L., Deeds 7271; P.R.O., SC 6/967/27, m. 12): cf. R. E. Zupko, *Dict. of Eng. Weights and Measures* (1968), s.vv. sack, stone; D. Postles, 'Fleece weights and the wool supply, c. 1250–c. 1350', *Textile Hist.* xii. 96–103.
[93] J. H. Munro, 'Wool-price schedules and the qualities of Eng. wools c. 1270–1499', *Textile Hist.* ix. 121, 131, 137, 141, 147, 154; above, Domesday Book to 1300 (Livestock and pastoral farming). [94] *Cal. Pat.* 1334–8, 480.
[95] *V.C.H. Salop.* ii. 53; T. H. Lloyd, *Eng. Wool Trade in*

Middle Ages (1977), 54–5, 115; *Cart. Haughmond*, p. 10.
[96] P.R.O., E 356/8, mm. 4d.–5.
[97] L.J.R.O., B/C/5, Lilleshall abbey acct. r. 1428–9, 1436–7.
[98] P.R.O., SC 6/967/27, mm. 10–12; SC 6/1304/17.
[99] *V.C.H. Staffs.* vi. 23.
[1] S.R.O. 552/1A/3, 8; N.L.W., Chirk Cast. D 26; ibid. Aston Hall 5308, 5771, 6918.
[2] S.R.O. 552/1A/8. [3] S.P.L., Deeds 9777.
[4] S.R.O. 1093, box 1, view of acct. ?1310–13; Davies, *Lordship and Society*, 119; L. F. Salzman, 'Property of the Earl of Arundel, 1397', *Suss. Arch. Collns.* xci. 34.

TABLE V: RUYTON-XI-TOWNS: VALUE OF
FLEECES

	no. of fleeces	value	value per fleece
		£ s. d.	d.
1365–6	217	9	10
1366–7	220	10	11
1370–1	212	10	11
1379–80	270	11	10
1386–7	247	6 13 4	6½
1387–8	241	8	8
1391–2	243	6 13 4	6½
1392–3	233	6 13 4	7

Sources: S.P.L., Deeds 7325, 7327, 7338, 7340–1, 7343–4, 9766.

the earl of Arundel at least the rewards of sheep farming in the 14th century were evidently worth the high level of organization involved.

Herds of pigs were kept on the demesnes but they are mostly found at the beginning of the period before many manors were given over to specialized sheep farming. There were 74 pigs and 8 goats among the demesne stock at Clun in the early years of Edward II's reign and 101 pigs at Ruyton in 1313, of which 39 died of murrain.[5] Pigs were moved between the FitzAlan manors for fattening: in 1313–14 there were 145 pigs at Shrawardine of which 20 had come from Ruyton, 33 from Clun, and 7 from Whitchurch, and by the end of the year they had reached the lord's larder, 75 of them in the form of flitches of bacon.[6] A small herd of pigs was kept at Adderley as a commercial enterprise in the unusual conditions of 1318–24. In 1318 the herd was established with the purchase of 33 pigs for £3 10s. 6d.; they were sold next year for £5 15s. and 18 more bought for £2 15s. In 1321–2 six were sold from the herd of 30 for 3s. 1d. each and next year the price reached 4s. for each pig sold but fell in 1323–4 to 2s. 1d. each.[7] The demesne herd at Dodington rose from 21 in 1333–4 to 46 in 1341–2 and 61 in 1343–4; some of the young pigs were sold but most were destined for the larder.[8] There were 60 pigs on the demesne at Stokesay in 1395–6.[9] Demesne pigs were fed on peas and beans and, though a pigman was employed for part of the year at Adderley, it was usual to combine the care of the pigs with that of the dairy cattle; at the beginning of the 15th century there was a small herd of pigs at Blakemere in the dairy at Yockings Gate.[10]

Other foodstuffs were reared on the demesnes, sometimes for sale but more usually for lords' larders. There was a flock of geese and several dozen chickens at Acton Round in the early 14th century and in 1314 the bailiff paid Roger le Voulare 3½d. a day for 14 days to catch partridges and supplied him with 2 chickens for his falcon; at the same time the bailiff of Wroxeter was feeding 2 bu. of wheat to the partridges.[11] Later in the century there was a flock of geese and eight swans on the demesne at Dodington and in addition several hundred hens were received each year as a payment for being allowed to cut turves and most of them were handed over to feed the lord's household or his falcons.[12] At Kinnerley the hens received by the bailiff were sold but at Stanton Lacy they were kept and their eggs

[5] S.R.O. 1093, box 1, view of acct. ?1310–13; S.P.L., Deeds 7322.
[6] S.P.L., Deeds 7531.
[7] P.R.O., SC 6/965/2–5.
[8] S.R.O. 212, box 80, bailiffs' accts. 7–8, 15–16, 17–18 Edw. III.
[9] S.P.L., Deeds 7526.
[10] S.R.O. 212, box 81, bailiffs' accts. 3–4 Hen. IV, 6–7

Hen. V.; S.P.L., Deeds 7322, 7531 (Acton Round); P.R.O., SC 6/965/5, m. 2.
[11] S.R.O. 1093, box 1, view of acct. ?1310–13; S.P.L., Deeds 7531.
[12] S.R.O. 212, box 80, bailiffs' accts. 15–16, 17–18 Edw. III.

were sold.[13] Geese were bred for market at both Stanton Lacy and Cleobury Barnes in the late 14th century, and there were several dozen capons among the demesne stock at Stokesay at the same period.[14] The only stock accounted for at Kinnerley in the 1330s were pigeons; 232 were produced in 1336-7, of which 146 were sold, and they were being fed on oats in winter.[15] In 1379-80 a new dovecot cost 25s. 8d. at Stanton Lacy; it was much cheaper that the one built at Blakemere in 1431-2 for £6 10s. but Blakemere supplied 1,222 pigeons to Lady Talbot's household in 1410.[16] Warrens, too, continued to be a feature on many, if not most demesnes. In 1337 rabbits, hares, pheasants, and partridges were stolen from Joan Talbot's warrens in Richard's Castle, and those were probably the creatures most commonly kept.[17] In the 14th century rabbits apparently began to escape the warren's confines; in 1377-8 the reeve of Earnwood painted the trees there with tar to prevent their being eaten by rabbits,[18] and in 1454 William Newport of High Ercall promised to keep his rabbits off his tenants' crops provided that they agreed to keep their hunting dogs away from the rabbits.[19] Manorial stews and fisheries provided fish for the lord's household: at Myddle in the 1420s and 1430s several hundred eels were caught each year and sent to the household or sold, but the fishery was farmed out by 1443-4.[20]

Whether or not the lords chose to exploit their demesnes directly they had considerable control over the resources of the countryside. In the 14th century marcher lords were advancing, and largely establishing, the claim that 'the pasture, forest, waste and water of the lordship in general were also part of their demesne in the broadest sense'.[21] Such a claim, with the implication that others could be forced to pay for the use or abuse of those resources, was of great significance in a county that was largely pastoral and still extensively wooded. Pasture was the demesne resource which was most in demand by others and which was amenable to exploitation in the most flexible fashion. Meadows were usually the last part of the demesne to be leased and the hay which was produced in large quantities (162 cart loads from nine meadows at Blakemere in 1402-3 and nearly 50 wagon loads a year at Stanton Lacy in the 1380s) was used for the demesne stock or sold.[22] Hay was highly profitable, and in the lordship of Oswestry extra income came from the sale of the aftermath or *ruannum*.[23] Where pasture was not required for demesne herds considerable sums could be raised by the sale of herbage or by the agistment of tenants' cattle.[24] In the last quarter of the 14th century the manor of Stanton Lacy was being intensively exploited and pasture proved a valuable asset; the herbage of uncultivated demesne and of the orchards and gardens was sold and meadow was offered for sale by the acre. In 1374-5 36 a. fetched £6 4s. 10d. and in 1379-80 45 a. were sold for £9 1s. 9½d., two portions of 4½ a. significantly going to Ludlow butchers.[25] When there was sufficient demand agistment could be more profitable than herbage: at Cleobury Barnes in 1378-9 a field which had been sold for herbage for 4s. earned 10s. 6d. when agisted.[26] The parks which were expensively maintained for the lord's deer provided additional pasture for herbage and

[13] S.P.L., Deeds 7233; P.R.O., SC 6/967/27, mm. 1, 12.
[14] P.R.O., SC 6/965/12; SC 6/967/27, mm. 1-2; S.P.L., Deeds 7526.   [15] S.P.L., Deeds 7233, 7234.
[16] P.R.O., SC 6/967/27, m. 8; S.R.O. 212, box 85, bailiff's acct. 7-8 Hen. V and household accts. 11-13 Hen. IV.
[17] Cal. Pat. 1334-8, 448.
[18] P.R.O., SC 6/967/27, m. 4.
[19] S.R.O. 212, box 85, household accts. 11-13 Hen. IV; S.P.L., Deeds 7531 (Shrawardine); S.P.L., MS. 301, p. 38; Staffs. R.O., D. 938/692.
[20] S.R.O. 212, box 14, bailiffs' accts. 1-2, 3-4, 7-8, 10-

11, 21-2 Hen. VI.   [21] Davies, Lordship and Society, 120-1.
[22] Smith, 'Lordships of Chirk and Oswestry', 117-18, 120, 147; S.R.O. 212, box 81, bailiff's acct. 3-4 Hen. IV; P.R.O., SC 6/965/2; SC 6/967/27, mm. 4, 8; S.P.L., Deeds 7188; V.C.H. Salop. viii. 66; above (Assarting and inclosure).
[23] Smith, op. cit. 287; N.L.W., Aston Hall 5305, 6918; S.P.L., Deeds 7327.
[24] e.g. Smith, op. cit. 288; S.P.L., Deeds 7240; S.R.O. 212, box 14, ct. 3 Aug. 1380; N.L.W., Aston Hall 5770.
[25] P.R.O., SC 6/967/27, mm. 2, 5, 10.
[26] P.R.O., SC 6/965/24.

agistment.[27] At Adderley in 1318-19 the lord's animals were pastured in the small park but £2 17s. 4½d. was collected for the herbage of affers and cattle in the great park, and in the park at Cleobury Barnes 35 cattle were agisted for between 4d. and 1s. a head in 1377-8.[28]

Many lords kept one or more parks in the 14th and 15th centuries, especially in central and eastern Shropshire. Between 1350 and 1370 there was a flurry of park creations with 11 or so new ones being formed.[29] It seems likely that in many of the 11 cases imparkment was part of the readjustment by lords to the new conditions prevailing after the Black Death, although in no case is that certain. As before parks continued to be used as demesne enclosures for stock and woodland, and for hunting. When Myddle park was broken into c. 1314 not only deer, but 24 mares, 16 colts, and 80 oxen were stolen.[30] In some woods in the county there were large numbers of deer in the late Middle Ages, and stocks had perhaps risen appreciably since the early 14th century as the population level fell and the pressure on land, especially marginal land, lessened. In Hogstow forest, actually an extensive tract of private woodland in Minsterley, deer were so plentiful that the hilly ground around Hope could not be cultivated, and Hogstow still contained 600 fallow deer in 1521.[31] The woods around Clun were also well stocked with deer, and in the 14th century the FitzAlans could take at least 70 a year.[32] Those deer were better protected than the ones in the royal forest of Morfe where it was reported that the king's deer had no browsing because of the large numbers of sheep and pigs commoned in the forest by the surrounding townships.[33] Woodland resources were jealously husbanded by the parkers and forest officials of the marcher lords. Heavy fines were imposed for putting cattle on woodland pasture without licence and in 1344 five men were amerced £4 16s. in Clun for claiming that a wood was theirs alone 'to the prejudice of the lord'.[34] A charge of 1d. a horse or head of cattle was levied for winter agistment in Clun forest and the charge was doubled in the summer; payment was made for over 500 animals in 1387 and over 100 horses were agisted each year at the beginning of the 16th century.[35]

Throughout the county parks, woods, and forests provided food, in the form of nuts, acorns, and berries, for large numbers of pigs. Goats were detested for their destructiveness and were kept out of the woods,[36] but pigs were encouraged between Michaelmas and Martinmas, provided mast was available and pannage dues paid. The amount charged for pannage and the associated payment known as tack, wormtack, or greystack varied according both to the manor and to the number and ages of the pigs, and payment was made both in money and in pigs for the lord's larder. The rules governing pannage appear complex and often obscure but it is clear from the accounts that pannage yielded a regular and considerable income from the 14th[37] to the 16th[38] centuries.

[27] V.C.H. Salop. viii. 107, 204; Leland, Itin. ed. Toulmin Smith, iv. 2; Cal. Pat. 1334-8, 448; N.L.W., Aston Hall 5356, 6918; S.P.L., Deeds 9071, 9766; S.R.O. 212, box 73, receivers' accts. 13 and 37 Hen. VI; P.R.O., SC 6/967/9.
[28] P.R.O., SC 6/965/2, 21. See also V.C.H. Salop. viii. 297-8; S.R.O. 212, box 14, parker's acct. 1-2 Ric. II; 956/1; S.P.L., Deeds 9768, ct. 9 Aug. 1384; Staffs. R.O., D. 641/1/2/240.
[29] L. Cantor, Med. Parks of Eng.: Gazetteer (Loughborough, 1983), 63-4. [30] Cal. Pat. 1313-17, 250.
[31] V.C.H. Salop. viii. 298.
[32] Two Est. Surveys of Earls of Arundel, 52; Leland, Itin. ed. Toulmin Smith, ii. 27. [33] P.R.O., DL 39/1/26.
[34] T.S.A.S. 3rd ser. i. 214-15; S.R.O. 552/1/11, m. 1; ibid. /1/20, ct. 18 Oct. 1380.

[35] S.R.O. 552/1/4, 9, 20, 50-1, 53-4.
[36] B.L. Add. Ch. 54387, m. 3; S.P.L., Deeds 6171, ct. 6 May 1451; Cal. Chart. R. 1427-1516, 213.
[37] Two Est. Surveys of Earls of Arundel, 51, 65, 76, 79, 81 (Acton Round, Clun forest, Oswestry, Shrawardine, and Upton Magna 1301); S.R.O. 552/1/4, 9, 20, 22; /1A/5, 13 (Clun forest 1334-1422); T.S.A.S. 3rd ser. i. 226 (Ruyton 1353-1412); S.R.O. 567/2A/40 (Longnor 1356); S.R.O. 212, box 14, parker's acct. 1-2 Ric. II, bailiff's acct. 9 Hen. V-1 Hen. VI (Myddle); V.C.H. Salop. xi. 41 (Madeley 1379-1449); S.P.L., Deeds 16330 (Albrighton 22 Oct. 1422, Lilleshall 16 Oct 1422), 19394 (Wrockwardine 7 Dec. 1397); S.P.L., MS. 345, ct. 27 Sept. 1425 (Prees).
[38] Clwyd R.O. (Hawarden), DD/WY/5483, p. 7 (Hogstow forest 1519-20); S. Garbet, Hist. Wem (Wem, 1818), 116.

The woods had other resources which could be exploited. Standing timber was a convenient capital reserve for landlords, and at the end of the 14th century Richard, Lord Talbot, sold over £800 worth of timber from Blakemere in 13 years.[39] Brushwood and branches were sold for firewood and supplementary winter feed for stock, and those who attempted to help themselves were heavily fined.[40] Licences were required to dig clay and cut peat or turves.[41] Even the birds and the bees were appropriated to the lord's use. Bird traps in the woods were leased out and swarms of bees were the lord's property.[42] Beehives (bykes) were kept in the woods and women employed to collect the honey. Sometimes the hives were leased in return for half the produce: in 1395–6 the bailiff at Blakemere accounted for 46 hives, 4 of which were in the hands of tenants. In 1313 the bailiff of Ruyton sold 3 gallons of honey from 4 bykes and a century later 13 bykes at Blakemere produced 8 gallons of honey and 16 gallons of mead.[43] In the 1380s over 20 gallons of honey were produced and consumed at Clun each year and 50 gallons of honey at Oswestry in 1397 were valued at 7d. a gallon.[44]

The building, maintenance, and use of a mill was another way in which the lord controlled and exploited his tenants and one which had been recently imposed on the Welsh communities of the march.[45] In 1301 the bond tenants of the lordships of Clun and Oswestry were obliged to cart millstones and timber for repairs and as late as 1401 a fine of £1 was imposed on a tenant in the Upper Gorddwr in the welshry of Caus who refused to carry timber to the mill.[46] The building of a new mill represented a considerable investment of money and labour and the cost was recouped by the maintenance of a monopoly of grinding corn or fulling cloth for the lords' mills.[47] Shrewsbury abbey's monopoly of grinding in Shrewsbury was the cause of a lengthy dispute and was not broken until 1328; it is not surprising that mills were singled out for attack in the Welsh raids of the 15th century.[48] The valuation placed on mills fluctuated with changing economic conditions and many were reported to be in a ruinous condition in the mid 14th century.[49] Even so it was not difficult to find tenants who were prepared to take long leases with heavy rents, sometimes—in the 14th century at least—paid in corn, and with the obligation to keep the mills in good repair.[50] Although the income from mills probably declined on most estates with the erosion of seigneurial authority and monopoly, as it certainly did on those of the Talbot family, it formed for the monastic houses a small but useful source of revenue throughout the period.[51] At the Dissolution the revenue from Haughmond abbey's 26 mills made up over 7 per cent of the total income of the house.[52] Five of the mills were fulling mills,[53] and it appears that, perhaps especially in the 14th century, there had been a considerable increase in the number of such mills in the county serving its

[39] Pollard, 'Fam. of Talbot in 15th cent.' 375–6.
[40] Mumford, *Wenlock in Middle Ages*, 164–6; *T.S.A.S.* 3rd ser. i. 226; S.R.O. 552/1/4, 9; *Cal. Pat.* 1301–7, 545–6.
[41] Mumford, op. cit. 164–5; S.R.O. 212, box 14, bailiff's acct. 19–20 Ric. II.
[42] Mumford, op. cit. 169–70; S.P.L., Deeds 13477, m. 5; S.R.O. 665, box 33, bailiff's acct. 21–2 Ric. II; P.R.O., SC 6/967/27, m. 3.
[43] S.P.L., Deeds 7234, 7322; P.R.O., SC 6/965/3–4; S.R.O. 212, box 80, bailiffs' accts. 48–9 Edw. III, 18–19 Ric. II; box 81, bailiff's accts. 10–11 Hen. IV.
[44] S.R.O. 552/1A/8; *Cal. Inq. Misc.* iv, p. 113.
[45] Davies, *Lordship and Society*, 127–8.
[46] Ibid. 390; *Two Est. Surveys of Earls of Arundel*, 53–4, 56, 64.
[47] S.P.L., Deeds 7531; *Cart. Haughmond*, p. 120 (no. 565);

Staffs. R.O., D. 938/718; *T.S.A.S.* 3rd ser. i. 230; Mumford, *Wenlock*, 167–8; Garbet, *Wem*, 241.
[48] *V.C.H. Salop.* i. 418; Pollard, 'Fam. of Talbot in 15th cent.' 359; Smith, 'Lordships of Chirk and Oswestry', 397.
[49] *V.C.H. Salop.* viii. 321; xi. 316; B.L. Add. MS. 6165, pp. 69, 77, 81–2.
[50] e.g. *Cart. Haughmond*, pp. 23 (no. 20), 63 (no. 237), 80–1 (no. 333), 116–17 (no. 543), 145 (no. 698), 202 (no. 1075), 228–9 (nos. 1249, 1256), 236 (no. 1306); *T.S.A.S.* 3rd ser. i. 231; S.R.O. 465/2/59; 552/1/20, ct. 18 Oct. 1380; S.P.L., Deeds 18650; S.P.L., MS. 341, ct. 11 Oct. 1326; Staffs. R.O., D. 1733/19, ct. 8 July 1426.
[51] Pollard, 'Fam. of Talbot in 15th cent.' 373; *V.C.H. Salop.* ii. 20.
[52] *Cart. Haughmond*, p. 11.
[53] Ibid. pp. 11–12.

textile industry. Certainly it has been claimed that the mid 14th century saw a 'mushrooming' of fulling mills in the lordship of Chirk, on Shropshire's north-western border, with much of the cloth being marketed at Oswestry.[54]

The lords also attempted to profit from the trade in animals and the marketing of agricultural produce by their tenants and others. Markets and fairs were created at nine places in Edward I's last years and during his son's reign: Albrighton (1303), Cheswardine (1304), Wistanstow (1306), Prees (1307), New Ruyton (1311), Shifnal (1315), Adderley (1315), Chetwynd (1318), and Leebotwood (1320).[55] Sometimes a new market or fair gained by being less restrictive. The profits of Whitchurch market and fair declined in the 15th century and it has been suggested that Prees, Market Drayton, and Wem were preferred as less regulated marts by the Talbots' tenants in Whitchurch.[56] On the whole, however, the newly created markets and fairs of the early 14th century, like those of the 13th century, indicate more the extent of seigneurial ambition than of local trade. Few of them became firmly established or even managed to survive into the 16th century.[57] The market and fair established at Chetwynd in 1318 may have been intended to allow Sir Philip de Chetwynd to profit from the cattle being driven from Wales to relieve the famine but they failed to rival nearby Newport's, and the market obtained for Adderley in 1315 proved to be no threat to Market Drayton.[58] The earl of Arundel's new borough of New Ruyton, where he obtained a Wednesday market and a 5-day fair in 1311, was for instance always overshadowed by Oswestry where his market and two fairs were valued at £20 a year in 1301. In the later Middle Ages Oswestry became the leading market for cloth and cattle in the area and it eclipsed the smaller markets around.[59] At Oswestry the royal charter of 1330 was one of those that merely confirmed or varied the exercise of existing market and fair rights.[60] Other mid 14th-century charters served similar purposes. At Church Stretton a charter (1337) was necessitated by the passing of a Crown manor into private hands,[61] and at Ludlow and Halesowen charters of 1328 and 1344 do not seem to mark the beginnings of regulated trade in those places.[62]

The leasing of the demesnes

The decline in demesne profits was a consequence of the withdrawal of the larger landlords from direct involvement in agriculture of any sort. The process had begun on some estates before 1300 and the unsettled economic and political conditions of the 14th and early 15th centuries made demesne administration increasingly difficult and the steady income which could be produced by leasing the demesne arable and pasture increasingly attractive. After the early 15th century direct exploitation of the demesnes ceased almost entirely and, although monastic landlords retained home farms to support their communities, the great lay lords, who rarely visited the county except to hunt, were content to retain a few parks and meadows for the support of their studs.[63] On the earl of Arundel's estates arable farming was never conducted on a large scale, and in 1301 most of the small

[54] Smith, 'Lordships of Chirk and Oswestry', 354–5.
[55] Cal. Chart. R. 1300–26, 35, 43, 70, 78, 183, 283, 389, 426.   [56] Econ. H.R. 2nd ser. xxv. 559.
[57] Above, Domesday Book to 1300 (Marketing); Ag. Hist. Eng. iv. 471.
[58] T.S.A.S. 2nd ser. ix. 93; xlvi. 105.
[59] Cal. Chart. R. 1300–26, 183; T.S.A.S. ix. 244–6; 2nd ser. iii. 243; Two Est. Surveys of Earls of Arundel, 65; Smith, 'Lordships of Chirk and Oswestry', 355–6, 369–71.

[60] Cal. Chart. R. 1327–41, 161.
[61] Ibid. 421; above, Domesday Book to 1300 (Marketing).
[62] Cf. Cal. Chart. R. 1327–41, 94; 1341–1417, 31; Eyton, v. 282–3, 290; above, Domesday Book to 1300 (Marketing); Z. Razi, Life, Marriage and Death in a Medieval Parish: Economy, Society and Demography in Halesowen 1270–1400 (1980), 5–6 esp. n. 21.
[63] V.C.H. Salop. ii. 32, 44, 57, 67, 76; viii. 317; Smith, 'Lordships of Chirk and Oswestry', 148.

arable demesnes were reported to be in the hands of the villeins while the 5 carucates in Oswestry were held by three prominent burgesses.[64] As new estates were acquired the arable demesnes were leased and the meadows used to support stock. The demesne arable at Lydley, which had been the centre of a flourishing estate when the Templar preceptory was suppressed in 1308, was disposed of on a stock-and-land lease to a syndicate of four tenants in 1324, and the exploitation of the demesne arable at Aston, Sandford, and Kinnerley did not survive their absorption into the lordship of Oswestry. Even where, as at Ruyton, the amount of demesne arable was being increased by assarting in the earlier 14th century it was with the intention of swelling the rent roll.[65] The earls, however, were reluctant to lease demesne meadows, which were kept in hand as long as there were demesne herds and flocks to be fed.[66] At Caus the whole demesne was kept in hand longer and the Staffords did not lease the arable until the early 1380s; there was still mixed farming at the same period on the Mortimer manors of Stanton Lacy and Cleobury Barnes but there is no evidence that such relatively small-scale agricultural activity was profitable enough to be prolonged far into the 15th century.[67] There was a more idiosyncratic pattern of sporadic exploitation on the estate around Whitchurch acquired by the Talbot family in 1383. Prompted either by an interest in agriculture or by an ill conceived belief that more money could be made out of direct exploitation than from varieties of leasing, each new holder of the estate exploited a small part of the demesnes directly for a few years, but those experiments in 1383-7, 1391-1401, and 1413-22 were not at all successful and by the mid 15th century the entire income from the demesne came from rents and sales of pasturage.[68]

On monastic estates the general pattern was a contraction in arable farming in the face of the 14th-century crises, a switch wherever possible to stock rearing, and the leasing of those parts of the demesne which were no longer worth exploiting. The pattern of leasing by Haughmond abbey is probably typical of most of the monastic demesnes. The first lease was in 1316, of an estate outside Shropshire; it was followed by leases of small demesne holdings and buildings mostly at some distance from the abbey. Haughmond began to lease its granges from the 1340s but often retained part of the buildings for its own use; by the late 14th century only the demesne round the abbey was retained as a home farm.[69]

As the greater landlords withdrew from direct involvement in agriculture and leased their demesnes there were plenty of opportunities for those in a position to take advantage of changing conditions. Their activities can usually be traced only imperfectly in the leasing policies of the landlords whom they replaced in the cultivation of the soil.

Evidence survives from several parts of the county of a practice by which part of the demesne arable was annually let for sowing in return for a money rent or a part—the third or fourth sheaf—of the proceeds. A similar practice was used for customary land for which tenants could not be found,[70] but when applied to demesne arable, or even meadow, it could be a convenient and profitable way of exploiting that part of the demesne which the lord did not have the resources or inclination to farm directly. At Stanton Lacy between 1373 and 1390 up to 66 a.

[64] *Two Est. Surveys of Earls of Arundel*, 51, 63, 65, 68, 79; Smith, op. cit. 118.
[65] *V.C.H. Salop.* ii. 86; Smith, op. cit. 120-3; above (Assarting and inclosure). [66] Above (Demesne agriculture).
[67] *V.C.H. Salop.* viii. 317; above (Demesne agriculture).

[68] Pollard, 'Fam. of Talbot in 15th cent.' 346-55.
[69] *Midland Hist.* viii. 18-20. Cf. *V.C.H. Salop.* ii. 32-3, 43-4, 57, 76, 82; xi. 82, 156-7.
[70] P.R.O., SC 6/965/5, mm. 1, 4; N.L.W., Aston Hall 5768; Pollard, 'Fam. of Talbot in 15th cent.' 350-1.

was let annually for sowing, at 12d. an acre for winter wheat and 6d. an acre for other crops.[71] A similar system of share cropping was in operation in the lordship of Blakemere where between 1399 and 1403 the lord's share, the third sheaf, of oats from a field previously worth £5 6s. 8d. as pasturage was sold for an average of £13 a year. The returns from the third sheaf dropped after the Welsh raid on Whitchurch in 1410 but it was a way of raising revenue from land which would not otherwise have been cultivated and it seems to have remained in use on the estate until 1468.[72] Sowing for the fourth sheaf was used in parts of the lordship of Oswestry as a way of attracting back tenants and raising revenue from the demesnes after the Welsh raids.[73] It is found also in the lordship of Caus: in 1366–7 the parker of Worthen accounted for 7 bu. of mixed corn received for land leased for the third sheaf and in 1383 the demesne arable at Caus was leased with the oxen in return for the third sheaf as a preliminary to leases for years and money rents.[74]

Some Shropshire demesnes were in the hands of tenants by the early 14th century.[75] Although it is rarely possible to discover the date of the first leases, rentals and accounts suggest that initially the demesnes were leased to the tenants as a whole or to groups of tenants. By the 1380s most of Fulk Corbet's demesnes were in the hands of the tenants: at Cardeston the tenants paid a joint corn rent for the arable demesne, at Yockleton c. 283 a. were held by the customary tenants and cottagers, and at Habberley the demesne arable was leased as nooks held at will.[76] The demesne arable at Ruyton was leased in 1346–7 to various tenants for 25s. a year, and in 1409 a group of tenants, headed by the vicar, paid 20s. a year.[77] Alberbury priory's grange at Pecknall was leased to a group of four peasants in 1373 and in 1406 six tenants took the demesne at Malinslee to hold at will for 43s. 2d. a year.[78] At Church Pulverbatch the tenants were willing to pay a rent of £18 2s. 1d. a year for the demesne and the mill, even in the unsettled years of the early 15th century when other rents were being reduced.[79] Demesne meadow and pasture were usually kept in hand longer than arable but when leased could command much higher rents though the tenants usually sought the security of long leases and the right to hold in severalty and inclose. When the demesne meadows at Pontesbury were leased in 1425 the common rights of other copyholders were excluded and at Condover at the same time meadow and pasture were being leased for terms of 20 to 100 years with permission to inclose.[80]

No single form of lease appears to have gained predominance but there was a tendency for the term to become longer. On Haughmond abbey's estates the lease for lives found in the earlier 14th century had been replaced by the mid 15th century by the lease for years. Haughmond is unusual in that the leases in force at the Dissolution were for a uniform 60 or 61 years; elsewhere there was considerable variation in the length of terms. Although lay lords were not prepared to grant such long leases as monastic landlords, their leases seem to have lengthened during the 15th century.[81] One unusual feature of Shropshire leases in the period was the widespread condition that lessees should pay a heriot of the best beast on

[71] P.R.O., SC 6/967/27, mm. 1–4, 8, 10–11; SC 6/1304/17.
[72] Pollard, op. cit. 350–1, 355.
[73] N.L.W., Aston Hall 5319, bailiff's acct. 7–8 Hen. IV; 5812–14.
[74] V.C.H. Salop. viii. 317; Staffs. R.O., D. 641/1/2/240.
[75] Above, Domesday Book to 1300 (Lords and tenants).
[76] S.P.L., Deeds 6172; V.C.H. Salop. viii. 204, 240, 320.
[77] S.P.L., Deeds 7192; 7311, ct. 13 Feb. 1409.
[78] V.C.H. Salop. viii. 206; S.R.O. 513, box 1, ct. 30 June

1406.
[79] S.R.O. 482/21; 665, box 33, bailiff's acct. 8–9 Hen. IV; see also V.C.H. Salop. viii. 120, 163, 258, 272.
[80] V.C.H. Salop. viii. 272; S.P.L., Deeds 9136, ct. 29 June 1429.
[81] Midland Hist. viii. 20–2, 24–5; V.C.H. Salop. ii. 20, 57; xi. 157, 189; S.P.L., Deeds 9136, ct. 21 Nov. 1442; ibid. 19397, ct. 28 Apr. 1457; Staffs. R.O., D. 593/O/2/1/1–2, 5; P.R.O., C 1/878/17; SC 6/Hen. VIII/3009, mm. 2d., 14–30.

the death of each tenant; that evidently provided useful additional income.[82] Sometimes the lessor retained an interest in part of the demesne buildings: when leasing half the vill of Cotwall in 1441 Thomas Newport reserved for his own use the large barn and two sheepcots, and Haughmond abbey reserved the use of the sheepfold at Downton grange in 1465 and imposed on the tenant the obligation of providing hay and straw for the abbey's sheep there.[83] More usually the demesne buildings were included in the lease and the lessees were required to maintain them in good repair and replace them when necessary; they were often given help in the form of timber and rent allowances when substantial rebuilding was required.[84]

The lessees were varied, but most of those who took leases were already tenants of the lessor.[85] Sometimes it is clear from the terms of the lease that the farmer was the equivalent of a demesne servant. In 1341 the lessee of Haughmond abbey's grange at Beobridge was responsible for collecting rents, accounting for the profits of the court, and maintaining a hall, chapel, abbot's chamber, two barns, and a bakehouse; in 1483 the grange was still leased on substantially the same terms though the lease was for years rather than lives and the rent was paid in money rather than wheat, oats, and barley.[86] The husbandmen who took the lease of Lady Clopton's Broseley demesnes in 1426 were to collect her rents and other manorial profits, maintain the inclosures around the demesne land, and bring in the harvest using the services of the customary tenants.[87] Sometimes, however, the lessees of the more substantial demesnes were of a more elevated rank, entitled to call themselves esquires or gentlemen.[88] Margaret Gresley, who leased Chelmarsh manor with all its lands and buildings in 1454–5, was far removed from a demesne servant, and Philip de Medewe, the farmer of Longnor from whom 14 oxen, 10 bullocks, and a heifer were stolen in 1403, was clearly a substantial stock breeder.[89] In the 1530s Prior Bayley of Wenlock leased Madeley to Hugh Leighton, esquire, of Rodenhurst, and Oxenbold to Richard Lee, esquire, of Wattlesborough, bailiff of the franchise of Wenlock 1542–3.[90] By the 16th century it was the local gentry families who were both farming the demesnes and supplying estate officials for the larger monastic houses and for the Stafford family in the lordship of Caus.[91] The most upwardly mobile of the lessees of demesnes in the later Middle Ages were the burgesses of Shrewsbury and Oswestry. Shrewsbury merchants were some of the most important of Haughmond abbey's tenants and were prepared to take leases of not only the abbey's fulling mills but also the granges within reach of the town; there was, however, some falling off in their enthusiasm in the early 16th century and rents which were buoyant in the 15th century had to be reduced.[92] Among the lessees of the Haughmond demesne at Aston, in Oswestry, were two Oswestry merchants. Prosperous Oswestry burgesses, such as Richard Ireland c. 1400, took advantage of the availability of demesne leases and acquired large holdings in and around the town and became the 'heirs of the soil'.[93]

[82] Midland Hist. viii. 21–2.

[83] Cart. Haughmond, p. 75 (no. 300); Staffs. R.O., D. 938/694.

[84] e.g. P.R.O., E 315/94, ff. 12v.–13; SC 6/966/12 (Hughley); Staffs. R.O., D. 593/B/2/2/1B; D. 938/694, 706; Cart. Haughmond, pp. 46 (no. 143), 68 (no. 267), 123 (no. 581), 168 (no. 830).

[85] Above.

[86] Cart. Haughmond, pp. 49–50 (no. 156); Midland Hist. viii. 19; Staffs. R.O., D. 593/B/2/2/1C/1–2.

[87] S.R.O. 1224/3/191.

[88] B.L. Eg. Roll 8456; Midland Hist. viii. 22–3; V.C.H. Salop. viii. 66.

[89] Salop. Peace Roll, 1400–14, 70; S.R.O. 1224/2/298.

[90] P.R.O., C 1/878, nos. 17–18, 20; C 1/936, nos. 35–6; E 321/1/21 and 51; SC 6/Hen. VIII/3021, mm. 5, 18; V.C.H. Salop. xi. 38; S.P.R. Lich. xxi (2), p. iii; T.S.A.S. vi. 101–2.

[91] Midland Hist. viii. 25; V.C.H. Salop. ii. 35; B. J. Harris, Edw. Stafford, 3rd Duke of Buckingham (1986), 224–5; A. H. Anderson, 'Hen., Ld. Stafford (1501–63), and the Lordship of Caus', Welsh Hist. Rev. vi. 7, 14–15.

[92] Midland Hist. viii, 21, 24; Cart. Haughmond, pp. 72–3 (nos. 286–7); V.C.H. Salop. viii. 29.

[93] Midland Hist. viii. 23–4; Smith, 'Lordships of Chirk and Oswestry', 155, 313–17, 323; N.L.W., Aston Hall 2227; Visit. Salop. 1623, i (Harl. Soc. xxviii), 269.

Peasants

The surviving records inevitably focus attention on the landlords' activities but during the period peasant holdings accounted for more land than the demesnes, and rents and the profits of lordship made up a larger part of seigneurial incomes than revenues from the demesnes, whether exploited directly or leased. At the beginning of the 14th century rents from tenants formed on average 46 per cent of the income expected from the FitzAlan estates in Shropshire and the march, and in the 15th century five sixths of the Talbots' estate around Whitchurch were in copyholders' hands and their rents accounted for a third of the total income, compared with a quarter from the exploitation of the remaining sixth which formed the demesne.[94] Beneath the formal nomenclature of bond or free, customary or copyhold, tenant at will or in advowry, lay the basic needs of the tenants in the arable, meadow, and pasture of their villages and townships and the constant interaction of landlord and tenant in the details of daily life. Changes in nomenclature during the period indicate that the balance was shifting slowly in favour of the tenant as the lords were forced to relax or reduce their demands for services and customary dues and payments in order to retain tenants and fill vacant holdings. Underpopulation and peasant mobility in the face of war and natural disaster or of excessive demands from lord or king were potent forces for change, and poverty as well as prosperity made for an active peasant market in land. Shropshire was predominantly a county of small holdings in the period, and economic conditions, though more favourable to tenants than to lords, were not so conducive to rapid peasant enrichment as in other regions. The pace of change was slow and uneven but the opportunities to acquire more land and a larger share of the resources of the countryside were there for those in a position to take advantage of them.

Peasant society in the 14th-century march has been described as 'not so much a pyramid in terms of wealth, but rather a broad plateau above which rose a few peaks',[95] and that probably applies to most of Shropshire for most of the century. At Adderley in 1322, when 14 bond tenants held half virgates and 18 held quarter virgates, services were calculated on the half-virgate unit.[96] At Little Wenlock 29 tenants held 34 customary holdings in the 1320s; they consisted of 15 half virgates, 17 quarter virgates, and 2 half nooks, and until Wenlock priory had leased its demesne in the manor at the beginning of the century each half virgate had owed the same labour services.[97] On Minsterley manor 26 tenants who were described in 1300 as tenants at will, or 'penimen', held half or quarter virgates and 10 bond tenants held half virgates at a rent of 2s. a year, but that rent had risen to 10s. by 1348 when labour services had probably been commuted.[98]

The erosion of any basic uniformity in holdings or rents, which had begun before the opening of the period, accelerated during the 14th century as opportunities increased for tenants to commute labour services and to rent portions of the demesne arable and meadow or small assarts in the wastes and woodlands.[99] In 1301 many of the customary holdings at Westhope in Clun and at Acton Round were supplemented by small portions of demesne arable and meadow, and at Little Wenlock the tenants could rent additional land as 'acres' from the former demesne or as acres of 'new' land, probably taken from the waste.[1] A survey of High Ercall

94 *Two Est. Surveys of Earls of Arundel*, 65, 74, 76, 79–80, 84, 89; *Econ. H.R.* 2nd ser. xxv. 554.

95 Davies, *Lordship and Society*, 395. Cf., however, cautionary remarks above, Domesday Book to 1300 (Lords and tenants).

96 P.R.O., SC 12/14/17.

97 *V.C.H. Salop.* xi. 81.

98 Ibid. viii. 318.

99 Above (Assarting and inclosure; Leasing of demesnes).

1 *Two Est. Surveys of Earls of Arundel*, 63, 80; *V.C.H. Salop.* xi. 82.

in 1399 reveals that over half of the tenants were willing to pay up to four times the customary rent for extra meadow or small assarts to add to their half or quarter virgate.[2] An extent of Condover in 1363 lists the customary holdings of 90 tenants of the manor: 56 held less than a half virgate of 'old-hold' land and only two held one virgate or more. The 1363 extent did not, however, include assarted land; a further extent drawn up in 1421 shows that, while the pattern of 'old-hold' holdings had not greatly changed, most tenants held in addition small parcels of demesne or assarted land. The rent received from the parcels was almost double that from the customary holdings, which had become fixed before 1363 at 8s. a virgate in Condover township and 6s. 8d. elsewhere.[3] The importance to both lord and tenant of assarts as an addition to customary holdings can also be seen in the lordship of Oswestry. Whatever its origins,[4] the *gwely* had developed by the 14th century into a unit of rent assessment. Each *gwely* was divided into a number of individually rented holdings, forming part of a virgate or half virgate; in 1393 hundreds of small holdings were contained in the lordship's 49 *gwelyau*. Land assarted during the 14th century was not, however, allowed to be absorbed into the *gwelyau* and was arrented separately.[5]

The growing complexity of peasant holdings revealed by 14th-century extents indicates a vigorous peasant land market. Deeds, where they survive, illustrate the transactions in detail, as at Brockton and Larden, where hundreds of conveyances record the buying and selling of small parcels of land by free peasants in the 14th century.[6] The peasant land market was fuelled both by a buoyant demand for small pieces of land and by peasant mobility in the face of poverty and other misfortunes. Some peasants evidently just abandoned their holdings, but court rolls frequently record the formal surrender of holdings and the payment of a 'fare fee' (or 'varneth' on the lands of Wenlock priory), the converse of an entry fine. A tenant who gave up his lands at Aston in 1354 was charged only 11d. as fare fee because he was a pauper, but surrender fines were usually much larger and brought in £5 from Wenlock priory's tenants in Madeley in 1321–2.[7] Few custumals were as liberal as that of Pontesbury which allowed a tenant to leave his tenement for the lord to enjoy the profits until he wished to reclaim it,[8] but mortgages and similar arrangements made it possible for tenants to transfer land without permanently alienating it. The market in Welsh land was facilitated by the refinement during the 14th century of the *prid* deed, or Welsh mortgage, which made it possible to evade restrictions placed by the kindred or the lord on the alienation of land. Land was conveyed in return for an agreed sum of money, the *prid*, for a term of years, renewable until the mortgage was redeemed but usually amounting to alienation.[9] By means of such mortgages Haughmond abbey advanced money to starving peasants on its estate in Aston and Hisland during the agrarian crisis of 1314–18 and acquired in return small parcels of land.[10] The *prid* deed brought a much needed flexibility to the market in Welsh land and its advantages can be seen in operation in the lordship of Oswestry at the end of the 14th and the beginning of the 15th century. It enabled adjustments to be made in family

[2] *T.S.A.S.* lxii. 23–4, 78–9.

[3] *V.C.H. Salop.* viii. 45; *T.S.A.S.* l. 112–24.

[4] Above, Domesday Book to 1300 (Lords and tenants).

[5] Smith, 'Lordships of Chirk and Oswestry', 269–76; W. J. Slack, *Lordship of Oswestry, 1393–1607* (Salop. Arch. Soc. 1951), 153–4.

[6] S.R.O. 1037/3; 1080, parcel 43, cal. of More deeds; 3195/1; S.P.L., MS. 2342; N.L.W., Dobell 1 (refs. owed to Dr. D. C. Cox).

[7] *V.C.H. Salop.* xi. 43, 82; N.L.W., Aston Hall 5328 (ct. 5 Feb. 1354), 5365 (ct. 7 Nov. 1478); S.R.O. 212, box 11c; 552/1/20, Bicton ct. 11 Oct. 1380; S.P.L., MS. 340, esp. ct. r. 24 Edw. III; Mumford, *Wenlock*, 156, 159; Smith, op. cit. 305–7.

[8] *V.C.H. Salop.* viii. 272; S.P.L., Deeds 6784.

[9] Davies, *Lordship and Society*, 408–9; *Cart. Haughmond*, p. 14.

[10] *Cart. Haughmond*, pp. 13–14; see also Staffs. R.O., D. 938/736; S.R.O. 552/1/11, 27; 1514/65.

territorial arrangements and also gave an opportunity for small tenants to increase and consolidate their holdings and for more ambitious investors, such as Richard Ireland and his fellow burgesses of Oswestry, to build up substantial rural holdings from vacant Welsh tenements.[11]

The increased availability of land, in combination with economic conditions that on the whole favoured the tenant rather than his lord, resulted in increased stratification within the ranks of the peasantry, although the structure of holdings continued to vary greatly from manor to manor. Some peasant families accumulated large holdings made up from one or more customary holdings with the addition of extra holdings of pasture or meadow and parcels of the demesne or old assarts. At Hopton Wafers in 1412 there were three such composite holdings: one consisted of a messuage, half virgate, and nook, a quarter messuage and half virgate, and a messuage and half virgate; the second comprised two messuages and half virgates; and the third a messuage and 3 nooks, a toft and nook, and a cottage. Such accumulations were not always stable and long-lasting. At Hopton Wafers 15 years later two tenants paid rent for more than one holding: one of them held the former demesne, two messuages and half virgates, and a quarter of 'Lewytefeld', and the other held a messuage, half virgate, and nook, a quarter of 'Pillokes land', and a parcel of meadow.[12] At Willey in 1446 there was one holding of 4 virgates, one of 2½ virgates, one of 2 virgates, seven of 1 virgate, five half virgates, and two holdings of 1 nook.[13] There was an even wider variation in the size of holdings at Chelmarsh in 1445 when a new rental was drawn up which incorporated recent changes in rents.[14] The accumulation of large holdings in the hands of one man was easier in vills or townships where there were few tenants. At Allfield in Condover, for example, there were six tenants holding 10 nooks in 1363 but by 1421 seven of the nooks were in the hands of one man.[15] In Cardeston parish the hamlet of Great Bretchell, where there had been eight tenants in 1379, was leased as a pasture to a single tenant in the 15th century, and in Alberbury parish Thomas Thornes built up a substantial estate between 1516 and 1535 on the site of Little Wollaston which, with Amaston, had contained at least eight families in 1327.[16] At the other end of the scale were the cottagers who appear with increasing frequency in rentals and court rolls and who held only a garden or a few acres of land. At Wroxeter in 1350 a third of the tenants held only cottages and between 3 and 6 a., and at Malinslee in 1406 there were six landed tenants and four cottagers.[17] These cottagers could not have supported themselves and their families from such small holdings and would have contributed to the pool of agricultural labourers.[18]

Peasant farm buildings in Shropshire probably varied widely in form and appearance according to the status of the occupier and the farming bias of the area. Documentary references suggest that the main components of a virgater's or half-virgater's messuage were a house of perhaps three bays and a barn of three or four.[19] The latter would presumably have provided winter housing for the plough beasts as well as storage for produce. Cottagers and wage labourers may have had no buildings besides a one- or two-bay house, and mention of a shepherd's hut at

[11] Davies, op. cit. 410–13; Slack, *Lordship of Oswestry*, 142–3, 158, 165; Smith, 'Lordships of Chirk and Oswestry', 312–15.
[12] S.R.O. 356, box 267, cts. 13 Oct. 1412, 26 Apr. 1430.
[13] S.R.O. 1224/2/536, ct. 9 June 1446. [14] Ibid. /2/298.
[15] *V.C.H. Salop.* viii. 45; *T.S.A.S.* l. 116, 123.
[16] *V.C.H. Salop.* viii. 192.

[17] *T.S.A.S.* xi. 282–6; S.R.O. 513, box 1, ct. 30 June 1406; see also S.P.L., Deeds 5455, ct. 29 Sept. 1334; ibid. MS. 340, esp. ct. r. 23 Edw. III; *T.S.A.S.* lxii. 78–9; *Cart. Haughmond*, pp. 135–7 (nos. 649, 654), 236–7 (no. 1310).
[18] Davies, *Lordship and Society*, 397–8.
[19] e.g. *Cart. Haughmond*, pp. 50–1, 54, 216, 236; *V.C.H. Salop.* viii. 307.

Caus in 1445[20] suggests how rudimentary accommodation might be for the poor countryman.

Relationships and contracts between peasants are difficult to assess as few written records of them survive. Study of marcher society, however, suggests that there the number of undertenants could be considerable, and the lord's authority over them minimal. In Clun it was asserted that any landholding tenant could accept another into his protection to become his tenant or servant, and it was even claimed that the goods of an undertenant who died without an heir should be forfeit not to the lord but to the tenant who was his immediate superior.[21]

Together with changes in the size and composition of peasant holdings went changes in the terms of tenure and the nature and amount of rent. Although progress was slow and uneven and there are some signs of seigneurial reaction, the general trend was towards an improvement in the status of the peasantry, a reduction in rents and customary dues and payments, and—in the marcher lordships—a blurring of the distinction between Welsh and English tenants. A variety of tenures could co-exist on one manor both at the beginning and end of the period.[22] Hereditary freeholds tended to disappear, as at High Ercall from the later 13th century, Church Preen by the mid 14th century, and Kenley between the 13th century and the 15th.[23] Between 1319 and 1331 several freeholds were bought back into the Langley manorial estate by Ralph Lee, and the lord of Whitton, William Spenser, took advantage of the Welsh raids in the early 15th century to increase his demesne by buying up freeholds.[24] Some monastic landlords seem to have followed the same policy for freeholds had disappeared at Lilleshall (except for one at Muxton), Madeley, and Little Wenlock by the end of the Middle Ages.[25] Leaseholds, however, a significantly different sort of free tenancy, were a common feature in most parts of the county and continued to increase in number during the 14th century with the encouragement of assarting.[26] At the other end of the spectrum of peasant tenures there were in the western lordships tenants in advowry who paid a small tax, usually 4d., for the lord's protection and permission to remain on the manor for a year; in 1362 advowry payments in the lordship of Oswestry were farmed for £2 a year. Most tenants in advowry were probably seasonal labourers or craftsmen or women and once they took land they ceased to be in advowry and became tenants. In the lordship of Clun in 1372 a tenant in advowry, a free man, offered to pay double rent for a messuage and 12 a. and to become a villein 'with all his brood'.[27] Elsewhere villeins were willing and able to pay large fines for their personal freedom. At the beginning of the 15th century members of the Houle family of High Ercall paid a total of over £50 in manumission fines.[28]

The conversion of customary villein tenures to leasehold or their gradual redefinition as copyholds[29] began first on those manors where the demesnes had been leased and labour services were no longer required. After Wenlock priory ceased to cultivate its Little Wenlock demesne at the beginning of the 14th century customary holdings were either converted to leaseholds (for some of the larger ones)

[20] V.C.H. Salop. viii. 306.
[21] Ibid. 395.
[22] e.g. V.C.H. Salop. xi. 82-3, 223.
[23] T.S.A.S. lxii. 14-17; V.C.H. Salop. viii. 93, 95, 126.
[24] V.C.H. Salop. viii. 144, 319.
[25] Ibid. xi. 43, 80, 83, 155.
[26] Ibid. viii. 111, 120, 320-1. Cf. above, Domesday Book to 1300 (Woodland, assarting, and commons).
[27] V.C.H. Salop. viii. 318; Davies, Lordship and Society, 138-9; Smith, 'Lordships of Chirk and Oswestry', 351-3;

S.R.O. 552/1/16, cts. 14 Apr., 5 May 1352.
[28] T.S.A.S. lxii. 24-5; see also S.R.O. 212, box 73, receiver's acct. 13-14 Hen. VI.
[29] Copyhold, according to Fitzherbert, 'was anciently tenure in villeinage' and 'is but a new name': G. Jacob, New Law-Dictionary (5th edn. 1744). The gen. hist. of the tenure and its diverse development during this period remains to be written. See M. Campbell, Eng. Yeoman Under Eliz. and Early Stuarts (1960), 118 sqq.

or began to develop into various forms of copyhold. In the 1320s all the tenants there held for three lives (the tenant's, his wife's, and their eldest child's), and in 1540 most of the thirteen copyholds were still for lives but a few, like the seven leaseholds, were for terms of between 50 and 81 years.[30] Leaseholds for life are also found on the manors of Haughmond abbey from the early 14th century,[31] and the conversion of customary tenures to leasehold took place on lay estates such as those at Cressage and Wattlesborough during the 14th century.[32] When the manorial estate at High Ercall was surveyed in 1399 only one tenant still held by simple customary tenure; 36 tenements were held at will and 17 tenants held by a hybrid tenure described as 'at will and according to custom'. In addition leases had been granted during the late 14th century to unfree tenants for messuages and land previously held by custom, and 21 such leases were still in force in 1399.[33] Changes in tenure were also taking place in the marcher lordships. They could be a source of profit if the tenants were prepared to pay for the privilege. In the late 1350s the tenants of Kinnerley were prepared to double their rents for the concession of being allowed hereditary tenures,[34] but in the early 16th century the Stafford family met great resistance when they tried to persuade their remaining customary tenants in the lordship of Caus to convert to copyhold—probably for terms of years.[35] More often changes were prompted by difficulties in attracting tenants to vacant holdings, as can be seen in the use of the *quousque* lease in the lordship of Oswestry and the surrounding FitzAlan manors from the late 14th century. Lands were granted 'until another better lease can be found for the lord's greater profit'; frequently the lease specified that the land was to be held at a lowered or 'old' rent, the entry fine was often waived, and a clause relating to the upkeep of buildings was usually inserted. During the 15th century 'for term of life' and 'to his heirs and assigns' was added to the *quousque* formula, and the term copyhold was well established by the 16th century.[36] Similarly the rents paid for the Whitchurch demesne lands remained so static throughout the 15th century that by the 1520s they seemed to the earl of Shrewsbury and his council indistinguishable from customary rents.[37]

There are other indications that landlords were prepared to adjust to changing conditions and make concessions in order to attract and retain tenants. The wide variations in the rents paid for virgate and half-virgate holdings on the same manor suggest that individual bargains were being struck between lord and tenant, and in some cases rents were said to have been reduced.[38] Rents at Ruyton, where the rent roll had been swollen in the late 14th century by rent from assarts, were reduced after the Welsh raids in the early 15th century.[39] Entry fines also varied widely but do not appear to have been high and were sometimes waived altogether if the tenement or land was in a bad state.[40] Contrariwise when the earl of Shrewsbury decided in 1525 to take advantage of the increased demand for land from the rising population and to attempt to increase revenue from the estate around Whitchurch, where rents had fossilized during the 15th century, he did it by imposing entry fines. The bids the tenants made in 1525 for renewing their

[30] *V.C.H. Salop.* xi. 82–3.
[31] *Midland Hist.* viii. 17; Staffs. R.O., D. 593/B/2/2/1A/7–10.
[32] *V.C.H. Salop.* viii. 76, 205.
[33] *T.S.A.S.* lxii. 23, 78–80.
[34] Smith, 'Lordships of Chirk and Oswestry', 216; N.L.W., Aston Hall 5305, reeve's acct. 42–3 Edw. III.
[35] Harris, *3rd Duke of Buckingham*, 119–20; *Welsh Hist. Rev.* vi. 2.
[36] Smith, op. cit. 339–41; N.L.W., Aston Hall 5813, 5345–6, 5364–7; S.P.L., Deeds 8393.
[37] *Econ. H.R.* 2nd ser. xxv. 558.
[38] e.g. S.R.O. 356, box 267, ct. 13 Oct. 1412; 1224/2/298; /536, ct. 9 June 1446.
[39] Smith, 'Lordships of Chirk and Oswestry', 210–11, 430.
[40] e.g. S.P.L., Deeds 5455, ct. 29 Sept. 1334; ibid. MS. 340, ct. r. 23 Edw. III, 6 Ric. II; S.R.O. 212, box 1, ct. r. 19 Edw. III; P.R.O., SC 2/197/130–1.

leases of demesne lands and mills amounted to £72 on top of an annual rental of £52.[41] At the same period the Stafford family were attempting to increase receipts in a similar fashion as they sought to fill vacant tenements on their Shropshire estates. In 1520 the duke of Buckingham proclaimed that anyone willing to take on farms and copyholds at increments or entry fines agreed with his surveyor and auditor should pay 'the old rent', and in 1527 his son Lord Stafford instructed that his Shropshire estates, whether held as copyhold or otherwise, were to be relet 'by indenture or bill' and copyholders were to pay agreed increments or entry fines.[42]

Both threats and inducements were employed by the lords to try to ensure that tenants kept their holdings in a good state. Those who allowed their buildings to become ruinous were presented in court and ordered to repair them under pain of forfeiture and those who failed to cultivate their holdings were forced to surrender them.[43] Leases frequently contained exhortations to keep buildings in good repair and land in a good state and were sometimes granted on condition that the tenants put up new buildings.[44] Inducements to build and repair were offered in the form of timber, rent reductions, and allowances. At Clun in 1411, for example, the rent paid for three holdings was halved during the first one or two years on condition that the tenants built houses at their own expense, and the farmer of the manor and demesne at Hughley was allowed 46s. 8d. for building a new hall and chamber.[45]

Labour services, whether commuted or not, and other customary dues and payments could increase considerably both peasant outgoings and seigneurial incomes, but they became increasingly difficult to exact and collect during the period. Most of the labour services which still remained in force in 1300 were commuted during the 14th century, apart from haymaking and harvest services which could be used to supplement full-time labour as long as the demesnes continued to be exploited directly.[46] Economic conditions were not conducive to the continued exaction of more than minimal labour services from customary tenants and made even the collection of commuted payments difficult. It was reported in 1519–20 that the 51 hens which were due from the customary tenants at Minsterley instead of labour services since the first visitation of the Black Death had not been collected since the Welsh raids over a century earlier, nor had any payments been received instead of ploughing and summer and autumn works.[47] To judge from entries in court rolls, carrying and carting were the residual services which the lords were most interested in exacting and which met with the most resistance; in 1357 four townships in the lordship of Clun were ordered to find someone to perform carting services within four days under pain of a hefty £5 amercement.[48] Any attempt to depress the status of the peasants by reimposing lapsed services met concerted resistance. In 1385 the customary tenants of Ford manor, which was ancient demesne,[49] obtained an exemplification of the Domesday

[41] Econ. H.R. 2nd ser. xxv. 557–8.
[42] Harris, 3rd Duke of Buckingham, 121; V.C.H. Salop. viii. 381; B.L. Add. MS. 36542, f. 27.
[43] e.g. Mumford, Wenlock, 158, 160, 163–4, 166–7.
[44] e.g. Staffs. R.O., D. 938/661, 691–2; S.R.O. 20/1/7, 10; S.P.L., MS. 343, ct. r. 15 Ric. II; B.L. Add. Ch. 54388, ct. r. 10 Hen. VI.
[45] S.R.O. 552/1/39; P.R.O., SC 6/966/12, receiver's acct. 12–13 Edw. IV; Cart. Haughmond, p. 108 (no. 488).
[46] Above (Demesne agriculture).
[47] Clwyd R.O. (Hawarden), DD/WY/5483, p. 8.

[48] S.R.O. 552/1/15, ct. 9 Aug. 1357; cf. Mumford, Wenlock, 155.
[49] There was virtually no Salop. terra regis in 1086 (V.C.H. Salop. i. 290, 341 n. 106; Eyton, ii. 149, 185) and the later privileges of ancient demesne seem to have been attached instead to those manors of royal demesne inherited by Hen. II in 1154 (V.C.H. Salop. iii. 48–9; Eyton, iii. 64). For ancient demesne elsewhere cf. R. S. Hoyt, Royal Demesne in Eng. Constitutional Hist. 1066–1272 (1950), 135–6, 171–207; E. M. Hallam, Domesday Bk. through Nine Centuries (1986), cap. 4.

Book entry, and their subsequent withdrawal of services led to the appointment of two commisions of oyer and terminer in 1386 and a further commission in 1410 when they renewed their resistance.[50]

Customary payments such as tallage seem to have been uneven in incidence and few records of their payment are found after the earlier 14th century.[51] A due which was unusually widespread in its incidence was the heriot of the best beast due to the lord at the death of a tenant; heriots were exacted from copyholders, leaseholders, freeholders, and even from tenants in advowry, and were collected conscientiously by the lord's officials.[52] Even more valuable was terciary, the right on death to a third of the goods of a tenant, bond or free, which is found on Wenlock priory's estates, where there is evidence that the tenants resisted by concealing the goods of dead relatives. Terciary had been commuted to a money payment by the time of the Dissolution but the heriot survived much longer.[53] The Welsh food rents and cow renders had been commuted to money payments by the beginning of the 14th century, and other renders in kind such as hen and goose rents were not of high value and few, apart from the 'tack' pigs associated with pannage, survived uncommuted into the 16th century.[54] The archaic nature of many customary tenures and the associated payments by the early 16th century did not deter the Stafford family from attempting to revive them in the lordship of Caus. The duke of Buckingham (d. 1521) revived bond services and forced the tenants of 3 townships in the Nether Gorddwr to pay a rent called *porthyant bagell*; the tenants claimed that it had been granted to the lord when the country was wild and disordered[55] for him to find a cattle guard and that it had not been levied 'time out of mind'.[56] Buckingham's policies were continued and extended with 'antiquarian enthusiasm' by his son Lord Stafford, whose revival of tallages and attempts to revive forest jurisdiction and restrict commoning rights caused disorder and conflict in border society.[57]

Only a faint and fragmentary impression can be received of the nature of peasant farming in later medieval Shropshire. The surviving documents are mainly concerned with the constraints imposed by landlords and local communities on the activities of individuals, rather than with change and innovation, which can only be guessed from the occasional inventory of a rich peasant's goods. Peasants' interests mirrored those of their landlords in that peasant pastoral farming was expanding in this period. Arable farming provided for the basic needs of the peasant and his family but it also provided support in the form of feed and grazing for the animals which were a source of profit, either in themselves or in their products of meat, wool, and hides. The peasant farmer's main concern was to find enough pasture for his animals, and there were signs of pressure when both landlord and tenant were competing for a share in the same resource, a pressure which was eased when the greater landlords withdrew from direct involvement in pastoral farming and released meadow and pasture for their tenants to rent and sometimes to inclose.[58]

[50] *Cal. Pat.* 1385-9, 54, 171, 178; 1408-13, 173; see also *T.S.A.S.* lxii. 24.

[51] *Two Est. Surveys of Earls of Arundel*, 53-4, 56-7, 61, 64; S.R.O. 1514/4A; S.P.L., Deeds 5455, ct. 29 Sept. 1334.

[52] *Midland Hist.* viii. 21-2; *V.C.H. Salop.* xi. 43, 81, 223; S.R.O. 552/1/2, cts. 18 Jan., 2 Aug. 1333.

[53] *T.S.A.S.* lviii. 68-70; *V.C.H. Salop.* xi. 43, 81-3.

[54] Davies, *Lordship and Society*, 134; Smith, 'Lordships of Chirk and Oswestry', 224-9, 243-4; Slack, *Lordship of Oswestry*, 26-9; cf. above (Demesne agriculture).

[55] It was being paid by 1388-9.

[56] Harris, *3rd Duke of Buckingham*, 109, 113-14; *Welsh Hist. Rev.* vi. 9; W.S.L. 1721/1/1, ff. 202-3; cf. *V.C.H. Salop.* viii. 317. The rent probably represents contributions to the food or maintenance (*porthiant*) of a guard bearing a staff or crook (*bagl*): *Geiriadur Pryfisgol Cymru: Dict. of Welsh Language* (Cardiff, 1950-). Miss M. B. Jenkins is thanked for linguistic advice.

[57] *Welsh Hist. Rev.* vi. 2-4, 6-15.

[58] Above (Assarting and inclosure; Leasing of demesnes).

The crops found in inventories of peasant goods confirm the subordination of arable to pastoral farming in that they are small in amount, low in value, and lacking in variety. Vegetables and fruit were doubtless grown in the garden attached to every peasant house but they are rarely mentioned; in 1306 the goods of a felon who abjured the realm included 1d. worth of cabbages growing in the curtilage.[59] In the fields the main crops were wheat and oats, with smaller quantities of barley, rye, vetch, peas, and beans. Of the 21 terciary payments from the estates of Wenlock priory recorded 1336-61 and 1377-9 and including crops, 5 mention only wheat and 15 both wheat and oats; 4 mention beans or peas, 6 either vetch or barley, and rye occurs only once.[60] Differing combinations of crops are found in other parts of the county at different times. The forfeited goods of a felon at Prees in 1324 included an acre sown with wheat, another sown with beans, and half an acre sown with rye, and there were 10 bu. of beans and 3 bu. of barley in his barn.[61] In the lordship of Clun it is more usual to find oats as the sole crop. A Welsh tenant at Bicton who died in 1357 had only an ox and 6 a. of land sown with oats, while a Welsh widow who died in 1372 had 4s. worth of standing oats which amounted to less than 6 per cent of the total value of her goods.[62] Further north more variety occurs. Two tenants who died at Ruyton in 1332 and 1353 had a few bushels of wheat, oats, and rye among their possessions; a Welsh tenant who died intestate in the lordship of Ellesmere in 1345 had 6 bu. of wheat, 6 bu. of oats, and an acre sown with wheat, oats, and beans; a prosperous Welsh tenant who died at Sandford in 1381 had stacks of wheat, rye, and oats valued together at £3 17s. 9d.; two tenants whose confiscated goods were sold by the bailiff of Blakemere in 1410-11 both had barley and oats among their possessions.[63] Seed is mentioned only occasionally. In 1321 a bond tenant at Stoke St. Milborough paid for permission to marry with a quarter of 'good seed'; in 1332 a tenant at Ruyton owned a fourth part of the seed of 2 bu. of wheat 'for increase'; wheat in the ground due as terciary at Hatton in 1354 was estimated in seed, and at Lilleshall the tenants of the abbey bought seed from the lord for 3d. a bushel in 1423.[64]

Although many peasants possessed affers, they probably used oxen for ploughing, as happened on the demesnes; draught horses were more expensive to maintain and were probably reserved for harrowing, hauling, or carting.[65] To judge from the evidence of heriots, strays, and reports of stolen animals, ownership of oxen and affers was widespread among the peasantry.[66] Between 1400 and 1414 nearly 150 oxen were stolen from 23 different places in Shropshire.[67] Such records, however, rarely give an indication of the total number of animals owned by individuals. Of the 23 tenants of Wenlock priory whose terciary payments are known, 10 owned oxen, 5 owned two or more oxen, and 4 had affers, all but one in addition to oxen. William Broun of Huntington, for example, owned four oxen and two affers when he died in 1377 and Agnes of Deuxhill (d. 1379) had seven oxen and an affer.[68] It is probable that a certain amount of co-aration was practised as few peasants can have owned enough animals even for a ploughteam of four

[59] *T.S.A.S.* 3rd ser. v. 173.
[60] Ibid. lviii. 71-6.
[61] S.P.L., MS. 341, cts. 17 Mar., 12 May 1324.
[62] S.R.O. 552/1/15, ct. 28 Apr. 1357; /1/16, ct. 18 Aug. 1372.
[63] *T.S.A.S.* 3rd ser. i. 57; Smith, 'Lordships of Chirk and Oswestry', 336; S.R.O. 212, box 1, ct. 25 Apr. 1345; box 81, bailiff's acct. 10-11 Hen. IV.
[64] Mumford, *Wenlock*, 155; *T.S.A.S.* 3rd ser. i. 57; lviii. 73; S.P.L., Deeds 16330, ct. 20 Jan. 1423

[65] Langdon, *Horses, Oxen and Tech. Innovation*, 176, 228; and see above (Demesne agriculture).
[66] For heriots see e.g. S.R.O. 552/1/26 (cts. 15 Dec. 1396, 19 July 1397), 31 (cts. 9, 30 Apr. 1399); S.P.L., MS. 342, ct. r. 43 Edw. III; ibid. Deeds 7280. For strays see e.g. S.P.L., Deeds 5455, cts. 5 Oct. 1335, 17 Dec. 1360; 19398; ibid. MS. 341, ct. 22 Oct. 1323.
[67] *Salop. Peace Roll*, 60, 65-6, 70, 72-3, 77, 81-3, 86, 88, 90, 92, 95, 103, 106, 109, 115; *E.H.R.* xcix. 549.
[68] *T.S.A.S.* lviii. 71-6.

oxen, a suggested likely size of peasant team in the period.[69] Most substantial peasants probably possessed one or more of the major pieces of farm equipment—ploughs, harrows, carts, and wagons—found in the surviving inventories, together with the occasional coulter, axe, or winnowing fan.[70]

Leland observed that the sandy soils of some parts of Shropshire would not bear good corn crops unless marled,[71] and there is evidence that, as in the preceding period,[72] marl was put on peasant holdings to improve their yield. Marlpits are found in field names and as the cause of accidental deaths, and leases occasionally specify that land must be marled at the tenant's expense or that the landlord will provide access to a supply of marl.[73] When Haughmond abbey acquired a piece of land called 'Skyneresmore' in Morfe forest in 1304 a 1-a. marlpit and the way leading to it were reserved for the use of the tenants of the royal manor of Claverley and the abbot allowed them to take marl when they wished.[74] In 1320 the lessees of an inclosed plot of land at Sandford, in Prees, were allowed to take mould and marl to improve the land when necessary, and the new tenant of an acre of land at Prees in 1323 had to pay 6s. 8d. to the previous tenant for his expense in marling it.[75]

All but the smallest peasant holdings supported a variety of animals. In addition to draught animals there were usually at least one cow (after oxen and horses the most commonly found heriot), a few sheep and pigs, the occasional goat, and some poultry, although the latter are seldom recorded except as rent hens or when geese strayed on crops.[76] There are, however, signs of change in the period with larger flocks and herds found concentrated in fewer hands. It is unusual in the 14th century to find references to peasants owning more than a dozen cattle or pigs or over a hundred sheep, although it is difficult to gauge the size of individual holdings from the surviving evidence of theft or trespass. Among the Wenlock priory terciary records peasant flocks ranged from 12 to 45 sheep.[77] Tenants of the manor of Sutton upon Tern were amerced for allowing flocks of between 15 and 60 sheep to stray into growing crops.[78] Inquests into the number of sheep kept in Morfe forest illustrate the growth in the size of flocks. In 1362 the average size of the flocks from Claverley and Worfield commoned in the forest was 13 with the largest flocks numbering no more than 40 sheep.[79] In 1497 the foresters reported that the king's deer could have no browsing because of the number of sheep commoned in the forest by the inhabitants of eight townships around Claverley and Worfield: over 2,000 sheep in 27 flocks were listed. Nearly 1,400 sheep in 19 flocks were said to be pastured daily in the bailiwick of Claverley and over 3,000 sheep from around Bridgnorth were kept in the forest throughout the year with the flocks averaging nearly 100 sheep.[80]

Herds of pigs also seem to have become larger during the 15th century, though individual herds varied greatly in size. In the 14th century herds of pigs are seldom found in more than single figures but in 1497 over 1,200 pigs from townships around Claverley and Worfield were listed by the foresters of Morfe in 115 herds averaging 11 swine, and agistment payments for swine in the same year show herds

[69] Smith, 'Lordships of Chirk and Oswestry', 286; Langdon, *Horses, Oxen and Tech. Innovation*, 176, 228.
[70] *T.S.A.S.* lviii. 72–6; Smith, op. cit. 336; S.R.O. 212, box 81, bailiff's acct. 10–11 Hen. IV; P.R.O., SC 6/967/9.
[71] Leland, *Itin.* ed. Toulmin Smith, iv. 2.
[72] Above, Domesday Book to 1300 (Arable farming).
[73] e.g. Eyton, iii. 309; *Cal. Inq. p.m.* xvi, p. 217; *Cart. Haughmond*, pp. 68 (no. 267), 158 (no. 778); *T.S.A.S.*

2nd ser. xi. 183; 3rd ser. v. 168, 171–3; lxii. 25–6; S.R.O. 567/2A/20.   [74] *Cart. Haughmond*, p. 49 (nos. 154–5).
[75] S.R.O. 2/7; S.P.L., MS. 341, ct. 16 Mar. 1323.
[76] For poultry see e.g. S.P.L., Deeds 5455, ct. 5 Oct. 1335; *T.S.A.S.* lviii. 72, 75–6.
[77] *T.S.A.S.* lviii. 72–6.
[78] S.P.L., Deeds 5454, ct. 17 Apr. 1367.
[79] P.R.O., E 32/308/5.   [80] P.R.O., DL 39/1/26.

varying in size from three to over a hundred animals.[81] At Little Wenlock 23 tenants made pannage payments for 200 swine in 1397, and in the 15th century the herds increased in size and one of 37 pigs is found in 1449.[82] In 1422 the park and woods at Lilleshall contained 400 pigs in 73 herds of up to 18 animals and at the same time the bailiff at Myddle was collecting £6 3s. 6d. in pannage payments for several hundred swine in 84 herds.[83] Goats are found less frequently and in much smaller numbers; in 1325 two men were amerced for pasturing ten goats and a kid in woodland at Prees, and a Welsh tenant in the lordship of Clun who died in 1514 had a herd of 15 goats.[84]

There is also evidence, admittedly fragmentary and often difficult to interpret, to suggest some specialization in cattle rearing and a growing trade in cattle and cattle products among the peasantry. Payments for agisting cattle and amercements for allowing animals to stray into growing crops and private pasture suggest that more cattle were being kept than were necessary for subsistence.[85] The impression is confirmed by lists of peasants' goods, especially from north and west Shropshire. In 1381 a Welsh tenant at Sandford had 12 head of cattle, worth twice as much as his flock of 30 sheep; in 1410–11 a prosperous tenant at Blakemere had 16 cows, 18 calves, 1 bullock, and 16 steers which, together with his two horses, were valued at over £5; a more modest herd of 6 cattle, including a young bull, was owned by a tenant at Ruyton in 1427–8; Ralph Bostocke of Hodnet, whose goods were valued in 1534, had 14 cattle worth £8 and 16 sheep worth £1.[86] Cattle were often the target of thieves, especially those from Wales, and criminal records provide further evidence of cattle rearing and trading. In the early 14th century Worcester merchants buying stock at Clun fair were held until compensation was paid to one of the earl of Arundel's tenants who dealt in cattle and from whom four oxen had been stolen at Clun and taken to Worcester market.[87] The crimes of Robert of Middleton in the early 1350s included stealing cattle in Shropshire and driving them into Wales, and in 1380 three Welsh tenants of the earl of Arundel were accused of stealing seven oxen which they had distrained for him in Herefordshire.[88] Many of the hundreds of cattle reported stolen in Shropshire between 1400 and 1414 were presumably reared by peasant farmers. In 1400 the Welsh rebels were said to have stolen 84 cattle from the tenants of the lord of Wem. In 1401 six men at Bridgnorth suffered the theft of 53 animals worth £20, and in 1408 a herd of 16 cattle was abducted from Millenheath and held to ransom. An even larger herd of 47 oxen and cows was stolen at Winsbury in 1410 and driven into Wales.[89] Pontesbury suffered from the attentions of Welsh cattle thieves in 1411 when 24 oxen and cows were stolen from the tenants of Moorwood and 38 bullocks and heifers from John Dod at Woodhouse.[90] In 1414 £20 worth of cattle were allegedly taken by force from four tenants at Shrawardine by John Skynner of Shrewsbury and one of Sir William Clinton's servants.[91] The licence granted in 1425 to a group of four tenants who had leased two of the common fields at Farley to build a pound there large enough to hold 40 cattle reveals both the existence of specialized cattle rearing and the need for co-operative action

[81] Ibid.; E 32/308/5; SC 2/197/97, ct. 28 Nov. 1342.
[82] V.C.H. Salop. xi. 82.
[83] Ibid. 157; S.P.L., Deeds 16330, ct. 16 Oct. 1422; S.R.O. 212, box 14, bailiff's acct. 9 Hen. V–1 Hen. VI.
[84] S.P.L., MS. 341, ct. 20 May 1325; S.R.O. 552/1/54, ct. 21 June 1514.
[85] S.P.L., Deeds 5455, ct. 17 Dec. 1360; S.R.O. 212, box 14, ct. r. 2–3 Ric. II; P.R.O., SC 6/965/21, agist. acct. 1–2 Ric. II; and see above (Demesne agriculture).

[86] Smith, 'Lordships of Chirk and Oswestry', 336; S.R.O. 212, box 81, bailiff's acct. 12–13 Hen. IV; T.S.A.S. 2nd ser. xii. 195; 3rd ser. i. 75.
[87] R. H. Hilton, A Medieval Society: W. Midlands at end of 13th cent. (1967), 261.
[88] Cal. Pat. 1350–4, 346; S.R.O. 552/1/20, ct. 17 Dec. 1380. [89] Salop. Peace Roll, 53, 67, 86–7, 95.
[90] Ibid. 103–4.
[91] E.H.R. xcix. 549.

perhaps to protect cattle from thieves who were a constant threat.[92] The tenants of Winnington in Alberbury paid for a hayward to guard their cattle on the Long Mountain from outlaws, and *c.* 1700 there was a tradition that in earlier times the townships around Myddle guarded their cattle in fortified enclosures at night.[93]

An increase in the number of animals kept by the peasantry was possible only if there was pasture enough to support them. Although there are signs of continued pressure[94] in the early part of the period, the combination of a declining population with the gradual withdrawal of the greater landlords from direct exploitation of their demesnes meant that sufficient resources of pasture and meadow were available to those who could afford them; the main problem was one of regulating the use of those resources that were still common to all members of the manorial community. The means of control were available in the manor court where ordinances and bylaws were agreed and enforced and anti-social behaviour was reported and punished. It is another sign of the predominantly pastoral concerns of the peasantry that ordinances found in the court rolls of the period are less concerned with arrangements for the common cropping of the arable fields and ensuring an adequate supply of labour at harvest time[95] than with pasturing routines. Tenants were ordered to close the fences around the arable fields at agreed dates, to keep the hedges and ditches around the common fields and closes in good repair, not to put animals into the common fields to graze at night or during harvest, and not to allow pigs into the common fields at all.[96] Those who broke their neighbours' hedges and allowed their animals to stray into growing crops were heavily amerced.[97] When permission was given to inclose woodland and waste the commoning rights of tenants were usually carefully safeguarded,[98] and there were protests in the manor court against those who were thought to have inclosed pasture without licence and thus reduced the common pasture. At High Ercall in 1338-9 there is evidence to suggest that an attempt by the lord to reduce the amount of land available for general grazing resulted in a concerted campaign of disobedience by his tenants.[99] In the early years of the 15th century the abbots of Lilleshall and Shrewsbury and the priors of Wenlock and Wombridge were all presented in Wrockwardine manor court for inclosing pasture that was claimed as common to all tenants.[1] Protests against those who overburdened the common pastures with their animals, who kept more animals than their land would support, or who allowed outsiders to bring their animals into the manor seem to increase during the 15th and early 16th centuries, and that jealous attitude to pasture is another indication of increasing specialization in cattle rearing among the peasantry.[2] Sometimes stints were fixed in an attempt to limit the abuse of common pasture. In the earlier 15th century limits were placed on the number of horses kept on the common pasture in Condover and Eaton-under-Heywood, and the

[92] *V.C.H. Salop.* viii. 272.
[93] Ibid. 317; R. Gough, *Antiquities & Memoirs of Par. of Myddle* (Shrews. 1875), 27.
[94] Above, Domesday Book to 1300 (Woodland, assarting, and inclosure); above (Assarting and inclosure).
[95] Though the familiar prohibitions of gleaning and leaving the manor during harvest do appear: see e.g. Mumford, *Wenlock*, 161-3; S.R.O. 20/1/6.
[96] e.g. Mumford, op. cit. 162-3; S.R.O. 212, box 10C; 611/421; 1224/2/6, ct. 16 Aug. 1412; S.P.L., Deeds 9136, ct. 21 Dec. 1453; 16330, ct. 16 Oct. 1422; Staffs. R.O., D. 593/J/17/2, ct. 1 Oct. 1527.
[97] e.g. Mumford, op. cit. 160-4; S.P.L., Deeds 7298, ct.

7 Oct. 1395; 16330, ct. 6 Oct. 1422; S.R.O. 20/1/3, ct. 24 Feb. 1355; Staffs. R.O., D. 1733/19, ct. r. 24 Edw. III; P.R.O., SC 2/197/131, ct. 21 Nov. 1409.
[98] e.g. *Cart. Haughmond*, pp. 45 (no. 140), 92 (no. 405), 115 (no. 535), 119 (no. 560); S.R.O. 2919/2/13.
[99] *T.S.A.S.* lxii. 24.
[1] Ibid. 28-9; S.P.L., Deeds 19395-6; see also ibid. 9136, cts. 11 June, 20 Oct. 1439; S.R.O. 566/1, ct. 13 Dec. 1333.
[2] e.g. Mumford, *Wenlock*, 161-2; *T.S.A.S.* 3rd ser. i. 219; B.L. Add. Ch. 54387, m. 1; Staffs. R.O., D. 593/J/9/1; /J/17/1-2; D. 1733/19, ct. r. 24 Edw. III, 23 Hen. VI; S.P.L., Deeds 9072, ct. 15 Oct. 1409; S.R.O. 1224/2/535, ct. r. 31-2 Hen. VI.

tenants of Dorrington, in Condover, agreed in 1449 to limit the number of sheep commoned to 40 for each half virgate.[3]

Although there are signs of increasing pressure on pasture resources, they are not as frequent or widespread as in some other counties because there was still a plentiful supply of waste, woodland, and forest for piecemeal inclosure or common grazing. The inhabitants of the area covered by the former Clee forest were allowed commoning rights within the remaining waste lands of the forest, and the movement of cattle on Brown Clee by the Clee strakers has been said to amount almost to transhumance.[4] Occasionally there were disputes between tenants from neighbouring townships over commoning rights, and individuals were accused of taking unfair advantage of rights common to all. In 1386 an ordinance was made in the court of Aston that the tenants of Sandford, Woolston, and Aston should not prevent the tenants of Felton from pasturing their sheep and small horses on the waste or on the common pastures of the townships.[5] In 1413 it was found that 34 tenants of Lord Ferrers of Groby and 4 tenants of the dean of St. Mary's, Bridgnorth, had kept pigs continuously in the royal forest of Morfe for two years, ruining the common pasture and destroying the forest agistment.[6] There were also protests when tenants' rights were threatened by their lords' desire to increase their income from rents. In 1368 the burgesses of Ruyton complained that parts of Allans wood which had been granted to them in common for a rent of 6d. an acre were being leased to outsiders at a higher rent, and in 1502 the inhabitants of the township of Bucknell in the lordship of Clun complained that the lord of Jay had inclosed the common of the township called Jay Morsse.[7] In 1413 Lord Furnivalle's tenants defended an inclosure made by the prior of Wenlock at Powkesmoor near Ditton Priors against an attack by the earl of Arundel's men, but that dispute had more to do with political rivalry for domination of the county than with threatened tenants' rights.[8] In the early 16th century four Shrewsbury butchers and graziers acquired the townships of Loton and Hayes (in Alberbury and Cardeston) by paying large entry fines; then, having driven out the tenants by raising their rents, they converted the arable to pasture.[9] The inclosure of Harley and Cressage woods at the same period led to one of the few recorded incidents of hedge burning in early 16th-century Shropshire.[10] Considerable ill will was engendered by Lord Stafford's attempts to increase income from the forests in his lordship of Caus in the 1530s and 1540s. He increased the number of inclosed pastures in Hogstow forest but had to compensate the freeholders of Minsterley and other manors for the loss of their well documented common rights. His restriction of rights of common herbage in Hayes forest and his attempt to revive ancient herbage rents from the townships around the forest was resisted by his tenants before the Council in the Marches of Wales, and his inclosure of the forest pastures was seen as an obvious threat to the way of life of those peasants who 'had no other living but only upon their cattle'.[11]

[3] Mumford, op. cit. 164; S.P.L., Deeds 9136, ct. 3 Apr. 1446, 2 July 1449.
[4] T.S.A.S. lviii. 48, 57-62.
[5] Smith, 'Lordships of Chirk and Oswestry', 289; N.L.W., Aston Hall 5343, ct. 14 July 1386.
[6] Cal. Inq. Misc. vii, p. 250.
[7] T.S.A.S. 3rd ser. i. 215; S.R.O. 552/1/51, ct. 7 Feb. 1502; 1514/433, ct. 1 Mar. 1368.
[8] E.H.R. xcix. 538-40.
[9] V.C.H. Salop. viii. 191; P.R.O., STAC 2/26/105.
[10] V.C.H. Salop. viii. 73, 85-6; P.R.O., STAC 2/27/182; STAC 2/30/32. [11] Welsh Hist. Rev. vi. 4, 8-9, 12-15.

1540–1750

THE period between the dissolution of the monasteries and the middle of the 18th century was an important one for the development of Shropshire agriculture, as it was nationally. There were vast changes in landownership. Many estates, especially in the first half of the period, were run more profitably. Shropshire farmers became more commercially minded and specialized in producing those commodities best suited to the areas where they worked. The growth of dairy farming on the north Shropshire plain is particularly noteworthy but other livestock and mixed-farming enterprises developed elsewhere in the county. Farm produce helped to supply more than the merely local markets and as inter-regional trade expanded new and more flexible means of doing business evolved; more trade bypassed the established markets and fairs. The agents of change, the middlemen, gradually tightened their grip on the market and if for long their efforts were largely unappreciated, they did a vital job in moving goods around the country.

Pressure on food supplies in the first half of the period increased the value of land, and in Shropshire thousands of acres of waste and common were brought into regular cultivation. Farming efficiency was also promoted by the tidying away of the strips in many of the residual open fields and by more systematic adoption of convertible husbandry. Some of the major landowners led the way in making improvements, hoping thereby to augment their income: higher entry fines were demanded and rack renting made some headway after the Restoration. Tenants in general had an interest in inclosure and if they disliked the rent rises of the late 16th and early 17th century, they seem nevertheless to have paid them.

Crises, however, did occur and harvest failures in the 1590s and 1620s were particularly severe. The agricultural depression which set in after the Restoration did not affect Shropshire to the same degree as it did those counties where mixed farming was more pronounced. Indeed more corn was grown locally, though much of it as animal fodder. Rent arrears built up from time to time, especially among the smaller farmers in the hundred years after the Restoration and that stimulated a move towards larger farms. Cattle plague in the 1740s led to the dislocation of Shropshire's livestock trade. Nevertheless the early modern period was in general one of progress for Shropshire agriculture and the benefits reached a wider section of the rural population than just the gentry and substantial farmers.

Inclosure

In mainly wood-pasture areas like Shropshire, where arable farming was subordinate to livestock husbandry, the open fields were less extensive and important than those in open-field mixed-farming communities. Much agricultural land had never been organized into open fields, having been inclosed directly from woodland. Normally laid to grass, those closes provided the basis of the largely pastoral economy. Accordingly there was not the same pressure to maintain the open fields and they tended to be inclosed early by private agreement. In Shropshire the attack on the open fields began before 1540 and intensified over the next two centuries so that by 1750 open-field cultivation had virtually disappeared, though in places a few strips remained until the early 19th century.

In some parts of England inclosure of the open fields was often a single cataclysmic event, whereas in pastoral areas it tended to be a more drawn-out and less convulsive business. To highlight differences in the timing and pace of the movement glebe terriers can be used,[12] and in Shropshire they show the gradual nature of the change. In 1612 the vicar of Montford's glebe lay largely dispersed in open-field strips, but during the 17th century they were gradually exchanged, consolidated, and inclosed, a process that was completed by the opening years of the 18th century.[13] Naturally there were variations between parishes, depending on social as well as economic and geographical differences. On the north Shropshire plain early inclosure was often associated with dairy farming and in villages like Adderley little open-field arable survived into the 17th century.[14] In south Shropshire the movement seems to have been initiated by the yeomen farmers and advanced quickest in places free of manorial control. Around the Brown Clee inclosure had been in progress since the 15th century and in townships with absentee landlords such as Cold Weston and Abdon the strips had largely disappeared by the early 17th century. At Ditton Priors, where the Cannings kept firm control, open fields survived until they were largely inclosed in the 18th century.[15]

Some large landowners, however, did begin to take positive action and their involvement was a major contribution to the acceleration of inclosure in the 17th century.[16] At Cantlop Thomas Owen owned the whole manor from 1587 and inclosed the open fields in the next few years. At Corfton William Baldwyn initiated exchanges with Charles Foxe, the manor's other major landowner, and by the mid 17th century the township was almost entirely inclosed. The family adopted a similar policy in Diddlebury and Siefton in the 1630s. On the Craven estate, however, little had been done by 1652–3 though some piecemeal inclosure had been carried out by the tenants.[17]

The inhabitants took the lead at Highley: c. 1626 the freeholders exchanged and inclosed their open-field land to 'their more commodious use' and the vicar joined in. Evidently the inclosure of the open fields did not meet the same opposition as was encountered in mixed-farming communities. At Lilleshall in the late 17th century William Leveson-Gower's tenants petitioned him that their field ground lay inconveniently dispersed and would benefit from inclosure; first, however, exchanges would be needed 'in order to lay their ground together and to make each others' farms convenient to them'.[18]

More common were the small-scale improvements made by peasant farmers and recorded in manor court rolls, such as those for which the inhabitants of Sleap and Eyton upon the Weald Moors were being presented in 1547. In 1588 John Harper *alias* Henson was said to have inclosed 'divers parcels of ground' in Kynnersley's leet fields; thirteen others from the parish were presented at the same time. The nibbling away at the edges of the fields continued throughout the 17th and early 18th century. At Longdon upon Tern in 1632 Jerome Bathoe was presented for taking in and inclosing part of the leet fields without the lord's licence. Six years later Hugh Wright was fined 6*d*. for encroaching on the open field in Muxton (in Lilleshall) at Alexander's dole.[19] The names of such closes often indicate their origin in the open fields. Thus among the fields farmed by

[12] M. W. Beresford, 'Glebe Terriers and Open Field Leics.' *Trans. Leics. Arch. Soc.* xxiv. 83.

[13] L.J.R.O., B/V/6, Montford.

[14] P. R. Edwards, 'Farming Econ. of NE. Salop. in 17th Cent.' (Oxf. Univ. D.Phil. thesis, 1976), 233–4.

[15] R. T. Rowley, 'Hist. of S. Salop. Landscape 1086–1800' (Oxf. Univ. B.Litt. thesis, 1967), 104–10, 134; K. W. G. Goodman, 'Hammerman's Hill: Land, People, and Inds. of Titterstone Clee Area 16th to 18th Cents.' (Keele Univ.

Ph.D. thesis, 1978), 140 sqq., 169–70. The hist. of Ditton Priors will be found in *V.C.H. Salop.* x.

[16] Rowley, op. cit. 126–7.

[17] Ibid. 107–8; *V.C.H. Salop.* viii. 22; Bodl., Craven dep. 16–17, 19–21.

[18] H.W.R.O.(H.), Heref. dioc. rec., Highley glebe terrier 1626; Staffs. R.O., D. 593/D/3/23.

[19] Staffs. R.O., D. 593/J/11/1/26; /J/13/2/1.

William Bishop, who leased a holding in Broadstone (in Munslow) in 1652, was a 2-a. arable close called Long furlong, which abutted on Hill field.[20]

Manorial lords seem in fact to have condoned piecemeal inclosure of open fields, only unlicensed activities coming before the manor court. In 1579 a pain was laid on all tenants of Sheriffhales manor who inclosed land without licence; all who had already done so were to cast them open again unless they had obtained the lady's permission. Much later, at a court held in 1716, the main concern was to ensure that those who had inclosed land should keep their hedges and ditches in repair.[21]

One effect of inclosure was to reduce grazing on the aftermath and fallows. Smallholders and cottagers were hardest hit but even so the effects were not as bad as in mixed-farming areas where there was less common land. Stinting, however, was often necessary. Cherrington and Kynnersley open fields were stinted as early as 1551 and 1558 and around the Weald Moors other stints were agreed at Waters Upton (1611), Lilleshall (1617, 1652), Kynnersley (1654), and Leegomery (1664). The growth of fattening in the area exacerbated the problem despite the existence of so much inclosed grassland and open pasture. Local people bought stores for feeding and some overstocked the fallows and stubble. The same problems were experienced elsewhere in the county. At Uckington, a manor in the Severnside parish of Wroxeter, a professional surveyor was appointed in 1632 to work out a stint in Marsh field and land recently inclosed from it.[22]

The piecemeal inclosure of Shropshire's open fields during the early modern period accounted for only a fraction of the land that was inclosed. Far more important was the improvement of thousands of acres of waste by tree felling, drainage, and inclosure. In general the greatest amount of improvement took place on the heavier soils that underlay the woodland or on the wet peaty soils. Pools were drained too. Piecemeal inclosure was carried out in the less fertile sandy heaths and on the thin soils of the upland commons but large-scale undertakings tended to be carried out later at the time of parliamentary inclosure.[23]

Cultivation had long been extended by inclosure of waste but the period from the mid 16th century was especially important as population grew and many landowners began to improve their estates. The rise in agricultural prices in the late 16th and early 17th century and the pressure on land encouraged improvements, which raised rents and land values. There was an active land market in the county in the late 16th century, and many of the new owners were determined to exploit their investment. Some purchasers were new to landowning like the Levesons, Egertons, and Welds, who had made fortunes in trade or the law, but it would be wrong to assume that the old established families played no part in the movement. The Talbots, earls of Shrewsbury, the Howards, earls of Arundel and Surrey, and the Corbets, for instance, were also involved in considerable inclosure and drainage schemes. Other families were less enterprising: on the loosely administered Craven estates in south Shropshire, for instance, not only did strip cultivation survive in some manors well into the 18th century but also large areas of common remained untouched.[24]

Inevitably the larger landowners were responsible for major undertakings. At Myddle, once 'beautified with many famous woods', officials of the le Stranges and their successors the Stanleys organized woodland clearance. Inclosure began

[20] Bodl., Craven dep. 16.
[21] Staffs. R.O., D. 593/J/17/3/6; /J/17/4.
[22] Edwards, 'Farming Econ. of NE. Salop.' 232–3.
[23] For this para. and the next see ibid. 235–7.
[24] Rowley, 'S. Salop. Landscape', 135.

in the late 15th century with the felling of Divlin wood, followed by Brandwood and Holloway Hills wood a generation later. About the mid 16th century systematic clearance of Myddlewood began and so much wood was felled that by 1563 Myddle's 'many inclosures' were said to be likely 'to destroy the woods'. In Wem the felling of Northwood, begun in Henry VIII's reign by Lord Dacre (d. 1563), was completed by his grand-daughter the countess of Arundel (d. 1630).[25] At the same time the upland wastes were improved. In 1575-6 an octogenarian recalled over 600 a. of Clun forest, part of the FitzAlans' lordship, being inclosed and brought into severalty.[26] On Wenlock Edge much woodland was cleared in the 16th century and in Corve Dale the work was almost complete by 1600.[27] In 1625 the 2,300 a. of wood and common constituting Shirlett forest was divided among the surrounding manors;[28] some inclosures were made then but the pace of change varied and final inclosure came only in 1775.[29]

Parks too were being split up by landlords in the later 16th and 17th centuries to profit from the new high rents that could be realized. Disparkment was often foreshadowed by an increased emphasis on cattle rearing or dairy farming in the park, whether by the lord or a tenant; that happened at Cardeston in the mid 16th century and at Minsterley a century later.[30] In 1617 the Council in the Marches of Wales recorded that Sir Charles Foxe refused to show 'by what title he doth hold Oakly Park and keepeth more sheep and cattle than deer'.[31] In Shropshire, as elsewhere, lords were 'making their deer leap over the pale to give bullocks place'.[32] In such cases, little change in land use followed final disparkment. Sometimes, however, disparkment could lead to sudden and radical changes involving woodland clearance and the creation of a patchwork of hedged closes. That happened at Tilstock and the process is vividly caught on a map of c. 1600 that shows two tenants felling trees in the former park.[33]

Generally, however, many more parks were created than destroyed. In some cases imparkment seems to have been the seizure of an opportunity, when allotment of common wood or waste suddenly invested a landowner with exclusive ownership of a large tract of what was often marginal land. Thus when Shirlett forest was allotted and partly inclosed in 1625 John Weld of Willey immediately imparked his 410-a. share, although he already had one park barely a kilometre away; the new park's management went hand in hand with the old one's and Weld's investments in them demonstrate the economic role of parks at that time. It remained much what it had been in the Middle Ages. Separately inclosed within the pale were extensive tracts of valuable woodland, which were pannaged in autumn; they contained both coppices and timber. There were also areas of pasture, which could be grazed either by cattle or by the deer and horses that Weld was putting into the park. He also made fishponds, and bought swans and bees.[34] Hence one of a park's two main economic functions was to ensure a ready supply of food—meat, fish, and honey for instance— for the lord's table. The other was to provide as secure an environment as possible for demesne stock management and

[25] R. Gough, *Antiquities & Memoirs of the Parish of Myddle* (Shrews. 1875), 23-5, 29-30; S.R.O. 167/51; 212, box 345, no. 1; S. Garbet, *Hist. Wem.* (Wem, 1818), 336.

[26] *T.S.A.S.* xi. 260-1.

[27] Rowley, 'S. Salop. Landscape', 112, 114.

[28] S.R.O. 1093/2/453-4; 1224/1/14-18; 1224, box 163, arts. of 1625; S.P.L., MS. 8891.

[29] Under 13 Geo. III, c. 105 (Private): S.R.O. 1224, box 147, award and Act; 1952/11-12.

[30] *V.C.H. Salop.* viii. 205, 298, 306, 318. Cf. also the cases

of Caus (ibid. 297), Hadley (ibid. xi. 257), Kenwick (S.R.O. 212, box 345, nos. 15, 17), and Oswestry (W. J. Slack, *The Lordship of Oswestry 1393-1607* (Salop. Arch. Soc. 1951), 20, 56-7). [31] *T.S.A.S.* 2nd ser. xii. 154.

[32] Ric. Carew's pithy observation in the *Surv. of Cornwall* (1603), cited by T. Williamson and Liz Bellamy, *Property and Landscape: Social Hist. of Landownership and the Eng. Countryside* (1987), 136.

[33] T. Rowley, *Salop. Landscape* (1972), 122.

[34] *T.S.A.S.* lxv. 71-3.

for the valuable reserves of wood: not surprisingly therefore, lords usually employed a parker who lived in a park lodge.

Nevertheless parks were invariably a drain on resources and a far from economic form of land use. Indeed they were not created for purely economic reasons. A park conferred prestige and drew attention to the owner's social rank; many in the later 16th century were made or extended to embellish new or remodelled houses, as at Plaish, Moreton Corbet, and Upton Cressett.[35] The work might involve the removal of tenants' houses or the diversion of roads and in such cases the park was designed to be more than protection for the lord's beasts and woods. It was also conceived as a wide surrounding paradise, almost invariably furnished with deer, the intended sport of the owner and his most favoured guests.[36] From the mid 16th century, moreover, there was clearly a growing appreciation of the aesthetic pleasures of a parkland view: at Frodesley a new lodge was built in the earlier 17th century on a rocky eminence,[37] while at Lilleshall a balcony overlooking the park was added to the lodge before 1679.[38]

Landowners were involved in drainage operations too, especially in north Shropshire. In 1539 Sir Richard Brereton, tenant of Harnage Grange,[39] bought Dogmoor, 200 a. of marsh in Prees, and reclaimed it. In Wem Lord Dacre was again the instigator: he began the drainage of the Old Pool, another enterprise completed by his grand-daughter. In Myddle Harmer Moss and Myddle Pools and in Ellesmere Tetchill Moor were among the marshy lands brought into regular cultivation during the late 16th and early 17th century. The largest project of all was the reclamation of the Weald Moors where by 1650—as the inhabitants of Wrockwardine claimed— 2,730 a. had been inclosed by tenants of neighbouring manors. The Levesons, as the major landowners, led the way, but other families participated too.[40]

Such improvements involved much expense and labour: Brereton spent 600 to 1,000 marks in buying Dogmoor and 'stocking, ditching, and mending' it.[41] Even if costs did not often run that high it was in the landowner's interest to involve his tenants in his projects, not only to reduce labour costs but also to head off opposition. The first attempts at draining Wem Old Pool were made by six of Dacre's tenants who had a joint lease of the land at a rent of 9d. for every acre made firm ground. Tenants of the newly improved land in Tetchill Moor had to make their own ditches and a road from Tetchill to Kenwick Park. The new ditches made in the Weald Moors were dug by the Sheldons' and Levesons' tenants. When Sir Walter Leveson had the Strine widened from Rodway to Crudgington he appointed that the river should be kept six yards wide and gave the men of Kynnersley a measure for the purpose.[42] To help with the felling of Northwood the countess of Arundel brought in outsiders but local labour was often used. It was normal, for instance, for tenants to grub up stumps and make hedges and ditches; in return they customarily had the stubbings and enough timber for fencing. About 1561 it was decided to inclose part of the Nether Marbury Heys, Whitchurch, and to let it for years, the tenant to stub it and 'have the rammel [barren earth] for his labour'. In 1590 Thomas Farmer acquired the

[35] E. Mercer and P. A. Stamper, 'Plaish Hall and Early Brickwork in Salop.' (forthcoming ibid. lxvi); Rowley, *Salop. Landscape*, 121–4.

[36] As 17th-cent. maps often emphasize: see e.g. S.R.O. 972, bdle. 233, item 1 (Lilleshall 1679); 1275/1 (Pitchford 1682).

[37] *V.C.H. Salop.* viii. 80 and pl. facing p. 82.

[38] Ibid. xi. 154.

[39] And of pools and rough pasture in the Condover demesne: *V.C.H. Salop.* viii. 44, 65.

[40] Edwards, 'Farming Econ. of NE. Salop.' 241–4, 246– 8, 250–4; D. G. Hey, *An Eng. Rural Community: Myddle under Tudors and Stuarts* (1974), 37–9 and pl. 1–3.

[41] J. R. W. Whitfield, 'Enclosure Movement in N. Salop.' *T.C.S.V.F.C.* xi. 54.

[42] S.R.O. 167/51; 212/92; Staffs. R.O., D. 593/E/6/10.

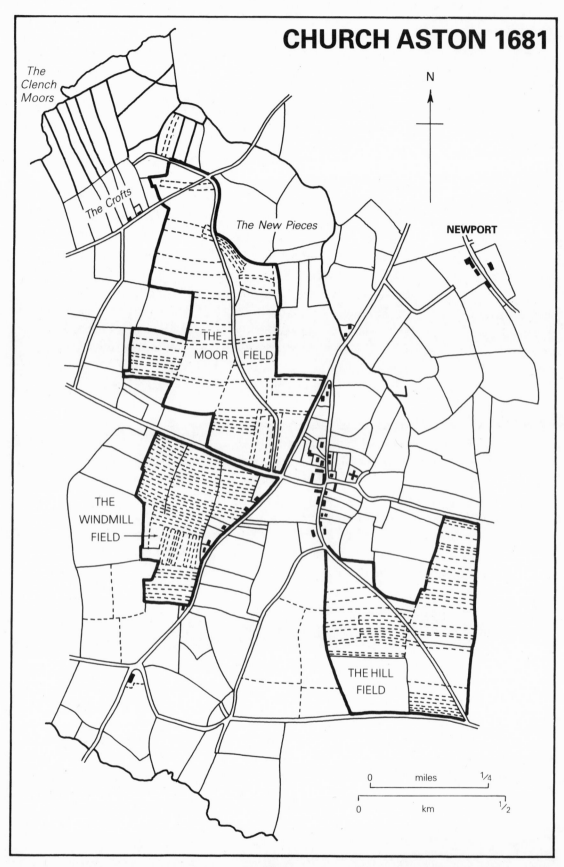

CHURCH ASTON 1681

N

The Clench Moors

The Crofts

The New Pieces

NEWPORT

THE MOOR FIELD

THE WINDMILL FIELD

THE HILL FIELD

| 0 | miles | ¼ |
| 0 | km | ½ |

Fig. 10

The manor's three open fields were inclosed in the early 18th century. Their long strips ran from furlong to furlong, as in open fields elsewhere in the county. The area outside the heavy line was ancient closes or former meadow, pasture and woodland. In the north much of the moorland had already been inclosed by 1681; no woodland survived.

lease of a farm at Cantlop (in Berrington) together with a 12-a. allotment in Cantlop wood, then being parcelled out; if Farmer inclosed this piece, the lease stated, the work had to be done at his expense.[43]

Clearly landowners hoped for a return on their investment and inclosure did raise the value of land. Dogmoor, which before reclamation was so 'miry and deep of water that no cattle could feed or pasture thereon nor any profit could be taken thereof', rose in value from 12*d.* a year to 40 marks. Similar improvements were made in the Weald Moors and rents increased. Nevertheless such low lying marshy areas needed constant attention, and in the Weald Moors some of the gains appear to have been lost by the beginning of the 19th century.[44]

In woodland clearances landowners benefited from the sale of timber, in increasingly valuable commodity as population grew and local mines and ironworks developed. On some estates that may have been a major stimulus to improvement. In the mid 16th century the earl of Shrewsbury had his wood at Diddlebury surveyed and sold the trees there, and William Savage did the same in Corfton wood in 1575. At Netchwood in the early 17th century much of the timber was cleared for the local iron furnaces; the same seems to have happened at Cleobury Mortimer and perhaps Shifnal.[45] Timber sales were important on the Bridgwater and Forester estates too: besides the power to raise occasional large sums Sir William Forester (d. 1718) enjoyed an average income of £250 a year from wood sales. To protect their position landowners normally reserved the right to the timber growing on their property whenever it was leased out.[46]

Landowners or their agents occasionally felt it prudent to justify inclosure as generally beneficial. About 1600 it was claimed that inclosure of commons and wastes in Whitchurch manor would do no harm 'for whereas before an acre of this waste did not yield 6*d.* to the commonwealth now being inclosed the farmer payeth 3*s.* 4*d.* the acre and maintaineth well a family on the same'.[47] Generally Shropshire attitudes to inclosure were quite favourable. In mixed-farming communities elsewhere in the country inclosure often meant conversion of open-field arable to pasture and caused depopulation and distress; loss of commons in those areas was also a cause of much concern as they were often small in extent and their extinction upset a delicately balanced economy. In Shropshire, on the other hand, inclosure did not change the rural economy and waste was still readily available. Many commons, especially upland wastes, remained largely unimproved partly because they were agriculturally unattractive but also partly because commoners preserved their rights by preventing total inclosure. Even in lowland parishes like Myddle, where much inclosure took place in the early modern period, patches of waste survived. Manorial lords might inclose their wastes provided they left their tenants sufficient common.[48] While not everyone observed that condition and disputes occurred, many did take the law into consideration. In 1639 it was said on behalf of Henry Powell of Worthen that, although he had inclosed 60 a. out of the Forest of Hayes, that was far less than a tenth of the common; that his family had held it separately from time immemorial; and that enough common remained for the tenants.[49]

[43] Garbet, *Wem*, 59, 336; S.R.O. 103/1; 212, box 346, no. 36; G. F. Jackson, *Salop. Word-Bk.* (1879), 343.
[44] *T.C.S.V.F.C.* xi. 55; Staffs. R.O., D. 593/J/11/2/3; /J/22/18/8; P. R. Edwards, 'Drainage Operations in the Wealdmoors', *Evolution of Marshland Landscapes* (Oxf. Univ. Dept. for External Studies, 1981), 139–40.
[45] Rowley, 'S. Salop. Landscape', 111 sqq.; L. Stone, *Crisis of the Aristocracy 1558–1641* (1965), 347–8, 350–1.
[46] E. Hopkins, 'Bridgewater Est. in N. Salop. in First

Half of 17th Cent.' (Lond. Univ. M.A. thesis, 1956), 123–4; S.R.O. 1224, box 297, rent r. of Sir Wm. Forester's Watling St. and Dothill est. [1689 × 1718]; *T.S.A.S.* 3rd ser. ii. 334.
[47] S.R.O. 212, box 60, acct. of commons and wastes in man. of Whitchurch.
[48] Under Stat. of Merton, 1236, 20 Hen. III, c. 4.
[49] Rowley, 'S. Salop. Landscape', 136–7; Hey, *Myddle under Tudors and Stuarts*, 34, 39; S.R.O. 837/56.

Inclosure improved the quality of grassland, an important consideration in an area dominated by livestock husbandry, and many new meadows and pastures were created. The amount of arable increased too. Wastes had always been liable to intermittent cultivation—in the 1690s tenants of Ratlinghope and Stretton manors were ploughing parts of the Long Mynd—but yields may not have been very high, especially after a couple of years. Civil War grain shortages led to the cultivation of Myddlewood common where the first crop was a very strong crop of winter corn; the next was a crop of barley so poor 'that most of it was pulled up by the root, because it was too short to be cut'. After inclosure, however, a regular course of husbandry could be adopted and with improvement the land gave better corn crops.[50] When Albrighton heath, near Shrewsbury, was inclosed in the early 17th century the lord of the manor Thomas Ireland claimed to have used his 20 a. 'for raising of more store of corn and grain for the good of the commonwealth'.[51]

By and large tenants seem to have been treated fairly by landowners in their improvement schemes. Newly inclosed land was often incorporated into their leases in lieu of common rights or alternative common grazing was found. Sometimes a rent charge was added, as when the tenants in Myddle and Marton townships were allowed to rent clearances from Myddlewood for 1s. an old customary acre (i.e. 6d. a statute acre). Individual closes could be leased and the extra holdings formed provided access to land for a growing population. Thus in the 1560s when William Leighton inclosed 100 a. of Holt Preen wood (in Cardington) he divided the land and let it to a number of tenants.[52] Farms generally remained small in the early modern period and that made it easier for comparatively lowly men to obtain a lease. Some engrossing of holdings did occur, and the process seems to have accelerated in the early 18th century as landowners sought to rationalize their enterprises, but in general the problem was not a serious one in the period 1540–1750.

Smallholders and cottagers may have viewed inclosure of the wastes with less pleasure than more substantial men, for the commons were relatively more important to them. Moreover such people may not have been able to rent newly inclosed ground and, even apart from a reduction in the area of common, they were simultaneously faced with restricted grazing on the shrinking fallows and aftermaths. As in the residual open fields, stints were introduced on some commons and constant care was needed to prevent overstocking by the commoners or others.[53] There was opposition: Sir Richard Brereton's efforts to drain and inclose Dogmoor, begun in 1539, provoked a violent clash with locals and the matter was not settled until Mary I's reign. At Oswestry in 1602 the surveyor, recommending large-scale inclosure of the wastes, observed that, although the action would be 'to the great benefit of the country and profit of your lordship', 'some perverse people . . . will hinder the best course of common good'.[54]

Protest against individual exploitation of the common waste, however, was often incited by rival gentry disputing rights of ownership.[55] In a conflict involving Holt Preen wood (1627–41), partly inclosed by the Leightons, lords of the manor, Francis Wolryche, lord of Hughley manor, gained his own ends by successfully inciting his tenants to pull down the fences.[56] Most of the opposition to improvement

[50] S.R.O. 93/26; S.P.L., Deeds 17419; Gough, *Myddle*, 33.
[51] S.R.O. 1514/608.
[52] Edwards, 'Farming Econ. of NE. Salop.' 253–4; S.R.O. 2922/1/1/1.
[53] Edwards, op. cit. 255–6.
[54] *T.C.S.V.F.C.* xi. 54–6; Slack, *Lordship of Oswestry*, 68.
[55] S.R.O. 665/1/256; 2922/1/5/1–19; Goodman, 'Hammerman's Hill', 119–20.
[56] S.R.O. 2922/1/1/1. Cf. C. J. Harrison, 'Fire on the Chase: Rural Discontent in 16th-Cent. Staffs.' (unpubl. paper to Joint Winter Conf. of Brit. Agric. Hist. Soc. and Hist. Geographers' Res. Group, 1979). Thanks are due to Dr. Harrison for kindly making his paper available.

of the wastes seems in fact to have been due to intercommoning disputes rather than conflicts between tenants and improving landlords. In the early 16th century many township boundaries in unimproved woodland and waste were marked by merestones and the commons were intercommoned by two or more communities. As population grew, and with it pressure on land, clashes were inevitable. That was the situation in the Weald Moors from the mid 16th century as each township adopted a more restrictive and exclusive policy contrasting with the casualness of earlier arrangements.[57] Similar cases elsewhere in the county are not hard to find.

In the lordship of Oswestry the motive behind the opposition to the inclosure recommended in the 1602 survey seems to have been one of self-interest. At that date 669¼ a. of waste had been inclosed, much of it as small encroachments by tenants and freeholders. They presumably had their eye on the remaining 5,596½ a. too![58] Nor were they alone. Many peasant farmers and cottagers throughout Shropshire, acting alone or in concert with their neighbours, were responsible for a good deal of inclosure. Numerous cottages were built on patches of waste with an acre or two of land added to them. Such encroachments could amount to a considerable acreage. On Prees and Whitchurch heaths the tenants had encroached on and improved 133¾ a. by 1593. On the Craven estates, where seigneurial initiative was lacking, the same tenants and small freeholders who were encroaching on the common fields were also taking in pieces of waste. In Stanton Lacy a number of commons were gradually whittled away during the 17th and early 18th centuries. In 1732 there were fourteen squatters on Hayton's Bent and twelve on Rock Lane, six on Green Lane and two on Vernolds Common. Fifteen years later there were well over forty cottagers in the manor.[59]

Particular concentrations occurred in industrial areas. On the Clee Hills mining had been practised since the Middle Ages, though haphazardly, and the miners, often part-time farmers, dug bell pits and built squatter cottages on the commons. In Ditton Priors a rise in the number of squatters was associated with mining and quarrying: a 1728 rental included eleven cottages on the Brown Clee with 22 a. of land and eleven encroachments (totalling 7 a.) along Bent Lane, the road leading from Ditton to the quarries. On the east Shropshire coalfield a similar development took place. In 1650 there were 34 cottages in Pain's Lane and Wrockwardine Wood, and c. 1688 41 householders in Coalpit Bank (in Wombridge) petitioned for exemption from the Hearth Tax.[60]

Cottages were occupied not only by locals but also by immigrants to Shropshire, attracted by the availability of land and opportunities of employment. References to squatters can be found in court rolls and other records throughout the early modern period but there seem to have been several bouts of increased activity, namely c. 1600, in the Civil War and Interregnum period, and c. 1700. The earlier two waves, at least, coincided with periods of increased mortality, so the immigrants were likelier to be welcomed as useful additional labour.[61]

Landowners had ambivalent attitudes to squatters; they opposed unlicensed cottages and inclosures but reserves of common were ample and encroachments, once regularized, might keep the very poor from destitution or, in more favourable circumstances, yield additional income. Six cottages in Little Drayton in 1648 paid

[57] Edwards, 'Farming Econ. of NE. Salop.' 247; *T.S.A.S.* lxiii. 1–9.
[58] Slack, *Lordship of Oswestry*, 44–95.
[59] S.R.O. 212, box 346, no. 9; Rowley, 'S. Salop. Landscape', 135–6.
[60] Rowley, op. cit. 138; idem, *Salop. Landscape*, 212–13; Goodwin, 'Hammerman's Hill', 159–62, 391–402; Staffs. R.O., D. 593/H/14/2/16; /N/3/10/17; *V.C.H. Salop.* xi. 151, 269, 323.
[61] Edwards, 'Farming Econ. of NE. Salop.' 263.

only 2s. 8d. a year altogether. Their inhabitants had taken in small pieces of common for gardens or closes but lived 'so lamentably poor' that they could be charged only an acknowledgement, though labourers or poor tradesmen might be got who could pay 10s. a year for a cottage.[62] Landlords were doubtless often reluctant to improve their rental so thoroughly that poor people were thrown on the rates;[63] at Whixall c. 1680, however, 16 cottages and 23 intakes (65⅜ a.) yielded rent of £25 4s. 11d.[64] In mining districts landowners encouraged immigrant labour. In such areas cottagers were exempt from the Act of 1589 requiring new cottages to have at least 4 a. laid to them.[65] In 1729 there were c. 76 cottagers in the several squatter settlements in and around Barrow parish, where there were mines and ironworks. Of the 63 cottagers about whom something is known one had 3 cows, one had 2, seventeen had 1, and the remainder none.[66] The statute of 1589 was not regularly observed in Shropshire,[67] and that suggests a lack of concern for a situation which often caused great consternation elsewhere.

The agricultural labourer's wages, appropriate for consideration along with the provision of cottages, may have made some progress against prices during the 17th and early 18th centuries. In the Shrewsbury area by 1628 a male day labourer received 3d. a day with diet or 7d. a day without during the summer, the winter rates being 1d. lower. For mowing at the hay and grain harvests the daily rates were 6d. and 8d. respectively with food and drink, 1s. and 1s. 4d. without. Reaping, probably less skilful and productive, was paid at 1d. or 2d. less than the mowing rate, and the gathering rate was less than the mowing rate by 2d. or more. Haymaking was paid at about the ordinary rate for summer labour. The lower rates of pay had increased slightly by 1640. In January 1694 general labouring on the Newport estate seems to have been paid at 9d. a day, though whether that included diet or not is uncertain. Samuel Matthews had 1s. a day with ale and food for appointing the ploughteams that year 'and keeping 'em at work'; another man received 2s. a day for 3 days' carrying with his team. Two months later labourers at hedging were receiving 10d. a day, though they were apparently being assisted by workers paid 6d. a day. On the Bridgeman estates haymaking was paid at 8d. a day in 1697 and that was also the rate for general labour in the winter of 1703–4. The hay mower was paid 1s. a day in 1713. In the autumn of 1746 mowing hay on the Davenports' estate was paid at 1s. 2d. a day, general labour at 10d. a day. Men were reaping wheat as task work for 1s. 4d. an acre. Throughout the period many labourers, particularly women and children, received less than the prevailing rates even when at the same work. In 1746 women at unspecified work and at apple picking on the Davenports' estate received 6d. a day. Another female, perhaps a girl, received 3d. a day at haymaking.[68]

Landlord and tenant

While inclosure did not generally prove a socially divisive issue in Shropshire, pressure on land did create other tensions. As land values rose from the mid 16th century landowners sought to strengthen their hold over their tenants and increase their income from land. Inclosure and improvement apart, the landlord's readiest

[62] Arundel Cast. MS. MD 507.
[63] Ag. Hist. Eng. v (1), 150.
[64] S.R.O. 2/276.
[65] 31 Eliz. I, c. 7: Ag. Hist. Eng. iv. 409.
[66] S.R.O. 1224, box 81, tithe acct. of Jos. Barney.
[67] Edwards, 'Farming Econ. of NE. Salop.' 268.
[68] T.S.A.S. lv. 136–42 (also giving rates for servants like

the plough driver who were paid annually and presumably lived with the farmer); Staffs. R.O., D. 593/F/2/35; D. 1287/3/4, Salop. est. disbursements bk. 1687–99; /3/5, accts. 1697–8; /3/6A and B (Sir J. Bridgeman's disbursements bks. 1704–16); S.R.O. 2713, box 30, Thos. Griffiths's 3rd acct. (Sept.–Nov. 1746), not mentioning whether food and drink was given.

means of raising his rental lay in an attack on customary manorial tenures and, *pari passu*, the substitution of leasehold tenure or, in the last resort, rack rents. Landlords' use of their opportunities to pursue such policies, however, should be seen against the background of a period that opened with the redistribution of a vast amount of landed property. Between 1540 and 1640, perhaps to a greater extent than at any other time between the Norman Conquest and the 20th century, membership of the landowning class changed: some great estates disappeared or shrank, other new ones were created, and on a more modest scale many families substantially improved their position within the landowning hierarchy or entered it for the first time.

From the 1540s, following on the dissolution of the monasteries, collegiate churches, and chantries, their huge endowments in land and tithe were for the most part quickly sold on to the established gentry or newly rich merchants and lawyers. Few aristocrats bought ex-monastic lands in Shropshire. The last Lord Grey of Powis (d. 1551) bought Buildwas abbey,[69] the 5th earl of Shrewsbury consolidated his Shifnal property by buying former Wombridge priory lands in 1545,[70] and Lord Clinton and Say (cr. earl of Lincoln 1572) speculated in a small way,[71] but they were exceptional. There was indeed another redistribution in progress as the estates of the great aristocratic landowning dynasties, largely absentee, that had dominated Shropshire in the late Middle Ages[72] began to disintegrate. Well before James I's death their own Shropshire estates—in many cases, it is true, appendages to even greater estates elsewhere in the kingdom—had been largely sold off to those same classes which had so readily acquired the monks' and canons' lands. Unlike the dissolution of the monasteries this second process was only in part the result of royal policies. Lord Lovel (1485) and the 3rd duke of Buckingham (1521) had certainly forfeited their great possessions by falling foul of the Tudors,[73] but the dismemberment of other estates, most notably the earl of Arundel's in the mid 16th century,[74] flowed from those circumstances—failure of heirs, improvidence, re-settlement of estates—whose occurrence, though fortuitous in particular cases, seems nevertheless a recurring feature of the history of landed society.

The bishops' role as Shropshire landowners also diminished at that time as a result of Crown pressure and episcopal weakness. In the Middle Ages the bishop of Hereford had owned Bishop's Castle and the great manor of Lydbury North, while the extensive manor of Prees (which produced a considerable income in the late Middle Ages) had belonged to the bishop of Coventry and Lichfield.[75] In 1550, however, Bishop Sampson leased Prees to a Londoner for 80 years and his successors unfailingly renewed leases so that the see never recovered possession. By 1591 the leasehold belonged to the Mainwarings of Ightfield who kept it until 1708 when it was sold to Richard Hill, the owner of Hawkstone, whose heirs acquired the freehold too in 1794. Thus for almost 250 years Prees produced no more than £46 a year reserved rent[76] for the see, fortunate bishops scooping up

[69] *V.C.H. Salop.* ii. 58; xi. 188; *T.S.A.S.* 2nd ser. xi. 108.
[70] G. W. Bernard, *Power of Early Tudor Nobility: Study of 4th and 5th Earls of Shrews.* (1985), 142.
[71] *V.C.H. Salop.* viii. 25, 135, 153; xi. 291; P. Klein and A. Roe, *Carmelite Friary, Ludlow* (Ludlow Hist. Research Paper, vi [1988]), 33.
[72] The FitzAlan earls of Arundel, Stafford dukes of Buckingham, Talbot earls of Shrews., Lds. Audley, Bergavenny, Greystoke, Strange of Knockin, etc.: M. D. G. Wanklyn, 'Landed Soc. and Allegiance in Ches. and Salop. in 1st Civ. War' (Manchester Univ. Ph.D. thesis, 1976), 16–17.

[73] *Complete Peerage*, viii. 225; *V.C.H. Salop.* viii. 7, 38, 265; xi. 215; B. J. Harris, *Edw. Stafford, 3rd Duke of Buckingham* (1986), caps. 5, 7–8. Buckingham's son recovered some of his fr.'s ests. in 1522: *V.C.H. Salop.* viii. 202, 309, 311.
[74] Stone, *Crisis of Aristocracy* 151, 542; Bodl., Craven dep. 64–5, deeds of 1560, 1562–5, 1567; 66, deed of 1596.
[75] Eyton, ix. 244–7; xi. 194–201, 203–6; *V.C.H. Salop.* i. 311; *V.C.H. Staffs.* iii. 15–17; L.J.R.O., B/A/21, CC 123984; S.R.O. 3607/I/A/31; /IV/B/1.
[76] The site of the manor, with a small amount of land, was separately leased for a reserved rent of 26s. 5d. or 30s.

the renewal fines for themselves.[77] In 1559 Elizabeth I annexed Bishop's Castle and Lydbury North to the Crown by an exchange of properties;[78] the forms of law[79] were observed but some of the odium for the see's spoliation clung, perhaps justly, to Bishop Scory's name.[80] Bishop Heath of Worcester acquired property in south Shropshire for his see by exchange with the earl of Warwick in 1549,[81] but the manors concerned[82] were subject to a 200-year lease that Warwick had granted to William Heath the previous year and they produced only a small reserved rent. The see never recovered possession,[83] though presumably from the earlier 18th century at least the prospect of a renewal fine became an occasional delight for a lucky bishop.

There is little doubt that one long-term result of these redistributions of land, though a difficult one to quantify,[84] was the further endowment of the substantial gentry, a class then, as always, composed of old and new families. Between 1540 and 1620, it has been calculated, sixty families improved their position in Shropshire landowning society or entered landowning for the first time. Over the period 1570–1640, however, little more than a dozen families appear to have sold all, or a significant part, of their Shropshire estates without making compensating purchases.[85] It thus seems fairly clear that the gentry class improved its economic position relative to those classes above and below it in the social hierarchy.

Most notable among the purchasers of monastic and aristocratic lands in Shropshire and the adjoining counties were three founders of families that must be accounted newcomers to the landed gentry: James Leveson (d. 1547) of Wolverhampton, a merchant of the staple;[86] Sir Rowland Hill (d. 1561), lord mayor of London 1549-50;[87] and Sir Rowland Hayward (d. 1593), lord mayor 1570-1 and 1591.[88] Leveson's Shropshire purchases, some of them soon conveyed on to others, included manors formerly belonging to Lilleshall abbey and Wenlock and Wombridge priories.[89] His son Richard (kt. 1553), moreover, had made a good first marriage with Sir Rowland Hill's niece Mary Gratewood and Hill had endowed her well with purchases he had made from the former estates of Lilleshall and Shrewsbury abbeys and Wombridge priory.[90] In fact Hill bought great quantities of ex-monastic property, manors formerly belonging to Combermere, Haughmond, Lilleshall, Shrewsbury, and Vale Royal abbeys and Wombridge priory;[91] with them, besides charitable works and foundations,[92] he endowed the Hills of Hawkstone,[93] the Corbets of Adderley and Stoke,[94] and the Barkers of Haugh-

[77] L.J.R.O., B/A/21, CC 123968-77; S.R.O. 731, box 84, Sir Art. Mainwaring's answer to bp. of Coventry and Lichfield's objections 1631; box 101, conveyance of lease 6 Aug. 1708 and renewal of lease 29 Jan. 1712; V.C.H. Staffs. iii. 52; 34 Geo. III, c. 106 (Priv. Act); cf. C. Hill, Econ. Problems of the Church from Abp. Whitgift to the Long Parl. (1956), 20-1.

[78] Cal. Pat. 1558-60, 440.

[79] It was done under the Bishoprics Act, 1559, 1 Eliz. I, c. 19. Cf. Hill, op. cit. 14-15.

[80] Eyton, xi. 201; Hill, op. cit. 19-20.

[81] Cal. Pat. 1547-8, 252-4; 1548-9, 255, 298.

[82] Holdgate and Rushbury (forfeited by Vct. Lovel: Cal. Pat. 1485-94, 236) and Stanton Long (former Hospitaller property: V.C.H. Salop. ii. 86), which Warwick had obtained 1533-47: sources cited ibid. viii, 7 n. 29; x (forthcoming).

[83] Cf. S.P.L., Deeds 6116, 10195; S.R.O. 933, box 16, abstr. of title of Eccl. Com. 20 Feb. 1861.

[84] Wanklyn, 'Landed Soc.' (esp. pp. 292-305, 418-32), reviews the sources for determining changes in landowner-ship.

[85] Ibid. 435-6.

[86] S. Shaw, Hist. Staffs. ii (1801), 169, 185.   [87] D.N.B.

[88] W.S.L. 350(3)/40, L. Wenlock pp. 2 sqq.; W. Jay, 'Sir Rowland Hayward', Trans. Lond. & Mdx. Arch. Soc. N.S. vi. 509, 513, 520, 522.

[89] Staffs. R.O., D. 593/B/2/7/4, 7-8; /B/2/8/2; /B/2/12/15, 25-6; /C/4, inq. p.m.; /D/3/1; /J/22/21/11-12; T.A.S.S. 2nd ser. xi. 171; V.C.H. Salop. xi. 80, 153, 166, 290.

[90] Staffs. R.O., D. 593/B/2/4/3. The property was evid. diverted from Mary Gratewood's dau. and heiress in favour of Leveson's son by a 2nd marr.: cf. V.C.H. Salop. xi. 219; Visit. Salop. 1623, i (Harl. Soc. xxviii), 245; Shaw, Staffs. ii. 169, 185.

[91] T.S.A.S. lv. 143; Staffs. R.O., D. 593/B/2/4/3; /O/2/1/2.

[92] D.N.B.; V.C.H. Salop. i. 416 (corr. ibid. ii. 316); ii. 145; iii. 73; xi. 220.

[93] T.S.A.S. lv. 143-4, 158; S.R.O. 731, box 166, settlement 16 Sept. 1560.

[94] Heirs of his neph. Wm. Gratewood: A[ugusta] E. C[orbet], The Fam. of Corbet: its Life and Times, ii [1918], 267-9, 350 sqq., chart facing p. 357; J. B. Blakeway, Sheriffs of Salop. (Shrews. 1831), 91, 111; Visit. Salop. 1623, i. 245; Wanklyn, 'Landed Soc.' 49-56, 97, 277, 308, 373.

mond.[95] Hayward too bought monastic estates at first[96] but he later invested mainly in the estates of the earl of Arundel and the Stafford family, both being broken up in the mid and later 16th century.[97]

Few other families acquired lands on the scale that the Levesons did,[98] or so promptly, and probably none could have bought as lavishly as Hill or Hayward. Most purchasers of former monastic lands seem to have been established gentry or minor landowners improving their position by the careful acquisition of properties adjoining their own, or else they were newly rich merchants and lawyers establishing new or cadet landowning families. In the first category were such families as the Actons of Aldenham,[99] the Charltons of Apley Castle,[1] the Corbetts of Longnor,[2] the Herberts of Lymore (Mont.),[3] the Lawleys of Spoonhill,[4] the Lees of Langley,[5] the Mackworths of Meole Brace and later of Betton Strange,[6] and the Steventons of Dothill.[7]

Merchants, in the second category, were men such as Thomas Ireland (d. 1554), the Shrewsbury mercer who bought Albrighton[8] and other former church lands;[9] Thomas Lawley (d. 1559), merchant of the staple, who bought Wenlock priory site and demesnes in 1545;[10] Robert Longe (d. 1552), the London mercer who bought Condover in 1544,[11] Norton in 1550,[12] and some adjoining ex-monastic property;[13] Roger Pope (d. 1573), the Shrewsbury draper who bought Woolstaston[14] in 1544 and the three Shrewsbury friaries;[15] and Roger Smyth (d. 1557), the Bridgnorth burgess who bought much former church property around Bridgnorth.[16]

Notable legal families investing in land were the Bromleys, the Brookes of Madeley, and the Foxes. All were in fact established, moderately well endowed landowning families, the Brookes with a pedigree of some length.[17] Sir Robert Brooke (d. 1558), chief justice of Common Pleas, bought the manor and rectory of Madeley, a former Wenlock priory estate.[18] His contemporary Sir Thomas Bromley (d. 1555), chief justice of King's Bench, bought Aston and Eyton on Severn, Shrewsbury abbey manors,[19] but his cousin's sons, who both also became judges,[20] acquired land in other ways. Sir George Bromley added to the paternal inheritance[21] by marrying the heiress of Hallon;[22] and Sir Thomas, lord chancellor 1579–87,[23] bought much property in Shropshire from the earl of Arundel's estates, as well as lands in other counties, and founded a line long seated at Shrawardine

[95] *T.S.A.S.* 3rd ser. vi, pp. *xviii–xix*; *Visit. Salop. 1623*, i. 26–9.

[96] e.g. Tugford man.: Bodl., Craven dep. 64, deed of 1555; cf. *Hist. Parl., Commons, 1558–1603*, ii. 284.

[97] Bodl., Craven dep. 64, deeds of 1560; *V.C.H. Salop.* viii. 63, 77, 101, 309, 311; xi. 80, 113–14, 188, 192; Wanklyn, 'Landed Soc.' 410–11; *Two Elizabethan Women* (Wilts. Rec. Soc. xxxviii), p. xix; *T.S.A.S.* 3rd ser. iv. 115–16; 4th ser. v. 43, 53; l. 179–80.

[98] For Jas. Leveson's Staffs. purchases see *V.C.H. Staffs.* vi. 79.

[99] *Visit. Salop. 1623*, i. 9–10; *V.C.H. Salop.* ii. 128; viii. 330 (purchasers of Morville prebend and Yockleton tithes).

[1] *V.C.H. Salop.* xi. 216, 221, 290–1 (purchasers of Wombridge man. and rectory and ½ Wellington rectory).

[2] *V.C.H. Salop.* viii. 101, 112 (purchasers of Cress grange).

[3] Edw. Herbert acquired Chirbury 1553: *Dict. Welsh Biog.* 348.

[4] Heirs of Ld. Wenlock (d. 1471) and purchasers of Bourton and Callaughton (incl. Spoonhill), former Wenlock priory properties, and Bradeley: *Complete Peerage*, xii (2), 479–80, 484 note k, 486 note b; *L. & P. Hen. VIII*, xviii (2), p. 239; Hull Univ., Brynmor Jones Libr., DDFA(2) /26/2.

[5] Who acquired Hawksley, a Shrews. abbey property:

[5 cont.] *V.C.H. Salop.* viii. 143. Cf. ibid. ii. 106.

[6] *T.S.A.S.* 2nd ser. i. 384, 390 sqq.; viii. 113–19; *V.C.H. Salop.* viii. 19 (purchasers of Betton Abbots).

[7] Purchasers of Wrockwardine rectory 1609: *V.C.H. Salop.* xi. 216, 313.   [8] *T.S.A.S.* 2nd ser. i. 100.

[9] Betchcott and its tithes, Cothercott (incl. Sheppen Fields), and (from Rob. Longe: see below) Lythwood: *V.C.H. Salop.* viii. 42, 134, 153, 158, 160.

[10] Cf. *L. & P. Hen. VIII*, xx (1), pp. 666–7; xx (2), p. 124; xxi (2), 167; *T.S.A.S.* 3rd ser. ii. 309.

[11] One of Vct. Lovel's forfeitures acquired from the Crown by Sir Hen. Knyvett in 1533: *V.C.H. Salop.* viii. 38.

[12] Ibid. 41.

[13] Lythwood (which was, however, soon resold: above n. 9) and the tithes of Yocklaton: ibid. 42, 330. Longe's son-in-law Hen. Vynar bought cottages formerly Shrews. abbey's in 1557: ibid. 44.

[14] Another est. forfeited by Vct. Lovel in 1485.

[15] Cf. ibid. ii. 91, 93, 97; viii. 172; *T.S.A.S.* l. 38–9.

[16] *V.C.H. Salop.* ii. 30, 100, 127; *T.S.A.S.* 4th ser. v. 44.

[17] *Visit. Salop. 1623*, i. 79–81.   [18] *V.C.H. Salop.* xi. 35.

[19] Which his dau. and heir carried to the Newports: ibid. 217–18; *T.S.A.S.* 2nd ser. i. 15–18.

[20] *T.S.A.S.* 2nd ser. i. 1.

[21] In Hodnet: ibid. 13.

[22] *Hist. Parl., Commons, 1558–1603*, i. 490.   [23] *D.N.B.*

and Holt (Worcs.).[24] The foundations of the Foxes' fortunes seem to have been laid by Roger Foxe, recorder of Ludlow in the 1460s,[25] and his grandson William (d. 1554) acquired two hospitals with property in Ludford (where his heirs were seated) and Ludlow.[26] William's second son Charles (d. 1590) was even more prominent than his great-grandfather: recorder of Ludlow and a greedy, none too scrupulous lawyer-administrator, he bought Bromfield priory and its estates, including Oakly Park, and the Carmelite friary in Ludlow.[27] Even a successful career in the new protestant church could raise up a new landowning family. In 1567 Archbishop Young of York, perhaps descended from minor landowners at Shelvock in the later Middle Ages, bought the earl of Arundel's manors of Ruyton-XI-Towns, Kinnerley, and Melverley and the advowson of West Felton as an inheritance for his descendants.[28]

It is by no means clear that the new families entering landowning from a mercantile or legal background were outstanding as a group in setting new standards of efficient estate administration to maximize their return on investment. Of the dozen or so identifiable gentry families whose Shropshire landed possessions shrank 1570–1640, half were from those new to landowning. The Haywards, among the most prominent mid 16th-century investors, also offer the most spectacular example of failure. In the 1620s Sir Rowland's second son, Sir John, dissipated all those of his father's acquisitions that had come to him; most went to the Cravens,[29] and thereafter Sir Rowland's only descendants among the Shropshire landowners were the Thynnes of Caus and Longleat.[30] Another London merchant dynasty that failed in landownership was that represented by Henry Vynar of Condover. Vynar (d. 1585) and his father-in-law[31] had worked hard to improve the value of the estate by buying up adjacent properties and attacking tenants' rights, but it was all in vain and the Vynars were forced to sell in 1586.[32] The Cromptons of Acton Burnell, another family that rose from obscurity in the mid 16th century,[33] sold up in 1597[34] and the Youngs of Ruyton-XI-Towns did so in 1612–13.[35] In 1628 Sir Thomas Jervois sold the Shropshire estates (Chelmarsh and Quatt) that his ancestor, a London alderman, had bought round about the 1540s,[36] and the Foxes of Ludford, who could still afford to buy monastic land from the Crown in 1589,[37] had parted with their estates before Edward Foxe's death c. 1630.[38] The Foxes of Bromfield lasted longer but, racked by disputes and lawsuits,[39] fared little better in the end.[40] Some other prominent new families narrowly escaped a similar fate: the Levesons of Lilleshall, for example, were heavily in debt in the late 16th century and were saved only by a well discharged trusteeship in the early 17th century.[41] A similar number of old established landowning families suffered comparable decline 1570–1640: the Greys of Buildwas,[42] the Hordes of Hoards

[24] Cf. *Hist. Parl., Commons*, 1558–1603, i. 492; *T.S.A.S.* 2nd ser. vii. 130, 132–41; *V.C.H. Worcs.* iii, 404–5.

[25] *T.S.A.S.* 2nd ser. xi. 301, 307–8; xii. 115.

[26] Ibid. 2nd ser. vii. 9, 11–12; xii. 113, 116–18, 120, 122–5, 133–6, 189–90; *V.C.H. Salop.* ii. 101, 104.

[27] *T.S.A.S.* 2nd ser. vii. 10–11; xi. 307, 316–18; xii. 113, 137–41; Penry Williams, *Council in Marches of Wales under Eliz. I* (1958), 159–60, 163–5, 333, 348–9; *V.C.H. Salop.* ii. 29; Klein and Roe, *Carmelite Friary, Ludlow*, 33.

[28] *T.S.A.S.* 3rd ser. i. 85; Bodl., Craven dep. 66, deed of 1596; cf. *D.N.B.*; Emden, *Biog. Reg. Oxf. 1501–40*, 652–3.

[29] Above; Wanklyn, 'Landed Soc.' 369, 412 n. 3; Bodl., Craven dep. 64–70; *V.C.H. Salop.* viii. 8, 63, 311; xi. 80–1, 113, 188.

[30] *Two Elizabethan Women*, pp. xix–xx; *T.S.A.S.* 3rd ser. iv. 116–17; *V.C.H. Salop.* viii. 309, 311; B. Botfield,

Stemmata Botevilliana (Westminster, 1858), 145.

[31] Rob. Longe, another Lond. merchant, who had bought Condover in 1544.

[32] *V.C.H. Salop.* viii. 38, 40, 43–4, 46, 48–9, 51–2, 330; below.

[33] S.P.L., MS. 2794, p. 586; *Visit. Salop. 1623*, i. 159.

[34] *V.C.H. Salop.* viii. 7–8, 20.

[35] *T.S.A.S.* 3rd ser. i. 90–1, 94.

[36] Blakeway, *Sheriffs*, 103; S.R.O. 1224, box 127, brief in Childe v. Brown for Salop. assizes 24 July 1752.

[37] *T.S.A.S.* 2nd ser. xii. 133.   [38] Ibid. 135–6.

[39] Ibid. 137–43, 154–61.   [40] Ibid. 161–70.

[41] *Hist. Parl., Commons*, 1558–1603, ii. 465–6.

[42] Descended from an illegit. s. of the last Ld. Grey of Powis: cf. Wanklyn, 'Landed Soc.' 310; *V.C.H. Salop.* iii. 61 (corr. below, Corrigenda), 76.

Park,[43] the Lacons of Willey and Kinlet,[44] the Leightons of Plaish,[45] the Mainwarings of Ightfield,[46] and the Vernons of Stokesay.[47] There were also others who sold Shropshire estates but retained land in other counties.[48]

The failure of some gentry families, and particularly that of the Haywards, with the continued erosion of the remaining aristocratic estates, released much land on the market in the early 17th century and facilitated the establishment of another generation of new landowning families. The most outstanding of them bought, or were granted, peerages and so founded a new aristocracy at the apex of landowning society. First and foremost were the Cravens who, from the City profits of trade and moneylending,[49] bought many of the old FitzAlan estates,[50] in particular most of those that had been acquired by the Haywards and Youngs;[51] £7,000 was laid out on a peerage in 1627.[52] Many of the family's purchases were made by the 1st Lord Craven's mother Elizabeth (née Whitmore), widow of Alderman Sir William Craven and perhaps the richest woman in England. She probably acted on the advice of her City relatives, the Whitmores and the Welds,[53] and her son was one of the richest English peers: in 1652 Lord Craven's estate was valued at a quarter of a million pounds.[54] Somewhat earlier than the Cravens Sir Thomas Egerton, lord keeper 1596–1603 and lord chancellor 1603–17,[55] began to buy up lands in his native Cheshire (by 1582),[56] in Shropshire, and in other counties.[57] In Shropshire he united the principal medieval estates of the Stranges of Blakemere and the Stranges of Knockin by buying first, in 1598, the Talbots' Whitchurch estate (including Blakemere)[58] and secondly, in 1600, the Ellesmere estate (including Colemere, Hampton, and Myddle) from his three step-daughters (one of them his daughter-in-law), coheirs of the 5th earl of Derby.[59] He was created Baron Ellesmere in 1603, and his son's Northamptonshire acquisitions[60] enabled Ellesmere to take the title Viscount Brackley on his promotion in 1616. In 1617 he died on the eve of being created earl of Bridgwater, a dignity immediately conferred on his son.[61] The Egertons' estates in Shropshire, Cheshire, Lancashire, and north Wales were organized in six receiverships[62] and there were estates in other counties too.[63]

The Cravens and Egertons, like the FitzAlans and Stanleys they supplanted, were absentee landowners in Shropshire, but the third newly ennobled family among Shropshire landowners, the Newports, were long established in the county and resident. By marriage and purchase they built up the largest landed estate in the county:[64] Sir Francis Newport was probably Shropshire's richest gentleman

[43] V.C.H. Salop. iii. 244; Wanklyn, op. cit. 409, 428.

[44] Wanklyn, op. cit. 319, 369, 410–11, 433, 499.

[45] Cf. ibid. 435; Visit. Salop. 1623, ii (Harl. Soc. xxix), 322–4.

[46] Wanklyn, op. cit. 310, 412 n. 3; Bodl., Craven dep. 66–7, 69–70. They had been buying in the 1590s but were selling in the 1620s.

[47] T.S.A.S. i. 325–7; Visit. Salop. 1623, ii. 471–2.

[48] Clare of Stanton Lacy (cf. T.S.A.S. liii. 207; Bodl., Craven dep. 67, deeds of 1606; V.C.H. Worcs. iii. 314) and Clifford of Broseley (cf. S.R.O. 1224/3/192 sqq., 303 sqq.; Wanklyn, 'Landed Soc.' 369; V.C.H. Glos. x. 145).

[49] Stone, Crisis of Aristocracy, 146, 535–6.

[50] Notably, in 1624, Oswestry ldship. from Arundel's half-bro. Suffolk, to whom Jas. I had granted it (away from the FitzAlan blood) in 1603; T.S.A.S. vii. 52; 2nd ser. vi. 143–4.

[51] Bodl., Craven dep. 69–70; T.S.A.S. 3rd ser. i. 94–5.

[52] Stone, Crisis of Aristocracy, 106, 120, 190, 632.

[53] Ibid. 607; Wanklyn, 'Landed Soc.' 412–13; T.S.A.S. 3rd ser. i. 94–5.

[54] Stone, op. cit. 146, 362, 761.

[55] D.N.B.; Hopkins, 'Bridgewater Est.' 3–5.

[56] Hopkins, op. cit. 5; G. Ormerod, Hist. of Co. of Chester (1882), ii. 299, 301, 847. He was illegit. s. of Sir Ric. Egerton of Ridley.

[57] Hist. Parl., Commons, 1558–1603, ii. 83.

[58] Hopkins, op. cit. 4, 23–32; B. Ross, 'Accts. of Talbot Household at Blakemere 1394–1425' (Australian Nat. Univ., Canberra, M.A. thesis, 1970), i. 111–12; cf. H. le Strange, Le Strange Records (1916), 288–322.

[59] Hopkins, op. cit. 4–5, 14–23; Mary C. Hill, Guide to Salop. Rec. (1952), 86–7; R. Gough, Antiquities & Memoirs of Par. of Myddle (Shrews. 1875), 25–6; cf. le Strange, op. cit. 323–47.

[60] The inheritance of Ellesmere's dau.-in-law Frances: Hopkins, op. cit. 5.

[61] Allegedly for £20,000: Stone, Crisis of Aristocracy, 116. See also Complete Peerage, ii. 271–2, 311–12.

[62] Stone, op. cit. 285.

[63] See e.g. V.C.H. Herts. ii. 203, 209–10. Harefield, where the ld. keeper lived, belonged to his wife: V.C.H. Mdx. iii. 240–1.

[64] Eyton, ix. 97; V.C.H. Salop. iii. 254–5.

by the beginning of James I's reign[65] and in 1642 his son Sir Richard bought the title of baron from Charles I, pressed for money at the beginning of the Civil War.[66] Before the end of the century the Newports were advanced to the earldom[67] justified by their landed wealth.

The invention of baronetcies (1611) enabled the Crown to sell hereditary titles to those whose estates, though substantial, yet did not rate a peerage. There were safeguards to prevent corruption of the new order by those too newly rich—three armigerous generations and an estate worth £1,000 a year were required—and perhaps only three of the twelve Shropshire landowners so dignified before the Civil War[68] were recognizably newcomers to the landed gentry. Of the four creations of the 1620s Sir Humphrey Lee (1620) and Sir John Corbet (1627) were gentlemen of ancient landed descent,[69] while Sir Thomas Harris of Boreatton (1622) and Sir Thomas Harries of Tong (1623) were successful lawyers of no pedigree, the first of those two creations giving very great offence in the county.[70] In 1641–2 eight further creations dignified members of five well established landowning families,[71] two more who were apparently qualified by armigerous descent and wealth,[72] and one new one. The newcomer was Sir Thomas Whitmore (kt. and bt. 1641);[73] he and his father had invested their City fortune in a large landed estate in south-east Shropshire between 1605 and 1631.[74]

Thus in the earlier 17th century the aristocratic crust on landed society in Shropshire was being re-formed from new materials. To some extent, however, the changes were disguised by the survival or resurrection of the older families and their prestigious titles and names among the newcomers. Although, for instance, the last FitzAlan earl of Arundel (d. 1580) lost all his Shropshire inheritance,[75] the earls of Arundel remained substantial Shropshire landowners on and off for over three quarters of a century. The lordship of Oswestry passed to the last FitzAlan's grandson Philip Howard, earl of Arundel. He forfeited it in 1589,[76] but his son Thomas (d. 1646), the traveller and collector (to whom the earldom had been restored in 1604),[77] inherited a very considerable Shropshire estate (Wem, Loppington, and Hinstock) from his mother (d. 1630), a co-heir of Lord Dacre of Gilsland. The Dacre inheritance, with a capital value of £73,818 in 1648,[78] must have gone far to settle Arundel's debts (scheduled at £93,234 in 1641) as sales proceeded through the 1650s.[79] The earls of Shrewsbury also remained substantial Shropshire landowners in the 17th century and beyond. Despite the sales of the 16th century,[80] a period which saw a shift in the centre of gravity of the Talbot estates

[65] V.C.H. Salop. xi. 97.
[66] D.N.B.; Complete Peerage, ix. 554.
[67] Bradford (1694): Complete Peerage, ii. 274.
[68] For the background see Stone, Crisis of Aristocracy, 82 sqq.; Wanklyn, 'Landed Soc.' 96 sqq.
[69] Visit. Salop. 1623, i. 138; ii. 320; V.C.H. Salop. viii. 8, 143.
[70] Visit. Salop. 1623, i. 224; T.S.A.S. 2nd ser. x. 77 sqq.
[71] Sir Thos. Wolryche, Sir Thos. Lawley, Sir Vincent Corbet, Sir Edw. Corbett, and Sir Adam Littleton: G.E.C. Baronetage, ii. 124, 140, 156, 184, 204; Visit. Salop. 1623, i. 137, 139–40; ii. 313–14, 508–10; T.S.A.S. 4th ser. iii. 302 sqq., 320 sqq., 331–2.
[72] Sir Hen. Fred. Thynne and Sir Moreton Briggs: G.E.C. Baronetage, ii. 92, 102, 134 n.; Visit. Salop. 1623, i. 68–9; ii. 460–1, 499–500; V.C.H. Salop. iii. 244; Botfield, Stemmata Botevilliana, 40–1, 59–60, 66–7; S.P.R. Heref. xix (5), pp. i–ii.
[73] T.S.A.S. 4th ser. v. 56; Wanklyn, 'Landed Soc.' 112.
[74] Wanklyn, op. cit. 409–10, 428; V.C.H. Salop. iii. 244.
[75] Apart from the sales to Sir Rowland Hill in 1559, Sir Rowland Hayward in 1560, and Ld. Chancellor Bromley in 1583 (above), Wroxeter and Clun passed to the Crown in

1561 and 1572 respectively (S.P.R. Lich. xi (1), p. iii; T.S.A.S. xi. 261). In 1603 Jas. I granted Clun away from the FitzAlan blood to Ld. Howard of Walden (cr. earl of Suffolk 1603) and Hen. Howard, respectively half-bro. and uncle to Arundel (d. 1595). In 1604 Hen. Howard (cr. earl of Northampton) acquired it; he entailed it on Suffolk's younger sons and the Howards sold it in 1677. See Arundel Cast. MSS. MD 1286–7; T.S.A.S. xi. 261; 2nd ser. x. 43–5; Burke, Peerage (1949), 1937.
[76] T.S.A.S. vii. 51–2; 2nd ser. vi. 143–4; Complete Peerage, i. 255; above, n. 50.
[77] D.N.B.; D. Howarth, Ld. Arundel and his Circle (1985); Complete Peerage, i. 255.
[78] Complete Peerage, i. 255; S. Garbet, Hist. Wem (Wem, 1818), 50 sqq.; S.R.O. 167/1–11, 51; 972, bdle. 232, descr. [map and bounds] of man. of Wem 1631; Arundel Cast. MSS. MD 507–8.
[79] Arundel Cast. MSS. MD 59, 536, 1289.
[80] e.g. of Alberbury at the beginning (1500) and Whitchurch and Blakemere at the end (1598): V.C.H. Salop. viii. 196; above.

away from Shropshire,[81] and despite the settlements which split up the estate in 1618,[82] the earl's Shropshire lands were worth perhaps £1,000 a year c. 1640, more than any gentry estate in the county but two.[83] Some of the Talbot estates passed in 1618 to the 8th earl of Shrewsbury's niece Alethea, countess of Arundel (d. 1654), and in due course to her fifth son, created Viscount Stafford in 1640; as a result the Stafford title and name figure again among Shropshire landowners[84] after the death of the last male Stafford.[85]

The changes in landownership that had been so marked a feature of the later 16th and earlier 17th centuries were apparently succeeded—the events of the Interregnum apart—by years of greater stability. In the second half of the period few estates were broken up:[86] in the early 18th century Richard Hill, of Hawkstone, had to buy up a very miscellaneous collection of properties, whenever and wherever he had the chance, to build up the estate with which he endowed his nephews.[87] Few of the leading aristocratic or gentry families sold off significant parts of their inheritances to others,[88] though the Howards disposed of their manors of Bishop's Castle[89] and Clun[90] in the 17th century and Arthur Mainwaring sold Ightfield in 1707.[91] Such sales seem to have been exceptional. The Bridgwater, the Craven, and (despite the involved story after 1734) the Newport estates survived,[92] as did those of the earl of Shrewsbury[93] and Lord Stafford.[94] Lord Kilmorey's estate increased.[95] The survival of more modest landed estates was no less remarkable if the estates of Shropshire's twelve senior baronets[96] may be taken as typical. Only two of those estates were broken up during the period: the Harrises of Boreatton, whose creation had given such offence, sold up in the second generation[97] and the Littletons' estates were sold off after the death of the last baronet, childless, in 1710.[98] The ten other families who bought their titles before the Civil War prospered well enough to pass down their estates (if not always their titles[99] and names) in their families beyond the end of the period[1] and, in the cases of six[2] of

[81] Bernard, *4th and 5th Earls of Shrews.* 11.

[82] Hopkins, 'Bridgewater Est.' 24, 30–1; Stone, *Crisis of Aristocracy*, 253, 497; *T.S.A.S.* 4th ser. v. 246–8, 287–8.

[83] i.e. the Newports' and the Levesons', the two greatest: Wanklyn, 'Landed Soc.' 18.

[84] Cf. e.g. *V.C.H. Salop.* xi. 311 (for ⅓ Wrockwardine); J. Randall, *Shifnal and Its Surroundings* (Madeley, 1878), p. [20] (for Shifnal); Burke, *Peerage* (1949), 1886–7 (for the Howards' addition of the name Stafford in 1688 and enjoyment of the earldom of Stafford 1688–1762).

[85] In 1641. The Salop. lands restored to Buckingham's son in 1522 had been gradually sold off and in 1638 the last, impoverished, Stafford squalidly bargained his title away for £100 p.a.: see e.g. *V.C.H. Salop.* viii. 202, 309, 311; *Two Elizabethan Women*, pp. xx, xxii–xxiv; Blakeway, *Sheriffs*, 96; Stone, *Crisis of Aristocracy*, 117.

[86] Setting aside long drawn out sales like those of the Arundel trustees from the 1640s to the 1660s.

[87] *T.S.A.S.* lv. 143–58.

[88] Though there is some evidence of a downward spread of landowning to classes below the gentry: see below.

[89] Cf. *V.C.H. Salop.* iii. 248–9, 298.

[90] Cf. *T.S.A.S.* 2nd ser. x. 43–5; J. R. Burton, *Hist. of Fam. of Walcot of Walcot* (priv. print. Shrews. 1930), 51.

[91] It was settled on Ld. and Lady Kilmorey and their heirs male: Blakeway, *Sheriffs*, 133–4; H. D. Harrod, *Hist. of Shavington* (Shrews. 1891), 110; idem, *Muniments of Shavington* (Shrews. 1891), 54–62.

[92] Below, 1750–1875 (Large estates).

[93] At Albrighton, Cheswardine, Ford, Tasley, Wrockwardine, etc.: cf. *Arundel Cast. Archives*, ed. F. W. Steer, i (Chichester, 1968), 76–8; J. Bateman, *Gt. Landowners of Gt. Brit and Irel.* (1883), 406; *V.C.H. Salop.* viii. 230; xi. 311, 326.

[94] e.g. around Shifnal: cf. Bateman, op. cit. 418; *V.C.H. Salop.* xi. 292, 296.

[95] By the acquisition of Ightfield in 1707: above n. 91.

[96] See above.

[97] *T.S.A.S.* 2nd ser. x. 91–2 (Onslow and Boreatton sold in 1658 and c. 1661).

[98] *S.P.R. Heref.* xix (5), pp. ii–iii; G.E.C. *Baronetage*, ii. 204.

[99] The only surviving title is that held by Ld. Bath, heir and namesake of Sir Hen. Fred. Thynne (cr. 1641): Burke, *Peerage* (1967), 187. One other (Lawley) lasted into the 20th cent.: L. G. Pine, *New Extinct Peerage 1884–1971* (1972), 291–2. The other 10 titles died out in the 17th (5) and 18th (5) cents.: G.E.C. *Baronetage*, i. 143, 217–18; ii. 34, 92, 124, 135, 156, 184–5, 204.

[1] For the Harrieses of Tong and their heirs the Pierreponts see Blakeway, *Sheriffs*, 119; *Hist. Parl., Commons, 1754–90*, ii., 370; for the Thynnes (marquesses of Bath) see *V.C.H. Salop.* viii. 309, 311–12; *T.S.A.S.* 3rd ser. iv. 116–17; for the Whitmores see *V.C.H. Salop.* iii. 244, 275, 311 n. 56, 335; for the Wolryches see below, 1750–1875 (Large estates). For the other six fams. see the next note. An eccentric legacy briefly (1911–18) restored some perhaps of their ancient Salop. lands to the Thynnes: below, 1750–1875 (Large estates).

[2] For the Briggses and their heirs, the Brookes and others, cf. *S.P.R. Heref.* xix (5), p. ii; Burke, *Land. Gent.* (1914), 243; for the Corbets of Moreton Corbet and of Stoke and the Corbetts see Corbet, *Fam. of Corbet*; *V.C.H. Salop.* viii. 110; for the Lawleys (Lds. Wenlock) cf. S.R.O. 3510/56, ff. 69, 97; 3898/Sc/6, pp. 331–2 (sales by 3rd baron and his neph. Ld. De Vesci); Burke, *Peerage* (1949), 589; for the Lees and their heirs the Smythes see *V.C.H. Salop.* viii. 8, 143.

the families (five of them old established when their titles were first created),[3] well into the 19th century or beyond.

After 1660 large, slackly administered estates like the Cravens'[4] survived as effortlessly as those whose efficiency and profitability had been fostered by improving landlords like the Levesons.[5] Perhaps not surprisingly in a period of agricultural depression, when profits from land were low and opportunities for non-landed investment were multiplying, some estates passed from the one condition to the other without breaking up. One such was the Welds'. The Whitmores' relative John Weld (kt. 1642, d. 1666), town clerk of London 1613–42, laid out his fortune in the earlier 17th century on an estate around Willey, bought principally from the Lacons, the Slaneys, and the Jervoises. He ran it, as he had acquired it, efficiently and with an eye to profit,[6] but by the 1740s it had long been mismanaged and was heavily encumbered.[7] In spite of that it was carried entire by an heiress to the Forester family in the mid 18th century and, with the investment of Forester money, it was then restored to profit.[8]

Apart from the vicissitudes of the principal landed families, other shifts in the pattern of landownership were taking place at a lower level as freehold estates were broken up and sold piecemeal and copyholders purchased enfranchisement of their lands or fought to establish hereditary titles to them. The changes are hard to quantify over the county as a whole, nor was change all in one direction. In the 1560s, for example, the earl of Arundel and the Lumleys were able to sell off many small estates in the manors of Ruyton, Kinnerley, and Melverley before the manors themselves were sold to Archbishop Young in 1567[9] while contrariwise, at the same period, Rowland Hayward (kt. 1570) was buying up small properties that lay convenient to the larger estates he was acquiring.[10] Some of the small properties sold by Arundel and the Lumleys were rejoined to the manor of Ruyton in the earlier 1620s when the Cravens bought it[11] (meanwhile probably depleted again by piecemeal sales of the Youngs)[12] as well as much Hayward property.[13] Around Church Stretton Bonham Norton (d. 1635) assembled a considerable estate out of small purchases,[14] while throughout the period and beyond the Leveson-Gowers pursued a consistent policy of consolidating their estates by buying up smaller ones.[15]

In some areas the fragmentation of large estates was perhaps a more important long-term development than changes in the squirearchy and nobility. By the later 18th century, for example, the manor of Melverley (1,397 a.) had no tenantable land, only 171 a. of commons, cottages, and encroachments; Kinnerley manor (2,602 a.) had only 42 a. of tenantable land, with 587 a. of commons, cottages, and encroachments; and although Ruyton manor had 2,281 tenantable acres with 821 a. of commons, cottages, and encroachments, that was only a modest proportion of the manor's 9,238 a.[16] The lands attached to the manors of Broseley and Madeley

---

[3] The exception was the Briggs fam.
[4] Below, 1750–1875 (Landlords and tenants) for the late survival of leasing.
[5] See e.g. T.S.A.S. lxiii. 9; below, for Geo. Plaxton's policies.
[6] Blakeway, Sheriffs, 120; Visit. Salop. 1623, ii. 495–6, 499–500; T.S.A.S. 3rd ser. i. 186–8, 191–4.
[7] S.R.O. 1224, box 171, memos. re condition of est. on d. of Geo. Weld; bk. of the state of Weld's affairs; valuation of lands in hand; rent r. of late Geo. Weld's est.
[8] Below, 1750–1875 (Large estates); T.S.A.S. 3rd ser. i. 208–9.
[9] T.S.A.S. 3rd ser. i. 84–5; Bodl., Craven dep. 64–5, deeds

of 28 May 1563, 13 May and 6 July 1564, 24 Nov. 1565; ibid. 66, deed of 22 May 1596; Cal. Pat. 1563–6, 46; 1566–9, 99; above.
[10] See e.g. Bodl., Craven dep. 64–5, deeds of 30 Apr., 1 May, 18 July 1564, etc.
[11] Hence the presence of the deeds in Bodl., Craven dep. (above, n. 9).
[12] T.S.A.S. 3rd ser. i. 94.   [13] Above.
[14] See e.g. P.R.O., C 66/2059, no. 6; Shrews. Sch. libr., James deeds nos. 44, 73–4. He had inherited other ests. in Salop.: P.R.O., C 142/535, no. 119.
[15] Staffs. R.O., D. 593/B/2; V.C.H. Salop. xi. 155.
[16] S.P.L., MS. 2482.

were broken up in the early 17th and early 18th centuries respectively, after the failure of their lords to profit from their industrial enterprises; the lands were never reunited.[17] After 1660 Sir George Saville (later Lord Halifax) sold off his estate in Wrockwardine Wood in small lots to tenants, and about the same time the Hills sold parts of Walcot, in Wellington.[18] Wem, Loppington, and Hinstock were surveyed and valued for piecemeal sale in 1648.[19] In Wem sales of portions of the manorial lands continued throughout the 1650s and when Daniel Wycherley bought the manor in 1665 he became trustee for conveying the freeholds on to their purchasers. By then the manorial property was by no means the extensive estate it had been in 1648[20] and Wycherley set about the 'improvement' of his own newly purchased manor by an attack on the copyholders.[21]

With regard to customary land, much depended on the copyholders' status since those holding at the lord's will had far less tenurial and financial independence than those who had heritable estates.[22] In Shrawardine manor tenure was for lives, renewable at the lord's will, and he could therefore obtain from the holdings a return related to their value. At a court held in 1639, for example, Richard Shorey was admitted to a messuage and 1½ virgate of customary land in Forton township for an entry fine of £100 and an annual rent of £1 2s. 10d; three years later his wife and son paid an instalment of a £125 fine for the reversion of the property.[23]

Copyholds of inheritance, on the other hand, provided little income for lords since fines, rents, and services, fixed by custom, were inadequate, even derisory, in an inflationary period.[24] At Wrockwardine and Edgmond tenants fined half a year's rent, though at Edgmond there was also a surcharge of 12d. an acre for parcels of land that had anciently belonged to any other messuage. At Prees and Ford a year's rent was given and at Worfield £1 for a yardland and 10s. for half a yardland.[25] Even if fines were arbitrary, at the lord's will, they had to be reasonable enough not to hinder the heir's succession, and a fine's reasonableness was agreed by both parties and the manorial tenants; two, occasionally three, years' improved value of the holding came to be regarded as the maximum.[26] Of course copyholders tried to claim that their fines were fixed, and much scope existed for dispute and litigation. In 1600 21 Whitchurch tenants complained of an 'unlawful' increase in their fines. They alleged a custom of only one year's rent, whereas the officers of Sir Thomas Egerton, lord of the manor, claimed never to have taken less than two years' rent. The outcome is unknown but 17th-century surveys and rentals of the estate show that income derived from the copyholders, the largest class of tenant, formed a small proportion of total receipts. Significantly, the dispute occurred within two years of Egerton's purchase of the manor and perhaps reflects an attempt to maximize the return on his investment. At Wem and Church Stretton later in the century tenants fought similar battles with their lords, who were trying to establish that the copyholds were held at will. At Wem the dispute dragged on for eight years, ruining both sides; Daniel Wycherley, the lord, eventually won a pyrrhic victory through his opponents' exhaustion not because of any merits of his case. At Church Stretton on the other hand the copyholders won. The dispute had 16th-century origins, and more recently Sir Henry Thynne and his steward

[17] V.C.H. Salop. xi. 36-7. The hist. of Broseley man., based largely on S.R.O. 1224/3, will be found in V.C.H. Salop. x.　　[18] V.C.H. Salop. xi. 218, 326, 328.
[19] Arundel Cast. MSS. MD 507-8.
[20] Ibid. MD 59.　　[21] Below.
[22] E. Kerridge, Agrarian Problems in 16th Cent. and After (1969), 35-7; C. G. A. Clay, Econ. Expansion and Social

Change: Eng. 1500-1700 (1984), 87-9.
[23] Edwards, 'Farming Econ. of NE. Salop.' 24-5.
[24] R. H. Tawney, Agrarian Problem in 16th Cent. (New York, 1967), 304-5.
[25] T.S.A.S. 4th ser. i. 228-9; S.R.O. 81/599; 2028/BO/1/8/8, customs of Worfield man., 1602; S.P.L., MSS. 348-51.　　[26] Kerridge, Agrarian Problems, 38-9.

had attempted to undermine the manor's customs by preventing access to the court rolls and inserting words like *ad voluntatem domini* after *secundum consuetudinem manerii* in records of transfers. In 1670, however, a Chancery decree affirmed the security of, and the titles to, the copyholds of inheritance.[27]

The period was critical for the system of copyhold tenure in general and, in Shropshire as elsewhere, the amount of customary land declined as it was enfranchised or converted to leasehold.[28] At the same time extension of cultivation to commons and wastes further reduced the proportion of copyhold land since in many cases the new land was leased from the outset.[29] Many lords whose manors included copyholds of inheritance, as Whitchurch did, concentrated on improving the income from demesne and leaseholders, despairing of ever obtaining much from their copyholders. At Madeley in the later 16th century over 70 per cent of the lord's rent came from leaseholders, barely a quarter from copyholders.[30] Because of the poor returns some landowners raised capital by agreeing to clarify conditions of tenure such as the level of entry fines or the services due. In the late 16th century the lord of the manor of Ford tried to raise rents and exact higher entry fines from the copyholders but his failure led him to make an agreement with them in 1608, later embodied in a Chancery decree. In return for a composition of £1,880 13s. he confirmed ancient customs of the manor that gave his copyholders a virtual freehold interest.[31] Others enfranchised copyholds. At Pontesbury the lord's decision to enfranchise in 1615 ended half a century of dispute. The earl of Arundel's trustees gave the copyholders the same opportunity; some took it but many, to their later discomfiture, refused, believing that copyholds of inheritance were as good as, or better than, freeholds. At Whixall in 1704 the copyholders were allowed to buy out their fines, heriots, and services at three years' improved rent as an inducement to agree to inclosure of the common.[32]

The development of leasehold proceeded apace too. Even on copyhold estates held at will, the lord benefited from the change by the formalization of tenants' rights and duties, the better enforcement of good husbandry, the elimination of free bench, and the control of sub-letting.[33] Leases made in 1533 and 1541 of former copyhold land held at will in the manor of Whittington are early examples of the change. In the 1540s Robert Longe, the London mercer who had bought Condover manor, was opposed by his copyholders when he tried a similar transformation. The copyholders accused Longe of refusing access to court records so as to override customs by compelling them to treat anew for their holdings which were to be held by leases for lives and on terms decided by Longe. The Ellesmere copyholders had estates for lives at the lord's will but, though numerous in 1560, had disappeared by the opening years of the 17th century. Leaseholds were created either as properties fell in with the extinguishing of lives or—because that could be a long drawn out process—by forcing the tenants to come to terms whenever an individual life dropped. In 1602 the surveyor of the lordship of Oswestry advised the lord to 'grant no more copies but as they fall grant them by lease because the copyholders are so few, and upon their leases to reserve a heriot'.[34]

[27] Edwards, 'Farming Econ. of NE. Salop.' 26–9; Garbet, *Wem*, 74, 83–4; P.R.O., C 3/268/10; C 3/275/12; Loton Hall MSS., Chanc. decree *re* man. customs of Ch. Stretton 1670.
[28] *Ag. Hist. Eng.* v (2), 198–9, 203–4, 208.
[29] Edwards, op. cit. cap. 4.
[30] Ibid. p. 30; *V.C.H. Salop.* xi. 43.
[31] *Ag. Hist. Eng.* v (2), 208; Kerridge, *Agrarian Problems*, 54–5; *V.C.H. Salop.* viii. 231, 273.
[32] *V.C.H. Salop.* viii. 272–3; Gough, *Myddle*, 85; Garbet, *Wem*, 65; Staffs. R.O., D. 593/B/2/12/23, arts. of agreement 1704.
[33] C. G. A. Clay, 'Lifeleasehold in W. Counties of Eng. 1650–1750', *Agric. H.R.* xxix. 91, 93, 95.
[34] Ibid. 90–1; S.R.O. 894/155–6; *V.C.H. Salop.* viii. 38, 46; P.R.O., STAC 3/4/80; Edwards, 'Farming Econ. of NE. Salop.' 30–1; Slack, *Lordship of Oswestry*, 81.

In order to adjust the level of their rents more effectively, from the mid 16th century landlords also shortened the period of their leases or copies. In Shropshire earlier in the century leases of more than 50 years had been common but thereafter they were rarely granted for longer than 21 years.[35] In Halton (in Bromfield) 21-year leases were granted in the later 16th and earlier 17th century,[36] but in the county as a whole it was more usual to let for lives. The typical lease was for three lives but indentures for one or two lives were also sealed. On Earnwood manor in 1643 ten of the nineteen copyholders held for three lives, four for two, and one for one, while five of the eleven leaseholders held for three lives, three for two lives, and one for one.[37] Twenty-one-year leases were reckoned to equal those for three lives, and calculations were made on that basis, although when the Ellesmere estate was being re-leased in 1637 a multiplication figure of ten was used for the former and eleven for the latter. By the late 17th century improved life expectancy had lengthened the duration of leases and made them an even better proposition for the tenants. About 1640 John Gough took a three-lives lease of land in Myddle parish and sixty years later two lives were still in being. Moreover his grand-nephew Richard, the historian of the parish, recalled hearing of a lease which had fallen in because the 99 years had elapsed and one of the three lives was still in being.[38]

Unlike the situation in the midlands and eastern England where economic annual rents were introduced at an early date, western landowners obtained the bulk of their income from large entry fines, with only small reserved rents and some rent chickens or bushels of corn coming in annually.[39] In 1652–3 tenants of 79 holdings on the Craven estate in south Shropshire were paying £197 5s. 4d. a year in reserved rents but had paid out £10,210 1s. 4d. in entry fines. Fourteen of the fines included an allowance for the surrender of an existing lease, a device which—with the adding of years or lives—enabled a landowner to update the terms he offered and a tenant to extend his interest: in 1729 a farm lease in Kynnersley allowed the tenant to exchange a life for £30 and add one for £60.[40]

Fines increased dramatically as land values soared, a rise due only in part to inflation. In Ellesmere in 1637 the re-leasing of the estate brought in £10,398 13s. 4d. in fines as compared with £660 19s. 11d. in 1602 and £404 7s. 2d. in 1560. Even that improvement did not satisfy Bridgwater and over the next four years his commissioners were ordered to get even better terms. On the Leveson estate in and around the Weald Moors receipts trebled in the years 1600–40.[41] The fact that tenants paid such greatly increased rents indicates the profitability of farming in early 17th-century Shropshire.[42]

As elsewhere in western England the system of life leaseholds persisted in Shropshire throughout the period.[43] A survey of leases made in the manor of Linley (in More) in 1699 shows that all but one of the nineteen granted in the previous fifty years were for three lives. In the mid 18th century the Foresters and the Lawleys regularly granted leases for three lives, and they were reintroduced by Lord Gower in 1755 in order to raise capital quickly from entry fines. In 1793 it was observed that Lord Craven's farms in Stanton Lacy 'as in other places in

[35] See e.g. *V.C.H. Salop.* xi. 83–4, 157, 224–5.
[36] S.R.O. 5/1/6–7, 9–10, 21–3, 25, 30.
[37] S.R.O. 20/1/78; 322/2/2; 567/1/229; 1037/11/5; 3320/58/2 (transcript in 4744/1, pp. 53 sqq.); Staffs. R.O., D. 593/J/11/2/4; Bodl., Craven dep. 14–22.
[38] *Agric. H.R.* xxix. 83–4; Hopkins, 'Bridgewater Est. in N. Salop.' 136–8; Gough, *Myddle,* 100.
[39] *Agric. H.R.* xxix. 83.
[40] Bodl., Craven dep. 14–23; Staffs. R.O., D. 593/I/1/14.
[41] Hopkins, 'Bridgewater Est.' 68, 71–2; Edwards, 'Farming Econ. of NE. Salop.' 34.
[42] Edwards, op. cit. 34–5.   [43] *Agric. H.R.* xxix. 83.

Shropshire' were let for lives at very low rents.[44] The depression that affected farming in the century after the Restoration may have helped to preserve the system for, apart from the short- and middle-term fall in receipts that would have accompanied a change to rack renting, it made it easier for landlords to maintain the level of their rents. Moreover a life leaseholder had normally to pay taxes and repair his holding,[45] so saving the landlord much expenditure.[46] Landlords who racked, however, could hardly avoid such charges. Thus in the early 18th century Richard Hill was told that 'tenants at rack in this country will not be tied to any repairs'.[47]

Letting at economic rent was not unknown in Shropshire in the early modern period. There were many tenants at will, for instance, though they tended to occupy smaller properties such as cottages, industrial premises, and parcels of land. That was the situation in Great Bromfield manor in 1635 where there was an obvious distinction between the messuages, normally leased for lives, and other forms of property.[48] A few of the messuages were being held at will but, as on the Bridgwater and Leveson estates at the time, that device appears to have been a temporary measure to bring recalcitrant tenants to heel.[49] In the manor of Cardington and Lydley Hayes too, a number of farms let annually in the early 1620s had been leased by the end of the decade.[50] On the earl of Bridgwater's Whitchurch estate, however, the number of tenants at will increased in the early 17th century as the landlord deliberately set about improving his receipts at a time of rising prices. Bridgwater was to some extent compensated for the loss of entry fines by the simultaneous introduction of leaseholds on the Ellesmere estate. Entry fines were reintroduced in the harsher climate of the later 17th century but, as they tended to be small, there was no abrupt change of direction.[51]

In areas where rents were not already racked the consequences of the Civil War may have stimulated an interest in economic rents. Much royalist land fell to the state and either because former leases were disallowed or because there were difficulties in negotiating new ones, many properties, as on the confiscated Craven estate or the Brookes' manor of Madeley,[52] were let at annual tenancies.

Development continued after 1660, though clearly the situation varied from estate to estate. The desire for modernization and greater efficiency seems to have been an important influence in favour of racking when it happened. From the 1680s the Leveson-Gowers' agent George Plaxton completely reversed the former leasing policy and insisted on letting only at will, perhaps influenced by practice on the family's Stittenham estate (Yorks. N.R.). In effect Plaxton showed that it was necessary to face severe short-term difficulties to secure a large and steadier return in the future. He also introduced modern methods of estate administration: tenants were encouraged to consolidate their holdings and general improvements of the estate were carried out.[53] The change can also be seen on Lord Kilmorey's estate in north-east Shropshire. A 1686 survey lists properties held for lives and at rack rents: it is clear that leases were not being renewed as lives ended for the

[44] S.R.O. 1037/11/5; Hull Univ., Brynmor Jones Libr., DDFA/26/27, 31–2, 34, 36, 39, 51, 57; DDFA(2)/15/8; S.P.L., Deeds 1384, 1864; V.C.H. Salop. xi. 84, 159; T. Rowley, Salop. Landscape (1972), 158.
[45] Staffs. R.O., D. 1287/18/15.
[46] Agric. H.R. xxix. 86–7.
[47] S.R.O. 112/1/2698; cf. ibid. 2697.   [48] S.R.O. 20/1/78.
[49] Edwards, 'Farming Econ. of NE. Salop.' 32, 34.
[50] S.R.O. 567/1/228–9.

[51] Hopkins, 'Bridgewater Est.' 156, 195, 200–1; Edwards, 'Farming Econ. of NE. Salop.' 32.
[52] Bodl., Craven dep. 14–22; C. O'Riordan, 'Sequestration and Social Upheaval: Madeley, Salop. and the Eng. Revolution', W. Midland Studies, xviii. 22, 24.
[53] J. R. Wordie, Est. Management in 18th Cent. Eng. (R.H.S. Studies in Hist. xxx), 29–30; idem, 'Rent Movements and the Eng. Tenant Farmer, 1700–1839', Research in Econ. Hist. vi. 197.

vast majority of people named were over sixty. In Shifnal manor a similar change was being carried out in the early 18th century.[54]

Tenants often preferred rack rents in economically troubled times, such as the late 17th and early 18th century, since they did not have to spend on taxes or repairs and rent reductions were easier to obtain. Farmers in Shropshire, a mainly pastoral county, did not suffer the same degree of hardship as those in mixed-farming areas did. Nevertheless conditions did worsen: arrears of rent built up from time to time and in the late 1740s a severe outbreak of cattle plague[55] did much damage to the farming economy.

Arable farming

Shropshire was mainly pastoral: only eight out of the 297 holdings covered by inventories of the 1550s[56] had more capital in crops than in animals (Table VI). Most farmers, however, grew some corn and it would be wrong to think that arable cultivation was of little account. In the mid 16th century—outside the northern dairy area where the management of cattle predominated—corn was often grown on more than a purely subsistence basis. The greatest acreages were grown on the Eastern Sands and in the Severn-Tern area, for the seemingly high level of capital investment on the east Shropshire coalfield reflects the smallness of the sample and the lack of specialization by that region's comparatively modest farmers. Wills show that good crops were gathered in south Shropshire too. There were many legacies of crops in field or barn; thus in 1548 Margery Atcherley of Onibury made bequests of all her growing crop (except 4 a. of the best corn), while her son William was to take possession of her fallow ground as soon as she died.[57]

In 1612 Shropshire's soil was said to be rich 'and standeth upon a red clay, abounding in wheat and barley'.[58] The point was reiterated in 1673 when, besides its good cover of woods, Shropshire's fertile tilth was described as 'abounding in wheat and barley' and its pasture as feeding 'store of cattle'.[59] In fact arable production increased in the 17th century as land was inclosed and a more flexible husbandry developed. The change seems to have been triggered by a subsistence crisis of the sort that wracked the forest of Arden (Warws.), a similar wood–pasture region, in the early 17th century.[60] Certainly by 1649 Shropshire was said to be one of those woodland counties that before inclosure 'were wont to be relieved by the fielden with corn of all sorts, and now are grown as gallant corn countries as be in England'.[61]

[54] S.R.O. 946/B. 640; S.P.L., MS. 2600, surv. of Shifnal man. 1720s; Staffs. R.O., D. 641/2/F/4/1, rental of Shifnal man. 1750.

[55] *Orders of Q. Sess.* ii, preface to orders 1741–57, 118–47, 152.

[56] Some 5,000 probate invs. were used for Edwards, 'Farming Econ. of NE. Salop.' (see pp. 19, 321). For this art. *c.* 3,000 more have been used, mainly for S. Salop. (in H.W.R.O.(H.)). Transcripts of over 300 (for Bp.'s Cast., Bitterley, Bromfield, Clee St. Margaret, Cleobury Mortimer, Culmington, Diddlebury, Holdgate, Hopton Wafers, Lydbury N., Lydham, More, Munslow, Norbury, Ric.'s Cast., Shifnal, Stanton Lacy, Stanton Long, Stoke St. Milborough, Stottesdon incl. Farlow, Tugford, Wentnor, Cold Weston, and Wheathill) were kindly lent by Dr. B. S. Trinder, of 247 more (for M. Wenlock) by Mr. S. P. Mullins, and of *c.* 100 others (for Bridgnorth) by Dr. M. D. G. Wanklyn. For Tables VI–VII 1,073 invs. were used, largely of Apr.–Oct. in the 1550s, 1660s, and 1740s. So few pre-1660 invs.

survive for S. and NW. Salop. that no inf. for the 1550s could be quantified for those regions in Tables VI–VII. Some hundreds of S. Salop. wills were, however, used to form an impression of mid 16th-cent. farming there and so allow comparisons with other areas and later periods. Invs. are less abundant in the 1740s, and those from the 1730s and later 1730s respectively have been used to reinforce the data for S. and NW. Salop. For 6 pars. (Adderley, Ellesmere, Kynnersley, Stanton upon Hine Heath, Worfield, and Wroxeter) all 17th-cent. invs. were looked at, for 2 others (Albrighton and Donington) all for the whole period.

[57] H.W.R.O.(H.), Heref. dioc. rec., will of Margery Atcherley, 1547.

[58] J. Speed, *Eng., Wales, Scotland, and Irel. Described* (1612), cap. 35.   [59] R. Blome, *Britannia* (1673), 192.

[60] V. H. T. Skipp, *Crisis and development: an ecological case study of the Forest of Arden, 1570–1674* (1978), 48–54.

[61] W. Blith, *The English Improver, or a New Summary of Husbandry* (1649), 72.

TABLE VI: LIVESTOCK, CROPS, AND FARM TACKLE IN THE 1550S, 1660S, AND 1740S
Percentage by value of total farm stock (T) and of livestock (L)

		Livestock			pigs	Crops		Tackle
		cattle	sheep	horses		hay	other crops	
1550s								
N. Plain	(T)	63.3	11.3	8.3	1.7	2.1	10.9	1.9
	(L)	74.8	13.4	9.8	2.1			
Severn–Tern &	(T)	54.3	12.2	7.1	1.6	1.7	17.6	3.1
Weald Moors	(L)	71.5	16.1	9.4	2.2			
Heathlands	(T)	53.6	19.0	6.9	1.7	2.5	12.6	2.0
	(L)	65.5	23.3	8.5	2.1			
E. Sands	(T)	51.2	16.5	5.5	2.4	2.0	16.2	2.4
	(L)	65.8	21.2	7.1	3.1			
E. Coalfield	(T)	53.5	11.4	5.7	1.8	1.5	19.5	4.0
	(L)	72.4	15.4	7.8	2.5			
1660s								
N. Plains	(T)	52.3	4.0	7.6	2.4	2.8	15.2	3.7
	(L)	78.2	6.0	11.4	3.6			
Severn–Tern &	(T)	46.8	7.8	8.0	2.3	2.6	24.4	5.5
Weald Moors	(L)	72.0	12.0	12.3	3.6			
Heathlands	(T)	39.0	14.2	10.4	2.7	3.4	24.0	3.3
	(L)	58.6	21.3	15.6	4.1			
E. Sands	(T)	32.9	10.5	7.2	2.8	2.3	35.1	6.1
	(L)	62.2	19.9	13.7	5.2			
E. Coalfield	(T)	52.7	4.6	8.0	3.1	4.7	16.3	5.0
	(L)	77.4	6.7	11.8	4.5			
NW. Uplands	(T)	51.4	9.9	6.9	2.0	1.2	21.6	4.1
	(L)	72.8	14.0	9.8	2.8			
S. Salop.	(T)	47.6	8.2	8.7	2.9	4.8	18.5	4.7
	(L)	70.2	12.1	12.9	4.3			
SW. Salop.	(T)	32.7	27.5	6.2	1.3	2.0	11.2	4.9
	(L)	47.9	40.3	9.0	1.8			
1740s								
N. Plain	(T)	48.8	5.0	13.3	2.7	2.1	16.4	6.3
	(L)	69.9	7.2	19.0	3.9			
Severn–Tern &	(T)	38.9	6.1	15.0	3.6	3.2	22.8	6.8
Weald Moors	(L)	61.1	9.6	23.6	5.6			
Heathlands	(T)	28.2	10.5	12.3	3.4	1.8	28.5	5.9
	(L)	51.8	19.3	22.6	6.2			
E. Sands	(T)	28.8	10.1	14.0	2.5	1.0	36.4	6.5
	(L)	51.9	18.3	25.3	4.4			
E. Coalfield	(T)	40.0	4.7	20.4	3.1	5.1	19.6	5.8
	(L)	58.6	6.9	30.0	4.5			
NW. Uplands	(T)	42.5	13.6	14.2	5.1	0.9	13.2	5.4
	(L)	56.3	18.0	18.8	6.8			
S. Salop	(T)	39.8	11.7	9.7	2.7	2.6	21.5	6.7
	(L)	62.3	18.3	15.2	4.2			
SW. Salop.	(T)	47.5	29.3	8.3	1.8	1.5	6.3	3.0
	(L)	54.6	33.7	9.6	2.1			

Source: Probate inventories: see p. 141 n. 56.

The percentages of total farm stock do not amount to 100 because produce is excluded from the table though not from the farm-stock values on which the percentages are based; in different regions products like cheese and wool were often of considerable value. In the figures for livestock, poultry values are usually negligible. For the 1550s figures for the NW. Uplands (St. Asaph diocese) and S. Salop. and SW. Salop. (Hereford diocese) are not available.

In the mid 16th century, though the inventories give no acreages, it seems that a rough balance existed between winter and spring corn. At Edgmond in the summer of 1548 Thomas Rofe had 20 strikes' seedness (12 a.) of wheat and rye, 9 strikes' seedness (5 a.) of barley, and 11 strikes' seedness (6½ a.) of oats growing.[62] Later that year at Sutton Maddock John Littleford sowed 10 strikes' seedness (6 a.) of winter corn and the following spring 12 strikes' seedness (7 a.) of dredge, barley, and oats.[63] The normal sowing rate in Shropshire varied between two strikes an acre and 3 strikes over 2 a., though winter corn tended to be sown less thickly than spring grain.[64] Where the arable area was organized in three open fields the division between winter and spring corn was simple. At Cleobury North in 1600 winter corn was growing in Oakwood field, oats in Stable field, while Haymers field lay fallow.[65]

In the mid 16th century oats was the most prominent spring corn in all regions covered by the inventories. Barley was also common, except in the south-west region, and it sometimes alternated with oats. In a 1588 lease of the capital messuage of More it was stated that barley or oats was to be sown on land that had previously grown rye.[66] Spring corn increased in importance and during the 17th century barley clearly became the leading Lent grain, more widespread than oats, and often the most popular grain of all. Barley comprised 68 per cent of the cereals winnowed from the Barkers' demesne lands around Haughmond between 1623 and 1625, compared with 15 per cent oats, 6.7 per cent rye, 10 per cent muncorn, and 0.3 per cent wheat.[67] In the century up to the Restoration barley's increasing popularity was most notable in north Shropshire, particularly in the northern dairy and Severn–Tern areas and to a lesser extent on the Eastern Sands. Farther south it had to share the land with oats and pulses. Small acreages of French wheat and vetches made up the balance of crops growing in the fields.

In the Severn–Tern area barley's emergence as the most important spring corn can be seen in the cattle–corn parishes of Atcham and Wroxeter, and barley pushed oats into second position even in places like Great Ness and Fitz where oats had been prominent in the early 17th century.[68] Much barley was malted, especially in and around towns such as Shrewsbury, Newport, and Ludlow. On the Lilleshall estate the Levesons' agent reported in 1615 that all the barley grown was malted.[69] After bad harvests, when barley was used as a bread corn, maltsters tended to fall foul of town authorities who wished to keep the market supplied with grain to prevent unrest. In the early 1620s Shrewsbury corporation officers searched malthouses for barley and forced the maltsters to send it to market for baking into bread.[70] Barley's popularity in wood–pasture counties like Shropshire lay in its adaptability: not only was it used as a bread and malting corn but increasingly as animal feed too.

The cultivation of oats not only gave way to that of barley but also tended to lose ground to pulses, especially peas, as the 17th century progressed. 'Green' and 'grey' peas comprised an eighth of the total crops from the Barkers' demesne lands around Haughmond winnowed between 1623 and 1625.[71] Oats nevertheless remained popular in some places: one day in March 1677 forty teams, sowers, and harrowers were employed to sow 145 strikes' seedness (85 a.) of oats in Lubstree

[62] L.J.R.O., B/C/11, Thos. Rofe 24 July 1551.
[63] Ibid. John Littleford 16 May 1549.
[64] Cf. V.C.H. Salop. xi. 157 n. 41; S.R.O. 167/51, f. 10v. The acre-equivalents here suggested are mid way between the two sowing rates.
[65] T. Rowley, Salop. Landscape (1972), 141.
[66] S.R.O. 1037/9/19.
[67] S.P.L., Deeds 18288. Total strikes of cereal winnowed 3,512.
[68] Edwards, 'Farming Econ. of NE. Salop.' 98.
[69] Ibid. 61, 128, 212–13.
[70] Ibid. 212–13.
[71] S.P.L., Deeds 18288.

park, Lilleshall.[72] In certain areas oats was the most practicable cereal: it was well adapted to the inhospitable conditions of the south-west for instance, though generally arable farming was of little importance there.

In north Shropshire the commonest winter corn in the mid 16th century was rye.[73] Some wheat was grown but inventory references to it in the 1550s are outnumbered by those to rye by almost four to one. In Tudor and early Stuart England barley seems to have been the usual bread corn, and undoubtedly barley bread was eaten in Shropshire. Rye bread, however, was eaten by a larger proportion of the county's population than was the case in many other parts of England. In 1575 barley was sown as a bread corn but only because of bad weather at the time of the rye sowing; the substitution was made again fourteen years later when the rye harvest failed once more.[74] In the 1660s rye was naturally an important corn on the light soils of the Eastern Sands, the main arable area, though some wheat also was grown. Rye remained the normal winter corn in north Shropshire in the later 17th century, though wheat was more widely grown than before and the overall proportion of winter- rather than spring-sown crops was declining.

Some wheat had always been grown, especially on the south Shropshire clays: wills of the 1550s suggest that in some areas, including those where it was later to be prominent, wheat was more extensively sown than elsewhere in the county. In the century before the Restoration the acreage of winter corn held up better in the Severn–Tern area and south Shropshire (though the balance between spring and winter crops varied) than it did in the north. That is confirmed by the few inventories and other records that give acreages, even if often they relate only to rather small areas. In 1626 Edward Cressett had 140 a. of cereals at Coates, in Holdgate: 20 a. of wheat, 30 a. of mixed corn, 20 a. of rye, 20 a. of barley, and 50 a of oats.[75] Thomas Dun of Eyton on Severn had 8 a. of wheat, 5 a of rye, 6 a. of barley, and 9 a. of peas, oats, and vetches growing at the time of his death in 1662.[76] At Halford John Carter left 12 a. of corn, 6 a. of barley, and 13 a. of peas and oats in July 1669.[77] More wheat was sown in those regions and it improved its position generally in the late 17th century. Inclosure, felling of woods, and the draining of mosses and meres in the preceding hundred years had brought more heavy land into cultivation and that inherently fertile soil grew good wheat crops. Wheat was often grown as a cash crop, and improvement of the ordinary man's diet resulted from extension of the acreage under hard corn, a mixture of rye and wheat.

The expansion of the spring-sown acreage was one of several developments which complicated the pattern of arable farming between the 1550s and 1660s as cropping arrangements—in any case complex in an old-inclosed county like Shropshire—became more flexible. The open-field system, never as extensive as in more champaign counties, was in full decline in the 17th century[78] and even where it survived reasonably intact there was often, as on the Craven estate in south Shropshire, a multiplicity of fields.[79] Inclosure of the open fields facilitated ley farming, and a form of convertible husbandry was often practised on inclosed land, especially that taken out of the open fields. In 1600 the inhabitants of High Hatton manor agreed that whenever Adam Peate's pasture called the New leasow,

[72] Staffs. R.O., D. 593/F/2/35.
[73] Cf. Edwards, 'Farming Econ. of NE. Salop.' 208–9.
[74] Ibid. 60–1; T.S.A.S. iii. 273, 315.
[75] S.R.O., Cressett fam temp. deposit, case, John James v. Edw. Cressett.
[76] L.J.R.O., B/C/11, Thos. Dun 1 Sept. 1662.
[77] H.W.R.O.(H.), Heref. dioc. rec., inv. of John Carter 1669.
[78] Above (Inclosure).
[79] Bodl., Craven dep. 14–23.

in Worrall field, was sown with corn no more than one or two persons at a time would go through with their oxen to get to the Wallbrook.[80] In a tithe dispute of 1602 the inhabitants of Eaton township (in Baschurch) claimed not to have ploughed part of their inclosed arable land, until then in the open fields, but had mown it for hay.[81] Land designated arable and pasture ground is listed in the parliamentary surveys of the Craven estate in south Shropshire.[82] Similarly at Lilleshall in 1683 William Leveson-Gower leased out a parcel of arable or pasture ground called the Upper Park field; the tenant covenanted not to impoverish it by over-tillage and to spread sufficient manure whenever the land was ploughed, though no part of it was to be ploughed during the last five years.[83]

The point of such covenants was to prevent loss of fertility by over-tilling in the last few years of a lease. Leases often included premiums to be paid if the land was so ploughed. It was known at the time that temporary grass leys renewed fertility. In 1637 it was said of land in Blakemere park, Whitchurch, held by Philip Cotton and 'wonderfully ill husbanded by over tilling', that the best way of restoring it was to let it lie 'five or six years with rough winter grass'.[84] Little is known about yields. Evidence is sparse and incidental, as is that revealed by the dispute between Thomas Adams of Barrow and John Weld, the tithe owner there. In October 1650 Adams sowed a 30-a. close with wheat, rye, and mixed corn; in 1651 Weld claimed the yield had been tenfold, but Adams said it had been slightly less. Whichever it was, such a yield was better than most contemporaries achieved.[85]

Thus by the mid 17th century convertible husbandry and ley farming were promoting a genuine form of mixed farming in places most suited to it. The Eastern Sands region, then Shropshire's leading corn district (judged by the value of the crops grown there), led the way with the development of an economy based on sheep–corn husbandry. Crops were important in the Severn–Tern area too and also in parts of south Shropshire, normally in conjunction with cattle keeping and sometimes with sheep rearing as well. In favoured parts of south Shropshire, especially in Corve Dale and in the Teme valley, mixed farming had taken hold, though in Lord Craven's manors much of the large arable acreages were still in open fields.[86] At Stanton Lacy, for instance, almost half (47.9 per cent) of the land surveyed in 1652 was arable.[87] Of course south Shropshire's hills and valleys gave rise to a considerable variety of farming practice, much depending on a farm's location, soil type, and access to commons and wastes. A similarly varied pattern seems to have characterized the north-west uplands.

By c. 1750 regional specialization had accentuated the difference between regions and the uniformity of farming practice within them. On the Eastern Sands the level of investment in sheep and corn remained the same as in the 1660s but the arable acreage had increased and its importance can be seen in the careful appraisals of crops. In 1739 the region was said to have a fine dry sandy soil suited to rye and barley, and so 'commonly distinguished by the name of the rye-land' from Shropshire west of the Severn.[88] Barley was certainly the most important spring grain and according to the acreages given, the most popular crop of all. Peas were probably the second spring grain but oats were extensively sown and a number of farmers favoured it. Clover had been incorporated in the rotation by 1700. Barley was used as a fodder crop but when in July 1737 the appraisers of the goods of

[80] Edwards, 'Farming Econ. of NE. Salop.' 64.
[81] Ibid. 88.   [82] Bodl., Craven dep. 14–23.
[83] Edwards, op. cit. 64.
[84] S.R.O. 212, box 346, survey of 1637 (Liber A), f. 24r.–v.
[85] P.R.O., C 3/467, no. 29; D. Palliser, Age of Eliz. (1983), 200.
[86] Bodl., Craven dep. 16–17, 20–1.
[87] Ibid. 17.   [88] T.S.A.S. ix. 205.

George Smith of Bridwick (in Shifnal) valued his winter corn and barley at £16 10s. and the peas and oats and the hay at £11,[89] they may have been distinguishing crops meant for human consumption from those to be fed to the animals. Some of this barley was made into bread but mostly it was consumed as beer. Rye bread was generally eaten but increasingly in the early 18th century bread was being made out of rye mixed with wheat. In Albrighton, Donington, and Shifnal parishes[90] fewer references to rye appear from c. 1700 and there was a corresponding increase in listings of hard corn.

In the Heathlands arable cultivation spread to the lighter soils in the post-Restoration period, a process typical of developments affecting similar land in the country at large.[91] As a result a system of farming was created akin to that practised on the Eastern Sands,[92] though with more emphasis on cattle and even dairying. Characteristically the post-Restoration period saw the beginning of heath inclosures, attention beforehand having largely been concentrated on the heavier soils. The stimulus in the country as a whole seems to have been the need for efficiency in an age of depressed corn prices, and it made sense to extend cultivation to the lighter and more easily worked soils.[93] Barley and rye were the commonest grains in the Heathlands, though wheat increased in popularity. Thus Griffith Spender of Great Sowdley (in Cheswardine) had a stack of wheat worth £18 in October 1740 and like many others also sowed rye mixed in with it.[94] By the 1740s clover was an established part of the rotation.

Elsewhere in north Shropshire cattle rather than sheep formed the basis of the mixed-farming economy, though sheep had some importance.[95] As there were fewer physical differences than in the south, so there was a greater uniformity of husbandry. In 1704 Wroxeter's black soils were noted as particularly fertile,[96] but there was excellent arable in many other parts. The relative valuations of winter and spring corn listed in inventories of the 1690s and 1740s indicate a move in the direction of the latter. Barley, already the most important Lent crop in the 1660s, steadily improved its position; oats had given way to pulses, especially peas. Farmers, however, did not neglect winter corn: wheat continued to expand its acreage at the expense of rye but, as elsewhere, a lot more hard corn was being grown.

In south Shropshire and in the north-west uplands large sheep flocks were kept on the hills[97] but mixed farming on the lower land was firmly based on a system of cattle–corn husbandry. That development was led by a class of prosperous yeomen who emerged in the mid 17th century and who invested much capital in the farms. They had large acreages under crops, ran substantial herds of cattle, and in many cases kept sizeable flocks of sheep too. The land was kept in good heart by dung and, as in the case of Thomas Stedman of Stanton Lacy, was also marled and limed. In July 1725 Stedman had 26 a. of corn and wheat (£26), 75 a. of lent grain (£30), and lime and earth worth £3 10s. His land was ploughed by 16 oxen while his herd of 50 head provided him with stores and dairy produce. He also reared and fattened pigs and sheep and bred horses.[98]

Where acreages were recorded, as in the above example, it seems that spring

[89] L.J.R.O., B/C/11, Geo. Smith 4 Nov. 1737.
[90] Prob. invs. *passim.*
[91] *Essays in Agrarian Hist.* ed. W. E. Minchinton (1968), i. 208, 212–17.
[92] Below (Livestock and dairy farming).
[93] Minchinton, op. cit. i. 208, 212–17.
[94] L.J.R.O., B/C/11, Griffith Spender 2 Apr. 1741, listing hard corn.
[95] Three quarters (76.3 per cent) of the invs. list sheep, which provided valuable income for many farmers.
[96] R. Morden, *New Descr. and State of Eng.* (1704), 70.
[97] Below (Livestock and dairy farming).
[98] H.W.R.O.(H.), Heref. dioc. rec., inv. of Thos. Stedman 1726.

corn tended to predominate. Nevertheless a good deal of winter corn was grown and some farmers gave it equal weight. Edward Jones of Ruckley (in Stanton Lacy), for instance, had corn worth £18 (c. 18 a.), 12 a. of vetches, 6 a. of oats, 2 a. of beans and peas, and 19 a. fallow in March 1737.[99] Winter corn was particularly important in the Teme valley; there mixed farming had made a considerable advance and it was in many ways very similar to that being practised on the central plain of Herefordshire.[1] Clover had been introduced into the rotation by the turn of the 17th century and there are odd references to turnips as a field crop. Anne Cooke of Richard's Castle planted 5 a. of winter corn in 1689 and a few months later 18 a. of spring crops, including 2 a. of turnips.[2]

On the east Shropshire coalfield numerous small farms, normally pastoral, continued in existence, and dairying was of some importance. On the fringes of the area larger farms could be found and they provided much of the corn brought to market. In the summer of 1749 William Picken of Donnington (in Lilleshall), a cattle–corn farmer, had a mixed herd of 25 head and growing corn and grain worth £40.[3] Spring corn predominated; the leading grain was barley, followed by oats and then peas. Rye was still cultivated but, as elsewhere, increasingly mixed with wheat. Clover was introduced to the area in the early 18th century, being first mentioned in the inventories of farmers dying in the 1720s.

Over most of the northern dairy area arable farming counted for little by c. 1750; only the farmers of the south-west had a lower proportion of capital in crops. Rye and wheat were generally grown mixed as hard corn, though they were also sown separately. Spring grain was emphasized with barley the leading crop, followed by oats and pulses, especially peas. Barley was malted and Wem was noted for its excellent malt liquors.[4]

Of the industrial crops, hemp and flax were the most widely grown. Cultivation was normally on a small scale but many holdings had a hemp plot by the house. Continual presentments of individuals, and even of whole townships, for watering hemp and flax in streams show that the practice was common, and indeed the processing of the crops was an important cottage industry.[5] Of the dye crops such as saffron, woad, and madder, so much discussed by contemporaries,[6] there is little evidence, though saffron was being grown on reclaimed land in Prees by c. 1549[7] and there was a 'saffron croft' among the fields of Cheswell Grange, Lilleshall, in 1580.[8]

Hop growing, though less common than that of hemp and flax, also developed from small beginnings: hops were grown in Prees by c. 1549, at Stoke upon Tern in 1588, at Chirbury in 1603, and at Madeley and in the Teme valley by c. 1650.[9] Inventories, however, suggest that cultivation was not very common before the mid 17th century; thereafter it began to expand more rapidly, especially in south Shropshire. Some hop growing was on a large scale. In 1746 Walter Pooler, a substantial cereal grower from Neen Sollars, had 12,000 hop poles valued at £30 on Mr. Carver's land[10] and four years later John Smith of Boraston (in Burford) had 20,000 poles worth £20 and hops worth £30.[11]

[99] Ibid. inv. of Edw. Jones appraised 18 Mar. 1737; cf. S.P.R. Heref. iv (2), 138.

[1] Ag. Hist. Eng. v (1), 172–7.

[2] H.W.R.O.(H.), Heref. dioc. rec., inv. of Anne Cooke 1690.

[3] L.J.R.O., B/C/11, Wm. Picken 12 Oct. 1749.

[4] S. Garbet, Hist. Wem (Wem, 1818), 230.

[5] Edwards, 'Farming Econ. of NE. Salop.' 62.

[6] Ibid. 63.

[7] i.e. Dogmoor: J. R. W. Whitfield, 'Enclosure Movement in N. Salop.' T.C.S.V.F.C. xi. 55; above (Inclosure).

[8] S.R.O. 38/124.

[9] T.C.S.V.F.C. xi. 55; S.R.O. 327, box 114, lease of 27 June 1588; T.S.A.S. vi. 286; V.C.H. Salop. xi. 43; Goodman, 'Hammerman's Hill', 175.

[10] H.W.R.O.(H.), Heref. dioc. rec., inv. of Wal. Pooler 1746.

[11] Ibid. inv. of John Smith 1750.

There were many orchards and in the early 17th century Shropshire hedgerows were stocked with fruit trees. Sometimes leaseholders covenanted to plant such trees.[12] Of course much of the produce was eaten as fruit—Edmund Mansell of Preston Boats (in Upton Magna) left a small quantity of apples, verges, onions, and garlic valued at 3s. 4d. in 1640 and seven years later William Brown of the same parish had apples and onions worth the same amount.[13] In south Shropshire, however, cider apples were grown and in the second half of the period a substantial brewing industry emerged which mirrored a similar development over the border in Herefordshire.[14]

Of the new crops, turnips[15] had made little impact on crop rotations by 1750 and their cultivation seems to have been largely restricted to the demesnes of gentlemen enthusiasts. Even in such favourable areas as the Eastern Sands there are few inventory references, though they were being grown at Coton Hall farm (in Alveley) in the 1740s.[16] Similarly potatoes were just beginning to appear by 1750, also, it seems, at the instigation of the gentry or with their encouragement. In 1738 potatoes were growing on the Davies estate at Brompton (in Church Stoke),[17] and in the 1740s they were being planted by the Davenports of Worfield[18] and the Waltons of Walton.[19] In 1756 the Foresters paid a labourer 6s. 4d. for nineteen days' work planting potatoes.[20] A problem common to all new crops was that of tithes and their assessment for such a purpose caused endless disputes.[21] In 1748, for instance, George Watson, a tenant on the Attingham estate, agreed to plant potatoes on a piece of boggy land that he wished to drain but only on condition that the vicar would waive his tithe on them.[22]

Oxen were universally used for ploughing in 16th-century Shropshire and the highest proportions of draught animals inventoried were in the chief arable areas: the Eastern Sands and Severn–Tern areas had most in the 1550s, and those two areas, with the Heathlands too, had most in the 1660s. Shropshire inventories often list considerable numbers of oxen, sometimes a reflection of the size of team needed to pull through the heavy soil. In June 1550 the team belonging to John Perton of Ledwyche (in Ludford) comprised eight oxen and two steers.[23] To acquire and keep that number involved considerable expense and smaller farmers naturally hired at least some of their draught animals. Thus in 1550 John Reynolds of Down (in Lydbury North) owed money to two men for the hire of two yokes of bullocks.[24] By the 1660s plough horses were occasionally recorded but they were rare. Robert Kilvert of Booley (in Stanton upon Hine Heath) left two draught nags as well as four oxen in 1627;[25] perhaps the horses led the oxen but they are just as likely to have pulled the harrow or cart. Richard Dabbs of the Wyke (in Shifnal) did use horses to till for in 1661 he left corn and draught horses but no ox.[26] Similarly Michael Thomas, rector of Stockton 1642–61, ploughed his glebe with horses.[27]

By the 1740s the move towards ploughing by horse is particularly apparent in the main arable areas. The change had proceeded furthest on the Eastern Sands and by the mid 18th century oxen had virtually disappeared. Indeed in parishes

[12] Edwards, 'Farming Econ. of NE. Salop.' 64.
[13] L.J.R.O., B/C/11, Edw. Mansell 27 Nov. 1640, Wm. Brown 22 Dec. 1647.
[14] Ag. Hist. Eng. v (1), 157, 162, 172–7; Goodman, 'Hammerman's Hill', 175–6.
[15] Known to Salop. gardeners by c. 1603: T.S.A.S. 2nd ser. iv. 249, 255.   [16] Ag. Hist. Eng. v (1), 156.
[17] S.R.O. 631/2/1.
[18] S.R.O. 2713, box 30, Betty Clemson's bill 8 July 1743.
[19] Ag. Hist. Eng. v (1), 156.

[20] S.R.O. 1224, box 164, acct. bk. 1755-7, 10 Apr. 1756.
[21] E. J. Evans, The Contentious Tithe (1976), cap. 3, esp. pp. 46-9.
[22] Ag. Hist. Eng. v (1), 151 n. 55.
[23] H.W.R.O.(H.), Heref. dioc. rec., inv. of John Perton 1550.   [24] Ibid. inv. of John Reynolds 1550.
[25] L.J.R.O., B/C/11, Rob. Kilvert 6 Dec. 1627.
[26] Ibid. Ric. Dabbs 9 May 1661.
[27] Ibid. Mic. Thomas 15 Oct. 1661; cf. T.S.A.S. 3rd ser. v. 355, 372; S.R.O. 3067/1/1, bur. 21 Aug. 1661.

like Albrighton and Worfield the transition had occurred fifty years before. The median number of horses per farm, eight, was the highest by far of any region. Apart from draught horses the stock included brood mares and young animals. Unlike other mixed farming areas in the country, on the Eastern Sands horse breeding and rearing were not yet separate activities, though some people did buy in stock. Joseph Parker of Chesterton (in Worfield) for instance, bought good quality draught horses and trained colts in the collar; in 1746 he left five horses and two colts worth £35.[28] Some Severn-Tern farmers continued to plough with oxen but the move to horses is indicated by the rise in the median head per farm from two in the 1660s to five in the 1740s. Some of those draught horses were the large powerful animals that had appeared on English farms after the Restoration.[29] Thomas Calcott of Allscott (in Wrockwardine) had three mares and a horse worth £6 each in 1744, apart from a (riding) mare worth £7; they ploughed and took Calcott's corn to market in his two wagons.[30] Horses ploughed on some south Shropshire farms but, as in the south-west, the ox remained the main draught animal. That is reflected in the high proportion of oxen and working bullocks and steers recorded in the inventories.

Shropshire farmers in the early-modern period used various fertilizers. Farmyard muck was the commonest, though sheep were folded on the lighter soils. In the years 1600-60 almost half (45.2 per cent) of the farmers' inventories in Worfield, a sheep-corn parish, include references to hurdles or fold hatches. In the mid 16th century poor sandy soils were marled in Shropshire,[31] though fifty years later it was beginning to be realized that marl appropriate to the type of soil being treated had to be used.[32] At Moreton Corbet castle in 1623 there was an 'iron marling auger of three rods', which suggests that there at least good quality marl was systematically searched for.[33] According to Fitzherbert's continuator, 'if you manure your grounds once in seven or twelve years, it is sufficient, and look how many years he beareth corn, so many years he will bear grass, and that plenty'.[34] Many farmers dug marl from the wastes. In a suit concerning Meeson heath in 1576 the plaintiff Thomas Cherrington claimed to have carried away 'clods, marl, and mud to amend his other lands about six years last past'.[35] Shropshire was among the counties where farmers limed cold or moist ground, building kilns in the fields to burn the limestone and then dressing the land 'to great advantage'.[36] Lime's main function was to neutralize the acidity inhibiting the growth of most crops and widely prevalent in Shropshire soils.[37] To be effective, however, lime had to be used with manure since, like marl, it was not a plant food, a fact not fully understood until the 19th century.[38]

In the 1550s the main farm vehicle was the two-wheeled wain. Most farmers had one. A farmer who had two, like Thomas Townsend of Quatt in 1555, would use one to muck, the other to carry the corn.[39] Tumbrils were also used around the farm and those who had a cart, a mainly horse-drawn vehicle, used it *inter alia* to take produce to market. By the 1660s there were more farm carts, though wains remained more numerous. Thereafter carts supplanted wains for all farm work.

[28] L.J.R.O., B/C/11, Jos. Parker 21 Nov. 1746.
[29] Peter Edwards, *Horse Trade of Tudor and Stuart Eng.* (1988), 6.
[30] *Yeomen and Colliers in Telford*, ed. B. Trinder and J. Cox (1980), p. 452.
[31] Leland, *Itin.* ed. Toulmin Smith, iv. 2.
[32] Norden, *Surveior's Dialogue*, 22.
[33] S.R.O. 322, box 59, inv. of goods at Moreton Corbet castle 1623.
[34] [Jas. Roberts], *Fitzharberts Booke of Husbandrie ... newlie corrected* (1598), 29.
[35] Staffs. R.O., D. 593/B/2/1/7.
[36] Norden, *Surveior's Dialogue*, 223.
[37] Below, 1875-1985 (Livestock rearing and feeding).
[38] Edwards, 'Farming Econ. of NE. Salop.' 66; *Rural Change and Urban Growth 1500-1800*, ed. C. W. Chalklin and M. A. Havinden (1974), 109.
[39] L.J.R.O., B/C/11, Thos. Townsend 15 July 1555.

In the early 18th century, moreover, the heavy four-wheeled wagon appeared in Shropshire. Far more expensive than cart or wain and rather cumbersome for use in the fields, its main purpose was to carry corn and other commodities to market. Naturally only prosperous farmers could afford it (and its team) and were busy enough to keep it fully used. With it they could dispose of their produce in bulk, marketing it as efficiently as possible.

Livestock and dairy farming

Animal husbandry formed the basis of Shropshire farming in the two centuries 1540–1750, even though many holdings grew considerable acreages of crops. Farmers' inventories[40] reflect the emphasis: livestock and animal products were almost invariably worth more than the crops (Table VII) and were listed in greater detail too. For most farmers the imbalance was quite marked: in the 1550s, for instance, four out of five farms (79.5 per cent) had three times as much capital in livestock as in crops. In the 1660s and 1740s only three farms out of five had the same 3:1 stock–crop ratio (58.5 and 61.6 per cent respectively) for the arable acreage had risen. Nevertheless livestock remained the most important commodity throughout the period.

Cattle were the most valuable animals in the 1550s and also the commonest on Shropshire farms. Even where sheep predominated, as on the Heathlands and the Eastern Sands, very few farmers had no cattle. In no region were cattle appraised at under 50 per cent of the value of farm stock. The picture is incomplete because of the absence of south Shropshire inventories, but cattle were clearly important there too. Many southern parishes had valley-bottom land as well as upland pasture and, according to the evidence of 16th-century wills, were well stocked with cattle. In 1548, for instance, Richard Browne of Stanton Lacy left, among other things, 36 head of cattle and 56 sheep.[41]

Cattle were used in various ways and, despite considerable overlapping of function, differences of emphasis can be glimpsed. Dairy farming was most pronounced in the northern dairy area (Table VII), especially in the parishes bordering Cheshire. Without doubt farmers there had been influenced by those to the north. Half (49.4 per cent) of the cattle consisted of cows and heifers, a figure approached only on the eastern coalfield (48.9 per cent): there the demands of a growing industrial population had already stimulated dairy production and incidentally provided a steady income for the many small farmers.

In the mid 16th century dairy farming was closely connected with cattle rearing[42] and in the western part of the northern dairy area, in parishes like Baschurch, the link is more apparent. In the Severn–Tern area and on the Heathlands and Eastern Sands dairy farmers mingled with rearers, the difference of emphasis varying according to who had first call on the milk, the milkmaid or the calf. Cattle were least important on the Eastern Sands with its emergent sheep–corn economy, but the two largest amounts of cheese were recorded there: the farmers, adding dairying enterprise to their sheep–corn farms, left cheese worth £4 and £5.[43]

A mixed form of cattle management seems to have been followed by south Shropshire farmers too, though the popularity of bequeathing cows and calves might exaggerate the importance of dairy farming there. In the south-west the

[40] Above, n. 56.
[41] H.W.R.O.(H.), Heref. dioc. rec., will of Ric. Browne 1548.
[42] Prob. invs. passim.
[43] L.J.R.O., B/C/11, John Blockeley (Shifnal) 7 Oct. 1556, John Strynger (Stockton) 2 Oct 1555.

TABLE VII: HERDS AND FLOCKS IN THE 1550S, 1660S, AND 1740S

	Cattle				Horses		Sheep
	median herd	% of value recorded in inventories			median herd	% of value recorded in inventories	median flock
		dairy	other	draught		adult	young	
1550S								
N. Plain	9–10	49.4	32.0	18.6	2	76.0	24.0	30
Severn–Tern & Weald Moors	11	42.2	36.1	21.7	2	73.8	26.2	30
Heathlands	11	44.4	37.7	17.8	2	76.4	23.6	30–5
E. Sands	7	39.3	32.6	28.1	2	67.7	32.3	30
E. Coalfield	10	48.9	33.7	17.4	2	53.8	46.2	23
1660S								
N. Plain	9	50.0	44.1	6.0	2	74.5	25.5	17
Severn–Tern & Weald Moors	11	45.7	40.9	13.4	2	72.2	27.8	21
Heathlands	7–9	39.2	46.9	13.9	2	74.0	26.0	21–4
E. Sands	8–9	43.4	40.4	16.2	2	79.5	20.5	40–6
E. Coalfield	7	59.1	35.7	5.3	1	86.1	13.9	37
NW. Uplands	17	45.9	43.6	10.5	4	81.8	18.2	20
S. Salop.	11	44.9	43.9	11.1	2	67.2	32.8	20
SW. Salop.	10	42.7	48.9	8.5	2	59.7	40.3	51
1740S								
N. Plain	18–19	61.6	35.5	2.9	4	70.4	29.6	10–12
Severn–Tern & Weald Moors	16	37.8	55.7	6.5	5	76.8	23.2	30–5
Heathlands	12–15	35.9	58.7	5.4	4	79.6	20.4	c. 50
E. Sands	12	43.7	48.8	7.5	8	72.8	27.2	69
E. Coalfield	6	47.8	50.6	1.6	4	72.3	27.3	25
NW. Uplands	12	42.1	46.3	11.6	5	72.4	27.6	40
S. Salop.	15	32.7	52.3	15.0	2	66.5	33.5	40
SW. Salop.	16	27.7	55.7	16.7	3	60.0	40.0	79+

Source: Probate inventories: see p. 141 n. 56.

Types of sheep are not distinguished regularly enough to permit classification. For the 1550s figures for the NW. Uplands (St. Asaph diocese) and S. Salop. and SW. Salop. (Hereford diocese) are not available.

raising of stores certainly predominated. South Shropshire wills do show the widespread custom of cow hiring, a device enabling smallholders to obtain milking animals cheaply while at the same time reducing the owner's need for pasture. In 1552 John Mytton of Kinnerton (in Wentnor) had his kine and heifers set either to parts or at hire, and he made specific bequests of all of them except five kine in Henry Davies's hands and a heifer in Richard Bullock's custody.[44] Cattle were also agisted. In 1551 Roger Gynnell of Bishop's Castle had two three-year-old steers in the custody of William Phillips of Kerry,[45] an example of the annual westerly movement of large numbers of stock from the west midlands to Montgomeryshire's extensive open pastures.[46]

By the 1660s there had been a tremendous increase in dairy production in the northern dairy area and output there must have approximated to that of the county's more famous neighbour, Cheshire. In fact it formed part of the same dairying country.[47] By the 1720s 'great quantities' of Cheshire cheese were made

[44] H.W.R.O.(H.), Heref. dioc. rec., will of John Mytton 1557.
[45] Ibid. will of Rog. Gynnell 1550.
[46] Edwards, 'Farming Econ. of NE. Salop.' 152.
[47] P. R. Edwards, 'Development of Dairy Farming on N. Salop. Plain in 17th Cent.' *Midland Hist.* iv. 175–90.

in the parts of Shropshire, Staffordshire, and Lancashire that bordered Cheshire.[48] In the eastern part of the northern dairy area, the earliest and most thoroughly affected by the development, the median value of cheese listed by the appraisers rose from 10s. in the 1600s to £2 13s. in the 1650s and 1660s.[49]

The median-sized herd in the region in the 1660s, as well as the proportion of capital in cattle, remained the same as it had been in the 1550s; in fact the figures reflect the continued involvement of small farmers in the dairy business and the wider section of rural society who were leaving inventories. Dairying did attract small farmers because of the lower capital investment needed in stock and equipment and also because it provided a regular income. Such people, however, had at most only a small surplus to sell, and the expansion of dairy production was brought about by the substantial farmers.[50] How large the scale of operations could be is shown by the inventory of Richard Furber, a yeoman from Shavington, in Adderley, the foremost cheese-making parish in the region: in May 1660 he had several tons of cheese in store, worth £168, and a dairy herd of 62 cows, a bull, 3 bull calves, 30 sucking calves, 25 yearlings, 15 two-year-olds, and 2 oxen.[51] Such men could provide the capital needed to maintain the comparatively high standards of stock breeding and careful grassland management necessary for effective dairy farming. That was best done in inclosed pastures rather than on open commons, and Adderley had been inclosed by the end of the 16th century.[52]

Dairy farming took longer to establish itself in the western half of the region. At the beginning of the 17th century the rearing of stores for market was probably the most widespread pursuit, though dairy production and the fattening of old and barren cows were associated interests. Towards the mid century, however, the emphasis shifted from stock rearing to a greater concentration on dairy production. Although the rearing of stores continued, the change is discernible in the greater number of milch cows grazing on the farms and in the larger stores of cheese.[53]

There were dairy farms elsewhere in the county, especially on the eastern coalfield and around Shrewsbury, where it was quite important, if on a lower level than in the northern dairy area. They existed in south Shropshire too and some inventories record reasonable stocks of cheese. In that region, however, it is difficult to assess the value of the dairy produce because appraisers commonly lumped it together with other provision. In south Shropshire more butter was made and near towns like Shrewsbury and Wellington liquid milk was important.[54]

By the mid 17th century more cattle were being fattened on riverside pastures and in improved peaty areas like the Weald Moors. Around Shrewsbury there were excellent feeding grounds[55] and the Newports, for instance, used the Severnside and Ternside meadows of their estate to fatten cattle.[56] Many cattle and sheep were grazed on pastures along the Severn and the Tern, in places like Atcham, Upton Magna, High Ercall, and Wrockwardine and the other Weald Moors parishes.[57] Hercules Felton, who left milch kine, barren cows, and stores in 1668, combined dairy farming with rearing and fattening, using the lush grass of the Weald Moors.[58] The moorland hay there was said to 'feed an ox to admiration';[59] inhabitants of the surrounding manors therefore brought in stock

[48] D. Defoe, *Tour through the Whole Island of Gt. Brit.* ed. R. Rogers (1971), 394–5.
[49] *Midland Hist.* iv. 177–8. [50] Ibid. 181–2.
[51] L.J.R.O., B/C/11, Ric. Furber 1 May 1660.
[52] *Midland Hist.* iv. 182, 184. [53] Ibid. 178–9.
[54] Edwards, 'Farming Econ. of NE. Salop.' 91; Trinder and Cox, *Yeomen and Colliers in Telford*, pp. 77–8.

[55] Edwards, 'Farming Econ. of NE. Salop' 89–90.
[56] P. R. Edwards, 'Cattle Trade of Salop. in late 16th and 17th Cents.' *Midland Hist.* vi. 77.
[57] Ibid.; Edwards, 'Farming Econ. of NE. Salop.' 102–4; prob. invs. *passim*.
[58] L.J.R.O., B/C/11, Hercules Felton (Wrockwardine) 29 July 1668. [59] *T.S.A.S.* lxiii. 1.

from outside to fatten over the summer, though the resulting pressure on the common meant that it had to be stinted.[60]

The attention Shropshire farmers gave to their livestock led to improved grassland management, for which there is considerable evidence from the mid 17th century. First and foremost there was much inclosure, which enabled farmers to improve the quality of grass and livestock.[61] The technique of floating meadows may have been known in the county before the end of the 16th century,[62] even if the first real evidence of it occurs only fifty years later. In 1649 Shropshire was among the counties in the woodland part of England where much progress had been made by this innovation.[63] Significantly, in that year meadows were being drowned in Little Wytheford.[64] The expense could be considerable and gentry like the Davenports, Harrieses, and Whitmores took the lead in the development of water meadows.[65]

Clover seems to have been introduced to north-east Shropshire in the mid 17th century: in 1663 a great part of the land in Worcestershire, Staffordshire, and Shropshire was said to be fit for its cultivation.[66] The earliest known inventory reference shows that in 1673 Richard Minton, a Felton Butler yeoman, left 'clover and other hay' worth £5.[67] At first it was largely grown on demesne land or on the farms of substantial yeomen but by the mid 18th century, partly as a result of landowners' encouragement, it was being planted by a wider cross-section of the farming population.[68] In December 1739 Sir John Bridgeman told his Shropshire agent to look at a tenement whose lease was shortly to fall in to ascertain those pieces of arable most suited for sowing with artificial grasses for the last three years of the term 'that the farm may come to hand in good heart to any succeeding tenant'.[69] Of the other rotational grasses there is little evidence, though they were clearly being grown. The Kynastons of Sundorne planted rye grass on their demesne in the 1720s[70] and, at a humbler level, Richard Shukar of Horton Lane (in St. Chad's, Shrewsbury) grew it in the 1740s.[71] In 1745 sainfoin was sown on Coton Hall farm in Alveley and had no doubt long been known in the county: almost eighty years earlier it had been grown in Denbighshire and seed had perhaps been shipped via Shrewsbury.[72]

Improved grassland management, together with the development of spring-sown fodder crops, helped to provide additional feed for the rising animal population of the county. Cattle were the main beneficiaries. Rearing had long been the traditional cattle enterprise of Shropshire and continued to provide a major focus of interest throughout the whole period. Dairy farmers were often engaged in cattle rearing as an ancillary occupation, but with increasing specialization there was a tendency to sell off all animals surplus to requirement, keeping only dairy replacements. Stores left Shropshire in considerable numbers for fattening but with the increase of grazing in the county there was a corresponding rise in local demand. Animals had always been valued for their carcass—beef and bacon are regularly inventoried— but until the 17th century the meat market was largely supplied with old or inferior animals. Greater numbers of fatstock were listed after 1660 and the trend continued

[60] Edwards, 'Farming Econ. of NE. Salop.' 103.
[61] Ibid. 44-5; *Midland Hist.* iv. 182-4; above (Inclosure).
[62] Edwards, 'Farming Econ. of NE. Salop.' 44.
[63] Blith, *Eng. Improver*, 54-5.
[64] S.R.O. 322, box 68, Humph. Pidgeon's acct.
[65] S.R.O. 2713, box 29, agreement betw. Hen. Davenport and John Shallcross and Thos. Higginbothom 29 Mar. 1679; Goodman, 'Hammerman's Hill', 171; *V.C.H. Salop.* viii. 278; *Ag. Hist. Eng.* v (1), 156.

[66] A. Yarranton, *The Improvement Improved by a Second Edn. of the great Improvement of Lands by Clover* (1663), 31.
[67] S.R.O. 522/3/2.
[68] Prob. invs. *passim*.
[69] Staffs. R.O., D. 1287/18/15, Sir John Bridgeman's letter bk. beginning 1 Aug 1739, letter of 8 Dec. 1739.
[70] S.P.L., Deeds 18290, disbursements 1721-3.
[71] L.J.R.O., B/C/11, Ric. Shukar 29 Apr. 1742.
[72] *Ag. Hist. Eng.* v (1), 156; *Pre-Industrial Eng.: Geographical Essays*, ed. J. Patten (1979), 132.

to the mid 18th century. The gentry were among the first to be involved, naturally developing an interest in commercial grazing as an extension of the fattening of stock for their own households.[73] Nevertheless others took part too. Samuel Wood for instance, a prosperous cattle, sheep, and corn farmer from Bockleton, reared and fattened his own animals and in 1749 left a herd comprising a bull and 16 cows (£80), 12 oxen (£54), 11 yearlings (£21), 11 rearing calves (£10), and 16 feeding beasts (£60).[74]

Although there was no distinct county breed, the Shropshire ox was remarkable for a large dewlap.[75] Shropshire lay across the drove routes from north Wales and north-west England and the local stock contained the blood of cattle from both.[76] About 1750 the cattle of north-east Shropshire were said to be 'middle size somewhat less than the Lancashire, but much larger than the Welsh breed'.[77] The milk of the black cattle of Cheshire and the other northern counties was excellent for making cheese,[78] and those Longhorns played a major part in the development of Shropshire dairy farming in the period, especially on the northern plain.[79] At Shrewsbury fair, a major centre for the sale of animals from Wales and the Welsh borderland, most of the cattle were black.[80] In south Shropshire, where dairy farming was less prominent, the stock varied more, black cattle mingling with red and brown animals from Herefordshire and central and south Wales.[81]

By the 1740s dairy farming had taken an even firmer hold in the northern dairy area's core parishes bordering Cheshire. About 1750 the pastures and meadows there generally produced good grass and hay 'and thereby maintain great dairies, which supply the markets with plenty of butter, and the factors with vast quantities of cheese, in goodness not much inferior to those of Cheshire'.[82] Stocks of cheese were on average far larger there than elsewhere in the county. Surprisingly, only a third of the farmers had produce inventoried, perhaps an indication of the efficiency of marketing facilities. Farmers did not rear so many young beasts, concentrating instead on increasing milking herds and keeping only dairy replacements. Herds were nonetheless larger than before: despite the absence of stores the median herd doubled from nine head in the 1660s to eighteen or nineteen by the 1740s. John Harries (d. 1732) of Adderley had a typical herd comprising 14 cows and a bull, 4 heifers coming up to three years old, 3 calves a year younger, and 3 young calves perhaps of that year.[83] Towards the west, around Baschurch, the edges of the dairy region had become a little blurred and the soils supported good mixed farms.[84]

Dairying was also significant elsewhere. It was important on the eastern coalfield where the size of herds and the number of dairy animals in them were rising in the 1730s and 1740s. In the parishes around Wellington cheese was made by a large number of farmers and it was a valuable product on the bigger farms. In Wellington most of the milk seems to have been drunk or churned for local consumption. The area's dairy farmers, however, were not always as single minded as those farther north and were likelier to rear stores as well. The small farms on the industrial belt were normally pastoral. In the Severn–Tern district too, with an agricultural economy based on cattle and corn, herds generally comprised dairy

[73] Midland Hist. vi. 76–8; Goodman, 'Hammerman's Hill', 172, 174–5.
[74] H.W.R.O. (H.), Heref. dioc. rec., inv. of Sam. Wood 1749.
[75] J. Plymley, Gen. View of Agric. of Salop. (1803), 241.
[76] Edwards, 'Farming Econ. of NE. Salop.' 47–8.
[77] Garbet, Hist. Wem, 9.
[78] G. Markham, Cheap and Good Husbandry (1631), 88–90.
[79] Midland Hist. iv. 178–9; vi. 74–5.
[80] Edwards, 'Farming Econ. of NE. Salop.' 49.
[81] Garbet, Hist. Wem, 9.
[82] Ibid. 8.
[83] L.J.R.O., B/C/11, John Harries 26 Apr. 1732.
[84] Prob. invs. passim.

animals and stores, while along the banks of the Severn and Tern they included fatstock. Smaller farmers gave greater emphasis to dairying and around Shrewsbury that continued to be a widespread activity.[85]

Cattle also remained numerous in most other areas of the county, where dairying was not of the first importance. In the south Shropshire vales a system of cattle-corn husbandry continued to grow. Apart from the draught oxen, still employed in large numbers on the land there, many stores were kept. Indeed inventories suggest that rearing became more prominent in the area during the earlier 18th century; herds increased in size but the proportion of dairy animals fell. Prosperous yeomen like Thomas Stedman of Stanton Lacy[86] had the largest herds but virtually all farmers possessed at least one or two beasts.

Pig keeping on a commercial scale began to develop in the 17th century partly in association with the increase in dairy production.[87] Already in the mid 16th century, however, many pig keepers were rearing more than they needed for domestic consumption and were selling at local markets and fairs. The largest herds even then tended to belong to substantial farmers with a dairy interest, though pig keeping as revealed by inventories of the 1550s, varied from region to region. Every inventory in the eastern coalfield lists them, though the median valuation was low; in the Heathlands, on the other hand, they are recorded in only two out of every five inventories.

Most people used their pannage rights on neighbouring commons, and in wood–pasture areas such as Shropshire swine had long been reared on acorns and mast. Many presentments for the perennial nuisance of unringed swine appear in court rolls: in 1586, for instance, Thomas Thomas had seven unringed swine rooting in the fallow field and on Prees heath.[88] In Elizabeth I's reign the tenants of Ellesmere manor could put their pigs into the woods, paying the lord their third best swine.[89] Nevertheless shortage of pannage in some manors in the early 17th century did lead to an abridgement of rights. In 1622 the inhabitants of Myddle manor were forbidden to gather mast or acorns or to pannage 'any swine other than such as were . . . there reared or bought the winter before'.[90]

Pigs were kept elsewhere in the county and on the large south Shropshire commons pannage was still available. In 1652 the inhabitants of Edgton manor could put their swine on the common, paying 1d. for every pig over a year old and ½d. for every younger one.[91] Pigs were important on the Eastern Sands and in south-east Shropshire in parishes such as Clee St. Margaret, Coreley, Stottesdon, and Wheathill.[92] The most valuable herds tended to be kept on larger farms, where cattle and corn formed part of the agricultural economy.

Inclosure was reducing the commons, wastes, and woodlands but later in the 17th century, as dairy farming developed and more fodder crops were grown, pig keeping increased again. The incremental value gained in feeding pigs (inclusive of costs) can be gauged from the inventory of William Lovekyn, a tanner and farmer from Tilley (in Wem), drawn up in December 1639: apart from his sow and 4 pigs worth £1 3s. 4d., he left 2 lean hogs (18s.), a hog feeding (12s.), and 2 fat hogs (£2 14s.),[93] an indication that about two months' feeding trebled values. Smaller men also fattened pigs for market, taking advantage of the reputation of the local product. Of course many of them did confine themselves to domestic

85 Ibid.   86 Above (Arable farming).

87 *Midland Hist.* iv. 181.

88 S.P.L., MS. 348, Prees ct. r. 14 Apr. 1586.

89 S.R.O. 212, box 345, no. 2, f. 21v.

90 Hey, *Myddle under Tudors and Stuarts*, 31–2.

91 Bodl., Craven dep. 23.

92 Prob. invs. *passim*.

93 L.J.R.O., B/C/11, Wm. Lovekyn 25 Jan. 1640.

production, and they included retired farmers like the elder John Butcher of Hopton Wafers. At the time of his death in 1664 he was growing one or two acres of corn and keeping a couple of cows; he also had beef and bacon worth 2s. and a hog worth 15s.,[94] presumably next year's provision. By the 1660s many of the larger dairy farmers, like Richard Furber of Shavington (in Adderley), kept pigs as an integral part of their operation—he had swine worth £6 6s. 8d.[95]—and, apart from dairy waste, pigs were also fed on fodder crops, especially peas. About 1750 Shropshire hogs were claimed as England's best: those of the north-eastern part of the county were 'large, broadset, and weighty, which may be owing to their being fed with peas'.[96] For brawn[97] pigs were fed on barley mash followed by raw malt and dried peas, washed down with sweet whey or the dregs of ale barrels.[98] Those who took most pigs to market were large-scale farmers who fitted pig keeping into their overall enterprise. Some, like John Cureton of Hordley, with (in 1741) a sow and 8 pigs (£1 15s.), 15 (feeding) swine (£26 5s.), and 34 store swine (£11 18s.),[99] were commercial dairy farmers. Others were sheep–corn farmers such as Edward Baker of Hilton (in Worfield), whose stock of pigs in 1749 comprised 2 sows with their pigs and a boar seg (£3 15s.), 11 store pigs (£3 10s.), and 4 feeding pigs (£5 12s.).[1]

Shropshire sheep were nationally renowned for their very fine wool. The best wool was produced around Shrewsbury and Bridgnorth and at the time only the product of the Ryeland sheep of Herefordshire was deemed superior. Shropshire wool maintained its fame throughout the period,[2] though the development of the new draperies, requiring coarser long-stapled wool, affected demand.[3] At the same time a growing interest in mutton production helped to maintain flock sizes, as did the development of a sheep–corn system of husbandry on the county's lighter soils. The old Shropshires were horned and had black or mottled faces and legs. They were about as large as the Southdown with rather longer necks but a less compact carcass. Extremely hardy, they never needed dry food except when heavy snow lay a long time. Another indigenous sheep was the Longmynd, nimble, hardy, and black faced.[4]

Many kept sheep in the various regions of the county in the mid 16th century, and flocks were grazed wherever there were commons; even smallholders and cottagers might graze animals on patches of waste. In 1557 Thomas Nagelon, a small farmer living on Wytheford Heath, Shawbury, left a flock of 12 old sheep and 8 lambs. Typically he was also engaged in dairy farming, pig keeping, and horse breeding on a small scale,[5] using the heath to keep his animals. Even in parishes where sheep were not very numerous inventories occasionally reveal much larger flocks. In Adderley, for example, only one inventory in five mentions sheep[6] and fourteen was the highest number kept by anyone, except for John Curdworth who left 58 head in 1624.[7] Flocks of over 50 head were not uncommon in mid 16th-century Shropshire and some were much larger. John Stringer, a sheep–corn farmer from Stockton, had a flock of 300,[8] the largest recorded, but others had over 100. Farmers with access to the vast commons of north-west and south Shropshire must also have kept large flocks but they are only hinted at in their

[94] H.W.R.O.(H.), Heref. dioc. rec., inv. of John Butcher 1664.   [95] L.J.R.O., B/C/11, Ric. Furber 1 May 1660.
[96] Garbet, *Hist. Wem*, 9.
[97] A Shrews. speciality: *V.C.H. Salop*. i. 422.
[98] *Ag. Hist. Eng*. iv. 193.
[99] L.J.R.O., B/C/11, John Cureton 3 Apr. 1741.
[1] Ibid. Edw. Baker 26 May 1750.

[2] Edwards, 'Farming Econ. of NE. Salop.' 52–3, 191–7.
[3] Ibid. 52–3.
[4] Plymley, *Agric. of Salop*. 260.
[5] L.J.R.O., B/C/11, Thos. Nagelon 21 May 1557.
[6] Prob. invs. *passim*.
[7] L.J.R.O., B/C/11, John Curdworth 20 Sept. 1624.
[8] Ibid. John Strynger 2 Oct. 1555.

wills. Thomas Adams of Barrow, for instance, disposed of 60 of his best sheep in 1546.[9]

The median-sized flocks are remarkably similar in the areas covered by the inventories but undoubtedly there were regional differences in the emphasis placed on these animals. They were proportionately most valuable in the Heathlands, being the best suited of all farm stock to the sandy commons. On the Eastern Sands sheep were folded on the arable, on farms like Thomas Thomas's in Hopstone (in Claverley): in 1558 he left a flock of 60 sheep worth £5 and corn valued at £10; he also had four draught oxen and kept two kine for milk and a heifer.[10]

Most flocks comprised breeding stock and stores. John Hill, a gentleman from Buntingsdale (in Market Drayton), had 62 ewes, 42 lambs, and 135 wethers in 1558,[11] and on a humbler but more typical level Richard Cowper of Sheriffhales had 20 couples and 20 wethers in 1559.[12] John Davies of Clungunford kept a similar flock, leaving in his will (May 1544) 10 couples, 2 lambs, 5 hog sheep, and 21 others.[13] In the Eastern Sands sheep may have been valued primarily for their dung but the farmers prized the wool clip too. Thus Humphrey Hallon of Beobridge (in Claverley) left rye, barley, and oats worth £10, 60 sheep, and wool appraised at £2 13s. 4d.[14] Similarly graziers gained additional income from the sheep they fed. John Young, gentleman, of Helshaw (in Stoke upon Tern), had 87 wethers grazing at Cherrington cote in the Weald Moors in 1551 and they had provided him with the 30 stones of wool (£21) listed in his inventory.[15] Few references to wool, however, appear in the inventories, an indication that it did not stay long in store: the Newport wool staplers, for example, regularly sent their agents round the farms.[16]

By the mid 17th century sheep breeding and rearing was carried on most notably in the uplands and on the Heathlands and Eastern Sands. In the south-west only one farmer in a sample of twenty-six had no sheep[17] and in terms both of flock size and capital investment, the area stands out from the others. Charles Edwards of Pentre Hodre (in Clun), whose farm stock in 1665 comprised a mare worth £1 10s. and sheep worth £12 10s.,[18] illustrates the husbandry practised by hill farmers throughout the county. Others with valley-bottom land kept cattle too. William Harris of Bettws-y-crwyn ran a flock of 137 sheep and also a mixed dairy and rearing herd of 21 head; he grew no corn but bred horses on a small scale.[19] In the north-west uplands dairying was commoner than it was in the south-west,[20] doubtless owing to the influence of the neighbouring dairy district. There was a higher median flock on the Coal Measures but fewer than one person in three (31 per cent) kept them and, apart from the northern dairy area, there was less capital tied up in them than in any other part of the county.

The Weald Moors had become a notable summer fattening area for sheep, as well as other stock, by the mid 17th century. In the 1650s the Wrockwardine copyholders complained about the practice of buying in stock from outside to fatten over the summer: the graziers who did that[21] oppressed the common 'by putting in great store of sheep' on it 'and suddenly eating up the grass upon the

[9] H.W.R.O.(H.), Heref. dioc. rec., will of Thos. Adams of M. Wenlock, 1546.
[10] L.J.R.O., B/C/11, Thos. Thomas 19 Oct. 1558.
[11] Ibid. John Hill 19 Oct. 1558.
[12] Ibid. Ric. Cowper 12 Apr. 1559.
[13] H.W.R.O.(H.), Heref. dioc. rec., will of John Davys 1544.
[14] L.J.R.O., B/C/11, Humph. Hallon 7 Oct. 1556.
[15] Ibid. John Young 4 Jan. 1552.
[16] Edwards, 'Farming Econ. of NE. Salop.' 192-3.
[17] Prob. invs. passim.
[18] H.W.R.O.(H.), Heref. dioc. rec., inv. of Chas. Edwards 1665.
[19] Ibid. Wm. Harris 1669.
[20] Prob. invs. passim.
[21] Staffs. R.O., D. 593/E/6/35.

... common not keeping their sheep upon their several tenements in the wintertime'. In fact large numbers of stock were being bought in the spring, fattened, and sold before winter. It seems to have been a long standing practice for in 1615 Kynnersley manor court had laid a pain on all who put more sheep on the commons than they could winter on their tenements.[22]

Regional systems continued to diverge as farmers specialized and by the mid 18th century sheep contributed in different ways to the local economies. The largest flocks, as always, roamed the upland commons of south and north-west Shropshire, parts of which had been turned into extensive sheep walks. The Stiperstones, the Long Mynd, Clun forest, the Clee Hills, Morfe forest, and surviving fragments of the Long forest, for instance, had all long been intercommoned by farmers from neighbouring manors.[23] In a dispute over grazing rights on the Long Mynd in the 1690s, involving the lords of Ratlinghope and Stretton, it was stated that one Ratlinghope tenant had kept 900 sheep there.[24] Elsewhere substantial flocks were folded on the arable land of the heathlands and of the Eastern Sands.

In the south-west the sheep-oriented economy had intensified. Even fewer acres were devoted to crops. The median flock of sheep rose to at least 79 and of the twenty entries in the inventories of the 1740s, nine (45 per cent) were of over 100 head. Roger Bryan of Bicton (in Clun) left the largest flock, of 800. He farmed on a big scale, keeping cattle worth £228 as well as his sheep,[25] and the combination was typical of the class of farmer whose inventories survive. It is left to John Jones of Clungunford with his flock of 23 sheep to represent the way the area's smallholders lived. Apart from his sheep, Jones cultivated a hemp plot and kept a breeding mare. Four swine rooted round the yard and last year's animals appear as 108 lb. of bacon at 3d. a pound. He also had an old gun, perhaps for a little shooting on the hills.[26] On the hills of south Shropshire and the north-west uplands too there were large flocks of sheep. Prosperous farmers with valley land combined sizeable flocks with a system of cattle–corn husbandry.[27]

The importance of sheep in the sheep-corn economy of the Eastern Sands can be seen in the size of flocks. The average number was 69 and of the nineteen entries, six were of at least 100 head. Edward Baker, a large sheep-corn farmer from Hilton (in Worfield), had 500.[28] Sheep naturally formed an essential part of the farming system of the Heathlands too and fine wool was produced around Stoke upon Tern.[29]

In the Severn–Tern area three quarters (76.3 per cent) of the holdings carried sheep and provided valuable income for many farmers. About 1700 Great Ness and Baschurch were singled out as the parishes producing the best wool.[30] The average flock size increased between the 1690s and the 1740s, probably to meet the demand for mutton,[31] but in general sheep were given less prominence than on the uplands.

Poultry keeping was universal: it was so commonplace that appraisers increasingly ignored it or lumped fowl in with other items of small value as 'things forgot'. Even the poorest peasant had one or two chickens scratching round the yard. The usual stock were chickens, though there were many ducks and those with common

[22] Ibid. /J/11/2/2.
[23] S.R.O. 93/25-6; 112, box 23, Thos. Bell to Thos. Hill 8 Apr. 1770; 1037/1/170; S.P.L., Deeds 17418-23; H.W.R.O.(H.), Heref. dioc. rec., Diddlebury glebe terrier 1589?; Bodl., Craven dep. 20; T.S.A.S. xi. 259-62; lvi. 48-67; J.R.A.S.E. xvi. 236.
[24] S.P.L., Deeds 17418.

[25] H.W.R.O.(H.), Heref. dioc. rec., inv. of Rog. Bryan 1744.   [26] Ibid. inv. of John Jones 1749.
[27] Prob. invs. passim.
[28] L.J.R.O., B/C/11, Edw. Baker 26 May 1750.
[29] Prob. invs. passim.
[30] R. Gough, Antiquities & Memoirs of the Parish of Myddle (Shrews. 1875), 175.   [31] Prob. invs. passim.

rights could rear geese too. On some estates the tenants customarily gave rent chickens or capons at the half-yearly audit and thus families like the Corbetts and Levesons obtained useful provision. Turkeys, introduced to Europe from Mexico in the early 16th century,[32] were kept by a few. In 1605 William Bettinson, yeoman, of Woodcote (in Sheriffhales), left 8 geese, 9 turkeys, 8 chickens, and a cock, altogether worth 13s. 10d.[33]

Some farmers living near commons kept goats. Occasional references in wills and inventories suggest that they were most popular in the south-west, though they were never numerous. In many places a strong prejudice persisted against the animal, whose close cropping and voracity was said to ruin the commons and prevent regeneration of vegetation.[34] In 1546 Baschurch manor court laid a pain on any who kept goats and owners were to get rid of them before All Saints'.[35]

Small game, though its preservation and culling should perhaps be seen as no more than an adjunct to agriculture, yielded a significant amount of provision and occasions of social conflict. Much poaching went on, and numerous presentments to manor courts testify to landowners' concern to preserve game. In 1593, for instance, the inhabitants of Crudgington were forbidden to shoot or trap wildfowl in the Weald Moors.[36] After 1660 legislation aimed at tighter control and so the legal pursuit of game was effectively restricted to the upper classes.[37] Offenders against the law included farmers such as William Patshull, John Davis, and Edward and William Harris, presented at the manor court of Hernes, Chilton, and Atcham in 1693 for owning fowling guns illegally.[38]

As the county was well endowed with rivers, streams, lakes, and marshes, fishing and fowling were vigorously pursued: boats, nets, fowling pieces, and a variety of other devices are listed in inventories. The poorer countryman had a chance thereby to supplement his meagre diet. In some places the inhabitants had the right to fish the local waters, in others, as on the Leveson estate, the privilege could be obtained only by buying a lease.[39] In 1575 the commissioners of sewers noted 28 fishing weirs and a bylet (barge gutter) on the Severn in Shropshire. By then the number of weirs may have been in decline, possibly hastened by a major flood in 1634 which 'broke all the weirs on the Severn'. A few weirs continued to stand until the later 19th century, but increasingly freshwater fishing was on a more personal, less commercial, basis.[40] Throughout the period and beyond fishponds continued to be a normal provision of any house with any pretensions and even of many farmhouses.[41]

Free warren normally belonged to the lord of the manor and because warrens were usually located on sandy heaths, rabbits generated income from land that had little other value. Inevitably the stock was stolen, a practice that was encouraged by the widespread belief that poaching was no theft.[42] In 1602 John Norden, surveyor of the lordship of Oswestry, noted that in the Traian 'every man spoiled the game and that hares, pheasants, and partridges would be plentiful if they were preserved'.[43] Manorial juries were induced to pass bylaws against poaching. In

[32] Edwards, 'Farming Econ. of NE. Salop.' 58; cf. *Ag. Hist. Eng.* iv. 194, 682–3.

[33] L.J.R.O., B/C/11, Wm. Bettinson 26 Apr. 1608.

[34] *Ag. Hist. Eng.* iv. 138.

[35] S.P.L., Deeds 16548.

[36] Staffs. R.O., D. 593/J/11/2/1.

[37] *Ag. Hist. Eng.* v (2), 366–71.

[38] S.R.O. 840/1.

[39] Edwards, 'Farming Econ. of NE. Salop.' 56, 110–12, 124–5.

[40] *Med. Fish, Fisheries and Fish Ponds in Eng.* ed. M. A. Aston (Brit. Arch. Rep. clxxxii), 371–89; Plymley, *Agric. of Salop.* 84–5, 88.

[41] S.R.O. 840, box 117, acct. of fish put into stews at Sandford 1810; 1681, box 32, (?) Wm. Ferriday's notebk.; 3385/5/4; J. Randall, *Hist. Madeley* (Madeley, 1880), 267–71; idem, *The Severn Valley* (1882), 499–504; Plymley, op. cit. 89.

[42] J. A. Sharpe, *Crime in Early Modern Eng. 1550–1750* (1984), 124–31. [43] Slack, *Lordship of Oswestry*, 81.

1570 the inhabitants of Longden manor were forbidden to kill the lady's rabbits or to dig out any of their earths under a pain of 1s. For their part the inhabitants not only objected to the creation of warrens on common land but were also aggrieved at the rabbits' depredation of their crops.[44] In 1610 the tenants of Cold Hatton complained of great destruction of their fields by rabbits bred and kept there; they also presented the warrener for unstopping earths in their corn fields and for refusing to allow them to be stopped up again.[45] The inhabitants of Stoke upon Tern had a similar problem at the end of the century and therefore agreed with Sir Robert Corbet that he might inclose a corner of Stoke Heath in return for the destruction of his warren.[46]

Horse breeding was widespread though normally small in scale. Many breeders were small farmers with access to commons where they could keep the animals cheaply, making good use of marginal land. Horse breeding thus provided them with useful additional income, even if they sold only one or two animals a year. Inventories of the 1550s record numerous mares and young horses, a pattern persisting for much of the 17th century. By the 1740s the higher proportions of horses and colts recorded suggest greater use of horse power on the farm rather than any decline in breeding. In general the largest herds were kept by the substantial farmers, men such as Edward Griffiths of the border parish of Church Stoke, who could make use of their extensive common rights: in 1740 his stock amounted to 16 mountain colts valued at £16, apart from 5 working horses and 3 sucking colts (£25), 2 grey riding mares (£16), and 4 yearling colts (£7).[47]

In 1540 the government, fearing that the size and strength of the native horse stock was being diminished, legislated to forbid the keeping of stallions over two years old and under fifteen hands on any common or waste outside the northern counties.[48] Shropshire court rolls record numerous offenders—in 1581 William Murroll, for example, was accused of grazing an undersized colt on Prees Lower Heath for two years[49]—but the Act did not stop the practice. Indeed with the growth of trade and industry such animals were needed in greater numbers.

Many caples, small horses found throughout the county in the 16th century,[50] were bred in the Weald Moors and they may have resembled the rough hardy horses that roamed the uninclosed Lincolnshire fens.[51] The largest herd recorded in the 1550s numbered seven; it was kept by Thomas Adams of Buttery (in Edgmond), a farm partly inclosed out of the moors.[52] Similar stock grazed the upland commons around the county. In Hogstow forest horses were kept throughout the summer but had to be off the common by Martinmas.[53] Farther south the inhabitants of the whole of south-west Shropshire pastured their beasts in Clun forest. Horses and cattle of the freeholders of Kerry (Mont.) were regularly found there too, straying off their own contiguous uninclosed commons.[54]

Most farmers kept one or two horses in the mid 16th century, owners being most numerous in the Severn-Tern area, especially in the Weald Moors where only one farmer in ten had no horse. Most farm horses would have been all-purpose animals, employed for the saddle as well as for work. Some farmers did keep a riding nag and of course the best animals belonged to the gentry. In 1551 Thomas Colfox of Merrington (in Preston Gubbals) had three geldings, valued at

[44] S.P.L., MS. 5457. [45] Staffs. R.O., D. 593/J/11/2/2.
[46] S.R.O. 327/64/64.
[47] H.W.R.O.(H.), Heref. dioc. rec., inv. of Edw. Griffiths 1740. [48] 32 Hen. VIII, c. 13.
[49] S.P.L., MS. 345, Prees ct. r. 4 Oct. 1581.
[50] Prob. invs. passim.
[51] W. H. Wheeler, Hist. of Fens of S. Lincs. (Boston, 1868), 411.
[52] L.J.R.O., B/C/11, Thos. Adams 11 May 1558.
[53] T.S.A.S. 4th ser. iv. 82-6. [54] T.S.A.S. xi. 260-2.

£3–£4 each,[55] well above the average price for the time. Apart from the riding nag, horses on farms before 1660 were cart or pack horses rather than plough beasts. Many of the pack horses that carried produce to market were of the border type: very small, hardy, and agile. They resembled the famed Montgomeryshire *merlins*, semi-wild mountain ponies that roamed the vast open commons of that county and were rounded up and broken in at the age of three.[56] Many other such pack horses took cloth to be finished in towns like Oswestry or Shrewsbury or were used extensively in trade, carrying goods across country.[57] In the 1580s, for instance, over a hundred householders in and around Oswestry and Shrewsbury lived wholly by the weekly carriage of Welsh cloths from Oswestry to Shrewsbury and thence up to London; some kept 12, 16, or even 20 horses or geldings.[58]

Larger horses were also bred in Shropshire, especially in the vales and on gentry estates. The gentry valued their superior horses both for use and ostentation. The Bridgemans and the Levesons were among those families interested in racing,[59] while others had fine coach teams.[60] Many leading families bred their own horses. Sir Walter Acton (d. 1665) of Aldenham left a herd of 23 worth £122 3s. 4d. and consisting of 3 mares and followers (£25), 3 old mares (£7 10s.), 2 twinter colts (£6 13s. 4d.), and 3 yearlings (£6), as well as 4 stallions (£60) and 5 geldings.[61] Gentlemen and dealers could also buy and sell good stock at local fairs such as Bridgnorth and Shrewsbury,[62] at Penkridge across the Staffordshire border,[63] or even farther afield in the east midlands:[64] in the 17th century numbers of Shropshire dealers appeared at Market Bosworth and Derby fairs and Leicestershire and Derbyshire remained the county's chief source of draught horses beyond the close of the period.[65]

Marketing

In 1540 Shropshire's main outlets for farm produce were its regulated markets and fairs. Two centuries later the situation was far more complex; many markets and fairs still functioned but there had been an undoubted decline as more flexible means were developed to deal with increasing commercial activity stimulated by a rapidly growing population. Some places fared better than others, drawing trade to them; those that failed fell into disuse or insignificance. The main agents of change were the specialist middlemen, increasingly numerous and important as inter-regional trade developed.

The increasing commercialization of agriculture affected especially those Shropshire farmers who concentrated on producing the commodities best suited to local conditions and aimed at a wider market. In 1597, when Sir Thomas Coningsby secured Shropshire's exclusion from the Tillage Act,[66] he put the case in effect for regional specialization and economic interdependence. Shropshire he said, consisted 'wholly of woodland, bred of oxen and dairies' and he hoped that 'as Herefordshire

[55] L.J.R.O., B/C/11, Thos. Colfox 17 June 1551.
[56] Defoe, *Tour*, 383; 'Montgomeryshire Horses, Cobs and Ponies', *Mont. Colln.* xxii. 19, 29.
[57] *Horses in European Econ. Hist.* ed. F. M. L. Thompson (1983), 117–18.
[58] S.R.O. 1831, box 21, petition of citizens of Chester for a staple of friezes & cottons [1583] (ref. owed to Mr. J. B. Lawson).
[59] Staffs. R.O., D. 593/P/16/1/3; D. 1287/3/8c (Sir J. Bridgeman's disbursements bk. 1716–47) 22 Jan. 1719.
[60] Ibid. D. 1287/3/6b (Sir J. Bridgeman's disbursements bk. 1704–16) 28 Sept. 1713; /8c (Sir J. Bridgeman's disbursements bk. 1716–47) 3 Dec. 1718; S.R.O. 2/135, 20 July 1679;

1224, box 299, accts. 1734–6, 1737–8.
[61] H.W.R.O.(H.), Heref. dioc. rec., inv. of Sir Wal. Acton 1665.
[62] S.R.O. 1224, box 297, rent bk. 1686, p. 60 (15 Jan. 1687); 3365/2645–68; 4001/Mar/1/268–71; Staffs. R.O., D. 593/F/2/11, 37, 40.
[63] Staffs. R.O., D. 593/F/2/8, 6 Sept. 1676.
[64] Ibid. /F/2/6, 19 Nov. 1674; /F/2/11, 3 Oct. 1678; S.R.O. 112, box 20, Bell to Hill 18 Mar. 1748/9, 28 Feb. 1749/50.
[65] P. R. Edwards, 'Horse Trade of Midlands in 17th Cent.' *Agric. H.R.* xxvii. 95.
[66] In opposition to Rob. Berry: *V.C.H. Salop.* iii. 246; *Hist. Parl., Commons, 1558–1603*, i. 639; 39 Eliz. I, c. 2, s. 14.

and the other countries adjoining, were the barns for the corn, so this shire might and would be the dairy house to the whole realm'.[67] Even allowing for hyperbole, dairy produce and cattle were certainly two of Shropshire's most important exports but to them must be added horses, sheep, and pigs as well as commodities like wool, woollen cloth, linen, skins, and leather.[68]

Animals could easily move long distances on the hoof but other goods had to be carried. Land carriage was expensive and wherever possible water transport was used. Thus Shropshire skins, linen, and cheese went down the Severn[69] and the river ports of Bridgnorth (where a fair-day's sales were alleged in 1597 to reach £10,000 on occasion) and Shrewsbury became markets for dairy produce. Other loads went down the Trent or through Cheshire ports. Goods also travelled overland and in the early 18th century the Davieses of Brompton regularly sent cheese to Hereford fair and occasionally to Leominster and Kingsland too,[70] neatly illustrating the point Coningsby had made in 1597. Cloth, especially linen, went down the Severn but textiles were as likely to go by road: they were light and of high value, so transport costs were more easily absorbed and damage by damp avoided. Thus packhorses took wool to the south-western and East Anglian textile areas and cloth to Blackwell Hall in London.[71]

Animals were traditionally sold at fairs, and those that flourished did so because they had geographical or economic advantages and were well stocked. Fair towns normally kept several fairs during the year and extra ones were often added. Ludlow obtained a third fair in 1596 (extended in 1604), a fourth in 1604, and a fifth in 1692; Shrewsbury obtained a fifth and sixth in 1638 and a seventh was established in 1702.[72] Specialization helped to maintain their position and the commodities sold changed with the seasons. In the mid 18th century Albrighton's fairs were held on 23 May, 18 July, and 9 November and horned cattle, sheep, and swine were sold 'at the proper season'. Stores and breeding stock were sold at spring and early summer fairs, while fatstock predominated later in the year. The pattern is clearest in the cattle trade but apparent too in the sale of other animals. Thus swine were usually killed in November and the Martinmas fair at Wem and St. Andrew's fairs at Shrewsbury and Oswestry were important for fat hogs. Other specializations included wool and cheese at Shrewsbury, cheese at Bridgnorth, and linen cloth at Wem. So trade concentrated at fewer centres despite a rise in the number of markets. By the 1750s many places with formal market rights were unimportant: thus the May and October fairs at Hodnet and the Easter Monday fair at Halesowen were said to be insignificant.[73]

Fairs, dealing largely in animals and held seasonally, had wider catchment areas than weekly markets. In 1552 Ludlow wanted ratification of Monday as market day, not Thursday which conflicted with Knighton and Kidderminster markets, ten and fifteen miles away; the only other Monday markets in Shropshire, Herefordshire, Radnorshire, and Worcestershire were at Oswestry (32 miles) and Evesham (36 miles).[74] Evesham's May-day fair, however, was thought to be near

[67] A. F. Pollard and M. Blatcher, 'Hayward Townshend's Jnls.' *Bull Inst. Hist. Res.* xii. 16.
[68] Edwards, 'Farming Econ. of NE. Salop.' cap. 3.
[69] Ibid. 137–8.
[70] Ibid. 187–9; *Bull Inst. Hist. Res.* xii. 16; *Midland Hist.* iv. 185; S.R.O. 631/2/1.
[71] Edwards, 'Farming Econ. of NE. Salop.' 196; P. J. Bowden, *Wool Trade in Tudor and Stuart Eng.* (1971), 75–6; J. A. Chartres, *Internal Trade in Eng. 1500–1700* (1977), 27–8.
[72] *Copies of Charters and Grants to Town of Ludlow*

(Ludlow [1821?], 75–8, 97–100, 135–40, 211–12; S.R.O. 356/2/1, ff. 50v., 51; 3365/2658; [H. Owen], *Some Acct. of Ancient and Present State of Shrews.* (Shrews. 1808), 457.
[73] Wm. Owen, *Authentic Acct. of Fairs in Eng. and Wales* (1756 edn.), s.v. Shropshire; Gough, *Myddle*, 176, 179; Garbet, *Wem*, 228.
[74] Alsop's 'opinion' (see next note) ignored the Mon. mkt. at M. Wenlock (cf. W. F. Mumford, *Wenlock in the Middle Ages* (Shrews. 1977), 121; *Cal. Chart. R.* 1226–57, 17), presumably of little acct.

enough to clash with Ludlow's, and in fact Ludlow's were being held 9–11 August and 24–6 November—much better dates, it was claimed, since they did not coincide with any other within fifty miles.[75] Differences between fairs depended on the reputation of individual centres and the number of alternative outlets in the area. Shrewsbury was particularly important, drawing custom from afar.[76] South Shropshire fairs like Ludlow and Bishop's Castle tended to serve wider areas than those in the north because settlement was more dispersed.[77]

Some of the animals sold at fairs were from outside the county. Cattle regularly came along the drove roads from Wales for sale in Shropshire, notably at Shrewsbury, Bishop's Castle, and Ludlow. Others came from north-west England,[78] or from Ireland until legislation suspended that trade 1664–79 and abolished it in 1681.[79] The gentry, with their scattered estates and their agents working for them, added to the county's stock of animals by integrating their activities and buying at widely separated fairs. Leveson agents from Trentham bought animals in Staffordshire, Cheshire, and Derbyshire, some of which were sent to Lilleshall for fattening in and around the Weald Moors.[80] Most animals sold, however, were Shropshire bred, a fact reflecting the importance of livestock in the county's economy. Over five sixths of the cattle sold at Shrewsbury fairs in the 17th century came from north Shropshire; at Bridgnorth almost two thirds of the beasts sold in 1631 and 1644–79 were from south Shropshire. Many of the horses were home bred too, though some large horses originated in the north midlands or Montgomeryshire. Montgomeryshire men also brought small work horses to the fairs. Similarly Shrewsbury, Wem, and Oswestry fairs, which specialized in the sale of pigs, drew on local supplies, especially hogs.[81]

Many buyers were local and they included the gentry who obtained stock at nearby fairs. The Bridgemans and the Newports, with estates centred on Knockin and High Ercall in the late 17th and early 18th centuries, bought store cattle primarily at Shrewsbury but also at Albrighton, Newport, Oswestry, and Wellington in Shropshire as well as at Welshpool (Mont.) and Leek (Staffs.). Sheep were bought at Shrewsbury and Oswestry and at Llanfyllin (Mont.).[82] Nevertheless buyers did travel farther than sellers, attracted to the leading fairs by the quality and number of stock. At Shrewsbury and Bridgnorth the proportions of buyers from that half of the county where each town lay were less than a third and just over a quarter respectively,[83] virtually the converse of the proportions of sellers.[84]

In the 16th century purveyors acting for the king (and themselves) travelled down from south-east England. By the following century such men, 'being found a great nuisance to the king and country, were laid aside'.[85] Nevertheless the metropolitan link survived, for estate records like those of the Tokes of Kent refer to Welsh and Border animals. Dealers serving those distant markets tended to be local men living near their sources of supply. Thus Thomas Johnson of Chester and Richard Higginson of Wem, early 17th-century droving partners, bought cattle

[75] S.R.O. 356, box 297, John Alsop's opinion for the mkt. days and fair; cf. *Copies of Charters and Grants to Ludlow*, 10–11, 75–8.
[76] *Midland Hist.* vi. 72–4.
[77] *Ag. Hist. Eng.* v (2), 421; Owen, *Fairs in Eng. and Wales*. [78] *Midland Hist.* vi. 72–5.
[79] 15 Chas. II, c. 7, ss. 13, 15; 18 Chas. II, c. 2, ss. 2, 4; 32 Chas. II, c. 2: *Ag. Hist. Eng.* v (2), 346–56; C. A. Edie, 'Irish Cattle Bills', *Trans. American Philosophical Soc.* N.S. lx (2), 5–66; *Midland Hist.* vi. 74.
[80] Staffs. R.O., D. 593/F/2/4–9, 14, 37; /F/3/1/1.

[81] *Midland Hist.* vi. 75, 90–1; Edwards, 'Farming Econ. of NE. Salop.' 142–4, 161; Thompson, *Horses in European Econ. Hist.* 116–18, 121; for swine see above (Livestock and dairy farming).
[82] For the Bridgemans see Staffs. R.O., D. 1287/3/5, accts. 1670, 1697–8, 1698–1701; /3/6A and B (Sir J. Bridgeman's disbursements bks. 1704–16). For the Newports see ibid. /3/4 (Salop. est. disbursements bk. 1687–99).
[83] *Midland Hist.* vi. 87–9.
[84] Edwards, 'Farming Econ. of NE. Salop.' 144–5.
[85] Gough, *Myddle*, 74.

in Wales and at Shrewsbury, Whitchurch, and Newport fairs and took herds of eleven score and more up to Epping and Blackmore fairs in Essex and to other places in the south-east. Higginson, probably the drover of that name licensed 1615–28, would almost certainly have employed servants to drive his animals; such a man was Samuel Lloyd, a Shrewsbury labourer employed c. 1600 in 'driving cattle into the nether country'.[86]

Other animals went in easy stages and the livestock trade was 'a flow rather than a once-and-for-all single move'.[87] In the 17th century dealers from Gloucestershire, Wiltshire, and Berkshire regularly came to buy cattle at Shrewsbury. William Brounker, a yeoman from Whaddon (Wilts.), stated in 1623 that he frequented Shropshire and Radnorshire fairs to buy cattle to stock his ground, as other local graziers did. Some of the animals would have stayed in the locality but others went to Thames-side meadows to fatten for the capital. Richard Ebourne operated in a similar manner. He was a large-scale cattle and sheep dealer from north Warwickshire and at the turn of the 17th century, he bought stock at Bridgnorth and Wellington and at Derbyshire and Staffordshire fairs; some was moved on to fairs in the south and east midlands or farther to the Home Counties but most of his customers seem to have been local butchers and graziers.[88] Such people supplied fatstock to the developing west midland industrial areas, probably the most important external market for Shropshire farmers. Other buyers from that area patronized fairs—at Bridgnorth, Ludlow, and Shrewsbury for instance—to acquire store cattle, sheep, and small work horses. Larger draught horses on show were taken elsewhere, notably to the mixed-farming horse-rearing districts of south-east Worcestershire and north Oxfordshire. Draught oxen, the speciality of Shrewsbury's midsummer fair, attracted buyers from south Shropshire and Herefordshire.[89]

Livestock was sold at weekly markets too. The numbers involved were smaller than at fairs and people did not travel so far, but the markets evidently did reasonable business. In the 1750s 'Rig Fair', the Ascension day market at Wem, was 'not much inferior to a fair in terms of concourse of pigs and the great variety of cattle and goods'. There were also good livestock markets at Shrewsbury, Oswestry, Market Drayton, Bridgnorth, and Ludlow. In 1673 cattle and all sorts of provisions were sold at Shrewsbury market 'in great plenty' and the same had been true a century earlier, when cattle, sheep, and pigs were sold and local butchers were among the buyers.[90]

The staple commodities of the markets, however, were corn and provisions. In 1673 Oswestry, Wem, Newport, Shrewsbury, Church Stretton, Much Wenlock, Bridgnorth, Bishop's Castle, and Ludlow were notable centres for those goods. Ludlow had a very good market for corn and provisions (and cattle) on Monday and its eminence was based on its proximity to the mixed farms of the south Shropshire vales and north Herefordshire. On the border Bishop's Castle market served the surrounding area of Shropshire and also the adjoining part of Wales. Conversely families like the Davieses of Brompton, with estates along the border, sent grain to Welsh markets.[91]

[86] *Acct. Bk. of a Kentish Est. 1616–1704*, ed. E. C. Lodge (Brit. Acad. Rec. of Social and Econ. Hist. of Eng. and Wales, vi, 1927); P.R.O., E 134/11 Chas. I East./20; S.R.O., q. sess. rec. parcel 254, badgers', drovers', and alesellers' licensing bk.; S.R.O. 3365/2211. [87] *Ag. Hist. Eng.* v (2), 441.
[88] *Midland Hist.* vi. 80–2; J. H. Bettey, *Rural Life in Wessex 1500–1900* (Bradford-on-Avon, 1977), 84; Warws. R.O., CR 1291/519.

[89] S.R.O. 356, box 297, mkt. papers 1607–1774; parcel 466, fair toll bks. for horses 1646–9, 1686–94; 3365/2645–68; 4001/Mar/1/268–71; Thompson, *Horses in European Econ. Hist.* 121.
[90] Garbet, *Wem*, 227–8; Blome, *Britannia*, 193–4; S.R.O. 3365/2645, 2647–8.
[91] Blome, op. cit. 193–4; *Midland Hist.* vi. 73; S.R.O. 631/2/1.

Towns in particular relied on the weekly market for essential foodstuffs, and the maintenance of a regular supply at reasonable prices became a matter of growing concern as population rose in the late 16th century. Until the Restoration there must have been very little surplus grain in the county and when harvests failed supplies had to be brought from outside. Shropshire, like most of the country, was affected by the series of disastrous harvests in the 1580s and 1590s, for instance, and if conditions at Shrewsbury were typical there was much distress in the county. The corporation often had to act urgently to keep the market supplied with corn during those years and to see that the poor did not starve. In 1586 and 1597 foreign imports were needed to alleviate the situation. About 1600 Richard Gardiner, a prominent burgess, urged the growing of more vegetables as a way of helping to employ and feed the poor; in the earlier 1590s he himself had fed hundreds from vegetables he had grown on 4 a.[92]

Suppliers of grain to the markets varied greatly in their scale of business. At a modest level were the three women who sold eight strikes of oats at one of Shrewsbury's Saturday markets in 1606.[93] Larger amounts were brought in by the servants of gentlemen and yeomen. In the 1740s Thomas Hill's steward, Thomas Bell, kept a close eye on corn prices at local markets so as to get the best price.[94] Badgers—dealers in corn and victuals licensed under Acts of 1552 and 1563[95]— were particularly important in predominantly pastoral counties like Shropshire since they sought out supplies wherever they could be found. Ralph Guest of Myddle, 'a sober peaceable man', was one, buying corn in one market town to sell in another 'which is called badging'. Under the early Stuarts badgers could be found all over the county. Shrewsbury naturally had most. Shropshire badgers were evidently active in Herefordshire in 1556–7, replenishing their stocks at Leominster, a noted corn centre, in the aftermath of two years' dearth. In 1631 they were buying corn and grain at the well provisioned market at Caerwys (Flints.) for sale at Whitchurch and Ellesmere.[96]

Internal trade increasingly came under the control of such middlemen, entrepreneurs alert to the opportunities created by growing commercial activity. Hampered, at least until the late 17th century, by legislation and by public hostility, they nevertheless throve, extending their contacts and filling the gaps in the trading network. They ranged from wholesalers dealing regionally or even nationally down to humble badgers and broggers active in one locality. Together, however, they made the market more efficient and ensured that supplies moved round the country in greater quantities. Many of the cattle sold at Shrewsbury fairs in the late 16th and early 17th century were taken there by country drovers who had bought stock from farmers or at other fairs. They achieved a dominant position in the horse trade too. Horse dealers living along the Montgomeryshire border or in the southern uplands brought hill ponies to centres like Shrewsbury, Bridgnorth, and Ludlow, while others living near the county's north-eastern boundary supplied the fairs with larger horses brought from the north and east midlands.[97]

Dealing was often a family business. Families like the Dickens of Ellesmere and Loppington, the Grooms and Tilers of Myddle and Wem, and the Moodies of

[92] Edwards, 'Farming Econ. of NE. Salop.' 61, 68, 206; *T.S.A.S.* iii. 304–5, 307, 315, 335–6; *Eng. Landscape Past, Present, and Future*, ed. S. R. J. Woodell (1985), 144–5; *T.S.A.S.* 2nd ser. iv. 241–63.

[93] S.R.O. 3365/2214.

[94] S.R.O. 112, box 20, Bell to Hill 28 Feb. 1749/50.

[95] 5 & 6 Edw. VI, c. 14; 5 Eliz. I, c. 12.

[96] Gough, *Myddle*, 115; S.R.O., q. sess. rec. parcel 254, badgers' etc. licensing bk. (manifestly incomplete); *V.C.H. Salop.* iii. 99–100; Edwards, 'Farming Econ. of NE. Salop.' 207.

[97] *Midland Hist.* vi. 75; S.R.O. 356, boxes 297, 466; 3365/2645–68; 4001/Mar/1/268–71; Thompson, *Horses in European Econ. Hist.* 122.

Ellesmere brought many of the large numbers of cattle from those parishes sold at Shrewsbury fair. Similarly the Bradleys of Lilleshall, the Walkers of Newport, and the Skitts of Lilleshall, Prees, and Newport had long-standing connexions with the horse trade. Dealers also established business and personal links with each other and reliance on trusted kith and kin was a characteristic of the way trade was conducted to minimize commercial risk.[98]

The dealers recorded in toll books represent the solid, respectable traders who had standing in their communities. Many had an agricultural holding, often similar in scale to those farmed by small yeomen or middling husbandmen. Richard Winsor, a prominent early 17th-century horse dealer, lived at Donnington (in Lilleshall) and leased a cottage, yard, garden, and orchard and five days' math of meadowing there; also in his lease was pasture of six beasts' gate (8 a.), formerly part of the moors, which his father had had to rent separately.[99] Unlike the substantial dealers, the poorer ones did not specialize in a commodity but traded in anything they could profit by. Thus at Shrewsbury in 1600 Joyce Clark, a seamstress, sold her own wares and travelled from market to market 'to buy and sell to get a penny to help to maintain her'.[1] The government was concerned about such people and a proclamation of 1618 complained about the number of vagabonds with trifles to sell, like pedlars or petty chapmen.[2] Nevertheless small dealers continued and, if some were disreputable, in general they did useful service, particularly in providing country folk with cheap items not made locally.

Middlemen continued to use markets and fairs but fewer commodities went through the traditional outlets after the Restoration as private dealing, away from the market place, was found easier. Shops, houses, and particularly inns became the scene of great activity. As early as 1618 Shrewsbury corporation proclaimed that strangers not keeping scot and lot in the town and bringing malt to sell 'should sell the same in the open market but not in the shops nor houses'. Shrewsbury cloth market was held on the first floor of the new market house; only the drapers were allowed upstairs, but their rivals tried to lure the clothiers to nearby houses and inns for clandestine sales and in 1645 the drapers sought legal advice. In other market towns too the authorities were concerned for the integrity of the open market; at Whitchurch, for example, bylaws governing the marketing of corn, malt, dairy produce, and hides were made in 1636.[3]

Corn badgers could buy grain privately and many did. In 1635-6 Richard Higginson of Creamore, in Wem (licensed as badger and drover in 1628), agreed with his fellow parishioner John Sherratt to buy 300 measures of wheat at 5s. a measure.[4] Until the regulations were relaxed after the Restoration the intention was that corn would be sold in the market place and, as noted above, middlemen did good service in that respect. Nevertheless, given the importance of grain in the diet and the great fluctuations in its price, there were golden opportunities for profiteering. Hoarding was a problem, especially during shortages. When the harvest failed in 1621, for instance, Shrewsbury corporation sent round the farms in the Liberties to ensure that all surpluses came to market immediately. In 1629 Thomas Carpenter, a Rushbury corn badger who bought at Ludlow, was accused of hoarding 40-50 strikes of wheat until the price rose.[5]

[98] P. R. Edwards, 'Horse Trade of Chester in 16th and 17th Cents.' *Jnl. Chester Arch. Soc.* lxii. 94-5.
[99] S.R.O. 38/143-4; Staffs. R.O., D. 593/G/1/1/13; cf. *V.C.H. Salop.* xi. 157 n. 41.
[1] S.R.O. 3365/2211.
[2] *Ag. Hist. Eng.* iv. 580.

[3] Edwards, 'Farming Econ. of NE. Salop.' 213-14; S.R.O. 212, box 59C, bye-laws 1636.
[4] Edwards, op. cit. 213; L.J.R.O., B/C/11, John Sherratt (Wem) 21 Mar. 1636/7; S.R.O., q. sess. rec. parcel 254, badgers' etc. licensing bk. East. 1628; Garbet, *Wem*, 263.
[5] Edwards, op. cit. 208, 211.

At Shrewsbury, Whitchurch, Market Drayton, and Newport—towns in or near the northern cheese-producing area—measures were taken against the forestalling of dairy produce. The market in dairy produce was particularly vulnerable because of its great importance in the area and the intrusion of a whole class of middlemen organizing distribution on a national rather than a local scale.[6] Thus Shropshire factors acted as agents for cheesemongers in London and elsewhere. They frequented local fairs but also toured the countryside to make contracts with farmers like John Archer of Dudleston: he left household provision worth 15s. and cheese for the factor worth £4 5s. 6d. in 1687. Agents took large quantities of cheese from the farmers of Wem. In fact the dairy trade was organized similarly to the wool trade, whose staplers, living in towns like Newport and Shrewsbury, had long employed factors to buy parcels of wool, generally in small lots, from farmers.[7]

The by-passing of markets and fairs in the 17th century is discernible in the livestock trade too. In the early 17th century unlicensed drovers like Cowper of Cymmerau ferry were alleged to have pushed up cattle prices in Shropshire and Montgomeryshire markets. At the 1654 Shrewsbury midsummer fair 221 cattle were sold, well over four fifths (85.9 per cent) of them at three suburban inns, the Swan, the Hatchet, and Widow Harper's. Such inns, with ample feeding along the Severn banks, probably attracted drovers who needed pasture on the eve of the fairs. Buyers doubtless came to the inns to inspect the stock, so avoiding the press of the town on fair day and also the payment of toll. The trade in Shropshire hogs at Wem followed a similar pattern; in the early 18th century dealers sending hogs to London for the navy forestalled the market on the eve of the Martinmas fair.[8] Nevertheless fair days were the occasions of such transactions. When Celia Fiennes visited Shrewsbury in 1698 she found the fair thriving, as did Thomas Hill's steward Thomas Bell in the 1740s.[9] So they remained important dates in the calendar even if buyers and sellers found more flexible means of dealing.

The wholesale market was more thoroughly affected than the retail one with its typical pattern of small transactions; nevertheless large scale purchases did affect the level of supplies for retail. The trend to wholesale dealing was particularly evident in commodities influenced by industrial demand, like wool, barley, and hops. Brewers were among the biggest buyers in many corn markets and there must have been constant temptation to forestall. In the harvest crisis of the early 1620s the Shrewsbury authorities, concerned to avert unrest, clashed with the town's large brewers and maltsters. In St. Julian's parish a search of malthouses revealed much malt and barley and one of the purchasers was Mr. Rowley, said in 1635 to have a 'vast' brewhouse with vessels 'capable of 100 measures'. Maltsters and brewers also fostered a futures market, buying corn before harvest: one farmer involved was Joseph Parker of Chesterton (in Worfield), who in June 1746 had barley (£8), peas (£4), and winter corn (£6 10s.) sold on the ground.[10]

Credit underpinned the expansion of internal trade and was used by all sections of the community. Farmers habitually gave and took credit and some indication of the amount of business they conducted in that way can be gauged from probate records of the 16th and early 17th century, particularly informative when they discriminate between money debts and commodity transactions. Much casual trade

[6] Ibid. 214.
[7] Ibid. 188–9, 192; *Midland Hist.* iv. 185–6; Garbet, *Wem*, 8. [8] Edwards, op. cit. 214–15; Garbet, *Wem*, 228.
[9] *Illustr. Journeys of Celia Fiennes c. 1682–c. 1712*, ed. C.

Morris (1984), 186; S.R.O. 112, box 20, e.g. Bell to Hill 4 May 1747, 7 Mar. 1747/8, 3 Dec. 1748, 15 Jan. 1749/50.
[10] Edwards, op. cit. 211–13; L.J.R.O., B/C/11, Jos. Parker (Worfield) 21 Nov. 1746.

took place in the village street. In 1546, for instance, William Clempson's neighbours in Wroxeter parish owed him 4s. 2d. for a horse, 3s. 4d. for barley, and 1s. and 4d. as part payments for oxen and a mare respectively. Most of the debts owed to William Weston of Shawbury, on the other hand, seem to relate to dealing at Whitchurch market: in 1545 he was owed £3 11s. 9d., of which Whitchurch men owed £1 17s. 11d. for cattle, corn, cheese, and hay. Middlemen also got credit at the farm gate or at markets and fairs, and such arrangements grew in importance as the trading network filled out. In 1646 William Browne, a Newport badger, owed John Lockley of Sheriffhales £4 18s. 4d. for barley. It was not unusual for drovers to take animals on trust from farmers, paying after the stock was sold: the £8 owed by John Higginson, drover, to Richard Leyte of Weston-under-Redcastle in 1553 may have been such a debt.[11]

To minimize the risks in credit dealing it became common for a buyer to give the seller a bond, though the bills, bonds, and specialties mentioned in wills and inventories are rarely described in sufficient detail to discern their purpose: such, for example, are those of William Skitt, a noted horse dealer from Willaston (in Prees), who died in 1670 leaving specialties worth £210.[12] Often the bulk of the money owed was to be paid on a specified day, frequently on an important calendar date, or at a fair, and perhaps only a small earnest was given at the sealing of the bargain. Easy terms could be arranged, especially for small transactions or those between friends and neighbours. Thus people of fairly humble means could get goods they needed—perhaps corn or even a horse to help them earn a living. Richard Wells of Wem accepted both forms of repayment: in December 1602 three of his fellow parishioners owed him for horses and of these Humphrey Pinsell had until Whitsun to find £3 12s., the price of the animal, while George Higginson the younger was being allowed to clear his debt of £2 6s. in weekly instalments of 1s.[13] Debts for part of the price of particular items[14] indicate other examples of the latter practice.

1750–1875

THE second half of the 18th century and the first three quarters of the 19th were a period of relative prosperity for British agriculture. At first export bounties helped grain prices to recover from the low levels of the earlier 18th century.[15] Subsequently population growth[16] (stimulated locally by industrialization)[17] and almost a quarter of a century of war (1793–1815) increased domestic demand for food and raised prices, rents, and land values to unprecedented levels. Inclosure was stimulated, arable farming expanded, and the new farming techniques devised in the arable parts of the kingdom spread widely; their adoption, perhaps later and more unevenly in Shropshire than in some other regions,[18] amounted to an agricultural 'revolution' which increased the productivity of the land and has given its name to the period. After the war the protection enacted in 1815[19] kept up

[11] L.J.R.O., B/C/11, Wm. Weston (Shawbury) 26 Nov. 1545, John Lockley (Sheriffhales) 21 May 1647, Wm. Clempson (Wroxeter) 7 July 1547, Ric. Leyte (Hodnet) 1 Oct. 1554.   [12] P.R.O., PROB 4/12355.
[13] L.J.R.O., B/C/11, Ric. Wells (Wem) 14 May 1603.
[14] Referred to in probate rec.
[15] D. Ormrod, *Eng. Grain Exports and the Structure of Agrarian Capitalism 1700–1760* (1985), cap. 4; W. G. Hoskins, 'Harvest Fluctuations 1620–1759 and Eng. Econ.

Hist.' *Agric. H.R.* xvi, fig. 1 (facing p. 15).
[16] E. A. Wrigley and R. S. Schofield, *Population Hist. of Eng. 1541–1871* (1981), 183–5, 576 sqq.
[17] *Compton Census*, ed. Whiteman, pp. cviii, cxii.
[18] J. P. Dodd, 'Salop. Agric. 1793–1870' (London Univ. Ph.D. thesis, 1981), 15–16, 30–40, 49.
[19] Corn Laws Amendment Act, 55 Geo. III, c. 26. W. Cunningham, *Growth of Eng. Ind. and Commerce in Modern Times* (1921), ii. 723–31, reviews the corn laws 1773–1846.

confidence in British farming; protection was strongly supported in the county[20] where, however, repeal of the corn laws in 1846[21] did not, except perhaps briefly,[22] sap that confidence. Investment in feeds and fertilizers, buildings and machinery continued. Many of the succeeding generation of Shropshire farmers earned a good livelihood in the 1850s and 1860s from 'high farming', well suited to the county's mixed husbandry.[23] The great improvement in transport effected by the building of railways in the 1850s and 1860s[24] made distant markets more accessible to Shropshire produce. High farming, with its emphasis on the rearing and feeding of livestock, seems to have brought about some reduction of the county's arable acreage, particularly that under wheat,[25] a foreshadowing of the more drastic changes (arising from different causes) that came with the deepening depression of the 1870s.[26] Towards the end of the period, from 1865 to 1867, a very severe outbreak of foot and mouth disease caused much hardship in the north Shropshire dairying district, particularly among the smaller farmers.[27]

In Shropshire, as perhaps elsewhere, the period marks high summer in the influence of landed society.[28] The most prominent landowners controlled the county's representation in parliament,[29] took a leading role in county and local government,[30] and even continued to influence the affairs of the larger boroughs;[31] they led in sport and fashion.[32] Their influence rested mainly on agricultural prosperity and in turn, during George III's reign[33] and later, the example of the improving landlord came to contribute greatly to the progress of agriculture. The landlord's influence, however, was most effective when he resided on his property or was at least represented by an efficient agent. The dullness[34] and inconvenience[35] of country life in the later 18th century caused many landowners to spend part or (more rarely) all of the year in London or other fashionable towns. In the late 18th and early 19th century Joseph Plymley (later Corbett), landlord, magistrate,[36] churchman, and author of the 1803 *General Survey of the Agriculture of Shropshire*, pondered the varieties of social intercourse in the countryside, deplored such absenteeism, and noted the beneficial results of a good landlord's residence.[37] Gradually during the period, as transport and communications were improved, the disadvantages of living in the country were diminished. Prestige came to attach to agricultural improvement. Horses, ploughteams, cattle, and estate landscapes were painted by artists such as Thomas Weaver of Shrewsbury (1775-1844)[38] and, somewhat later, William Gwynn of Ludlow. Many landlords who set good examples of modern farming and breeding techniques were by no means averse to the acclaim they received.

[20] Dodd, 'Salop. Agric.' 151-3, 158, 173-4, 184, 263-6, 289, 323; V.C.H. Salop. iii. 313-14, 328, 341.
[21] Corn Laws Amendment Act, 9 & 10 Vic. c. 22.
[22] Dodd, op. cit. 292-3, 310. [23] Ibid. caps. 7, 9.
[24] V.C.H. Salop. i. 416 (corr. ibid. ii. 316); R. K. Morriss, Rlys. of Salop.: brief hist. (Shrews. 1983).
[25] Dodd, op. cit. 231-2, 317-18, 328-32.
[26] Below, 1875-1985.
[27] V.C.H. Salop. iii. 162-3; T.S.A.S. lix. 137-8; 3rd Rep. Com. to inquire into Cattle Plague [3656], map facing p. 244, H.C. (1866), xxii.
[28] G. E. Mingay, Eng. Landed Soc. in 18th Cent. (1963), 11-14; F. M. L. Thompson, Eng. Landed Soc. in 19th Cent. (1963), cap. 2. [29] V.C.H. Salop. iii. 308-43.
[30] Ibid. 135-63, 166-7, 172.
[31] Ibid. 296, 328, 330-3, 340, 343; J. F. A. Mason, Boro. of Bridgnorth 1157-1957 (Bridgnorth, 1957), 33-4.
[32] V.C.H. Salop. ii. 165 sqq.; Mingay, Eng. Landed Soc. in 18th Cent. 215 sqq.; E. W. Bovill, The Eng. of Nimrod

and Surtees (1959); F. M. L. Thompson, 'Upper class culture in 19th cent. Eng. and the aristocratic legacy', Comité International des Sciences Historiques, 16e Congres International des Sciences Historiques, Rapports (Stuttgart, 1985), ii. 505-8.
[33] A. Young, On the Husbandry of Three Celebrated Brit. Farmers, Messrs. Bakewell, Arbuthnot, and Ducket (1811), note on pp. 29-31.
[34] Hist. Parl., Commons, 1754-90, iii. 591; S.P.L., MSS. 6863, pp. 5-6, 30; 6865, p. 163. [35] T.S.A.S. lix. 139-42.
[36] V.C.H. Salop. iii. 119-20, 127, 130; viii. 110.
[37] S.P.L., MSS. 6860-5 (much of the inf. in these MSS. will also be found in B.L. Add. MS. 21018); J. Plymley, Gen. View of Agric. of Salop. (1803), esp. 95-101.
[38] For him see W. S. Sparrow, 'Thos. Weaver of Salop.: a Yeomanist in Paint', The Connoisseur, xciv. 386-91; Bryan's Dict. of Painters and Engravers, ed. G. C. Williamson, v (1921), 347. There is a very fine collection of cattle paintings in Attingham Hall.

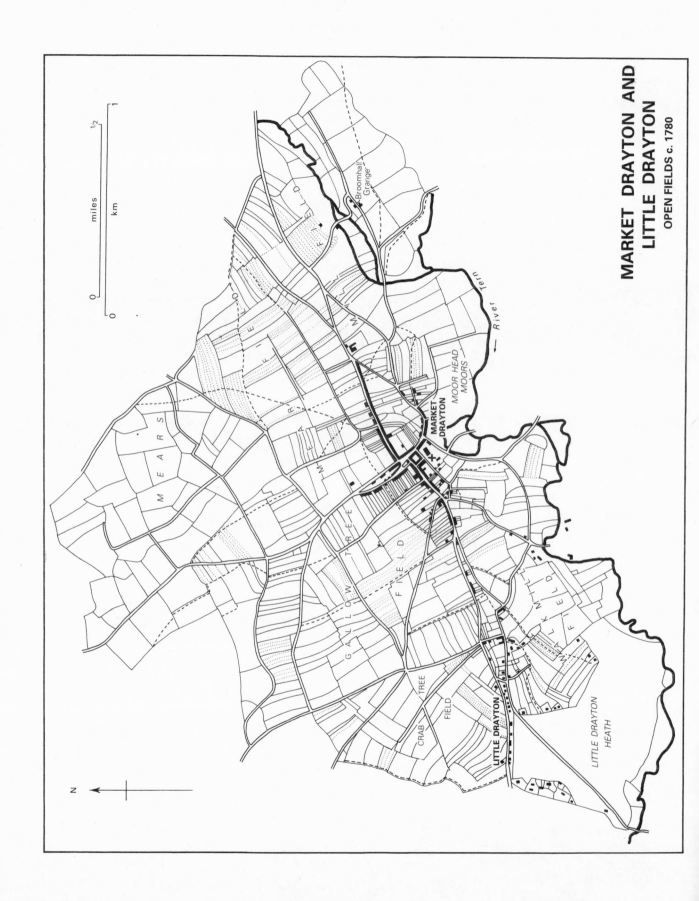

MARKET DRAYTON AND
LITTLE DRAYTON
OPEN FIELDS c. 1780

In many instances the improving landlord probably earned more in reputation than in cash profit, for many inventive and respected farming landlords—such as William Childe of Kinlet, William Wolryche Whitmore of Dudmaston, and the 2nd Lord Hill—left heavy mortgages to their successors. Only one large Shropshire estate, however, was broken up during the period[39] and one or two of the largest continued to expand.[40] Some smaller squires sold up or had retrenchment forced on them; paradoxically the fact that they were usually those who had lived beyond their means or inherited heavily encumbered estates is evidence of over-confidence in the considerable recuperative powers of the landed estate. Land that came up for sale did not wait long for purchasers. Few country houses went out of use;[41] indeed new ones were built and many older ones rebuilt or altered.

Shropshire farmers, whether freeholders or rack tenants, enjoyed a share in the period's prosperity. Many farmhouses were built or altered, and better furnished, for a more genteel type of family.[42] Many farmers spoke at agricultural meetings on equal terms with their landlords,[43] and by the 1870s they were beginning to take an independent line even in politics.[44]

Save in exceptional circumstances the farm labourer did not share in the prosperity. Wages were kept low and the general standard of housing was very bad. The working life was long, and after 1834 the threat of the workhouse overshadowed the old age or impotence of all but those who had been most fortunate or rigidly provident. Almost all other work was more eligible than farm labouring and, whether or not mechanization was involved in the process, most rural parishes (especially in the south) lost population.[45]

Inclosure

Even at the end of the Middle Ages Shropshire was an area of old inclosure, and by the mid 18th century the work of two more centuries had further diminished the extent of the open fields and common wastes.[46] Thus it is hardly surprising that parliamentary inclosure was relatively insignificant in the county, as it was in all the counties on the western border of England.[47] Nevertheless, in what was to be the last phase of inclosure,[48] a very considerable quantity of Shropshire land was dealt with. By parliamentary methods almost $7\frac{1}{2}$ per cent (63,775 a.) of the county area was inclosed (Table VIII) and, as in earlier periods, there were many inclosures by private agreement. Fifteen private agreements leading to awards made 1787–1835 and deposited with the clerk of the peace dealt with 4,874 a.[49] Eleven of those agreements belonged to the years 1806–15,[50] and the war years had seen many other small inclosures without recourse to parliament or trace in the clerk of the peace's records. Indeed during the war private agreement seems to have been the normal method.[51] A thousand acres in the manors of Child's

[39] Ld. Craven's.
[40] e.g. Ld. Bradford's and Ld. Forester's.
[41] P. Reid, *Burke's and Savills Guide to Country Hos.* ii (1980), 71. Cf. Loton Hall MSS., Sir B. Leighton's diary 27 Oct 1865.
[42] Dodd, 'Salop. Agric.' 88, 188–91, 319.
[43] See e.g. *T.S.A.S.* lix. 135–6.
[44] Ibid. 170–80; *V.C.H. Salop.* iii. 323–4.
[45] Dodd, 'Salop. Agric.' 16, 63–72, 88, 161–6, 172, 178, 192–4, 257–63, 320–1, 323–6, 334 (fig. 41).
[46] Above, 1540–1750 (Inclosure); M. Turner, *Eng. Parl. Enclosure: Its Hist. Geog. and Econ. Hist.* (1980), 37, 142.
[47] Turner, op. cit. cap. 2, esp. pp. 35, 59, 61.

[48] Beginning nationally with the mid 18th-cent. recovery in corn prices (ibid. 106), the parl. inclosure movement reached Salop. in 1765: below.
[49] To 14 listed in *T.S.A.S.* lii. 37 (cf. S.R.O., incl. awards B 15–20, 23, 26–7, 30, 32, 37, 41, 50, C 5/45) should be added the Forton heath award (1787): S.R.O., q. sess. rec. parcel 283, reg. of enrolled incl. awards, pp. 77–81; S.R.O. 89/1.
[50] i.e. all but those for Forton heath (470 a.), Wollerton wood (39 a.), Loughton common (361 a.), and Duparts man. (926 a.), made 1787, 1821, 1824, and c. 1835 respectively.
[51] *Rep. Sel. Cttee. on Commons' Inclosure*, H.C. 583, pp. 474–5 (1844), v.

Ercall and Howle, for example, were privately inclosed in 1801,[52] while at Bronygarth, in St. Martin's, a 'large quantity' of waste land, and at Aston on Clun a 160-a. common, were similarly divided and allotted.[53] Such inclosures, however, unrecorded by the clerk of the peace, were by no means confined to the war years: for instance, the only record of the disappearance of Farley common (58 a. inclosed in 1818), in Much Wenlock, is a private deed.[54] Dates are sometimes hard to establish: all that is known of the end of Presthope common in the same parish, 14 a. in 1769, is that it was inclosed by 1846.[55] If all inclosure agreements that did not find their way to the clerk of the peace's office may reasonably be supposed to have brought the total of Shropshire land inclosed between 1765[56] and 1891[57] to approach 10 per cent of the county area,[58] then that was an acreage approximating to that of the southern division of Bradford hundred.[59]

TABLE VIII: PARLIAMENTARY INCLOSURE AWARDS 1765–1891

	number of awards	acreage
1765–1854 under Local etc. Acts		
(i) including open-field land	7	5,500
(ii) not including open-field land	44	46,255[a]
1850–91 by provisional Order confirmed by annual general Acts:	21	12,020
TOTAL	72	63,775

Sources: below, Table IX; Tate, *Domesday of Eng. Encl. Acts*, 223–7, supplemented by S.R.O., incl. awards A 13/2, 14/5, 5/13, 18/51, 17/53, B 11–12, 14, 24, 29, 33–5, 38–40, 42, 44, 46, 49, C 4/36, 3/43. Where no extant award is known acreages have been estimated from S.R.O. 81/309; 1900/3/29–36 (for Newport); S.R.O. 1709, box 203, copy map and ref. on incl. of Long Mynd and Picklescott Hill; 299/1/1, nos. 4–5, 14–16, 35–6, 41–3, 150–260; /1/2, no. 1411 (for Ch. Stretton); S.R.O. 32/1–2 (for Siefton forest); and S.R.O. 3121/1 (for the Weald Moors). The acreage for Hine and Shawbury heaths, etc., is that stated in 37 Geo. III, c. 109 (Priv. Act), that for Upton common, Shifnal, is that stated in 53 Geo. III, c. 17 (Local and Personal, not printed).

[a]Including 579 a. inclosed in Sheriffhales, part of which parish was in Staffs. until 1895, but excluding inclosures in Oldbury, transferred to Worcs. in 1844.

Shropshire open-field land inclosed by Act amounted to some 2,500 a. (Table IX).[60] The figure, though to an extent artificial,[61] is unlikely to have been exceeded very greatly in fact. Two considerable areas of open-field land were inclosed by private agreement in 1775–7 (at Siefton) and 1813 (at Sheinton),[62] but by the late 18th century changes on such a scale normally made it desirable to have an Act. Where there were numerous freeholders a pattern of landowning sometimes survived which preserved the shapes of the open-field strips. That seems to have happened in Minton where, in 1822, 41 a. of strips were abolished by exchanges

[52] Cf. S.R.O. 327, map 4; 2151/769. W. E. Tate, *Domesday of Eng. Enclosure Acts and Awards*, ed. M. E. Turner (1978), 225, wrongly accounts it an inclosure by Act (of 1824); it is here omitted from Table VIII.

[53] *Trans. Soc. of Arts*, xxiv. 41, 43; *Rep. Sel. Cttee. on Commons' Inclosure*, 171–2.

[54] S.R.O. 1681, box 144, deed of 1818.

[55] Cf. S.R.O. 294/6; 3657/2/7, 12.

[56] When Newport marsh was inclosed under 4 Geo. III, c. 59 (Priv. Act): S.R.O. 81/309; 1900/3/29–36.

[57] When, in the last Salop. award, the hills in Llanfair Waterdine were inclosed: S.R.O., incl. award A 2/72.

[58] The estimate that *c.* 11 per cent of the co. was waste *c.*

1800 (cf. *T.S.A.S.* lv. 7–8; Dodd, 'Salop. Agric.' 23) seems too low. Cf. below, 1875–1985 (Agrarian economy and society), for the *c.* 11,700 a. of commons (1.2 per cent of the 1891 area of Salop.) registered under the Commons Registration Act, 1965, c. 64.

[59] For hund. and co. areas see *Census*, 1841; 1891; cf. *V.C.H. Salop.* xi. 94.

[60] Cf. below n. 63.

[61] Based on incl. Acts that G. Slater found in B.M. (*T.S.A.S.* lii. 2) and summarized in his *Eng. Peasantry and Encl. of Common Fields* (Studies in Econ. and Political Science xiv, 1907), 298.

[62] S.R.O. 4064; incl. award B 32.

LODGE FARM, QUATT MALVERN

Boundary ditches of Iron Age or Romano-British enclosures seen in fresh plough. Together the two main enclosures (perhaps one for farm buildings, the other a home paddock) cover about the same area as the largely 19th-century farm buildings to the south.

CAER-DIN RING, NEWCASTLE, CLUN

Oblique view south. The hill-top enclosure (c. 0.8 ha.), assumed to be prehistoric, invites comparison with the banjo enclosures of central southern England. The outward-flaring ditches presumably funnelled stock along the sunken approach road to the entrance.

CROWLEASOWS FARM, MIDDLETON, BITTERLEY
View north-west into the yard. Crowleasows was one of several farms rebuilt by Sir C. H. Rouse-
Boughton, Bt., of Downton Hall. His initials appear several times on the farm buildings, with '1863' in
blue brick headers on the end of the right-hand range.

CATHERTON COMMON
View west over Catherton common, a landscape of irregular squatters' inclosures and pock-marked
with infilled bellpits. The squatter settlement was sarcastically nicknamed Lubberlands after an
imaginary land yielding plenty to those too lazy to labour. The 17th- and 18th-century landscape
contrasts vividly with the regular Farlow Enclosure beyond, created c. 1815 by Lord Craven's
inclosure of common.

under an Act of 1816.[63] When no Act was procured, as in the case of Market Drayton,[64] a complicated pattern of landowning might well survive for very many years.[65] The late survival of open fields, however, cannot be assumed from every example of intermixed landowning[66] or of rationalization by exchange.[67] The inclosure of 2,500 a. of open-field land in the county was spread over six decades (Table IX), extents of land and time that do not corroborate the suggestion that parliamentary inclosure of open fields was a rapid response to a general crisis in open-field agriculture,[68] though corroboration could hardly be expected from Shropshire where such a crisis would have had minimal effects.

TABLE IX: PARLIAMENTARY INCLOSURES INCLUDING OPEN-FIELD
LAND 1773–1828

Townships grouped by parish	Date of award	Acreage inclosed	Open-field land acreage	% of total
Bucknell	1828	798	51	(6.39)
Clungunford				
Shelderton	1828	287	48	(16.72)
Donington	1774	340	130	(38.23)
Kinnerley				
Dovaston & Kynaston	1813	318	74	(23.70)
Edgerley	1789	418	132	(31.57)
Kinnerley	1789	158	39	(24.68)
Upr. & Lr. Maesbrook	1813	270	21	(7.77)
Tyr-y-coed	1789	137	91	(66.42)
Melverley	1789	505	371	(73.46)
Shifnal	1794	722	722	(100)
Stanton Lacy				
W. Hamlet(s)	1828	42	9	(21.43)
Lr. Hayton	1828	94	11	(11.70)
Upr. Hayton	1828	304	80	(26.31)
Stanton Lacy	1828	256	121	(47.26)
Much Wenlock	1777	704	551	(78.26)
		5,500[a]	2,451	(45.79)

Sources: S.R.O., dep. plans B 1, B 9, C 1/48, C 2/47; q. sess. rec. parcel 283, reg. of enrolled incl. awards, pp. 25–49; S.R.O. 3879/Enc/1–3; 3880/Enc/1–3.

[a]Not counting land inclosed before the awards but included in them. Three townships in the 7 awards here tabulated had no open-field land inclosed; though not tabulated here, their acreages contribute to the total of 5,500 a. inclosed under the awards. They are Knockin (where 27 a. were inclosed in 1813), Morton in Oswestry (66 a. in 1813), and Hopton in Stanton Lacy (54 a. in 1828).

Thus almost all Shropshire land inclosed during the period was common waste, and the sequence of inclosures in the county helps to substantiate the suggestion that commons inclosure spread from one region to another as its effectiveness was demonstrated locally.[69] If, as seems reasonable, the sequence of parliamentary inclosures may be held to represent that of all inclosures, by whatever method, then from the 1760s to 1820 there was almost four times the amount of inclosure in north Shropshire as in the south (Fig. 12).[70] Despite the serious drainage costs

[63] S.R.O., incl. award C 3/43. The 41 a. should perh. be added to the 2,451 a. in Table IX.
[64] For Mkt. Drayton cf. Fig. 11 and O.S. maps 6", Salop. XVI. NW. (edns. of 1888, 1902, and 1929), which show 20th-cent. traces of the old open-field strips.
[65] There were said to be 500 a. of surviving open fields in 12 Salop. pars. in 1873: T.S.A.S. lii. 24.
[66] J. Bishton, Gen. View of Agric. of Salop. (Brentford,

1794), 8; Rep. Sel. Cttee. on Commons' Inclosure, 346.
[67] S.R.O. 112, map 5.
[68] J. Chapman, 'Extent and Nature of Parl. Encl.' Agric. H.R. xxxv. 34.
[69] Ibid.; Rep. Sel. Cttee. on Commons' Inclosure, 174–5.
[70] 'North' here means east and north of the Severn (cf. above, Physical Environment), from Morfe forest to Whittington and Selattyn.

involved in some cases, the heavier clay soils and the peat mosses in the north seem to have been inclosed first, doubtless because of their great potential fertility. One of the largest of those tackled was the extensive Baggy Moor in the Perry valley; 1,283 a., formerly under water every winter, were drained under an Act of 1777 and made valuable. In a later phase of inclosure in the north, as war and dearth forced up grain prices, the less fertile but more easily tackled heathlands were dealt with.[71]

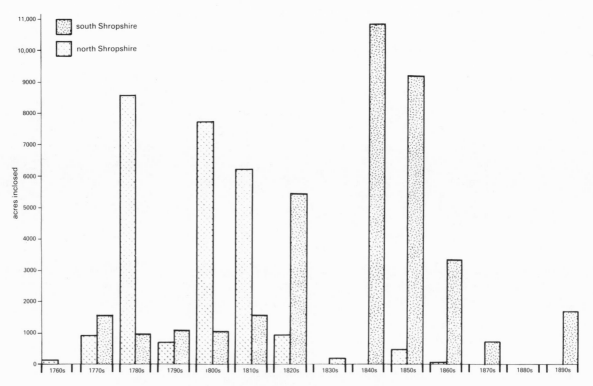

Fig. 12: PARLIAMENTARY INCLOSURE 1765–1891
Based on sources cited for Table VIII.

By 1820 north Shropshire landowners had inclosed more than 24,000 a. by Act (Fig. 12). Thereafter, as the Shrewsbury solicitor and banker Thomas Salt testified in 1844, there were very few commons left in the north though large uninclosed areas survived in the south.[72] During the seventy-odd years from 1820 almost all parliamentary inclosure was confined to the extensive hills of the south-west and the south-east where, earlier, inclosure had seemed unprofitable.[73]

The profitability of inclosure in the south was not in doubt by the 1840s. Much was then being done: nearly 11,000 a. were inclosed by parliamentary means during the decade, and there were high expectations of profit. The possibilities had been long forseen. In 1760 Clun forest had been advertised to be 'as profitable a sheep walk as any in England' and it was claimed that 'great advantage' might be made of it by 'inclosing, ploughing, and sowing acorns, granting sheep walks, or making advantageous leasows for improvements'. Expectations of profit after inclosure were apparently well founded. Good land inclosed from Clun forest increased in annual value from 2s. or 3s. an acre when it was open sheep pasture to 10s. or 12s.

[71] Dodd, 'Salop. Agric.' 24–9, 54, 56, 128, 139–40; S.R.O. 671/1; Plymley, *Agric. of Salop.* 223.
[72] *Rep. Sel. Cttee. on Commons' Inclosure*, 453–4. Salt
helped to manage Ld. Powis's est.
[73] Dodd, 'Salop. Agric.' 16.

by 1844 when inclosure was nearly complete; some of it was then growing oats, rye, and turnips or, in lower situations, wheat.[74] Francis Marston of Aston on Clun, a landowner and farmer with much experience of inclosure,[75] considered that open commons were worth nothing, indeed—conventional wisdom by Plymley's time—that they had a deteriorating effect on neighbouring inclosed lands. That was partly because they discouraged farmers from thinking of their closes as anything but winter pasture, so that they were left uncultivated, and partly because sheep commoned on open land could not effectively be fenced out of the neighbouring closes where they did much damage.[76] Crime, particularly the theft of livestock, was alleged to be another characteristic of the open commons that was injurious to farming.[77] Inclosure, Marston testified, more than doubled the value of the closes adjoining the former commons because they could then grow green crops, an important new element in improved livestock husbandry.[78]

Improvement of livestock by good feeding and controlled breeding was a most important development in 19th-century farming,[79] and there too the open commons obstructed progress. The small 'common sheep' of Shropshire did not prosper when turned out on the common; farmers never sent breeding ewes there, only wethers, and they came down 'very poor indeed', often in worse condition when they were gathered in at Michaelmas than when they had gone out in the spring. In south-west Shropshire the farmer's motive for pasturing his sheep on open land was not an economic one: all had to do it in order to preserve their common rights as long as the land remained open.[80] At Aston on Clun sheep profits more than trebled after inclosure.[81]

Particularly in the uplands of south Shropshire the greater part of the newly inclosed commons became separate pastures,[82] but some common land, even in the hilly districts, was capable of cultivation or conversion to meadow. Good grain was grown c. 1800 on parts of the Long Mynd inclosed in 1790[83] and, as has been seen, cultivation was extended into Clun forest in the 1840s. Francis Marston, an enthusiast for inclosure, urged the cultivation of oats on high land; the conversion of wild land on the slopes of hills to water meadows, as had been done with the lord of the manor's permission in Clun forest even before inclosure was completed; and, wherever there was soil and an absence of rock, the extension of cultivation up the slopes even of commons as high as Clunbury common and the Long Mynd.[84]

Parts of one or two inclosures made during the period were used to round off a park or extend plantations, as at Sansaw in 1783, where the western side of Sansaw heath was added to Sansaw park, and at Wootton Fawnog near Oswestry, part of which was planted after inclosure in 1789. The Revd. Samuel Wilding, owner of a substantial estate at All Stretton, planted part of the newly inclosed northern edge of the Long Mynd with oak after the inclosure of 1790. At Leaton a small part of the southern edge of Leaton heath (inclosed 1813) seems to have been incorporated in the Leaton Shelf plantations stretching north from Leaton Knolls[85] and in a similar way perhaps part of Winscote heath was added to Apley Terrace

[74] *Rep. Sel. Cttee. on Commons' Inclosure*, 179–80; S.P.L., MS. 110, s.v. Clun, MS. and printed sale partics. for John Walcot's est. 1760.

[75] *Rep. Sel. Cttee. on Commons' Inclosure*, 171–2, 174–5.

[76] Ibid. 172–4; Plymley, *Agric. of Salop.* 144.

[77] *Rep. Sel. Cttee. on Commons' Inclosure*, 180.

[78] Ibid. 172.

[79] Below (Livestock breeds).

[80] *Rep. Sel. Cttee. on Commons' Inclosure*, 172.

[81] Ibid. 174.

[82] Dodd, 'Salop. Agric.' 56–7, 158–9, 249–53.

[83] Plymley, *Agric. of Salop.* 222.

[84] *Rep. Sel. Cttee. on Commons' Inclosure*, 171–9.

[85] Dodd, 'Salop. Agric.' 30; S.R.O., incl. awards B 3, B 8, B 35; S.R.O. 3375/96; Plymley, op. cit. 148; R. Baugh, *Map of Salop.* (1808); O.S. map 1″, sheet 118 (1953 edn.).

plantations extending south from Apley Park.[86] Plymley, enthusiastic advocate of inclosures though he was, yet acknowledged his regret that 'a great deal of beauty' was often spoiled by them:

it seems a pity to lose scenes of pure Nature, in a country so artificial as that of South Britain. This applies chiefly to very large wastes, for instance, Clun forest...is a fine specimen of smooth and extended turf, with every variation of swelling banks and retired dingles.

A later age might agree with his aesthetic sentiments[87] but in the utilitarian 1840s Francis Marston uttered a perhaps more prevalent opinion, that inclosure and plantation made the land more useful and no less fair: he considered that the side of Clunbury Hill and the whole top of the Long Mynd should be planted to increase their utility and beauty and at the same time to improve the local climate.[88]

The main deterrent to inclosure was expense.[89] In 1796, when Andrew Corbet of Acton Reynald had the open wastes on his estate surveyed and found that some 2,380 a. might be inclosed for him, it was noted that some of the smaller landowners were against inclosure by Act. Tact and caution were necessary[90] and four of the twelve townships were left out of the Act procured next year and were dealt with privately.[91] During the early 19th century professional and legal costs, especially perhaps those involved in parliamentary inclosure, were increasing. The smaller owners were those who faced the most difficulty over costs. In the private inclosures of the early 19th century very many small owners evidently failed to secure fair treatment, though at Aston on Clun, where the large commoners kept the small ones off the common, it was only at inclosure in 1804 that the small men's rights were duly acknowledged by allotments inclosed from the common.[92] Sometimes road making cost a good deal.[93] Fencing was another potentially large expense[94] for all owners of newly inclosed land, though local resources occasionally reduced the cost: on the Baggy Moor, for example, wide drainage ditches were made to serve as fences in the late 18th century,[95] and at Bronygarth there were plentiful supplies of stone to hand in 1804.[96]

In rural England at least[97] it might still be maintained in the earlier 1840s that the public—as distinct from the lord of the manor, the owner of the soil, and the commoners—had no rights deserving consideration on inclosure.[98] There was nevertheless a growing feeling that some part of common land, even when it was far from large towns, should be devoted to public and recreational purposes at inclosure. In Shropshire an early voluntary example of such provision was Richard Reynolds's assignment of parts of his manorial waste and woodland around Coalbrookdale for public recreation.[99] The 1845 Inclosure Act empowered the Inclosure Commissioners to allot recreation ground when unstinted commons were inclosed,[1] and out of the 8,208 a. of Clun forest inclosed in 1847, besides the

[86] Dodd, op. cit. 30, citing no evidence of inclosure. It is also stated ibid. that inclosures at Burwarton and Willey were imparked or planted, but no Burwarton inclosure is known during the period and the farmland imparked at Willey after 1811 (T.S.A.S. lxv. 72-3) was not newly inclosed.
[87] Cf. Plymley, op. cit. 145; G. Shaw Lefevre, Eng. Commons and Forests (1894), 4. Clun forest's smooth turf was of course also artificial rather than 'pure Nature'.
[88] Rep. Sel. Cttee. on Commons' Inclosure, 173-4.
[89] Plymley, op. cit. 145.
[90] As on Sir Watkin Williams Wynn's est. c. 1770: below (Landlords and tenants).
[91] Cf. S.R.O. 322, box 61, 'Particulars of Waste Lands [on And. Corbet's est.]' 4 May 1796; 731, boxes 36, 197-9,

incl. papers; 37 Geo. III, c. 109 (Priv. Act).
[92] Tate, Domesday of Eng. Enclosure Acts, 31, 36; Rep. Sel. Cttee. on Commons' Inclosure, 172, 175-6.
[93] See e.g. below for the Clun forest roads.
[94] Plymley, Agric. of Salop. 145-51, offers much advice on fencing.   [95] Ibid. 223.
[96] Trans. Soc. of Arts, xxiv. 42-3, 45, 47-8.
[97] The 1836 Inclosure Act showed some care for public interests in the neighbourhood of large towns: Tate, Domesday of Enclosure Acts, 31.
[98] Thos. Salt's view, emphatically stated: Rep. Sel. Cttee. on Commons' Inclosure, 474.
[99] Tate, op. cit. 31-2; B. Trinder, Ind. Rev. Salop. (1981), 220; V.C.H. Salop. xi. 41.
[1] 8 & 9 Vic. c. 118, s. 30.

provision of 35 miles of public roads 30 ft. wide and the allotment of 21 a. to the highways surveyors as stone quarries, gravel pits, and public watering places for cattle, 5 a. were allotted for the building of a parochial chapel and curate's house at Newcastle, plots amounting to 1½ a. for schools at Newcastle, Whitcott Keysett, and Mainstone, and 1 a. for a public recreation ground in the Vron promontory fort, Newcastle.[2] Such provision, though small, was probably fairly typical of the standards prevailing in the mid 19th century.[3] Only one Shropshire inclosure was effected after the passing of the 1876 Commons Act which, for the first time, required the Inclosure Commissioners to make provisions for the benefit of the neighbourhood.[4] It was that for the Llanfair hills (1,634 a.) in 1891, in which 15 a. were allotted for labourers' 'field gardens', 10 a. beneath the summit of Llanfair hill were allotted as a parish recreation ground, and the 1½-mile stretch of Offa's Dyke that passed through the newly inclosed land was preserved as a public footpath.[5]

The Agricultural Revolution

Inclosure of land and rational consolidation of estates by exchange were essential prerequisites for the advancement of arable and livestock-breeding techniques. Without convenient field boundaries the progressive farmer could neither improve his livestock nor derive any advantage from new crops and crop rotations, underdraining schemes, or the expense of applying fertilizers. With fences in position, however, the county's agriculture was set for 19th-century progress as improved scientific farming began to displace outmoded methods. In Shropshire, as elsewhere, convertible, and eventually alternate, husbandry[6] were practised more widely and skilfully as the new feeding and breeding[7] techniques and new fertilizers became available. The consequent increase in the productivity of the land—the very essence[8] of the Agricultural Revolution—led to the mid 19th-century period of high farming, for which Shropshire's mixed farming practices were peculiarly well adapted.

On the lighter soils of eastern England the practice of alternate husbandry, interspersing temporary grass and clover leys and turnips[9] with the more demanding corn crops, had been employed from the late 17th century.[10] In a typical four-course rotation the well manured turnip crop prepared the soil for the following season's barley, after which a one-year clover ley restored nitrogen to the ground[11] for use by the next year's wheat. Such a system kept the soil in good heart, provided valuable fodder for livestock, and eliminated fallowing. The new techniques spread from east to west; that seems no less true of Shropshire, whose light eastern soils were best adapted to the improved husbandry, than of the country as a whole.[12] At the time of Arthur Young's visit to Shropshire in 1776 elements of alternate husbandry were already present, and it was particularly in the east that he found

[2] S.R.O., incl. award A 17/53; cf. *V.C.H. Salop.* i. 355–6; SA 1191.

[3] Tate, *Domesday of Enclosure Acts*, 32–3; Shaw Lefevre, *Eng. Commons and Forests*, 23, 286; J. L. and B. Hammond, *The Bleak Age* (1934), cap. 5.

[4] Tate, op. cit. 33; 39 & 40 Vic. c. 56, s. 7.

[5] S.R.O., incl. award A 2/72; Shaw Lefevre, op. cit. 372.

[6] Below, n. 9.

[7] Below (Livestock breeds).

[8] J. D. Chambers and G. E. Mingay, *Agric. Revolution 1750–1880* (1966), 4–5, 54.

[9] The introduction of roots, with the shortening of the long ley characteristic of convertible husbandry, distinguish alternate husbandry: ibid. 61–2.

[10] Col. Rob. Walpole, of Houghton (Norf.), grew large quantities of turnips and a regular acreage of clover as early as 1673, and was followed in that practice by others, including his better known son-in-law 'Turnip' Townshend: G. E. Fussell, 'From the Restoration to Waterloo', in intro. to Ld. Ernle, *Eng. Farming Past and Present* (6th edn. 1961), p. lxvii.

[11] Its practical benefits were realized, without being understood, by 18th-cent. farmers: Chambers and Mingay, op. cit. 56.

[12] Ibid. 36–7.

clover leys on the farms which he visited and turnips cultivated on the lighter soils. At Benthall, for example, turnips were sown in well prepared ground that had been ploughed four times and received heavy dressings of dung and lime.[13] In some other places, however, the fallows were still being preserved and taking as much fertilizer as the growing turnips: at Cruckton and Petton they received 1-1½ wagon load of lime an acre in addition to farmyard manure.[14] Nowhere in the county did Young record the strict Norfolk four-course rotation, though then, or soon after, John Bishton of Kilsall was using it on the eastern edge of the county and it was in use in the hilly south Shropshire parish of Hope Bowdler by 1793.[15] By the 1790s in fact various rotations were in use and adjustments to suit terrain and the farmer's preferences had lengthened them to six or seven courses.[16]

In the years following Young's tour the new rotation crops, which had been known in Shropshire before, gained further popularity, though dissemination of new ideas was uneven.[17] Clover in 'old' and 'new' ricks had been offered for sale at Edgmond in November 1778 while rye grass, in two stacks, was on sale at Ensdon House, Montford, in March 1781.[18] It was after the late 1780s, however, that stacks of rye grass, and especially clover, formed a regular part of farm-based dispersal sales. Advertisements for turnip seeds, of the Norfolk Ox and Stubble varieties, appeared in the local press,[19] and their cultivation was no doubt stimulated by the offer of awards for the best crops, such as those given by the 2nd Lord Clive to his turnip-growing tenants on the Walcot and Montford estates.[20] Peas, which had been included in several of the rotations noted by Young, continued to spread in popularity in a manner not seemingly matched in other counties. Plymley, when discussing commonly cultivated crops, claimed that peas were 'more grown upon our sound soils than any other county'.[21] Like turnips they could be hoed, so restricting weed infestation, while they also shared the nitrogen-fixing benefits of the clover ley.

From the 1790s Bishton, Plymley, and others lent support to the enlightened system of alternate husbandry. It was, however, more in the nature of a recommendation than an observation of the county's common standard. Several alternative rotations were noticed, generally of five to seven courses, along with one designed to improve wheat lands that ran to nine years and was one of several to retain a fallow and three summer ploughings, harrowings, and rollings. To that requirement was often added an earlier ploughing during the previous winter, so elevating a 'tolerable' fallow to the status of a good one.[22]

The successful cultivation of turnips within a rotation was never an easy task on those Shropshire farms with a heavy, unyielding soil. The potato, which was gaining in popularity for both animal and human consumption, was suggested as one alternative by John Cotes of Woodcote in two letters to the Board of Agriculture in 1800-1. He drew on personal experience, having partly planted his fallow with potatoes, and he contended that with adequate manure they would not impoverish the soil.[23] Within a generation further alternatives were provided by the more adaptable swede and the hardier mangold-wurzel: in December 1832, in the earliest noticed reference to Swedish turnips and mangold-wurzels, Lord Kilmorey offered

[13] A. Young, *Tours in Eng. and Wales Selected from the Annals of Agric.* (Reprints of Scarce Tracts in Econ. and Political Science, xiv; 1932), 146, 154, 159, 162.
[14] Ibid. 146, 154, 163.
[15] Bishton, *Agric. of Salop.* 11 sqq.; S.P.L., MS. 6865, p. 105.
[16] S.P.L., MSS. 6860-5 *passim*.
[17] Dodd, 'Salop. Agric.' 39.
[18] The earliest noticed adverts. for these crops: *Shrews. Chron.* 31 Oct. 1778; 17 Mar. 1781.
[19] Ibid. 26 June 1795; 28 June 1799.
[20] Ibid. 1 Jan. 1796.
[21] *Agric. of Salop.* 172-3.
[22] Ibid. cap. 7.
[23] Ibid. 162-9.

700 measures of mangolds and 11 a. of Swedish and Scotch turnips for sale at Shavington farmyard.[24] Both roots were to gain in popularity during the 19th century.

Elsewhere in the county other fodder crops were being tried. By the 1770s cabbages were being grown for stall feeding to cows, as Arthur Young observed at Mr. Badder's farm at the Bank, between Cruckton and Shrewsbury.[25] Subsequent newspaper advertisements attested the seedsmen's claim that 50–60 lb. specimens were attainable.[26] Vetches, mentioned c. 1800 as being used for the soiling of horses,[27] were another leguminous crop capable of improving land and being made into hay; a crop was offered for sale at Condover in 1798, the earliest noticed mention in a farm sale advertisement.[28]

The 1801 crop returns,[29] though deficient for large areas of eastern and north-west Shropshire,[30] show that turnips and rape were then being grown in appreciable quantities virtually everywhere in Shropshire. So were peas, but peas were a well established rotation crop in the county[31] and it is clear that they preponderated over turnips and rape in the south-eastern parts of the county—the hop-growing district adjoining Herefordshire and the higher, relatively backward Wheatland to the north. The largest quantities of turnips and rape were naturally grown on east Shropshire's light sandy soils, and it was there that they greatly outweighed peas in importance. Beans were recorded in only two dozen of the 141 places for which returns survive; only eight places grew 10 a. or more. Potatoes were grown in 131 of the places with extant returns and in most parts of the county. Though potatoes were useful as animal feed and a rotation crop, acreages were fairly small.[32] The largest acreages were grown conveniently near the populous areas of Shrewsbury and the east Shropshire coalfield, probably an indication of the potato's increasing use to feed the poor: 'it has been the chief means of their support', it was reported from Longford, for bread corn and butcher's meat were beyond them 'and nothing will tend more to check the exorbitancy of the farmer than attention to the cultivation of this nutritious root'.[33]

During the years 1793–1815 there was a great extension of cereal farming, notably of barley growing on the newly inclosed heaths of the north[34] and of wheat in the Wheatland of the south-east;[35] even steep former waste land, as high as 200 m. or more and in the wetter north-west, could be made to yield profitable crops of wheat and oats.[36] War and bad harvests, pushing corn prices up to unprecedented levels, were the causes.[37] By 1801 wheat (40,425 a.) was much the most important cereal crop in Shropshire, and in the south-eastern parishes, even in the hop country, it occupied very high proportions of the cereal acreage. Oats (22,520 a.) were grown widely in south Shropshire and apparently in the north-west too; in those areas they occupied the biggest proportion of the cereal acreage in areas of high land where cereal acreages were small and other grains would not do. In the northern dairying district, another area where arable acreages were

[24] *Shrews. Chron.* 21 Dec. 1832.
[25] Young, *Tours in Eng. and Wales*, 161.
[26] Hamburgh Giant cabbage seed, in 4-oz. packs costing 10s. 6d. each, was available by post from an address in Oxford St., London: *Shrews. Chron.* 30 June 1797.
[27] Plymley, *Agric. of Salop.* 173. For soiling see *Rural Cyclopedia*, ed. J. M. Wilson, iv (1849), 269–71, 587; *Eng. Dialect Dict.* ed. J. Wright, v (1904), 609.
[28] *Shrews. Chron.* 7 Sept. 1798.
[29] For this and the next para. see the Salop. figs. in *Home Office Acreage Returns Pt. II* (List and Index Soc. cxc), 178–95.

[30] The map in *T.S.A.S.* lv. 17, has some small errors but gives an accurate impression.
[31] Above.
[32] Potatoes and beans were of course a regular cottage garden crop, grown for food rather than sale: *H.O. Acreage Ret. Pt. II*, 185 sqq.
[33] Ibid. 190; below; below (Labourers and cottagers).
[34] Above (Inclosure); *T.S.A.S.* lv. 25, 27–9.
[35] Above, Physical Environment; *T.S.A.S.* lv. 2–4, 21–3; Dodd, 'Salop. Agric.' 54 (fig. 4), 139–40.
[36] *Trans. Soc. of Arts*, xxiv. 43 sqq.
[37] Ibid. 44; Dodd, 'Salop. Agric.' 21–3 and cap. 3.

THE FORDS FARM, TWYFORD, 1797

Vignette, naïve in style, of farm work in north-west Shropshire. The harvest is being got in, cart-horses watered, pigs fed, and a cow milked. The Fords (120 a.), had belonged to the Lloyds, a yeoman or minor gentry family, for generations; Samuel Lloyd owned it in 1797. The drawing is on the edge of a map.

small, oats were grown perhaps as horse feed or as a bread corn for Cheshire and Lancashire.[38] In 1801, as in earlier periods,[39] rye seems to have been grown mainly in east, central, and north Shropshire, areas where barley too was grown, though rye (probably under-recorded at 556 a.) was the least important cereal[40] and barley (23,466 a.) the second most important and increasing in importance;[41] barley was also grown in the south-west around Bishop's Castle and Hopesay.

Arable extension during the years of dearth and war, 1793–1815, greatly assisted the progress in Shropshire of that mixed farming which combined cereal growing with the keeping of sheep or cattle or both and which, because there was no general arable shrinkage in the county after 1815, was to lead eventually to the high farming of the mid 19th century.[42] Though the techniques of alternate husbandry were practised with more and more sophistication as the new root and green rotation crops spread, the story revealed by local evidence is not simple. Ford, for instance, was chiefly an arable parish in the 1790s,[43] and one of the best farmers in the area regularly grew enough potatoes to feed his livestock and, during the famine of 1799, to sell several thousand bushels for pauper consumption. In 1800 the perpetual curate campaigned for more potato growing to relieve famine, provide animal food, and prepare the soil for wheat,[44] but in 1801 only 4 a. in the parish grew potatoes.[45] The undoubted conservatism of the local farmers' attitude to the potato[46] cannot wholly explain the discontinuities of the local story. The heavy dunging which the potato required caused some prejudice against it as an 'exhausting crop',[47] but even that does not seem to explain the grassing down which appears to have been taking place. In 1801, a year of excellent harvests, a succession of disastrous crop failures with consequently high cereal prices was still a recent experience; even so in Baschurch the tillage was estimated at only one third of the average, and the perpetual curate of Ford opined that nationally the diminution of arable by grassing down more than balanced the additions made by inclosure: in his own parish and many adjoining ones he observed that 'great quantities' of land formerly growing grain had lately been converted to pasture and hop-yards, the latter engrossing the local supply of dung so that arable lands suffered from want of manure.[48] The truth seems to be that farmers were very ready to cultivate whatever seemed to promise quick profits. Hops were planted in Ditton Priors too, though with disappointing financial results, and the increasing importance of barley as a north Shropshire crop seems to have owed something to the maltsters' needs.[49] Nevertheless, in spite of local fluctuations and notwithstanding the vagueness of the available evidence,[50] there does seem to have been a steady general increase of arable. In Ford it may have tripled between 1801 and 1847[51] and the parish was by no means untypical: for example the balance was tipping in favour of arable in Wrockwardine 1801–37,[52] and at Woolstaston the arable acreage more than tripled in the last quarter of the 18th century and almost doubled again 1801–40.[53]

[38] Dodd, op. cit. 57 (fig. 10); T.S.A.S. lv. 26.
[39] Above, 1300–1540 (Demesne agriculture).
[40] Muncorn, wheat and rye grown together, was said to be the county's common bread corn (H.O. Acreage Ret. Pt. II, 186) but it brought the rye acreage to only 1,038. Perh. returns of wheat sometimes failed to mention rye growing with it: cf. ibid. 195.
[41] Dodd, 'Salop. Agric.' 149.
[42] J. P. Dodd, 'High Farming in Salop. 1845–70', Midland Hist. viii. 152.
[43] V.C.H. Salop. viii. 233.
[44] T.S.A.S. lv. 24–5.
[45] H.O. Acreage Ret. Pt. II, 180.
[46] T.S.A.S. lv. 25.
[47] Plymley, Agric. of Salop. 165; Dodd, 'Salop. Agric.' 36.
[48] H.O. Acreage Ret. Pt. II, 185, 188.
[49] Corn went to the distillers too: ibid. 187, 190; Dodd, 'Salop. Agric.' 41, 48, 58, 99–101; T.S.A.S. lv. 26–7.
[50] It seems clear e.g. that local commentators, the clergy making returns in 1801, and the later tithe surveyors had varying criteria for classifying land as arable. See e.g. R. J. P. Kain and H. C. Prince, Tithe Surveys of Eng. and Wales (1985), 195.
[51] V.C.H. Salop. viii. 233.
[52] Cf. H.O. Acreage Ret. Pt. II, 195; V.C.H. Salop. xi. 315.
[53] V.C.H. Salop. viii. 174.

With the fall in cereal prices after the end of the war some of the new arable lands seem to have been returned to grass; probably, however, they were the rougher, more marginal ones impoverished by overcropping. In fact far from there being any general post-war grassing down of arable it seems rather that tenants had often to be forbidden to replough the newly grassed marginal lands. Landlords who supervised rotations had often to prohibit tenants from ploughing up permanent pasture for, as corn prices fell after 1815, many farmers who had come to rely on corn crops for cash during the years of high prices were trying to keep up their income by extending tillage.[54]

Maintenance of the arable acreage helped to accommodate the techniques of alternate husbandry which, along with all forms of agrarian improvement,[55] were making headway in the post-war period. Already by 1820 it seems that Norfolk practices—the crop rotation and ploughing technique—were coming in,[56] even in parts of south and west Shropshire,[57] though presumably only on farms suited to it. There, by the 1830s, land lettable at only 8s. an acre was cultivated on a three-course rotation, though sometimes with two white crops in succession. It had for the most part been first cultivated after c. 1760 and some of it had paid 16s. rent during the war. It was the lowest quality land cultivable (annual rent for Shropshire arable then averaged 25s. an acre), yielding 9 bu. of wheat an acre (after a bare summer fallow) or 12–15 bu. of oats, and growing green crops and (after liming) turnips, though peas and beans only indifferently. Eight-shilling land could not be made to pay its rent but it hardly ever made up a whole farm and in the new mixed-farming systems it could contribute to the overall profitability of a farm by, for instance, providing straw for livestock.[58] By the 1840s much of the overcropped land that had had to be grassed down in the county after 1815 was evidently considered fit to be ploughed again and incorporated in a balanced system of alternate husbandry.[59]

By the 1850s unwieldy rotations had been replaced in almost all parts of the county by Norfolk or Northumberland ones of four or five courses in which no land had to endure corn crops in successive years. Nevertheless the amount of fallow ground long remained extensive, especially on the stiffer, heavier soils in the west and south-east. Bare fallows seem to have amounted to over 14 per cent of the county's arable acreage in the 1830s and to just over 7 per cent in the 1850s. It was then declining in virtually every area except the Wheatland of the south-east, to be replaced by roots—mangolds, swedes, potatoes, and turnips—on drier ground, and green crops, such as rape and vetches, where the land was wetter. Peas and beans were less frequently found and were often grown only as an alternative to a clover and rye-grass ley. By the early 1870s bare fallows accounted for little more than 4 per cent of arable. The more productive rotations and techniques, developed first on light lands, had been extended more and more generally as a result of improved methods of fertilizing and draining and the consequent extension of the growing and working seasons.[60]

The late 18th-century farmer had a range of traditional fertilizers to draw on. In the 1790s dung, highly prized, was applied to fallows or root ground at 10 cu.

[54] T. H. Thursfield, *Wenlock Farmers' Club 1842–1902* [c. 1902], 9–10 (copy in S.P.L.); Dodd, 'Salop. Agric.' 139–46, 150–1, 159; *V.C.H. Salop.* xi. 106, 225. 'Nimrod' [C. J. Apperley], *Hunting Reminiscences* (1843), 15, recalls the great extent of ploughland.
[55] C. Hulbert, *Hist. and Descr. of Salop.* ii (1837), 96–7.
[56] *V.C.H. Salop.* xi. 225; below (Motive power, tools, and mechanization).
[57] Dodd, 'Salop. Agric.' 30–1.
[58] *Rep. Sel. Cttee. on Agric.* H.C. 612, pp. 31–4 (1833), v.
[59] Thursfield, *Wenlock Farmers' Club*, 9–10.
[60] *J.R.A.S.E.* xix. 8–20, 32–8, 48–55; *V.C.H. Salop.* xi. 160; Kain and Prince, *Tithe Surveys*, 227; R. J. P. Kain, *Atlas and Index of Tithe Files of mid-19th-cent. Eng. and Wales* (1986), 298, 300, 307; *Midland Hist.* viii. 158.

yd. an acre,[61] and additional supplies were often sought to supplement the farm's own production. The street soil and night soil of towns and populous places was collected for farm land: by 1776 farmers in Petton were accustomed to buy manure from Shrewsbury, 15 km. away, at 5s. a cart load, and in Great Dawley a farmer was contracting to take the street soil away c. 1781.[62] About 1800 lime, though costing between 10s. and 12s. a wagon load (of 40–50 bu.), was used extensively on arable land, where it was usually spread at 72–80 bu. an acre.[63] Also used were soot, as a dressing for wheat (as at Benthall) and grass (as at Petton) in the 1770s,[64] and marl; the labour of digging marl, however, and the cost of its transport were persuading farmers to try lime instead, though marling was kept up around Preston Brockhurst, for example, where the soil was sandy.[65]

From the 1840s a combination of agricultural science and improved sea transport brought the farmer new alternatives in soil treatment. The experiments of a German chemist, publicized in 1840,[66] attracted attention at about the same time that J. B. Lawes began to produce superphosphate at his Deptford factory in 1843.[67] That low-cost substitute for crushed bone spread into the county early. Its presence no doubt stimulated two of Shropshire's progressive agriculturists, T. C. Eyton[68] of Donnerville and William Wolryche Whitmore of Dudmaston, into conducting their own experiments in bone-based manures: Eyton (like Lawes) tried the action of sulphuric acid on bones to make a fertilizer, reputedly costing $\frac{1}{4}d.$ a bu., for turnip crops, while Whitmore produced various artificial manures from bones and charred vegetable refuse. Both men communicated their results to the Royal Agricultural Society.[69]

Rising to popularity as a fertilizer during the same period was guano, which consisted largely of sea birds' droppings; imported from the Peruvian coast, on many Shropshire farms it provided the organic partner for superphosphates. Sir Baldwin Leighton and his father-in-law T. N. Parker, of Sweeney, saw it at the Royal Agricultural Society's Liverpool show in 1841 and Leighton then thought that, at £25 a ton, it was 'almost too high' to come into general use. Nevertheless guano's rise to popularity was swift, with national imports increasing from just 1,700 tons in 1841 to 220,000 tons only six years later.[70] During that period it had already made its way into the county,[71] where it was commonly applied to root land and as a top dressing for wheat at a rate of 2–3 cwt. an acre.[72] By 1844 African guano from Liverpool docks cost just over £9 a ton.[73] Along with guano, British ports were also admitting increasing quantities of Chilean nitrates, and, from the 1860s, German potash as the pace of the fertilizer revolution quickened.[74] Despite the undoubted benefits of the new fertilizers, farmyard manure was still highly prized, and highly spoken of, for its contribution to the rotation. Nevertheless in 1858 Tanner considered that the management of dung was generally 'too much neglected'[75] and its management and application formed the subject of a talk to

[61] Bishton, *Agric. of Salop.* 15.
[62] Young, *Tours in Eng. and Wales*, 163; *V.C.H. Salop.* xi. 126.
[63] Plymley, *Agric. of Salop.* 153, 156, 232; Young, *Tours in Eng. and Wales*, 160.
[64] Young, op. cit. 147, 166. The sowing of soot and malt dust on meadow and pasture is noted in Plymley, op. cit. 233.   [65] Young, op. cit. 162–3.
[66] J. von Liebig, both by his experiments and by his bk. *Organic Chemistry in its applications to Agriculture and Physiology*, ed. L. Playfair (1840), is generally regarded as stimulating many of the mid 19th-cent. developments in agric. science: Ernle, *Eng. Farming Past and Present*, 368–9.

[67] *D.N.B.*
[68] Compiler of the Heref. cattle herd bk.: below (Livestock breeds).
[69] *Shrews. Chron.* 23 Sept. 1836 (fm. sale); 5 Apr. 1844; 9 June 1848.
[70] *T.S.A.S.* lix. 135; Ernle, *Eng. Farming Past and Present*, 369.
[71] First noticed in a fm. sale at Ratlinghope: *Shrews. Chron.* 26 Apr. 1844.
[72] H. Tanner, 'Agric. of Salop.' *J.R.A.S.E.* xix. 13, 16, 33–4, 51.   [73] *Shrews. Chron.* 19 Apr. 1844.
[74] Chambers and Mingay, *Agric. Revolution*, 170.
[75] *J.R.A.S.E.* xix. 30.

the Wenlock Farmers' Club in 1868.[76] It was applied to green crops in the 1850s at 7–8, and to roots at 12–16, cu. yd. an acre. To supplement this home-produced fertilizer, guano and superphosphate were commonly applied by broadcasting and drilling respectively.[77]

On the heavier land the full benefit of expensively purchased new fertilizers could be realized only after draining, when root growth was no longer checked by cold waterlogged conditions. Underdraining had been practised in Shropshire since the later 18th century. At first, however, it was undertaken only by the 'gentlemen' and 'best farmers', who could afford the high costs associated with the improvement.[78] For the installation of stone drains a cost of 6d. per 8 yd. was given c. 1800.[79] Despite that, and despite the far from prosperous years that followed the peace of 1815, large drainage schemes were undertaken by, for example, the marquess of Stafford's tenants, with Cheswell Grange farm receiving 34,000 yd. of new drains in the three years before 1820.[80] William Childe of Kinlet extended his demesnes and drained his large home farm, thereafter, in the years 1817–21, applying some 15,000 cartloads of burnt clay to cold fallows (for wheat, turnips, and cabbages) and to meadow and pasture; the effects were very good and were well publicized by the Kinlet annual sale and agricultural meeting. Later the Hon. R. H. Clive carried out extensive drainage schemes on his estates around Bromfield and in lower Corve Dale, and his progress was regularly reported to the Royal Agricultural Society in the late 1830s and early 1840s.[81] By 1843 Sir Francis Lawley too had achieved much in the way of draining on his Bourton estate near Much Wenlock.[82]

Most of the heavy land in need of draining was incapable of benefiting from the timber- or stone-filled drains which were liable either to collapse or to become clogged and eventually to require attention. During the 1840s, however, and contemporaneously with the changes in the use of fertilizer, there came a new era of underdrainage. In 1843 a cylindrical clay land-drainage pipe was produced, and two years later a pipe-making machine was patented that enabled its large-scale manufacture.[83] In 1846, moreover, the government introduced drainage loans at the cheap rate of 3½ per cent and repayable over 22 years.[84] In such a technical and financial climate much of the county's heavier land was improved. Subsoiling was similarly encouraged by local interest groups including the Shropshire Agricultural Society, which the Hon. R. H. Clive addressed on the subject in 1844; it was then claimed that subsoiling could be satisfactorily achieved with 4–6 horses.[85] By the late 1850s tile and pipe drains, 3–4 ft. in depth, were to be found in most areas of the county.[86]

The seeds sown in the enriched and drained soil were increasingly identified by name from the 1850s and so enabled the discerning farmer to select the strain that performed best on his land. Not surprisingly optimum yields of wheat and barley climbed during the period. In 1776 Arthur Young was told of a wheat sowing at Petton of 2½ bu. an acre that realized a crop of 20 bu. and of a barley sowing of 3 bu. an acre that yielded 30 bu.[87] Those yields were perhaps high for the time. In

[76] *Shrews. Chron.* 1 May 1868.

[77] *J.R.A.S.E.* xix. 9, 12–13, 33, 48, 51.

[78] Young, *Tours in Eng. and Wales*, 163; Plymley, *Agric. of Salop.* 228.   [79] Plymley, op. cit. 229.

[80] J. Loch, *Acct. of Improvements on Estates of Marquess of Stafford* (1820), App. IX, pp. 89–90.

[81] S.P.L., Salop. Miscellanea, v (accession 2757), pp. 6–14; *J.R.A.S.E.* i. 33–7, 248–52; ii. 346–53; iv. 172–6.

[82] *Eddowes's Jnl.* 21 June 1843.

[83] Ernle, *Eng. Farming Past and Present*, 367.

[84] Chambers and Mingay, *Agric. Revolution*, 176–7.

[85] *Shrews. Chron.* 11 Oct. 1844; cf. *Midland Hist.* viii. 157.   [86] *J.R.A.S.E.* xix. 31, 44–5, 61–2.

[87] *Tours in Eng. and Wales*, 162. Young's figs., reported here, are actually expressed as 9½-gallon strikes—near enough perh. to the (8-gallon) Winchester bushel to permit comparison with later bushel figs. For variations in the strike see R. E. Zupko, *Dict. of Eng. Weights and Measures* (1968), s.v.

1801, a year of exceptionally good harvest, wheat seems to have yielded on average some 16½ bu. an acre, perhaps rather more in the north and rather less in the south, though the best yield (21 bu. an acre) was recorded at Sidbury in the south-eastern Wheatland. Barley yields averaged *c.* 19 bu. an acre that year, once again more in the north and less in the south.[88] In 1858 Tanner found the wheat yield to vary in the county's different regions: 22–24 bu. an acre in the Wheatland and 25–30 bu. in Corve Dale (30–36 bu. in a season of ideal weather) for a sowing of 2–2½ bu., and 35 bu. average on the best parts of the rest of the county, though 40-bu. crops were known on the best land and rare 48-bu. crops had been recorded. William Childe claimed that his improvements to Kinlet home farm produced 46 bu. of wheat an acre in 1820 on some land that had never before yielded more than 16. Nowhere, however, could the county match the 40–48 bu. averages of eastern England. Barley yields seem to have risen less, though with similar regional variations, and it is perhaps significant that Tanner recorded insufficient attention to a change of seed. In the late 1850s 30 bu. an acre was produced in the Wheatland and western Shropshire, 30–35 bu. in Corve Dale (40 bu. in a dry season), and 35–45 bu. in north and east Shropshire from sowings of 2½–3 bu.[89]

Increased cereal yields were an important result of the revolution in agricultural techniques, at first for the increased profits realized from cash crops but later for the part they played in the 'high feeding' of livestock. In the later 1850s, after the end of the Crimean War, wheat prices began steadily to fall.[90] Meanwhile, from the 1840s, 'high farming' was increasingly seen as the substitute for protection.[91] It was a mixed-farming regime of alternate husbandry and high feeding; it aimed at maximum soil fertility and productivity; and it implied the efficient management of manure and regular use of the new, purchased, fertilizers and of the new feeds— oil cake, for example, besides roots and green crops grown on the farm. Where the system was most consistently employed some redesign of farmyard might be necessary, partly for reasons of general efficiency[92] and partly (in some instances) to achieve covered feeding and so avoid waste of manure: the latter, however, as some critics alleged, might involve unacceptably high capital and labour costs.

Model farm buildings in England, apt symbols of the revolution in agricultural practices, are found most thickly in the eastern grain-growing counties and on the large estates of the north.[93] Central and eastern Shropshire, however, contain many early examples, though improvements to farm buildings were by no means confined to those areas. Elegant Gothick farms were built at Stoke upon Tern (Woodhouse Farm 1754–6) and Acton Scott (Home Farm 1769), and in 1782 a classical farmhouse was built at Boreton, in Condover. At Kilsall, where John Bishton farmed, new farm offices and cattle sheds were built *c.* 1790.[94] Most notable of all was the rebuilding campaign of 1811–22 on the marquess of Stafford's Lilleshall estate, directed by James Loch and financed by the Bridgwater fortune. At an average cost of £1,500–£1,600, 14 farmsteads were rebuilt in the parishes of Lilleshall, Edgmond, Ercall Magna, Longdon upon Tern, Longford, and Sheriffhales. Plain neo-classical farmhouses stand beside highly organized, logically

[88] Yields (but no sowing rates) given in *H.O. Acreage Ret. Pt. II,* 185–9, 191–3. The rector of Willey considered the 1801 harvest ⅓ greater than the previous yr.'s (ibid. 194), a fairly typical view.

[89] *J.R.A.S.E.* xix. 16, 20, 36–7, 53–5; *Shrews. Chron.* 2 Nov. 1821 (letter of Wm. Childe); cf. Kain, *Atlas and Index of Tithe Files,* 300, for crop yields *c.* 1836.

[90] Dodd, 'Salop. Agric.' 231 sqq.

[91] As the title of Jas. Caird's bk. attests: *High Farming*

under *Liberal Covenants the best substitute for Protection* (1849). For this para. generally see Chambers and Mingay, *Agric. Rev.* 170 sqq.; Dodd, 'Salop. Agric.' cap. 7; *Midland Hist.* viii. 148–68.

[92] Mechanization of threshing, for example, might affect fm. plans, esp. the size and siting of the barn: J. M. Robinson, *Georgian Model Farms* (1983), 82 sqq.

[93] Ibid. 15–16.

[94] Ibid. 113, 117, 129, 146.

PLAN & ELEVATION OF A HOUSE AND FARM OFFICES,

at the *DAYHOUSE* Erected 1812-3.

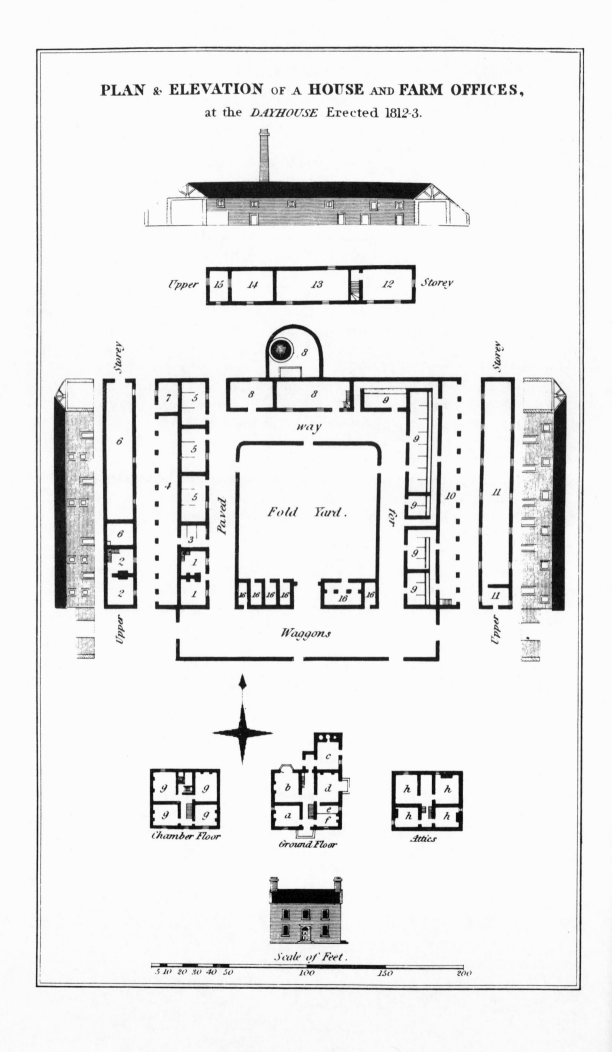

Chamber Floor.   Ground Floor.   Attics.

Scale of Feet.

planned farmyards, practical and utilitarian in conception[95] and without decoration or disguise[96] of any kind. Such plain improvements characterized the whole period. In 1786–7 Sir Robert Leighton was putting up new farm buildings in Alberbury and Cardeston. New barns, stables, cart houses, granaries, cow and calf houses, pigsties, and drift houses[97] were erected. Sometimes the work was done on a contract between the landlord and the builder; then the farmer seems to have paid extra rent as an interest charge on the investment. Sometimes the farmer contracted to have the work done for a corresponding rent reduction.[98] Similarly farmhouses and outbuildings were being improved or newly erected by Sir Francis Lawley on his Bourton estate c. 1840, by Sir Baldwin Leighton on the Loton and Sweeney estates, and by Lord Powis at Montford, where the 1st Lord Clive had reorganized the farm boundaries.[99] Later Sir C. H. Rouse-Boughton was building on his estates in the south: the outbuildings (but not the house) of Crowleasows farm, Middleton, for example, bear the date 1863 and the landlord's initials; about the same time Rouse-Boughton also rebuilt others, such as Upper Wood Farm, Hopton Cangeford.[1]

High farming in the county, the local culmination of the Agricultural Revolution, may be considered, merely technically, as a mixed-farming regime based on high feeding and aimed at maximizing the productivity of the farm.[2] James Caird, however, saw high farming in starker financial terms—as high capital investment to achieve high productivity,[3] and there was much to invest in: inclosure, fencing, draining, fertilizers, feedstuffs, new buildings,[4] and new tools and machines.[5] Did high farming repay the necessary investment? The question is as difficult to answer for Shropshire as it is generally. Few Shropshire families have left accounts sufficiently revealing to give the complete financial background to their agricultural holdings and enterprises. Estate accounts alone rarely give a full account of the sources of investment in agriculture or the destination of agricultural profits. The

[95] Ibid. 8, 13, 26–7, 130–1, 141–2. Stafford's agent (Loch) and steward supervised the est. architect's designs very closely.
[96] So much deplored by Plymley: *Agric. of Salop.* 109–10.
[97] Covered way out of fm. yd. for loaded wagons: G. F. Jackson, *Salop. Word-Bk.* (1879), 126.
[98] Loton Hall MSS., bdle. of Sir Rob. Leighton's fm. bldg. agreements 1786–7.
[99] *Eddowes's Jnl.* 21 June 1843; *T.S.A.S.* lix. 139, 144;

Loton Hall, Lady Leighton's album; R. A. D. Cameron and D. J. Pannett, 'Hedgerow Shrubs and Landscape Hist.' *Field Studies,* v. 179–80; inf. from Mr. Pannett, who is thanked for making his unpublished wk. on Montford available.
[1] S.R.O. 99/1, pp. 9–10 (no. 46); inf. from Mr. G. E. Morgan, Crowleasows Fm.
[2] Above.
[3] Chambers and Mingay, *Agric. Revolution,* 183–4.
[4] Above (Inclosure); above.
[5] Below (Motive power, tools, and mechanization).

DAY HOUSE FARM, CHERRINGTON (*opposite*)

One of the numerous farms rebuilt on the marquess of Stafford's estate in the early 19th century. The courtyard farm, with its central fold yard and steam powered machinery, then typified modern farm design.

1 Men servants' day rooms
2 Men sevants' sleeping rooms
3 Hackney stable
4 Implement shed
5 Wagon horse stable
6 Hay loft
7 Tool house
8 Barn and steam engine
9 Feeding and cow tyings
10 Turnip house
11 Great granary and pay room, used for the annual agricultural dinner given by Lord Stafford
12 Small granary
13 Corn loft
14, 15 Straw lofts
16 Pig sties, hen houses over

a Parlour
b Family room
c Brewhouse
d Kitchen
e Pantry
f Milk house
g Bedrooms
h Attics

Leveson-Gowers' records are exceptionally abundant[6] and there were other Shropshire landlords who, like them, had substantial surplus incomes from non-agricultural sources which they could invest in their land, as the Hon. R. H. Clive did in his Oakly Park estate. Among them, naturally, were some of the families new to landowning, such as the Fosters of Apley Park or the Wrights of Halston, with fortunes made in industry or commerce. Their position, however, by no means resembled that of many of the heavily encumbered Shropshire squires, and their motives for high investment were often in part social as much as financial: high farming was prestigious[7] and men who invested lavishly, like W. O. Foster on his Apley Park estate,[8] doubtless aimed at making a big impression, in his case on the landed gentry whose ranks he had just joined. Apley was over-priced when Foster bought it in 1867 and its capital value fell over the next thirty years. Foster, like the dukes of Sutherland, could have earned a greater income from his capital had he invested it judiciously in stocks or the funds, but a generation was yet to pass before landownership lost its social mystique.[9]

The 2nd Lord Hill (d. 1875) was well known as an agriculturist and was a successful breeder on the scale that required commitment of capital, but his Hawkstone estate was run without financial control or discipline, a state of affairs in which high-farming investment was likely to be burdensome rather than beneficial. By contrast his kinsman the 5th Lord Berwick, living inexpensively and in strict retirement from society, probably made his farming enterprises pay: certainly the investment which built up his celebrated herd of Herefords[10] enabled him eventually to export stock to France, the U.S.A., and Australia. Men with less capital, many of them tenant farmers, built up renowned flocks of Shropshires, in which there was also a vigorous export trade. The answer to the question 'Did high farming pay?' seems to be trite: investment paid where financial control was strict, as it was, to take a landlord as example, on Sir Baldwin Leighton's Loton Park estate.[11] Among the Shropshire tenantry, who also had an investment in the success of high farming, enterprising skills and financial discipline were equally important and seem, in the thirty or so years after the repeal of the corn laws, to have brought them the rewards of higher profits and an improved standard of life.

Motive power, tools, and mechanization

The decades around 1800 marked the eclipse of the working ox by the more intelligent and versatile horse. Until the mid 18th century ploughing with 5 yoked pairs of oxen had been a regular sight.[12] The size of team had been commonly reduced to 3 pairs by the 1770s[13] and to 5 oxen, working in line and wearing horse gears, by the early 1800s. Some farmers preferred a team of 4 oxen with a horse to lead them,[14] and by the time that the Shropshire General Agricultural Society offered a prize for working oxen in 1816 the specified size of the team had been further reduced to 4.[15]

---

[6] J. R. Wordie, 'Rent Movements and the Eng. Tenant Farmer, 1700–1839', *Research in Econ. Hist.* vi. 194–5, 215, 237–8; E. Richards, 'Anatomy of Sutherland Fortune: Income, Consumption, Investments and Returns 1780–1880', *Business Hist.* xxi. 45–78. For the rest of this section see Dodd, 'Salop. Agric.' cap. 9; cf. Chambers and Mingay, *Agric. Revolution*, 176–7.　　　　[7] Dodd, op. cit. 225.
[8] *T.S.A.S.* lix. 145.
[9] Loton Hall MSS., Sir B. Leighton's diary 17 Jan. 1870; N. Mutton, 'The Foster Fam.: Study of a Midlands Industrial Dynasty 1786–1899' (London Univ. Ph.D. thesis, 1974), 213–14, 216.
[10] Below (Livestock breeds, Large estates).
[11] Loton Hall MSS., Sir B. Leighton's diary *passim*; cf. *T.S.A.S.* lix. 134–43; *V.C.H. Salop.* iii. 140, 150–1.
[12] Plymley, *Agric. of Salop.* 264, referring to 18th-cent. practice.
[13] Young, *Tours in Eng. and Wales*, 147.
[14] Plymley, op. cit. 264.
[15] *Shrews. Chron.* 26 July 1816.

JOHN COTES OF WOODCOTE, M.P. (d. 1821)
Agriculturist, advocate of potato cultivation, and founder member of Shifnal Agricultural Society.
Beside him, presumably, is his agent or bailiff. The labourers are adjusting a swing plough, and the
horses wear tall leather housen on their collars to keep rain off their withers.

HEREFORD-TYPE CATTLE AT BUILDWAS ABBEY, 1841
The painting probably shows Thomas Jones, outgoing tenant of Abbey Farm (390 a.), and his
landlord Walter Moseley (d. 1850). The red-bodied cattle are probably Herefords, but the herd book
first appeared only in 1845.

TWIN WHITE OXEN

A pair owned by James Ackers, M.P., of Heath House near Leintwardine, painted by William Gwynn of Ludlow in 1845. A few working oxen were then still to be found in Shropshire, but Ackers probably kept these for show.

A SHROPSHIRE PIG

William Gwynn's picture of a Berkshire cross owned by Sir C. W. Rouse-Boughton, Bt. (d. 1821), of Downton Hall. The 20-month-old pig weighed 33 score 15 lb., just over 6 cwt.

Reductions in the size of ploughteams were made possible by improvements in technology and in plough design. Those developments, however, only hastened the ox's demise. Though the ox was considered to thrive on poorer quality food and provided a more useful carcass than its equine rival, and despite the reputed difficulty of shoeing the latter, the balance of advantage tipped from the ox to the horse, for the ox was unable to tackle a range of the newly mechanized farm tasks. Apart from ploughing, the ox's only commonly recorded duty was wagon haulage, although that use of oxen was never as common as in the southern counties of England.[16]

The speed of the ox's decline was not uniform throughout Shropshire; in 1776 Arthur Young reported that oxen were 'commonly used' in the Benthall area, although, if a second team was kept, it was a horse team. Around Cruckton, farther west, many oxen had been used some years before but there were 'scarce any' then; in the north, around Petton, there were 'very few'.[17] Several instances of the ox's survival into the 19th century were on large estates or in the hands of keen advocates of a particular breed. For instance Farmer Flavel used them at Alberbury, on the Loton estate, c. 1800.[18] William Childe of Kinlet regularly included working Devon bullocks in his annual stock sales until his death in 1824,[19] while at Shrawardine Castle 2 teams of 5 oxen were introduced in the late 1820s. They were regarded as something of a novelty, being Indian cross-bred stock, and remained there until 1835;[20] they may well have been the half-bred oxen advertised for sale at Montford on Lord Powis's behalf in 1836.[21] Finally the 5th Lord Berwick, who took a number of prizes for Hereford cattle in the Royal Agricultural Society's shows, was still breeding oxen for sale in 1860, when he entered two 3-year-old draught oxen in W. G. Preece's fatstock sale.[22] By the later 1860s draught oxen were probably unknown in Shropshire.[23]

The horses of the early 19th century were a disparate collection. Stallions of the 'cart breed' were kept, but their breeding was indifferent: they were small, hardy, and useful for work but lacking consistency and conformation.[24] Such inattention to breeding seems odd in a county that was all but pre-eminent in the breeding of hunters,[25] but even that distinction was lost during the 19th century. In 1853 R. A. Slaney expressed the hope that Shropshire horse breeding would regain its former eminence, but there was a great lack of good thoroughbreds to cover inexpensively for the farmers. That lack, and Shropshire's decline as a breeding county, continued beyond the end of the period[26] and working stock with any claim to a recognized pedigree, such as the Suffolk Punches in William Childe's annual Kinlet sale of 1808,[27] remained a rarity until the last quarter of the 19th century.

Initially the horses were harnessed in line, with 4 or 5 commonly being used to haul a single-furrow plough: in 1776 Arthur Young found that to be common practice on the farms he visited in Shropshire.[28] Three quarters of a century later Tanner reported that a similar practice still prevailed in parts of south-eastern Shropshire, although he explained that it was often used as a means of exercising

[16] Plymley, op. cit. 264–5.
[17] Young, *Tours in Eng. and Wales*, 147, 157, 164.
[18] *T.S.A.S.* lix. 140; cf. *V.C.H. Salop.* viii. 189, 209.
[19] See e.g. adverts. in *Shrews. Chron.* 11 Sept. 1812; 15 Sept. 1820.
[20] *Bye-Gones*, 25 Mar. 1903.
[21] *Shrews. Chron.* 11 Mar. 1836. Powis (then Ld. Clive) had been in India 1798–1803: cf. *D.N.B.*; *V.C.H. Salop.* iii. 131.
[22] *Shrews. Chron.* 8 June 1860.

[23] *T.S.A.S.* lix. 140.
[24] Plymley, *Agric. of Salop.* 262–4.
[25] Only Yorks. bred better hunters acc. to 'Nimrod' [C. J. Apperley], *Hunting Reminiscences* (1843), 5–6.
[26] *Eddowes's Jnl.* 19 Oct. 1853; Earl Cathcart, 'Half-bred Horses for Field or Road: their Breeding and Management', *J.R.A.S.E.* 2nd ser. xix. 30 sqq.
[27] *Shrews. Chron.* 26 Aug. 1808.
[28] *Tours in Eng. and Wales*, 147, 157, 164.

animals normally held in reserve for the busier periods.[29] Many farmers on heavier land had by that time progressed to ploughing with only two horses abreast, a Norfolk practice.[30] Colts were introduced to work at 4, sometimes 3, years old, and many would leave the farm for the town or manufacturing district before their sixth year. That remunerative trade, which in the late 1850s brought the farmer between £40 and £50 for each good horse,[31] was to grow steadily throughout the late Victorian age as more attention was paid to selective breeding.

In addition to haulage, horses were also used on Shropshire farms to operate horse engines or horse works, and thus to power a widening range of barn machinery. In the early 19th century horse engines were often large, cumbersome structures with the main wheel positioned above the working horses. They were generally used to drive the early designs of threshing machine that would take up to 4 horses to operate.[32] By the mid century more sophisticated, ground-level engines were available in a portable form. They typically used 2 horses: one in 1865 retailed at 11 guineas and powered root cutter, corn mill, and chaff cutter.[33]

With the popularity from the mid 19th century of the larger designs of portable thresher came an increased demand for steam engines to provide the required power. Although the smaller fixed engines of 3 and 4 hp continued to have a limited role,[34] it was the portable engine of between 6 and 12 hp that met the demands of the threshing machine and the ancillary equipment. Numbers of portable engines were brought into the county during the later 19th century (the Lincoln firm of Clayton & Shuttleworth, for example, contributed nearly a hundred between 1852 and 1880)[35] and a flourishing market in second-hand engines also developed.[36]

The use of steam power for ploughing and cultivation in the county was less popular. Never endowed with a large arable acreage on terrain suitable for steam ploughing, Shropshire was not to witness the complexities of the technique on a widespread scale. The high cost of the necessary engines and ancillary equipment made such a use of steam beyond the means of all but the wealthiest. During the mid 1860s companies were established at Whitchurch,[37] Market Drayton,[38] and Shrewsbury[39] to provide steam ploughing facilities for the interested farmer. Nevertheless the failure of that use of steam power to match the success of the threshing contractors is symbolized in the brief existence of the Shrewsbury company which was liquidated in 1868, a little over four years after its foundation; the company's equipment, to be auctioned in the Smithfield, included a Howard's patent double-action steam cultivator and a set of Howard's patent steam harrows as well as Garrett winding engines and Howard's patent double-action four-furrow plough. Steam ploughs were still a novelty in Shropshire in the mid 1860s.[40]

[29] H. Tanner, 'Agric. of Salop.' *J.R.A.S.E.* xix. 29.

[30] J. Loch, *Acct. of Improvements on Estates of Marquess of Stafford* (1820), App. IX, pp. 86, 88; *V.C.H. Salop.* xi. 160.

[31] *J.R.A.S.E.* xix. 29. In some of the industrial parts of the county there was a long tradition of rearing horses for industrial wk.: *V.C.H. Salop.* xi. 118.

[32] e.g. a 4-hp threshing machine advertised for auction at the Hill, Cheswardine, and a 4-hp threshing machine and kibbling mill for sale at Aston Pigott: *Shrews. Chron.* 20 Mar., 15 May 1812.

[33] Bentall's of Maldon 1865 cat. p. 29 (copy in Inst. of Agric. Hist. and Mus. of Eng. Rural Life, Reading Univ.).

[34] In 1872 e.g. a 3-hp horizontal engine (an early design) was offered for auction at J. Edwards's fm., Eyton upon the Weald Moors, and Thos. Everall, of Halford, advertised a vertical engine of similar size: *Shrews. Chron.* 1 and 29 Mar. 1872.

[35] Inst. of Agric. Hist. and Mus. of Eng. Rural Life, Reading Univ., rec. of Clayton & Shuttleworth; cf. *V.C.H. Lincs.* ii. 395.

[36] e.g. Brown & Lock, engineers, Smithfield Ironwks., Shrews., advertised 2 second-hand steam engines at £140 and £100 in *Shrews. Chron.* 1 Jan. 1868.

[37] Whitchurch Steam Ploughing, Cultivating & Thrashing Co. Ltd., inc. 1864: P.R.O., BT 31/895/989c.

[38] Mkt. Drayton Steam Ploughing, Cultivating & Thrashing Co. Ltd., inc. 1865: P.R.O., BT 31/1079/1997c.

[39] Shrews. Steam Cultivation Soc. (later Shrews. Steam Cultivation Co. Ltd.), est. 1864: *Shrews. Chron.* 8 Jan. 1864.

[40] Ibid. 26 June 1868; Loton Hall MSS., Sir B. Leighton's diary 11 Sept. 1865.

The tools and implements owned by the Shropshire farmer of the mid 18th century did not vary significantly from those of his ancestors. Most originated in the workshops of the village blacksmith and wheelwright and combined traditions, local preferences, and sturdy workmanship in an object usually well designed for its simple task. The transmission of new ideas on the design and construction of tools was as slow to reach the county as were the improved communications that were to bring the mass produced implements of the mid 19th century, and for the first decades of the period Shropshire farmers continued in their well trodden paths. A valuable indicator of the rate of progress of new technology is provided by advertisements for dispersal sales of farm stock and implements in the local press.[41] Such advertisements, entered by local auctioneers, would naturally list those larger or more modern items that would draw more people to a sale. Their appearance in quantity in such a prominent county paper as the *Shrewsbury Chronicle* provides a source from 1772 with a good coverage of most classes of farmer throughout the whole county.[42]

In addition to the plethora of hand tools on the late 18th-century farm—hay rakes, pitchforks, flails, shovels, spades, and wheelbarrows—the vast majority of dispersal sales specified ploughs, rollers, and harrows. Originally the ploughs were locally produced from wood, with iron used only for share and coulter. Ploughs of all-iron construction were not offered in farm sales until the 1840s[43] and in 1858 Tanner mentioned the Wheatland farmer's reluctance to buy new ploughs to replace the traditionally made wooden ones.[44] Swing ploughs were initially widespread, but as craftsmanship improved so the wheeled versions were favoured. Plymley referred to the use of double-furrow ploughs at the turn of the century, although he regarded single-wheel ploughs as more widespread.[45] Sophisticated mole ploughs were less common, although one early example was being sold from Stanton Lacy in 1812 and a hollow drain plough of Yorkshire origin was advertised in the local press the same year.[46]

Other implements on farms of most sizes were rollers and harrows of various sizes and types. Being of more straightforward construction than the plough they were produced in iron at an earlier date; cast-iron rollers, for example, were advertised as early as the 1780s: William Waller, of Chetwynd Hall, had one 26 in. in diameter in 1781[47] and Abraham Darby (III) had another large one at the Hay, Madeley, when he died in 1789.[48] Nevertheless simple tree-trunk rollers presumably continued in use alongside their cast-iron counterparts, and wooden-beamed harrows similarly persisted. Consistently appearing and described in farm sales were the various wooden vehicles, carts, and tumbrils.

The first significant mechanization came with new methods of threshing and winnowing corn. That winter activity centred on the barn where the hinged wooden flail was used to knock the corn from the straw lying on the threshing floor. The winnowing of the newly threshed corn depended on a convenient wind blowing through the barn to remove the chaff and husk from the grain. The unreliability of such a draught encouraged the development of the winnowing fan, comprising sails fitted to four or more radial arms resting on a stand and revolved by hand to

[41] See e.g. P. Perry, 'Source for Agric. Hist.—Newspaper Adverts.' *Local Historian*, ix. 334–7; *Change in the Country-side: essays on rural Eng. 1500–1900*, ed. H. S. A. Fox and R. A. Butlin (Inst. Brit. Geographers Special Publn. x; 1979), 23–42.
[42] A sample (2,358) of fm. sale notices was taken from *Shrews. Chron.* 1772–1880.
[43] e.g. *Shrews. Chron.* 10 Jan. 1840 (Geo. Davies of Lythwood offering '4 iron ploughs'); 9 Feb. 1844 (Edw. Steedman of High Ercall offering '10 iron and wood ploughs'). [44] *J.R.A.S.E.* xix. 29.
[45] Plymley, *Agric. of Salop.* 141.
[46] *Shrews. Chron.* 3 May, 25 Sept. 1812.
[47] Ibid. 19 May 1781. [48] Ibid. 5 May 1789.

create an artificial wind. In Shropshire over 20 per cent of early 19th-century farm sales, where implements were listed, included a fan in their inventory (Fig. 13). The number of fans on farms declined with the advent of the more complex winnowing machine, a box-like contrivance of shakers and screens that ensured a cleaner grain; it was initially hand powered. With remarkably little alteration to its basic design it became widely adopted and was to be found at over 60 per cent of farm sales until the 1870s.

If the developments in winnowing were welcomed by the labourers, the advent of the threshing machine was not always similarly appreciated. It is easy, however, to understand their disquiet when even a small machine at the beginning of the century was reputed to thresh 5 sheaves a minute.[49] Mechanical threshing was seen by some rural workers as depriving them of much-needed winter work, although there is little evidence that Shropshire labourers protested in the organized manner of their fellows in southern England: some stacks were fired in 1831-2, but the fires were almost entirely in the Whitchurch area and motivated partly by political feeling against the Hills after John Mytton's withdrawal from the county election in 1831 and partly by personal animosity for one or two farmers.[50] The threshing machine developed into one of the most complex pieces of apparatus on the Victorian farm. George Ashdown believed that his father, who had farmed in the Hopesay district, had introduced the first threshing machine thereabouts in 1790, and there were several in the county c. 1800;[51] probably they, like others of

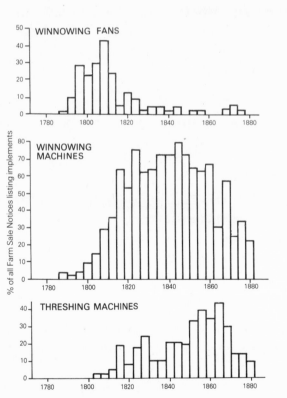

Fig. 13: ADOPTION OF WINNOWING AND PROCESSING MACHINERY 1772–1880

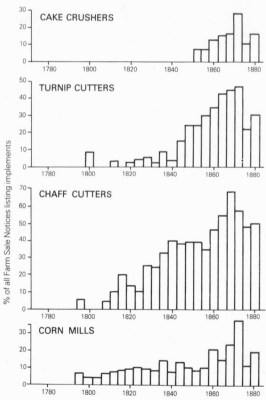

Fig. 14: ADOPTION OF BARN AND PROCESSING MACHINERY 1772–1880

Based on a sample of 2,358 farm sale notices in *Shrews. Chron.* 1772–1880.

[49] Advert. for threshing machine patent from John Palmer, Maxstoke (Warws.): ibid. 16 Nov. 1804.
[50] *Salopian Jnl.* 2 Feb., 4 Apr., 14 Sept. 1831; 21 Mar., 4 Apr. 1832; Kain and Prince, *Tithe Surveys*, 27; *Rep. Sel. Cttee. on Agric.* H.C. 612, p. 288 (1833), v; *V.C.H. Salop.* iii. 263-4.
[51] Kain, *Atlas and Index of Tithe Files*, 297; Plymley, *Agric. of Salop.* 141.

the period, were fixed installations in farm buildings. Early hand-powered machines gradually gave way to larger machines powered by water or horses. In 1820, for example, James Loch cited examples of irrigation streams being used to drive threshing machines at Lilleshall Grange and Honnington Grange on the Leveson-Gower estates.[52] Nevertheless the majority of the early examples of the machine advertised in the *Shrewsbury Chronicle* required 3–4 horses working a horse engine to provide the necessary power.[53]

A threshing machine cut the wages bill but required considerable capital: in 1812 a portable thresher, made by William Martin of Bedale (Yorks. N.R.) and powered by two horses, was advertised at 40 guineas.[54] The development of the portable machine enabled several farmers to share the cost or a contractor to serve a group of farms. By 1812 machines were being manufactured locally: seven were sold at Hazeldine, Rastrick & Co.'s works at Bridgnorth; each needed four horses to pull it.[55] Initially the portable machines used horses for power, but as the 19th century progressed they became ideal partners for the early portable steam engines which Tanner called 'frequent' in 1858, adding—with reference to his own district, the Wheatland—that most corn was threshed in that way.[56] With the advent of steam from the 1860s the necessary investment meant that more contractors sprang up. As a consequence the numbers of threshing and winnowing machines at farm dispersal sales fell back to the levels prevailing earlier in the century.

Winnowers and threshing machines were not the only mechanical inhabitants of Shropshire barns. During the earlier 19th century agricultural engineers developed machinery to process a widening range of stock food. Frequently such barn machinery was able to use the same source of power as the threshing machines, so adding to its popularity with cost-conscious farmers.

Cutting straw into chaff for feeding livestock had long been practised in the county[57] and was a natural candidate for mechanization (Fig. 14). Straw engines, or chaff cutters, were already on farms by 1796, although those with the wheel-mounted knives that were to become customary were probably not sold until 1812.[58] Large numbers were later brought to the county from works as far apart as Manchester (Richmond & Chandler) and Ipswich (Ransomes) to be sold through their local agents. Turnip cutters, common once the feeding of roots to stock had been popularized, came largely from Gardners (later Samuelsons) of Banbury.[59]

At the time when the expanding railway network might have helped the import of machinery from other counties, Shropshire began the manufacture of implements. Of several manufacturers in the county the most successful was Thomas Corbett of Shrewsbury.[60] Corbett's products included winnowers, oil-cake breakers, and other barn machinery. The son of Samuel Corbett, a Wellington agricultural engineer, Thomas began his career in 1863 as manager of the Samuelson Implement Depot in Shrewsbury. Four years later he had taken his own workshop in Chester Street, where he produced the 'Eclipse' winnower. It was awarded second prize at the Bury St. Edmunds meeting of the Royal Agricultural Society[61] and created a sound start to Corbett's venture.

In 1868 Corbett bought land in Castle Foregate for his Perseverance Ironworks

---

[52] Loch, *Acct. of Improvements*, App. IX, pp. 85, 88.
[53] *Shrews. Chron.* adverts. for fm. sales 1804–24.
[54] Ibid. 25 Sept. 1812. [55] Ibid. 28 Feb. 1812.
[56] *J.R.A.S.E.* xix. 29.
[57] Young, *Tours in Eng. and Wales*, 147, 157, 164.
[58] One 'worked with a wheel' was offered for sale at the Hill, Cheswardine, in 1812: *Shrews. Chron.* 20 Mar. 1812.

[59] Cf. *V.C.H. Oxon.* x. 66. Samuelsons took Gardners over in 1849: ibid. ii. 268–9; x. 66–7; B. Trinder, *Victorian Banbury* (1982), 34, 82 sqq.
[60] For the rest of this para. and the next see *Shrews. Chron.* 29 Dec. 1876, p. 7; *Implement Manufacturers' Rev.* iii (1877), 1287–8; *V.C.H. Salop.* i. 476–7; xi. 229–30.
[61] *J.R.A.S.E.* 2nd ser. iii, p. lxxiii.

which, in its final state, was the largest works of its type in the west midlands. His success can be attributed as much to his design and creation of a self-contained factory to provide both castings and wooden components as to his vigorous export drive. As a result of the oversea promotion and exhibition of the firm's products in most west European countries over 400 first prizes had been gained by the end of 1876, and Corbett's ploughs, horse hoes, drills, and rollers were in widespread use both at home and abroad.

An oil-cake breaking machine was in use on Lilleshall home farm as early as 1830[62] and improved designs followed in the next decade. Fragments of the residue following the extraction of the oil from linseed and rape seed had long been used as a manure. When those residues began to be used as a highly nutritious livestock food, a strong crushing machine was required to break the large slabs into edible pieces. The first prize to be offered by the Royal Agricultural Society for such a machine was won at the Shrewsbury meeting of 1845 by Alexander Dean of Birmingham.[63] By the early 1850s oil-cake breakers were being advertised at farm sales. Given the initially high price associated with an unproven product, it was often the landowner or gentleman farmer, relatively well read and widely travelled, who introduced an innovation to an area; that was the pattern with cake-breakers, where three of the first four advertised for sale were the property of titled owners, Lord Liverpool,[64] the duke of Sutherland,[65] and Lord Granville.[66]

While designs of barn machinery were developed promptly to meet the demands of the farms and the crops to be processed, the evolution of the seed drill was an altogether lengthier affair. The subject of experiment by the close of the 17th century and publicized by one of its chief advocates in 1731,[67] it was nevertheless a rarity in the county until after 1825 (Fig. 15). Time-honoured methods of broadcasting seed remained normal on Shropshire farms, despite 18th-century advertisements in the local press urging the benefits of the drill technique: James Cooke, for example, who patented a seed drill in 1788, published a booklet on drill husbandry which was advertised in the county paper and claimed that his drill enabled a man, a boy, and one or two horses to sow 8 a. a day.[68] As late as 1820 James Loch regarded use of a seed drill on the marquess of Stafford's Shropshire estates as worthy of special comment[69] along with its ally in row cultivation, the horse hoe. By that time seed drills had eventually begun to appear in the farm sales advertisements in the local press. Initially drills for sowing turnips and other root crops were the most widespread (Fig. 15), although as the century progressed corn drills of the Suffolk type appeared more regularly. Commonly specified makes included Garrett of Leiston and Smyth of Peasenhall. Smyth was producing drills as early as 1800 and supplied over 180 to Shropshire customers between 1838 and 1871.[70] The company expanded steadily, with members of the Smyth family leaving their Suffolk base to establish similar concerns elsewhere. A son-in-law of the Smyths, Woodgate Gower, went to Hook (Hants), and one of his sons was established as an agricultural engineer in Market Drayton by 1850. During the 1860s he was sufficiently well established to challenge the East Anglian makers for a share of his local market.[71]

[62] *Midland Hist.* viii. 158.   [63] *J.R.A.S.E.* vi. 306.
[64] Pitchford Hall: *Shrews. Chron.* 12 Mar. 1852.
[65] New Lodge Fm., Lilleshall: ibid. 26 Mar. 1852.
[66] Croft Fm., Morville, on the est. of his stepson, Sir John Dalberg-Acton, who had recently come of age: ibid. 22 Feb. 1856; cf. D. Mathew, *Acton: the Formative Years* (1946), 28.

[67] Jethro Tull, *The New Horse-Houghing Husbandry* (1731).   [68] *Shrews. Chron.* 13 Mar. 1784.
[69] *Acct. of Improvements*, App. IX, p. 88.
[70] Rec. of J. Smyth & Sons, Peasenhall: Suff. R.O., Ipswich, HC 23/F1/1–5.
[71] *E. Anglian Daily Times*, 6 July 1901; Slater, *Nat. Com. Dir.* (1850), Salop. p. 18; *V.C.H. Salop.* i. 478.

Although harvest was the most labour-intensive farming occupation, it was the last to receive the benefit of horse-powered mechanization (Fig. 16). About 1800 wheat was normally reaped with broad hooks or saw sickles while barley and oats were mown with a scythe. Where conditions were suitable wheat was sometimes mown and Plymley recommended that.[72] Such had been the general pattern for the previous fifty years and for the next half century mowing remained commonplace. Reports of trials of experimental reapers reached the local press in the 1820s but, despite the claim that their hourly rate of progress was equal to one man's daily output with a scythe,[73] the age of the mechanical harvest was still forty years distant.

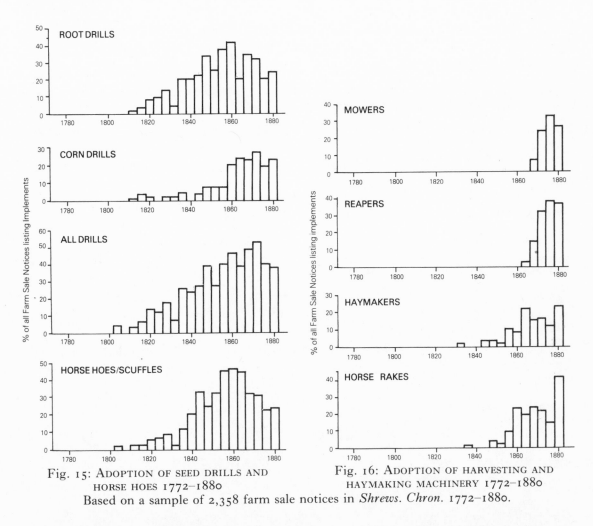

Fig. 15: ADOPTION OF SEED DRILLS AND HORSE HOES 1772–1880

Fig. 16: ADOPTION OF HARVESTING AND HAYMAKING MACHINERY 1772–1880

Based on a sample of 2,358 farm sale notices in *Shrews. Chron.* 1772–1880.

From the 1840s the mechanization of the hay harvest began as haymakers, or tedding machines, were used to turn the drying crop. Tanner considered such implements to be good investments as they introduced a degree of efficiency seldom found in the county's casual harvest workers.[74] With the horse hay rake, favoured from the later 19th century, came the speed of operation required for successful hay harvests in a fickle climate, and both implements soon became standard.

It is likely that the cutting of the hay and corn crops remained essentially a manual task on many Shropshire farms until the 1870s and even longer on the smaller or marginal holdings. A Royal Agricultural Society judge doubtless spoke

---

[72] Plymley, *Agric. of Salop.* 142–3.
[73] e.g. *Shrews. Chron.* 3 Oct. 1828, reported a trial of

Bell's reaping machine in Forfarshire: it was claimed to cut 1 a. of corn an hour. [74] *J.R.A.S.E.* xix. 23.

for many farmers when, in 1852, he said that they would never be able to rely solely on a reaping machine to cut their corn, although it made a useful addition to the scythe. Reaping machines were still a novelty in Shropshire in 1865.[75] For innovative farmers, with cash available, Hornsbys' and Samuelsons' reapers and mowers could be bought from local agents at prices ranging from £15 10s. for a reaper to £24 10s. for a combined reaper-mower. The more efficient self-delivery reaper, where a series of rakes removed the cut corn from the machine's path, was available in 1876 at nearly twice the price of the standard model.[76]

Livestock breeds

During the first half of the period Shropshire can be regarded as a melting-pot for a variety of sheep types. Into the county came a wide selection of strains, from the nimble Welsh at 6 lb. a quarter to the improving Leicestershire of 30 lb. a quarter, and from the horned Dorset to the highly bred polled Southdown. The range of stock types suited both the county's varied terrain and the differing tastes of the county's landowners. More significantly, it stimulated the more adventurous breeders to improve their local stock, and in some cases the imported breeds provided the means for that improvement.[77]

During the late 18th century Shropshire's indigenous sheep were still mainly in the southern uplands and commons. On both Morfe common in the east and the Long Mynd range in the west they were recorded as being nimble, hardy, and horned, with face colour ranging from black through brown to speckled. When fat the ewes weighed 9–11 lb. a quarter and gave between 2 and 2½ lb. of 'superior quality' wool; the wethers weighed 11–14 lb. a quarter.[78] Already c. 1800 Plymley referred to this type as the 'old Shropshire sheep', which, when crossed with the Dorset, produced 'excellent stock'.[79] The Dorset was one of the earliest identifiable breeds noted in farm sale advertisements in the county's press. Mentioned in a sale in Shifnal parish in 1778, the breed was recorded increasingly further west along the Severn Valley, in Atcham (1789), Bicton (1793), Montford (1796), and Alberbury (1808). The diffusion of the Dorset breed was largely assisted by the dispersal sale on the Attingham estate of the 1st Lord Berwick in 1789 when c. 700 Dorset and Wiltshire sheep were sold.[80] Elsewhere in the county landowners played an important role in improving the county's sheep: at Sweeney Hall, Oswestry, and Walcot Hall, Lydbury North, various established types of sheep were kept, including Merino rams for crossing with unimproved ewes.[81]

During the first quarter of the 19th century two breeds of national repute, the New Leicester and the Southdown, were found in increasing numbers on Shropshire farms. Sheep from Leicestershire had been mentioned in farm sales well before the results of Bakewell's longwool improvement were first advertised in 1797 as New Leicesters, belonging to Mr. Hawley of Aston Rogers.[82] Limited numbers of the compact, short-woolled Southdowns too were found in the county at that time, but the rise to popularity of both breeds can be traced to the period 1800–20 (Fig. 17). Several of the more progressive farmers and landowners assisted

[75] Ibid. xiii. 316 n.; Loton Hall MSS., Sir B. Leighton's diary 11 Sept. 1865.

[76] *Shrews. Chron.* 2 June, 4 Aug. 1876.

[77] Plymley, *Agric. of Salop.* 259; 'The Druid' [H. H. Dixon], *Saddle and Sirloin* (1895), 434 sqq.

[78] Plymley, op. cit. 260; rep. on sheep of Eng. to Bristol Wool Soc. 1792, quoted in J. Wilson, 'On the various Breeds of Sheep in Gt. Brit.' *J.R.A.S.E.* xvi. 36. Cf. 'Nimrod', *Hunting Reminiscences*, 7, for the 'little black sheep' of the Clees.   [79] Plymley, op. cit. 260.

[80] *Shrews. Chron.* 18 Apr. 1778; 21 Mar. 1789; 15 Mar. 1793; 2 Feb. 1796; 26 Feb. 1808.

[81] Ibid. 3 Mar. 1812; Plymley, op. cit. 260-1.

[82] *Shrews. Chron.* 20 Oct. 1797.

the process with regular sales of good quality breeding stock: William Childe supported the New Leicester breed from his Kinlet estate, William Beddoes of Diddlebury and Mr. Tench of Bromfield both advocated the Southdown, while at Hawkstone Park examples of both breeds were offered for sale on a regular basis.[83]

The improved sheep breeds, standing in marked contrast to slow-maturing indigenous stock, invited cross-breeding experiments. By 1800 the use of a Southdown ram on the hill ewes of the Long Mynd was noted as improving the wool and carcass weight of the local breed without loss of hardiness.[84] The extent to which pure-bred rams other than Southdowns were used in refining the breeding stock of the new race of Shropshire sheep is less certain. Some 19th-century commentators said that rams from the improved Leicester and Southdown breeds had generally been employed, others that at least some breeders had used only native stock and selective breeding to eliminate unwanted traits and fix the characteristics sought.[85]

Although the Shropshire breed was the world's first to be catered for by a breed association and flock book society (founded in 1882),[86] the interval between the efforts of the early breeders and the recording of their rams in the first flock book of 1883 does little to unravel the mysteries of the breed's origins. Nevertheless there was sufficient standardization by 1853 for Shropshires to be included in a new class at the Royal Agricultural Society's Gloucester show and for the judges there to describe the breed as 'very successful'.[87] By 1860 the society had rewarded the Shropshire sheep with its own class, and the Bath and West of England society first listed Shropshires as a separate class at its 1864 show in Bristol.[88] Such national recognition by no means implied that the Shropshire was bred just for show; it remained the choice of practical farmers in the county.

Shropshire farmers usually put ewes to the ram from mid October[89] and lambed from mid February onwards.[90] The lambs were weaned by June and, following a summer on good quality clover, they were fed roots during the winter and generally sold the following spring. By that time pure-bred hoggets usually weighed 20 lb. a quarter, and if left until 20 months old an average of 35 lb. a quarter was typical. Breed improvements had not reduced the wool's high quality but had increased the average weight of a ewe's fleece to between 5 and 8 lb.[91]

Not all of the many sheep described as Shropshires in auctions and newspaper accounts would necessarily have been considered pure-bred by the later standards of the flock book society, but mention of the breed in farm sales after 1850 usually implied an improved strain. In 1875, with the breed's heyday at home and abroad still to come, a Royal Agricultural Society judge commented that 'there is not a single breed of sheep which has made greater or more rapid improvement'.[92] In the face of the Shropshire breed's dominance few other breeds were able to maintain their popularity in the county after the mid century. Numbers of Leicesters and Southdowns declined from the 1840s. The indigenous Clun and Longmynd types persisted in small numbers, the former to evolve into an improved,

[83] e.g. ibid. 11 Sept. 1812 (Childe); 29 Aug. 1828 (Beddoes); 30 Mar. 1832 (Sir Rowland Hill, Hawkstone).
[84] Plymley, *Agric. of Salop.* 261.
[85] *J.R.A.S.E.* xvi. 236; W. C. Spooner, 'On Cross Breeding', ibid. xx. 308.
[86] R. Hill, *Shropshire Sheep: A Hist.* (Salop. Co. Mus. 1984), 5. The formation of a Shropshire Sheep Club had been proposed in 1860: *Eddowes's Jnl.* 12 Dec. 1860, p. 6.
[87] Rep. on Glouc. mtg.: *J.R.A.S.E.* xiv. 458.

[88] Hill, *Shropshire Sheep*, 4; Bath City R.O., D/BW 2/4.
[89] Young, *Tours in Eng. and Wales*, 168. At Drayton Lodge fm., Shifnal, the ewes were mated from 12 Oct. (1824) and 13 Oct. (1826): acct. bk. in Reading Univ. Libr. SAL 7.1.
[90] *J.R.A.S.E.* xix. 60.
[91] Ibid. 43, 59–61.
[92] C. R. Pitman, 'Rep. on Exhibition of Live-Stock at Taunton', ibid. 2nd ser. xi. 617–19.

well respected, hardy race, and the latter to become extinct in 1926.[93] The fine-woolled Ryelands, although of national repute, suffered a local retreat into their Herefordshire heartland (Fig. 17).

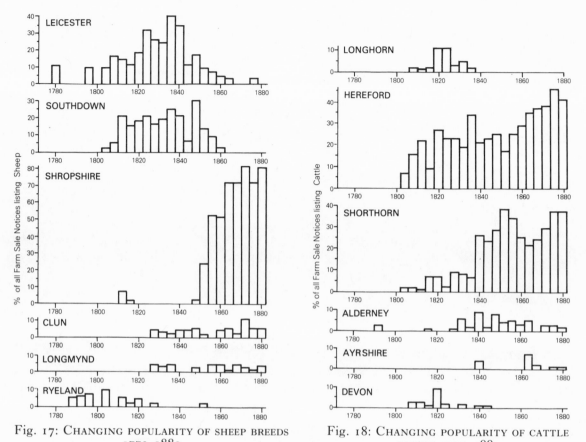

Fig. 17: CHANGING POPULARITY OF SHEEP BREEDS 1772–1880

Fig. 18: CHANGING POPULARITY OF CATTLE BREEDS 1772–1880

Based on a sample of 2,358 farm sale notices in *Shrews. Chron.* 1772–1880.

Late 18th- and early 19th-century commentators found it hard to describe the native cattle of Shropshire. Plymley admitted that they could not be ascribed to an identifiable breed, but indicated that they were similar to the original longhorned stock of Warwickshire and Staffordshire. Both Plymley and Arthur Young considered that some native stock had already been improved by the use of better animals from Cheshire and Lancashire, and suggested that the purchase of a better bred Leicester Longhorn bull, at between £15 and £25, would continue the upgrading of local cattle.[94] Several such bulls from the east midlands were present in the county before 1800 (Fig. 20), with five examples changing hands in farm sales during the 1790s.[95] Their use is likely to have improved the conformation and fattening qualities of the local Longhorns and is even recorded as having increased the milk yield to 3 gallons 'at a meal'. Such cattle were allowed up to 1½ a. of summer grazing each but did not receive any additional food. In winter they were housed and fed on turnips and straw, an example of unusually enlightened management.[96]

As the 19th century progressed interest in selective cattle breeding grew. Enterprising farmers were encouraged by the results of earlier improvements to

[93] At Long Meadowend fm., Aston on Clun. See R. Trow-Smith, *Hist. of Brit. Livestock Husbandry 1700–1900* (1959), 280–3.

[94] Plymley, *Agric. of Salop.* 241, 258; Young, *Tours in*

Eng. and Wales, 155, 163, 166–7.

[95] *Shrews. Chron.* 15 Mar., 5 Apr. 1793; 7 Mar. 1794; 3 Mar. 1796; 21 Mar. 1797.

[96] Young, op. cit. 155, 167.

look afresh at other local breeds. The Hereford beef breed had already begun to rise from its unimproved state by the time of its Smithfield club successes from 1799. It continued with the standardization of the breed's colour as the mottle-faced, dark and light grey strains eventually gave way to those with red bodies and white faces, and received further impetus with the publication of the first volume of the breed's herd book in 1845.[97]

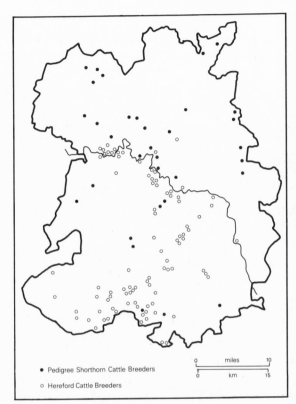

• Pedigree Shorthorn Cattle Breeders

o Hereford Cattle Breeders

△ Pre 1800   ◆ 1810–19
▲ 1800–09   ◇ 1820–29   ● 1830–39

Fig. 19: LOCATION OF PEDIGREE CATTLE BREEDS 1870–9
Based on the Hereford and Shorthorn herd books.

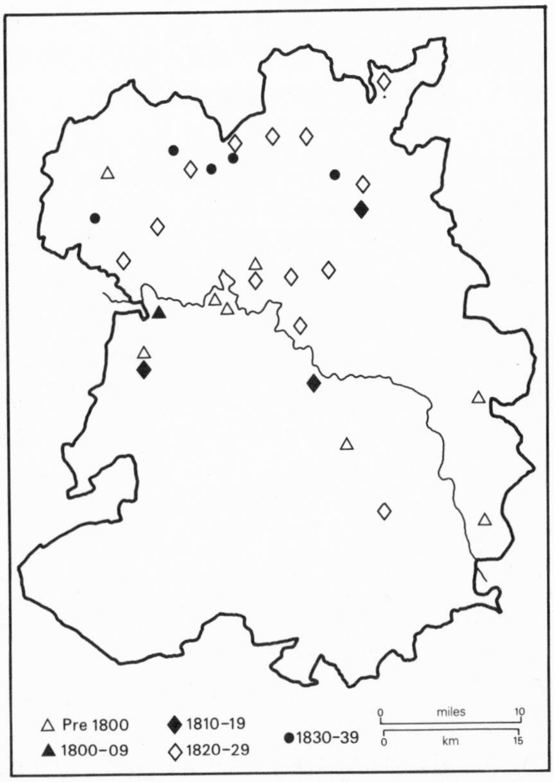

Fig. 20: DISTRIBUTION OF LONGHORN CATTLE 1772–1839
Based on a sample of 2,358 farm sale notices in *Shrews. Chron.* 1772–1880.

The fact that the responsibility for compiling the herd book fell to a Shropshire man, T. C. Eyton of Eyton Hall,[98] demonstrates the links between the county and the Hereford breed. The ability of the cattle to thrive in only moderate conditions, together with the their early maturity, made them a profitable choice for Shropshire farmers intent on producing good beef stock. In the Corve Dale region cows calved in winter or early spring so that the calves were weaned on spring grass. The cows when dry could then be adequately fed on the poorer hill pastures until their calving time approached again, while the calves could be wintered on hay and turnips. Under that system two-year-old stock typically fetched between £18 and £20 at market, the best animals selling for up to £25.[99]

Besides Corve Dale the important areas for the breed in Shropshire were the fertile Severn valley and the southern hill and dale land adjacent to Herefordshire (Fig. 19). In the 1870s only one breeder of registered Hereford cattle was located well to the north of the Severn valley.[1] The distribution of Herefords, registered

[97] T. Duckham, 'Hist., Progress and Relative Merits of Heref. Breed of Cattle', *Eyton's Herd Bk. of Heref. Cattle*, vi (1865), 3–32.
[98] *D.N.B.*; *V.C.H. Salop.* i. 54 (corr. ibid. xi. 375); xi.
140.
[99] *J.R.A.S.E.* xix. 25–7, 38–9, 56–7.
[1] *Herd Bk. of Heref. Cattle*, i–xv, cover the period to 1880.

and 'commercial' stock, in farm sale notices confirms that pattern, with the great majority in south Shropshire. Several dispersal sales contained cattle descended from the stock of such successful Herefordshire breeders as Knight, Tully, Price, and Tomkins,[2] although before long Shropshire could boast its own breeders of repute. Foremost was the 5th Lord Berwick, who won nearly £400 in prize money with Herefords at the Royal Agricultural Society's shows between 1849 and 1857.[3]

Although the Hereford breed satisfied the beef farmers' requirements it never won widespread respect as a producer of milk. Dairy farmers seeking quality and yields that the improved Longhorn failed to deliver had eventually to look farther afield than a neighbouring county for better stock. At the close of the 18th century at least three farmers in the county tried Holderness cattle. Before 1776 Edward Maurice of Petton had had them, and one of the cows had given over $4\frac{1}{4}$ gallons at one milking. He gave them up, finding that they were difficult to feed and 'tender' because of their thin hides, which were consequently of little value after slaughter; nor did he consider their milk rich.[4] Despite Maurice's disappointing experience Holderness cattle were recorded later: a 'very large' animal was offered for sale at the Bank, near Shrewsbury, in 1785,[5] and in 1792 a Holderness cow in calf, formerly Richard Birkinshaw's, was offered for sale at Berwick Maviston, in Atcham.[6] Such stock, together with the Durham and Teeswater strains, were later to provide the raw materials for the Shorthorn improvers of the north. Although the Shorthorns could boast a herd book by 1822,[7] a combination of continued Longhorn popularity and the distance between Shropshire and the Shorthorn's homeland delayed their appearance in numbers in farm sale notices until the 1840s.

Typically, the earliest breeders of Shorthorns in the county were gentlemen farmers of substance. The first four known Shropshire breeders were E. W. Smythe Owen at Condover (1836), Lord Hill at Hawkstone (1840), Edward Corbett at Longnor (1845), and the Hon. Henry Noel-Hill at Berrington (1846).[8] Their means and their ability to breed prize-winning stock are reflected in the fact that by 1851 three of the four had been successful at Royal Agricultural Society shows ranging from their county town to Northampton and from Windsor to York.[9]

By c. 1875 the breeders of pedigree Shorthorns were generally located in the northern half of the county (Fig. 19). It was there that the dairy farms turned to Shorthorns in increasing numbers, with the breed's greatest popularity occurring after 1875. Few other breeds of dairy cattle made much impact in the county, and none achieved the numerical position of the Shorthorn (Fig. 18). Alderney, or Channel Islands, breeds had been present since the early 19th century[10] but were widely kept only after regular sales of breeding stock were organized around the county by E. Parsons Fowler from the 1840s, as at Bridgnorth and Shrewsbury in 1848.[11] A similar supportive role was performed for the Ayrshire by a Mr. Cotterell, who by 1860 was conducting sales throughout the county; that year his annual Ayrshire sale was at the Raven and Bell, Shrewsbury.[12] The Alderney and Ayrshire, however, were to remain minority breeds in the shadow of the Shorthorn's success.

[2] See e.g. *Shrews. Chron.* 20 Sept., 4 and 11 Oct. 1816; cf. Trow-Smith, *Brit. Livestock Husb. 1700–1900*, 101, 253.
[3] *J.R.A.S.E.* xix. 56.
[4] Young, *Tours in Eng. and Wales*, 163, 166–7.
[5] *Shrews. Chron.* 16 Apr. 1785. [6] Ibid. 9 Nov. 1792.
[7] G. Coates, *Gen. Short-Horned Herd Bk.* (1822). Coates published 4 more vols. 1829–44 and H. Strafford continued the wk. as *Coates's Herd Bk.: containing the pedigrees of improved short-horned cattle*, vi–xx (1846–73). Vols. xxi (1876) sqq. were publ. by Shorthorn Soc. of Gt. Brit. Vols.

i–xxx cover the period 1822–80.
[8] Strafford, *Coates's Herd Bk.* vi–xii.
[9] Lists of prize-winners and commendations: *J.R.A.S.E.* vi, pp. xxvi, xxxii (Shrews. 1845); viii, p. xxv (Northampton 1847); ix, p. xxxii (York 1848); xii, pp. xi, xix–xx (Windsor 1851). [10] Plymley, *Agric. of Salop.* 260.
[11] *Shrews. Chron.* 17 Mar., 12 May 1848. Sales were also held at Bp.'s Castle and Ludlow.
[12] Ibid. 9 Mar. 1860. Subsequently sales were also held in Bp.'s Castle, Craven Arms, and Ludlow.

Few indigenous cattle breeds of the county survived to the later 19th century in an original form. The dark red Bishop's Castle breed, first noted in a farm sale notice in 1799[13] and mentioned *c.* 1800,[14] maintained a sporadic presence until 1828, by which time they had spread east to Cressage[15] and north to West Felton.[16] Of more continued importance as a local strain was the Montgomeryshire Smoky Faced breed, which could be found on the county's western margins from 1804, when a two-year-old bull was on Thomas Roberts's farm at Wilmington, in Chirbury,[17] to 1876, when Mr. Pugh of the Beach offered 12 bullocks for sale at Bishop's Castle fair.[18]

In the later 18th century a large proportion of the county's pigs were to be found in the sties of smallholders and cottagers. To Arthur Young a pig appeared to be a regular member of each family in the Severn Gorge,[19] consuming household waste and scraps to provide a much prized source of protein when killed. Plymley considered home produced pork and bacon to be a desirable part of the diet of labourers in the county, although he lamented the fact that farmers did not sell small quantities of wheat to their workers any more, so depriving them of the by-product of the milling, the bran, for feeding to their pigs.[20]

During the 18th century a breed of white pig, loosely referred to as the Shropshire, was to be found over a wide area of western England. It was reputed to be the largest British pig, with drop ears, a coarse and wiry coat, and a long body.[21] By the end of the century that native type was being improved by a cross with the Berkshire to produce the spotted type immortalized in the portrait of 'A Shropshire Pig'.[22] Such cross-bred pigs were reported to fatten on less food than the original hogs of the county, and so were looked upon as being more profitable.[23] Weights of bacon pigs of between 16 and 20 score were typical, and a final figure of 37 score was not unknown.[24] What is not recorded is the time taken to get the pig to that weight, although the finished pigs would be unlikely to be less than two years old when killed.

The average litter size of an improved cross-bred pig was seven, with two litters from each sow during the course of a year. Some farmers disposed of the weaned piglets at ten weeks, presumably to local cottagers for fattening. The price obtained for such weaners was 10s. 6d. in the 1780s.[25] In the mid 19th century Tanner considered that with the use of a good boar the weanlings should fetch £1 when sold on for fattening from the farms of south-eastern Shropshire.[26]

The Berkshire breed, used to improve the local stock of the 18th century, maintained its popularity within the county throughout the following century. At a time when few pigs were easily identified by breed over 60 per cent of those sold at farm sales before the 1870s were described as Berkshires. There were nevertheless sufficient strains available to satisfy breeders like Lord Hill and Lord Berwick, who were successful at Royal Agricultural Society shows with their Shropshire-bred, and locally named, exhibits: Lord Hill at Northampton in 1847 with a boar and sow of Hawkstone breed and Lord Berwick at Norwich in 1849 with a Cronkhill boar.[27] Comparatively few representatives of the Chinese or Neapolitan

[13] Ibid. 26 Apr. 1799, when a bull was offered at Fitz.
[14] Plymley, *Agric. of Salop.* 241.
[15] *Shrews. Chron.* 11 Mar. 1808, when a bull was incl. in the fm. sale of a Mr. Hayward.
[16] Ibid. 21 Mar. 1828, advertising a bull at the Fords.
[17] Ibid. 2 Mar. 1804.   [18] Ibid. 6 Oct. 1876.
[19] *Tours in Eng. and Wales*, 145.
[20] Plymley, *Agric. of Salop.* 267.
[21] J. Lawrence, *Gen. Treatise on Cattle* (2nd edn. 1809),

439.
[22] Plymley, op. cit. 266; Rothamsted Agric. Research Stn., Rothamsted colln., painting of pig belonging to Sir C. W. Rouse-Boughton, of Downton Hall.
[23] Plymley, op. cit. 267.
[24] Young, *Tours in Eng. and Wales*, 147. The score was 20 lb.: Zupko, *Dict. Eng. Weights and Measures*, s.v.
[25] Young, op. cit. 164.
[26] *J.R.A.S.E.* xix. 29.   [27] Ibid. viii, p. xxvi; xi, p. xxiv.

lines, so revered by improvers elsewhere in the country,[28] were recorded in Shropshire, though the Revd. John Hill, of the Citadel, Weston-under-Redcastle, was highly commended (twice) and commended (twice) for his Essex and Neapolitan cross-bred sows at the Royal Agricultural Society's 1845 show in Shrewsbury and Neapolitan pigs descended from his stock were offered for sale at Stanton upon Hine Heath in 1852.[29]

The large estates

The large, well documented landed estates, with which Shropshire was so well endowed (Table X), yield ample details of the vagaries of landlord management during a period that, save for the uncertainties of the 1820s and 1830s,[30] was marked by steadily increasing agricultural prosperity. Some large estates received very heavy capital investment with the ultimate objective of increasing the rental. Some, on the other hand, were mortgaged to finance conspicuous expenditure, and when that happened too frequently without intervals of retrenchment or the acquisition of new capital or income, sale was the inevitable end. The very large estates naturally withstood extravagance best; only two such were sold during the period, though in other cases outlying properties had to be relinquished. Some large estates, well run by owners who lived within their ample means, increased. The varying histories of the largest estates help to illuminate those of the more modest estates, which succumbed more quickly to extravagance: many were sold as old landed families were ruined. There was no lack of buyers among the newly rich industrial and commercial men.

TABLE X: SHROPSHIRE LANDOWNERS 1872-3

Parliamentary return:			Bateman:		
number	classification by acreage	total acreage	number	classification by rank	total acreage
8	over 10,000	142,863	8	peers	195,276
129	1,000–10,000	359,279	109	gt. landowners and squires	333,929
746	100–1,000	219,687	669	yeomen	186,990
3,955	1–100	65,566	3,841	smaller proprietors	57,738
7,281	under 1	4,544	7,281	cottagers	4,544
12,119		791,939	11,908		778,477

Sources: Summary of Returns of Owners of Land in Eng. and Wales, H.C. 335, p. 12 (1876), lxxx; J. Bateman, Gt. Landowners (1883).

The two large Shropshire estates sold were the Craven and Apley Park estates. The latter was sold entire in 1867[31] and the Cravens' Shropshire properties, outliers to a great English estate that extended into many counties, thus formed the only large estate in the county to be broken up during the period. Put together in the 1620s,[32] it amounted to 19,642 a.[33] worth some £9,000 a year in 1770-1. The 5th Lord Craven died in 1769, and in 1770-1 the Shropshire estates were surveyed for the 6th baron, evidently with a view to sale: by 1772 Capability Brown was spending thousands of pounds for Craven at Benham Park (Berks.) and Combe

[28] Trow-Smith, Brit. Livestock Husbandry 1700–1900, 154 sqq., 288 sqq.
[29] J.R.A.S.E. vi, p. xxxiii; Shrews. Chron. 20 Feb. 1852.
[30] E. Richards, '"Leviathan of Wealth": W. Midland Agric. 1800–50', Agric. H.R. xxii. 113.
[31] Below.
[32] Above, 1540–1750 (Landlord and tenant).
[33] Including 4,821 a. of uninclosed common.

Abbey (Warws.).[34] Piecemeal sale of the estate in the north-west—*c*. 4,000 a. mainly in the manors of Kinnerley, Melverley, and Ruyton-XI-Towns—began in the 1770s and continued in the 1780s;[35] the Pradoe estate, acquired and built up by the Kenyons from 1803, was formed partly from Craven properties sold at that time.[36] The 2nd earl of Craven (succ. 1825, d. 1866) resumed sales:[37] Little Dawley, in the east Shropshire coalfield, was sold in the 1850s[38] and the south Shropshire estates were broken up: notable purchasers there were the Botfields on the southern slopes of the Clees,[39] C. O. Childe-Pemberton on the northern slopes,[40] and J. D. Allcroft in lower Corve Dale.[41] By 1873 the 3rd earl owned only 803 a.[42] in Shropshire, of which about half were in Coreley.[43]

Three of the largest estates that had been assembled in earlier centuries—the Newports', the Leveson-Gowers', and the Egertons'—lasted throughout the period. The vast estate of the Newports, 23,430 a. lying in most parts of the county,[44] was for a time (1734–62) divided[45] but fell eventually to the Pulteneys (as trustees until 1783), passing from them *c*. 1808 to the Vanes of Raby Castle (co. Dur.). The Newports' estates were thus lost to their legitimate heirs, the Bridgemans. The Bridgemans, however, had considerable estates of their own in Shropshire and they added to them in the mid 18th century,[46] when they also inherited Weston under Lizard (Staffs.) near the eastern county boundary. In 1855 Lord Bradford's consequence as a Shropshire landowner was greatly increased by his purchase of the 2,900-a. Tong estate for £170,000.[47] The Leveson-Gowers' Lilleshall estate[48] had been built up, largely from monastic properties, in the 16th century, and the Egertons' Ellesmere estate had been a creation of the late 16th and early 17th century.[49]

The owners of such estates were non-resident but their agents and officials were substantial and influential men in the county,[50] though highly centralized estate managements, such as the 2nd duke of Kingston's[51] or the 2nd marquess of Stafford's, probably restricted the influence of local officials.[52] Agents often belonged to, or founded, landed families or official dynasties. Offshoots of minor landed families who prospered locally as land agents or stewards included men such as Hugh Pigot who acquired Peplow in the early 18th century,[53] John Ashby of the Lynches, Yockleton,[54] Thomas Wingfield of Alderton,[55] and the Lewises of Marshall & Lewis, the Bridgnorth attorneys who worked for the Foresters and others in the late 18th century; the Lewises bought estates in Deuxhill (the manor)

[34] S.P.L., MSS. 2480–2; J. B. Blakeway, *Sheriffs of Salop.* (Shrews. 1831), 207 note a; *Complete Peerage*, iii. 503–4; *V.C.H. Berks.* iv. 105; *V.C.H. Warws.* vi. 73; N. Pevsner, *Berks.* (Bldgs. of Eng. 1975), 36, 225; idem and A. Wedgwood, *Warws.* (Bldgs. of Eng. 1966), 238; *Memoirs of Margravine of Anspach* (1826), ii. 88, 92.

[35] S.P.L., MS. 2482; *T.S.A.S.* 2nd ser. viii. 357; 3rd ser. i. 100–1, 224, 232, 249; ii. 138–9, 361, 367, 383; S.R.O. 497/5.

[36] *T.S.A.S.* 3rd ser. ii. 138–41; cf. S.P.L., MS. 2482, pp. 22–8 and map; S.R.O. 2106/T/5.

[37] *T.S.A.S.* 2nd ser. ix. 369.   [38] *V.C.H. Salop.* xi. 114.

[39] Catherton; Earl's Ditton, etc., in Cleobury Mortimer; Farlow; and Hopton Wafers: B. Botfield, *Stemmata Botevilliana* (Westminster, 1858), pp. ccxlviii, ccli.

[40] Heath and Tugford: cf. S.R.O. 3651, parcel 17C, sched. of old deeds relating to ests. of C. O. Childe-Pemberton, pp. 151–9; S. Bagshawe, *Dir. Salop.* (1851), 552–3; *P.O. Dir. Salop.* (1856), 133.

[41] Culmington, Onibury, Stanton Lacy, and Stokesay: cf. *S.P.R. Heref.* xvii (3), p. iv; xviii (2), p. iv; *Kelly's Dir. Salop.* (1870), 46, 146.

[42] Bateman, *Gt. Landowners*, 111.

[43] Long retained: cf. S.R.O. 426/44–5; *P.O. Dir. Salop.*

(1870), 45; *Kelly's Dir. Salop.* (1941), 82.

[44] S.R.O. 168/1–2, 4; Barnard MSS., Raby Castle, boxes 6 and 8, abstr. of writings relating to Salop. est. (earl of Bath v. Newport); ibid. steward's rm. box 81, maps.

[45] Some descended with Cressage: see e.g. *V.C.H. Salop.* viii. 75; cf. Barnard MSS., Raby Castle, box 4, bk. containing accts. of Chas. Bolas, receiver of John Newport's est. in Salop., Staffs., and Ches. descending from Thos., earl of Bradford [d. 1762]. Some descended with Harley: see e.g. *V.C.H. Salop.* viii. 88, 95; xi. 99, 218, 313.

[46] When Hughley and Presthope were bought.

[47] *V.C.H. Salop.* iii. 254–5; *V.C.H. Staffs.* iv. 173; S.R.O., q. sess. rec. box 260, reg. of gamekeepers 1742–79, 1 Feb. 1746/7; Loton Hall MSS., Sir B. Leighton's diary 18 Aug. 1855.   [48] S.R.O. 972, bdle. 238.

[49] Above, 1540–1750 (Landlord and tenant).

[50] *V.C.H. Salop.* iii. 310; *T.S.A.S.* lix. 53–4, 62.

[51] Mingay, *Eng. Landed Soc. in 18th Cent.* 69–70.

[52] *Agric. H.R.* xxii. 105–8.

[53] Below; Blakeway, *Sheriffs*, 202.

[54] His property, not his residence: *T.S.A.S.* 4th ser. vi. 279–80; lix. 53–62; below.

[55] Below; *T.S.A.S.* 4th ser. iv. 101; *V.C.H. Salop.* iii. 129.

and Chelmarsh for example.[56] Robert Pemberton, attorney, younger son of the family seated at Wrockwardine Hall, legatee of Millichope, and agent to the Attingham estate in the 1790s, was closely connected with several landed families. His son, the Revd. R. N. Pemberton, builder of Millichope Hall, increased his landed inheritance by purchase and, dying childless in 1848, left it away from his heir at law, Miss Cludde of Orleton, to the Salusburys[57] and the Childes (later Childe-Pembertons).[58] By no means all the landless sons of landed families succeeded as agents: in 1859 Charlton Leighton worked for a year with William Smith, the duke of Sutherland's agent at Lilleshall; he then went on to the agricultural college at Cirencester but thereafter never exerted himself to find employment, a failure that would have justified the suspicions of gentlemen agents put to James Loch in 1814.[59] The monument to John Mytton's agency for the eccentric 2nd earl of Kilmorey in the 1830s was a deserted and dilapidated estate.[60] Nevertheless from 1855 kinsmen were employed as resident agents for the Ellesmere estate by the 2nd and 3rd Earls Brownlow: Capt. H. F. Cust (later Cockayne-Cust) came in 1855 and was succeeded in 1884 by his son-in-law Brownlow R. C. Tower (d. 1932).[61]

During the Pulteneys' trusteeship of the Newport estate[62] the agency was given to the Peeles who founded a dynasty of prominent county officials,[63] and leading county magistrates such as Charles Bolas and the Revd. Edmund Dana seem also to have been involved in the affairs of the estate.[64] The Levesons were represented in the county by an almost continuous succession of very able administrators from the Revd. George Plaxton 1685–1720,[65] through Thomas Gilbert 1760–88,[66] John Bishton (author of the 1794 *General View of the Agriculture of Shropshire*) 1788–1803,[67] John Bishton the younger 1803–9, and his incompetent brother George 1809–12,[68] to the ruthless Scot James Loch 1812–55.[69] During the younger Bishtons' and Loch's stewardships the family's income was greatly (if temporarily) enlarged: from 1803[70] to 1833 the 2nd marquess of Stafford (cr. duke of Sutherland 1833), head of the Leveson-Gower family, also enjoyed an income averaging £77,345 a year from the great inheritance of the Egertons, which in Shropshire included the 20,000-a. Ellesmere estate worth £17,500 a year in 1802. It was that windfall that enabled Loch to invest very large amounts of money in his master's estates in order to rack up his rental.[71] The dowager countess of Bridgwater's agents at Ellesmere were said in 1837 to spend over £20,000 a year on 'the improvement of estates, houses, roads, &c.'[72]

Two large estates came into existence by the fusion of families: Foresters and Welds in the one case, Herberts and Clives in the other. The dynastic alliances

[56] S.P.L., MS. 6864, ff. 28, 43; *V.C.H. Salop.* iii. 296.

[57] Kinsmen of E. W. Smythe Owen (formerly Pemberton) of Condover.

[58] Below; S.P.L., MS. 2793, pp. 219–21; S.R.O. 1011, box 241, Pemberton pedigree and draft settlement (11 Aug. 1849) of est. devised by the Revd. R. N. Pemberton; bdles. 247–9, rentals 1842–8; box 255, Pemberton's will pr. 1849; Burke, *Land. Gent.* (1914), 368, 372, 1652; Loton Hall MSS., Sir B. Leighton's diary 18 Dec. 1848, 2 Oct. 1857, 27 Jan. 1862, 23 Sept. 1869.

[59] Loton Hall MSS., Sir B. Leighton's diary 28 Mar. 1865; *Agric. H.R.* xxii. 107.

[60] H. D. Harrod, *Hist. of Shavington* (Shrews. 1891), 122.

[61] *V.C.H. Salop.* iii. 138; Loton Hall MSS., Sir B. Leighton's diary 17 Sept. 1866; *P.O. Dir. Salop.* (1879), 320; *Kelly's Dir. Salop.* (1885), 850; Burke, *Peerage* (1949), 277.

[62] Above.

[63] *V.C.H. Salop.* iii. 129.

[64] Ibid. 119. For Bolas cf. above, n. 45.

[65] Above, 1540–1750 (Landlord and tenant).

[66] P. Lead, 'Thos. and John Gilbert: Study in Business Enterprise and Social Mobility in 18th-Cent. Eng.' (Keele Univ. M.A. thesis, 1982), 46. Cf. *D.N.B.*; *Hist. Parl., Commons, 1754–90,* ii. 499–501.

[67] *Research in Econ. Hist.* vi. 208; B. Trinder, *Ind. Rev. Salop.* (1981), 44–5. Bishton evidently took responsibility for the Lilleshall est. 3 yrs. before becoming (1791) Ld. Stafford's chief agent and auditor.

[68] *Research in Econ. Hist.* vi. 208.

[69] Ibid.; *V.C.H. Staffs.* vi. 93; *D.N.B.*

[70] When the 3rd duke of Bridgwater died.

[71] *Research in Econ. Hist.* vi. 213–14; E. Richards, 'Anatomy of Sutherland Fortune: Income, Consumption, Investments and Returns, 1780–1880', *Business Hist.* xxi. 48–52; below (Landlords and tenants).

[72] Hulbert, *Hist. and Descr. of Salop.* ii. 242.

were made more effective by the contribution of the Foresters' mercantile and industrial wealth and of the Clives' nabob fortune. The Foresters' medieval estate near Wellington had been enlarged in the 16th[73] and 17th[74] centuries but in 1714 the younger William Forester married the heiress of William Brooke, a rich Londoner (d. 1737), and in 1734 their son Brooke married George Weld's heiress.[75] William Brooke's East India Co. stock realized almost £18,000, virtually all of which was invested in the improvement of the dilapidated Willey estate[76] that came to the Foresters on George Weld's death in 1748.[77] Brooke Forester's interest in the Willey estate (arising from the investment of his inheritance) was kept separate from his son George's after 1756,[78] Brooke living at Dothill and George at Willey.[79] On Brooke's death in 1774, however, the Forester properties and his interest in the Willey estate were all added to George's inheritance.[80] It was a rich and partly industrial estate[81] with a surplus income that supported the Foresters' political activities, paid for the new Willey Hall (built 1812-20), justified the conferment of a peerage in 1821,[82] and allowed the acquisition of more land, though purchases consolidating the estate were sometimes financed by sales of outlying properties;[83] in 1870 the 2nd Lord Forester was said to have added more farms to his inheritance than any other Shropshire landowner.[84]

By 1750 Henry Arthur Herbert, earl of Powis, owned an extensive estate inherited from his father (d. 1719) and centred on Dolguog (Mont.) and Oakly Park.[85] He had more recently also inherited the estates of two kinsmen, Lord Herbert of Chirbury (d. 1738)[86] and the 3rd marquess of Powis (d. 1748) whose daughter he married in 1751; besides the Powis castle estate in Montgomeryshire the marquess's lands had included the lordship of Oswestry.[87] In 1784 the earl's daughter married the 2nd Lord Clive, owner of Styche[88] and of the many estates which his father, Clive of India, had bought, mainly for the political influence they gave him over Bishop's Castle and Ludlow[89] or for the enhancement of his new status as an aristocratic landowner: properties bought for the latter reason included the manors of Kinnerley, Melverley, Munslow, and Ruyton-XI-Towns and the hundreds of Clun, Munslow, and Purslow, which brought him several lordships but very few acres.[90] After Lady Clive's brother had died unmarried in 1801 the great estates strung out along the county's western border—Clun, Walcot, Bishop's Castle, Chirbury, Montford, and Oswestry[91]—with others in Wales[92] and north-east Shropshire[93] were united;[94] with the exception of the Oakly Park estate[95] they

[73] V.C.H. Salop. xi. 220.
[74] By the purchase of L. Wenlock 1623 and the acquisition of the est. of the Steventons of Dothill: ibid. 80, 215-16.
[75] Ibid. iii. 294; T.S.A.S. 3rd ser. ii. 338; Gent. Mag. vii. 637.
[76] S.R.O. 1224, box 284, settlement, agreement for timber, etc., 7 Jan. 1757.
[77] Ibid. box 155, Geo. Weld's will pr. 1748; T.S.A.S. 3rd ser. ii. 336, 340.
[78] When Geo. came of age. See sources in n. 76, above. Separate rentals were made 1757-74: S.R.O. 1224, boxes 183-4.
[79] They were not on good terms after 1759: S.R.O. 112, Noel Hill's letter bk. 1774, Geo. Forester to Hill 10 Apr. 1774; ibid. box 23, Thos. Bell to Thos. Hill 5 Dec. 1759; T.S.A.S. 3rd ser. ii. 340, 342-3; V.C.H. Salop. xi. 216.
[80] For Geo. see T.S.A.S. 2nd ser. iii. 173-4; lviii. 221-2; J. Randall, Old Sports and Sportsmen (1873), esp. 76 sqq., 198.
[81] The ind. enterprises on the main part of the est. will be found descr. in V.C.H. Salop. x-xi.
[82] Ibid. iii. 294-7, 339-43; L.J. xlix. 42; S.R.O. 1224, box 165, drafts of bill and petition; H. M. Colvin, Biog. Dict.

Brit. Architects 1660-1840 (1978), 954.
[83] e.g. property in Wellington for the Caughley est. 1822: cf. V.C.H. Salop. xi. 215 and n. 66; S.R.O. 1224, box 175, acct. of John Pritchard & Sons 1823.
[84] T.S.A.S. lix. 145-6.
[85] T.S.A.S. 2nd ser. xii. 168-9; Dict. Welsh Biog. 348, 779; V.C.H. Salop. iii. 255 and pl. facing p. 176.
[86] Burke, Peerage (1938), 2014.
[87] Left to the 2nd marquess by his gt. uncle Ld. Craven in 1697: T.S.A.S. vii. 52-3.
[88] Visit. Salop. 1623, i (Harl. Soc. xxviii), 121-5; S.R.O. 1635/1-2; Burke, Peerage (1949), 1631.
[89] V.C.H. Salop. iii. 255-6, 288, 303-4.
[90] S.R.O. 497/5; S.P.L., MS. 6865, pp. 148, 150; V.C.H. Salop. iii. 45.
[91] S.R.O. 552, 735, 1043, 2561, 4303; N.L.W., Powis Cast. Man. Rec. [92] V.C.H. Salop. iii. 310.
[93] The Styche est.: see e.g. S.R.O. 552/8/51-3, 500-6.
[94] Strictly, not until the death of Edw. Clive, earl of Powis, in 1839: Complete Peerage, x. 652-3.
[95] Settled on the Hon. R. H. Clive, for whose grandson the earldom of Plymouth was re-created in 1905. See V.C.H. Salop. iii. 311.

were preserved largely intact by a new line of earls of Powis descended from the Indian proconsul.[96] From the 1760s Clive needed efficient agents to manage his rapidly growing estate and other affairs. At first he used Thomas Wingfield but in 1769 he made Thomas Ashby his chief estate and political agent.[97] Both Wingfield and the highly competent[98] Ashby (who married a kinswoman of Wingfield)[99] were also involved in Lord Powis's affairs, and the patronage of Clive and Powis secured the county clerkship of the peace (1779–1802) for Wingfield and the town clerkship of Shrewsbury (1767–79) for Ashby.[1]

The Hills of Hawkstone owed their enhanced status during the period to the 'Great Envoy' Richard (d. 1727),[2] uncle of the 1st baronet, and to that baronet's grandson Rowland, a distinguished soldier[3] who left a viscountcy to the owner of Hawkstone at his death in 1842.[4] Richard Hill's benefactions, however, had also included the endowment of two other nephews, Thomas Harwood and Samuel Barbour, who both took the name Hill. When Samuel died in 1758 almost all his settled estates passed to his cousin Thomas (d. 1782), of Tern,[5] and the combined inheritance, though more scattered[6] than the large compact estate eventually formed around Hawkstone,[7] sufficed for the conferment of a peerage on Thomas's son Noel (Lord Berwick 1784)[8] and for the building (1783–5) of Attingham Hall.[9] The Tern (later Attingham) estate and its owners were long and well served by Thomas Bell, land and house steward there 1734–73,[10] though Thomas Hill was a very careful manager of his own affairs and a prudent investor in the funds and additional land.[11] Hill also drew on the services of professional men. John Olivers (later Oliver), a Shrewsbury attorney, acted for him in financial and other matters, to some extent as a banker.[12] Such men's usefulness consisted not merely in their business ability and professional skill: involved in the affairs of several estates at once, they could supply confidential information when required. Thus in 1756 Oliver, employed by the Leightons of Loton,[13] advised Thomas Hill on Sir Charlton Leighton's affairs and the ability of the Loton estate to pay interest on £16,000,[14] and in 1774 Noel Hill was able to oblige his friend Charlton Leighton (Sir Charlton's son, newly possessed of the paternal estate) by taking over the mortgage for a few years.[15] Like others of his profession Oliver hoped that his clients could help him to extend his business but in 1757–8 Hill's patronage did not avail him for the stewardship of Lord Montfort's estate or for the county militia registrarship.[16] Nor in 1779 could he secure the town clerkship of

[96] V.C.H. Salop. iii. 255–6, 310–11. The 2nd and succeeding earls bore the name Herbert under a licence of 1807: Burke, Peerage (1949), 1631.

[97] T.S.A.S. lix. 55, 58–60.

[98] Adviser to many other county fams., incl. the Foresters: ibid. 53–62, esp. 60–1.

[99] S.P.L., MS. 4081, pp. 2299, 2303.

[1] V.C.H. Salop. iii. 129 and n. 28; T.S.A.S. lix. 55; H. Owen and J. B. Blakeway, Hist. Shrews. (1825), i. 544.

[2] Above, 1540–1750 (Landlord and tenant).

[3] Commander in chief 1828–42: D.N.B.; E. Sidney, Life of Ld. Hill (1845).

[4] Complete Peerage, vi. 521; G.E.C. Baronetage, v. 66.

[5] S. Shaw, Hist. Staffs. ii (1801), 44–6. The exception was Whitmore Pk. (Warws.) which passed to the Hills of Hawkstone, who exchanged it for the freehold of Prees man. in 1794: cf. ibid. 45; T.S.A.S. lv. 152; 34 Geo. III, c. 106 (Priv. Act); V.C.H. Warws. viii. 58, 77 (some errors).

[6] S.R.O. 112, vol. of rent receipts and accts. 1755–75.

[7] See e.g. S.R.O. 731, bdle. 351, maps of 1890s.

[8] Complete Peerage, ii. 167–8; V.C.H. Salop. iii. 263.

[9] N. Pevsner, Salop. (Bldgs. of Eng. 1958), 66–7.

[10] S.R.O. 112, box 25, [Edw. Jones?] to Thos. Hill 2 Nov.

1734; S.P.R. Lich. xiv (2), 111. Bell's letters to Hill 1734–71 are in S.R.O. 112, boxes 20, 23. S.R.O. 112, vol. of rent receipts and accts. 1755–75, incl. Bell's accts. 1755–71.

[11] See S.R.O. 112, box 42A, Noel Hill to Thos. Hill 15 Feb. 1771; ibid. boxes 20, 23, bdles. 21–2 (Bell's and Hill's corresp.); and e.g. V.C.H. Salop. viii. 19, 43, 198, 200. Barbara Coulton kindly contributed her knowledge of Bell's and Hill's characters. See her Salop. Squire: Noel Hill, 1st Ld. Berwick (Shrews. 1989).

[12] S.R.O. 112, box 27, Oliver's letters 1747–75. For the Olivers see T.S.A.S. 4th ser. iv. 97–8; Shrews. Burgess Roll, ed. H. E. Forrest (Shrews. 1924), 219.

[13] Blakeway, Sheriffs, 26–7; Loton Hall MSS., bdle. of abstrs. of title, legal opinions, etc., re mortgages 1750–88 and 1825; vol. of Copies of deeds, etc., p. 215.

[14] S.R.O. 112, box 27, Olivers to Hill 29 Nov. 1756.

[15] From Ld. Plymouth's executors: Loton Hall MSS., assignments of mortgages in trust for Charlton Leighton 1774–80.

[16] Jobs that Powis and Bath secured for their respective agents Wingfield and Bolas: cf. S.R.O. 112, box 27, Oliver to Hill 9 and 20 Feb. 1757, 15 Mar. 1758; V.C.H. Salop. iii. 129 n. 25; above, n. 45.

Shrewsbury or the county clerkship of the peace for his son Bold.[17]

After Bell's death in 1773 his duties seem to have been divided between a house steward, Richard Partridge, who died in 1809 and was succeeded by his son of the same name,[18] and a land steward or agent, John Hurd of Hatton Grange. Hurd (d. 1792) evidently began by receiving and accounting for rents as Bell had done[19] but by 1786, probably the date of his retirement in favour of his assistant Thomas Hurd the younger,[20] that side of the work was being done by the Olivers, first John the younger (d. 1789) then his brother Bold (d. 1791). In 1787 John Oliver hoped that Lord Berwick's interest would make him receiver general of the county[21] but, like his father thirty years before, he was disappointed.[22] Early in the 1790s efficient advice was needed as the sale of outlying properties began.[23] Thomas Hurd was expensive and perhaps dilatory. In 1792 therefore the 2nd Lord Berwick's cousin Edward Burton, a trustee of the estate whose advice and care proved invaluable until his death in 1827, recommended the appointment of Robert Pemberton, a Shrewsbury attorney.[24] Pemberton took over in 1793[25] and much of the work soon seems to have passed to John Dodson, probably Pemberton's deputy but called agent in 1797–8. John Southern, a surveyor who had worked with Pemberton on Lord Berwick's business, became agent in 1799[26] but Pemberton (d. 1816) continued to advise on administration and policy:[27] in 1804 he recommended that Southern be restricted to rent receipt and payment on account.[28] A new agent, Francis Walford, was appointed. He settled in Nash's new house at Cronkhill[29] and remained through difficult years, playing his part in the progress of William Hitchcock's 1807 survey[30] and in subsequent sales to finance Berwick's extravagance. Berwick later received management advice from a firm of Gray's Inn lawyers, but Walford's independent views were also conveyed to him.[31]

The variety and quality of advice applied to Attingham estate affairs helped to limit the damage inflicted by Berwick's extravagance between 1791 (when he came of age)[32] and 1827. In the latter year the contents of Attingham were sold to pay his debts and during his last five years Berwick (d. 1832) lived cheaply in Italy.[33] Attingham was shut up or let to tenants, Berwick's three successors lived unostentatiously, and by 1861 the debts had been cleared.[34] An unhappier fate awaited the Hills of Hawkstone who seem to have been less well served by their

[17] S.R.O. 112, box 40, corresp. of John [snr.] and Bold Oliver and Thos. Loxdale with Noel Hill Jan.–Mar. 1779.

[18] Formerly in service with Godolphin Edwards (d. 1772) of Frodesley. See *S.P.R. Lich.* xiv (2), 111, 140; Attingham Hall, Partridge's memo. bk. 1760–1806; S.R.O. 112, Wm. Hill's letter bk. 1826–7, Aug. 1827. Partridge collected Thos. Hill's rents.

[19] S.R.O. 112, vol. of rent receipts and accts. 1755–75, incl. Hurd's gen. accts. 1773–5 and accts. for Sutton (nr. Shrews.) alone 1775–82; ibid. box 25, Hurd's letters to Thos. Hill 1773–80; S.R.O. 1335/Rg/3, bur. 10 Dec. 1792.

[20] S.R.O. 112, box 40, vouchers 1782–3; box 66A, Edw. Burton to Ld. Berwick 13 Apr. 1792.

[21] S.R.O. 112, duplicate rentals 1786–91; box 42A, John Kynaston to [Ld. Berwick] 26 Feb. 1787; *T.S.A.S.* 4th ser. iv. 98.

[22] Sir Ric. Hill, with evil consequences for his successor at Hawkstone, obtained the office for Thos. Eyton: below.

[23] e.g. Willenhall (Warws.) and Weston Jones (Staffs.): cf. S.R.O. 112, box 66A, Edw. Burton to Ld. Berwick 13 Apr. 1792, with deficient acct. in *V.C.H. Warws.* viii. 116; *V.C.H. Staffs.* iv. 159 (some errors).

[24] Son of the eminent attorney mentioned in *V.C.H. Salop.* iii. 260: see sources there cited.

[25] S.R.O. 112, box 49, Thos. Hurd's acct. Feb. 1795; box 66A, Burton to Berwick 13 Apr. 1792; Wm. Hill's letter bk.

[26] 1826–7, 20 May 1827; Burke, *Land. Gent.* (1914), 281.

[26] S.R.O. 112, box 49, Jos. Phillips's acct. bk. with Ld. Berwick's agents. For Southern see S.R.O. 112, boxes 43 sqq., bills, vouchers, etc.; box 49, receipt of J. Southern, surveyor, 4 July 1795.

[27] S.R.O. 112, box 66A, Pemberton to Berwick 3 Oct. 1808; R. C. B. Pemberton, *Pemberton Pedigrees* (Bedford, 1923), chart 16.

[28] S.R.O. 112, box 70, Pemberton to Berwick 21 May 1804.

[29] Ibid. Nash to Walford 25 Mar. 1812; Pevsner, *Salop.* 116.

[30] See e.g. S.R.O. 112, map 5; ibid. box 66A, John Southern to Ld. Berwick 10 Apr. 1808.

[31] See e.g. ibid. box 66A, Pemberton to Berwick 3 Oct. 1808 and memo. of Lythwood and Brockton sales 1810; box 66B, Chas. Tennant to Berwick 27 Aug. 1827; box 70, Ld. Berwick's acct. with Sir John Hill *re* sales of lands 1815–23.

[32] *Shrews. Chron.* 28 Oct. 1791.

[33] '£200,000 has been thrown away, nobody knows how!!!': S.R.O. 112, Wm. Hill's letter bk. 1826–7, 15 and 20 May 1827; Attingham Hall, sale cat. Aug. 1827; *Complete Peerage*, ii. 168.

[34] *T.S.A.S.* lix. 147; *Attingham Pk.* (Nat. Trust 1981), 28; 'The Druid' [H. H. Dixon], *Saddle and Sirloin* (1895), 439–40.

agents. In 1790 Sir Richard Hill's steward, George Downward, was found negligent.[35] At Attingham the efficiency and economy of agents had been kept under review and changes made, but the owner of Hawkstone did not discharge Downward.[36] Extravagance continued: in 1796 Hill did not flinch from a very expensive parliamentary contest with his Attingham kinsmen[37] and in 1816 the Hawkstone estate was hit hard by the failure of Thomas Eyton, receiver general of Shropshire.[38] Lack of financial control continued to afflict Hawkstone, and Sir Rowland Hill's marriage to a Manchester fortune, Ann Clegg, failed to achieve[39] what retrenchment and sales[40] did for Attingham: by the early 1870s Hill's estate, though thrice the acreage of Berwick's, had a gross annual value barely twice the size and was very heavily encumbered.[41]

An estate comparable to the combined inheritance of Welds and Foresters in the later 18th century was the Whitmores' Apley Park estate. Formed in the early 17th century,[42] and increased by Catherine Pope's property in 1754 and the Wolryches' Dudmaston estate in 1774, it then extended to some 14,800 a.[43] As the Clives and Herberts used Oakly Park so the Whitmores' Pope and Wolryche estates served to endow a cadet line.[44] The main part of the estate, however, remained intact until Thomas Whitmore's time (1803–46). Whitmore inherited an income of £20,000 but with it the increasingly expensive burden of controlling a parliamentary borough (Bridgnorth); his fortune was less equal to the task than were the greater resources of the Clives and Foresters in their boroughs, and in 1811 it had also to pay for a new house. Whitmore is said to have sold £100,000 worth of land and to have left a mortgage of £180,000. The heir, T. C. Whitmore (d. 1865), was left with only £4,000–£5,000 a year after payment of interest, his mother's jointure, and his brothers' and sisters' portions: he had to live very quietly and to stop treating the Bridgnorth voters, his only extravagances being a large game preserve and 300 head of deer.[45] After his death, however, the estate had to be sold, and in 1867 it was bought lock, stock, and barrel for £550,000 by W. O. Foster, a Stourbridge ironmaster.[46]

The sale of the Craven and Apley Park estates, the permanent undermining of the Hawkstone estate and the temporary undermining of the Attingham estate, the survival of the Vanes' (formerly the Newports'), the Leveson-Gowers', and the Egertons' (later the Custs') estates, and the expansion of the Weld-Foresters' and Bridgemans' estates all display the various effects of carelessness, conspicuous expenditure, retrenchment, capital investment (in improvement or expansion), and careful management. The same themes may be detected in less well documented estates and the estates of the squires and lesser landowners. N. O. Smythe Owen of Condover, for example, came into £15,000 a year in 1790 but half of his property had soon to be sold to pay his debts.[47] Charles Baldwin (d. 1801) so mismanaged his affairs that he had to sell Aqualate (Staffs.) in 1797, and his son William,

[35] Papers in S.R.O. 731, box 226.
[36] Ibid. box 200 corresp. re Prees incl. 1797–1801.
[37] V.C.H. Salop. iii. 271–2; 'The Druid', Saddle and Sirloin, 441.
[38] S.R.O. 665/1/468; 731, box 248, Exchequer judgement, costs papers, etc.
[39] T.S.A.S. lix. 147–8; S.R.O. 731, bdle. 358, marr. settlement 1831; Shropshire Mag. Sept. 1977, pp. 26–7.
[40] e.g. Redrice (Hants), sold for £112,500 in 1844: S.R.O. 112, box 86, Thos. Salt to Ld. Berwick 2 Apr. 1844.
[41] Bateman, Gt. Landowners, 40, 221; V.C.H. Salop. iii. 140, 319, and sources there cited; T.S.A.S. lix. 148; S.R.O. 731, bdle. 351, maps of 1890s.
[42] Above, 1540–1750 (Landlord and tenant).
[43] V.C.H. Salop. iii. 280, and sources there cited. The falling in of the Dudmaston est. was delayed by Lt.-Col. Thos. Weld's longevity (1678–1774): B.L. Add. MS. 38469, f. 284r.-v.; T.S.A.S. 3rd ser. ii. 336.
[44] V.C.H. Salop. viii. 101, 152, 173; Burke, Land. Gent. (1914), 2015.
[45] Loton Hall MSS., Sir B. Leighton's diary 24 Oct. 1848; Burke, Land. Gent. (1914), 2014–15; Pevsner, Salop. 60; T.S.A.S. lix. 145; V.C.H. Salop. iii. 281–3, 330–4.
[46] V.C.H. Salop. iii. 335; Sir B. Leighton's diary Mar. 1867, 17 Jan. 1870; T.S.A.S. lix. 145.
[47] Leighton's diary 2 Oct. 1857; V.C.H. Salop. viii. 38.

succeeding to his mother's inheritance of Kinlet, took her name Childe. William Childe (d. 1824), the well known agriculturist, left a mortgage debt of £25,000, and his large home farm lost money in the hands of his son William Lacon Childe; by 1862 the Kinlet estate, despite housekeeping economies, was believed to be encumbered to the extent of £150,000 while the extravagant and unbusinesslike Childe was borrowing to pay the interest charges 'and muddling away his money with little or no show for it'.[48] William Wolryche Whitmore was another inventive agriculturist and 'schemer in things on his own property'; when he died childless in 1858, however, the Dudmaston estate was encumbered with £40,000 of debt, perhaps nine years' income.[49] The Myttons of Halston were wrecked by the career of that eccentric sportsman John Mytton (d. 1834), and Halston, their last landed possession, was sold in 1848. Mytton's son John, gaoled c. 1856 for a tavern debt of £1,500, was reduced to trying to raise money on his chance of the reversion of the Sundorne estate.[50] Sir Corbet Corbet (d. 1823), despite harsh dealing with his tenants, left the Adderley estate so heavily encumbered that even after 25 years, during which his trustees had had to spend almost the whole income (£12,000 a year) on repairs and debt repayment, there was still a large debt.[51] The Sundorne estate was so 'involved' that Andrew Corbet (d. 1856) had to live 'very retired' at Pimley, keeping only two servants at Sundorne Castle to open windows and light fires.[52] The estates of the 2nd earl of Kilmorey (d. 1880), which included the 3,000-a. Shavington estate in Shropshire, were heavily mortgaged from 1863, principally by his grandson (and eventual successor) Lord Newry, who came of age that year. By 1874 the mortgages amounted to £180,000, and in 1885 the 3rd earl sold the Shavington estate (subject to his mother's and aunt's jointures) for £125,000.[53]

Recklessness and bad judgement might bring a family down as when, during the American War of Independence, Robert Pigott became so 'terrified' at the prospect of imminent revolution and ruin in Britain that he sold the Chetwynd estate cheaply (1779) and retired with the proceeds to Italy, losing much of it there and dying at Toulouse in 1794.[54] Politics helped to bring down others, like the Warings of Owlbury and the Walcots of Walcot who both had to sell their estates to Lord Clive in the 1760s.[55] A much commoner cause of trouble, however, was the widespread assumption among genteel landowners at every level that estates could be endlessly milked for levels of expenditure considered necessary to maintain their place in society but unrelated to the income the land could yield. That was as true of the Sutherland-Leveson-Gowers, who had the resources to continue the game so much longer than most,[56] as of many small landowners like the Griffithses who mortgaged their Braggington estate eight times between 1769 and 1821[57] or the Wildings who repeatedly mortgaged their All Stretton property until forced to sell in 1856.[58] Thomas Harries (d. 1848) of Cruckton, typified their improvident habits: by 'not looking into his affairs and a careless habit of allowing his expenditure

[48] Leighton's diary 19 Nov. 1850, 27 Jan., Feb., and 8, 23, and 25 Apr. 1862; *T.S.A.S.* lix. 136; *V.C.H. Salop.* iii. 119; *V.C.H. Staffs.* iv. 106; Burke, *Land. Gent.* (1914), 367–8; S.P.L., Salop. Miscellanea, v (accession 2757), pp. 6–14. Kyre (Worcs.), inherited in 1832 (*V.C.H. Worcs.* iv. 283) free of debt, was mortgaged for £33,000 by 1862 when £4,000 more was about to be raised.

[49] Leighton's diary 24 Aug. 1858; *T.S.A.S.* lix. 135 and n. 12.

[50] Leighton's diary 8 Dec. 1856; *T.S.A.S.* lix. 145; Burke, *Land. Gent.* (1914), 433; cf. 'Nimrod' [C. J. Apperley], *Memoirs of Life of late John Mytton, Esq.* (1837).

[51] Leighton's diary 16 Nov. 1848; below (Landlords and tenants).   [52] Leighton's diary 8 Dec. 1856.

[53] H. D. Harrod, *Muniments of Shavington* (Shrews. 1891), 89–95; idem, *Hist. of Shavington*, 126; Bateman, *Gt. Land-owners*, 251.

[54] Blakeway, *Sheriffs*, 207; S.R.O. 1696, box 22, deed of 16 Aug. 1791; Leighton's diary 18 Jan. 1841.

[55] *V.C.H. Salop.* iii. 303–4.

[56] *Business Hist.* xxi. 45–78.

[57] Leighton's diary Oct. 1848; *V.C.H. Salop.* viii. 199.

[58] Leighton's diary 4 Oct. 1864; Botfield, *Stemmata Botevilliana*, p. ccli.

to exceed his income' over the years he ran up a debt of £80,000 and *c.* 1844 was forced to sell his Benthall estate, which was bought by Lord Forester for £60,000.[59] Henry Lyster (d. 1863) of Rowton Castle was 'a very bad manager' and when his widow advertised the place to let in 1866, putting it about that life there was 'so dull', her neighbour Sir Baldwin Leighton suspected 'very heavy book debts' as her real reason for leaving.[60] In 1863, when his debts caught up with him, J. W. Dod had to retire from his house at Cloverley to Rhyl; he died soon after and in 1864 the Cloverley estate had to be sold.[61] E. L. Gatacre left Gatacre in 1870 to live in London 'owing . . . to expenditure exceeding income', and the Oakeleys' Oakeley estate was heavily mortgaged by the 1870s.[62] No lessons seem to have been learnt from the reckless courses of others. Dod, as a trustee of the Adderley estate, must have known the consequences of Sir Corbet Corbet's overspending, and he was certainly aware of the precarious condition of the Hawkstone estate; yet for fifteen years before he had to give up his home his own estate was progressively encumbered with debt.[63] William Lacon Childe knew 'everyone's income' and was fond of comparing housekeeping costs with his fellow squires, yet he did not avoid very heavy embarrassments himself.[64]

There were of course careful and provident landowners. For his retrieval of the family fortunes John Oakeley (d. 1811) of Oakeley was remembered as the 'Old Retriever' by his descendants, who soon undid his work.[65] Other prudent landowners were the efficient C. K. Mainwaring (d. 1862) of Oteley, enabled *c.* 1850 to continue doing everying in the 'grand style' by a 'windfall' of £2,000 a year; the very businesslike (though autocratic) E. W. Smythe Owen (d. 1863) of Condover and his 'inexpensive' kinsman Reginald Cholmondeley who owned the estate 1864-96; William Sparling (d. 1870) of Petton, who saved all his life and lived to be 94; Sir Baldwin Leighton (d. 1871); and the 2nd Lord Forester (d. 1874). John Wingfield (d. 1862) of Onslow added seven or eight farms to his inheritance and left £80,000 in money, and C. O. Childe-Pemberton (d. 1883) added £60,000 worth of land bought from Lord Craven, as well as other smaller farms, to the Millichope estate. Purchase of land, however, required prudence. In the mid 1830s the Hon. H. W. Powys of Berwick bought the Rossall estate for the high price of £30,000, which he had to borrow. By 1850, when he was living as a guest in his own house (evidently let), the prospect of falling rents made it likely that his income would not suffice to pay the interest on his mortgages. Rossall was sold in 1852 for £22,500 and immediately after Powys's death in 1875 his nephew Lord Denbigh sold Berwick too.[66] It was such imprudence that enabled newcomers to acquire land and with it the entrée to society.

The investment of industrial, commercial, and other fortunes in land was well under way by the later 18th century.[67] Peplow, for example, bought from Sir Richard Vernon by his steward in 1715, was sold *c.* 1795 to Thomas Clarke, a Liverpool slave trader, for £45,000. After Clarke's death it was sold for £60,000, being acquired by Joseph Clegg, a Manchester merchant whose daughter became Lady Hill. In 1873 Lord Hill sold it to Francis Stanier Phillip Broade, a north

[59] Leighton's diary 3 Oct. 1848; *V.C.H. Salop.* viii. 274.

[60] Leighton's diary 1 Sept. 1866; *V.C.H. Salop.* viii. 201-2.

[61] Leighton's diary 11 June, 8 July 1863; *T.S.A.S.* lix. 148; below.

[62] Leighton's diary 17 Jan. 1870; *Salop. Landowner: Diary of Hen. Oakeley, 1869-71*, ed. G. Rhodes (priv. print. Capel St. Mary, 1980), 8-9, 65-6.

[63] Leighton's diary 16 Nov. 1848; *T.S.A.S.* lix. 148; Harrod, *Muniments of Shavington*, 130-2.

[64] Leighton's diary 6 Jan. 1845, 2 Oct. 1857, 15 Sept. 1858; above.

[65] Rhodes, *Salop. Landowner*, 1; above.

[66] Leighton's diary 23 June, 19 Nov. 1850, Apr. 1852, 9 Sept. 1862, 17 Apr. 1863, 19 Sept. 1864, 23 Sept. 1869, Oct. 1870, and *passim*; *T.S.A.S.* lix. 136, 146; *V.C.H. Salop.* viii. 39; Burke, *Peerage* (1949), 569-70; below.

[67] Mingay, *Eng. Landed Soc. in 18th Cent.* 101-5; S.P.L., MSS. 6860-5 *passim*.

Staffordshire ironmaster.[68] George Durant, enriched by his paymastership of the 1762 expedition against Havana, bought the duke of Kingston's Tong estate in 1764.[69] In the early 19th century the Bensons of Liverpool,[70] apparently slave traders,[71] bought much of the Lutwyche estate and some adjoining properties.[72] The Liverpool merchant John Sparling (d. 1800), who bought Petton from a Chambre heiress, may have made his money in a similar way.[73] In 1804 the Irelands sold Albrighton, which they had owned since 1543, and it passed through several hands before being bought in 1853 by W. H. Sparrow of Penn,[74] the Staffordshire ironmaster. He settled it on his eldest son; other Shropshire estates which he had bought in the 1840s from 'old county families now ruined'—Church Preen (with properties at Eaton under Heywood and Rushbury) and Habberley—he settled on younger sons.[75] Thomas Wells, another Staffordshire ironmaster, bought Eaton Mascott and Berrington in the 1860s.[76] J. P. Heywood, a millionaire banker, bought the Cloverley estate in 1864 and on his widow's death in 1887 it was added to the estates which his nephew A. P. Heywood-Lonsdale had begun to buy in the 1870s.[77] J. D. Allcroft, partner in the Worcester glovers Dent, Allcroft & Co., bought Lord Craven's Stokesay estate in 1869[78] and James Watson, a Birmingham businessman, bought Lord Denbigh's Berwick estate in 1875.[79]

Not all newcomers to landed society came from outside the county or from industry or commerce. The Botfields, the Warters, and the Pritchards were examples of home-grown gentry. The Botfields claimed descent from a minor landowning family (ancestors also of the Thynnes) settled at Botvyle near All Stretton,[80] but Thomas Botfield (d. 1801), of Dawley, laid the foundations of their wealth in the Shropshire coal and iron trades. He and his sons invested wisely in land, though some estates, such as the Wildings' in All Stretton, were bought for reasons of family sentiment;[81] in the Clee Hills area much was bought from the Craven estate. Thomas's grandson Beriah, the county's 'richest commoner' and one of the minority of Shropshire landowners who were free traders, married into landed society (the Leightons of Loton) in 1858 but died childless in 1863. The Botfield estates were subsequently divided, passing to the Garnett-Botfields of Decker Hill (7,670 a.), the Woodwards of Hopton Court (4,024 a.), and, after the death of Beriah's widow Mrs. Seymour (2,940 a.)[82] in 1911, Lord Alexander Thynne (d. 1918).[83]

The Warters of Longden were copyholders in Ford manor by 1308 and began steadily to accumulate additional lands in the later 17th century. In the 1790s they became manorial lords and by the early 1870s Henry de Grey Warter owned 3,453 a. in Shropshire, most of it in Pontesbury parish where, between 1863 and 1866 and largely to his own design, he built Longden Manor, a big Tudor house.[84]

68 S.P.R. Lich. xi (2), p. vi; V.C.H. Salop. iii. 305; Blakeway, Sheriffs, 236; Shrews. Chron. 12 Oct. 1900, p. 5; 19 July 1901, p. 6.
69 Hist. Parl., Commons, 1754–90, ii. 370.
70 V.C.H. Salop. iii. 142 n. 39 (perh. suggesting rather too early a date for the purchase of Lutwyche).
71 Inf. from Capt. Ralph Benson, Minton Ho.
72 S.R.O. 809, box 10, est. acct. of M. Benson, deceased; S.P.R. Heref. xix (4), pp. ii–iii; H. E. Forrest, Old Hos. of Wenlock (Shrews. 1914), 41–2.
73 There were W. Indian connexions: Loton Hall MSS., Sir B. Leighton's diary Oct. 1870; Burke, Land. Gent. (1914), 479; Blakeway, Sheriffs, 238[71] T.S.A.S. 2nd ser. i. 98–101.
75 W. Hughes, Sheriffs of Salop. 1832–86 (Shrews. 1886), 84–5; V.C.H. Staffs. ii. 99, 131 n. 81, 132 n. 90; V.C.H. Salop. viii. 126, 240; A. Sparrow, Hist. of Ch. Preen (1898), 61–6; Loton Hall MSS., Sir B. Leighton's diary 30 Dec. 1866; Burke, Land. Gent. (1952), 2364–5.

76 V.C.H. Salop. viii. 18, 21.
77 Harrod, Hist. of Shavington, 4, 122–3; idem, Muniments of Shavington, 94–5, 124, 126–8, 172; V.C.H. Salop. iii. 322; Shrews. Chron. 26 Feb. 1897, p. 8.
78 J. F. A. Mason, Stokesay Castle [1963]; H. W. Gwilliam, 'Old Worc.: People and Places' (1977), i. 28 (TS. in Worc. City Libr.).   79 V.C.H. Salop. iii. 352.
80 For the rest of this para. see Botfield, Stemmata Botevilliana; Trinder, Ind. Rev. Salop. 46; T.S.A.S. lix. 131; V.C.H. Salop. iii. 314, 338–9, and sources there cited.
81 Loton Hall MSS., Sir B. Leighton's diary 4 Oct. 1864.
82 Bateman, Gt. Landowners, 49, 402, 489.
83 Burke, Peerage (1949), 146, 1199; Kelly's Dir. Salop. (1913), 64; (1917), 57; Loton Hall MSS., Sir B. Leighton's diary 13 Aug. 1863.
84 V.C.H. Salop. viii. 230, 247, 256, 259, 263, 266–7, 270–1, 273, 285, 290, 320; Bateman, op. cit. 466. There was also a Notts. est.

John Pritchard (d. 1837), of Broseley, made a fortune as solicitor and (from 1799) banker. From 1794 he was George Forester's 'law agent' and came to do much work for many of the principal landowners around Broseley and Bridgnorth. His sons and partners George and John gave up the law in 1846 and 1836 respectively but stuck to the more gentlemanly occupation of banking.[85] They bought land and George (d. 1861) became a magistrate, deputy lieutenant, and in 1861 high sheriff. His share of the estates passed to John, M.P. for Bridgnorth 1853–68. The brothers, though 'very worthy men', were too recently landed to be in county society. In the early 1870s John owned 3,254 a. scattered over south Shropshire but with 1,300 a. around Stanmore Hall, in Worfield, a house he built (1868–70) in the Italian style with John Ruskin's advice.[86]

As communications improved, particularly with the coming of the railways in the last twenty years of the period, small or middling landed estates became especially attractive: without having to be the main source of income or being troublesome to run, they conferred the social cachet that brought their new owners into society.[87] Such perhaps were the Woodhill estate, near Oswestry and accessible from Whittington railway station (opened 1848), bought by John Lees from Lazarus Venables for £22,000 in 1852, or Henry Justice's 550-a. Hinstock Hall estate on the main road to Wolverhampton bought for £42,200 by a Black Country banker in 1862.[88] After the end of the period agricultural depression reduced still further the desirability of land[89] and perhaps what the successful banker wanted in the 1880s was a place like Overley Hall, a big new Tudor mansion built in 48 a. of grounds conveniently near Wellington and the railway.[90]

Landlords and tenants

As the new rich were infiltrating established landed society relationships between landlords and tenants were changing, though there is no evidence that the one process caused the other. Perhaps the most important changes affecting the tenant's relationship with his landlord were those conditioning his liability to pay rent and to a lesser extent tithe.

Rent was the tenant farmer's biggest outgoing. It was believed in general to represent about a quarter of a farm's gross produce, though perhaps increasingly as the period wore on it may often have come nearer to a third.[91] After rent the farmer's main outlay was normally tithe, frequently owed to more than one tithe owner. In the mid and later 18th century impropriate tithes on the Leveson-Gower estates probably amounted to little more than 3 per cent of a farm's gross produce. Landlords who were also impropriators could collect their tithes with the rent.[92] The farmer, however, often had other tithes to pay and in the late 18th century cash payments, with a compounding rate per acre related to rent, were replacing collection in kind. In some districts tithe was valued annually and, if occupiers declined to buy it at that valuation, the tithe was then taken in kind.[93] A rule of

[85] *V.C.H. Salop.* iii. 296; S.R.O. 1190/3/734.

[86] For over £40,000; it replaced Stanmore Grove ('Gitton's Folly'), a 'mean-looking' modern brick ho. See S.R.O. 1190/3/567–8, 734, 782–814, 826–996; *Salopian Jnl.* 12 July 1837, p. 1; *Eddowes's Jnl.* 28 Feb. 1866, pp. 5, 8; Hughes, *Sheriffs*, 53–4; Loton Hall MSS., Sir B. Leighton's diary 25 Aug. 1857; Burke, *Land. Gent.* (1894), 1659–60; Bateman, op. cit. 370; *Shrews. Chron.* 21 Aug. 1891, p. 8 (obit.; ref. owed to Dr. R. H. Moore).

[87] 16ᵉ Congres International des Sciences Historiques, *Rapports*, ii. 507.

[88] Loton Hall MSS., Sir B. Leighton's diary Apr. 1852, 1 May 1862, 25 Sept. 1866; *P.O. Dir. Salop.* (1856), 57, 132; *T.S.A.S.* lxiv. 95.

[89] See Thompson, *Eng. Landed Soc. in 19th Cent.* 319–20, for the repeated failures to sell Millichope (Childe's, formerly Childe-Pemberton's) and Oakeley (Oakeley's) in the 1880s and 1890s.   [90] *V.C.H. Salop.* xi. 309.

[91] *Research in Econ. Hist.* vi. 198, 219.   [92] Ibid. 197–8.

[93] Hulbert, *Hist. and Descr. of Salop.* ii. 98; Kain and Prince, *Tithe Surveys*, 12, 14; cf. E. Evans, *The Contentious Tithe* (1976), 26–8.

thumb used by the vicar of Madeley in 1756 suggests that he was securing composition at a tenth of the landlord's rent, i.e. between a fortieth and a thirtieth of gross produce;[94] the Madeley farmers had also to pay the impropriate rectorial tithe[95] and their total obligation may have been between a thirteenth and a tenth of gross produce.[96] Moduses depressed many incumbents' tithe income, and many had probably to accept less than their legal due. Often perhaps tithe was only the largest single item that brought a farmer's total outgoings to an average 33 per cent of gross produce after 25 per cent had been paid in rent. Other items were taxes and local rates, and among the latter poor rates were very high for some years after the end of the war against France in 1815.[97]

The farmer's prosperity therefore depended largely on the relationship between the rent he had to pay and the value of his annual produce, and there seems little doubt that in the later 18th century most landlords were able to maintain their real income in the face of rising prices: that happened even on the Lilleshall estate where leases for three lives granted (for political reasons) in 1755 were not renewed before they expired.[98] Where landlords continued to sell renewals their real income was doubtless maintained the more easily. Racking naturally made it even easier to keep rent up with prices and increasing numbers of landlords were in fact abandoning leases in favour of rack rents. Tenure at will, in place of freehold or chattel leases,[99] was making progress on the Newport estate by the 1740s; after control of the estate had fallen into the hands of the notorious miser William Pulteney, earl of Bath, leases seem not to have been renewed and in the 1760s and 1770s many fell in.[1] Already by 1793 in south Shropshire the survival of leases on Lord Craven's estate was noted as an oddity.[2] The change to rack rents highlights the final phase of 18th-century agrarian 'improvement' that may be equated largely with improving the rent roll by efficient management.[3] Improvement of the rental, however, often implied at least the enlargement and greater consolidation of farms and the inclosure of common wastes, and much was achieved in that way by the end of the 1830s.[4] Such matters were often long and carefully planned as part of the campaign to raise rents. About 1770 John Probert valued Sir Watkin Williams Wynn's Much Wenlock estate and recommended a reorganization of the farms that included enlargement of the biggest ones. He also advised a cautious canvass of the other freeholders about the desirability of inclosing Westwood common by an Act under which the inconveniently interspersed freeholds of Williams Wynn and others could be consolidated;[5] that part of the programme, however, was not achieved until 1814.[6]

A second phase of landlord investment began c. 1790 and was characterized by the sinking of considerable amounts of capital in improvement of the land and in new buildings in order to enable the farmer to pay more rent.[7] The idea of such investment was not new. In 1767 that tireless propagandist Arthur Young had urged Lord Clive to convert some of his 'immense' new fortune from monied to

[94] S.R.O. 2280/2/11, [p. 1] memo., elucidated by the ensuing accts.

[95] Mostly then owned by the Ashwoods: V.C.H. Salop. xi. 38.

[96] In view of the ratio of vicarial to rectorial tithes on (e.g.) Audley Bowdler's est. in the 1840s: S.R.O. 2280/2/48, p. 8.

[97] Kain and Prince, Tithe Surveys, 16, 26; Research in Econ. Hist. vi. 197–8, 219; Evans, Contentious Tithe, 28–9.

[98] Research in Econ. Hist. vi. 206–8.

[99] i.e. those for life and those for yrs. respectively: Cal. Antrobus Deeds bef. 1625 (Wilts. Arch. and Nat. Hist. Soc.

Rec. Branch, iii), p. xl.

[1] S.R.O. 168/4; V.C.H. Salop. iii. 254. On the whole Salop. and Welsh est. there were 167 tenants at will and only 111 leaseholders in the mid 18th cent.

[2] S.P.L., MSS. 6860, p. 53; 6862, ff. 109v., 115, 127v.

[3] Research in Econ. Hist. vi. 212.

[4] S.P.L., MSS. 6860–5; Plymley, Agric. of Salop. 120–3; above (Inclosure); Hulbert, Hist. and Descr. of Salop. ii. 96.

[5] N.L.W., Wynnstay, box 43/3.

[6] S.R.O., incl. award B 38.

[7] Research in Econ. Hist. vi. 212.

landed property and to invest in an experimental farm to be made from newly inclosed 'barren land'. Equally with military exploits, argued Young, and for an initial outlay of only £26,000, such an enterprise would confer 'immortal fame' and yield a profit.[8] Clive did buy land and the family estates were improved,[9] but it was the appointment in 1789 of the elder John Bishton as chief agent for the Leveson-Gower estates that inaugurated the most spectacular Shropshire example of landlord investment as a rent-racking device.[10]

Between 1789 and 1804 landlord expenditure on the Lilleshall estate more than trebled and there was a dramatic increase in the rental: rents had risen by c. 50 per cent 1750–90 and by 1805 they were double the 1750 figure. There were further big increases under James Loch. Between 1805 and 1809 the marquess of Stafford spent an average £1,767 a year (13 per cent of the rental) on the Lilleshall estate, nine times the 1789 figure; the rental was correspondingly racked—by 60 per cent between 1804 and 1810. Landlord expenditure and rent racking continued and between 1817 and 1822 expenditure averaged £9,316 a year, or 48 per cent of rent receipts, on the Lilleshall estate.[11] By 1822 low agricultural prices had forced Loch to concede that half of a tenant's rent should vary with the price of wheat. Within two or three years, however, rising wheat prices brought the rents up again, and between 1825 and 1833 average rent levels on the Lilleshall estate exceeded those of the years 1810–20 when wheat prices had been over 50 per cent higher.[12]

Tenant farmers on the Leveson-Gower estates were very hard pressed by the 1830s. In 1815 the Lilleshall estate was rented at roughly 20s. an acre, slightly higher than a probable national average (18s.) but slightly lower than one suggested for Shropshire (20s.–24s.). By 1833 the Lilleshall estate rents, after an abnormally steep increase, averaged 26s. 8d. an acre compared with a probable national average of 18s. 4d. Shropshire was perhaps an area where rent increases after 1815 were greater than average,[13] and there were other estates in the county where the landlord's investment, even if not on the scale of the Leveson-Gowers', was nevertheless considerable. The Hon. R. H. Clive's tenants paid a percentage on his capital expenditure,[14] and tenants had to do so wherever extensive improvements were carried out, as they were on the Bourton estate of Sir Francis Lawley (7th bt. 1834, d. 1851). By 1843 Lawley had rapidly improved his land by drainage schemes, introduced better systems of cultivation, put up new farm buildings and labourers' cottages, and built new roads;[15] the last-mentioned improvement probably extended cultivation on the estate for in 1793 the remoter parts of Monkhopton parish had lain untilled owing to the impossibility of carting manure there.[16] The Lawleys had perhaps accumulated capital during the lifetime of Sir Francis's childless elder brother,[17] and Sir Francis, childless himself, had married an heiress.[18]

How typical of Shropshire was the position of the tenant farmer on the Leveson-Gower estates? There were certainly other hard-pressed farmers. In 1799 Sir Corbet Corbet of Adderley was unpopular with his tenants on account of his

[8] Young, Letter to Ld. Clive (1767).

[9] But largely by Clive's successors. His elder son encouraged turnip growing on the Montford and Walcot estates; new fm. bldgs. were erected at Montford, and Walcot became a centre of experimentation: above (Agricultural Revolution); Dodd, 'Salop Agric.' 45–6. On the Oakly Pk. est. Clive's grds. was a notable pioneer of underdraining: above (Agricultural Revolution).

[10] Though Loch seems to have disparaged his predecessors' wk.: cf. Research in Econ. Hist. vi. 208; 212; Agric.

H.R. xxii. 103.

[11] Research in Econ. Hist. vi. 206, 208–9.

[12] Ibid. 209–10.   [13] Ibid. 215–17.

[14] Midland Hist. viii. 157.

[15] Eddowes's Jnl. 21 June 1843.

[16] S.P.L., MS. 6865, p. 143.

[17] Sir Rob., cr. Ld. Wenlock 1831, legatee of half of the Brearley est. 1795: V.C.H. Staffs. xvii. 101.

[18] L. G. Pine, New Extinct Peerage 1884–1971 (1972), 291.

'rapacity'[19] and it has been argued that the phasing and level of the Leveson-Gowers' rent increases and the amount of investment can be matched on other great estates. It is nevertheless unlikely that many landlords were prepared to face the social consequences of applying policies like the Leveson-Gowers'.[20] There is, moreover, evidence to suggest that, whatever the case elsewhere in the country, some other large Shropshire landowners had priorities and responsibilities that prevented them from investing in their estates in order to rack rents up to the level attained by James Loch for the Leveson-Gowers. There were, for example, heavy debts charged on the Hawkstone[21] and Attingham estates, in the latter case owing to the extravagance of the 2nd Lord Berwick between 1791 and 1827. The Attingham debts were cleared off by 1861[22] but the Hawkstone debts remained until Lord Hill was made bankrupt in 1894.[23] The Leveson-Gowers eschewed political expenditure from 1825[24] but some leading Shropshire landowners persisted much longer. The Whitmores did not stop treating voters at Bridgnorth elections until after Thomas Whitmore's death in 1846,[25] and his grandson was forced to sell the Apley Park estate in 1867 to pay off the heavy encumbrances.[26] After 1832 the Clives continued to use corruption to control Ludlow and the Foresters kept up their political interest at Wenlock.[27] The Bridgemans[28] and Foresters seem to have invested heavily in extension of their estates, and in the Foresters' case at least that seems to have been done at the expense of their improvement.[29] In the later 1830s the dowager countess of Bridgwater (d. 1849), life tenant of the county's third largest estate (over 20,000 a.), was said to invest over £20,000 a year in the property but even so was considered 'a very low letter of land'.[30]

By the early 19th century, with the onset of scientific farming, tenants had more opportunities of investing in their farms—primarily in new fertilizers, grains, and livestock.[31] In such circumstances tenant right, an outgoing farmer's entitlement to compensation for unexhausted improvements, became a more urgent matter. It had been discussed by farming writers certainly since the 17th century,[32] but the subject became more widely canvassed as leases gave way to rack renting and tenant investment increased. William Pinches, president of the Wenlock Farmers' Club and living on 400 a. of his own at Ticklerton, considered the subject for many years and his estimates of improvements deserving compensation ranged from liming (exhausted after 2 years) to fencing (20 years) and draining (30 years). In a period of rack renting the most important improvements, such as fencing and draining, were unlikely to be undertaken by the tenant, even if he had sufficient capital. Pinches stated that racked land in Shropshire was the least improved, but a landlord's reputation counted for much and in Shropshire as elsewhere tenant investment was in practice covered by landlord–tenant agreements.

[19] S.R.O. 3916/1/1, p. 44.

[20] *Research in Econ. Hist.* vi. 215–17 (the examples given are not Salop. ones); E. Richards, 'Social and Electoral Influence of the Trentham Interest, 1800–60', *Midland Hist.* iii. 118, 120, 126.

[21] S.R.O. 731, box 207, partics. of Hawkstone unsettled ests. 1897; bdle. 351, maps of 1890s.

[22] Above (Large estates).

[23] *Shrews. Chron.* 20 July, 31 Aug., 28 Sept. (editorial) 1894; 5 Apr. 1895.

[24] *Midland Hist.* iii. 138–43.

[25] *V.C.H. Salop.* iii. 333.

[26] Loton Hall MSS., Sir B. Leighton's diary 14 Mar. 1865, Mar. 1867, 17 Jan. 1870.

[27] *V.C.H. Salop.* iii. 336–43.

[28] Above (Large estates).

[29] *T.S.A.S.* lix. 146.

[30] Cf. *2nd Rep. Sel. Cttee. on Agric.* H.C. 189, p. 236 (1836), viii (1); Hulbert, *Hist. and Descr. of Salop.* ii. 242; Bateman, *Gt. Landowners*, 61, giving the acreage (by then Ld. Brownlow's) as 20,233, an area exceeded only by Ld. Powis's and the duke of Cleveland's: ibid. 94, 367. For the good condition of Brownlow's property in the 1880s see below, 1875–1985 (Agrarian economy and society).

[31] P. J. Perry, 'High Farming in Victorian Brit.: Financial Foundations', *Agric. Hist.* lii. 374.

[32] For this para. and the next two see *Rep. Sel. Cttee. on Agric. Customs*, H.C. 461, pp. 363–9 (1847–8), vii; J. H. Pinches, *Fam. of Pinches* (1981), 21–2, 49–50; G. E. Fussell, 'Tenant Right and Salop. Farming in 1848', *Salop. Agric. News*, v. 41, 43; H. H. Dixon, *Law of the Fm.* (1858), 21; ibid. (4th edn.), ed. H. Perkins (1879), 26–7, 43–9; S.R.O. 807/273–9; 2868/164.

By c. 1850 it had become the custom either for the landlord to do all the work of draining (except haulage of materials) and charge the tenant 5 per cent or for the landlord to supply pipes and the tenant to lay them at his own expense under the bailiff's supervision. Surviving agreements fill out the details: in 1823 the owner of Sweeney agreed to provide the incoming tenant of one of his farms with drainage stones; the tenant was to carry them and the landlord was to allow him two thirds of the expense of cutting the drains and back-filling. Legislation on tenant right came only at the end of the period, but the Act,[33] officially recognizing Lincolnshire customs,[34] was permissive and its procedures complicated and potentially expensive. In Shropshire, as elsewhere, it was probably a dead letter.

It seems not to have been the custom in Shropshire for an outgoing tenant to be compensated by his successor for the use of manure or the newer feeds. No doubt such matters, as at Atcham in 1795, on the Sutherland estates until 1859,[35] and at Sweeney in 1823, were regulated according to custom by the landlord. So were the general relations between incoming and outgoing tenants: payment for seed sown, the sharing of growing white crops and their straw, the use of boosy pastures,[36] and the general sequence of handing over sown land, stubbles, meadows, and the house and farm buildings. Standard arrangements were introduced on the Hawkstone estate in 1786[37] and next year were embodied in standard two-life farm leases printed on parchment. The late 18th-century Hawkstone arrangements[38] seem to agree well with the generalized accounts of Shropshire agricultural customs recorded in the mid 19th century: clearly those customs were widely observed and of long standing by 1848.

Landlord–tenant relations were by no means governed exclusively, or even principally, by economic considerations and the clauses of leases and tenancy agreements. Many Shropshire landlords were on the friendliest terms with their tenants, and against the advantages of enlarging farms they weighed 'the honour and respectability conferred by a numerous tenantry': farmers of £50 a year or more were parliamentary electors and increased their landlord's consequence in the county in proportion to their numbers.[39] Though leasing gave way almost everywhere to rack renting during the period, it remained true that on many large estates the same farm was held by one family for generations.[40] In Shropshire the large owners were said to be as good landlords as any in the country[41] and, so far as it affected the improvement of the land, confidence in a landlord made up for the influence of tenure at will on the tenant's willingness to lay out capital.[42] One land agent writing in the 1830s, when leasing was largely going out, claimed to know on the one hand of some freehold farms that had deteriorated from generation to generation and on the other of many farms under good landlords long occupied by the same family and in a high state of cultivation.[43] Sir Baldwin Leighton, though strict, was a meticulously fair landlord,[44] and the dowager countess of Bridgwater was known to be 'always ready to assist a tenant'.[45] There was in fact much mutual respect between landlord and tenant. Robert Luther held 1,000 a.

[33] Agric. Holdings (Eng.) Act, 1875, 38 & 39 Vic. c. 92.
[34] J. R. McQuiston, 'Tenant Right: Farmer Against Landlord in Victorian Eng.' Agric. Hist. xlvii. 108, 112.
[35] S.R.O. 112, box 49, Thos. Hurd's acct. Feb. 1795; Agric. H.R. xxii. 116.
[36] i.e. those available to an outgoing tenant for a time after the end of his tenancy: H. D. G. Foxall, Salop. Field-Names (Salop. Arch. Soc. 1980), 34.
[37] S.R.O. 731, parcel 222, agreement 1786.
[38] Ibid. boxes 213-17, printed fm. leases.

[39] Hulbert, Hist. and Descr. of Salop. ii. 96; cf. Mingay, Eng. Landed Soc. in 18th Cent. 186-8; Thompson, Eng. Landed Soc. in 19th Cent. 196 sqq.
[40] Dixon, Law of Fm. (1858), 21; ibid. (4th edn.), ed. Perkins, 26; 2nd Rep. Sel. Cttee. on Agric. 245.
[41] Rep. Sel. Cttee. on Agric. Customs, 364-6.
[42] Rep. Sel. Cttee. on Agric. 24.
[43] Hulbert, Hist. and Descr. of Salop. ii. 96.
[44] T.S.A.S. lix. 142.
[45] 2nd Rep. Sel. Cttee. on Agric. 236.

at Acton, in Lydbury North, under Lord Powis who, it was said, 'had no farmer of whom he felt more proud'.[46]

Generally the social forces uniting the ranks of landed and farming society were stronger and more varied than the causes of dissension. Sport was a powerful bond, field sports in particular providing those occasions of 'unceremonious intercourse' between gentry and farmers that engendered 'mutual admiration and respect'. Some local hunts were led by yeomen; the mastership of the United (mainly a farmers' hunt), for instance, passed on William Pinches's death in 1849 to Lord Powis's tenant Luther. 'Nimrod' asserted that no other county in England showed more respect for the 'noble science' or had more sportsmen and wellwishers among the 'higher orders' and the yeomen, the result being an 'excellent feeling' between tenant and landlord.[47]

The tenant farmers of the earlier 19th century were, if contemporary comment may be trusted, superior in intellect and education to many of their predecessors. In 1833 Richard White attributed the general improvement in agriculture to the farmers' activity and to the spirit of emulation among them. Samuel Bickerton thought that education had greatly improved the younger farmers and that tenants showed a great deal more intelligence and knowledge of their business than in the past.[48] In 1841 the Wenlock Agricultural Reading Society was formed; it established reading rooms and a library in which priority was given to the provision of books on agriculture, thus accessible to local farmers in return for an annual subscription of 6s. It was at Much Wenlock too that one of the leading farmers' clubs in the county was formed next year; its membership of farmers and gentlemen could discuss and write about matters of common interest to all involved in agriculture.[49] Ironically it was also at Much Wenlock that the squire's wife, Lady Catherine Milnes Gaskell, cherished condescending notions of the ideal farming family. In 1884 she depicted the tenants of 'a farm that pays' as simple people educated narrowly for the work they had to do and leading a life of incessant toil, domestic drudgery, and cheeseparing frugality; without intellectual interests (beyond regular Bible reading) and strictly attentive to the habits of their forefathers, they disclaimed—in homely unpolished speech—any political or other wider interests, content simply to affirm their reverence for the queen. This snobbish effusion, revealing an outlook more than half a century out of date, was skilfully deflated by John Bowen-Jones, the leading Shropshire farmer of his day. He depicted 'a farm that really pays', run with more profit to all classes by a modern tenant living 'a life of comfort and culture' who was at the same time 'a useful member of society'. 'As well try to restore the heptarchy', he concluded, as to 'resuscitate the smock-frock farmer'.[50]

In the earlier part of the period there were political bonds between the landlords and their tenants, notably the protectionist cause as the free-trade movement gathered strength in the 1840s. The protectionists organized particularly well in central Shropshire[51] and almost all the landlords[52] and 8 of the county's 12 Tory M.P.s[53] were solidly against repeal of the corn laws.[54] Thus for perhaps the first

[46] 'The Druid', Saddle and Sirloin, 447.
[47] 'Nimrod' [C. J. Apperley], Hunting Reminiscences (1843), 2–3, 5, 31; V.C.H. Salop. ii. 173–5.
[48] Hulbert, Hist. and Descr. of Salop. ii. 95; Rep. Sel. Cttee. on Agric. 23–4, 27, 240, 243.
[49] E. B. Higgs, 'Wenlock Agric. Reading Soc. Libraries' (TS. [c. 1980] in town clk.'s office, M. Wenlock); below. Attempts to unite the club with the Reading Soc. failed.
[50] The Nineteenth Cent. Oct. 1884, 568–75; May 1885,

847–56. For the Gaskells see L. Edel, Hen. James: The Conquest of London 1870–83 (1962), 336; for Bowen-Jones see V.C.H. Salop. iii. 166, 185–6, 323, 348, 351 and n. 34, 360.
[51] Dodd, 'Salop. Agric.' 151–3, 158, 173–4.
[52] The most vociferous exception was Wm. Wolryche Whitmore of Dudmaston: V.C.H. Salop. iii. 282, 314, 331.
[53] Most notably Benj. Disraeli.
[54] Ibid. 314, 328.

time the intelligent and prosperous tenant farmers came forward to speak on a political subject on more or less equal terms with their landlords;[55] Samuel Bickerton of Sandford was one such[56] and there were many others. That bond, however, was removed after the free traders triumphed in 1846, and in the last 30 years of the period some diminution of tenants' deference is discernible on the increasing number of occasions when they had a forum for their views. Indeed even before 1846 there were early signs of independence: a few Whig or Liberal landowners did not join the Shropshire Agricultural Protective Society formed in 1844, but their tenants joined without them.[57]

Protectionist organization probably gave an impetus in the 1840s to the formation of farmers' clubs. Two early ones (c. 1800) were on the eastern, more agriculturally advanced, side of the county at Market Drayton and Shifnal; John Cotes of Woodcote was probably the leading spirit in the latter, which was founded in 1800 and lasted over a century; it was well supported by the landowners and both societies evidently included Staffordshire farmers too.[58] By 1838 there was a practical farmers' society at Ellesmere.[59] The Wenlock Farmers' Club, however, founded in 1842,[60] came to be regarded as first and foremost, and its meetings evinced strong protectionist feeling.[61] The club arranged regular discussion meetings and lectures and soon established itself as a model for others, such as those formed at Atcham (1843), Baschurch and Ruyton (by 1846), Ludlow (c. 1847), and Wellington (1843). There was an agricultural society at Oswestry by 1865. Some of the clubs were short-lived. In 1863, for example, farmers and gentlemen living around Bridgnorth wanted to join the Wenlock club when their own suspended operations, and in fact the Wenlock club's membership came to include gentlemen and farmers from many different parts of the county. The club thus maintained its leading role and in 1866 was asked to assist in the formation of an agricultural association for Shropshire and Montgomeryshire.[62]

There was no county agricultural society in Shropshire until 1810 when the Shropshire General Agricultural Society was formed.[63] It organized, as did its successors, an annual stock show with prizes, but the events were restricted to subscribers with the result that the prize competitions were effectively closed to tenants. That exclusiveness, and the inconvenience of a July show, led to the society's dissolution in 1823.[64] A later society, the Shropshire Agricultural Association, was evidently in a poor way by 1838 when Lord Darlington cancelled its annual dinner.[65] The name of the Shropshire Practical Farmers' Association, which held its first show in 1840, indicates an intention to avoid the exclusiveness that had earlier proved so harmful. Known, however, as the Shropshire Agricultural Society by the late 1840s, the society and its annual show were then failing to attract the support of either the gentry (mainstay of the earlier societies) or the townspeople of Shrewsbury. The show ground there, near St. Julian's Friars, was cramped and difficult of access and by 1850 the society's future seemed doubtful; the society was, however, revived or re-established in 1853-4 and continued to hold a winter cattle

[55] S.P.L., MS. 3040.
[56] S. Bagshaw, Dir. Salop. (1851), 204.
[57] Dodd, 'Salop. Agric.' 174.
[58] Plymley, Agric. of Salop. 351; D. H. Robinson, The Sleepy Meese (Albrighton, 1988), 29-30, 32. Wm. Ward's engraving (1810) of Thos. Weaver's portrait of John Cotes (at Pitchford Hall) was dedicated to members of the Shifnal Agric. Soc.
[59] Salopian Jnl. 3 and 10 Oct. 1838.
[60] T. H. Thursfield, Wenlock Farmers' Club 1842-1902

[c. 1902], 1, 3 (copy in S.P.L.).
[61] Ibid. 3, 6, 15.
[62] Ibid. passim; S.R.O. 836/70; Speeches, articles &c. of Edw. Jas. Herbert, 3rd earl of Powis, ed. R. C. and W. H. Herbert (1892), 263-72; S.P.L., MS. 3040, newscutting 2 Oct. 1850.
[63] Plymley, Agric. of Salop. 351; Salopian Jnl. 3 Oct., 14 Nov. 1810.
[64] Salopian Jnl. 9 July, 19 Nov. 1823.
[65] Ibid. 10 Oct. 1838.

and poultry show in Shrewsbury for a few years more.[66] The Shropshire Chamber of Agriculture, formed in 1866, was destined to endure. It was paralleled by county chambers all over the country under a Central Chamber, in whose formation R. J. More of Linley, Liberal M.P. for South Shropshire 1865–8, had played a leading part.[67] In 1874–5 the Shropshire Chamber, with More, one of the county's leading farmers J. Bowen Jones,[68] and Thomas Corbett of the Perseverance Ironworks,[69] assisted the formation of the Shropshire and West Midlands Agricultural Society. At first the Chamber evidently hoped that the Wenlock Farmers' Club would form the basis of the new society, which in the event, however, was formed independently. It held its first annual agricultural show in Shrewsbury in 1875.[70]

The early county agricultural associations, the local farmers' clubs, and the Shropshire Chamber provided forums that were perhaps more welcome to the farmers than the squires, some of whom found the farmers' growing self-confidence brash and irritating. In 1849 Sir Baldwin Leighton had much difficulty in preventing John Meire from inflicting a second long speech on the Shropshire Agricultural Society after an earlier, 'very violent', after-dinner harangue.[71] A meeting of the Shropshire Chamber of Agriculture in 1869 was said to be attended by a 'very large muster' of the county's 'most influential tenant farmers', and next year the Chamber's dinner, presided over by Lord Bradford, was attended by very many farmers but just 15 gentlemen, only 5 of whom were squires. Leighton, there to support Bradford, considered the Chamber unpopular with the landlords and its meetings likely to engender bad feeling against them.[72] Nevertheless Leighton himself had not been averse to studying the farmers in the interests of his own political career, and near the end of the period there were clear signs of the farmers occasionally exercising political choices in opposition to their landlords. In the 1865 general election they helped R. J. More, who stood as their candidate, to beat Leighton in the Southern division,[73] but only at the end of the period was a political clash between landlords and tenants provoked. That was done by Leighton's younger son Stanley, victor in the 1876 North Shropshire by-election. The immediate effects of that contest, however, seem not to have lasted long and party-political rivalries among the squires disappeared after the Liberal split of 1886. Nevertheless the two county members, Leighton (1876–1901) and More (1865–8 and 1885–1903), continued to boast of being 'the Farmer's Friend'.[74]

Two subjects on which landlords almost invariably found that their own views diverged from those of their tenants were game preservation[75] and the letting of labourers' cottages.[76] Preservation was organized with increasing efficiency from the mid 18th century and some well documented estates, such as Apley Park, Hawkstone, and Walcot, show a sustained revival of interest after c. 1850 when landowners' anxieties about a possible repeal of the game laws were dissipated.[77] Rabbits were not a highly regarded bag and were indeed destroyed by gamekeepers and other agents of the landlord; nevertheless they were a particular irritant to

[66] Ibid. 14 Oct. 1840; *Eddowes's Jnl.* 8 Oct. 1845; 11 Oct. 1848; 19 Oct., 30 Nov. (p. 5) 1853; 4 Oct. (p. 4), 29 Nov. 1854; 12 Dec. 1855, pp. 6–7; Herbert, *Speeches of Powis,* 74–82; *Shrews. Chron.* 12 Oct. 1849; 11 Oct. 1850.

[67] *V.C.H. Salop.* iii. 316–18, and sources cited ibid. 317 n. 49.

[68] Above.

[69] The Soc.'s first sec. For him cf. above (Motive power, tools, and mechanization).

[70] Thursfield, *Wenlock Farmers' Club,* 29–30; *Cent. of Progress 1875–1975: Salop. & W. Midlands Agric. Soc.* ed. R. Kenney (Shrews. 1975), 4 sqq.

[71] *T.S.A.S.* lix. 135–6; *Shrews. Chron.* 12 Oct. 1849.

[72] Loton Hall MSS., Sir B. Leighton's diary 15 Jan. 1870; *Eddowes's Jnl.* 10 Feb. 1869; 19 Jan. 1870.

[73] *V.C.H. Salop.* iii. 143, 311, 316–17. More was seconded by John Meire: *T.S.A.S.* lix. 166.

[74] *V.C.H. Salop.* iii. 318, 323–4, 344–5, 347; *T.S.A.S.* lix. 170–80. In 1877 Stan. Leighton's elder bro. Sir Baldwyn became M.P. for S. Salop. with farmers' support.

[75] Dodd, 'Salop. Agric.' 176–7.

[76] Below.

[77] *V.C.H. Salop.* ii. 188–90. For the Apley Pk. est. cf. *T.S.A.S.* lix. 145.

farmers and others.[78] Sir Baldwin Leighton enforced strict preservation on his Loton Park estate in the 1850s and secured the passing of the 1862 Poaching Prevention Act. That and a prosecution of his own gamekeeper in 1855 for stealing a couple of rabbits later harmed his political career.[79] The keenest game preserver of all was probably the 2nd Lord Forester, and his Willey estate was so highly preserved that A. H. Brown, the Liberal M.P. who divided the representation of Wenlock with the Conservative Foresters, brought in a Bill in 1870 to repeal the 1862 Act. Col. Edward Corbett, M.P. for South Shropshire, was absent from the Commons when they voted on it because he feared that a vote against Brown would harm him with the farmers.[80] In 1870 Lord Bradford was compelled to strike a defensive note about game preservation when addressing farmers in the Shropshire Chamber of Agriculture.[81] Despite farmers' grumbles, however, preservation continued long after the close of the period, and the gentry's enthusiasm for shooting was unchecked before 1914.[82]

Farmers wished to have cottages for their workers included in their farm tenancies but landlords were well aware that it was not in the labourer's best interests,[83] and most of them seem to have resisted the farmers' demands. Farmers also complained generally of a shortage of cottages,[84] but the perennial obstacle to building and improving cottages was the low return on the investment, a consequence of the farm labourer's low wages.[85]

Labourers and cottagers

About 1775 a Shropshire labourer could probably earn 1s. a day with beer. In 1776 Arthur Young considered that labourers' wages had grown by thirty per cent since c. 1760, and his view may probably be taken as an indication that wages fluctuated in the earlier 18th century.[86] There was a slight tendency for wages to rise after the mid 1770s, albeit slowly and probably more slowly than elsewhere.[87] By 1793, when Joseph Plymley visited his archdeaconry and made detailed records of the civil as well as the ecclesiastical character of every south Shropshire parish under his jurisdiction, the average daily wage for ordinary work on south Shropshire farms seems to have been 8d. if the farmer provided meat and drink, 14d. if he did not.[88] Wages, however, varied with the season and the work being done: by 1793 the daily wage in the 'dark quarter' was often no more than 6d. with meat and drink, though that rate (which was sometimes also the rate for old labourers) seems to have been objected to and was going out.[89] At harvest 1s. a day with meat and drink was evidently normal and double that rate was known.[90]

It was an advantage to have 'constant work, wet or dry': those who did in Barrow, Much Wenlock, and Wistanstow, for example, were better off than men who earned higher rates for work 'by measure' or from 'occasional employers'.[91]

[78] V.C.H. Salop. iii. 324; Thursfield, Wenlock Farmers' Club, 7; R. M. Grier, John Allen (1889), 187–8, 247.
[79] V.C.H. Salop. iii. 316; T.S.A.S. lix. 127, 142.
[80] Loton Hall MSS., Sir B. Leighton's diary July 1870; T.S.A.S. lix. 145–6; V.C.H. Salop. iii. 342.
[81] Eddowes's Jnl. 19 Jan. 1870.
[82] Thursfield, Wenlock Farmers' Club, 33; V.C.H. Salop. ii. 188–90.
[83] Plymley, Agric. of Salop. 113–14; Midland Hist. iii. 123.
[84] 2nd Rep. Emp. Children and Women in Agric.: App. Pt. II [4202–I], p. 74, H.C. (1868–9), xiii.
[85] Shrews. Chron. 12 Jan. 1872, p. 6.

[86] Wage rates c. 1700 were not much lower than those of the 1770s: above, 1540–1750 (Inclosure).
[87] Dodd, 'Salop. Agric.' 65–7 (here, as elsewhere, misdating Young's tour of 1776); Young, Tours in Eng. and Wales, 148, 158, 164–5.
[88] This and the next 10 paras. are based on S.P.L., MSS. 6860–5. There is no comparable contemporary evidence for N. Salop.
[89] Cardington, Chirbury, Habberley, Stanton Lacy, Monkhopton.
[90] Eaton-under-Heywood, Mainstone, Ratlinghope.
[91] Cf. Beckbury.

As in Wistanstow, so elsewhere it was presumably 'good masters' from among the 'large farmers' who gave constant work and helped their men with gifts of firewood and milk for their families. That seems to have happened even in low-wage parishes like Acton Scott. Nevertheless the farmers, even where they were considerate, could do nothing to improve their labourers' cottages; they belonged to the landlords, and in Wistanstow, for example, many were semi-ruinous c. 1805.[92] Plymley, though he gave much thought to labourers' wages and housing standards, never connected the two questions in the way that his Madeley statistics might have prompted him to do. There industrial wages were good and domestic comfort increasing in the 1790s.[93] Elsewhere, however, farm labourers' low wages set low limits to cottage rents. Cottage improvement thus remained an act of benevolence on the landlord's part rather than a normal investment of capital.

Even within south Shropshire there were considerable differences in labourers' living standards between one parish and another. In Habberley the cottagers were wretchedly poor,[94] whereas in Ashford Bowdler, Clunbury, Hope Bowdler, and Stanton Lacy, for example, they were comparatively comfortable, either because wages were higher than average or because the farmers were considerate. Agricultural improvement seemed to enhance the labourer's prospects. In Middleton Scriven the newly resident lord of the manor[95] had recently taken 400 a. in hand 'to set an example of good husbandry to a neighbourhood that wants it', and perhaps as a result of his improvements the labourers had 14d. a day in winter (without drink), 18d. a day in summer, 'and they are advancing'.

A landowner's liberality could make much difference to the labourers' condition. In Astley Abbots, where 'the poor' (i.e. labouring families)[96] were 'supposed to fare hardly', they were also said to benefit greatly from the 'kind consideration' of Mrs. Phillips, the only resident among the parish's nine landowners, and in Cleobury North the lord of the manor Thomas Knight, though not resident there,[97] did much to improve the poor's lot. In Badger Isaac Hawkins Browne, lord of the manor and much the greatest landowner, allowed the labourers 8s. a week all year, with beer at harvest and a guinea a year to each family for coal. Moreover Browne often continued allowances to labourers in sickness and old age. In Beckbury, where the Badger Hall estate extended but Browne was only one of eight landowners, most labouring was done 'by measure' on a contract between farmer and labourer. Where that was not so labourers got 1s. a day and beer. There was pressure to raise that rate and Plymley believed it could not have been kept so low but for Browne's allowance of 1s. 6d. to 2s. 6d. a week to many poor families in the parish.

An important influence on farm labourers' wages was the opportunity for alternative work, for industrial wages were always higher. In Beckbury it was only Browne's benevolence that kept farm wages down, because the parish lay between the east Shropshire coalfield and Wolverhampton, within the influence of manufactories, collieries, and furnaces 'on almost every side'. In parts of the east Shropshire coalfield wages at the mines and ironworks (1s. 6d. a day in Benthall) and potteries (Barrow) pushed farm labourers' daily rates up to 10d. and 1s. with maintenance (Barrow and Willey) or even 16d. (Benthall). In Linley too wages were rising, and

[92] S.R.O. 1986/9, 14, 16-17, 19-20, 23, 29, 34, 36- 7, 43-4, 46.
[93] S.P.L., MS. 6865, pp. 128, 132; cf. e.g. ibid. pp. 161-3; MS. 6863, pp. 179-81; Plymley, *Agric. of Salop.* 344.
[94] *V.C.H. Salop.* viii. 241.
[95] Ric. Rowley, also patron of the living and curate for

the absentee rector.
[96] Plymley (s.v. Woolstaston) equates 'the poor' with 'day labourers'; that is his general usage, reflecting that of contemporary and later writers.
[97] He lived at Henley Hall in Bitterley. Plymley considered there was no more useful country gentleman.

farmers wanting occasional men without maintaining them had to pay 18d. In the industrial parish of Madeley[98] farmers had to pay 9s. a week in winter and 10s. in summer, for at the furnaces wages were 11s. or 12s. a week and even (presumably for the more highly skilled) up to 40s. Across the Severn in Broseley, where the mines and ironworks paid 20s.-24s. a week, the least able farm labourer could get 10s. at common work. Around the Titterstone Clee industrial wages had an effect. Coal and lime works raised the Coreley farm labourer's daily rate to 2s.-2s. 6d. In Hopton Wafers paper-makers' earnings (10s.-10s. 6d. a week) and miners' (12s.-15s.) meant that ordinary farm work cost as much as 16d. a day, 2d. more than the prevailing rural rate. Farm labourers in Hope Bagot could hope for 18d. a day because of the lime-rock workers' 2s.

Inexplicably industrial wages had less effect in some parishes. In Stoke St. Milborough 2s. or 3s. a day could be earned in the coal and lime works but farm labourers' rates were if anything slightly below average. West of Shrewsbury industry's effects varied: lime and coal works[99] and trials for lead had more effect in Alberbury for instance than in heighbouring Cardeston. In Great Hanwood, where there was a drapers' manufactory, labourers seem to have got about 1d. a day more than average but farther south in the mining district no such influence can be detected: coal miners in Pontesbury[1] and Westbury[2] and lead miners in Minsterley[3] earned a guinea in a short week[4] but farm workers there and thereabouts[5] could get only the average rates, as they did in Wentnor, despite the presumably recent influx of 100 miners to work the Bog mine,[6] most of them living in sheds and tabling at small farmhouses.

There is little evidence that the proximity of towns influenced farm labourers' wages. Near Shrewsbury their earnings in Meole Brace (where there was a woollen manufactory) and Sutton seem only average, and at Tasley, outside Bridgnorth, wages had only just begun to rise from 14d. a day with drink.

More vivid indications of the farm labourer's standard of living in south Shropshire in 1793 are provided by comments on his diet and housing. With regard to diet the greatest division appears between men who could kill a pig for their family and those who could not. In a few parishes virtually no labourer could keep a pig,[7] or at least not for his own consumption.[8] Even in the numerous parishes where 'several', 'some', or 'a few' labourers had one, it often seems that such phrases meant a small minority: in Farlow fewer than 1 in 6. In Wistanstow only the 'industrious' kept a pig and in Church Pulverbatch 'fewer kill pigs than used to', a change most marked in the previous seven years: 'scarce any labourer has a pig this year and all used to kill one against Christmas formerly'. In a few parishes 'most' or 'many' of the labourers could keep a pig for their family, and that was normally an indication of exceptional local prosperity with particular causes, such as the influence of industry,[9] considerate farmers,[10] or a resident landowner.[11] In Alberbury it was the vicar's sale of tithe pigs to the labourers at 3s. and 4s. apiece that enabled them to rear the animals. The poor of Church Stretton were said to buy flesh meat 'seldom'; elsewhere, when there was no pig (perhaps an increasingly common state of affairs),[12] meat was beyond the labourer's

[98] Cf. V.C.H. Salop. xi. 22, 45 sqq.
[99] Cf. ibid. viii. 211. [1] Cf. ibid. 279-80.
[2] Cf. ibid. 322. [3] Cf. ibid. 322-4.
[4] i.e. reserving Sun., Mon., and sometimes Tues. for drinking: Pontesbury.
[5] e.g. at Habberley: cf. V.C.H. Salop. viii. 241.
[6] Which had passed to new owners c. 1789: F. Brook and
M. Allbutt, Salop. Lead Mines (Buxton, 1973), 46.
[7] Clee St. Margaret, Culmington (except the cottagers near the wastes), Greete, Munslow. [8] Bettws-y-crwyn.
[9] Barrow, Coreley, Gt. Hanwood, Pontesbury; cf. Young, Tours in Eng. and Wales, 145; above.
[10] Acton Scott, Clunbury. [11] Middleton Scriven.
[12] Chirbury, Ch. Pulverbatch.

family.[13] Their diet, as at Stretton, was bread and potatoes[14] with a little cheese[15] and, more rarely, butter;[16] in Bishop's Castle dripping was used instead of butter. In the poorest parishes, like Habberley, the labourer could not buy even cheese for his wife and family: it had nevertheless to be afforded for the labouring man who could not work on bread and potatoes alone. Some Habberley farmers gave the poor a weak broth called 'supping',[17] and many labourers, when not at task work, ate at the farmhouse.

By 1793 cottage brewing was almost unknown,[18] though in Hope Bowdler, some brewed 'a little small beer now and then'; that also happened in Barrow and perhaps Bromfield. In Middleton Scriven the squire thought the higher wages then coming in would permit brewing, 'but it is not done'. In Chirbury the poor were remembered generally to have had small beer and 'plenty' of cheese but by 1793 there was no brewing and they had little cheese.

There were various ways of earning a living in the countryside[19] but by the 1790s two main groups of rural poor, most easily defined by their respective types of housing, were becoming increasingly distinctive. First there were the cottagers and small occupiers dwelling on or near the commons, owing little beyond an acknowledgement to the lord of the manor and using the common and small inclosures taken from it; for them day labour was perhaps only an occasional supplement to their basic living. Secondly there were the full-time labourers, both the village day labourers who paid proper rents for their cottages and gardens and the living-in farm servants.

Progressive opinion was hardening against the commons squatters. John Bishton inveighed against them and the holdings that afforded them only a trifling income but worked on their minds as 'a sort of independence' productive of idleness and immorality.[20] Plymley often noted how ineligibly the squatters lived compared with the regular labourers. In Clee St. Margaret in 1793, for example, 22 of the 50 houses were cottages amerced as low as 8d. a year, but generally their occupants seem to have been unable to get a pig and were more expensive to the parish than the labourers who paid rent. In Cardington there were plenty of hills and commons and the cottagers generally paid only small amercements; nevertheless they were poor and getting poorer. Those who paid amercements in Hope Bowdler (6d. or more) and had 'most advantage' from the waste were 'indolent' and fared worse than the labourers paying rent and living in the villages.

Such views of the commons squatters survived as long as the commons themselves. A 160-a. common at Aston on Clun was inclosed c. 1804 by agreement between the lord of the manor and the freeholders; the initiative, however, had come from the new rector of Hopesay, principally concerned to see the immoral commons dwellers cleared off.[21] In 1844 the surveyor for the inclosure of Clun forest stated that 'one lot' of cottagers living about the waste were very bad, 'terrible sheep-stealers and pony-stealers'; many lived idly, being of such bad character that honest people would not have them on their premises. He believed

[13] Occasionally stated (e.g. for Acton Scott) and almost everywhere implied.
[14] Culmington, Mainstone, Myndtown. Cf. Dodd, 'Salop. Agric.' 71.   [15] Wistanstow.
[16] Acton Scott, Munslow, Ch. Preen.
[17] Not 'jupping' as in V.C.H. Salop. viii. 241.
[18] Other domestic brewing continued longer. Cf. 2nd Rep. Sel. Cttee. on Agric. 242; P. Mathias, Brewing Ind. in Eng.

1700–1830 (1959), pp. xxii, 376–7.
[19] See e.g. H. Green, 'Linen Ind. of Salop.' Ind. Arch. Rev. v. 114, 119–21; S.P.L., Geo. Broughall's fm. acct. bk. 1795–1811 (class f NU 22), recording ann. pmnts. to Geo. Baugh for catching moles.
[20] Bishton, Agric. of Salop. 24–5.
[21] Rep. Sel. Cttee. on Commons' Inclosure, H.C. 583, pp. 171–2 (1844), v; cf. S.P.R. Heref. xviii (1), p. ix.

inclosure might improve their condition but would anyway largely put an end to sheep stealing.[22] Whether the destruction of an idle way of life was always so consciously intended by inclosers is uncertain. Time, however, was certainly running against the squatters. Sometimes the imposition of rents in place of the old amercements was the first sign of change, though inclosure was usually associated. In the early 18th century the Preen common cottagers had been kindly treated by the lord of the manor and the farmers who helped them with their ploughing to keep them off the rates. Shortly before 1793, however, rents from 10s. to £4 were put on them so that the cottagers, though they had ground enough, could no longer keep a pig or cow, having instead to sell hay from their land to pay the rent. Preen common was inclosed in the 1790s and the cottage settlement then shrank.[23] Inclosure and the imposition of rents on ramshackle properties worked similar changes elsewhere, as in Astley Abbots and Barrow, both inclosed in 1775.[24] In Barrow cottages with land for a cow continued for a time to pay amercements of 3s. 4d. but by 1793 rents of 40s. or more had been set, and in Astley Abbots c. 40 occupiers of cottages and grounds worth from 40s. to £30 a year were fighting a rearguard action in claiming prescriptive freedom from rent, fines, and taxes of all kinds.

For the industrious rent-paying labourer in the village farming continued to provide a living, though one that was hard, precarious, and in fact deteriorating by the 1790s. In 1793 Plymley's most frequent comment was that the labourer lived 'worse' or 'much worse' than before.[25] The main cause was the high and rising price of corn[26] which brought prosperity to the landowner and farmer but poverty to the labourer. In Edgton the labourers were further impoverished by being forced to buy flour rather than wheat, the price of flour being kept high to retail customers. The same seems true of Woolstaston. In Church Pulverbatch some farmers regularly sold wheat to their labourers below the market price: never more than 7s. 6d. a bushel even if the market went to 10s. 6d. or more. The Pulverbatch labourers earned 9d. a day with meat and drink in summer, and if their families consumed what one Shropshire commentator considered the average of ½ bu. of wheat a week,[27] then even the farmers' concessionary price meant only that their labourers were enabled to subsist: a week's wheat would take a 3s. 9d. out of the man's 4s. 6d. wage. In Munslow parish no labourer's family kept a pig, brewed beer, or bought butcher's meat; they managed to get a little cheese when the family was small but the wheat or flour for a large family took all the man's wages. In some parishes[28] a large labouring family could not survive without parish pay added regularly to the man's wage.

Agricultural wages in the county perhaps increased by 67 per cent over the years 1790–1803, an increase that was much smaller than the rise in prices. By 1800 the prices of 1794 seemed like 'a report from ancient times'; all provisions had at least doubled in price and some had quadrupled.[29] The wild fluctuations in corn prices during the 1790s stimulated profiteering by farmers and millers, and the poor bore the brunt of it. A particularly mean fraud practised on them by millers around Oswestry in 1800 was to exact toll, or payment in kind, amounting to 2s. 6d. worth of wheat instead of the 6d. or 9d. due.[30] After

[22] Rep. Sel. Cttee. on Commons' Incl. 180.
[23] Though Preen Common was eventually to become the par.'s main settlement: cf. V.C.H. Salop. viii. 125, 127.
[24] S.R.O. 1224, box 147, copy award 17 Oct. 1775.
[25] e.g. Bettws-y-crwyn, Chelmarsh, Edgton, Rushbury.
[26] It had been rising since the mid 18th cent.: Ashton,
Econ. Hist. Eng.: 18th Cent. 39-40, 197-8, 239.
[27] J. L. and B. Hammond, The Village Labourer (1978 edn.), 67.
[28] Astley Abbots, Greete, Stoke St. Milborough, Tasley.
[29] Dodd, 'Salop. Agric.' 66, 103; Plymley, Agric. of Salop. 271.
[30] T.S.A.S. lv. 14-15.

1803, it has been suggested, wages made little real progress, though there seems to have been some increase of rates up to c. 1807.[31]

When peace came in 1815 wages fell as farmers cut their costs: in 1833 it was claimed that labourers' wages went from 2s. 4d. a day in 1815 to 1s. 6d. in 1822, little more than the rate of thirty years before.[32] If Church Stretton parish was typical c. 1833, the daily rates then remained unchanged since 1822: 9s. a week in summer (with keep in harvest time) and winter. There it was then believed that a labourer's annual earnings (excluding parish relief) averaged £24 or £25.[33] In one respect Stretton labourers may have been luckier than some others: they were rarely out of work, and indeed some labour had to be imported to the parish in spring and at harvest;[34] they were said to 'subsist very well' on their earnings, allegedly enjoying bacon, bread, potatoes, cheese, milk, tea, and coffee;[35] cheap tea had been affordable by the poor since at least the 1770s but c. 1800 coffee had been almost unknown to the mass of the population.[36] It may by then have become commoner for farmers to sell their men grain below the market price.[37]

The farm labourer's wife and children could earn something to add to the family income. Nevertheless in the late 18th and early 19th century, and for long after, the countrywoman's earnings were small and unreliable, and many Shropshire women sought summer work in the market gardens around London, picking fruit and carrying it to market. The carrying was 'unparalleled slavery', but the 8s. or 9s. a day they earned was unobtainable at home; if a woman stayed on near London for the lower paid vegetable picking she might, having lived frugally, return with £15 as a small dowry or for the support of old parents.[38] A labourer's sons were generally taken off his hands (aged c. 11) before they could earn by being informally apprenticed (unpaid until perhaps the last year of service) to farmers who kept them until they could earn; then they were normally allowed to go, or they ran away.[39] Girls went into farm service younger than their brothers, and owing (as one commentator remarked in 1869) to 'the great evil' of a want of female chastity farm service often led to bastardy.[40] In Shropshire, as in much of the west, male as well as female farm servants lived in the farmhouses as they always had, though their numbers were probably diminishing during the period and their earnings are hard to chronicle. They included ploughmen, wagoners, and cowmen.[41]

In many parts of the county in the 1830s a labourer's wife and four children might earn £8–£9 a year,[42] and thirty years later women (apart from Irishwomen from the towns) were not commonly employed, though in the south-west some took low paid winter work like turnip cutting or stone picking on condition of being allowed to glean. Young children helped with stone picking too.[43]

The poverty and bad housing of most labouring parents made them indifferent to their children's schooling, though by the 1790s thoughtful commentators, including the clergy, increasingly deplored their want of education. In that respect

[31] Dodd, op. cit. 66–7, 88, 104.
[32] G. E. Fussell, 'Salop. Farming in 1833', Salop. Agric. News, iii (2), 11.
[33] Rep. Com. Poor Laws Eng. and Wales, H.C. 44, p. 388a (1834), xxx. [34] Cf. ibid.; Salop. Agric. News, iii (2), 11.
[35] Rep. Com. Poor Laws, p. 388b (1834), xxxi.
[36] Cf. Young, Tours in Eng. and Wales, 148, 158, 164; T.S.A.S. lv. 26.
[37] A privilege confined to the W. counties acc. to Ric. White, agent to the Hon. R. H. Clive (Oakly Pk.) and others: Salop. Agric. News, iii (2), 11; cf. above.
[38] Bridget Hill, 18th-Cent. Women (1984), 193–5, 221.
[39] S.P.L., MSS. 6860–5 passim; Rep. Com. Poor Laws

Eng. and Wales, p. 662A (1834), xxviii (2).
[40] 2nd Rep. Emp. Children and Women in Agric.: App. Pt. I [4202], pp. 12–13, H.C. (1868–9), xiii; App. Pt. II [4202-I], pp. 74–84 (esp. 77–8).
[41] Ibid. App. Pt. I, 13; App. Pt. II, 81; Rep. Sel. Cttee. on Agric. 31–2; W. Hasbach, Hist. of Eng. Agric. Labourer (1908), 176–8, 262–3; Dodd, 'Salop. Agric.' 172, 192–3.
[42] Rep. Com. Poor Laws Eng. and Wales, 385a–396a. Higher earnings for women were claimed in Baschurch, Edgmond, and Kinlet, with varying degrees of plausibility. Many parishes could make no estimate.
[43] 2nd Rep. Emp. Children and Women in Agric.: App. Pt. I, 12; App. Pt. II, 74–6.

J. W. Davis, vicar of Loppington, was probably untypical of his clerical brethren. In 1869 he uttered what was probably a more prevalent rural prejudice when he revealed the plan he adopted in his parish by agreement with the land-owners: since it was found that the best paid labourers were the illiterate ones, labourers' children were encouraged to begin farm work 'as young as possible' (about 10 years old) and 'by this means it is hoped that the children of the smaller farmers will keep ahead of their labourers in respect of education'.[44]

In parts of Shropshire by the mid 19th century there were some labourers who were more prosperous and better housed than most. Mainly they lived on estates whose owners were prepared to let smallholdings or allotments to the more enterprising labourers and to improve cottages with little hope of recovering the capital outlay. The allotments were small farming enterprises, usually pastoral and quite distinct from the gardens, plecks, and headlands where they grew their potatoes, vegetables,[45] and hemp.[46] Advocacy of the allot-ment system in the county went back at least to Plymley's day when inclosure of commons and enlargement of farms were widening the social and economic gap between farmers and labourers. Archibald Alison, incumbent of Kenley, began a scheme on the 30-a. glebe awarded to him at inclosure in 1793: ten 3-a. holdings were let at 7s. an acre to 'the poor people of the common' with the largest families. A jury of farmers inspected the holdings annually and the tenant who had improved his land most was excused the year's rent. By 1796 the scheme was working well, benefiting both the tenants and their land, and the 'experiment' was praised c. 1830. In the mid 1790s Edward Harries of Arscott, in Pontesbury, undertook a similar scheme, though by 1840 that hamlet had apparently been reduced to two farmhouses and a private house.[47] Plymley regretted the 1775 repeal of the 1589 Cottages Act[48] and asserted unequivocally that to deny labourers the chance of renting land was an 'evil'.[49] Some landowners[50] and most tenant farmers—perhaps increasingly as they themselves became rack tenants—disap-proved of letting land to labourers, and in the poverty-stricken south-west (it was alleged in 1844) labourers did not want it.[51] Nevertheless the practice never died out. In north Shropshire it was given an impetus by the 2nd Lord Kenyon, owner of large Welsh estates adjoining Shropshire. About 1833 he subscribed a paper from the Labourer's Friend Society that advocated lettings to labourers, and his agent at Malpas (Ches.) persuaded many other gentlemen to subscribe and circulate it. The agent considered that the plan could do more to improve the labourer's condition than anything else. Sir Rowland Hill (2nd Viscount Hill 1842), a friend of the Kenyons,[52] was evidently sympathetic[53] and labourers' smallholdings were a feature of the Hawkstone estate,[54] though many of them seem to have been created by the labourers' own exertions on Prees[55] and Stanton heaths, two of the largest north Shropshire commons until 1801;[56] probably that had

[44] Ibid. *App. Pt. I*, 12; *App. Pt. II*, 78; S.P.L., MS. 6865, p. 130; G. Nicholls, 'On the Condition of the Agric. Labourer', *J.R.A.S.E.* vii. 11-16; *V.C.H. Salop.* iii. 176-7.
[45] Young, *Tours in Eng. and Wales*, 146, 155, 162; H.O. *Acreage Returns Pt. II*, 185-6, 188, 190-2, 194-5.
[46] Young, op. cit. 146, 155, 162; *Ind. Arch. Rev.* v. 114 sqq. Cottagers grew such small quantities that claiming the govt. bounty (1784-94) was probably not worthwhile: ibid. 117.
[47] Plymley, *Agric. of Salop.* 114-19; *V.C.H. Salop.* viii. 95-6, 255-6.
[48] Forbidding the bldg. of new cottages without at least 4 a. set to them: cf. above, 1540-1750 (Inclosure); Plymley,

op. cit. 117; 15 Geo. III, c. 32.
[49] Plymley, op. cit. 114; cf. Hammond, *Vill. Labourer*, pp. xvi, 102-7.
[50] e.g. J. B. Minor: Dodd, 'Salop. Agric.' 261, 266. Cf. *J.R.A.S.E.* vii. 20.
[51] *Rep. Sel. Cttee. on Commons' Inclosure*, 177-9; cf. below, n. 69. [52] *V.C.H. Salop.* iii. 139.
[53] *Rep. Sel. Cttee. on Agric.* 283.
[54] *2nd Rep. Emp. Children and Women in Agric.: App. Pt. II*, 78-80. [55] Grier, *John Allen*, 243-6.
[56] In 1801 1,463 a. in Prees man. (mostly on Higher and Lower heaths) and 417 a. on Stanton heath were inclosed: S.R.O., incl. award B 10.

happened before the beginning of the period and was regularized by successive owners of the estate.[57] Hill was reputed a cottage improver, and as the owner of 300–400 north Shropshire cottages[58] he was well placed to do much good.[59]

The improvement of cottages often accompanied allotment letting. Some of the poor commons dwellers resettled on Kenley glebe in 1793 soon built themselves cottages in which they took pride, and ten years later Plymley prescribed standards for good cottages.[60] The estate where cottage improvement and the letting of land to labourers was perhaps most intelligently effected was the Loton estate west of Shrewsbury. In 1776 Charlton Leighton (4th bt. 1780) began to improve the amenities of Loton Hall by demolishing the western end of Alberbury village[61] and offering the dispossessed villagers[62] three-life leases to move to Wattlesborough Heath, taking land at 10s. 6d. an acre and building their own cabins and cow houses there.[63] At first sight the change seems against the trend of the times, but the subsequent history of settlement at Wattlesborough Heath shows clearly what the real trend was: villagers were not being made into squatters, but in the long run a squatter settlement was being given more of the social character of a village. In the 1770s the more respectable villagers[64] diluted an old squatter settlement dating from the 1540s, and when the heath was inclosed c. 1780 a more compact settlement was formed along the Shrewsbury–Welshpool turnpike road.[65] By 1793 the most ruinous cottages seemed likely to disappear: as they fell down their land was to be set to the large farms adjoining. In the mid 19th century, as the leases granted by his father's cousin fell in, Sir Baldwin Leighton was building new model cottages and moving the inhabitants of the old cabins into them, sometimes willy-nilly. There were few, perhaps only one, of the old squatter cottages left when Leighton died in 1871.[66] By the 1860s Leighton's parallel policy of letting land to labourers was also achieving remarkable results. Some of his cottages had several acres, the keep of a cow; they were let only to men with savings and Leighton succeeded thereby in his policy of fostering labourers' providence, for there were always applicants for vacant lettings.[67] Leighton's son Sir Baldwyn continued his father's policy of building good cottages, and in 1872 he addressed the nascent farm workers' union on allotments and cow pastures.[68]

It had been a constant preoccupation of those advocating labourers' smallholdings that a man's land should not 'interfere with his working for hire'. Landlords therefore tried to restrict landed labourers to pastoral enterprise.[69] Labourers' holdings on the Loton estate occupied their tenants for one month a year; even so the Alberbury farmers alleged that they made labourers unreliable, especially at busy seasons.[70] How far such claims were justified is impossible to estimate, though the system may have increased the local farmers' objections if the proportion of

[57] Standard smallholding leases (on printed parchment) were introduced in 1787: S.R.O. 731, boxes 213–17, leases.
[58] Rep. Sel. Cttee. on Agric. 283.
[59] 2nd Rep. Emp. Children and Women in Agric.: App. Pt. II, 82–3. [60] Agric. of Salop. 109–13, 118.
[61] And rerouting the Shrews.–Llanfyllin road farther off. V.C.H. Salop. viii. 189, dates the change 1780 × 83, but Plymley's date is right. Mr. Charlton Leighton owned the paternal est. from 1773 (Loton Hall, TS. hist. of Leighton fam. pp. 15, 24–5 (2nd nos.)), not from 1780 (as stated in V.C.H. Salop. viii. 196), and was planning Loton improvements in 1773–4 (A. E. Richardson, Rob. Mylne (1955), 93–4, 98).
[62] i.e. all but 'a residue of depravity in the village whom he did not wish to keep or settle elsewhere': they were taken off at night by a 'press-gang': Loton Hall, TS. hist. of Leighton fam. p. 36 (2nd nos.).
[63] Ibid. pp. 34–7 (2nd nos.) agrees with, and fills out,

Plymley's 1793 acct. (S.P.L., MS. 6863, pp. 4, 22), though putting the rent at 12s. rather than 10s. 6d.
[64] Craftsmen, limeworkers.
[65] Cf. V.C.H. Salop. viii. 187, 189–90, 193.
[66] Cf. Loton Hall, Lady Leighton's album of watercolours; TS. hist. of Leighton fam. pp. 35–6, 66 (2nd nos.); T.S.A.S. lix. 139–41.
[67] 2nd Rep. Emp. Children and Women in Agric.: App. Pt. II, 79–80. S.R.O. 783, parcel 194, specification and design for Tall Cottages, Alberbury, built 1875; R. Groves, Sharpen the Sickle! Hist. of Fm. Workers' Union (1949), 52, 56–7.
[69] Plymley, Agric. of Salop. 114–15; 2nd Rep. Emp. Children and Women in Agric.: App. Pt. I, 13 (noting also the absence of allotments in the SW.).
[70] 2nd Rep. Emp. Children and Women in Agric.: App. Pt. II, 79–80.

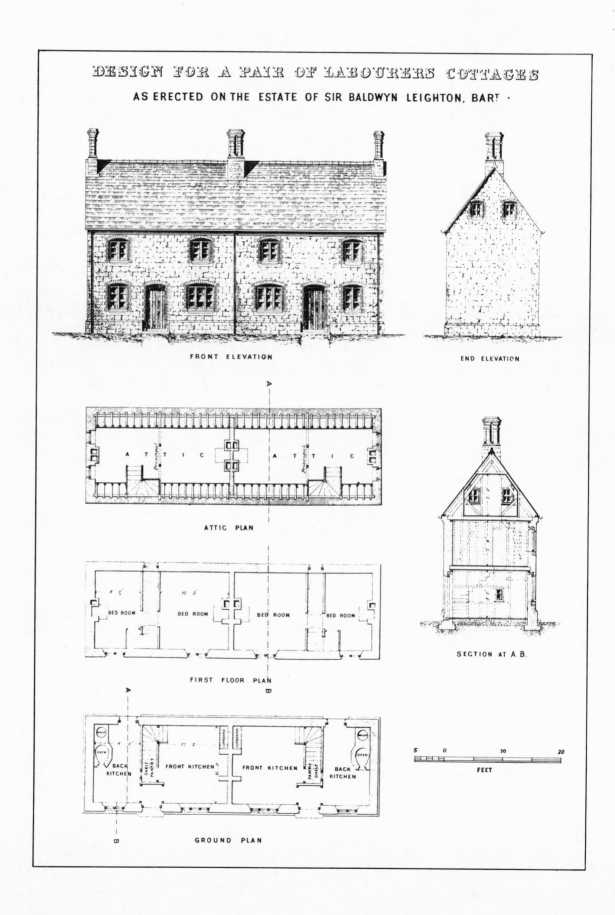

DESIGN FOR A PAIR OF LABOURERS COTTAGES

AS ERECTED ON THE ESTATE OF SIR BALDWYN LEIGHTON, BART·

FRONT ELEVATION

END ELEVATION

ATTIC PLAN

SECTION AT A.B.

FIRST FLOOR PLAN

GROUND PLAN

FEET

landed cottages was higher around Alberbury than elsewhere. In 1869 the Shrewsbury land agent Timotheus Burd stated that within 20 miles of the county town 49 (21 per cent) of the 278 farm workers' cottages on seven estates (20,000 a.) were let with 1–5 a.; the other 229 had only gardens of *c.* ¼ a.[71] Nevertheless it is likelier that the farmers' complaints originated in the belief that such labourers were 'better off than many of the small farmers'.[72] There was almost certainly more truth in that opinion[73] than in the allegation of Samuel Plimley, an Alberbury farmer and grazier on the edge of bankruptcy, that the landed labourers' relative prosperity was due to the fact that their holdings were let to them 'so low'.[74] It was generally thought that labourers could pay the same rent as farmers for a few acres,[75] and Leighton was not the man to mix charity with business.[76]

A few farmers did favour the scheme. From the time he began farming in the early 19th century Samuel Bickerton, of Sandford, found that allotments improved the labourers' moral character: 'a property at home' counteracted the allure of the public house.[77] Bickerton, however, may have been better placed than the rack-rented farmer more typical of the mid 19th century: occupying a lease of over 300 a. in Sandford and Woolston under Sir T. J. Tyrwhitt-Jones,[78] he had a longer interest in the property.

Other landlords did something to improve the labourers' conditions. A. C. Heber-Percy of Hodnet let ½-a. pieces of inclosed heath to them because the farmers charged high rent for potato ground.[79] Lord Craven built two-bedroomed cottages in Stokesay[80] but is not known to have let land to labourers. The farmers' almost universal disapproval of smallholdings may have influenced landlords who, though less strong-minded than Sir Baldwin Leighton, were otherwise disposed to improve the labourer's standard of living. On the Hawkstone estate, long run less vigorously and consistently than (for example) the Loton estate, farmers' complaints were said in 1869 to have secured discontinuance of the system, though in fact it was not discontinued.[81]

Any profits of high farming[82] generally failed to benefit the farm labourer. In 1869 the Hon. Edward Stanhope considered that the living conditions of the peasants of south-west Shropshire were 'deplorably low', worse than in Dorset. Weekly wages in the Clun area were 9s. or 10s.[83] without a cottage but with ½–2 chains of potato ground rent free; at hay harvest the labourer had part of his daily food and in the grain harvest (there was no piece work) all his food for a month or £1 cash.[84] Perquisites and payments in kind varied over time and even from farm to farm. Wages in north Shropshire in 1869 were rather higher at 11s.–12s. a week.[85] That may long have been the case. There is no systematic evidence for the area in the 1790s, but James Caird's mid 19th-century wages line had marked off north-east Shropshire as a higher-wages area.[86] In the matter of wages, as in other ways, the north-west uplands (where, at times, labour could be had 'for almost anything we please to give' in the 1830s) resembled the south.[87]

[71] Ibid. 80–1.

[72] Ibid. 80. Bagshaw, *Dir. Salop.* (1851), 204.

[73] Cf. Plymley, *Agric. of Salop.* 118 (favourably comparing Kenley labourers holding 5–10 a. with farmers of 20–30 a.).

[74] *2nd Rep. Emp. Children and Women in Agric.: App. Pt. II,* 80; Loton Hall MSS., Sir B. Leighton's diary 30 Oct. 1869; *Lond. Gaz.* 12 (p. 6084) and 30 (p. 6823) Nov. 1869.

[75] Plymley, *Agric. of Salop.* 117; *Rep. Sel. Cttee. on Commons' Inclosure,* 177.

[76] Even if privately charitable: 'Life of Sir B. Leighton' (TS. in S.R.O. 783, parcel 194), pp. 66–9.

[77] *2nd Rep. Sel. Cttee. on Agric.* 238–9.

[78] Ibid. 236; S.R.O. 4687/T/1, pp. 25–6, 46, 50, 52; S.

[79] *2nd Rep. Emp. Children and Women in Agric.: App. Pt. II,* 83.

[80] Ibid. 82.

[81] Ibid. 79–80; S.R.O. 731, boxes 218–21, letting agreements, above (Large estates).

[82] Above (Agricultural Revolution).

[83] *2nd Rep. Emp. Children and Women in Agric.: App. Pt. I,* 12–13.

[84] Ibid. *App. Pt. II,* 75.

[85] Ibid. *App. Pt. I,* 13.

[86] Chambers and Mingay, *Agric. Revolution,* 141–2.

[87] *Rep. Com. Poor Laws,* p. 393a (1834), xxx; above, Physical Environment.

Housing was intimately connected with wages in a number of ways: low wages depressed housing standards,[88] and where cottages were let to farmers labourers' earnings were depressed. Hiring terms were usually fixed vaguely and later the farmer might vary wages with the corn prices and require longer hours of work. Labourers in cottages under the farmer could not complain,[89] and in Stokesay parish, where almost all the cottages except Lord Craven's were let with farms, the cottagers bitterly criticized the system as 'slavery'.[90] Defects in the hiring system were not peculiar to south Shropshire: the rector of Whitchurch called the oral hiring agreements (with 1s. earnest) 'very unsound', and there was no general understanding in the county that pay was due for extra hours worked; overtime was generally paid in food, but as charity and at the employer's pleasure.[91]

Stanhope considered Shropshire cottages 'infamous': the mud houses occupied by Melverley labourers in 1851 may have been unknown to him but he learnt of similar ones at Whixall (unfit for human habitation), and in most parishes he visited in 1869 he found cottages that were tumbledown, leaky, insanitary, and with too few bedrooms. He attended a meeting of the Shropshire Chamber of Agriculture that called for 'great improvement' to cottages and (to many farmers' cheers) for the provision of more: at least three per 100 a. On some estates there were cottages that were a 'disgrace to a civilized country' and such places were not cheap: for the 'miserable' dwellings in Loppington parish the larger landowners took £3 10s. a year, the smaller proprietors £4 or £5. On some estates cottages pulled down were not replaced: two leading north Shropshire landowners demolished bad properties to escape the reproach of owning them, thereby causing the labourers of their district to 'herd' in 'open' villages.[92]

Some of the very poorest housing in the 1860s resulted from much earlier rural clearances. In the late 18th century, for example, the poor had been largely shifted out of Lydham parish by the demolition of cottages[93] and by 1869 there were no labourers' cottages there and none in the neighbouring townships of Lea and Oakeley. Thus many farm labourers had to live in Bishop's Castle and walk to and from their work. Their conditions combined the disadvantages of an urban slum with low agricultural wages. Their houses were of the worst kind: most had only one bedroom and gardens hardly amounted to clothes-drying space. One farm labourer's house in the town, let for 1s. 6d. a week in 1869, had only one room upstairs and one down and no back door; it was only 9 ft. square. Overcrowding was common in other small towns and villages, like Wem and Prees,[94] and one-bedroom cottages were common throughout central Shropshire too, and they were a great cause of pauperism, immorality, incest, and illegitimacy.[95]

The condition of the south Shropshire labourer was highlighted in 1872 at a meeting of the new North Herefordshire and South Shropshire Agricultural Labourers' Mutual Improvement Society, attended by c. 300.[96] The standard wage seems to have been 9s. a week (18d. a day) with an extra shilling if Sunday work was required. Even with the usual perks, then worth perhaps 3s. or 4s. a week, it was not enough according to those at the meeting. A labourer from Twitchen, in

[88] Above (Landlords and tenants).
[89] *2nd Rep. Emp. Children and Women in Agric.: App. Pt. II*, 77.
[90] Ibid. *App. Pt. I*, 12–13; *Pt. II*, 76, 82.
[91] Ibid. *App. Pt. I*, 13; *Pt. II*, 79.
[92] Ibid. *App. Pt. I*, 12; *Pt. II*, 74, 83; P.R.O., HO 107/1991, ff. 187v.–188 (ref. owed to Dr. R. A. Preston).
[93] S.P.L., MS. 6861, f. 118.

[94] *2nd Rep. Emp. Children and Women in Agric.: App. Pt. II*, 77, 83–4.
[95] F. Drake, *Rural Sanitary Auth.: Atcham Union: Rep. of Sanitary Survey* (1874), 14 (copy in S.P.L., accession 1098; ref. owed to Dr. Preston).
[96] This para. and the next two are based on *Eddowes's Jnl.* 10 Jan. 1872, pp. 2, 5; cf. below, 1875–1985 (Agrarian economy and society).

Clunbury, who had 10s. a week, a free house and garden (the keep of 2 pigs), and perks, admitted that he had more than many but also complained that it was not enough to keep a family. There were new expenses too: it was hard to afford schooling[97] out of 10s. a week. Even the most industrious labourer, it was claimed, could not in the long run avoid the workhouse. Such had been the fears of a generation or more of labouring men, since the formation of the poor-law unions in 1836–7 and the spreading influence of Sir Baldwin Leighton's[98] rigorous application of the poor-law principles underlying the Act of 1834. In the 1850s the commonest class of patient in the county asylum consisted of those deranged by the 'ceaseless labours and anxieties of the lowest rank of labouring independence'.[99]

Conditions appear worst when housing is described. The meeting was reminded that Shropshire was conspicuous for poor cottages. A labourer from Long Meadowend, Aston on Clun, thought some not fit for a pig, and the chairman William Jellicorse, vicar of Clunbury, referred to many that had a ladder instead of stairs, only one upper room, and no water supply but the river. Such conditions lend force to a less familiar version of the epigraph to Housman's poem:[1]

Clunton and Clunbury,
Clungunford and Clun,
Are the dirtiest places
under the sun.

The labourers wanted 15s. a week cash, without perks and with overtime after 6 o'clock; better cottages; a chance to keep a cow and rent ¼ a.; and help to emigrate for those willing to risk it. Respectable opinion was against them. A Kempton labourer keeping a family of eight on 9s. a week said he was under notice for 'sticking up for his rights' by asking 15s. The Conservative *Eddowes's Shrewsbury Journal*[2] attributed the labourers' complaints to the work of 'political agitators' seeking their votes at enfranchisement.[3] The *Shrewsbury Chronicle*, still nominally Liberal, adopted a more sympathetic tone but was sceptical of all the remedies proposed.[4] Even the chairman of the meeting thought labourers should continue to be paid partly in kind and should marry later and be thriftier, with young men spending less on pleasure (drink) and young women less on finery (clothes). The society's secretary offered the men addresses of employers in regions where wages were higher,[5] and many of the next generation abandoned a countryside that yielded so meagre a living. The population of Clun rural sanitary district fell by over 23 per cent in the 1880s,[6] much the largest drop of any Shropshire district and one that reinforces the other evidence of the area's great poverty.

[97] The universal availability of education had been enacted in 1870 and education became compulsory during the following decade; it was not generally free until 1891. See *V.C.H. Salop*. iii. 174, 176.
[98] About whom many harsh things were said, and (according to the chmn.) said unjustly, at the mtg. With the labourers Leighton's reputation as a strict poor-law administrator obviously outweighed his reputation as a landlord.
[99] *V.C.H. Salop*. iii. 161, 169, 171–2.
[1] Cf. *Salop. Folk-Lore*, ed. C. S. Burne (1883), 583 (another version has 'drunkenest'); A. E. Housman, *A Shropshire Lad* (1896), no. 50. [2] *V.C.H. Salop*. iii. 313.

[3] Town labourers had been enfranchised in 1868: Representation of the People Act, 1867, 30 & 31 Vic. c. 102. Rural labourers did not generally have the vote until 1885 (Rep. of People Act, 1884, 48 & 49 Vic. c. 3), though many in Wenlock parl. boro. and smaller nos. in Bridgnorth and Ludlow had had the vote since 1868: *V.C.H. Salop*. iii. 309–10, 335, 339, 341–2; Sir G. Leveson Gower, *Years of Content, 1858–1886* (1940), 211.
[4] *Shrews. Chron.* 12 Jan. 1872, p. 6 (for the rep. of the mtg. see ibid. 5 Jan. 1872, p. 5); *V.C.H. Salop*. iii. 312–13.
[5] Derb., Lancs., Northumb., and Scot.
[6] *V.C.H. Salop*. ii. 221. Cf. Grier, *John Allen*, 244–5.

1875–1985

THE two world wars, each in different ways, marked the major watersheds in the agrarian history of Shropshire in the 20th century, though fundamental change had been in progress for almost four decades before the first of those conflicts. In the last quarter of the 19th century farming at county and national level was affected by a variety of influences, some reflecting changes in the domestic economy and others developments in the international economy. Imports of cheap food from North America, Australia, and New Zealand undermined the competitive position of British producers and led to sharp price falls across the whole range of agricultural commodities, with an initial and most severe impact on cereal prices. That development set in motion important shifts in land use within the county as farmers abandoned corn growing to concentrate on pastoral farming wherever possible.[7] In 1875, nine years after the first national agricultural statistics were collected, arable and permanent grass acreages were approximately equal at 326,758 and 369,364 respectively. Starting in 1873, however, thousands of acres were converted to permanent pasture so that by 1913 the arable acreage had declined to 226,755 and that of permanent grass had risen by a third to 489,284.[8] To some extent changes in the ability to compete in international markets were masked by a succession of unusually bad seasons in the late 1870s and early 1880s, so that not until the 1890s did all owners and occupiers entirely appreciate the forces influencing them. Those years were marked by a dramatic acceleration in the rate of rural social change determined by developments mainly, though not wholly, within the national economy. There were wide divergences of experience not only between the pastoral north and south of the county and the more arable central and eastern districts, but also within those areas and even within individual parishes. Tenants' and landlords' access to capital and variations in farming ability, to say nothing of differences in the size of holdings or the nature of the soil itself, could evoke different responses in terms of cultivation methods applied or produce raised even within relatively small areas.

Farmers and landlords regarded the time as one of agricultural depression, especially severe before 1896 but with some signs of revival and readjustment thereafter. The start of the depression is difficult to pin-point in the 1870s: long afterwards some remembered it as a sudden collapse,[9] and in 1885 John Bowen-Jones recalled the 'acute stage' of the depression as having begun about ten years before.[10] In south Shropshire some estates had already granted farmers a 10 per cent rebate on their rents in 1879.[11] Initially farmers placed almost the entire blame for their difficulties on the wet weather. On the Sutherland estate farms bordering the river Tern had had their meadows and pasture land destroyed by flooding a number of years in that decade, and in mid August 1879 the lower portion of the whole estate, including the Weald Moors, was under water.[12] At the Shropshire and West Midlands Agricultural Society's 1879 show, held at the Quarry in Shrewsbury, the management committee's main anxiety was that the wet weather

[7] T. W. Fletcher, 'Gt. Depression of Eng. Agric. 1873–96', *Econ. H.R.* 2nd ser. xiii. 417–32.

[8] *Agric. Returns G.B.* The title of the ann. agric. statistics has changed several times since the returns began in 1866, but for simplicity the form *Agric. Returns G.B.* has been used. Cf. E. Turnbull, 'Farming in Salop. in 1875 and 1895', *Jnl. Bath and W. of Eng. Soc.* 4th ser. vii. 85.

[9] J. A. Bridges, *Victorian Recollections* (1919), 17.

[10] J. Bowen-Jones, 'A Fm. that Really Pays', *The Nineteenth Cent.* May 1885, 854; cf. *V.C.H. Staffs.* vi. 122. For Bowen-Jones see above, 1750–1875 (Landlords and tenants).

[11] *Agric. Gaz.* 10 Feb. 1879, p. 126.

[12] R. Perren, 'Effects of Agric. Depression on Eng. Estates of the Dukes of Sutherland, 1870–1900' (Nottingham Univ. Ph.D. thesis, 1967), 65–6.

would damage the turf and reduce attendance.[13] Farmers' reactions to the deepening depression were twofold: an increased emphasis on the most profitable sectors of agriculture and an anxious search for ways to cut production costs. Both required a response from landlords in the forms of new buildings to accommodate livestock and lower rents to lessen the fall in farmers' incomes. In February 1881 the appearance of foot and mouth disease, with the declaration of the county as an infected area and the consequent closure of livestock markets for the next few weeks, added to current difficulties of low prices and wet seasons.[14] In the 1880s assistance by landlords took the form of a temporary remission of rent, particularly on cold, clay, thin-soiled lands, and of allowances in manures, payment of drainage charges, and other permanent improvements.[15] By the 1890s the allowances and improvements were continuing but on many estates temporary remissions of rent had been converted to permanent reductions amounting to around 15 per cent for grazing and 20 per cent on arable farms. There were regional differences. The northern dairy district was hardly affected but in the central and south-eastern divisions of the county there were very considerable reductions; in the mainly arable Bridgnorth district, which suffered most, they varied from 10 to 40 per cent.[16]

Both wars saw something of a revival of cereal growing as a result of the rise in grain prices, reinforced by the government's encouragement to farmers to grow more cereals in order to reduce the amount of scarce shipping space devoted to imported grain. The 1917-18 ploughing-up campaign had best response from the central parts of the county, and reaction from some rearing and dairying districts like Cleobury Mortimer, Ludlow, and Whitchurch was slow.[17] Nevertheless the First World War resurgence can be regarded only as an interruption of the long-term decline in cereal growing where the acreage fell from 173,000 in the 1870s to just under 76,000 in the 1930s (Table XI). The increase in the Second World War was more permanently established by the government's continuation of deficiency payments and price guarantees in peace time, so that in the 1970s the corn acreage of over 193,000 was the highest since statistics had started.

Whereas the First World War and its immediate aftermath were seen as a brief revival of prosperity, not only for cereal growers but for most of the major sectors of agriculture, the years between the wars were regarded by those old enough to remember as an era of depression even more severe than those before 1914. At the annual general meeting of the South Shropshire branch of the National Farmers' Union in 1931 the president said that in looking back over the past year he thought farming was in a worse condition than ever before, and the secretary, John Norton, noted that every year lower price levels were reached.[18] Products with relatively buoyant prices in the 1890s and 1900s, such as milk and cheese, felt the impact of falling demand from the home market with increased imports from overseas. More than 30 per cent of the milk produced in the county was made into cheese at individual farms or small factories.[19] On occasions the price of cheese fell so far that, even with the advantages of cheap family labour and the valuable by-products from the whey-tub, the returns from cheese making were less than could be obtained by the sale of fresh milk; when that happened a vast flood was ready to

[13] *Wellington Jnl.* 26 July 1879, p. 3.
[14] Ibid. 19 Feb. 1881, p. 5.
[15] *Rep. R. Com. on Depr. Condition of Agric. Interests: Digest and App. to Pt. I* [C. 2778-II], pp. 272, 282-3, 303, 349-50, H.C. (1881), xvi.
[16] *1st Rep. R. Com. on Agric. Depr.: Mins. of Evid.* iii [C. 7400-III], pp. 1, 3, H.C. (1894), xvi (3); S.R.O. 2868/22-6; 3075/3/21.
[17] S.R.O. 207/2, rep. of 3 Dec. 1917 after p. 153.
[18] *Shrews. Chron.* 2 Jan. 1931, p. 8.
[19] *Agric. Output of Eng. and Wales, 1930-1* [Cmd. 4605], p. 28, H.C. (1933-4), xxvi.

TABLE XI: AVERAGE ACREAGES OF PRINCIPAL CROPS AND NUMBERS OF LIVESTOCK FOR SELECTED GROUPS OF YEARS, 1870–1979

	1870–9	1890–9	1910–14	1915–19	1920–9	1930–9	1940–4	1950–9	1970–9
Crops and grass (acres)									
Wheat	81,074	38,434	28,111	39,056	26,097	26,174	55,009	42,184	44,862
Barley	53,832	52,526	45,682	33,213	24,951	11,600	24,803	33,712	128,385
Oats	25,623	39,776	40,544	51,756	44,049	33,747	52,187	31,888	15,572
Other Corn	12,503	6,438	4,812	6,311	7,271	4,213	29,652	43,373	4,481
Total Corn	173,032	137,174	119,149	130,345	102,368	75,734	161,651	151,157	193,300
Potatoes	5,553	6,629	5,102	5,611	6,441	5,305	17,117	13,871	12,104
Turnips and Swedes	49,856	43,488	31,138	26,364	22,570	12,374	12,330	8,042	5,264
Mangolds	4,804	5,548	11,519	10,782	10,054	6,176	7,702	6,946	670
Sugar Beet	—	—	—	—	3,306	13,234	16,099	16,616	22,776
Other Green Crops	3,272	1,816	909	801	1,401	1,792	4,267	10,628	6,351
Total Green Crops	63,485	57,481	48,668	43,558	43,772	38,881	57,515	56,104	47,165
Clover and Rotation Grass	77,292	70,033	58,041	55,033	60,234	53,752	53,348	121,686	121,434
Total Arable	325,993	268,372	228,269	232,088	211,800	174,105	279,495	336,651	366,270
Permanent Grass	366,289	451,644	488,173	482,659	489,152	520,511	402,685	352,064	311,564
Total Crops and Grass	692,282	720,016	716,442	714,747	700,952	694,616	682,180	688,715	677,834
Livestock (numbers)									
Cattle in Milk or Calf	52,304	61,250	76,755	85,919	93,910	110,346	120,399	141,226	158,403
Other Cattle	82,223	108,508	121,303	131,734	117,903	128,678	131,335	153,790	198,082
Total Cattle	134,527	169,758	198,058	217,653	211,813	239,024	251,734	295,016	356,485
Sheep	485,099	477,102	486,241	463,488	408,240	533,064	416,130	462,161	620,770
Pigs	62,280	68,599	75,110	64,408	80,640	101,356	50,384	123,620	176,937
Horses	28,108	34,656	37,520	38,124	33,400	24,698	22,300	6,982	—

Source: Agric. Returns G.B.

pour into the liquid milk market, as in 1920 and 1931, further to depress prices there.[20] Once more farmers reacted by reducing their expenditure to the lowest possible level. In one respect circumstances had worsened since the war: large sales of land between 1910 and 1925, for the most part to the sitting tenants, had left parts of the country without the presence of a landowner[21] willing and able to ameliorate the situation by a timely infusion of capital in the form of fertilizers or new buildings. In the 1930s the government did provide some limited assistance to agriculture under the Agricultural Marketing Acts,[22] and the schemes for potatoes, pigs, and milk had some impact on Shropshire producers. The greatest number were affected by the Milk Marketing Board, which they supported in principle though they often criticized the details of its administration and always complained at the level of contract prices.[23]

In April 1939 the government, faced by the threat of war, announced a subsidy of £2 an acre for permanent grassland ploughed up before 30 September. Initial response was slow and by August only 2,970 a. had been notified from 167 farms for inclusion in the scheme. The scheme was administered by the Shropshire War Agricultural Executive Committee (1939–47), chaired by Capt. Edward Foster (kt. 1950) of Newton (in Worfield). Once war was declared farmers acted with more urgency, and promises to break up over 34,000 a. had been received by the end of October.[24] Between May 1939 and April next year 40,000 a. had been converted to arable, whereas the 1917–18 ploughing-up campaign had increased the 1917 arable acreage by only 26,985 a.[25] In succeeding years, and with increased financial inducements, the response was more positive as the exigencies of war tended to iron out differences in farming systems and all districts were subjected to the common strain of finding priority crops and meeting the needs of their own stock. In the eastern part of the county potatoes became a major crop. Before the war only around 5,000 a. were grown, but by stages the quota was raised to 20,000 a. In the northern dairying district some potatoes were grown but the trouble and labour taken by the crop were disproportionate to the returns obtained. One problem was that there was little native skill in cultivation there and on some farms hardly any tools. Contractors, however, sprang up in great numbers and, while their early work was sometimes unsatisfactory, they quickly acquired the ability to turn furrows and bury grass on even the most unpromising land. By far the greater part of the increased arable grew oats and mixed corn, though green crops and especially kale were increased considerably to compensate for the hay that could no longer be grown.[26]

Although the war had altered the more or less traditional emphasis on grassland, the return to peace did not see a swing away from arable. Continued subsidies for corn after 1945 and their permanent incorporation into government policy in the 1950s[27] was one reason for that. Subsidies also encouraged a greater use of fertilizer in arable farming, which resulted in substantially increased yields of all crops. The expansion in output meant that farmers were not faced with a choice between horn and corn, and they could carry larger numbers of all types of livestock despite a

[20] *Bridgnorth Jnl.* 6 Mar. 1920, p. 7; *Shrews. Chron.* 2 Jan. 1931, p. 8.
[21] Resident landowners had been virtually non-existent in SE. Salop. by the 1900s: *T.S.A.S.* 3rd ser. viii. 125 n. 1.
[22] 21 & 22 Geo. V, c. 42; 23 & 24 Geo. V, c. 31; 24 Geo. V, c. 1.
[23] *Shrews. Chron.* 4 May 1934, p. 4; 7 Aug. 1934, p. 4; 11 Jan. 1935, p. 4; 10 June 1938, p. 4; *Wellington Jnl.* 28 Apr. 1934, p. 7.

[24] K. A. H. Murray, *Agriculture* (Hist. of Second World War, U.K. Civil Ser. 1955), 57; *Shrews. Chron.* 11 Aug. 1939, p. 4; S.R.O. 207/19, 31 Oct. 1939; *S.C.C. Mins.* 1950–1, 104. [25] E. J. Howell, *Salop.* (Land of Britain, lxvi), 235.
[26] *Agric. Returns G.B.*; W. B. Mercer, 'Farming in W. Midlands', *J.R.A.S.E.* cix. 89–90.
[27] And into the common agric. policy of the European Econ. Community, which the U.K. joined in 1973: above, p. 00.

reduction in the amount of permanent grass. Cattle numbers increased in the war though sheep and pigs became fewer. Sheep numbers fell because dairy farmers were encouraged to specialize in milk production and so did not keep flying flocks.[28] Nevertheless by the 1950s both pig and sheep numbers had recovered to record levels. In the late 1940s intensive dairying was typical of the northern part of the county; it was still based largely on grassland but with an increased reliance on silage depending on grass for both summer and winter keep (Table XI).[29] In the upland breeding and rearing districts of south Shropshire the coming of the crawler tractor and mechanical spreader, along with improvement grants under the 1946 Hill Farming Act,[30] allowed the conversion to regular grassland of tracts where previously only bracken had flourished. In that respect many of these post-war changes were merely a continuation of developments that had been initiated under the county's War Agricultural Executive Committee.[31] By 1955 there was a new spirit of optimism in the uplands and scores of farmers in the Clun forest area had adopted these measures to achieve a tremendous increase in their stocking rates.[32]

The growth of industry had relatively little direct effect on farming in Shropshire, the limited extent of urban development having only a small influence on land use. Piecemeal industrial exploitation meant that towns were small and usually separated from each other by farming land. Only in the neighbourhood of the east Shropshire coalfield, between the Weald Moors in the north and Broseley in the south, did the extent of colliery cottages, pit workings, and spoil heaps restrict agricultural acreage.[33] Nevertheless although the geographical demarcation between agriculture and industry was a sudden one, with industry following the mineral deposits, the two co-existed with few problems in places such as Kemberton, where the colliery in the early 20th century abutted on cornfields.[34] Indeed by the 1960s there were signs that as industry declined agriculture was staging a counter offensive. Much mining and quarrying waste south of the Severn had been re-absorbed into the rural landscape, so that throughout the area there were islands of agricultural land reclaimed from the waste heaps.[35] In some districts near to settlements farmers experienced the nuisance of vandalism and petty theft, such as the loss of poultry around Wellington and Market Drayton in the 1950s.[36] In the 1960s marauding dogs from towns and post-war dormitory villages caused some farmers on their outskirts to stop keeping sheep.[37] Isolation, however, did not necessarily provide protection from major losses, as demonstrated by the experience of John Williams and a neighbour, farming on the Long Mynd, who had over 300 ewes heavily in lamb rustled early in 1984.[38] Later that year George Pearce, a pig farmer of long experience, discovered that his pens at Nesscliff were being systematically robbed by a thief whose skill suggested that a good stockman was at work.[39]

Whereas about 10 per cent of England and Wales is covered by areas of outstanding natural beauty, in Shropshire the proportion is perhaps 20 per cent. At various times after 1945 suggestions to make the south Shropshire hills a

[28] S.R.O. 207/34, 4 Sept. 1945, p. 2. 'Flying flocks' of wethers were bought in mid to late summer solely to eat up surplus roots or aftermath grass and then to be sold. For the fall in pig nos. see below (Livestock rearing and feeding).
[29] J. W. Reid, 'Farming in Salop.' Agriculture, lvi (4), 164. [30] 9 & 10 Geo. VI, c. 73.
[31] S.R.O. 207/19-25.
[32] J. W. Reid, 'Clun Forest Fm.' Agriculture, lvi (11), 513-17; D. R. Browning and H. Harland, 'Clun Forest Fm. progress rep.' ibid. lxi (11), 538-43.

[33] L. Dudley Stamp, Land of Britain (3rd edn. 1962), 235.
[34] W. W. Watts, Salop.: the Geog. of the County (Shrews. 1919), 3; cf. V.C.H. Salop. xi. 44, 48, 118.
[35] T. Rowley, Salop. Landscape (1972), 221-2.
[36] Shrews. Chron. 30 May 1958, p. 10.
[37] Ibid. 12 Feb. 1965, p. 2; 13 Feb. 1970, p. 6.
[38] B.B.C. Radio 4 broadcast 'On Your Fm.' 7.15 a.m. 23 June 1984.
[39] Pig Farming, xxxiii (7), July 1985, 34-5; cf. ibid. xix (8), Aug. 1971, 36-7, 39.

SHROPSHIRE YEARLING RAMS

Three fine rams bred in the 1920s by J. W. Lockhart (right), a Culmington farmer. They display the woolly face then demanded by the international market but later bred out.

A SHROPSHIRE WAGON, 1912

Among jobs undertaken by Richard Leath, a smallholder on the Gatacre estate, was hauling coal to Gatacre Hall. The wagon is a type traditional in the Bridgnorth area; its colouring (yellow body with blue and red detailing and salmon-red wheels and harvest ladder) is more typical of central south Shropshire.

THRESHING AT OVERWOOD FARM, NEEN SAVAGE, 1908

A typical set-up of steam engine, threshing box, and trusser. The grain is being bagged. The engine, a 4-hp Foster, has just arrived on the farm; the manufacturer's man, there for 10 days to check the engine, stands by its driving wheel.

PLOUGHING AT STOKE ST. MILBOROUGH *c.* 1902

Ploughing a headland in Kinson field, part of New House farm. The ploughman, Henry Burton (d. 1923), is using a plough made by Howards of Bedford. His grandson Albert Burton (d. 1984) leads the blinkered 'Telley'; she and her harness are in poor condition.

national park worried farmers, for amenity use might conflict with commercial agriculture. Nevertheless the county did not come under great pressure from visitors, and the absence (until 1983) of a link to the national motorway system preserved its remoteness from major towns[40] until the later 1980s.[41]

Arable farming

For the century and more from 1875 the greatest emphasis on arable farming was in the central and eastern part of the county with its western limits where the Severn flows out of Wales, its northern boundary a line thence to Market Drayton, and its southern boundary being where the Severn valley gives way to the uplands of south Shropshire. It was there that the decline of wheat growing after 1870 had its greatest impact, but to some extent that was cushioned before 1914 by the maintenance of the barley acreage. That was a feature of the sheep and barley farming found on the highly cultivated light soils towards the eastern boundary. In 1911 Shropshire possessed a greater acreage of barley than any other county in the western half of England. The heaviest concentrations were found east and north-east of Bridgnorth and another band of barley land ran from Newport, curving round by Shrewsbury, passing towards Whittington. On the lighter soils around West Felton and Shawbury fine malting barley was grown. Barley prices did not fall after 1880 to the same extent as those of wheat, a fact which helped to shield the Shropshire farmer from the worst effects of foreign grain imports and to preserve generally high standards of farming. In root growing, often taken as a test of good cultivation, Shropshire was surpassed by only one county in average yield of mangolds and by two or three northern counties in that of turnips.[42] The livestock enterprises of the central and eastern district were shared between sheep and cattle feeding, the former suffering a reverse in the wet seasons of the early 1880s when sheep rot added to the difficulties of that class of farm. The precise balance between cattle and sheep varied from farm to farm, but in general the preference before 1914 was, wherever possible, to fold the sheep directly on the lighter soils sown with roots, thus avoiding the cost of carting. There is no doubt that that form of mixed farming was under some pressure before the First World War. In addition to the hazard of sheep rot, the decline in wool and mutton prices and the vulnerability of roots to fly infestations added further uncertainties. Barley growers complained of the competition from substitutes for barley malt allowed after Gladstone's Inland Revenue Act of 1880.[43]

In the years between the world wars the acreage of the traditional root crops of turnips, swedes, and mangolds fell sharply and their area in the 1930s was only 43 per cent of what it had been in the five years up to 1914.[44] There were two reasons for the decline: first a fall in the number of folded sheep and secondly the unprofitability of winter feeding of cattle in yards, which had increased in popularity up to 1914.[45] Part of the decline was offset by an increase in the acreage of sugar beet, a new root crop first grown in the county in 1922, but becoming significant only after 1925 when the government introduced a subsidy guaranteed for 10 years, though diminishing to zero in the last five.[46]

[40] S.C.C. Salop Co. Structure Plan: Rep. of Survey (1977), 233 sqq.; Shrews. Chron. 7 Feb. 1958, pp. 9, 15; S. Salop. Jnl. Farming Suppls. Jan. 1978, p. 3; Jan. 1979, p. 2; V.C.H. Salop. iii. 220; xi. 12, 18.
[41] When attitudes to tourism began to change: above, p. oo.
[42] G. W. Robinson, Survey of Soils and Agric. of Salop. (Shrews. 1912), 29, 54; A. D. Hall, Pilgrimage of Brit. Farming (1913), 205.
[43] 43 & 44 Vic. c. 20; Newport and Mkt. Drayton Adv. 24 Dec. 1886, p. 6; 16 Nov. 1895, p. 8; 1st Rep. R. Com. on Agric. Depr.: Mins. of Evid. iii. 4–5.
[44] Agric. Returns G.B.   [45] Howell, Salop. 231.
[46] Ag. Hist. Eng. viii. 126.

The history of beet cultivation in Shropshire was closely connected with the growth of the Allscott sugar factory built near Wellington by the Shropshire Beet Sugar Co. Ltd. in time to deal with the 1927 crop, which had increased to 10,007 a. The Allscott factory served as a nucleus for beet growing in the lower Tern valley, on the arable land immediately west and north of Newport, and in the High Ercall-Shawbury district. In addition beet growers in the arable region around Claverley, Worfield, Shifnal, and Albrighton sent their crop to a factory opened in 1925 just over the border at Kidderminster (Worcs.).[47] In 1934, when the beet acreage in Shropshire was 16,017, 55 per cent of that total was grown within 15 miles of the Allscott factory and 26 per cent 25 miles away.[48] A feature further emphasizing the importance of proximity to the factory was that some farms in the dairy district contained a considerable arable acreage with a large area of sugar beet.[49] In the mid 1930s the crop was grown in about half of the 270 agricultural parishes in the county, though in many the acreage was trifling. In 1935 only five had more than 300 a.: Worfield (857), Ercall Magna (766), Claverley (696), Shifnal (632), and Chetwynd (381).[50] The most notable decline in the acreage was in 1932, following the halving of subsidy from 13s. to 6s. 6d. a cwt.; the area under beet slumped to 9,441 a. The three major determinants of production costs for the crop were labour, manure, and carriage to the factory. During the 1920s farmers experienced some difficulty in growing their first crops but their problems were eased by research done at the Harper Adams Agricultural College, which demonstrated the value of the correct spacing of plants during singling and the accurate deposition of fertilizers along with the seed. In 1934 the Allscott factory was supplied with 177,592 tons by 1,689 growers.[51] In 1965 it received 249,225 tons.[52] The introduction of sugar beet was an important agricultural stimulus. Shropshire was the only county in the western half of England to develop a substantial beet industry.[53] It came at a time when agricultural morale was low and it encouraged farmers to pay greater attention to peculiarities of soil fertility and to their profit and loss accounts. It also involved new marketing arrangements, though it did not entirely alter existing farming patterns even among those most heavily reliant on the crop.

There was a limited tendency throughout the county to replace root crops for animal feed by vegetables for human consumption, especially near the towns. Immediately around Newport carrots and parsnips were grown. The production of lettuces, peas, beans, parsnips, Brussels sprouts, and broccoli was localized in the Whixall district where smallholders with less than 20 a. produced early material for markets as far away as Liverpool, but chiefly for the neighbouring towns of Oswestry and Whitchurch.[54] Small undertakings with cultivation under glass were scattered throughout the county. At Roden the Co-operative Wholesale Society opened a small factory for jam and bottled fruits before the First World War; practically the whole village was given over to this occupation partly in the open and partly under glass. Nevertheless the general verdict at that time was that, apart from farmers' orchards and the market gardens near towns, fruit was not much in evidence. The greatest concentration of orchards was in the extreme south-east of the county, where the south-facing slopes of the Clee Hills sloped down to the Teme valley. That area was really the northernmost extension of the Worcestershire

[47] Howell, op. cit. 228-9; V.C.H. Salop. xi. 232; J. T. Coppock, Agric. Atlas of Eng. and Wales (1976), 95-9.
[48] J. B. Butler, Sugar Beet in Salop. 1926-38 (Shrews. 1939), 6.
[49] E. Druce, 'Agric. in Salop.' Agricultural Progress, viii. 37.
[50] P.R.O., MAF 68/3772.
[51] Butler, Sugar Beet in Salop. 6.
[52] Shrews. Chron. 2 Apr. 1965, p. 2.
[53] Vct. Astor and B. Seebohm Rowntree, Brit. Agric.: the principles of future policy (1938), 101.
[54] Regional Types of Brit. Agric. ed. J. P. Maxton (1936), 218; Howell, Salop. 231-2.

and Herefordshire fruit growing region. The peak acreage of 4,846 was reached in 1900 but during the war it declined, to 3,545 in 1919. In 1937 the county had 2,986 a. of orchard. Cider trees predominated but cherries and damsons were also grown.[55]

The introduction of a wheat subsidy under the Wheat Act of 1932[56] stimulated further change in arable farming. Between 1931 and 1935 wheat doubled from 16,100 a. to 32,300. Most of the extra wheat was grown in place of other corn and in those years there was a reduction of 12,200 a. in oats and barley.[57] The increased emphasis on crops for sale at the expense of fodder crops required changes in the customary rotations. In 1878 the most common systems on light land involved four or five courses. The former consisted of roots, spring sown barley, clover, and wheat. The five-field course was only a slight variation with the clover seed left down for two years instead of one.[58] In 1881 eight out of twelve farmers who submitted returns to the Royal Commission on Agricultural Interests were restricted to a four-course rotation and six were not allowed to sell off hay, straw, or roots under any circumstances.[59] That practice persisted until the the First World War and was the one most frequent in estate agreements, though there was some relaxation of restrictions on the sale of fodder crops.[60] In general the four-course rotation still provided the basis for cropping patterns, but most farmers were able to exercise their own judgement and be guided by circumstances over the precise details of rotations.[61] In the 1870s on strong land and inferior clays fallows were adopted and the pattern was generally fallow, wheat, clover, barley, fallow, wheat, peas or beans.[62] The commercial pressures of the 1880s reduced this less intensive cultivation and fallowing lost favour: in 1882 there were 13,188 a. of fallows or uncropped arable in the county but by 1895 land of that description had fallen to 2,286 a.[63] In the 1930s the ordinary four-course rotation was lengthened to increase the acreage under corn, beet, or potatoes. A five-course rotation of wheat, potatoes, sugar beet, oats, and clover was often used, giving a slight reduction in corn but an increase in roots which, in the form of potatoes and beet, increased total output of cash crops.[64]

The increase in cash crops both before and after 1939 required more machinery. For sugar beet the most economic way to grow it was on shallow ridges about twenty inches apart, and a local four-row drill, the Gower drill made by Gowers of Market Drayton, was used more widely than any other machine.[65] In 1942 there were 1,949 tractors, and 2,033 tractor-drawn ploughs. In 1944 those numbers had risen to 3,362 and 2,952 and in 1952 to 6,597 and 6,351 respectively.[66] The larger farms were usually the first and best equipped with machinery: combine harvesters, introduced into England in the early 1930s,[67] and combine drills became more common, and potato planters and lifters and sugar beet lifters came into general use.[68] Sugar beet was eminently suited to mechanization, and the introduction of precision drilling, pre-emergent spraying, and machine harvesting eliminated practically all hard work. In the 1950s harvesters were pulled by tractors, lifted

[55] Hall, *Pilgrimage of Brit. Farming*, 215; W. E. Bear, 'Flower and Fruit Farming in Eng.—III', *J.R.A.S.E.* 3rd ser. x. 84. [56] 22 & 23 Geo. V, c. 24.
[57] J. B. Butler, 'Cropping Changes in Salop.' *Farm Economist*, iii (4), 69–70.
[58] J. A. Clarke, 'Practical Agric.' *J.R.A.S.E.* 2nd ser. xiv. 604.
[59] *Rep. R. Com. on Depr. Condition of Agric. Interests: Digest and App. to Pt. I*, 296.
[60] J. Coleman, 'Fm. Prize Competitions 1884', *J.R.A.S.E.*

2nd ser. xx. 567; C. S. Orwin, 'Fm. Prize Competitions 1914', ibid. lxxv. 207, 217, 223.
[61] Robinson, *Soils and Agric. of Salop.* 54–5.
[62] *J.R.A.S.E.* 2nd ser. xiv. 604.
[63] *Agric. Returns G.B.*
[64] *Farm Economist*, iii (4), 70.
[65] *Agric. Progress*, viii. 36.
[66] *Agric. Returns G.B.*
[67] D. H. Robinson, *The New Farming* (1951), 203.
[68] *Agriculture*, lvi (4), 164.

single rows, and deposited the beet in a trailer driven alongside. Twenty years later the self-propelled beet harvester was a common sight on most arable farms, a giant that could lift as much as six rows at a time and cope with 10 ha. a day.[69] One consequence of the high cost of such mechanization was that in 1958 five farmers in the Edgmond–Newport district co-operated to purchase a harvester jointly to lift the 90 a. of sugar beet on their farms.[70] Even with such developments, by 1972 the crop was handled by fewer than 600 growers.[71]

The use of fertilizer rose over the 20th century, particularly after the Second World War. In the arable districts of east Shropshire, which had always used plenty of fertilizers, applications of nitrogen, phosphates, and potash rose by 31 per cent, 19 per cent, and 76 per cent respectively between 1944 and 1950.[72] This heavier use of chemical fertilizers was reflected in a substantial rise in grain yields after the Second World War, a sharp contrast to the virtual stagnation between the wars under the less capital-intensive farming systems that then prevailed (Fig. 21). The change was also apparent in livestock enterprises, and in the 1950s heavier stocking rates and high output of milk from grass were achieved only by the liberal and efficient use of fertilizers.[73] Nevertheless there was a perceptible growth of public unease about the strategy[74] and not all farmers adopted it. Sam Mayall, later joined by his son Richard, managed his 600 a. near Harmer Hill after 1947 relying wholly on compost and dung to maintain soil fertility and using no artificial fertilizers. He acquired an international reputation for such methods.[75] Another organic farmer was Arthur Hollins of Fordhall farm near Market Drayton, a farm

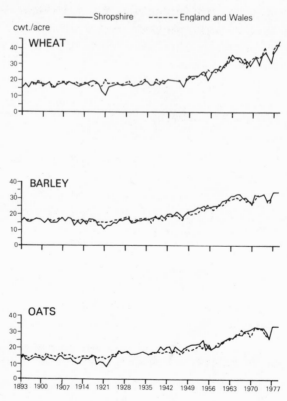

Fig. 21: COUNTY AND NATIONAL GRAIN YIELDS 1893–1979
Based on *Agric. Returns G.B.*

[69] *S. Salop. Jnl. 'The Farmer' Suppl.* Mar. 1979, p. 19.
[70] *Shrews. Chron.* 26 Dec. 1958, p. 5.
[71] E. Shaw, 'Farming in Salop.' *J.R.A.S.E.* cxxxii. 55.
[72] Rep. on 113th ann. mtg. of Brit. Assoc.: *Brit. Agric. Bull.* iv (16), 207.

[73] H. S. Davidson, 'Intensive Milk Production on Salop.-Ches. Border', *Agriculture*, lxii (5), 215–16.
[74] Above, p. 00.
[75] *Farmers Weekly*, 3 Aug. 1962, pp. 64–5; *Shrews. Chron.* 31 July 1970, p. 6.

that his father had almost ruined by the injudicious use of artificial fertilizers between the First World War and the early 1930s. In the mid 1950s, after almost 20 years' agricultural experimentation, Hollins and his wife began to sell yoghourt, cream, cheese, and other milk-based products from his herd of Jerseys at local markets. In 1972 he employed 40 people in his own dairy producing eighty speciality milk products, distributed to all parts of the country with London retailers taking three tons a week.[76] Such men, however, were exceptions earning special notice.

Dairy farming

For the latter part of the 19th and the whole of the 20th century the area where dairy enterprises were most important was north of a line beginning just south of Market Drayton and passing westwards through Shawbury, Stanwardine, and West Felton but excluding the upland area in the extreme north-west bordering Denbighshire, where farming had more in common with the uplands in the south. There was no sharp division between the northern dairying district and the arable and cattle feeding district of mid Shropshire. Indeed in 1912 it was observed that 'the dairy area is gradually extending south',[77] and a report of 1930 noted that 'in Shropshire, dairying has been introduced comparatively recently into the farming system as a substitute for cattle feeding'.[78]

The size of the dairy sector was determined partly by inherent soil characteristics and partly by the relative prices of dairy[79] and other agricultural products. The general soil type was heavier than in the east of the county and thus more suited to permanent pasture than to arable. In most dairy farms the root area before 1920 occupied a larger proportion than that demanded by the four-course rotation but roots were seen as cattle food rather than as a means to clear the land before cereal planting; indeed in 1895 much of the winter butter marketed in Shropshire was said to have an objectionable, though not unavoidable, 'turnip-flavour'.[80] In 1875 the lack of suitable rail links to the large centres of population from this area[81] meant that, apart from a small proportion used to supply local towns including Shrewsbury, production was used mostly for butter and Cheshire cheese made in farmhouse dairies. From the mid 19th century the increased demand for milk from the south Lancashire towns had pushed the centre of the Cheshire cheese making district southwards from Cheshire into Shropshire. Local markets reflected the importance of the cheese trade. Some was sold at the farm to travelling dealers, and a number of large cheese fairs were held periodically at Ellesmere, Market Drayton, Shrewsbury, Wem, and Whitchurch.[82] In 1915 a quarter of all Cheshire cheese was made in Shropshire.[83] In the 1920s Shropshire was one of the four largest cheese producing counties in England[84] and more Cheshire cheese was sold

[76] *Farmers Weekly*, 14 Apr. 1972, pp. 104–5; cf. A. Hollins, *The Farmer, the Plough and the Devil: The Story of Fordhall Fm.* (Bath, 1984); idem, 'My System of Organic Farming', *Agric. and Society: Procs. of Attingham Conf. 1967* (Soil Assoc., Haughley, 1968), 86–93.

[77] Robinson, *Soils and Agric. of Salop*. 56.

[78] Min. of Agric. and Fish. *Rep. on Marketing of Dairy Produce in Eng. and Wales, Pt. I—Cheese* (Econ. Ser. xxii, 1930), 22.

[79] Reviewed 1875–95 in *Jnl. Bath and W. of Eng. Soc.* 4th ser. vii. 98–100. One farm's hist. is recounted by A. J. Lockett, 'Dairy Farming in N. Salop. in late 19th Cent.' (TS. in S.R.O. 3526/3).

[80] Robinson, op. cit. 57; *Jnl. Bath and W. of Eng. Soc.* 4th ser. vii. 99.

[81] For the relative importance of liquid milk and cheese production and the influence of rlys. elsewhere in the country see D. Taylor, 'Growth and Structural Change in Eng. Dairy Ind. c. 1860–1930', *Agric. H.R.* xxxv. 50–2, 55 sqq.

[82] Min. of Agric. and Fish. *Marketing of Dairy Produce—Cheese*, 98–9; *Agric. H.R.* xxxv. 49–50, 59–60.

[83] S.R.O. 207/8, p. 165, 22 June 1915.

[84] *Agric. Output of Eng. and Wales, 1925* [Cmd. 2815], p. 68, H.C. (1927), xxv; *1930–1* [Cmd. 4605], p. 27, H.C. (1933–4), xxvi.

there than in Cheshire. The largest cheese fair was at Whitchurch where an annual average of 1,411 tons was sold between 1925 and 1929.[85]

There were small pockets of dairying in other parts but they did not approach the northern district in importance. In 1858 Henry Tanner's rather patchy survey, taken before the collection of national agricultural statistics, identified the south-east corner, where butter was made 'for the manufacturing towns', as 'the dairying district of Shropshire', barely mentioning its existence elsewhere.[86] Indeed in 1919 Watts dismissed Shropshire as 'not a great dairying county', remarking only on that portion of the northern plain from Market Drayton to Ellesmere as having dairying of any importance.[87] Even in Tanner's Wheatland in the south-east the extent of dairying increased considerably after 1930, although rearing and fattening beef cattle and lamb production still retained a predominant position.[88] In the 1930s a few dairy herds, mainly Friesians, did occur in the valleys of the south-west and milk was produced around the small towns like Church Stretton, Bishop's Castle, and Craven Arms.[89] Improved motor transport eased the problem of carriage for milk producers, but soil and climate remained as constraints so that similar conditions existed in 1972 when dairy farms were found in every part of the county except the remoter uplands, but their greatest concentration was still on the heavy land in north Shropshire.[90]

Only a very small proportion of Shropshire's total milk output could be absorbed by the county's small population through local markets. In 1925 it was estimated that 23.7 million gallons was sold off Shropshire farms, but only 3.7 million gallons (15.6 per cent) went to supply the county.[91] Before and after 1914 a small amount of milk was carried to London and the railway companies quoted rates from the stations at Newport (145 miles) and Ellesmere (182 miles). Nevertheless the county was at the limits for supplying the capital's milk market[92] and in the 1920s producers relied mainly on the Birmingham market for the sale of liquid milk.[93]

A great increase in the sale of liquid milk was the most notable change in Shropshire dairying between the wars.[94] That happened as milk processing off the farm was facilitated by improved roads and the opening of new rural factories. Two or three small cheese factories had been operating since the later 19th century and in 1906 the Birmingham dairy firm of Wathes Bros. (later Wathes, Cattell & Gurden Ltd.) opened a small creamery at Minsterley employing three or four people. After the war the site was enlarged when the government forage depot there was bought from Lord Bath. In 1932 the firm was one of the first to make tinned cream, spurred on by a government ban on imports of the article, and two years later it installed plant for the production of condensed milk. By 1934 milk was collected over a wide area covering Bishop's Castle, Church Stoke, Montgomery, Ford, Builthy Rock, Longden, and Habberley; over 40 people were regularly employed in processing over $1\frac{1}{2}$ million gallons into Cheshire and Cheddar cheese, creamery butter, and fresh cream, the last supplying the immediate neighbourhoods. Chocolate making provided another outlet for the increased quantity of milk produced: Cadburys of Bournville became one of the largest purchasers of milk in north-east Shropshire after their Knighton (Staffs.) factory opening in 1911, and the

[85] Min. of Agric. and Fish. *Marketing of Dairy Produce—Cheese*, 150.
[86] H. Tanner, 'Agric. of Salop.' *J.R.A.S.E.* xix. 25–6, 47.
[87] Watts, *Salop.: Geog. of the Co.* 74.
[88] P. E. Knight, 'S.E. Salop.—Bridgnorth', *Agriculture*, lxxvii (9), 444.
[89] Maxton, *Regional Types of Brit. Agric.* 217.

[90] *J.R.A.S.E.* cxxxii. 52.
[91] Min. of Agric. and Fish. *Fluid Milk Mkt. in Eng. and Wales* (Econ. Ser. xvi, 1927), 16.
[92] Ibid. fig. 1 and p. 31; E. A. Pratt, *The Transition in Agric.* (1906), 13, 22–3.
[93] Min. of Agric. and Fish. *Fluid Milk Mkt.* 15; cf. *Agric. H.R.* xxxv. 63–4.
[94] *Agric. H.R.* xxxv. 62–4.

firm had another milk factory at Stoke upon Tern 1935–8. In April 1934 another Birmingham firm, with the rural-sounding name of Dingle Dairies, invited local farmers to make milk contracts.[95] In the north the Wem milk depot, taken over by the Milk Marketing Board in 1935, concentrated mainly on the production of Cheshire cheese, though butter was also produced and some of the milk was pasteurized for the Manchester market. It processed *c.* 1 million gallons a year. The link with farmhouse production was not entirely extinguished as the manager of the cheese making department, J. Craddock, was an ex-farmer who, in his former occupation, had produced prize-winning cheeses for shows in Liverpool and other parts of the country.[96] By 1939 'Kraft' cheese was made at Whittington. There was a large milk factory at Ellesmere and there were several other smaller depots, mainly in the north where milk was either bottled or made into cream or cheese.[97] The Milk Marketing Board established another creamery at Crudgington, north of Wellington, in 1936 and by the 1960s it was making a wide range of products including 'Dairy Crest' butter, full cream concentrate, and a number of skim milk products.[98] In the 1970s the Board rationalized its operations, closing the Wem cheese factory in 1975: though it drew supplies from 150 farms and employed 45 people, with a daily output of only five to eight tons it was too small to be economic.[99] In 1979, however, the Board's purchase of the Unigate group's creameries brought it the Minsterley premises.[1] Further rationalization closed the Ellesmere creamery, with a loss of 272 jobs, early in 1987 when some operations were transferred to the Maelor creamery near Wrexham.[2]

The expansion of milk processing off the farm was facilitated also by the comprehensive sales organizations of the milk factories. Moreover the factories offered farmers a guaranteed monthly income from their milk rather than a gamble with the hazards of manufacture, fluctuating markets, and the whims of cheese factors. Nevertheless most farmhouse Cheshire cheese, especially that produced in the early part of the year, was the short-keeping variety with a production time of eight weeks[3] and it is unlikely that the switch to liquid milk did much to save farmers any delay in the receipt of money.

The growth of the liquid milk market and of milk processing off the farm posed a threat to the survival of farmhouse cheese making.[4] Even before the First World War some farmers around Shrewsbury already had milk contracts and, as that allowed them to sell their entire dairy output as liquid milk, they soon abandoned farmhouse cheese making in favour of rearing and fattening as alternatives to combine with milk production.[5] In fact, however, farmhouse cheese making survived until the 1930s. The farmer's own family contributed most of the labour and for that reason cheese making had been fairly resilient to the impact of wartime shortage of hired labour. By 1931, although sales of liquid milk had grown and a certain amount of it was made into cheese at central depots, the county agricultural organizer noted that the amount of home-produced cheese was certainly not decreasing. The demand for cheese making instruction—either at ten-day courses at a farmhouse, or to help individuals who were just starting, or to assist those

[95] S.R.O. 3763/18/1 corresp., Cadbury Bros. (7 and 12 Jan. 1950) and F. W. Foulkes (23 and 28 Jan. 1950) to W. J. Slack; *V.C.H. Salop.* viii. 324; *Shrews. Chron.* 6 April 1934, p. 4.

[96] *Shrews. Chron.* 6 Apr. 1934, p. 12.

[97] Howell, *Salop.* 256.

[98] Federation of U.K. Milk Marketing Bds. *U.K. Dairy Facts and Figs. 1963*, p. 143; *Shrews. Chron.* 23 Feb. 1968, p. 6.

[99] *Shrews. Chron.* 4 Dec. 1970, p. 6; *U.K. Dairy Facts and Figs. 1976*, p. xiii.

[1] *U.K. Dairy Facts and Figs. 1980*, pp. vii, 22.

[2] *The Times*, 31 Oct. 1986, p. 2; inf. from Dairy Crest Foods.

[3] J. P. Sheldon, *Livestock in Health and Disease* (1907), 353.

[4] *Agric. H.R.* xxxv. 62.

[5] Robinson, *Soils and Agric. of Salop.* 55.

with some problem—indicated that, if anything, farm cheese making was experiencing a modest revival.[6] Four of the five towns with a cheese fair[7] were in north Shropshire and most cheese made in the county was sold in the north midlands and the north of England. Each fair was held every three weeks throughout the year and, as the fairs were designed for the sale of farm-produced cheese, their healthy state was further evidence of its survival.[8]

The collapse of the milk marketing system in the summer of 1932[9] had a most serious impact on farm cheese making. The establishment of the Milk Marketing Board in September 1933 meant a nationally agreed system of guaranteed prices which, in Shropshire as elsewhere, removed one element of uncertainty from the liquid milk trade. The change in the farm routine of the northern districts was dramatic as former outbursts of seasonal activity were markedly reduced. Previously the cheese maker had calved his cattle in the spring, poured a great volume of milk into the dairy throughout the summer, and then virtually hibernated. By freeing the dairy farmer from heavy reliance on summer milk production, and from the need to find profitable outlets for the inevitable surpluses, the guaranteed price allowed him to develop a steadier level of output over the whole year and greater specialization in milk alone. Pigs had been an element in the farmhouse-cheese economy, but they survived its decline. Cheese production had been accompanied by the output of whey which, along with some purchased food, went to fatten pigs. In some years, before the advent of the Milk Marketing Board, pigs had yielded a bigger profit than cows,[10] and the sale of liquid milk and absence of whey did not necessarily bring a fall in the number of pigs. That came only in the Second World War with the general shortage of feed.[11] Up to 1939 pigs were still kept on many dairy farms as a relic of the days when whey provided plentiful pig food, but by then their owners had turned over to ordinary mash and dry feeding.[12]

By 1939 throughout the county most farmers with milking herds were committed to the sale of liquid milk. The change had been accompanied by an increase in the number of accredited herds and a move towards greater mechanization.[13] In 1942 there were 1,125 milking machines and their number rose steadily during and after the war and had reached 2,601 by 1950.[14] Farm cheese making still persisted on a few holdings but by then was on a very small scale. The change affected entries at the county agricultural shows. In 1933 the Whitchurch Dairy Farmers' Association noticed that the prize money offered at their annual show, which was mainly for cheeses, exceeded the entry fees by £40.[15] Disrupted during the Second World War farm cheese making declined further, although in the immediate post-war years it temporarily gained ground again. By the 1960s there were only some twenty cheese making farms around Market Drayton and Whitchurch.[16] In 1972 all were large milk producers and some took milk from co-operating farmers.[17] The character of the product, though not necessarily its methods of production, had changed markedly. A great deal of farm cheese in the 19th and (despite the Cheshire Cheese Federation's introduction of grading in 1927) in the earlier 20th

[6] Agric. Progress, viii. 34; F. W. Foulkes, Hooked on Cheese (Shrews. 1985), 12, 24.
[7] Bridgnorth, Mkt. Drayton, Oswestry, Shrews., Whitchurch.
[8] Agric. Progress, viii. 35; Min. of Agric. and Fish. Marketing of Dairy Produce—Cheese, 39, 97–8; Wellington Jnl. 27 Feb. 1932, p. 7; Foulkes, op. cit. 11–14.
[9] Ag. Hist. Eng. viii. 250.
[10] J.R.A.S.E. cix. 89.
[11] Agric. Returns G.B.
[12] Maxton, Regional Types of Brit. Agric. 216.
[13] W. A. Scriven, 'Accredited Milk in Cheese Production', Salop. Agric. News, iii (2), 22–3; idem, 'Management of Milking Machines', ibid. iii (1), 13, 15.
[14] Agric. Returns G.B.
[15] Shrews. Chron. 23 Feb. 1934, p. 4.
[16] Agriculture, lvi (4), 161; Foulkes, Hooked on Cheese, 11, 25.
[17] W. Rollo, 'Drayton, Salop.' Agriculture, lxviii (9), 502; Foulkes, op. cit. 28.

century had been of indifferent quality;[18] after 1945, however, cheese makers found that unless top-grade cheese was produced farmhouse cheese making showed no advantage over selling milk.[19]

The post-war world saw a dramatic rise in the size of herds as milking machines allowed a diminishing labour force to handle increased numbers of cows. In 1942 the average Shropshire dairy herd was 16.5 but by 1965 it had risen to 29.[20] The number of registered milk producers in the county fell from 3,921 in 1963 to 2,502 in 1973 and 1,460 by 1983, but milk sales in those years were 87.9 million gallons, 100.2 million gallons, and 125.6 million gallons respectively.[21] The pressures within the industry, reducing the number of producers by 63 per cent in twenty years, were the move towards more intensive systems, involving greater capital outlay, and the use of larger herds to produce economies of scale and meet increased costs. Friesians were the most popular dairy breed and increased from 77 to 83 per cent of dairy cattle between 1955 and 1965.[22]

Dairy farmers were severely affected by the outbreak of foot and mouth disease in 1967–8. Its first appearance in October 1967 was on Bryn farm, Nantmawr, near Oswestry, and the final case was not recorded until June 1968.[23] Only Cheshire experienced a worse epidemic than Shropshire, and around Ellesmere, Prees, and Wem more than half the dairy farmers whose stock was infected had not returned to milk production by 1970. Those who lost stock complained of inadequate compensation, but many who escaped suffered as much for they were forced to keep their cattle in the shippons for months, feeding them expensive hay, silage, and commercial feeds and actually watch them decline and lose market value.[24] Ministry and self-imposed restrictions on movement, in order to contain the epidemic, soon brought social and economic life almost to a standstill. Women's Institutes, Young Farmers' Clubs, and National Farmers' Union branches ceased to meet. All livestock markets were closed and trade was disrupted as country people stayed away from towns. Public houses, banks, toy shops, television suppliers, grocers, hairdressers, caterers all noticed a sharp fall in business before Christmas 1967, when Oswestry in particular became almost a ghost town.[25] The N.F.U. put the value of animals lost in the county at c. £10 million. In all there were 727 outbreaks in Shropshire, and stock losses, either from disease or slaughtered contacts, amounted to 65,722 cattle, 41,098 sheep, and 39,523 pigs.[26]

With the increase in herd size the other significant post-war change was from the delivery of farm milk in churns to its collection from farm vats by bulk tankers.[27] The change was completed by July 1979.[28] It was made easier by the presence at Ellesmere of R. J. Fullwood & Bland, who were major manufacturers of dairy equipment, producing both complete dairy systems and their range of 'Dari Kool' refrigerated farm milk vats. Progress in Shropshire was quite fast. The Milk Marketing Board began bulk collection in the 1950s and 27 per cent of the county's milk was handled in that way by 1966,[29] 45 per cent by March 1970.[30] In August 1970 the biggest single switch to bulk collection took place when 104 farmers in Shropshire and another 97 in Montgomeryshire gave up the daily chore

[18] *J.R.A.S.E.* cxxxii. 52; Foulkes, op. cit. 17–21.
[19] Min. of Agric. and Fish. *Marketing of Dairy Produce—Cheese,* 22, 143.
[20] Milk Marketing Bd. *Nat. Dairy Census 1965,* p. 56.
[21] *U.K. Dairy Facts and Figs. 1963,* 23, 78; *1973,* 12, 65; *1983,* 4, 58. [22] *Nat. Dairy Census 1955,* p. 30; *1965,* p. 46.
[23] *Rep. Cttee. of Inq. on Foot-and-Mouth Disease,* Pt. I [Cmnd. 3999], p. 41, H.C. (1968–9), xxx.

[24] *Shrews. Chron.* 10 Apr. 1970, p. 6.
[25] Ralph Whitlock, *The Gt. Cattle Plague: Acct. of Foot-and-Mouth Epidemic of 1967–8* (1969), 62, 65–6.
[26] *Shrews. Chron.* 7 June 1968, p. 6; 10 Jan. 1969, p. 6.
[27] Ibid. 27 Mar. 1970, p. 6.
[28] *U.K. Dairy Facts and Figs. 1980,* 22.
[29] *Shrews. Chron.* 1 July 1966, p. 6.
[30] Ibid. 27 Mar. 1970, p. 6.

of churn handling. That was made possible by the Express Dairy Co. which made major changes at the Minsterley creamery to allow it to accept bulk deliveries.[31]

Livestock rearing and feeding

Livestock rearing was heavily concentrated south-west of the Severn, with a smaller area in the north-west uplands where the lower slopes of the Berwyn Mountains extend from across the Welsh border. Practically all the districts were above the 122-m. contour, with areas over 244 m. and a few, notably in the Clun forest, on the Long Mynd, Wenlock Edge, and the peaks of the Clee Hills, above 366 m. There was little change in any of them from their traditional reliance on rearing, with the exception of the Clee Hills. They had formed the heart of the Wheatland where their strong loams and clay lands had, in the 19th century, been the most important wheat growing area, as opposed to the barley extensively cultivated on the lighter soils east of the Severn. Nevertheless the steep fall in wheat prices from the 1870s onwards, combined with high labour costs and only moderate fertility on the heavy soils, proved the region to be marginal for growing wheat. As a result the greatest part of the arable land was laid down to pasture, and raising store cattle became the major occupation.[32] During the depression's worst years, those before 1896, its effects were mitigated in Shropshire by the farmers' increased reliance on livestock husbandry.[33] The concentration on cattle breeding and rearing is shown by the fact that throughout the depression Shropshire had the greatest concentration of cattle under two years of age in all the west midland counties; their density rose from 7.8 per 100 a. in 1875 to 13.1 in 1914.[34] In all parts of the rearing country the tendency was to use cattle to stock the lower slopes while on the higher parts large numbers of sheep were reared. For the most part the upland sheep were either the Clun Forest or the Kerry Hill breed; the Shropshire breed, though widespread in the late 19th and early 20th century when many upland farmers kept pure flocks, was, like the other downland breeds, more properly suitable for the arable lowlands.[35] The numerical preponderance of the two former breeds over the Shropshires probably increased in the years between the wars, with the Clun Forest predominating.[36] Herefords were the chief breed of cattle: although the sprinkling of Welsh, Lancashire, Longhorns, Shorthorns, Ayrshires, and Devons of Tanner's day were also present in the 1880s and early 20th century, white-faced cattle were still the preponderant breed.[37]

Horse breeding was a further activity on rearing farms, though carried on in other places too. In the earlier 19th century 'the Shropshire type' of fine quality hunter had been produced to meet the demand from the abundant country seats around Shrewsbury and in the south, and for export to other countries. By the 1880s its reputation had declined because, it was argued, landowners no longer provided suitable stallions to cover for their tenant farmers at low fees.[38] Agricultural stallions and strong cart-horses were still produced, the latter highly sought after by the railway companies and brewers because of their ability to gain muscle when worked on good hard keep. Three societies—at Shrewsbury, Ellesmere, and Ludlow—were formed in the early 1880s to foster the breeding of such horses.[39]

[31] Ibid. 7 Aug. 1970, p. 6.

[32] Howell, *Salop.* 253.

[33] *Jnl. Bath and W. of Eng. Soc.* 4th ser. vii. 85, 94–6, 101.

[34] G. M. Robinson, *W. Midlands Farming 1840s to 1970s* (Univ. of Cambridge Dept. of Land Economy, Occ. Paper xv), 35.

[35] Hall, *Pilgrimage of Brit. Farming,* 200–1.

[36] Maxton, *Regional Types of Brit. Agric.* 217.

[37] W. Houseman, 'Rep. on Exhibition of Livestock at Shrews.' *J.R.A.S.E.* 2nd ser. xx. 642–3; H. Rider Haggard, *Rural Eng.* i (1902), 422.

[38] Above, 1750–1875 (Motive power, tools, and mechanization). [39] *J.R.A.S.E.* 2nd ser. xx. 617–18, 627–8.

The emphasis on breeding was maintained into the 20th century. At the Ludlow Agricultural Society's annual show in 1906 it was remarked: 'Again the horses were the most prominent feature of the show'.[40] In 1885 occupiers of land in the county possessed a total of 32,323 horses, of which 19,377 (59.9 per cent) were used solely for agricultural purposes, the rest being young horses and brood-mares. By 1935 the total number of horses had fallen to 24,177 (a decline of 25.2 per cent) with 14,838 used for agriculture (a decline of 23.4 per cent). That represented only a slight rise in the percentage kept for agriculture (to 63.6 per cent in 1935) and indicates that the relative emphasis on horse breeding in Shropshire had hardly changed since 1885.[41] J. M. Belcher of Tibberton Manor near Wellington was a noted horse breeder. His Harboro' Golfinder took the King's Champion Challenge Cup, the Society's Gold Challenge Cup, and the £25 Champion Cup at the 1935 Shire Horse Society's Show at Islington, London.[42] Between the wars the heavy horse societies at Bishop's Castle, Bridgnorth, Chirbury, Craven Arms, Rea Valley, and Wem were in a position to serve the greater part of the county. They travelled several stallions subsidized under the Ministry of Agriculture's livestock improvement scheme.[43] A number of breeders took part in the scheme, but there were still those who preferred to use any sire to avoid the trouble of obtaining a better quality subsidized one.[44]

Ludlow had formerly been a marketing centre for horses but in the late 19th century its position declined in favour of Kington and Leominster in Herefordshire. In 1890 the borough council tried to revive the June and October horse fairs but without lasting success.[45] In the north the monthly horse markets at Oswestry suffered a similar decline; they were nearly defunct by the 1920s and attracted only a few nags of various kinds. Craven Arms and Shrewsbury remained substantial centres for horse sales, at Craven Arms on the first Sunday of each month with twice yearly pony sales; at Shrewsbury there was a well equipped repository next to the Smithfield with accommodation for 200 animals.[46]

The feeding that was the complementary, indeed at times the dominant, activity on arable farms in the central and eastern districts was also subject to changes in emphasis over the years. Store cattle were bought in either from the rearing areas or from further afield. Shrewsbury retained its position as the largest store market in the country and most of the beasts fattened in the county passed through it at some point in their lives. In the 1890s some 43,000 cattle were sold there annually and that number increased up to 1914 and into the years between the wars. In 1922–3 the annual total was 53,200 of which 85 per cent were stores.[47] In addition to Welsh animals many Irish Shorthorns were sold there. Large store sales were also held at Oswestry and Wellington and Wellington was in addition the biggest fatstock market. The important store sheep sales took place between August and October at Bridgnorth, Much Wenlock, Cleobury Mortimer, Craven Arms, and Church Stretton, and there were others at smaller centres.[48] In the 1940s some of them were known for particular breeds: the chief sales of Cluns were at Craven Arms, Clun, and Kington, and for the Kerry Hill breed at Kerry, Craven Arms, Knighton, and Kington.[49] The cattle used for fattening in central Shropshire were Herefords

[40] *Ludlow Adv.* 11 Aug. 1906, p. 8.
[41] *Agric. Returns G.B.*
[42] *Wellington Jnl.* 2 Feb. 1935, p. 7.
[43] T. Wilding Davies, 'Improvement of Livestock Scheme of Min. of Agric.' *Salop. Agric. News*, v. 84, 87; S.R.O. 207/17, rep. betw. pp. 39 and 40.
[44] *Shrews. Chron.* 7 Jan. 1938, p. 4.
[45] *Ludlow Adv.* 25 Jan. 1890, p. 5.
[46] Min. of Agric. and Fish. *Rep. on Mkts. and Fairs in Eng. and Wales*, ii (H.M.S.O. 1927), 54, 72, 79.
[47] *Agric. Returns G.B.*
[48] S.R.O. 4752, sale cat. 9 Sept. 1915; Maxton, *Regional Types of Brit. Agric.* 217.
[49] J. F. Robinson, 'Sheep on Eng.–Welsh Border', *Agriculture*, lvi (4), 182–3.

and Shorthorns in almost equal proportions, with Shorthorns becoming commoner further north. Fattening cattle were turned out to spring grass in April and May, and were mostly cleared off by October, by which time the yards were occupied by cattle for winter fattening. Up to 1914 yard feeding tended to increase. In very few cases was it possible to fatten entirely on pasture, and cake and corn were nearly always required to supplement grass.[50] The larger farmers engaged in fattening often organized their own sales, like Henry Pooler of Tibberton Manor (429 a.) and John Belcher of Honnington Grange (426 a.), both near Newport; their farm sales in the mid 1890s realized between £5,500 and £7,000 and attracted buyers from Coventry, Birmingham, Wolverhampton, Tamworth, Stoke, Stafford, Hereford, and Craven Arms.[51] All that time more farmers were turning to fattening and that, together with the competition from imports, led to complaints from those in the area around Newport that the Smithfield there, which the smaller men relied on entirely, was overstocked. To relieve the situation local auctioneers arranged to hold the spring markets in 1895 and 1896 weekly instead of fortnightly.[52]

Between the wars there was some decline in the number of cattle and sheep fed off roots,[53] an inevitable consequence of the reduction in the acreage of turnips and mangolds. Nevertheless sheep still retained an important place in the livestock feeding economy and at 533,000 their average number in the 1930s was the highest for any decade since records began (Table XI).[54] The substitution of sugar beet for other roots did not constitute a total loss in the amount of home grown fodder available, since the tops formed a valuable food for both cattle and sheep. The practice of folding sheep on beet tops was very common in Shropshire, and progressive farmers regarded them as equal in feeding value to a crop of common turnips. By 1948 close folding on roots had declined so much that it was regarded as 'something of a spectacle', and open folding on beet tops and autumn catch crops was general.[55] The beet pulp, which until 1939 was available to growers at a reduced rate,[56] was also a valuable stock food used either alone or as Rowland W. Ward of Sambrook Hall farm, near Newport, used it: he took 75 tons a year from the Allscott factory and fed between 350 and 400 Herefords, mixing it with mangold to give even better results.[57] The tendency was for the old fashioned rations based on roots, hay, or straw to give way to a more modern feeding policy in which beet pulp, mostly blended with molasses, was used with concentrates and a reduced amount of hay to provide a balanced ration.[58] The change applied to both beef and dairy animals.[59]

In those years more emphasis was placed on feeding the livestock than on feeding the land. Shortage of capital as well as of labour may well account for the fact that, although the acreage of grass increased between 1920 and 1939, yields from both temporary and permanent grass were rather lower than they had been in the twenty years before 1913 (Fig. 22). Part of the explanation lay in the decline in liming after 1900. In the 1880s as much as three tons of lime an acre were applied to acid soils in the Ludlow and Much Wenlock areas every eight years.[60] There was a general belief in the early 20th century that chemical fertilizers made lime unnecessary.[61] The problem was most serious in the north where the soils were

[50] Robinson, *Soils and Agric. of Salop.* 55–6.
[51] Perren, 'Agric. Depression', 329–32.
[52] *Newport and Mkt. Drayton Adv.* 5 Jan. 1895, p. 1; 25 May 1895, p. 5; 1 June 1895, pp. 1, 5; 9 May 1896, p. 8.
[53] W. M. Davies, 'Soils of Salop.' *Agric. Progress,* v. 36.
[54] *Agric. Returns G.B.*
[55] *J.R.A.S.E.* cix. 87.
[56] Butler, *Sugar Beet in Salop.* 16.
[57] *Shrews. Chron.* 20 May 1938, p. 4.
[58] Butler, op. cit. 16–31.
[59] W. E. Usher, 'Summer Feeding of Dairy Cows', *Salop. Agric. News,* i (1), 23.
[60] *J.R.A.S.E.* 2nd ser. xx. 548–56.
[61] D. Lloyd George, *Organizing Prosperity* (1935), 76.

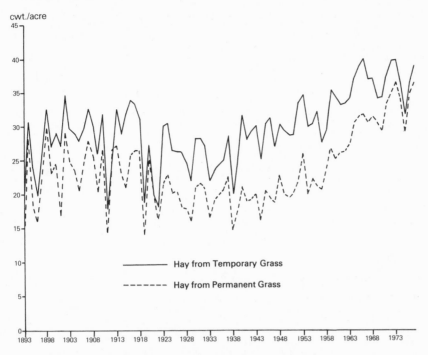

Fig. 22: HAY YIELDS IN SHROPSHIRE 1893–1977
Based on *Agric. Returns G.B.*

intensively farmed,[62] but by 1937 A. G. Street commented that 'Throughout the county the soil seems to be deficient in lime'.[63] Even when provided with the results of scientific soil analysis, farmers did not always find it easy to tackle the problem. When H. P. Reynolds of High Walton farm, Bromfield, in south Shropshire was informed by the county analyst that every field was deficient in lime to the extent of at least a ton an acre, and some as much as 55 cwt., he found that it took one man a whole winter to apply the necessary amount of burnt lime and slag.[64]

Wartime livestock policy was to avoid dual-purpose breeds as much as possible and encourage farmers to select cattle specifically suited to the environment and purpose. In the hill districts of Clun, Bridgnorth, Ludlow, and Oswestry the change was to rearing for the sale of heifers (or down-calvers) and beef stores, and to the discouragement of milk production in inaccessible places and on poor farms. For dairy animals the most popular breeds were Shorthorns and Friesians, and in the case of beef animals preference was given to pure herds of Hereford and Angus. In 1946 an artificial insemination centre was opened at Cheswardine with five Friesian and six Shorthorn bulls.[65]

After the war, although dairying crept further south into the more intensive arable districts around Newport, Wellington, Shifnal, and Bridgnorth, the winter feeding of sheep and cattle still remained the major livestock enterprise.[66] Here and there a minority of farmers gave up cattle altogether and adopted an unmixed arable system. Most, however, preferred to modify their style of management without abandoning the central emphasis on sheep and cattle feeding.[67] Lowland holdings based entirely on sheep farming could probably be counted on the fingers of one hand.[68] In eastern Shropshire the barley acreage, which had declined

[62] D. Turner, 'Lime Survey in W. Midland Cos.' *Jnl. of Min. of Agric.* xxxiii. 319.
[63] Street, *Farming Eng.* (1937), 68.
[64] *Shrews. Chron.* 8 July 1938, p. 4.

[65] S.R.O. 207/34, 4 Sept. 1943, 4 Sept. 1945, 5 Mar. 1946.
[66] *Agriculture*, lvi (4), 164.   [67] *J.R.A.S.E.* cix. 106.
[68] H. Hope, 'Down Under in Salop.' *Farmers Weekly*, 20 Mar. 1964, pp. 109–10.

between the wars, recovered in the 1960s because, as a major source of cattle feed, it became the district's basis for 'barley beef'.[69] Even where livestock was abandoned, barley barons and single enterprises were not the alternative: four-crop enterprises with wheat, barley, potatoes, and sugar beet were most common in the 1960s. Beef remained essentially a winter yarding exercise with stores from the south of the county and plenty of Irish. Sheep were mainly Cluns crossed with Down rams; much of their winter was spent on beet tops and kale and the summer on rape and turnips. Farms with pigs carried nearly all White, and the Old Spot had all but disappeared. In this branch, after a sharp fall in numbers 1940–7 (owing to government controls and shortage of feed), units tended to become larger; some specialized in breeding, others in feeding, but the really big units did the whole job. Even so, large numbers of store pigs were still brought into the county for fattening. Poultry, both for eggs and meat, were found over the whole county and that branch of farming, like pigs, increasingly adopted the modern features of the large unit.[70] In the rearing districts, whereas most of the cattle went as stores off grass, there was by the 1970s more finishing in good store condition for sale in spring or retaining to finish off grass the next summer. The reason for that particular break with tradition was the poor prices made by the lighter, less well grown, and late calves. On the arable farms, where it was formerly common to keep a resident flock of ewes for crossing with a Down ram to produce fat lambs, the ewes gave way to feeding tegs.[71]

Agrarian economy and society

The lead given to farming by the landed proprietors was already well established in the 1870s and their role was, if anything, enhanced during the difficulties of the next twenty years or so. From the repeal of the corn laws in 1846 most finance for British agriculture was provided by landlords and tenants. Government grants to land improvement companies for drainage works after 1846 never amounted to substantial subsidies. Only in the later 20th century did the state provide significant long term assistance to agriculture. In the late 19th and early 20th century landlords were often personally concerned to nurse their tenants through the adversities of disastrous seasons and poor prices, even though those events squeezed landowners' incomes harder than either tenants' or labourers'.[72] Large landowners were most likely to have enough money to finance such assistance, and Shropshire was comparatively well endowed with them. In 1874 peers and commoners with over 3,000 a. owned 51 per cent of the county, compared with 40 per cent of England and Wales as a whole.[73] The fact that so much of the county was in the hands of large landowners was certainly a stabilizing influence. In 1891 R. J. Barber of Barber & Sons, the Wellington auctioneers and estate agents, reported that property in that locality was unlikely to alter much in value because it was mostly in the hands of large landowners.[74] In 1872–3 eight men owned over 10,000 a. (Table X). They were Lord Powis with 26,986 a.; the duke of Cleveland, 25,604 a.; Lord Brownlow, 20,233 a.; the duke of Sutherland, 17,495 a.; Lord Hill, 16,554 a.; Lord Forester, 14,891 a.; Lord Windsor, 11,204 a.; and Lord Bradford, 10,833 a. In all there were 52 owners with over 3,000 a., and there were a further 65 'squires' who

[69] Robinson, *W. Midlands Farming 1840s to 1970s*, 98.
[70] W. A. Thurgood, 'E. Salop.' *Agriculture*, lxxiii. 236.
[71] *J.R.A.S.E.* cxxxii. 4.
[72] *Econ. Hist. of Brit. since 1700*, ed. R. C. Floud and D.
N. McCloskey, ii (1981), 176–8, 186–8.
[73] J. Bateman, *Gt. Landowners of Gt. Brit. and Ireland* (1883), 508, 515.
[74] *Ludlow Adv.* 24 Jan. 1891, p. 4.

possessed estates between 1,000 and 3,000 a. and accounted for 110,500 a. or 12 per cent of Shropshire, a similar proportion to the 13 per cent that such men owned nationally.[75]

Besides the most familiar form of assistance, reductions in rent,[76] landowners also provided new buildings or paid the cost of adapting existing ones to meet changed requirements. The general standard for the county was high, but in the 1880s Lord Brownlow's properties were noted as especially creditable; some of his homesteads verged on the extravagant. Those of Lord Powis, the dukes of Sutherland and Cleveland, Lord Stafford, Sir Thomas Boughey, and Mrs. Stapleton-Cotton came close in excellence. Nevertheless the relationship was one in which each side had duties, and tenants were encouraged to spend their own money too and take a pride in doing justice to the land.[77] In that respect landowners would offer guarantees to tenants that if they left their farms they would receive compensation for the unexhausted value of their improvements, and even where nothing existed in writing farmers were often satisfied that where an improvement was made with the owner's consent their interests would be protected.[78] There is also evidence that those farmers who practised a high standard of cultivation were able to get rent reductions greater in proportion to the fall in prices than could be obtained by those who let their farms go down.[79] Nevertheless the absence of legally enforceable rights to compensation was regarded with some disquiet by a number of farmers in the county, particularly those who gave evidence to the royal commissions on agriculture in the 1880s and 1890s.[80]

The social and economic position of landlords required them to take a part in the various local agricultural societies and the other public bodies representing the farming interest. The most important in Shropshire were the Chamber of Agriculture founded in 1866,[81] and the Shropshire and West Midlands Agricultural Society which had started in 1875;[82] in the 1880s Lord Powis attended meetings of the former and was president of the latter. Sir Baldwyn Leighton, M.P. for South Shropshire and with an estate of 4,085 a. at Loton Park, was a tireless campaigner to reduce the burdens of the poor law on farmers and landowners alike; he served a term as president of the chamber.[83] It is not known if such division of offices between aristocrat and politician was planned or fortuitous, but it was certainly appropriate, for agricultural societies were principally devoted to the improvement of livestock whereas chambers of agriculture mainly concerned themselves with legislation. In the 1900s Lord Windsor was elected president of the Ludlow Agricultural Society and in the 1920s Lord Kenyon was president of the Whitchurch Dairy Farmers' Association.[84] Where a landowner was not normally resident in the county his estate agent provided the familiar regular contact with tenants, as John Mackrory did when, in the 1880s, the 3rd duke of Sutherland's personal circumstances forced him to forsake his Scottish castle and his two English houses and live abroad. Contact with the estate agent meant that most farmers noticed little difference between periods of residence and absence. The 4th duke's succession in 1892 was followed by a more personal interest in the farming

[75] Ret. of Owners of Land [C. 1097-I], Salop. H.C. (1874), lxxii (2); Bateman, op. cit. passim. [76] Above, p. 000.
[77] J.R.A.S.E. 2nd ser. xx. 512.
[78] 1st Rep. R. Com. on Agric. Depr.: Mins. of Evid. iii. 373-4; above, 1750-1875 (Landlords and tenants).
[79] 1st Rep. R. Con. on Agric. Depr.: Mins. of Evid. iii. 11.
[80] Ibid. 11-12, 373-4; Rep. R. Com. on Depr. Condition of Agric. Interests: Digest and App. to Pt. I, 350.
[81] F. J. Ingleson, Salop. Chamber of Agric. 1866-1966: a
Cent. of Service (Salop. Chamber of Agric. [1966]).
[82] Cent. of Progress 1875-1975: Salop. & W. Midlands Agric. Soc. ed. R. Kenney (Shrews. 1975); Shrews. Chron. 17 (p. 17) and 30 (p. 17) May 1975; above, 1750-1875 (Landlords and tenants).
[83] Wellington Jnl. 29 Jan. 1881, p. 6; 28 Jan. (p. 6), 22 July (p. 8) 1882.
[84] Ludlow Adv. 16 Dec. 1905, p. 5; Foulkes, Hooked on Cheese, 10-11.

problems on the Lilleshall estate.[85] In 1896 he discussed with his Shropshire tenants how to alleviate the economic problems which all faced. One scheme seriously considered was the formation of a co-operative for the sale of farm produce. Although it proved impractical,[86] the duke and his tenants did form the Newport & District Agricultural Co-operative Trading Society Ltd. in the autumn of 1904 to obtain the advantages of bulk purchasing and also to combine small quantities of produce like cheese and eggs and so obtain cheaper carriage from the L.N.W.R. It was an advantage that the duke was a director of the railway as well as president of the society, and the railway provided the society with a warehouse next to Newport station at a moderate rent. At the end of the first year the society had 79 members and the year's trade exceeded £7,000.[87]

Many of the great estates in the county were sold during the great national land sales in the years immediately following the First World War. If owners were disenchanted with their properties and tired of such responsibilities, those feelings were not translated into action much before the 1890s. The poor market for land may have partly accounted for that. In June 1878 the Howards' Middleton Priors estate of over 4,000 a. in the south-east of the county was offered for sale, but the same London auctioneers were still trying to sell it in 1881, then specifying an upset price of £82,000.[88] As late as 1894 the *Shrewsbury Chronicle* confidently asserted that 'such a thing as a Shropshire estate offered for sale is an absolute novelty'; that of course was not true, but the sluggish land market of the 1880s and 1890s had faded recollections of the brisker times before that.[89] In the later 1890s there came the first indications of what was to follow. The 4,000-a. Condover estate, which in the 1870s had been 5,525 a., was auctioned on Reginald Cholmondeley's death in 1896. In 1895 the break-up and sale of Lord Hill's 16,554-a. Hawkstone estate began, but in that case the estate had been heavily mortgaged to finance the extravagances of two previous generations.[90] The process of dissolution was already at work on Lord Powis's south Shropshire estate when Rider Haggard visited the agent in 1901, as he recorded that the earl then owned only 21,000 a. in the county.[91] Powis's decision to sell the 5,800-a. Montford estate came in 1912. Made nervous by Lloyd George's 1910 Finance Act,[92] with its increased taxation and death duties, he felt compelled to disinvest in land. Although he was willing to sell to the sitting tenants, provided a majority would purchase their farms, he found too few were willing to incur the burdens of ownership. He was also unable to find a buyer for the entire estate at an asking price of £147,000, so it remained on his hands for the next five years.[93] When Montford was sold in 1917, with vociferous protests from the tenants (then eager to buy), it went over their heads to T. E. Dennis.[94] A 3,000-a. estate at Culmington was being broken up in 1911 and a sale effected in 1912 was of 8,600 a. on the western boundary of the duke of Sutherland's Lilleshall estate, for £278,000; the major part was sold to the sitting tenants.[95] In 1878 the estate was 19,714 a.,[96] or 2,219 more than was recorded in the 1873 *Return of Owners of Land*. Moderate reductions had been made in 1894 when 834 a. at Ketley had been

[85] Perren, 'Agric. Depression', 15-17, 47.
[86] Ibid. cap. 7.
[87] E. A. Pratt, *Rlys. and their Rates* (1905), 108-9; idem, *Transition in Agric.* 193-4.
[88] S.P.L., Sale Cat. 1/2; *Salopian Shreds & Patches*, iii. 63, 196.
[89] *Shrews. Chron.* 8 June 1894, p. 5; above, 1750-1875 (Large estates).
[90] H. A. Clemenson, *Eng. Country Hos. and Land. Est.* (1982), 103-4; *V.C.H. Salop.* viii. 39; above, 1750-1875 (Large estates).
[91] Rider Haggard, *Rural Eng.* i. 423.
[92] 10 Edw. VII, c. 8.
[93] S.R.O. 552/11/1533, 1539, 2066.
[94] Ibid. /1628-34, 1638-46.
[95] *Shrews. Chron.* 24 Mar. 1911, p. 7; S.R.O. 2505/1; J. Beard, *My Salop. Days on Common Ways* (Birm. [1948]), 60-1.
[96] Staffs. R.O., D. 593/H/14/2/10; Perren, 'Agric. Depression', p. ix.

CRAVEN ARMS, 61ST ANNUAL EWE SALE 29 AUGUST 1935

Craven Arms developed as a major regional livestock market in the later 19th century when it became a railway junction. A small town also grew up. In the background workmen put the final touches to the Regal cinema.

CHURCH STRETTON HORSE FAIR *c.* 1905

Horse breeding and rearing was part of the economy of upland Shropshire during the Middle Ages and later. In the earlier 20th century, partly as demand for pit ponies fell, the old horse fairs declined, among them Church Stretton's.

HAYMAKING AT NEWTON, STOKESAY, *c.* 1917
Family and employees gather round John Boulton (at bottom of ladder), small-scale farmer and
licensee of the Stokesay Castle Hotel, Craven Arms. The young men are away at the war; otherwise it
is a wholly traditional picture of communal effort.

SINGLING SUGAR BEET *c.* 1950
Seasonal farm work provided a useful supplement to family income in rural areas. The women, one
accompanied by a child, are working near Tibberton.

sold, but they were partly industrial or residential properties.[97] Some of the Lilleshall estate's remaining farmland was offered at a second sale in July 1914, and the remainder, including the House and the estate yard, at a third in 1917.[98]

A number of the early post-1914 sales were those of outlying portions of large estates that left the central portions intact. Sales from the Stanmore Hall estate began during the war but continued until five or six years after it, the central portion (1,300 a.) being offered in 1920.[99] In 1918 Lord Acton announced the sale of *c.* 3,600 a. of outlying parts of the Aldenham estate in Oldbury, Morville, Acton Round, and Aston Eyre parishes.[1] In 1873 the whole property had amounted to 6,321 a.[2] In 1920 a second portion of the estate amounting to 1,757 a. was sold.[3] Also in 1918 Lord Forester's Dothill estate (including the Little Wenlock manorial lands) and 1,325 a. of outlying lands of the Sparrows' Church Preen estate were advertised,[4] though the large Willey estate remained in the hands of Forester and his heirs. In other instances sales were complete and severed a long family connexion with the county. That happened in 1919 when H. D. Corbet sold the Sundorne Castle estate of 8,162 a. ending a descent in the Hill, Barker, Kynaston, and Corbet families dating from 1542.[5] The same year Mrs. Baldwyn-Childe put up for sale 4,930 a.: 14 sizeable stock-rearing and dairy farms, with several smaller farms, that formed outlying portions of the Kinlet estate.[6] Among small estates sold in 1919 were Market Drayton, 980 a. for £46,260, and Astley Hall near Shrewsbury, 666 a. for £45,345, equal to £68 an acre.[7] Later that year part of Lord Barnard's (formerly the duke of Cleveland's) Shropshire estate, which the Newport family had built up before 1734 as the largest landed estate in the county, was sold for £130,314. Most of it was disposed of privately to the sitting tenants but 1,400 a. were sold under the hammer for £30,314.[8] Another estate mostly sold by private treaty to the sitting tenants was Lord Bath's Minsterley estate.[9] In north Shropshire the Whitchurch portion of Lord Brownlow's Bridgwater estate, 4,000 a. out of 20,233 originally owned in the county, was sold for £150,000 in February 1920, over 3,000 a. going to sitting tenants.[10] Brownlow was in fact one of the most prominent vendors of land in the county and realized some £190,000 from sales before his death in 1921.[11] A conservative estimate of land sales in the county, based on surviving catalogues and press reports, suggests that over 80,000 a. were on offer between 1918 and the early 1920s.[12]

After 1921 the extent of property sales was reduced though they still continued in the years between the wars. Some properties were resold within a few years. In 1921 the trustees of the late T. H. Ward, a successful former tenant who had collected 1,700 a. around the parishes of Kynnersley and Lilleshall in the two Sutherland sales, offered his lands under the nostalgic title of the 'Lilleshall estate'.[13] In 1926 an outlying 1,200 a. of the Walcot estate was on offer.[14] The Hawkstone estate, reduced to 5,810 a., was resold in 1915 by the Hon. W. T. and

[97] Staffs. R.O., D. 593/G/1/24/22; Perren, op. cit. 55; *V.C.H. Salop.* xi. 267, 270.
[98] S.P.L., Sale Cat. 1/23, 83; S.R.O. 2141/1; *Wellington Jnl.* 28 July 1917.
[99] S.R.O. 1190/3/437-639.
[1] *Shrews. Chron.* 12 July 1918, p. 1.
[2] *Return of Owners of Land,* ii, Salop. p. 1.
[3] S.P.L., Sale Cat. 2/40.
[4] *Shrews. Chron.* 12 July 1918, p. 1; *V.C.H. Salop.* viii. 126; xi. 80, 216, 220.
[5] *Shrews. Chron.* 30 May 1919, p. 5; *T.S.A.S.* 2nd ser. vi. 217-19; 3rd ser. vi, pp. *xviii-xix*; J. B. Blakeway, *Sheriffs of Salop.* (Shrews. 1831), 95; *Visit. Salop. 1623,* i (Harl. Soc. xxviii), 27-8; Burke, *Land. Gent.* (1914), 433.

[6] Sale cat. in I.G.M.T. Libr., 1987.5750.
[7] *Estates Gaz.* 3 Jan. 1920, p. 13.
[8] Ibid. 3 Jan. 1920, p. 13; *Shrews. Chron.* 28 Nov. 1919, p. 5; Beard, *Salop. Days on Common Ways,* 60-1. For the descent of the Newports' est. after 1734 see *V.C.H. Salop.* iii. 254-5.
[9] *Shrews. Chron.* 12 Mar. 1920, p. 1; *Estates Gaz.* 1 Jan. 1921, p. 12; *V.C.H. Salop.* viii. 311.
[10] *Estates Gaz.* 1 Jan. 1921, p. 12; S.R.O. 119/31.
[11] *Shrews. Chron.* 25 Mar. 1921, p. 5.
[12] S.P.L., Sale Cat. 1-10; *Shrews. Chron.* 1919-21; *Estates Gaz.* 1919-21.
[13] S.P.L., Sale Cat. 2/25; cf. *V.C.H. Salop.* xi. 160.
[14] S.P.L., Sale Cat. 5/46.

the Hon. R. G. Whiteley when the Hall and adjacent farms and parkland, which amounted to 1,265 a., were bought by W. C. Gray.[15] Most of the section comprised the much reduced 'Hawkstone estate' of 1,102 a. that was for sale again in 1925.[16]

Transfer of ownership had considerable economic and social consequences. Tenants viewed the prospect of becoming owner-occupiers with much disquiet, and in 1919 the county branch of the N.F.U. spoke of farmers being saddled with farms for the rest of their lives at figures far beyond their true commercial value.[17] Landowners were anxious to take advantage of the buoyant real estate market after a generation of low land values and farmers' unwillingness to pay true economic rents. In many cases the money from sales earned more when invested in government and other securities than rents had yielded, and it was without the expenses and uncertainties of landowning.[18] In 1919 Lord Powis sold 4,400 a. of the Clun Forest and Bishop's Castle estates for £38,900. The gross rents had been £1,695 but the interest on the sale receipts, invested in government stock, came to £1,946, an increase of £251; in addition the cost of repairs and upkeep to the properties, estimated at £380, was also saved.[19] After the decline in prices from April 1920 farmers were extremely anxious not to lose the protective shield of those owners that remained. In December that year tenants on Sir Beville Stanier's 4,000-a. Peplow estate asked if there was anything they could do to avert the calamitous prospect of the sale of the Hall and estate. Stanier expressed concern for their welfare but maintained that he had no alternative but to sell the Peplow end of the estate, where costs were heavy, and move to a smaller house and less expensive surroundings.[20] Time was not on his side and the Hall was still in his family's hands on his death in 1922: it and 1,000 a. remaining were put on the market by F. A. H. Stanier in 1923.[21]

The decline of the gentry families and the country house was probably more obvious than that of the great landowners, a number of whom had seats outside the county. When the Sandfords of Sandford sold their estate of 950 a. near Prees in 1928 they severed a family connexion with the area dating from just after the Norman Conquest.[22] Of c. 90 country houses standing in the 1870s at least 35 had no trace left in 1952.[23] Land sales did not by any means eliminate the landlord from the county, though they did reduce the size of surviving estates. Nor did the surviving landowners entirely abandon their former functions. In 1934 when the Newport & District Agricultural Society was revived, after suspension during the depths of depression in 1931, the president was Lord Bradford.[24] The loss of many long-established proprietors, together with the generally depressed state of farm incomes, meant that buildings, hedges, drainage schemes, and the standard of cultivation as a whole often declined between the wars. Some of the loss was countered by the extension of the county council's activities to river and land drainage work and campaigns against injurious weeds and against vermin like the musk rat.[25] Nevertheless those efforts did not prevent a net deterioration in the fabric of the countryside.

Membership of the Shropshire branch of the Central Landowners' Association rose in the 1930s. In 1931 it had 109 members but through the activities of an official organizer in the county a further 64 were recruited in 1932.[26] By 1938

[15] S.R.O. 231/247.
[16] S.P.L., Sale Cat. 8/29.
[17] *Bridgnorth Jnl.* 25 Oct. 1919, p. 2.
[18] *Estates Gaz.* 1 Jan. 1921, p. 12.
[19] S.R.O. 1011/214.
[20] *Shrews. Chron.* 7 Jan. 1921, p. 5.
[21] S.P.L., Sale Cat. 7/23; *V.C.H. Salop.* iii. 358.
[22] S.P.L., Sale Cat. 2/71; Eyton, ix. 222.
[23] F. M. L. Thompson, *Eng. Landed Soc. in 19th Cent.* (1963), 342.
[24] *Wellington Jnl.* 2 Feb. 1935, p. 7.
[25] S.R.O. 207/2-14; W. H. H. 'Destruction of Rats and Mice', *Salop. Agric. News*, v. 15, 17-18; *V.C.H. Salop.* iii. 197-8.
[26] *Shrews. Chron.* 17 Feb. 1933, p. 8.

membership numbered 239. At the start of 1938 the president, Maj. E. R. T. Corbett of Longnor, noted that there were no instances in Shropshire where whole estates had been broken up to meet the cost of death duties, though there were several where portions of estates had been sold to pay such duties.[27]

After the Second World War there were further sales and break-ups of the older properties. The remnants of the Bridgwater estate, amounting to 2,000 a., were sold by Lord Brownlow to the duke of Westminster after 1951 but were resold by the 4th duke's executors in 1972. Lord Barnard sold some of the Cressage section of his estate before the war and the rest after, and land at Harley was sold in the 1950s and 1960s.[28] In 1947 Lord Acton, dispirited by the bureaucratic entanglement of farming, sold the 930-a. Aldenham estate to his father-in-law, Lord Rayleigh, and went to farm in Southern Rhodesia. Almost immediately Rayleigh disposed of 260 a. of the outlying farms.[29] Acton was not the only Shropshire landowner impelled by the atmosphere of post-war Britain to seek a more congenial residence or a more secure future overseas.[30] Col. C. R. Morris-Eyton, who sold his remaining Shropshire and Staffordshire estates in 1948, also went out to Southern Rhodesia,[31] and the 7th Lord Forester, though not under the necessity of selling his Shropshire estates, had an extensive tobacco plantation in the colony, where he died in 1977.[32] In 1954 Ronald Knox noted dryly that Southern Rhodesia 'seemed to be peopled entirely with Shropshire county families and Central European refugees'.[33] Some found other havens. At the end of the war Galfry Gatacre locked up Gatacre and went out to his estate in British Columbia, returning only in 1961 to find his property in a dismayingly dilapidated state.[34]

Some of the older families nevertheless remained substantial landowners in the 1980s. Among them were Lords Bradford (whose family estate had been increased by the purchase of the Leaton Knolls estate in 1947),[35] Forester, Harlech, and Plymouth. By 1972, though many of the large estates had been broken up, over a dozen representatives of the established landed families remained: beside the peers mentioned, they included Sir John Corbet, Sir Michael Leighton, Sir David Wakeman, and the owners of the Apley Park, Longnor, Onslow, Orleton, Plowden, Shavington, Stokesay Court, and Wenlock Abbey[36] estates. Many of the owners tended to take farms in hand as they became vacant and so were among the larger farmers in the county.[37] In south Shropshire Lord Plymouth's 8,000 a. in 1978 embraced the villages of Bromfield and Stanton Lacy, and the work on three dairy farms with 560 cattle was carried out under the direction of the estate manager and two assistants.[38] In 1981, after a successful career as a London restauranteur, Lord Bradford returned to manage the 17,000-a. Weston Park estate, not all of it in Shropshire.[39]

By the later 20th century some large agricultural estates were owned by institutions[40] rather than individuals or families. The county council smallholdings estate, for example, extended to just under 9,000 a. in the mid 1980s[41] and the

[27] Ibid. 4 Feb. 1938, p. 4.
[28] S.R.O. 2799/1; V.C.H. Salop. viii. 76, 89.
[29] E. Waugh, Life of Ronald Knox (1959), 305; The Times, 1 (p. 2) and 30 (p. 2) Aug. 1947; 25 Jan. 1989, p. 14.
[30] Nor was he the first: see above, 1750–1875 (Large estates), for Rob. Pigott's similar course in 1779.
[31] S.C.C. Ch. Exec.'s Dept. deed bdle. ED 170; V.C.H. Staffs. iv. 83, 93; Burke, Land. Gent. (1952), 791–2.
[32] Shropshire Star, 6 Jan. 1977, p. 3; The Times, 6 Jan. 1977, 14; S. Salop. Jnl. 7 Jan. 1977. [33] Waugh, Knox, 322.
[34] Daily Express, 17–18 July 1961; private inf.
[35] From the LLoyds: Burke, Land. Gent. (1952), 1543;

local inf. Ld. Newport had also bought much of the Morris-Eyton property in Staffs. after the war: V.C.H. Staffs. iv. 83, 93.
[36] The ho. was sold away from the est. in 1983: Shrews. Chron. 15 July 1983, p. [37] J.R.A.S.E. cxxxii. 48; local inf.
[38] S. Salop. Jnl. 2 June 1978, p. 18.
[39] Sunday Times Mag. 24 Feb. 1985, p. 74; Chartered Surveyor Weekly, 18 June 1987, 100 (advt., mentioning properties in the Welsh borders and Devon in addition to Salop. [and Staffs.]).
[40] Neglecting family estate companies.
[41] Inf. from S.C.C. Property and Planning Services Dept.; below.

National Trust owned several thousand Shropshire acres, including the valuable agricultural estates centring on Attingham Park and Dudmaston.[42] The Trust also acquired the lordship of the manor of Stretton-en-le-Dale in 1965 and with it one of the largest surviving open commons in the county—the Long Mynd (5,470 a.).[43] The Long Mynd illustrated the extremely difficult problems of managing an estate so as to reconcile the interests of numerous commoners possessing generously registered grazing rights, the general public in search of recreation, and the landlord as custodian of the land and its delicately balanced ecology.[44] Such problems were by no means confined to the Long Mynd, where they certainly antedated the Trust's ownership of it. The management of open commons indeed had become a progressively more difficult general problem as manorial management broke down, government aid made hill farming more profitable, and more of the public sought outdoor recreation in their leisure time. In 1987 the government was said to be preparing legislation to improve commons management.[45] About 1985 there were some 11,700 a. of uninclosed commons (1.2 per cent of the 1891 county area) in Shropshire, mostly (82.7 per cent) on the Long Mynd, the Clee Hills, and the high lands in the west around the Stiperstones.[46]

One development that had been causing increasing concern in the farming community for some years before 1980 had been the covert acquisition of agricultural land by financial institutions. From the later 1960s pension funds, insurance companies, unit trusts, and similar investors had been buying up large acreages, and Shropshire farms—for example in Onibury, Longford, Lilleshall, Crudgington, and the Ellesmere area—had not been exempt. The faltering of farm incomes in 1984, however, was followed by a sharp depression in the capital value of agricultural land. That brought problems for farmers who had borrowed when land values were high but it also served to reduce the financial institutions' interest in farm land as an investment.[47]

An important accompaniment of land sales was the growth of owner occupation. In 1911 its extent in Shropshire, as might be expected, was below the average of 13 per cent of holdings in England and Wales: 10 per cent of Shropshire farms, covering 8 per cent of farm land, were occupied by their owners. The greatest difference between county and national figures was for holdings over 300 a., of which 15.3 per cent were farmed by their owners in England and Wales but only 7.6 per cent in Shropshire.[48] By 1919 there had been a slight increase to 11 per cent of all farms and total acreage. Thereafter the rise in owner occupation was much more rapid and by 1922 16 per cent of farms and 18 per cent of farm land were wholly or mainly owned by their occupiers.[49] Between the wars the trend continued with some fluctuation so that 34 per cent of farms and 30 per cent of the acreage was owner-occupied by 1940–1.[50] After 1950 owner occupation increased rather faster than between the wars. By 1979 government statistics showed that 52 per cent of farms, covering 42 per cent of the acreage, were wholly owned by their occupiers and a further 13 per cent of farms were mainly owned

[42] Nat. Trust Handbk. (1985); cf. (for Dudmaston) B. Trinder, Hist. Salop. (1983), 108.

[43] Nat. Trust deeds; S.C.C. Ch. Exec.'s Dept., commons reg.

[44] J. S. Ellett III, 'Sheep Stocking Densities and Vegetation Change on the Long Mynd Common' (Univ. Coll., London, M.Sc. thesis, 1984), esp. pp. 3–4, 210–12, 217–18.

[45] Assoc. of County Councils Gaz. Sept. 1987, 195.

[46] S.C.C. Ch. Exec.'s Dept., commons reg.

[47] Inf. from local land agents and S.C.C. Property and Planning Services Dept.; above, pp. 1–2. Cf. Rep. Cttee. of Inq. into Acquisition and Occupancy of Agric. Land [Cmnd. 7599], H.C. (1979); Savills–RTP Agric. Performance Analysis [1982], esp. pp. 8–9 (for W. midlands); Daily Telegraph, 22 Dec. 1982, p. 6; AMC Review (Agric. Mortgage Corpn.), iv (1987), 2–3.

[48] Robinson, Soils and Agric. of Salop. 70; Agric. Returns G.B.   [49] Agric. Returns G.B.

[50] Min. of Agric. and Fish. Nat. Fm. Survey of Eng. and Wales (1941–3) (1946), 93.

by their occupiers; 60 per cent of the total acreage was occupied by owners. The proportion of wholly rented holdings in the county had shrunk to 28 per cent with a further 7 per cent mainly rented.[51] The buoyancy of the land market in the 1960s was enhanced by purchasers who were farmers from Lancashire and further north and had been dispossessed of their holdings by public works developments.[52]

Changes in the number and size of holdings again reflected national developments. In 1875 the average holding was c. 60 a.; in 1935 there had been a small increase to c. 66 a. By 1979 the average farm size had more than doubled since the 1930s to c. 122 a.[53] With the increase in the size of holdings there was naturally a fall in the number of farms. The only groups to increase in number were those of 300 a. and above. In 1935 they made up only 3.6 per cent of farms but by 1979 they accounted for 10.4 per cent of the total. Farm sizes varied between districts. In the 19th century the largest were among the sheep walks in the central and south-eastern divisions, the smallest in the dairying districts of the north.[54] That distribution persisted in the 20th century and was reflected in the fact that the majority of the county council's smallholdings schemes, established after 1908, were north of the Severn.[55] In 1950, of the 35 farms over 300 a., 30 were in the Southern, Bridgnorth, and Wrekin districts.[56] By 1970 there were 14 farms over 1,000 a. and 10 were in those districts.[57]

The numbers engaged in agriculture, both farmers and labourers, fell greatly. In 1871 there were 21,165 labourers and 6,102 farmers. By 1911 the number of labourers was 13,497 and the number of farmers was 5,543, which represented falls of 36 per cent and 9 per cent respectively.[58] At the beginning of the 20th century the farmers' main concern was not the weather, prices, or landlord–tenant relations but the general shortage of labour.[59] In 1881 the Shropshire Chamber of Agriculture complained that conditions of cleanliness and cultivation on many farms were 'defective'. That was partly due to a lack of juvenile labour owing to the legislation of 1876 and 1880 that made elementary education compulsory, but it was also caused by a loss of adult labour from rural areas to industrial ones, though a reverse flow could still be detected during periods of industrial slump.[60] Nevertheless that source disappeared after 1881 as Shropshire experienced an absolute decline in population from 248,111 in 1871 to 243,062 in 1921.[61] Emigration from the county is explained by the limited urban and industrial base within its borders. Shrewsbury, the largest town, remained an administrative and marketing centre throughout the whole period, with the industrial population concentrated in the slowly growing, and sometimes stagnant or declining, small towns between Wellington and Broseley. Agriculture therefore remained a major employer, but with wage levels too low to compete with those of other types of work. Sometimes changes in the farming system were blamed. In the Chirbury and Ellesmere districts in 1906 loss of population was ascribed to less capital-intensive methods with more arable land laid down to grass and the consequent employment of fewer hands. Although around Ellesmere the growth of Cheshire cheese making had maintained the demand for men capable of attending to stock and willing to milk, such men were scarce and commanded good wages. At Newport the small extent of such labour-intensive activities as fruit farming and poultry

[51] *Agric. Returns G.B.*
[52] *Shrews. Chron.* 11 Dec. 1970, p. 6.
[53] *Agric. Returns G.B.*
[54] Rider Haggard, *Rural Eng.* i. 422–3.
[55] S.R.O. 4449, est. papers; cf. *V.C.H. Salop.* iii. 197.
[56] P.R.O., MAF 68/4324.
[57] Ibid. /5190.
[58] *Census,* 1871, 1891.
[59] Rider Haggard, *Rural Eng.* i. 423–35.
[60] *Rep. R. Com. on Depr. Condition of Agric. Interests: Digest and App. to Pt. I,* 319–20, 333, 349–50.
[61] J. Saville, *Rural Depopulation in Eng. and Wales, 1851–1951* (1957), 56; *V.C.H. Salop.* ii. 219.

TABLE XII: NUMBER OF AGRICULTURAL HOLDINGS CLASSIFIED BY ACREAGE, 1875–1975

	Over 1 a. up to 5 a.	Over 5 a. up to 20 a.	Over 20 a. up to 50 a.	Over 50 a. up to 100 a.	Over 100 a up to 150 a.	Over 150 a. up to 300 a.	Over 300 a. up to 500 a.	Over 500 a. up to 700 a.	Over 700 a. up to 1000 a.	Over 1000 a.	TOTAL
1875		8,281		903	1,925		457	47		—	11,613
1880		8,528		918	1,934		444	47		1	11,872
1885	3,491	3,513	1,308	966	1,946		448	43		1	11,716
1890	4,245	5,061									
1895	3,070	3,624	1,427	999	2,000		421	39		1	11,581
1900	No returns collected										
1905	2,838	5,086			3,057			449			11,430
1910	2,783	5,117			3,072			459			11,431
1915	2,712	3,652	1,540	1,085	757	1,299		420			11,465
1920	2,488	3,614	1,656	1,124	779	1,295		395			11,351
1925	2,296	3,399	1,689	1,105	778	1,284		382			10,933
1930	2,223	3,295	1,778	1,117	805	1,268		375			10,861
1935	2,046	3,140	1,844	1,134	791	1,263	350	23	4	1	10,596
1940	1,742	2,919	1,839	1,166	800	1,269	325	23	8	1	10,092
1945	1,726	3,010	1,865	1,154	793	1,207	347	24	5	3	10,134
1950	2,046	2,934	1,847	1,155	815	1,208	353	28	7	1	10,394
1955	2,129	2,870	1,784	1,199	819	1,217	365	30	7	2	10,422
1960	1,962	2,527	1,702	1,166	827	1,255	398	43	20	3	9,903
1965	1,701	2,330	1,576	1,105	781	1,193	410	56	26	11	9,189
1970	409	1,527	1,288	975	663	1,115	412	101	41	19	6,550
1975	267	1,155	1,127	956	626	1,042	422	101	51	25	5,772

Sources: Agric. Returns G.B.; for 1890 *Return Agric. Holdings* [Cd. 3408], p. 4, H.C. (1907), lxvi, which does not include holdings over 50 a. In 1940 and 1942 slight changes were made in the official classifications, but they do not materially affect the figures from 1940 until 1967. In 1967 and 1968 many holdings under 10 a., with little production, were deleted: *Agric. Returns G.B.* 1968–9, page xii note a, and table 63A, notes a and b.

had failed to check the decline in the agricultural population, though vegetable growing did provide some seasonal increase in employment.[62] Shortage of new recruits became more serious between the wars, though in the eastern arable areas the lack of alternative employment gave school-leavers few chances of esape from farm work.[63] Near to towns, however, parents encouraged their sons to seek employment in other occupations and advertised vacancies on farms were sometimes filled by boys from other counties.[64]

The two wars each added to labour problems. The trend in favour of grassland was reversed after 1914 and 1939 with the result that the partial revival of corn growing demanded more labour while military service reduced the supply. In the First World War attempts were made to plug the gaps with soldiers stationed locally who were temporarily released for agricultural work, with members of the Women's Land Army, and, during the latter stages, with prisoners of war from the camps at Bromfield and Wem. The labour from all those sources, however, was not equal to the numbers of regular workers lost, and in many cases farmers said that the quality was poorer.[65] Before the outbreak of war in 1939 arrangements were made for recruitment into the Women's Land Army (1939–50), and a

[62] *Rep. on Decline in Agric. Pop. of Gt. Brit. 1881–1906* [Cd. 3273], pp. 38, 103–4, H.C. (1906), xcvi.
[63] J. B. Butler, 'The Fm. Workers Standard of Living: Study of Conditions in Salop. in 1939' (London Univ. M.Sc. thesis, 1946), 39.

[64] *Rep. of Procs. under Agric. Wages (Regulation) Act, 1924, for two yrs. ending 30 Sept. 1930* (H.M.S.O. 1931), 128.
[65] *Wages and Conditions of Employent in Agric. Vol. II* [Cmd. 25], pp. 283–4, H.C. (1919), ix.

committee was formed with Lady Boyne as chairman.[66] By 1944 there were 888 members on farms in Shropshire. The war years saw an increase in all groups of agricultural workers, and as late as 1950 the total agricultural labour force was larger than it had been in 1939.

Shropshire, like all other counties, experienced a rise in the number of regular and part-time workers in the early post-war years: demobilized men returned more quickly than prisoners of war and members of the Women's Land Army left. After 1949 the labour force declined yearly. In the sixteen years to 1965 the number of full-time workers fell by 39.6 per cent to 8,134 and part-time workers by 5.7 per cent to 2,979. The decline in full-time workers was the seventh lowest out of 60 county divisions of England and Wales. Nevertheless 40 counties lost more part-time workers, and Shropshire contradicted the national pattern that where counties lost more full-time workers they suffered smaller falls in the part-time labour force, which filled the vacuum left by the departure of full-timers. The relative stability of both sectors of the farm labour force was a reflection of the slow growth of secondary and tertiary employment in a decade and a half when such opportunities experienced greater growth elsewhere.[67] In 1969 the number of farmers, at 6,191, was superficially greater than a hundred years earlier, but 1,231 of them were part-time. The total of workers was 6,636 full-time and 1,446 part-time.[68] Greatest reliance on hired labour was in the arable districts, but on most hill farms family labour remained essential to success. In upland districts when extra hands were needed it was usual to seek assistance from neighbours and return the help when required.[69]

In the 19th century the standard of Shropshire farm workers' cottages varied but was mostly bad.[70] With a few glaring exceptions, those for which great landowners were directly responsible were better than average. Those sub-let by farmers ranged from good to deplorable. All agreed that the worst class of cottages were those belonging to tradesmen or speculators or owned by the labourer himself. Rents ranged from 1s. 3d. to 2s. a week in the 1880s, and from 2s. to 3s. by the end of the First World War. That included an adequate vegetable garden. Very often pigs and hens, and commonly a cow, were kept; they were mostly for home consumption, but in the 1890s Wellington retailers advertised cottage-fed bacon.[71] Owners and farmers blamed the poor housing on prevailing rent levels, which made building cottages an unprofitable investment so that many cottages were old and out-dated. In the Oswestry district shortages were caused by colliery owners who bought any offered for sale for their own workers.[72] By the Second World War cottage rents at around 3s. a week for the farm labourer compared favourably with the 6s. to 10s. paid by town workers,[73] but that was almost the only feature of the farm worker's life that was more eligible; local authorities had done little to improve rural housing.[74] The relatively uniform earnings of farm workers meant that living standards were markedly low in those families with three or more dependent children, though they rose once the children started work. Among families containing four or five people 50 per cent of the children were well clothed,

[66] Bridgnorth News, 14 July 1939, p. 3.
[67] Min. of Agric., Fish. and Food, Changing Structure of Agric. Labour Force in Eng. and Wales, 1949-65 (1967), 3, 17-18, 47; for the great increase in tractors, above (Arable farming).
[68] Agric. Returns G.B.
[69] S.P.L., T22 v.f., Weston Fm., Clun (Farm Adoption Scheme No. 2), n.d. but after 1948.
[70] Above, 1750-1875 (Labourers and cottagers).
[71] Wellington Jnl. 21 July (p. 4), 8 Sept. (p. 4) 1894, cited

by H. Knibb, 'Fm. Museum Profile—Blists Hill, E. Salop.' The Ark, xii (2), 54; cf. V.C.H. Salop. xi. 296.
[72] Rep. R. Com. on Depr. Condition of Agric. Interests: Digest and App. to Pt. I, 311, 326-7, 330; Wages and Conditions of Employment in Agric. ii. 287, 289.
[73] Shrews. Chron. 4 Feb. 1938, p. 4.
[74] Rest of para. based on Butler, 'Fm. Workers Standard of Living', 9-10, 19, 22, 35, 37-38. See also H. C. Miller, The Ageing Countryman (1963), cap. 7; V.C.H. Salop. iii. 174 n. 5, 177, 208-9.

TABLE XIII: WORKERS EMPLOYED ON AGRICULTURAL HOLDINGS, 1939–50
excluding the occupier, his wife, and family

| | Regular Workers: | | | Casual Workers: | | | |
	male	female	Women's Land Army	male	P.O.W.	female	TOTAL
1939	10,598		845	1,575	—	415	13,433
1940	10,084		797	1,486	—	674	13,041
1941	10,228		946	1,974	—	1,057	14,205
1942	10,243		1,693	2,150	—	1,532	15,618
1943	10,025		2,018	2,382	—	1,588	16,013
1944	10,232	1,331	880	2,248	837	1,292	16,820
1945	10,199	1,241	758	2,303	1,320	1,263	17,084
1946	10,586	1,065	403	2,061	1,910	836	16,861
1947	10,059	1,056	309	2,021	1,980	805	17,230
1948	11,067	1,153	293	2,337	328	782	16,500
1949	12,374	1,098	257	2,380	—	780	16,889
1950	12,364	1,059	138	2,486	—	812	16,859

Source: *Agric Returns G.B.* The figures are for 3 June in each year.

but among families containing six people the proportion was only 24 per cent. The largest single weekly expenditure was on food, while such items as clothing were paid for by the man's harvest earnings and, when available, potato and beet lifting by the wife. Cottages were sparsely furnished and social life was limited by lack of time and money. The weekly shopping trip to town was often the only break for housewives and attendance at church or chapel was unusual. For the men there were few social contacts outside the pub, which the majority visited only occasionally. The most popular entertainment was the wireless, often bought on hire purchase, which was preferred to magazines or books because of the smaller mental effort involved.

Agricultural wages rose in the 46 years after 1875, but progress was not constant. Average Shropshire earnings were 12s. 3d. a week 1867–70, rising to 17s. 5d. by 1898 and 18s. in 1908. Lowest wages were paid on the western side of the county.[75] Specialist workers earned most. In 1894 at Montford Bridge 16s. a week was paid to ordinary labourers, but between 18s. and £1 to waggoners and stockmen.[76] In north-east Shropshire in 1918 average wages had risen to 27s. a week, both for ordinary labourers and stockmen, whereas in the south-west traditional grading was still preserved with ordinary labourers at 25s. 3d. and stockmen at 27s.[77] During the war payments for harvest work increased also, though by then the groups of migrant Irish workers, employed every summer in the 1870s and 1880s, had ceased to appear in the county. The 'Irishman's Bothy' at Leighton, built to house migrant workers, was taken over in 1917 for the Women's Land Army.[78] The county Agricultural Wages Board was able to fix minimum wages 1917–21 but the power was then lost until 1924,[79] and meanwhile wages had been reduced in the wake of farmers' economic difficulties.[80] The usual hours throughout the county before the war were 59 in the summer and 52 in the winter, excluding meal breaks. Those long hours persisted as late as June 1918.[81] In the months immediately

[75] E. H. Hunt, *Regional Wages in Brit. 1850–1914* (1973), 30, 62.
[76] *1st Rep. R. Com. on Agric. Depr.: Mins. of Evid.* iii. 370.
[77] *Wages and Conditions of Employment in Agric.* ii. 285.
[78] *Rep. R. Com. on Depr. Condition of Agric. Interests: Digest and App. to Pt. I,* 320. For the Irish see also Beard, *Salop. Days on Common Ways,* 100.
[79] Cf. Corn Production Act, 1917, 7 & 8 Geo. V, c. 46, repealed by 11 & 12 Geo. V, c. 48; Agric. Wages (Regulation) Act, 1924, 14 & 15 Geo. V, c. 37.
[80] *Ag. Hist. Eng.* viii. 91, 153–4, 157–8.
[81] *Wages and Conditions of Employment in Agric.* ii. 284–5.

after the war the wages board reduced the weekly hours (for which the highest post-war county minimum of 46s. a week was paid) to 50 in the summer and 48 in the winter.[82] After 1921 farmers wanted to increase the hours of work to 54 and in many places that was achieved. In addition, between 1921 and 1924, wages were pushed as low as 30s. a week. In February 1925 there was some recovery and the wages board raised the county minimum to 31s. 6d. for a standard 54-hour week, increased to 32s. 6d. in June 1926. Further pressure for a reduction came with the fall in prices after 1929, and in August 1931 wages fell back to 32s., and 30s. a week was reached again in October 1933. A revival took place from June 1934 and 32s. 6d. was achieved by June 1936,[83] and 35s. by the Second World War.[84] There is evidence that in many cases farmers paid less than the legal minimum. In 1932 ministry officials inspected 30 farms in the county employing 96 workers, and they found 19 workers underpaid.[85] Wages increased during and after the Second World War. In March 1945 the county minimum for full-time workers over 21 was 70s. a week[86] and by 1958 it had risen to £7 10s. a week.[87] In the inflationary 1960s and 1970s increases were accompanied by further reductions of hours, so that by 1983 the national weekly minimum for a 40-hour week was £79.20,[88] equivalent to a real wage of £11.44 (£11 8s. 10d.) at 1958 prices.[89]

The amount of union activity in the county fluctuated with wage levels. The North Herefordshire and South Shropshire Agricultural Labourers' Mutual Improvement Society was formed in 1871. Its slogan was 'Emigration, Migration, but not Strikes', and it specialized in dispatching surplus labour from low-wage areas to better paid employment in northern England. At its peak it claimed a membership of 30,000 in six counties.[90] In spite of that pioneering venture Shropshire did not play an active part in the early history of conventional agricultural trade unionism. A county representative attended Joseph Arch's inaugural meeting of the first national union of farm workers at Leamington on Good Friday 1872,[91] but he was Sir Baldwyn Leighton, a sympathetic landowner who believed that the union movement could 'effect great permanent good, without inducing any feelings of hostility between employer and employed'.[92] Arch's Agricultural Labourers' Union had little initial success in the county, which had only very slight unionism in 1874, and even that had died out by 1881, though membership of friendly societies was quite common.[93] The first record of the National Union of Agricultural Workers[94] was in 1913 when Tom Mackley was appointed organizer and visited Shropshire to help in the formation of a number of branches. After the war it was the tenth largest county in the country in terms of union organization, with a county subscription of over £1,600 from 70 branches. The fall in wages 1921–3 affected union membership and, although there were

[82] 'Min. Rates of Wages of Agric. Labourers', *Labour Gaz.* xxviii. 479.

[83] *Procs. under Agric. Wages (Reg.) Act, 1924, for Yr. ending 30 Sept. 1925* (H.M.S.O. 1926), 57; *for Two Yrs. ending 30 Sept. 1930* (1931), 76; *Yr. ending 30 Sept. 1931* (1932), 48; *Yr. ending 30 Sept. 1934* (1935), 15; *Yr. ending 30 Sept. 1936* (1937), 12.

[84] *Shrews. Chron.* 4 Feb. 1938, p. 4.

[85] *Procs. under Agric. Wages (Reg.) Act, 1924 for Yr. ending 30 Sept. 1933* (H.M.S.O. 1934), 31.

[86] 'Agric. Wages in Eng. and Wales', *Min. of Labour Gaz.* liii. 45. [87] *Shrews. Chron.* 21 Mar. 1958, p. 5.

[88] *U.K. Dairy Facts and Figs. 1963*, 16; *1973*, 44; *1983*, 34.

[89] i.e. acc. to the gen. index of retail prices (1975 = 100). Change in the £'s purchasing power (1975 = 100) gives an equivalent of £11.46 (£11 9s. 2½d.) at 1958 prices. See *Econ.*

Trends, Ann. Suppl. vi (1981), 114; *Econ. Trends*, no. 385 (Nov. 1985), 42.

[90] *Victorian Countryside*, ed. G. E. Mingay (1981), ii. 582–3; above, 1750–1875 (Labourers and cottagers).

[91] *Autobiog. of Jos. Arch*, ed. J. G. O'Leary (1966), 49–51.

[92] Sheffield Univ. Libr., Mundella Colln., Leighton to A. J. Mundella 29 Apr. 1872, quoted in P. Horn, *Jos. Arch* (1971), 70–1.

[93] J. P. D. Dunbabin, 'Incidence and Organization of Agric. Trade Unionism in the 1870s', *Agric. H.R.* xvi. 117; *Rep. R. Com. on Depr. Condition of Agric. Interests: Digest and App. to Pt. I*, 337, 341; Perren, 'Agric. Depression', 308; Beard, *Salop. Days on Common Ways*, 17, 77–9.

[94] From 1968 Nat. Union of Agric. & Allied Workers, and from 1982 a trade section within the Transport and Gen. Workers' Union: inf. from T.G.W.U.

only three fewer branches in 1923 than in 1919, total conributions were then markedly less. Some branches ceased in the 1920s and by 1931 there were just over 40 branches with a total income of well under £1,000. The renewed prosperity of the industry after 1939 saw an improvement in union organization and by 1946 there were 85 branches in Shropshire. The 1950s saw a continued strengthening of union activity so that by 1958 the number of branches had risen to 120 with a subscription income of over £4,700. At local level the main activities were recovering arrears of wages and obtaining damages for members injured at work.[95]

Farmers too discovered the advantages of organization, and in 1908 Shropshire took a leading part in the formation of the National Farmers' Union. That year the National Federation of Meat Traders demanded that farmers should give them a warranty with their fatstock, indemnifying them against loss through condemnation of diseased carcasses. After a series of meetings beginning at the Wellington Smithfield, the county's largest fatstock market, Stephen Ward proposed to a gathering in the Shrewsbury Corn Exchange on 12 September that a farmers' association be formed to resist the butchers' demands. The Shrewsbury and District Farmers' Association held its first meeting a week later. Shropshire farmers contacted Colin Campbell, of the Lincolnshire Farmers' Union, and associations in other counties. As a result the butchers eventually withdrew their demands. Other farmers' associations were formed at Wellington, Oswestry, and Craven Arms and those, with the Shrewsbury branch, were among the earliest branches when the National Farmers' Union was formed the same year.[96]

Pioneers of the N.F.U. in Shropshire included William Everall of Forton, T. Powell Davies of Lydbury North, Stephen Ward of Kynnersley, T. C. Ward of Sambrook, Richard Kilvert of Kempton (later of Culmington), and Richard Evans of Shawbury; T. W. Bromley of Ford Mansion became its first county chairman. Initially progress was small and by 1914 membership was under 500. Growth was slow and sometimes faltered between the wars though in the 1920s the branch exerted itself to fight for cuts in county expenditure. In 1920 the paid-up membership in the county was 2,225,[97] but by the end of the Second World War there was a membership of 3,500. Progress was more spectacular after 1946 when a new policy of county and local branches staffed by full-time secretaries was inaugurated. A drive for new members, under the guidance of the then county chairman, Rowland W. Ward, of Sambrook Hall, was begun. Shropshire membership was brought up to 6,000 by 1958, with 20 local branches staffed by nine full-time secretaries with offices in the main market towns.[98] The county executive in Shrewsbury took responsibility for presenting a general voice on common issues, though that was not always an easy matter with the division between the arable and dairying north and the mainly livestock interests of the south and also the greater militancy of farmers in the north.[99]

The first Young Farmers' Clubs in the county were started at Bridgnorth in 1928 and (by T. C. Ward) at Newport in 1929, and a Shropshire Federation of Y.F.C.s operated after 1945.[1] By the later 1980s there were 29 clubs in the county.[2]

The years between the wars saw the decline of the Chamber of Agriculture, as farmers' interests were covered by the N.F.U. and landowners' by the C.L.A. In

[95] *Shrews. Chron.* 21 Mar. 1958, p. 5.
[96] Ibid. 30 May 1958, p. 10; cf. Ld. Ernle, *Eng. Farming Past and Present* (1961), 49.
[97] *Bridgnorth Jnl.* 29 Jan. 1921, p. 5; *V.C.H. Salop.* iii. 184, 191; S.R.O. 4531/1, pp. 35-7; *Kelly's Dir. Salop.* (1913),
380-404.
[98] *Shrews. Chron.* 11 Jan. 1935, p. 4; 30 May 1958, p. 10.
[99] Ibid. 6 Feb. 1970, p. 6.
[1] Ibid. 21 Feb. 1969, p. 6; *Salop. Young Farmers Handbk.* (1988), 62.
[2] *Salop. Young Farmers Handbk.* (1988).

1932 the chamber had 271 members and, though still lobbying parliament on agricultural matters, devoted more of its attention to organizing lectures.[3] Nevertheless the chamber did have staying power. When it celebrated its centenary in 1967 it was the only one left out of 67 county chambers formed in the 19th century; by then, however, it was entirely an educational and social organization.[4] In the later 1970s the chamber (revivified in 1977) had about 200 members and the C.L.A. over 1,200.[5]

Private co-operative enterprises were also part of farmers' reactions to difficult economic circumstances. One of the earliest was the Wem Cow Club, a cattle insurance society formed in 1866 and having 68 members in 1913.[6] In 1929 there were seven co-operatives based in the county with a combined membership of 2,219 and a turnover of £218,032. They ranged from the Market Drayton & District Agricultural and Small Holding Society, with 43 members and £13 worth of sales, to the Shrewsbury-based Shropshire Farmers with 1,226 members and £99,655 of sales. Other groups included the Llangedwyn Farmers' Co-operative Cheese Association, Oswestry, which manufactured dairy products, and the Burwarton Poultry Society marketing eggs and poultry.[7] Not all survived the war. Those that did and that expanded tended to be trading societies supplying farmers with a broad range of agricultural goods at a discount. Such was South Shropshire Farmers Ltd., formed by a group of N.F.U. members in 1917. Their first dividend was paid in 1926 and by 1979 they had a turnover of £11 million and supplied virtually everything that members needed from fertilizers, cereal seeds, and feedstuffs to heavy machinery.[8] Another organization with over £1 million turnover in the 1970s was Wrekin Farmers, which provided members with grain drying and storage facilities and was also agent for various fertilizers and feedstuffs. In 1977 their sales were £3.5 million.[9]

One way in which the county council attempted to stem the flow of labour from farming, albeit initially with some reluctance, was by the operation of the 1907 Small Holdings and Allotments Act.[10] In the first year of the new legislation 395 applications for 5,963 a. were received. There was little response to advertisements placed in the local press inviting offers of land, and as most applicants desired only to lease their holdings the council did not at first intend to purchase. When the Board of Agriculture pointed out the advantages of purchase, that soon became the preferred method of acquisition. By the end of 1909 land had been bought at Albrighton, West Felton, and Baschurch and further amounts leased at Llanyblodwel, Rodington, Lee Brockhurst, and Ellesmere. Most properties were in north Shropshire and the council was among the first to use the new powers of compulsory purchase. By 1909 it had been granted orders for 261 a. at Whixall and Wem and 80 a. at Hadley. The greatest progress before the First World War was made in 1909 and 1910. In 1909 the council undertook to acquire 1,056 a. At the start of 1910 there were only 11 smallholders settled on its schemes; by the end of the year there were 70. War slowed progress, but by the end of 1914 there were 11 properties covering 2,064 a., divided into 93 smallholdings.[11] Between the wars another 30

[3] Shrews. Chron. 3 Feb. 1983, p. 3.
[4] Ibid. 28 Jan. 1966, p. 2.
[5] Shrews. Chron. 20 Jan. 1978; S. Salop. Jnl. 7 July 1978, p. 15; 26 Jan. 1979, p. 17; local inf.
[6] Jnl. of Bd. of Agric. xix. 946-7.
[7] Yr. Bk. of Agric. Co-operation in Brit. Empire (1929), 330-48. [8] S. Salop. Jnl. 'Farmore' Suppl. Apr. 1979, p. 4.
[9] S. Salop. Jnl. Salop. Farming Suppl. Spring 1978, p.

5; 5 May 1978, p. 17.
[10] 7 Edw. VII, c. 54: V.C.H. Salop. iii. 197. It was replaced next yr. by a consolidating Act, 8 Edw. VII, c. 36.
[11] Rep. of Procs. under Small Holdings and Allotments Act, 1908, for 1908, Pt. I [Cd. 4846], p. 27, H.C. (1909), ix; 1909, Pt. I [Cd. 5180], pp. 2, 8, 27, 57, H.C. (1910), vii; 1910, Pt. I [Cd. 5615], p. 39, H.C. (1911), viii; 1914, Pt. I [Cd. 7851], p. 23, H.C. (1914-16), v.

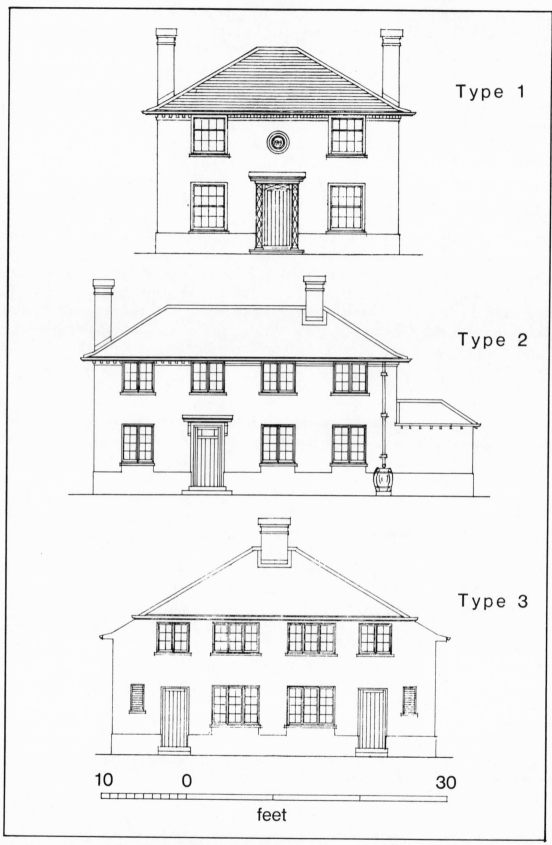

Type 1

Type 2

Type 3

10   0   30
feet

DESIGNS FOR SMALLHOLDINGS AT EMSTREY, 1919
In 1919 the county council bought 427 a. from Lord Berners at Emstrey, on the south-eastern outskirts of Shrewsbury. Twenty-seven smallholdings were created, and 21 new houses of three nationally approved types constructed: Type 1 (front elevation) for holdings over 20 a., Type 2 (front elevation) for holdings of 5–20 a., Type 3 (rear elevation) semidetached cottages.

properties were acquired, and 3 after 1945.[12] In 1957 the council owned 9,220 a., divided into 250 holdings over 15 a., which accounted for 7,902 a., with the remaining 1,318 a. in holdings under 15 a.[13] In the 1960s the council had c. 340 tenants[14] and the average size of holdings in 1965, excluding 39 cottage holdings of less than 2 a., was 32 a.[15]

Not all county council smallholdings sufficed to provide a full livelihood, and roughly a third of the tenants had part-time and cottage holdings.[16] The most favoured enterprise was intensive dairying with more than two thirds of the land under grass.[17] Typical of such holdings was the Shropshire Farm Institute's 36-a. smallholding at Baschurch, managed by one man, which initially carried 22 Ayrshire milkers and 8 followers. Such heavy stocking rates were achieved with silage making, heavy fertilizer applications, and high fixed costs.[18] In later years silage making was abandoned and the stocking rate raised to 50 milkers through intensive grazing and buying in all winter fodder.[19] The council encouraged its tenants to move to larger farms, either on its own estate or on privately owned estates, in order to make room for new entrants. Nevertheless in the years 1959–61 only 23 moved to larger county council holdings and 6 to private farms.[20] In 1965 the waiting time for applicants was 3 years and it seems that a number of suitably qualified agricultural workers did not apply for smallholdings because they believed the delay was even longer.[21] For most of the council's tenants progress up the farming ladder was blocked by the scarcity of farms to let and the high price of those for sale.[22]

Agricultural education

For most of the 19th century there was little enthusiasm for rural education and even considerable opposition. That state of affairs hardly altered after elementary education was universally provided under the 1870 Act[23] and made compulsory from 1877.[24] Between 1879 and 1899 school attendance rose only from 61 to 65 per cent, and magistrates, conscious of the priorities in a farming county, were unwilling to convict parents for infringements of by-laws. Even in the 1950s the problem still remained, especially at harvest which, in the potato and beet growing areas, extended well into November.[25] Small attempts at agricultural training were made in the 1880s, before the Technical Instruction Act of 1889[26] empowered county councils to provide post-school agricultural education, and in elementary schools gardens were begun in 1885.[27] The first interest in agricultural education at a higher level was shown by Sir Baldwyn Leighton. In 1880, in evidence to the royal commission, he had deplored the fact that Oxford and Cambridge colleges drew income from tithe rent charges but that neither university had seen fit to establish a school of agriculture.[28] In 1888 a privately organized Agricultural and Dairy Conference was held at Ludlow as part of a national campaign to arouse interest in better cheese and butter making. It was followed by a series of demonstrations,

[12] S.R.O. 4449, general/3A.
[13] Ibid. general/16, Cambridge Univ. Fm. Rent Surv. 1957.
[14] Ibid. general/16, G. R. Cooper to D. Long 22 Jan. 1962. [15] S.R.O. 4449, general/3A.
[16] Shrews. Chron. 18 Feb. 1966, p. 2.
[17] S.R.O. 4449, general/16, Cambridge Univ. Fm. Rent Surv. 1957.
[18] Farmers Weekly, 5 Jan. 1962, pp. 70–1.
[19] Shrews. Chron. 13 Aug. 1965, p. 2; 28 Oct. 1965, p. 2.
[20] S.R.O. 4449, general/16, Cooper to Long 1 Feb. 1962.

[21] Shrews. Chron. 12 Feb. 1965, p. 2.
[22] S.R.O. 4449, general/16, Cooper to Long 22 Jan. 1962.
[23] Elem. Educ. Act, 1870, 33 & 34 Vic. c. 75.
[24] Under the Elem. Educ. Act, 1876, 39 & 40 Vic. c. 79, s. 4. See V.C.H. Salop. iii. 174.
[25] J. P. Dodd, 'Rural Educ. in Salop. in 19th Cent.' (Birm. Univ. M.A. thesis, 1958), 140, 142–5; V.C.H. Salop. iii. 176–7. [26] 52 & 53 Vic. c. 76.
[27] Bridgnorth Jnl. 20 Sept. 1919, p. 5.
[28] Rep. R. Com. on Depr. Condition of Agric. Interests: Mins. of Evid. [C. 2778–I], p. 333, H.C. (1881), xv.

including one held in Willey park in 1889 for Lord Forester's tenants.[29] The county council was relatively slow to take advantage of the 'whisky money' offered for technical instruction of an agricultural or horticultural nature.[30] For the first four or five years the council adopted a policy of experiment.[31] In 1894, under the auspices of its Technical Instruction Committee, classes in butter making were conducted at two centres and classes in cheese making in five districts. In addition horticultural and veterinary lectures were given and a grant of £50 made to Childe's School, Cleobury Mortimer,[32] which had an agricultural curriculum. By 1896 the council extended similar grants for agricultural education to Oswestry and Ludlow grammar schools and had begun to support the proposed Harper Adams Agricultural College. Expenditure on all agricultural education, however, amounted to only £1,246 out of a total of £7,160 on all technical education.[33]

The provision of agricultural education was significantly extended by the opening of Harper Adams College at Edgmond, near Newport. Endowed under the will of Thomas Harper Adams (1816–92), the college was opened by the president of the Board of Agriculture in 1901.[34] The first principal was P. H. Foulkes.[35] Previously the west midland counties had been unable to consolidate the several schemes of agricultural instruction that each organized for itself.[36] At its outset the new college was primarily a centre for Shropshire (where it was the main channel of agricultural education) and Staffordshire, but eventually it played an important part in co-ordinating agricultural education for the region. The original endowment, providing rather less than £800 a year, was too modest to provide more than a fraction of the necessary support. In return for grants and scholarships, students from the two counties were admitted at reduced fees which, in the case of farmers' children, were less than half the usual amount. In 1915 and 1932 similar arrangements were made with Warwickshire and Herefordshire.[37] By 1938 the major part of the college's finance was from Shropshire, Staffordshire, and Warwickshire county councils and Ministry of Agriculture grants.[38] Between 1899–1900 and 1910–11 the county spent £25,560 on agricultural instruction. Over 60 per cent of that expenditure (£15,232) was for scholarships and grants to colleges and schools.[39] Between 1903 and 1908 Shropshire spent only £93 a year on agricultural education for every 1,000 males over 10 years old engaged in agriculture, but even that modest outlay made it the fourteenth highest out of 49 English counties.[40] From 1904 the council passed its responsibility for travelling lecturers on agriculture to the college staff, who developed that aspect with classes on dairying, horticulture, poultry keeping, and veterinary instruction. In 1910 the college's success induced the Technical Instruction Committee to engage its own lecturing staff again.[41] In 1913, to co-ordinate the lecturers' activities and to promote the investigation of farm problems by Harper Adams, the council appointed Edric Druce as its first agricultural organizer, a post he held until his retirement in 1937; his successors

[29] *Ludlow Adv.* 14 Sept. 1889, p. 5.
[30] Under the Local Taxation (Customs and Excise) Act, 1890, 53 & 54 Vic. c. 60: *V.C.H. Salop.* iii. 198-9.
[31] T. D. M. Jones, 'Development of Educational Provision in the Rural Co. of Salop. between 1870 and 1914' (Keele Univ. M.A. (Educ.) thesis, 1969), 115.
[32] *Rep. on Distribution of Grants for Agric. Educ. in Gt. Brit. 1895-6* [C. 8228], pp. 99-100, H.C. (1896), lxvii.
[33] *Grants for Agric. Educ. in Gt. Brit. 1896-7* [C. 8690], pp. 73, 99, H.C. (1898), lxxii; *V.C.H. Salop.* iii. 198.
[34] Jones, 'Educ. Provision in Salop.' 147-53.
[35] C. Crowther, 'Harper Adams Agric. Coll.' *Agric. Pro-*

gress, xxvii (1), 5-9.
[36] *Grants for Agric. Educ. and Research 1900-1* [Cd. 814], p. xv, H.C. (1902), lxxxii.
[37] S.R.O. 207/8, pp. 156-61; *V.C.H. Staffs.* vi. 148.
[38] C. Crowther, 'Work and Aims of Harper Adams Agric. Coll.' *Salop. Agric. News,* iv (4), 10.
[39] S.R.O. 207/8, accts. inserted at front endpaper.
[40] *Grants for Agric. Educ. and Research 1907-8* [Cd. 4802], pp. xxi-xxii, H.C. (1909), ix.
[41] Jones, 'Educ. Provision in Salop.' 341-3; *Grants for Agric. Educ. and Research 1906-7* [Cd. 3908], pp. 48-9, 121-2, H.C. (1908), xxii.

were called chief agricultural officer.[42] Although the war saw a fall in the numbers attending the various classes arranged by the county council, as well as a reduction in staff, its travelling courses in dairy instruction and poultry keeping were maintained throughout.[43] Even with those difficulties, between August 1914 and September 1918 the staff gave 751 lectures and demonstrations at day and evening centres to a total audience of 16,240, and they made 214 visits to secondary schools.[44]

Between the wars the county agricultural organizer's staff offered advice to farmers on general agricultural matters, horticulture, dairying, poultry, farriery, and beekeeping. They also continued to work closely with the advisory service at Harper Adams College.[45] It was felt that the needs of students from the larger holdings were well catered for by day classes, evening lectures, and the travelling dairy schools. Druce, however, found it was more difficult to assist the county's 9,600 smallholders,[46] who were slow to ask advice and often not easily able to afford to act on it when given.[47] By 1939 there were 10 members of staff besides the chief agricultural officer.[48]

The First World War curtailed the work of Harper Adams College even more severely than that of the county's agricultural advisory service. Staff numbered 17 in 1913 with over 70 long-course and c. 14 short-course students,[49] but staff and student numbers and income fell sharply after 1914. In the spring of 1915, at the Board of Agriculture's request, a series of fortnightly courses for women recruits to agriculture was begun, and in 1917 women were admitted to the college's standard courses. In spite of financial stringency, the college's educational activities expanded between the wars and staff numbers rose from 12 in 1922 to 26 in 1932 and 50 by 1939.[50] At its establishment the college had a home farm of 178 a.[51] The farm was extended over the years to c. 240 a. in 1910,[52] and 340 a. by 1938 with 110 a. arable, 210 a. of grass, and the remainder as gardens and orchards; 70 a. were devoted to poultry and experimental work, leaving c. 270 a. for ordinary farm work.[53]

The college extended its experimental work between the wars. That work had begun in 1911 when the Harper Adams egg-laying trials were started, and continued in an unbroken series of thirty years.[54] In 1925 the National Institute of Poultry Husbandry, occupying c. 50 a., was established on the college farm.[55] Although the greater part of the college's work was instruction, some experimental work on crops and livestock was conducted in association with other bodies. In 1926 a pig-feeding experimental station was established as part of a co-ordinated pig-feeding research programme developed by the Rowett Institute at Aberdeen and the Cambridge Animal Nutrition Research Unit.[56] Experiments in dairy husbandry and extensive series of trials of different varieties of corn and root crops with the National Institute of Agricultural Botany, Cambridge, were conducted at Edgmond and various sites in the west midlands. The experience thus gained was of value in the college's role in the 1920s and 1930s as the specialist advisory centre for

[42] *Salop. Agric. News*, iii (4), 9; *S.C.C. Mins. (Educ.)* 1912–13, 25–6, 38, 50–1, 66; *S.C.C. Mins.* 1912–13, 266–8; 1913–14, 5. [43] *S.R.O.* 207/9, pp. 9–10.
[44] *Bridgnorth Jnl.* 20 Sept. 1919, p. 5.
[45] *Salop. Agric. News*, i (1), 7, 9.
[46] *P.R.O.*, MAF 68/1283.
[47] *S.R.O.* 207/11, p. 85, 27 Sept. 1924.
[48] *Salop. Agric. News*, v (4), 102.
[49] *Grants for Agric. Educ. and Research 1912–13* [Cd. 7179], pp. 109, 114, H.C. (1914), xi; *1913–14* [Cd. 7450],

pp. 118, 126, H.C. (1914), xi.
[50] *Agric. Progress*, xxvii (1), 9. [51] *S.R.O.* 207/8, p. 160.
[52] *Grants for Agric. Educ. and Research 1910–11* [Cd. 6025], p. 28, H.C. (1912–13), x.
[53] *Salop. Agric. News*, iv (4), 10–11.
[54] *Agric. Progress*, xxvii (1), 9.
[55] W. T. Price, 'Harper Adams Agric. Coll.' *Agriculture*, lvi (4), 168.
[56] C. Crowther, 'Work of Harper Adams Coll. Pig Feeding Experimental Sta. 1926–31', *J.R.A.S.E.* xcii. 14.

Shropshire, Staffordshire, and Warwickshire. In that work it supplemented the county organizer and his staff in each of the three counties, through whom the college's services were available for particularly difficult problems of cropping or livestock management.[57] In 1939 the full range of courses offered was: London B.Sc. (Agric.), Intermediate and Final; National and College Diplomas in Agriculture (three years); Agricultural Certificate (two years); National Poultry Diploma and Institute Senior Certificate (two years), and Institute Junior Certificate (one year). Staff and student numbers fell again after September 1939. Residential accommodation was put at the disposal of the Women's Land Army for 4–8 weeks' practical training courses, but after two courses and 90 trainees the scheme was abandoned.[58]

The history of post-war agricultural education was one of steady growth. In 1945 the county council's Education Committee took responsibility for agricultural education and found itself with no general educational staff. Earliest efforts were concentrated on technical agricultural subjects, and in the first two years classes on tractor maintenance were established at a dozen centres in the county. In 1948, after consultation with the N.F.U. and N.U.A.W., a series of general courses was arranged on crop and animal husbandry, farm machinery, farm management, and manual skills; more specific courses were directed at the smallholder and hill farmer. Over a thousand attended, the programme ranging from mid-week and weekend to full residential courses at Harper Adams, Shrewsbury Technical College, and the new residential Shropshire Adult College at Attingham Park. In the autumn of 1949 the committee opened the Shropshire Farm Institute at Walford Manor 6 miles north-west of Shrewsbury to provide a focus of technical agricultural education.[59] It had 750 a. bought from the former Morris-Eyton estate for £75,000.[60] From its inception the institute pioneered the development of an extensive network of part-time courses in agriculture and related subjects. In the very early days, with money and manpower in short supply, much of the instruction was on an *ad hoc* basis. Some of the county's leading farmers provided practical tuition to supplement the work of the small team of lecturers. As more staff were appointed a more formal course structure was developed.[61] The institute played an important part in agricultural training in the county. Particular attention was paid to livestock regimes most suited to the small farmer, such as heavy dairy stocking and barley beef feeding.[62] In 1975 over 90 per cent of school leavers taking up farm work in the county attended day-release classes at Walford and various outlying centres, a proportion approached nowhere else in the country and well above the national average of 40 per cent for similar institutions. Nevertheless it is symptomatic of the small extent of agricultural employment that entry of county school leavers amounted to only 150, compared with 450 students when the institute opened.[63] The main foundation course, offered at seven centres in the county, was for one day a week over 30 weeks of the year, lasting for three years. In addition to the principal, the institute had a staff of 24 agricultural and two horticultural instructors: eleven were wholly engaged at the institute teaching full-time students; the remaining 13, including the two horticulturalists, were employed

[57] *Salop. Agric. News*, iv (4), 13–14.
[58] *Agric. Progress*, xxvii (1), 11.
[59] H. Martin Wilson, 'Agric. Educ. in Salop.' *Agriculture*, lvi (4), 184–5; *V.C.H. Salop*,. iii. 205.
[60] *Shrews. Chron.* 19 June 1970, p. 6.
[61] J. A. S. Brasier, 'Agric. Educ. in Salop.' *Agric. Progress*, li. 109.

[62] H. Hope, 'Plans on Paper Paid Fm. Inst.' *Farmers Weekly*, 5 Jan. 1962, pp. 70–1; A. G. Harris and R. W. Griffiths, 'Three Ways to Beef: a Cash and Grass Comparison', ibid. 28 Feb. 1964, pp. 93–4.
[63] *S. Salop. Jnl.* 26 June (p. 21), 2 July (p. 6) 1970; 16 June 1978, p. 21.

in extra-mural work in the county and were based at the Shirehall in Shrewsbury.[64]

The Farm Institute forged close links with the county's 50 secondary schools, giving careers advice, arranging visits to the Walford farms, and publicizing agricultural education courses available in the county. Older school pupils were also offered a five-day residential course at Walford on 'Learning from the Land', and adult non-vocational courses were offered on horse riding and country sports.[65] The one-year course for the National Certificate in Agriculture, introduced in 1954, was particularly popular. By 1975 just under 1,200 Walford students had been entered for it, more than from any other centre in the kingdom. In 1963 the institute offered a Regional Course in Farm Business Management and Advanced Husbandry, primarily intended to serve the needs of students from Shropshire, Herefordshire, Worcestershire, Warwickshire, and Staffordshire. In 1969 the Ordinary National Diploma in Agriculture was introduced.[66] From the start the institute had forged close links with Young Farmers' Clubs, providing, for instance, training in stock judging.[67]

In 1975 the county council opened an agricultural museum to illustrate farm work and rural life of the period 1875–1925. Uniquely it was a working farm: 23 a. leased from Acton Scott home farm (where appropriate buildings, hedgerows, and unsprayed pasture survived) were farmed according to local traditions of the pre-tractor age. Over 400,000 visitors were attracted 1975–85, many of them in school parties, and the museum's educational potential soon led to the appointment of an education officer.[68]

[64] *Agric. Progress*, li. 109-12.   [65] Ibid.
[66] G. Salmon, 'Philosophy of the Full-time Farming Courses, and Links with the Farming Community', *Agric. Progress*, li. 106.
[67] Inf. from Mr. R. D. Park, principal of Salop. Farm Inst.

1949-79, who is thanked for his comments.
[68] R. Hill, 'Fm. Museum Profile—Acton Scott Working Fm. Mus.' *The Ark*, xi (12), 395-7; S.C.C. Leisure Activities Cttee. Mins. 14 Mar. 1986; inf. from S.C.C. Leisure Services Dept.

INDEX

NOTE. A page number in italics denotes an illustration on that page or facing it. A page number followed by *n* is a reference only to the footnotes on that page.

INDEX

A HISTORY OF SHROPSHIRE

CORRIGENDA TO VOLUMES I–III

Earlier corrigenda to Volumes I and II were published in Volumes II and III. In references to pages printed in more than one column 'a', 'b', and 'c' following a page number denote the first, second, and third column.

Vol. I, page 181b, line 44, *for* 'Burnall' *read* 'Burnell'
,, ,, 313a, line 23, *for* '7½' *read* '7'
,, ,, 314a, line 20, *for* '2' *read* '4'
,, ,, 319a, line 14, *for* '2½' *read* '1½'
,, ,, 324b, line 13, *for* 'shillings' (*twice*), *read* 'pence' (*twice*)
,, ,, 329a, line 30, *for* '40' *read* '60'
,, ,, 334a, line 6, *for* 'shillings' *read* 'pence'
,, ,, 335b, line 13, *for* 'and Elward' *read* 'and Elmund'
,, ,, 345a, line 11, *for* '23' *read* '20'
,, ,, 346a, line 45, *for* '2' *read* '3'
,, ,, 495, line 49, *for* '1374' *read* '1377–8'

Vol. II, page 22, note 6, line 1, *for* '25' *read* '26'
,, ,, 39, note 1, *for* 'of St.' *read* 'of the translation of St.'
,, ,, 143b, line 22, *for* '1908' *read* '1909'
,, ,, 143b, line 23, *for* '11' *read* '14'
,, ,, 143b, line 23, *for* 'three' *read* 'four'
,, ,, 143b, line 25, *for* 'following' *read* 'same'
,, ,, 240b, line 30, *delete* '335,'

Vol. III, page 61, line 24, *for* 'grandson' *read* 'son'
,, ,, 61, note 42, *for* 'bros.' *read* 'sons'
,, ,, 68, note 74, *for* '440' *read* '40'
,, ,, 103, note 38, *for* '58' *read* '85'
,, ,, 247, line 31, *for* 'Priory' *read* 'Abbey'
,, ,, 395b, line 54, *delete* '(Priory)'